Pediatric Metabolic Syndrome

Steven E. Lipshultz • Sarah E. Messiah
Tracie L. Miller
Editors

Pediatric Metabolic Syndrome

Comprehensive Clinical Review
and Related Health Issues

Editors
Steven E. Lipshultz, M.D.
Departments of Pediatrics,
Epidemiology and Public Health
and Medicine (Oncology)
Leonard M. Miller School of Medicine
University of Miami
Holtz Children's Hospital of the University
of Miami-Jackson Memorial Medical Center
Batchelor Children's Research Institute
Mailman Center for Child Development
University of Miami Sylvester
Comprehensive Cancer Center
Miami, FL USA

Tracie L. Miller, M.D.
Departments of Pediatrics and
Epidemiology and Public Health
Division of Pediatric Clinical Research
Leonard M. Miller School of Medicine
University of Miami
Holtz Children's Hospital of the University
of Miami-Jackson Memorial Medical
Center
Batchelor Children's Research Institute
University of Miami Sylvester
Comprehensive Cancer Center
Miami, FL USA

Sarah E. Messiah, Ph.D., MPH
Departments of Pediatrics and
Epidemiology and Public Health
Division of Pediatric Clinical Research
Leonard M. Miller School of Medicine
University of Miami
Batchelor Children's Research Institute
Miami, FL USA

ISBN 978-1-4471-5853-0   ISBN 978-1-4471-2366-8 (eBook)
DOI 10.1007/978-1-4471-2366-8
Springer London Heidelberg New York Dordrecht

British Library Cataloguing in Publication Data
A catalogue record for this book is available from the British Library

© Springer-Verlag London 2012
Softcover reprint of the hardcover 1st edition 2012
This work is subject to copyright. All rights are reserved by the Publisher, whether the whole or part of the material is concerned, specifically the rights of translation, reprinting, reuse of illustrations, recitation, broadcasting, reproduction on microfilms or in any other physical way, and transmission or information storage and retrieval, electronic adaptation, computer software, or by similar or dissimilar methodology now known or hereafter developed. Exempted from this legal reservation are brief excerpts in connection with reviews or scholarly analysis or material supplied specifically for the purpose of being entered and executed on a computer system, for exclusive use by the purchaser of the work. Duplication of this publication or parts thereof is permitted only under the provisions of the Copyright Law of the Publisher's location, in its current version, and permission for use must always be obtained from Springer. Permissions for use may be obtained through RightsLink at the Copyright Clearance Center. Violations are liable to prosecution under the respective Copyright Law.
The use of general descriptive names, registered names, trademarks, service marks, etc. in this publication does not imply, even in the absence of a specific statement, that such names are exempt from the relevant protective laws and regulations and therefore free for general use.
While the advice and information in this book are believed to be true and accurate at the date of publication, neither the authors nor the editors nor the publisher can accept any legal responsibility for any errors or omissions that may be made. The publisher makes no warranty, express or implied, with respect to the material contained herein.

Printed on acid-free paper

Springer is part of Springer Science+Business Media (www.springer.com)

Preface

The new millennium is well underway and many parts of the world are appreciating arguably the most advanced prosperity in modern history—profound technological advances, housing explosions, transport systems that facilitate global travel in hours, ample food supplies, and medical advances that have both eradicated and controlled many diseases that once killed millions. Simultaneously, there are a significant number of families that live in poverty, adversely affecting their health status. These very riches and health disparities have compromised the most important ones of all—our youngest generation's health. In this millennium, these splendid advances should serve to increase average life expectancy by many years, yet it will not—unless the current trajectory for childhood nutrition is altered.

In just under three decades, the world has realized an unparalleled rise in overweight and obesity. Recent studies report an association between childhood obesity and the development of a cluster of cardiometabolic disease risk factors characterized by variable combinations of insulin resistance, dyslipidemia, and hypertension, known as the metabolic syndrome. In just under three decades, the world has unfortunately learned that this clustering of risk factors is associated with the early onset of both type 2 diabetes and atherosclerotic cardiovascular complications—conditions previously unheard of in children and adolescents. Yet in three decades, we have little knowledge of the global and cumulative detrimental health effects of childhood obesity—virtually no organ or system is left unscathed. As obese children age, not only will their health be negatively affected, but infertility and pregnancy complications associated with the metabolic syndrome will affect generations to come. The work force will undoubtedly be affected because of increased sick days and decreased work productivity. It may conceivably result in lower armed services recruits due to failing weight qualifications.

Identifying children and adolescents at the earliest stages of chronic disease onset should be the goal of clinical practice, yet there are no clear guidelines for defining the risk of metabolic syndrome or appropriate risk-factor thresholds among children and adolescents. If children are identified early in the disease process, lifestyle and clinical interventions can be instituted when they are potentially more effective.

This book approaches the pediatric metabolic syndrome in two dimensions: by elucidating its effects on specific organ systems and by considering the problem more holistically through understanding the social, psychological, and economic consequences of it. We have included an invited group of esteemed experts in the field to help provide the most timely and informative approaches on how to deal with this health crisis in our nation's youth. Through educating our practitioners, our future researchers, our health and community organizations, our legislators, and our families and children, we have the best chance at improving the health trajectory of the next generation.

Steven E. Lipshultz, M.D.
Sarah E. Messiah, Ph.D., MPH
Tracie L. Miller, M.D.

Contents

1 **Why Should We Write a Book on Pediatric Metabolic Syndrome?**
   Commentaries from Worldwide Experts   1
   Arthur S. Agatston, Shari Barkin, Gerald S. Berenson,
   Stephen R. Daniels, Tia Diaz-Balart, Matthew W. Gillman,
   Joel Edward Lavine, Brian W. McCrindle, Andrew N. Redington,
   Ralph L. Sacco, Donna E. Shalala, Julia Steinberger,
   Leonardo Trasande, Ann M. Veneman, and Michael L. Weitzman

2 **Epidemiology of the Metabolic Syndrome in Youth:
   A Population-to-Clinical-Based Perspective**. 37
   Sarah E. Messiah, Kristopher L. Arheart,
   and James D. Wilkinson

3 **Perinatal Epidemiology of Metabolic Syndrome
   Risk Factors**. 57
   Barbara Luke and Mary L. Hediger

4 **Metabolic Syndrome in Childhood as a Risk Factor
   for Type 2 Diabetes** 83
   Nicola Santoro, Cosimo Giannini, and Sonia Caprio

5 **Effects of Metabolic Syndrome on Atherosclerosis
   in Childhood** 93
   Muhammad Yasir Qureshi, Sarah E. Messiah, Tracie L. Miller,
   and Steven E. Lipshultz

6 **Metabolic Syndrome and Associated Kidney Disease** 117
   Carolyn L. Abitbol and Wacharee Seeherunvong

7 **Metabolic Syndrome and Related Liver Diseases** 137
   Aymin Delgado-Borrego

8	**The Relationship Between Asthma, Sleep Apnea, and Other Respiratory Disorders and Childhood Metabolic Syndrome**...	159
	Erick Forno and Annabelle Quizon	
9	**The Relationship Between Components of the Metabolic Syndrome and Bone Health**...................................	183
	Zeina M. Nabhan and Linda A. DiMeglio	
10	**The Relationship of Childhood Obesity with Cardiomyopathy and Heart Failure**..	199
	Muhammad Yasir Qureshi, James D. Wilkinson, and Steven E. Lipshultz	
11	**Childhood Metabolic Syndrome and Cancer Risk**................	217
	Stefanie R. Brown and Steven E. Lipshultz	
12	**Neurocognitive and Psychological Correlates of Metabolic Syndrome in Childhood**...........................	229
	Anna Maria Patino-Fernandez, Amber Daigre, and Alan M. Delamater	
13	**Genomics of Pediatric Metabolic Syndrome**....................	241
	Evadnie Rampersaud and Maria A. Ciliberti	
14	**Physical Activity Assessment and Intervention**..................	267
	Gabriel Somarriba	
15	**Nutritional Evaluation and Intervention**.......................	283
	Runa Diwadkar Watkins, Daniela Neri, and Tracie L. Miller	
16	**Pharmacological Therapies of Metabolic Syndrome**..............	311
	Adriana Carrillo-Iregui and Carley Gomez-Meade	
17	**Bariatric Surgery to Reverse Metabolic Syndrome in Adolescents**...	333
	Noor Kassira, Valerie Ann Marks, and Nestor de la Cruz-Muñoz	
18	**Moving Clinic- and Community-Based Practice into Policy to Address Child Healthy Weight (and Vice Versa)**...............	351
	Danielle Hollar, T. Lucas Hollar, and Michelle A. Lombardo	

Index... 369

Contributors

Carolyn L. Abitbol, M.D. Department of Pediatric Nephrology, University of Miami Miller School of Medicine, Holtz Children Hospital, Miami, FL, USA

Arthur S. Agatston, M.D., FACC Department of Medicine, University of Miami Miller School of Medicine, Miami, FL, USA

Cardiac Prevention Center, Mount Sinai Medical Center, Miami Beach, FL, USA

South Beach Diet, Miami Beach, FL, USA

Kristopher L. Arheart, B.S., M.S., EdD Division of Biostatistics, Department of Epidemiology and Public Health, University of Miami Miller School of Medicine, Miami, FL, USA

Shari Barkin, M.D., MSHS Marian Wright Edelman Professor of Pediatrics, Division of General Pediatrics, Monroe Carell, Jr. Children's Hospital, Vanderbilt, Nashville, TN, USA

Gerald S. Berenson, M.D. Center for Cardiovascular Health, Tulane University Health Science Center, New Orleans, LA, USA

Department of Medicine, Pediatrics, Biochemistry & Epidemiology, Tulane University Health Science Center, New Orleans, LA, USA

The Bogalusa Heart Study, Tulane University Health Science Center, New Orleans, LA, USA

Stefanie R. Brown, M.D., FAAP Department of Pediatrics (R-131), University of Miami Miller School of Medicine, Miami Beach, FL, USA

Sonia Caprio, M.D. Department of Pediatrics, Yale University, New Haven, CT, USA

Adriana Carrillo-Iregui, M.D. Division of Pediatric Endocrinology, Department of Pediatrics, Miller School of Medicine, University of Miami, Miami, FL, USA

Maria A. Ciliberti, MPH John T. MacDonald Department of Human Genetics, University of Miami Miller School of Medicine, Miami, FL, USA

Amber Daigre, Ph.D. Department of Pediatrics, University of Miami Miller School of Medicine, Miami, FL, USA

Stephen R. Daniels, M.D., Ph.D. L. Joseph Butterfield Chair in Pediatrics, Children's Hospital Colorado, Denver, CO, USA

Department of Pediatrics, University of Colorado School of Medicine, Denver, CO, USA

Nestor de la Cruz-Muñoz, M.D. Division of Laparoendoscopic and Bariatric Surgery, The DeWitt Daughtry Family Department of Surgery, University of Miami Miller School of Medicine, Miami, FL, USA

Alan M. Delamater, Ph.D. Department of Pediatrics, University of Miami Miller School of Medicine, Miami, FL, USA

Aymin Delgado-Borrego, M.D., MPH Division of Pediatrics/Gastroenterology, University of Miami, Miami, FL, USA

Tia Diaz-Balart Founder & President, EcoChamber, Miami, FL, USA

Linda A. DiMeglio, M.D., MPH Section of Pediatric Endocrinology and Diabetology, Department of Pediatrics, Riley Hospital for Children, Indiana University School of Medicine, Indianapolis, IN, USA

Erick Forno, M.D., MPH Division of Pediatric Pulmonology, University of Miami, Miami, FL, USA

Cosimo Giannini, M.D., Ph.D. Department of Pediatrics, Yale University, New Haven, CT, USA

Matthew W. Gillman, M.D., SM Department of Population Medicine, Harvard Medical School/Harvard Pilgrim Health Care Institute, Boston, MA, USA

Obesity Prevention Program, Harvard Medical School/Harvard Pilgrim Health Care Institute, Boston, MA, USA

Department of Nutrition, Harvard School of Public Health, Boston, MA, USA

Carley Gomez-Meade, D.O. Division of Pediatrics Endocrinology, Department of Pediatric, Jackson Memorial Hospital/Miller School of Medicine, University of Miami, Miami, FL, USA

Mary L. Hediger, Ph.D. Division of Epidemiology, Statistics and Prevention Research, Eunice Kennedy Shriver National Institute of Child Health and Human Development, National Institute of Health, Rockville, MD, USA

Danielle Hollar, Ph.D., MHA, M.S. Department of Pediatrics, University of Miami School of Medicine, Miami, FL, USA

Contributors

T. Lucas Hollar, Ph.D. Master of Public Health Program,
Nova Southeastern University, College of Osteopathic Medicine,
Fort Lauderdale, FL, USA

Noor Kassira, M.D. Department of Surgery, Jackson Memorial Hospital,
University of Miami, Miami, FL, USA

Joel Edward Lavine, Ph.D., M.D. Division of Pediatric Gastroenterology,
Hepatology and Nutrition, Morgan Stanley Children's Hospital, New York,
NY, USA

Department of Pediatrics, New York Presbyterian Columbia University
Medical Center, College of Physicians and Surgeons,
Morgan Stanley Children's Hospital, New York, NY, USA

Steven E. Lipshultz, M.D. Professor of Pediatrics, George E. Batchelor
Chair in Pediatrics, Chairman of the Department of Pediatrics,
Professor of Epidemiology and Public Health, Professor of Medicine (Oncology),
Associate Executive Dean for Child Health, Leonard M. Miller School
of Medicine, University of Miami

Chief-of-Staff, Holtz Children's Hospital
of the University of Miami-Jackson Memorial Medical Center

Director, Batchelor Children's Research Institute

Associate Director, Mailman Center for Child Development

Member, University of Miami Sylvester Comprehensive Cancer Center Miami,
FL, USA

Michelle A. Lombardo, DC The OrganWise Guys Inc., Duluth, GA, USA

Barbara Luke, ScD, MPH Department of Obstetrics, Gynecology,
and Reproductive Biology, College of Human Medicine,
Michigan State University, East Lansing, MI, USA

Valerie Ann Marks, B.A. The DeWitt Daughtry Family Department of Surgery,
University of Miami Miller School of Medicine, Miami, FL, USA

Brian W. McCrindle, M.D., MPH, FRCP(C) Department of Pediatrics,
CIBC World Markets Children's Miracle Foundation Chair in Child Health
Research, The Hospital for Sick Children, University of Toronto,
Toronto, ON, Canada

Sarah E. Messiah, Ph.D., MPH Research Associate Professor of Pediatrics,
Research Associate Professor of Epidemiology and Public Health, Division of
Pediatric Clinical Research, Department of Pediatrics, Leonard M. Miller School
of Medicine, University of Miami

Member, Batchelor Children's Research Institute Miami, FL, USA

Tracie L. Miller, M.D. Professor of Pediatrics, George E. Batchelor Endowed Chair in Pediatric Cardiology, Professor of Epidemiology and Public Health, Director, Division of Pediatric Clinical Research, Associate Chair for Clinical Research, Department of Pediatrics, Leonard M. Miller School of Medicine, University of Miami

Member, Batchelor Children's Research Institute Miami, FL, USA

Zeina M. Nabhan, M.D., M.S. Section of Pediatric Endocrinology and Diabetology, Department of Pediatrics, Riley Hospital for Children, Indiana University School of Medicine, Indianapolis, IN, USA

Daniela Neri, M.S. Division of Pediatric Clinical Research, Department of Pediatrics, University of Miami Miller School of Medicine, Miami, FL, USA

Anna Maria Patino-Fernandez, Ph.D. Department of Pediatrics, University of Miami Miller School of Medicine, Miami, FL, USA

Annabelle Quizon, M.D. Division of Pediatric Pulmonology, University of Miami, Miami, FL, USA

Muhammad Yasir Qureshi, M.D. Division of Pediatric Cardiology, Department of Pediatrics, University of Miami/Jackson Memorial Hospital, Miami, FL, USA

Evadnie Rampersaud, Ph.D. John T. MacDonald Department of Human Genetics, University of Miami Miller School of Medicine, Miami, FL, USA

Andrew N. Redington, M.B.B.S., MRCP(UK), M.D., FRCP(UK), FRCP(C) BMO Financial Group Chair in Cardiology, Department of Paediatrics, University of Toronto, Toronto, ON, Canada

Division of Cardiology, The Labatt Family Heart Centre, The Hospital for Sick Children, Toronto, ON, Canada

Ralph L. Sacco, M.D., M.S. Department of Neurology, University of Miami Miller School of Medicine, Miami, FL, USA

Department of Neurology, Epidemiology and Public Health, Human Genetics and Neurosurgery, Miami, FL, USA

Neurology Service, Jackson Memorial Hospital, Miami, FL, USA

President, American Heart Association 2011–2012, Dallas, TX, USA

Nicola Santoro, M.D., Ph.D. Department of Pediatrics, Yale University, New Haven, CT, USA

Wacharee Seeherunvong, M.D. Division of Pediatric Nephrology, Department of Pediatrics, University of Miami Miller School of Medicine, Holtz Children Hospital, Miami, FL, USA

Contributors

Donna E. Shalala, Ph.D. President, University of Miami, Coral Gables, FL, USA

Gabriel Somarriba, DPT Division of Clinical Research, Department of Pediatrics, University of Miami, Miller School of Medicine, Miami, FL, USA

Julia Steinberger, M.D., M.S. Department of Pediatrics, University of Minnesota Amplatz Children's Hospital, Minneapolis, MN, USA

Leonardo Trasande, M.D., MPP Department of Pediatrics, Environmental Medicine and Health Policy, New York University School of Medicine, New York, NY, USA

Ann M. Veneman, B.A., M.A., JD Bipartisan Policy Center, current member, Washington, DC

Previous Secretary, United States Department of Agriculture

Runa Diwadkar Watkins, M.D. Department of Pediatric Gastroenterology, University of Miami, Miami, FL, USA

Michael L. Weitzman, M.D. Department of Pediatrics, Environmental Medicine, and Psychiatry, New York University School of Medicine, New York, NY, USA

James D. Wilkinson, M.D., MPH Department of Pediatrics and Epidemiology, Leonard M. Miller School of Medicine, Miami, FL, USA

Chapter 1
Why Should We Write a Book on Pediatric Metabolic Syndrome? *Commentaries from Worldwide Experts*

Arthur S. Agatston, Shari Barkin, Gerald S. Berenson,
Stephen R. Daniels, Tia Diaz-Balart, Matthew W. Gillman,
Joel Edward Lavine, Brian W. McCrindle, Andrew N. Redington,
Ralph L. Sacco, Donna E. Shalala, Julia Steinberger, Leonardo Trasande,
Ann M. Veneman, and Michael L. Weitzman

Abstract One might ask "why write an entire book on the pediatric metabolic syndrome?" It is not operationally defined as of yet, and some even challenge its very existence. However, couched in the current worldwide obesity epidemic, the scientific literature indicates that this constellation of cardiometabolic disease risk factors is increasing in pediatric populations around the world without discrimination by age, sex, or race/ethnicity. This chapter provides unique perspectives from a select group of child health advocates and experts, many who have dedicated significant proportions of their careers, and in some cases their entire career, to pediatric preventative health and nutrition. Here, they provide their candid perspective on the pediatric metabolic syndrome from different positions, yet all emphasize the resolve of the scientific community to continue to pursue this area both in research and clinical care.

Keywords Metabolic syndrome • Pediatric • Preventive cardiology • Child health

---

A.S. Agatston, M.D., FACC
Associate Professor, Department of Medicine, University of Miami Miller School of Medicine, Miami, FL, USA

Director, Cardiac Prevention Center, Mount Sinai Medical Center, Miami, FL

President and Founder, South Beach Diet, Miami Beach, FL, USA

S. Barkin, M.D., MSHS
Marian Wright Edelman Professor of Pediatrics, Division of General Pediatrics, Monroe Carell, Jr. Children's Hospital, Vanderbilt University, Nashville, TN, USA

G.S. Berenson, M.D.
Chair of Preventative Cardiology, Director for the
Center for Cardiovascular Health, Tulane University, New Orleans, LA, USA

S.E. Lipshultz et al. (eds.), *Pediatric Metabolic Syndrome*,
DOI 10.1007/978-1-4471-2366-8_1, © Springer-Verlag London 2012

Department of Medicine, Pediatrics, Biochemistry & Epidemiology,
Tulane University Health Science Center, New Orleans, LA, USA

Principal Investigator, The Bogalusa Heart Study, Tulane University Health Science Center,
New Orleans, LA, USA

S.R. Daniels, M.D., Ph.D.
L. Joseph Butterfield Chair in Pediatrics,
Children's Hospital Colorado,
Denver, CO, USA

Professor and Chair, Department of Pediatrics Children's Hospital, University of Colorado,
Denver, Aurora, CO, USA

T. Diaz-Balart
Founder & President, EcoChamber,
Miami, FL, USA

M.W. Gillman, M.D., SM
Professor, Department of Population Medicine,
Harvard Medical School/Harvard Pilgrim Health Care Institute,
Boston, MA, USA

Obesity Prevention Program,
Harvard Medical School/Harvard Pilgrim Health Care Institute,
Boston, MA, USA

Department of Nutrition, Harvard School of Public Health,
Boston, MA, USA

J.E. Lavine, Ph.D., M.D.
Chief, Division of Pediatric Gastroenterology, Hepatology and Nutrition,
Morgan Stanley Children's Hospital,
New York, NY, USA

Department of Pediatrics, New York Presbyterian Columbia University Medical Center,
College of Physicians and Surgeons, Morgan Stanley Children's Hospital,
New York, NY, USA

B.W. McCrindle, M.D., MPH, FRCP(C)
Professor, Department of Pediatrics, CIBC World Markets Children's Miracle Foundation Chair
in Child Health Research, The Hospital for Sick Children, University of Toronto,
Toronto, ON, Canada

A.N. Redington, M.B.B.S., MRCP(UK), M.D., FRCP(UK), FRCP(C)
Professor and BMO Financial Group Chair in Cardiology,
Department of Paediatrics, University of Toronto,
Toronto, ON, Canada

Division of Cardiology, The Labatt Family Heart Centre,
The Hospital for Sick Children,
Toronto, ON, Canada

R.L. Sacco, M.D., M.S.
Professor and Chair, Department of Neurology, University of Miami Miller School of Medicine,
Miami, FL, USA

Professor, Departments of Neurology, Epidemiology and Public Health,
Human Genetics and Neurosurgery,
Miami, FL, USA

Chief of Neurology Service, Jackson Memorial Hospital,
Miami, FL, USA

President, American Heart Association 2011--2012,
Dallas, TX, USA

D.E. Shalala, Ph.D.
President, University of Miami,
Miami, FL, USA

J. Steinberger, M.D., M.S.
Professor, Department of Pediatrics, University of Minnesota Amplatz Children's Hospital,
Minneapolis, MN, USA

L. Trasande, M.D., M.P.P
Associate Professor, Department of Pediatrics, Environmental Medicine and Health Policy,
New York University School of Medicine,
New York, NY, USA

A.M. Veneman, B.A., M.A., JD
Bipartisan Policy Center, current member,
Washington, DC

Previous Secretary
United States Department of Agriculture

M.L. Weitzman, M.D.
Professor, Department of Pediatrics, Environmental Medicine, and Psychiatry,
New York University School of Medicine,
New York, NY, USA

Childhood Obesity: A Worldwide Health Emergency

Donna E. Shalala, Ph.D. is the President of the University of Miami in Coral Gables, FL. She served for eight years as Secretary of Health and Human Services (DHHS) under President William Clinton (1993–2001), the longest term ever served in this position. Previous to her DHHS appointment, she was Chair of the Children's Defense Fund (1992–1993). Dr. Shalala has been elected to the Council on Foreign Relations; National Academy of Education; the National Academy of Public Administration; the American Academy of Arts and Sciences; the American Philosophical Society; the National Academy of Social Insurance; the American Academy of Political and Social Science; and the Institute of Medicine of the National Academy of Sciences.

Today, when an overweight, middle-aged man stumbles into the emergency room clutching his chest, we react swiftly, urgently, and with grave concern.

Yet when a pudgy 8-year-old visits a pediatrician with a big belly, high blood pressure, and elevated blood sugar, we do not treat the child's condition as an emergency.

We must. Our future depends on it.

Over the past three decades—in a single generation—obesity rates for children in the USA have tripled. Today, more than one-third of the children and adolescents are morbidly obese, obese or overweight. Youngsters in the rest of our world are not in much better shape.

The ramifications are frightening.

Millions of children, many of them preschoolers, already have signs of one or more of the five risk factors for metabolic syndrome, a combination of disorders once associated only with adulthood. They are already on the road to developing diabetes and coronary heart disease, being felled by stroke, or a myriad of other diseases in the prime of life.

For the first time in history, children are not destined to live longer, healthier lives than their parents.

They will enter the workforce, not with the boundless energy and enthusiasm of the youth, but with dire and costly medical needs that will implode an already over-burdened health-care system.

This is untenable, unsustainable, and unthinkable.

We can, and must, reverse this trend. The task is formidable, but we have the tools. Starting in preschool, education and prevention campaigns can create a new mindset, a new culture of healthy eating and active living.

Obesity is a complex, multifaceted problem. It needs to be tackled from many fronts—cultural, environmental, physical, nutritional, as well as medical. But unlike cancer, we already know the cure. The solutions may be complicated, but the equation is simple. Our bodies need to burn up what we consume. We need to use food as it was intended, to fuel busy, active lives.

Children may not instinctively know how to eat well, but they are naturally active. They like to play. They have trouble sitting still. We cannot let them lose that bent. They and we must make exercise a daily habit. Computers are educational wonders, but video games are no substitute for playing softball before dinner, or taking a walk afterward.

Children can learn to make healthy food choices, too. We can teach them by eating right ourselves, by offering plums over donuts, water over cola. But we also have a duty to teach them early in life how the body functions, and why they are obligated to take care of theirs. I have seen preschoolers sing and dance with glee to songs about healthy hearts and other organs. The message is magical and, when reinforced, lasting.

Unfortunately, too many adults in the USA are nutritionally illiterate. Every parent wants the best for their children, but many never learned how to eat healthy themselves, or do not have the means. Many cannot buy fresh produce in their own neighborhoods.

It is our job—all of us, as a "village," as a society—to remedy that reality and create a new mindset. From Washington to City Hall, the government, in partnership with academia, must halt the epidemic of obesity, embracing education and prevention programs that work and research that translates into results. But the government and academia cannot do it alone. Parents, teachers, siblings, coaches, Scout leaders, restaurateurs, farmers, nutritionists, athletes, celebrities, and, not least of all, primary care physicians, nurses, and allied health professionals must sound the alarm—preaching and modeling healthy eating and active living—loudly, clearly, relentlessly.

Our health-care system is at a dangerous crossroads. We cannot let preventable diseases spawned by obesity cripple our nation and threaten our future. We cannot stand by and watch a chubby-cheeked 8-year-old become an obese man who stumbles into the emergency room clutching his chest.

Pediatric Metabolic Syndrome: A Concern

Gerald S. Berenson, M.D. is the Director for the Center for Cardiovascular Health and Chair of Preventative Cardiology at Tulane University in New Orleans, Louisiana. Additionally, he is a Professor with appointments in the Departments of Medicine, Pediatrics, Biochemistry & Epidemiology. Dr. Berenson is Principal Investigator of the Bogalusa Heart Study, the longest and most detailed study of a biracial (black-white) population of children in the world.

It is appropriate and timely to have a comprehensive overview of the metabolic syndrome beginning at the pediatric age. The occurrence of multiple risk factors consistent with the metabolic syndrome is now well known to be associated with atherosclerotic lesions in the coronary arteries of young individuals [1, 2]. Further, the severity of coronary atherosclerosis in the youth is noted to increase markedly with increasing numbers of risk factors; and risk factors at a young age are predictive of subsequent development of clinical cardiovascular disease and type 2 diabetes. However, the question remains whether early changes in the cardiovascular system associated with the metabolic syndrome set the stage for cardiac events much later in life, at middle to older ages; setting the stage for future heart disease is real. "Tracking" or persistence (at a given level) of risk factors, especially multiple risk factors, occurs at a high degree. The association of metabolic syndrome with cardiovascular disease has generated the term "cardio" metabolic syndrome, and the ravages from the "silent" burden of the cardiometabolic syndrome is much broader in the population than can possibly be shown by a limited number of autopsy studies.

Although current anatomic studies concern cardiac and carotid structures, cardiovascular systemic changes by metabolic syndrome involve other organs including kidney, liver, or even brain (cognitive function) and cancer risk.

Emphasizing the pediatric occurrence of the metabolic syndrome, which may have its origin in utero [3], in a broad perspective is important. Unfortunately, no consistent criteria are available to diagnose the metabolic syndrome in pediatric populations [4]. The comparison of the prevalence among pediatric populations, in terms of its components and cut points, either in absolute values or percentiles is problematic. Although not totally exclusive, just the inclusion of measures of central obesity, like waist/height ratio, BMI, and some measure of insulin resistance, provides the basis for the diagnosis, while recognizing that inflammatory, hemodynamic, and various other metabolic factors also play a role.

Initially, efforts regarding secondary and primary prevention of cardiovascular risk in the youth focused mainly on LDL cholesterol and its familial nature.

The advent of the obesity epidemic and the recognition of the limitations of controlling only LDL cholesterol in terms of lipoproteins led to emphasizing triglycerides, HDL cholesterol, and mixed dyslipidemia in adult cardiology. The recognition of the metabolic syndrome even at the pediatric age brings together more components for controlling and prevention of cardiovascular risk. Pediatricians now have the opportunity, more correctly the responsibility, to play an important role in encouraging and guiding primordial prevention—to begin preventing the development of risk factors at the childhood age. There is an urgent need for taking various avenues to address this problem.

Thus, two strategies have evolved: The high-risk or family approach, that is, for families and parents with high-risk, to develop healthy lifestyles and become important role models for their children [5]. Encouraging adult cardiology colleagues to refer families and offspring of such patients to enter a preventive cardiology program should be a goal [6]. The other strategy recognizes the diffuse nature of early cardiovascular disease beginning in childhood, as pointed out above, and the importance of the metabolic syndrome at the pediatric age. Pediatricians can play a leadership role by encouraging broad health education to be included in the public education system and help children in understanding healthy lifestyles while preventing poor and unhealthy behaviors [7]. Health education, like "Health Ahead/Heart Smart" is a prevention approach that can be directed to the elementary school age at the onset of development of obesity and the metabolic syndrome. This has been an effective approach for controlling obesity and addressing unhealthy lifestyles [8].

The authors are to be credited for drawing attention to a broad health problem that has emerged over the past two decades and still continues to increase. This book underscores the need for pediatricians to provide direction for primordial prevention of a major public health problem.

Childhood Obesity: Children Out of Balance

Shari Barkin, M.D., MSHS is the Director of the Division of General Pediatrics and the Marian Wright Edelman Professor of Pediatrics at Monroe Carell, Jr. Children's Hospital at Vanderbilt University in Nashville, Tennessee. At Vanderbilt, Dr. Barkin leads a group of pediatric obesity researchers to develop and test promising approaches to stem the tide of pediatric obesity.

Over the past three decades, overweight/obesity has risen dramatically, resulting in two-thirds of adults in the USA with excessive adiposity. The rise of overweight/obesity in adults is mirrored in children. Between 1976 and 1980, the overweight/obesity rate for children between 6 and 17 years old was 5.7%. Twenty-five years later, that rate tripled to 17.2% for boys and 15.9% for girls [9]. In fact, in some states the prevalence of overweight/obesity in childhood is closer to one in three children [10]. In the USA, childhood obesity appears to have reached a plateau at these high rates; however, morbid obesity continues to rise [11]. At these rates, 30–40% of today's children may eventually develop type 2 diabetes and reduce their life expectancy [12].

While the consequences of overweight/obesity may not be readily apparent until adulthood, overweight/obesity and its complications begin in childhood. Nader et al. demonstrated that children who were ever overweight during the preschool period were five times as likely to be overweight adolescents [13]. And the chances of overweight increase as the child ages. In that same study, 80% of school-age children who were ever overweight during this period went on to become overweight adolescents. The significance of mounting risk for sustained overweight/obesity and its consequences cannot be overstated. In the Harvard Growth Study, overweight adolescents as adults had a twofold increase in all-cause mortality and an increased morbidity due to cardiovascular disease [14]. It is not merely overweight/obesity in childhood that poses the risk for later increased mortality and morbidity as an adult, the slope of early weight gain is a potent predictor [15, 16]. For example, Leunisson et al. showed that rapid weight gain without concomitant growth in height during the first 3 months of infancy is linked with reduced insulin sensitivity in early adulthood. Furthermore, Barker et al. demonstrated that the risk of adult coronary events was more strongly related to the rapid childhood gain in BMI than to BMI attained at any particular age [15].

But obesity also confers increased risk for many other medical problems, including uterine cancer, cervical cancer, and breast cancer in women, and premature testosterone decline, liver cancer, and pancreatic cancer in men [17]. Moreover, these predictions are not unique to the USA, they are consistent with patterns of rising overweight/obesity seen in developing countries that have adopted "Western" lifestyles with lower levels of physical activity and increased consumption of processed, nutrient-poor food [18]. For example, the World Health Organization predicts that by 2030, India will be home to 80 million diabetics [19].

The biologic processes underpinning the connection between childhood and later adulthood overweight/obesity are unclear. The body attempts to maintain stability through change. It does this by maintaining narrow set points, such as body temperature through homeostasis, while more dynamically regulating large systems, such as the cardiovascular, immune, sympathetic nervous system, metabolic, hypothalamic-pituitary-adrenal-axis, and central nervous system; this concept is called "allostasis." Allostasis is a multifactorial biomarker model, which captures the complex regulation and relationship between multiple systems [20, 21]. While allostasis designates processes of bodily adaptation to stressful challenges, "allostatic load" refers to the cost of wear and tear on the body as a consequence of dysfunctional allostasis [22]. This concept is evident in the notion of the Metabolic Syndrome.

The Metabolic Syndrome, well characterized in adults, has been less characterized in children. However, over the past decade as rates of childhood overweight and obesity continue to exist at high levels, understanding how to best utilize the information presented by the metabolic syndrome becomes even more critical to the public's health. The definitions vary by study and are borrowed in large part from the adult world [23]. Most recommend that the metabolic syndrome for children continue to utilize the same components of dyslipidemia, elevated blood pressure, hyperglycemia, and BMI [24]. Some suggest examining our measurement strategies: waist circumference for visceral adiposity versus merely BMI, and impaired glucose tolerance versus fasting hyperglycemia [25]. Whatever markers we use, we need to be mindful of both what the information means for childhood and adulthood health as well as possess a clear strategy to employ once we identify the Metabolic Syndrome. For children, we have an opportunity to advance prevention of these processes.

While it is clear that overweight/obesity in childhood is associated with persistent overweight/obesity in adulthood and poor outcomes such as cardiovascular disease, there are also those overweight/obese children and adults without evidence of disease. So while overweight/obesity can be a powerful risk factor, it might be more of a symptom and not necessarily a mediator of disease. Some have discovered that insulin resistance, regardless of BMI, appears to mediate the process of the aforementioned common disease states [26]. This appears to be consistent with the finding that not all fat functions in the same manner. Cruz and Goran posit that ectopic fat storage plus a genetic susceptibility to insulin resistance is inversely related to glucose disposal and nonoxidative glucose metabolism [25]. It is likely that this is associated with the development of the metabolic syndrome in children and the continued progression to disease states either in childhood or, more commonly, in adulthood.

Once we determine what causes this metabolic syndrome, we are faced with the challenge of what to do with this information. We must strive to link diagnosis with effective treatment for this critical public health issue of childhood obesity.

Obesity is now epidemic among children in most of the industrialized world. While estimates vary by country and definition, increases in body mass index have been detected across all ages and even to the preschool years. The waves of this epidemic are now such that globally 9.1% of preschool children will be overweight or obese by World Health Organization norms by 2020, a doubling since 1990.

The future consequences for health in the twenty-first century are disheartening. Diabetes, hypertension and the metabolic syndrome are phrases commonly used by all child-health providers now. During this author's own pediatric residency, type 2 diabetes was still thought to be an adult disease though hospitalizations for new onset diabetics were already and alarmingly on the rise. In the USA, hard-fought increases in life expectancy are now slipping away. Myocardial infarctions in the fourth decade may reemerge as common events the way they did in the 1940s and 1950s.

The adult epidemic of cardiovascular disease was so swiftly overcome through identification of preventable risk factors, largely through the Framingham Heart Study, a large-scale longitudinal study of health in one Massachusetts community. Presently, it is well understood that childhood obesity is different and potentially more complex in its origins. Diet and physical activity in childhood remain leading suspected causes, but changing community structures and exposures to synthetic chemicals that may disrupt energy balance are also thought to have produced increases in unhealthy weights in children out of proportion to their heights.

Scientific knowledge will go far to improve upon interventions to improve nutritional balance and future cardiovascular health, as those interventions to date which have endeavored to prevent obesity before it occurs have achieved success only fleetingly, if at all. If implemented in the originally proposed and robust fashion across a population of 100,000 children, the National Children's Study has the potential to achieve similar gains in children's health to the Framingham Heart Study.

Yet the hidden secrets to the success in decreasing cardiovascular morbidity and mortality through the past three decades lie not only in individual interventions but also in the political will to implement regulation and legislation that limited harmful exposures. Pharmacotherapy and more intensive management by generalists and specialists no doubt were crucial, but reduction in tobacco smoke exposure and changes toward healthier diet should also be credited in part to policy activity, despite the long lag that sometimes followed strong and sound science that suggested the need for intervention.

Fortunately, we are now seeing greater attention and proactive effort by child health-care providers to identify and treat obesity-associated comorbidities in childhood. Unfortunately, the intervention documented to be most effective for reducing weight in extremely obese adolescents remains one fraught with unknown health and other implications—bariatric surgery. While these procedures clearly have their place, they represent increasingly common options of last resort.

A similar recipe to that described for adult cardiovascular disease is therefore needed for the childhood obesity epidemic. Policy experiments are being actively pursued, from calorie count posting in restaurants and other eateries to removal of sodas from schools and reemphasis on physical activity during and outside of schools. If chemical factors are identified to be contributors to childhood obesity and eliminated, even resulting in modest (1–3% shifts) in Body Mass Index across the population, the implications for removal of those risk factors for reductions in prevalence of childhood obesity and overweight are profound.

The stakes for combating the obesity epidemic are not just high for health but the economy as well. Obese and overweight children have higher health-care expenditures and are more likely to become obese or overweight as adults, with continued increases in health-care expenditures for comorbidities later in life. Whatever the scheme for insurance in a given country, a portion of the economic burden of childhood obesity is felt as increases in national health expenditures. Shorter life spans also mean reductions in lifetime economic productivity. Indeed, large investments (on the order of $2 billion annually) could be cost-effective even if they produce modest reductions in the prevalence of obesity (one percentage point, from 16.3% to 15.3%), using an example documented from the USA.

While great emphasis in global health rightly remains on human immunodeficiency virus, malaria, and tuberculosis, this text anticipates the rising need for increased attention to a major epidemic that may well wash out hard-fought gains in health and economic productivity for decades to come. Ministries in industrializing nations that take heed will reap great rewards for their nations if they take proactive steps to intercede before environmental and other factors reproduce the epidemic that has wrought havoc in the industrialized world.

Mixed Messages in Health Promotion

Brian W. McCrindle, M.D., MPH, FRCP(C) is a Professor in the Department of Pediatrics at The Hospital for Sick Children, University of Toronto, Toronto, Ontario, Canada. Dr. McCrindle has a strong interest in outcomes research and is a key member of the Data Center Research Team. His research interests include clinical aspects of lipid disorders and cardiovascular risk factors assessment and intervention and clinical trials as well as the psychosocial, neurodevelopmental and quality of life aspects relevant to pediatric cardiology.

Childhood obesity and its associated toll on mental health and social functioning are immediate factors influencing the healthy development of the youth worldwide and achievement of functional health and quality of life into adulthood. From this perspective, childhood obesity represents a symptom of a number of "societal ills" directed at a very vulnerable population. Foremost is the manipulation of innate and acquired physiologic and psychologic drivers for consumption and dependence leading to profit, at the expense of health and well-being. Industry marketing firms know a great deal more than health promotion experts about influencing behavior and consumption, and have enormous resources and an intense drive to achieve maximal profits. Current strategies to address childhood obesity with interventions aimed at changing individual behavior in the face of an obesogenic environment are unlikely to succeed, unless that behavior change also prompts paradigm-shifting changes in market forces and policy that influence that environment and protect our youth.

Pediatric metabolic syndrome represents the dominant physical morbidity associated with childhood obesity and is the primary point of engagement with the health-care system. However, current evidence suggests that health-care providers lack sufficient knowledge and skills to initiate discussion and effective counseling in practice. There is a general pessimism regarding effectiveness, and reluctance to engage with limited time and resources. As a result, overweight and obesity go unrecognized and unaddressed for the majority of the youth, unless specific adiposity-related morbidities become clinically evident. Assessment and management is then often focused on the specific morbidity, with little progress made regarding reductions in adiposity.

Rarely acknowledged, studied, and addressed are the mixed messages regarding health promotion given by the health-care system. Both health-care providers and health-care institutions have been subjected to the same market drivers influencing the childhood obesity epidemic. As a result, neither have been effective role models for health, which influences their enthusiasm for engagement and the public's perception of that engagement. Health-care providers often are no healthier than their patients. Early studies of cohorts of male physicians and female nurses were the first studies to show associations between obesity and cardiovascular disease. Recent surveys of pediatricians that have included self-reported height and weight have shown similar levels of overweight and obesity to that in the general population, with similar patterns of health behaviors with the exception of lower rates of smoking. There have been some gradual improvements. A health-care provider's personal health and health behavior have not only been shown to influence if and how they counsel their patients regarding healthy lifestyle, but also how their patients perceive the effectiveness of that counseling. Surveys of pediatric health-care institutions have found a high proportion with fast-food franchises and a plethora of vending machines on site, with some dependence on the income generated. Studies have shown that having these products and associated marketing within hospitals gives families and staff the impression that the products are healthy.

Clearly, any solution to childhood obesity must be complex, intensive, and system-wide. The health-care system is but one component, but a critical component. Health-care providers need to take ownership of their obligations as role models for health and health behavior, but to also recognize that just because they have expert knowledge about health does not necessarily lessen the challenge of making personal health behavior change. We need to be sympathetic and supportive to our peers, who are also challenged with living in an obesogenic environment and also susceptible to the same psychologic and physiologic drivers. Health-care institutions need to take ownership for the messages they are sending, and develop effective policy and action to provide environments that support health and health behavior. In the face of the childhood obesity epidemic, the proverb "Physician, heal thyself" rings truer than ever.

Reasons to Invest in the Health of Our Nation's Youth

Ann M. Veneman, B.A., M.A., JD is the immediate past Executive Director of UNICEF, a position she held from her appointment by the United Nations Secretary General in May 2005 until April 2010. As Executive Director, Ms. Veneman worked on behalf of the United Nations children's agency to help children around the world by advocating for and protecting their rights. Prior to joining UNICEF, Ms. Veneman served as Secretary of the U.S. Department of Agriculture (USDA) from 2001 until 2005. She is currently a member of the Bipartisan Policy Center, the only Washington, DC-based think tank that actively promotes bipartisanship.

This important work addresses a critical health trend among children, the rise of pediatric metabolic syndrome. The prevalence of childhood overweight and obesity is increasing dramatically and is associated with rising incidence of pediatric metabolic syndrome.

Worldwide, obesity rates have more than doubled since 1980. The World Health Organization estimated that globally 1.5 billion adults are overweight; 500 million of whom are obese. In the USA, according to the Centers for Disease Control (CDC), 68% of the US population is overweight, with 34% of those meeting the definition of obese. Among children (aged 2–19), approximately one third are overweight, of which 17% are obese. Obesity prevalence among children and adolescents in the USA has almost tripled since 1980, and there are significant racial and ethnic disparities embedded in these numbers.

And, according to *America's Health Rankings*®, if left unchecked or untreated, obesity will affect 43% of adults by 2018 and will add nearly $344 billion in that year alone to the nation's annual direct health-care costs, accounting for more than 21% of health-care spending.

Childhood obesity is associated with a higher chance of premature death and disability in adulthood. In addition to increased future risks, obese children experience breathing difficulties, increased risk of fractures, hypertension, and early markers of cardiovascular disease, insulin resistance and psychological effects.

Obese children are more likely to become obese adults. For example, one study found that 80% of children who are overweight between the ages of 10–15 were obese at age 25. And, as this book examines, high obesity rates correspond closely with not just high diabetes rates but a host of other health consequences as well.

There is increasing recognition that the first 1,000 days of a child's life—from conception to age 2—is a critical time for development. The nutrition of the pregnant mother affects development of the child. A child who is malnourished in the first 2 years of life is likely to have reduced cognitive and brain development thereby affecting the ability to learn in school and earn as an adult. This, then, can perpetuate the cycle of poverty. As a means of focusing national and international attention and improving outcomes, some experts are calling for dietary guidelines for this first 1,000-day period.

There is increasing evidence that children who do not receive adequate nutrition early in life risk overweight and obesity later in life, which puts them at greater risk of associated diseases.

The trend toward overweight and obesity is caused by a number of factors—particularly the quality and amount of food consumed and lack of physical activity. There must be a clear focus on wellness strategies to address this health-care crisis.

What the Childhood Obesity Epidemic Means

Michael L. Weitzman, M.D. is a Professor of Pediatrics and Psychiatry at the New York University School of Medicine in New York, New York where he previously served as the Chairman of the Department of Pediatrics. Prior to this, he was the Executive Director of the American Academy of Pediatrics' Center for Child Health Research and Professor and Associate Chair of Pediatrics at the University of Rochester, where he also served as Director of the Division of General Pediatrics and Pediatrician-In-Chief at Rochester General Hospital for 10 years, as well as the Director of the fellowship training programs in Academic General Pediatrics for 15 years. Before that he was Director of Maternal and Child Health for the City of Boston and Director of General Pediatrics and the fellowship training program in Academic General Pediatrics at Boston City Hospital and Boston University.

The childhood obesity epidemic is changing the nature of childhood and child health, healthcare for children, and it has implications for the training and practice of pediatrics and pediatric subspecialists, the organization of health and related services, as well as implications for the health of adults and the practice and cost of healthcare for all. This epidemic may result in the current generation of our children having a shorter lifespan than that of its parents, something that has never before occurred in our history, and will certainly result in a far less healthy adulthood with countless medical burdens.

Much or all of the profound increase in child obesity rates and the rates of its complications, such as the Metabolic Syndrome, are manmade, e.g., the development of fast foods, changes in eating patterns and serving sizes, advertising of calorie and fat dense foods to unwitting children and their parents, the built environment, alterations in family structure and functioning, reduced opportunities for children's unsupervised sports and calorie expenditures, and the ever increasingly sedentary lifestyle of our children due to profound increases in time spent watching television or using computers. Do we have the knowledge and the means to change individual behaviors and the social forces that shape the behaviors that contribute to this epidemic?

Twenty-five years ago, we were in the midst of understanding and beginning to devise and implement strategies to prevent and treat the HIV epidemic. Few, if any at that time, would have anticipated that just several decades later almost a third of our children would be overweight, or that almost half of all new cases of childhood diabetes would be Type II (formerly called "Adult Onset") Diabetes, that a substantial percentage of our children would have hypertension and dangerously high levels of lipids, that we would be facing hepatic, orthopedic and renal complications of obesity among our children, or that there would be serious discussion of considering extreme obesity as a form of child neglect or abuse, with all the ethical, practical, and quality of life implications that such a policy decision would have. No one would have anticipated increased lengths of stay and hospital costs for childhood appendicitis or asthma, or for childbirth because of complications caused by obesity and its countless comorbidities, or of considering bariatric surgery for large numbers of adolescents. We have barely begun to seriously think of how we will care and pay for vastly increased numbers of younger adults who are likely to suffer myocardial infarcts, renal failure, and ophthalmologic complications in early to middle adulthood, or how we will deal with a much larger percentage of young adults unable to be gainfully employed because of obesity-related complications, or the increased rates of depression and anxiety that accompany unemployment and the cascading effect that these alterations in parental mental health have on child development and function—and what about the educational and social implications of social attitudes toward those with obesity, and their own self-esteem and dreams?

Clearly, the childhood epidemic demands a broad-based and urgent effort to prevent and treat obesity and its complications. This requires acquiring and transmitting vast new amounts of knowledge, and the political will and social strategies to use this new information. This volume provides a much needed comprehensive compendium that addresses current knowledge of the biologic, medical, health service, social, psychological and economic consequences of the most common and serious complications of obesity, namely the Metabolic Syndrome. One has reason to hope and believe that it will help clinicians, administrators, policy makers and researchers to better prevent and treat the single most serious public health threat to our children and the adults they will become.

Yes—It Is Worse Than You Think. We Must Act Now

Tia Diaz-Balart is Founder & President of the EcoChamber, a Green "Chamber of Commerce" for Businesses, Non-Profits, Associations, and Governments whose goal is to support the next generation of environmental educationalists and innovators. She is married to the Honorable United States Congressman Mario Diaz-Balart, member of the US House of Representatives representing the 21st District of Florida.

According to an old American Indian proverb, everything we put in our mouths is either medicine or poison. Sadly, children today are being slowly poisoned by the quantity and quality of the foods they eat, as demonstrated by the alarming statistic that nearly 20% of today's kids are obese, up from 6.5% just 30 years ago.

The somber reality is that for the first time in recorded history, children are likely not to live as long as their parents. Our children's health and safety are at acute risk giving rise to long-term health and societal problems of unprecedented proportions.

Childhood obesity imposes severe obstacles on development and normal maturation, growth, and adult health. It often creates a vicious and even worsening cycle of slowing metabolism and decreased physical activity at an ever-increasing spiral.

All of this is accompanied by social and economic handicaps, such as low self-esteem, becoming the target of teasing and bullying, and as adults, having a much harder time competing in the workforce for the best jobs, irrespective of qualifications, thus earning less. Of course, the eventual acute health effects are generally well-known—from heart disease, stroke, type 2 diabetes, cancer, and osteoarthritis, to name a few.

These trends if unabated could eventually overwhelm society and future generations. Burgeoning health-care costs, breakdown of family units unable to support financially or emotionally ill or societally handicapped members, a partially crippled workforce with high absenteeism, and daunting medical costs (making employer provided insurance a dwindling benefit) are just some of the more dramatic future implications from today's clear trends.

But, there is a glimmer, maybe a beacon, of hope. Research being done by The University of Miami Miller School of Medicine Department of Pediatrics as well as other leading institutions, is giving us the road map to get back to a healthier child population since the causes of childhood obesity are now proven to be primarily products of the social environment—not genetic, not intractably biologic or scientifically complex or baffling. From soft drink vending machines being virtually commodities in our Nation's schools, to supersized fat, simple carbs and caloric bombs masquerading as "specials of the day" at many of the country's chain restaurants, virtually all of the problems have appeared in the last generation or two and can be reversed just as quickly, if not faster.

Thanks to recent research, we now know that by simply improving the quality of just one meal a day, children can not only reduce their blood pressure and cholesterol levels but also improve their levels of attention and grades. If these dramatic results can come from just one meal change, imagine what could happen with two or three. We also now know that by educating parents and giving them the tools to change, not only will the health of their child be improved, but the health of the whole family will as well.

The intensive research and hands-on community education provided by these and other world-class leaders are the kind of work it will take to start reversing these statistics and creating a healthier future for our children, country, and even world. This is an urgent issue, and this is a critical issue. It is one upon which we must now act across many fronts but starting right at our own dining table.

Understanding Pediatric Metabolic Syndrome: Current Challenges Facing the Field

Stephen R. Daniels, M.D., Ph.D. is Professor and Chair of the Department of Pediatrics at Children's Hospital, University of Colorado at Denver, Aurora, Colorado. Dr. Daniels' area of expertise is in preventive cardiology. He is interested in the causes of blood pressure elevation and cholesterol abnormalities in children and adolescents, particularly the role that obesity may play in these health issues; development of structural and functional abnormalities in the heart and vascular system, including cardiovascular abnormalities occurring in pediatric patients with diabetes mellitus; as well as the relationship of left ventricular hypertrophy to obesity and hypertension. The role of lifestyle factors, such as diet and physical activity, is central to many of Dr. Daniels' studies.

There is increasing awareness of the worldwide epidemic of obesity in both the medical and lay communities. While the prevalence of overweight and obesity has increased, there also has been an increase in the wide variety of adverse health outcomes associated with obesity. A major concern is the development of what has been called the metabolic syndrome. This is a cluster of factors including central obesity, insulin resistance, inflammation, atherogenic dyslipidemia, and hypertension that result in increased risk of type 2 diabetes and cardiovascular disease. This is an important clinical entity for adults. It has been less clear that it is important for children and adolescents. However, autopsy and other studies have shown that this cluster of risk factors results in accelerated atherosclerosis during childhood and adolescence.

While we have learned much about childhood obesity and the metabolic syndrome, much remains to be learned. It is difficult to know how to make the diagnosis of metabolic syndrome in the pediatric population. While many approaches have been proposed, they all essentially apply a percentile-based classification scheme to the clinical variable believed to be relevant. The proposed approaches for pediatrics are "hand-me-downs" from the adult definitions in that they use the same variables. What is really needed is an outcome-based definition, but this will require more longitudinal data. It will also be important to determine which outcomes are most important. Potential outcomes could include type 2 diabetes, cardiovascular outcomes, such as stroke and myocardial infarction, or the presence of metabolic syndrome in adulthood. In addition, when a continuous clinical variable is dichotomized by a cut point to classify a patient as normal or abnormal, real information is lost. It is never clear whether values just below the cut point are really normal or if those just above are really abnormal. Unfortunately, our clinical approaches often do not embrace continuous variables in a useful way.

We are gaining more information about the utility of using the metabolic syndrome in pediatrics as a predictor of health outcomes in adulthood. It does seem potentially useful for this purpose, at least from an epidemiologic perspective. However, we need more information on how to use the diagnosis of metabolic syndrome in a clinical setting when it is identified. We also need more information on how to respond clinically to the metabolic syndrome. We know that treatment of obesity and improvement in the BMI percentile can have important beneficial effects. We also know how to manage individual cardiovascular disease risk factors to improve risk status. Unfortunately, we do not yet know whether treatment of insulin resistance or inflammation will have an important beneficial effect.

A major question is the stability of the metabolic syndrome during childhood and adolescence. Studies have shown that some children will gain the diagnosis while others will lose it over time. Still other children may gain, lose and then regain the diagnosis even without specific intervention. It is not clear how to interpret these changes.

The metabolic syndrome variables also can be significantly different by race/ethnicity. African-Americans may have higher HDL-C and lower triglycerides compared to Caucasians. On the other hand, African-Americans may have higher blood pressure than Caucasians. Thus, there may be differences in how individuals in certain ethnic groups attain the metabolic syndrome diagnosis. Whether these differences by ethnicity reflect real differences in risk of diabetes and cardiovascular disease remains to be determined.

It is also unclear how broadly to define the metabolic syndrome. Should we include other co-morbidities of obesity, which may be in part related to insulin resistance, such as non-alcoholic fatty liver disease or steatohepatitis? Should we consider other obesity-related conditions, such as obstructive sleep apnea, abnormalities in bones and joints, and renal and cardiac abnormalities as part of the metabolic syndrome complex, or do they have other etiologic pathways and other implications for cardiovascular risk that put them in a different classification?

It seems that the more we learn about obesity and the metabolic syndrome, the more questions we have. Nevertheless, we must continue to study this syndrome and potential clinical interventions as the concern looms that because of obesity and its complications, our current generation of children will have a shorter life span than their parents. We must continue to seek ways to prevent diabetes and improve cardiovascular health beginning early in life, perhaps even in utero.

Adult Cardiovascular Disease Begins in Childhood

Julia Steinberger, M.D., M.S. is a Professor in the Department of Pediatrics, Division of Cardiology at the University of Minnesota Amplatz Children's Hospital Minneapolis, MN. She is the Director of the Pediatric Lipid Clinic at the University of Minnesota, Medical Director of the Pediatric Echocardiography Laboratory at the University of Minnesota Medical Center and Director of Research at the University of Minnesota National Center of Excellence in Women's Health. Dr. Steinberger's research interests are focused on clinical and epidemiologic studies of metabolic syndrome, insulin resistance and cardiovascular risk factors in children and young adults. She currently serves on several committees of the American Heart Association and on expert panels in areas of preventive cardiology.

Studies within the last two decades demonstrate that the process of atherosclerosis begins in early childhood and is strongly associated with various risk factors, including obesity, elevated blood pressure, abnormal serum lipids, and impaired glucose tolerance. The metabolic syndrome, a constellation of these interrelated risk factors, is a frequent subject of attention, discussion, and debate in medical research because of its connections to the growing problem of obesity on the one hand and both diabetes mellitus and cardiovascular disease on the other. It is also grounds for contention, as respected researchers disagree on its definition and even on its validity as a construct. However, the clustering of obesity, dyslipidemia, elevated blood pressure, insulin resistance and impaired glucose metabolism can be seen in children and shows significant longitudinal tracking. Ample evidence accumulated in recent years shows that clinical disease is more prevalent in adults who had elevated risk factors as children.

Since obesity and its metabolic complications occur at a young age and have long-lasting consequences, there are important implications for recognizing those children at risk and performing appropriate screening, so that lifestyle modification and at times medication may be used to reduce future cardiometabolic risk.

Obesity among the North American youth has risen to epidemic levels and is expected to result in costly and burdensome chronic health problems, most notably type 2 diabetes mellitus and premature cardiovascular disease. Failure to reverse these trends may result in significant consequences with respect to health-related quality of life and longevity, as we raise a generation of children whose life expectancy may be shorter than their parents. One cannot over emphasize that prevention should start in the beginning of life with parental education on healthy nutrition, physical activity, and role modeling. In addition to family-based intervention, community and school programs that promote healthy lifestyles are an integral part of successful prevention.

Pediatric Metabolic Syndrome

Arthur S. Agatston, M.D., FACC is an Associate Professor of Medicine at the University of Miami Miller School of Medicine and Director of the Cardiac Prevention Center at Mount Sinai Medical Center in Miami, Florida. Dr. Agatston's pioneering work in noninvasive cardiac imaging has resulted in computed tomography scanning methods and measures for screening coronary calcium that continue to bear his name. In 2004, Dr. Agatston founded The Agatston Research Foundation for the purpose of conducting and funding original research on diet, cardiac and disease prevention. His goal is to educate and empower both his patients and the public about healthy lifestyle choices and disease prevention, encouraging the practice of such prevention in America and throughout the world. The Agatston Research Foundation supported the research of school-based obesity prevention efforts in the State of Florida and around the United States. In addition, Dr. Agatston is founder of the South Beach Diet and maintains a full-time cardiology practice in Miami Beach.

As an adult cardiologist, you might wonder why I have become concerned about pediatric metabolic syndrome. The answer is that it has become clear to me that there is no more important issue for the future health of our country—from both the chronic disease and economic perspective.

The impact of pediatric metabolic syndrome on the adult population is already becoming apparent. Death from coronary artery disease has been on a downward trend since the 1960s, even as we have been experiencing a continuing epidemic of obesity, metabolic syndrome, and type 2 diabetes [27]. This decline has been attributed to a decrease in the incidence of smoking in the at-risk population, as well as to tremendous strides in pharmacologic treatment of high blood pressure, lipid abnormalities, and other cardiac risk factors. Better treatment of patients with myocardial infarction has led to much longer survival during and after the acute event [28].

But an interesting and disturbing new trend has become apparent. While overall mortality from coronary disease continues to decline, in the youngest relevant adult age groups—those between 35 and 44—the downward trajectory has plateaued and may now be turning upward [27]. In a post mortem study performed in 425 individuals who died from traumatic non cardiac causes in Olmstead County from 1981 to 2004 and between the ages of 16 and 64, coronary atherosclerosis was quantified. It showed that over the last 8 years of the study and especially in the younger age groups there was an *increase* in coronary atherosclerosis [27]. Those young adults, represent the age groups that constitute the first generations heavily exposed to our fast-food, sedentary culture during their childhood and adolescent years. These facts suggest that our toxic lifestyle is in fact trumping our advances in medical science. This has led some epidemiologist to predict that for the first time, we are looking at a decrease in longevity [29].

Pediatric metabolic syndrome is, as you will read, the medical manifestation of our fast food, sedentary habits beginning in childhood. The association of pediatric metabolic syndrome with atherosclerosis in the young [30], and its value as a predictor for preclinical and clinical disease in adults [31], is further proof that when it comes to coronary disease, we are sitting on a ticking time bomb.

Another unfortunate relationship has become apparent that also does not bode well for our future health. The metabolic "stew" that comprises the pediatric metabolic syndrome is associated with disease far beyond the vascular system. It affects just about every organ system, including the kidneys, liver, lungs, bones, and brain, as is well documented in this book. It also is a risk factor for cancer and infectious disease, which is why a large prospective study of type 2 diabetes showed it to be a predictor of all-cause mortality [32].

Currently, our obesity epidemic shows no sign of abating [33], and since we are rapidly exporting our fast-food, sedentary lifestyle around the world, the impact of pediatric metabolic syndrome is being felt well beyond our shores. Therefore, if we do not better understand and treat pediatric metabolic syndrome, we can expect a volume of chronic disease that will simply overwhelm our health-care systems both here and abroad. This is why this outstanding text is so timely and important.

The Relation of Pediatric Metabolic Syndrome to the Prevalence and Consequences of Fatty Liver Disease

Joel E. Lavine, Ph.D., M.D. is Chief of Gastroenterology, Hepatology and Nutrition at New York-Presbyterian Morgan Stanley Children's Hospital in New York, New York. Dr. Lavine is also on the faculty of Columbia University College of Physicians and Surgeons. Dr. Lavine has devoted his career to helping children with acute and chronic liver diseases. A noted clinician-scientist, his research focuses on fatty liver disease and viral hepatitis in children. Dr. Lavine is a National Institutes of Health-National Institute of Diabetes and Digestive and Kidney Disease (NIDDK) and NICHD Principal Investigator for a national, seven-year study on fatty liver disease in children and adults. Dr. Lavine serves on the Executive Committee and Chairs the Steering and Pediatric Committees for the national multi-center network.

Many gourmands of French fare are fond of foie gras, a delicacy that literally means "fatty liver." This expensive appetizer requires a great deal of preparation since confined geese are gavage fed high-calorie, high-fat diets over a few weeks prior to harvest. This force-feeding results in massive and diffuse fat accumulation in the liver, rendering the liver a buttery yellow consistency and color. In children, the equivalent of *foie gras* has become increasingly prevalent over the past three decades with modern diets that are high in calories, fat and refined sugar in children increasingly less active.

Fatty liver in children, albeit not a defined component of the metabolic syndrome, is nonetheless a frequent but uncommonly mentioned concomitant in children with obesity and metabolic syndrome. In fact, it may be a major and independent player in the etiopathogenesis of insulin resistance. Although it is difficult to ascertain its prevalence accurately due to the need for imperfect surrogate markers in population-based studies, it is likely that nearly 10% of American children have fatty liver disease. This disease, which appears microscopically similar to alcoholic liver, is termed nonalcoholic fatty liver disease (NAFLD) because in children it is unlikely that alcohol plays any role. A subset of children with NAFLD (40–60%) develops more severe liver problems in addition to fat accumulation. This subset has nonalcoholic steatohepatitis (NASH), characterized by hepatic inflammation, cell injury and scarring. The natural history of children with NASH is not yet well characterized, but if they behave like adults with NASH, a fifth will go on to develop cirrhosis of the liver after a decade or more. This predisposes to liver cancer. Indeed, indications for liver transplant in adults with NASH related end-stage liver disease has risen more than seven-fold in the past decade alone.

Heredity imparts susceptibility to fat accumulation in the liver in children and their relatives when controlled for body mass index, gender, age and ethnicity. Genotyping for certain variants shows that certain loci confer susceptibility. However, the rapid increase in prevalence over a few decades prompts identification of more concerning environmental adjuvants that may be modifiable.

Lifestyle intervention has been shown to improve NAFLD and NASH, although these interventions are difficult to implement and maintain. Lifestyle interventions also treat the accompanying co-morbidities of metabolic syndrome in many instances. For NASH, this includes loss of more than 10% of body weight in those who are overweight, achieved by a combination of decreased calories, less fat calories, elimination of refined carbohydrates (particularly fructose additives), and eating foods with more antioxidants. For those unable, unwilling, or unresponsive to such measures, recent randomized controlled trials demonstrate the statistically significant utility of supplemental vitamin E in improving NASH histology.

Metabolic syndrome is a burgeoning correlate of the global obesity epidemic. The current health burden is worrisome and the yet unfolding consequences are alarming. The hepatic manifestation of metabolic syndrome (NASH) in children will result in yet unrecognized and largely untreatable problems of cirrhosis, liver cancer and transplantation in these children in the years ahead.

The AHA 2020 Goal to Improve Cardiovascular Health: Starting with Children

Ralph L. Sacco, M.D., M.S. is Professor and Chairman of the Department of Neurology with additional faculty appointments in the Departments of Epidemiology and Public Health, Human Genetics and Neurosurgery at the University of Miami Miller School of Medicine in Miami, Florida. He is also the Chief of Neurology Service at Jackson Memorial Hospital in Miami, FL. Additionally, Dr. Sacco is the immediate past President of the American Heart Association. In 2007, he received the association's Chairman's Award for his pioneering role in Power To End Stroke, an initiative to heighten awareness of stroke risk among African Americans. He also is past chair of the association's Stroke Advisory Committee (2005–08) and was lead author of the 2006 publication, Guidelines for Prevention of Stroke in Patients with Ischemic Stroke or Transient Ischemic Attack. During his tenure as AHA President he stated "This is an exciting time to be involved with the American Heart Association. We are taking a bold approach to preventing cardiovascular diseases through our new initiatives and strategic plan for the coming decade. Our 2020 goal is to improve the cardiovascular health of all Americans by 20 percent, as well as continue to reduce death from cardiovascular diseases and stroke by 20 percent. Most of my professional life has been focused on preventing these illnesses, so I am really excited to be playing a leading role as the AHA takes on this ambitious goal."

The number of Americans with cardiovascular disease and stroke has grown to an alarming 81 and 6 million and they comprise 2 of the top 3 leading causes of mortality [34]. Over the last decade, mortality from heart disease declined by 36% and for stroke by 33% [35]. Major gains were made in the control of several cardiovascular risk factors with a 28% reduction in hypertension, a 22% reduction in uncontrolled cholesterol, and a 20% reduction in the prevalence of smoking. Despite these improvements, there are some major public health concerns regarding the much less successful control of physical activity, and an alarming rise of obesity and diabetes. Current cost estimates are that cardiovascular diseases and stroke are responsible for 17% of national health expenditures. Costs are projected to triple by 2030 when more than 40% of US adults, or 116 million people, will have one or more forms of cardiovascular disease [36].

The 2020 impact goal of the American Heart Association is to improve the cardiovascular health of all Americans by 20% while reducing deaths from cardiovascular diseases and stroke by 20% [35, 37]. A greater focus has been placed on promoting ideal health rather than avoiding disease. The goal has shifted toward a comprehensive entity of ideal cardiovascular health, composed of seven ideal factors. "Life's Simple 7" is a combination of ideal health behaviors and vascular health factors: non-smoking, and ideal physical activity, body mass index (BMI), diet, blood pressure, untreated total cholesterol, and fasting glucose. These health factors have all been shown to have independent contributions to cardiovascular health.

Many of these less than ideal health factors are embodied in the definition of the metabolic syndrome which is an increasingly recognized important precursor to diabetes, cardiovascular disease and stroke and is occurring more frequently among children [38]. This comprehensive and timely book titled "Pediatric Metabolic Syndrome: Comprehensive Clinical Review and Related Health Issues" reviews the evidence related to the causes and consequences of childhood obesity, and in particular the metabolic syndrome.

To achieve the AHA 2020 goal, it is understood that intensive programs will have to start as early as possible and must involve children. Currently, half of US children ages 12–19 years meet 4 or fewer criteria for the AHA definition of ideal cardiovascular health [34]. Childhood obesity has reached epidemic proportions in the USA, even among our infants and toddlers. In 2007–08, over 1 in 5 preschool children ages 2–5 were overweight or obese and the percentage of obese children ages 2–5 years increased more than 30% from 2001 to 2004 [39, 40]. Moreover, among children 12–19 years, 18% are obese and 56% do not meet the AHA ideal level of physical activity [34]. Substantial race and ethnic disparities have long been reported for cardiovascular disease and stroke, and are mirrored in the higher rates of childhood obesity and physical inactivity among American Indian, Hispanic, African American, and low-income children.

Early interventions starting in childhood is the perfect time to start encouraging healthy lifestyles including ideal diet and physical activity behaviors. Some studies have suggested that the propensity for obesity may even occur before age 2, when the child is learning how much and what to eat suggesting that interventions as early in life as possible may be critical in reversing the childhood obesity epidemic [41]. The AHA is working on programs to target children, reducing childhood obesity by limiting access to sugar-sweetened beverages, enhancing knowledge about healthy diets and fresh fruits and vegetables, and advocating for more physical activity in schools and communities. Creating positive habits and developing healthy patterns as early as possible among children may be our best hope to prevent childhood obesity and pediatric metabolic syndrome and avert the future cardiovascular disease crisis.

Pediatric Metabolic Syndrome: Comprehensive Clinical Review and Related Health Issues

Matthew W. Gillman, M.D., SM is a Professor in the Department of Population Medicine at the Harvard Medical School, Harvard Pilgrim Health Care Institute and a Professor in the Department of Nutrition at the Harvard School of Public Health in Boston, Massachusetts. Additionally he is the Director of the Obesity Prevention Program in the Department of Ambulatory Care and Prevention Harvard Medical School, Harvard Pilgrim Health Care. Dr. Gillman's current research interests are early life prevention of adult chronic disease, optimal nutrition for children and adults, and clinical epidemiology. He directs an NIH-funded cohort study of pregnant women and their offspring, focusing on effects of gestational diet on outcomes of pregnancy and childhood. He also directs a behavior change intervention to prevent obesity among preschool children, and he participates in several other federally-funded studies of diet, activity, obesity, and disease risk in children and adults.

Rates of childhood obesity are mushrooming across the world. While obesity rates in the USA and some other developed countries may have leveled off, especially within more privileged population subgroups, the prevalence remains disturbingly high. Further, racial/ethnic disparities abound in the USA, and obesity is becoming a major public health issue in low- and middle-income countries.

With obesity, especially visceral obesity, comes a constellation of abnormalities that includes insulin resistance and sometimes glucose intolerance, high blood pressure, and dyslipidemia comprising high triglyceride and low HDL-cholesterol levels. Together these abnormalities make up the metabolic syndrome. A lot of ink has gone into defining the metabolic syndrome in children and adolescents, focusing primarily on choosing threshold cut points for each of the criteria, and the number of "failed" criteria to qualify for the syndrome. This is an important exercise for clinicians, who need diagnostic clarity, and who will rightly ask whether the syndrome confers any additional prognostic value over and above the simpler measure body mass index, or BMI plus one or more of the syndrome's components. The most important issues for scientific investigation and public health, however, do not depend on the exact definition. They include questions like

- What adverse health outcomes does the pediatric metabolic syndrome predict?
- Do one or more components predict an outcome better than the other components do?
- What are the mechanisms of these observed phenomena?
- Can we target therapies to the pediatric metabolic syndrome or its components, beyond weight loss?
- What are the etiologies of pediatric metabolic syndrome?
- What are the best ways of preventing pediatric metabolic syndrome?

The chapters of this book address these questions. Five of the ten leading causes of death in the USA—heart disease, cancer, stroke, diabetes, and kidney disease—are plausible long-term consequences of the pediatric metabolic syndrome. Worldwide, similar non-communicable diseases are becoming the leading causes of death and disability. Hyperinsulinemia, insulin resistance, hypertension, and atherogenic lipid profiles play greater or lesser roles in the pathogenesis of each of these conditions. We know that obesity is the leading preventable cause of these risk factors and their ultimate consequences. The end game of lessening the burden of pediatric metabolic syndrome will surely involve preventing childhood obesity, including starting early in life when behaviors and physiology are most plastic. The most effective and cost-effective ways of achieving this goal are still elusive.

Pediatric Metabolic Syndrome

Andrew N. Redington, M.B.B.S., MRCP(UK), M.D., FRCP(UK), FRCP(C) is the Division Head of Cardiology at the Hospital for Sick Children in Toronto, Canada. Additionally he is a Professor of Pediatrics at the University of Toronto in Toronto, Canada. Dr. Redington's research interests include ventricular function and cardiopulmonary physiology, mechano-electric interactions in congenital heart disease, and the pathophysiology of late postoperative functional decline. Dr. Reddington's current research interests are in two major areas: the non-invasive assessment of myocardial contractility using tissue Doppler techniques, and the use of a novel remote ischemic pre-conditioning protocol to protect the myocardium and other organs from the ischemic insult of cardiopulmonary bypass and ischemia re-perfusion injury.

As someone that does not specialize in the field, I come to write this commentary very much as an observer of, rather than a participant in, the care of children with obesity and its secondary effects. Indeed, as I gathered my thoughts prior to penning this brief vignette, I thought I would be discussing the role of (or perhaps arguing the inappropriateness of) the specialist pediatric cardiologists in the management of childhood obesity.

But I was thrown a curveball this morning. As I sat with my morning coffee, and as is my routine early on a Sunday morning, I opened the website of my favorite British Sunday newspaper. The front page news was prescient *"Your children are too fat – you will never see them again: Nightmare of parents of seven whose four youngest will be put up for adoption."* (http://www.mailonsunday.co.uk/news/article-2033486/your-children-fat-again.html). This article describes the potential fate of the obese children of a family in the UK. In the first of its type, social services are taking the parents to the high court, threatening to remove, without further contact, four of the seven children from their family because of their ongoing obesity. Social services argue that the inability of their parents to manage their children's weight, despite years of advice, education and support, is akin to child abuse. At first I was outraged, but would I have been as outraged if the same parents had been starving their children and causing them equally damaging physical harm?

Obesity, then, appears to have transcended issues of medicine, perhaps even issues of societal responsibility, and has become a legal one. The vox pop responses from the readers of this article were equally thought provoking. Aggressive animosity toward the parents prevailed (it is their fault not the children's), but others blame the media, the advertisers, the fast-food industry, and a pantheon of usual suspects. Many do target the children however, "why should we pay for the care of these kids when they should just eat less." This response is not uncommon when the costs of adult obesity to the health-care system are discussed….for example, who should pay for gastric bands in a socialized health-care system, the patient or the system? The argument goes that the obese adult has made the choice to become obese, so why should the system pay for it. But where does such an argument stop, do we not treat victims of road traffic accidents because they chose to drink and drive, or refuse therapy to smokers with lung cancer?

A significant minority places the blame at the door of schools, government, and even the medical profession itself. The 'blame game' is, of course, the stuff of tabloid news and is usually irrelevant to the matter at hand. No individual, group, or agency is to "blame" for pediatric obesity. We all have a collective responsibility for the epidemic of childhood and adult obesity. Just as it has evolved as a societal issue, it will need to be resolved as one also. Governments, advocacy groups, healthcare workers, parents and children will need to be engaged in a process to reverse these worldwide trends.

This brings me back to what I thought I would be writing about. Such is the enormity of the problem, an individual pediatric cardiologist, or indeed the entire community of pediatric cardiologists, or the entire community of health-care professionals dealing with childhood obesity, cannot solve the problem alone. But we each can contribute by our example, our science, or our advocacy. As such, this book "Pediatric metabolic syndrome: Comprehensive clinical review and related health issues" is not only a tremendous description of the state of the art, but also a timely wake-up call that addresses one of today's biggest issues in world health.

The Health and Economic Urgency of the Pediatric Metabolic Syndrome

Leonardo Trasande, M.D., M.P.P. is an Associate Professor of Pediatrics, Environmental Medicine and Health Policy at New York University in New York, NY. Dr. Trasande published a series of studies which document increases in hospitalizations associated with childhood obesity and increases in medical expenditures associated with being obese or overweight in childhood, cited in the President Obama's 'White House Task Force on Childhood Obesity'.

Obesity is now epidemic among children in most of the industrialized world. While estimates vary by country and definition, increases in Body Mass Index have been detected across all ages, and even to the preschool years. The waves of this epidemic are now surging to the industrializing countries as well, such that globally 9.1% of preschool children will be overweight or obese by World Health Organization norms by 2020, a doubling since 1990.

The future consequences for health in the twenty-first century are disheartening. Diabetes, hypertension and the metabolic syndrome are phrases commonly used by all child health providers now. During this author's own pediatric residency, type II diabetes was still thought to be an adult disease, though hospitalizations for new onset diabetics were already and alarmingly on the rise. In the USA, hard-fought increases in life expectancy are now slipping away. Myocardial infarctions in the fourth decade may reemerge as common events the way they did in the 1940s and 1950s.

The adult epidemic of cardiovascular disease was so swiftly overcome through identification of preventable risk factors, largely through the Framingham Heart Study, a large-scale longitudinal study of health in one Massachusetts community. Presently, it is well understood that childhood obesity is different and potentially more complex in its origins. Diet and physical activity in childhood remain leading suspected causes, but changing community structures and exposures to synthetic chemicals that may disrupt energy balance are also thought to have produced increases in unhealthy weights in children out of proportion to their heights.

Scientific knowledge will go far to improve upon interventions to improve nutritional balance and future cardiovascular health, as those interventions to date which have endeavored to prevent obesity before it occurs have achieved success only fleetingly, if at all. If implemented in the originally proposed and robust fashion across a population of 100,000 children, the National Children's Study has the potential to achieve similar gains in children's health to the Framingham Heart Study.

Yet the hidden secrets to the success in decreasing cardiovascular morbidity and mortality through the past three decades lie not only in individual interventions but also in the political will to implement regulation and legislation that limited harmful exposures. Pharmacotherapy and more intensive management by generalists and specialists no doubt were crucial, but reduction in tobacco smoke exposure and changes toward healthier diet should also be credited in part to policy activity, despite the long lag that sometimes followed strong and sound science that suggested the need for intervention.

Fortunately, we are now seeing greater attention and proactive effort by child health-care providers to identify and treat obesity-associated comorbidities in childhood. Unfortunately, the intervention documented to be most effective for reducing weight in extremely obese adolescent remains one fraught with unknown health and other implications—bariatric surgery. While these procedures clearly have their place, they represent increasingly common options of last resort.

A similar recipe to that described for adult cardiovascular disease is therefore needed for the childhood obesity epidemic. Policy experiments are being actively pursued, from calorie count posting in restaurants and other eateries to removal of sodas from schools and reemphasis on physical activity during and outside of schools. If chemical factors are identified to be contributors to childhood obesity and eliminated, even resulting in modest (1–3% shifts) in Body Mass Index across the population, the implications for removal of those risk factors for reductions in prevalence of childhood obesity and overweight are profound.

The stakes for combating the obesity epidemic are not just high for health but the economy as well. Obese and overweight children have higher health-care expenditures, and are more likely to be obese or overweight as adults, with continued increases in health-care expenditures for comorbidities later in life. Whatever the scheme for insurance in a given country, a portion of the economic burden of childhood obesity is felt as increases in national health expenditures. Shorter life spans also mean reductions in lifetime economic productivity. Indeed, large investments (on the order of $2 billion annually) could be cost-effective even if they produce modest reductions in the prevalence of obesity (one percentage point, from 16.3% to 15.3%), using an example documented from the USA.

While great emphasis in global health rightly remains on human immunodeficiency virus, malaria and tuberculosis, this text anticipates rising need for increased attention to a major epidemic that may well wash out hard-fought gains in health and economic productivity for decades to come. Ministries in industrializing nations that take heed will reap great rewards for their nations if they take proactive steps to intercede before environmental and other factors reproduce the epidemic that has wrought in the industrialized world.

References

1. Berenson GS. Childhood risk factors predict adult risk associated with subclinical cardiovascular disease. The Bogalusa heart study. Am J Cardiol. 2002;90:3L–7L.
2. Natural history of aortic and coronary atherosclerotic lesions in youth. Findings from the PDAY Study. Pathobiological Determinants of Atherosclerosis in Youth (PDAY) Research Group. Arterioscler Thromb. 1993;13:1291–8. http://atvb.ahajournals.org/content/13/9/1291.long.
3. Gluckman PD, Hanson MA, Cooper C, Thornburg KL. Effect of in utero and early-life conditions on adult health and disease. N Engl J Med. 2008;359:61–73.

4. Chen W, Berenson GS. Metabolic syndrome: definition, and prevalence in children. J Pediatr (Rio J). 2007;83:1–3.
5. Johnson CC, Nicklas TA, Arbeit ML, Harsha DW, Mott DS, Hunter SM, Wattigney W, Berenson GS. Cardiovascular intervention for high-risk families: the heart smart program. South Med J. 1991;84:1305–12.
6. Berenson GS, Srinivasan SR, Fernandez C, Chen W, Xu J. Can adult cardiologists play a role in the prevention of heart disease beginning in childhood? Methodist Debakey Cardiovasc J. 2010;6:4–9.
7. Downey AM, Greensberg JS, Virgilio SJ, Berenson GS. Health promotion model for "Heart Smart": the medical school, university and community. Health Values. 1989;13:31–46.
8. Berenson GS. Cardiovascular health promotion for children: a model for a Parish (county)-wide program (implementation and preliminary results). Prev Cardiol. 2010;13:23–8.
9. Center for Disease Control and Prevention. Overweight children ages 6–17: increased from 6% in 1976–1980 to 17% in 2005–2006. www.cdc.gov/Features/dsOverweightchildren/. Accessed 30 Sept 2009.
10. Trust for America's Health (TFAH). F as in fat: how obesity policies are failing in America, 2009. Washington, DC: Robert Wood Johnson Foundation, Trust for America's Health; 2009.
11. Ogden CL, Carroll MD, Curtin LR, Lamb MM, Flegal KM. Prevalence of high body mass index in US children and adolescents, 2007–2008. JAMA. 2010;303(3):242–9.
12. Olshansky SJ, Passaro DJ, et al. A potential decline in life expectancy in the United States in the 21st century. N Engl J Med. 2005;352(11):1138–45.
13. Nader PR, O'Brien M, et al. Identifying risk for obesity in early childhood. Pediatrics. 2006;118(3):e594–601.
14. Must A, Jacques PF, et al. Long-term morbidity and mortality of overweight adolescents. A follow-up of the Harvard growth study of 1922 to 1935. N Engl J Med. 1992;327(19):1350–5.
15. Barker DJ, Osmond C, et al. Trajectories of growth among children who have coronary events as adults. N Engl J Med. 2005;353(17):1802–9.
16. Leunissen RW, Kerkhof GF, et al. Timing and tempo of first-year rapid growth in relation to cardiovascular and metabolic risk profile in early adulthood. JAMA. 2009;301(21):2234–42.
17. Brown WV, Fujioka K, et al. Obesity: why be concerned? Am J Med. 2009;122(4 Suppl 1):S4–11.
18. Hossain P, Kawar B, et al. Obesity and diabetes in the developing world—a growing challenge. N Engl J Med. 2007;356(3):213–5.
19. Wild S, Roglic G, et al. Global prevalence of diabetes: estimates for the year 2000 and projections for 2030. Diabetes Care. 2004;27(5):1047–53.
20. Surgeon general report on youth violence. 2001. http://www.surgeongeneral.gov/library/youthviolence/sgsummary/summary.htm. Accessed 1 Oct 2011.
21. Seeman T, Gruenewald T, et al. Modeling multisystem biological risk in young adults: the coronary artery risk development in young adults study. Am J Hum Biol. 2010;22(4):463–72.
22. McEwen BS, Seeman T. Protective and damaging effects of mediators of stress. Elaborating and testing the concepts of allostasis and allostatic load. Ann N Y Acad Sci. 1999;896:30–47.
23. Meigs JB, Wilson PW, et al. Prevalence and characteristics of the metabolic syndrome in the San Antonio heart and Framingham offspring studies. Diabetes. 2003;52(8):2160–7.
24. Cook S, Weitzman M, et al. Prevalence of a metabolic syndrome phenotype in adolescents: findings from the third National Health and Nutrition Examination Survey, 1988–1994. Arch Pediatr Adolesc Med. 2003;157(8):821–7.
25. Cruz ML, Goran MI. The metabolic syndrome in children and adolescents. Curr Diab Rep. 2004;4(1):53–62.
26. Cruz ML, Weigensberg MJ, et al. The metabolic syndrome in overweight Hispanic youth and the role of insulin sensitivity. J Clin Endocrinol Metab. 2004;89(1):108–13.
27. Nemetz PN, Roger VL, et al. Recent trends in the prevalence of coronary disease: a population-based autopsy study of nonnatural deaths. Arch Intern Med. 2008;168(3):264–70.

28. Ford ES, Ajani UA, Croft JB, et al. Explaining the decrease in U.S. deaths from coronary disease, 1980–2000. N Engl J Med. 2007;356:2388–98.
29. Olshansky SJ, Passaro DJ, Hershow RC, Layden J, Carnes BA, Brody J, Hayflick L, Butler RN, Allison DB, Ludwig DS. A potential decline in life expectancy in the United States in the 21st century. N Engl J Med. 2005;352:1138–45.
30. Le J, Zhang D, et al. Vascular age is advanced in children with atherosclerosis-promoting risk factors. Circ Cardiovasc Imaging. 2010;3(1):8–14.
31. Berenson GS, Srinivasan SR, et al. Association between multiple cardiovascular risk factors and atherosclerosis in children and young adults: the Bogalusa heart study. N Eng J Med. 1998;338(23):1650–6.
32. Emerging Risk Factors Collaboration, Seshasai SR, et al. Diabetes mellitus, fasting glucose and risk of cause-specific death. N Engl J Med. 2011;364(9):829–41.
33. Centers for Disease Control and Prevention. U.S. Obesity Trends by State, 1985–2009. http://www.cdc.gov/obesity/data/trends.html#State. Accessed 1 Oct 2011.
34. Roger VL, Go AS, Lloyd-Jones DM, American Heart Association Statistics Committee and Stroke Statistics Subcommittee, et al. Heart disease and stroke statistics–2011 update: a report from the American Heart Association. Circulation. 2011;123(4):e18–209.
35. Lloyd-Jones DM, Hong Y, Labarthe D, et al. Setting national goals for cardiovascular health. Circulation. 2010;121:586–613.
36. Heidenreich PA, Trogdon JG, Khavjou OA, American Heart Association Advocacy Coordinating Committee; Stroke Council; Council on Cardiovascular Radiology and Intervention; Council on Clinical Cardiology; Council on Epidemiology and Prevention; Council on Arteriosclerosis; Thrombosis and Vascular Biology; Council on Cardiopulmonary; Critical Care; Perioperative and Resuscitation; Council on Cardiovascular Nursing; Council on the Kidney in Cardiovascular Disease; Council on Cardiovascular Surgery and Anesthesia, and Interdisciplinary Council on Quality of Care and Outcomes Research, et al. Forecasting the future of cardiovascular disease in the United States: a policy statement from the American Heart Association. Circulation. 2011;123(8):933–44.
37. Sacco RL. Achieving ideal cardiovascular and brain health: opportunity amid crisis: presidential address at the American Heart Association 2010 scientific sessions. Circulation. 2011;123(22):2653–7.
38. Boden-Albala B, Sacco RL, Lee HS, et al. Metabolic syndrome and ischemic stroke risk: Northern Manhattan Study. Stroke. 2008;39(1):30–5.
39. Ogden CL, Carroll MD, Curtin LR, et al. Prevalence of high body mass index in US children and adolescents, 2007–08. JAMA. 2010;303(3):242–9.
40. Ogden CL, Carroll MD, Curtin LR, et al. Prevalence of overweight and obesity in the United States, 1999–2004. JAMA. 2006;295(13):1549–55.
41. Harrington JW, Nguyen VQ, Paulson JF, Garland R, Pasquinelli L, Lewis D. Identifying the "tipping point" age for overweight pediatric patients. Clin Pediatr (Phila). 2010;49(7):638–43.

Chapter 2
Epidemiology of the Metabolic Syndrome in Youth: A Population-to-Clinical-Based Perspective

Sarah E. Messiah, Kristopher L. Arheart, and James D. Wilkinson

Abstract Recent studies have reported an association between childhood obesity and the development of a cluster of cardiometabolic disease risk factors characterized by variable combinations of insulin resistance, dyslipidemia, and hypertension, which some have termed metabolic syndrome. In turn, this clustering is associated with the onset of type 2 diabetes and long-term atherosclerotic cardiovascular complications in both childhood and adulthood. In this chapter, we summarize the national prevalence estimates for metabolic syndrome in US youth based on various definitions that employ either a clinical threshold value for each component or a percentile threshold based on some combination of age, sex, and ethnicity. The national estimates are followed by a summary of large, key regional studies. The authors are aware that literally hundreds of small national and international clinical studies have estimated the prevalence of metabolic syndrome in youth, and summarizing them all is beyond the scope of this chapter.

Keywords Epidemiology • Childhood obesity • Metabolic syndrome • Pediatric • Adolescent

---

S.E. Messiah, Ph.D., MPH (✉)
Division of Pediatric Clinical Research, Department of Pediatrics,
University of Miami Miller School of Medicine, Batchelor Children's Research Institute #541,
1580 NW 10th Avenue, Miami, FL 33130, USA
e-mail: smessiah@med.miami.edu

K.L. Arheart, B.S., M.S., EdD
Division of Biostatistics, Department of Epidemiology
and Public Health, University of Miami Miller School of Medicine,
Miami, FL, USA

J.D. Wilkinson, M.D., MPH
Division of Pediatric Clinical Research, Department of Pediatrics,
Leonard M. Miller School of Medicine,
Miami, FL, USA

Introduction

Not too long ago, the terms "metabolic syndrome" and "child" would not have been mentioned in the same sentence. However, an entirely different scenario is rapidly unfolding before our society and our health-care system. Deeply rooted in the current childhood obesity epidemic are both the components of metabolic syndrome (elevated blood pressure and glucose levels, hypertriglyceridemia, low HDL cholesterol levels, and central adiposity) and the syndrome itself (three or more of these components in the same individual). Children are being diagnosed with metabolic syndrome at increasingly younger ages, including some as young as 8 years old [1]. The longer-term consequences of childhood obesity and its metabolic changes are now just starting to emerge [2–4].

Childhood overweight is a major public health problem. Virtually no age group is left unscathed; currently one in four US children *under the age of 5* is overweight [5] (Fig. 2.1). Even more alarming is the fact that the latest US pediatric obesity prevalence estimates for all children ages 2–18 for the first time now included levels of *morbid obesity* (a body mass index percentile for age and sex at or above the 97th percentile), whereas previous reports only included up to the 95th percentile (cutoff for obese) [5]. However, the latest news is that morbidity associated with childhood obesity is occurring at younger ages and is associated with adult diseases, including adult-onset obesity [3], atherosclerotic cardiovascular disease, and diabetes [7–10]. Autopsy results from the Pathobiological Determinants of Atherosclerosis in Youth (PDAY) study and the Bogalusa Heart Study have revealed that the atherosclerotic process begins in childhood, for example [8, 11–14].

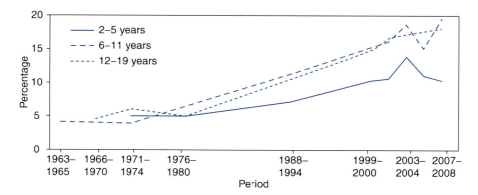

Fig. 2.1 Prevalence of obesity among children and adolescents, by age group, United States, 1963–2008 (Reprinted from Centers for Disease Control and Prevention [6])

Pathophysiology of the Metabolic Syndrome

The concept of metabolic syndrome in childhood can easily diverge into two different and, at times, opposing views. Epidemiologically, the literature indicates quite clearly that this cluster of abnormal risk factors exists in both clinic and population-based samples and is highly prevalent in the obese. However, the pathophysiological view suggests that this association is not so clear. For example, some have questioned the advantage of naming a syndrome that includes several different components. Instead, should each individual risk factor be treated independently? On the other hand, should a different set of criteria be based on racial-ethnic background? The literature consistently shows that certain ethnic groups display elevated risk factors at baseline. Among those children who are overweight or obese, insulin resistance is likely more important than overall adiposity in the development of the syndrome. Therefore, the accumulation of visceral fat, as opposed to subcutaneous abdominal fat, or alternatively, increased ectopic fat, may be important in the pathophysiology of the disorder. For example, Cruz and colleagues [15] report that visceral fat, in addition to total fat, is an important contributor to differences in insulin sensitivity among overweight Hispanic youth with a family history of type 2 diabetes.

Although a consensus has been reached in defining metabolic syndrome in adults [16], controversy nevertheless remains concerning the actual underlying causal factors. Currently, the most accepted hypothesis supported by prospective studies is that obesity and insulin resistance are the key underlying factors in the syndrome [17, 18], and both have been explored in children using both cross-sectional and prospective studies [15, 19] (Fig. 2.2).

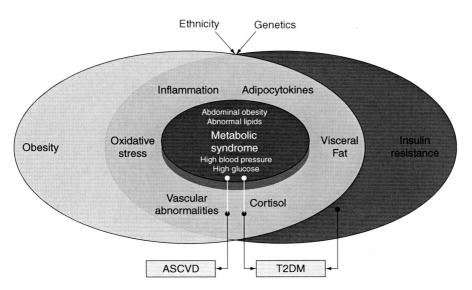

Fig. 2.2 Schematic of components of the metabolic syndrome (Reprinted from Steinberger et al. [16]. With permission from Lippincott Williams & Wilkins)

Controversy Surrounding a Universal Definition

Identifying children who are at risk for metabolic syndrome has remained elusive and as stated above, controversial as well. Because it is a recently emerged syndrome, its validity and purport have been questioned by organizations such as the Federal Drug Administration (FDA) and the American Diabetes Association (ADA) [20]. The most widely accepted opinion is stated in the International Diabetes Federation's (IDF) Joint Interim consensus report, which affirms that all components together are important for risk prediction [21] and that early diagnosis promotes preventative measures [22].

Much of the controversy surrounding the syndrome in children is its definition. Definitions of pathological processes are typically based on endpoints. The difficulty in defining these cardiovascular risk factors in childhood is that most children have not reached the endpoint (atherosclerotic cardiovascular disease) [23–25]. Thus, there is technically no single, widely accepted operational definition of metabolic syndrome in children. This confusion has led to more than 50 different definitions being proposed in the pediatric literature, with the American Heart Association and International Diabetes Federation definitions being used most prominently in the literature.

Many of the pediatric metabolic syndrome definitions are based on a modified adult definition [26] proposed by Cook et al. [25] and include the following components in variation: (1) waist circumference greater than the 90th percentile for age, sex, and ethnicity; (2) a fasting glucose level greater than 100 mg/dL; (3) a blood pressure (systolic or diastolic) greater than the 90th percentile for age and height; (4) fasting triglyceride levels greater than 110 mg/dL; and (5) HDL cholesterol less than 40 mg/dL (Table 2.1). More recently, attention has been paid to the definition published by the IDF in 2007. The report was compiled in Australia by a group of international doctors intending to create a "universally accepted diagnostic tool that is easy to use in clinical practice and that does not rely upon measurement only available in research settings" [22]. Adolescent metabolic syndrome defined by the IDF states that those below ten cannot be diagnosed, those aged 10–16 have specific thresholds for each of the components proposed by Cook, and those above 16 should be diagnosed with same criteria as adults.

The challenge in pediatrics lies in the difficulty of arriving at an appropriate threshold for each risk factor that takes into account age and sex as well as continuous growth, the onset of puberty, and perhaps ethnic background. This challenge has led several groups, including ours [1], to employ percentiles adjusted for age and sex. This approach then raises the issue of what percentile maximizes both sensitivity and specificity and what historical cohort is used to derive these thresholds: one before the current obesity epidemic, perhaps as far back as NHANES I or II, or one that is current and potentially skewed toward higher values?

Table 2.1 Various definitions of metabolic syndrome for children and adolescents

	Cook et al. [25]	De Ferranti et al. [27]	Cruz et al. [15]	Weiss et al. [28]	IDF[b] [22]
Obesity	WC ≥90th percentile (age- and sex-specific, NHANES III)	WC >75th percentile	WC ≥90th percentile (age-, sex-, and race-specific, NHANES III)	BMI–Z score ≥2.0 (age- and sex-specific)	≥90th percentile or adult cut-off if lower
HDL-C	≤40 mg/dL (all ages/sexes, NCEP)	<1.3 mmol/L (<50 mg/dL)	≤10th percentile (age- and sex-specific, NHANES III)	<5th percentile (age-, sex- and race-specific, NGHS)	<1.03 mmol/L (<40 mg/dL)
Blood pressure	≥90th percentile (age-, sex-, and height-specific, NHBPEP)	>90th percentile	>90th percentile (age- and sex-specific, NHANES III)	>95th percentile (age-, sex-, and height-specific, NGHS)	Systolic ≥130, diastolic ≥85 mmHg
Triglycerides	≥110 mg/dL (age-specific, NCEP)	≥1.1 mmol/L (≥100 mg/dL)	≥90th percentile (age-, sex-, and race-specific, NHANES III)	>95th percentile (age-, sex-, and race-specific, NGHS)	≥1.7 mmol/L (≥150 mg/dL)
Glucose	≥110 mg/dL	≥6.1 mmol/L (≥110 mg/dL)	Impaired glucose tolerance (ADA criterion)	Impaired glucose tolerance (ADA criterion)	≥5.6 mmol/L (100 mg/dL)

[a]AHA definition applies to ages 12–19
[b]IDF definition applies only to those aged 10–16; those younger cannot be diagnosed and those older use adult criteria

Ethnicity and the Prevalence of Metabolic Syndrome

The prevalence of obesity remains high among all age and ethnic groups in the USA. However, the prevalence of obesity among African-Americans and Hispanic and Mexican Americans is rising disproportionately (Fig. 2.3). Analysis of NHANES III found that the prevalence of metabolic syndrome varies more specifically between ethnic groups in the USA. The rate was highest among Hispanic (6–13%) and lowest among black adolescents (2–3%), with white adolescents in between 5% to 11% [25, 27]. Smaller clinical studies have estimated the prevalence to be between 4% and 9% in preadolescents and adolescents and also reported higher prevalence rates in minorities than in whites [15, 29, 30].

Few of these studies examined differences in prevalence of MS by race and ethnicity in children younger than 12 however. Although rates of overweight and obesity may vary by ethnicity, it is currently unclear if obesity alone is driving these differences in MS components. If individual MS components vary by ethnic group and are independent of obesity, then these findings could, in turn, be used to target prevention and treatment programs. Collectively, the authors of these studies concluded that the higher prevalence among Hispanic youth can most likely be attributed to their overall higher rates of overweight and obesity. Similarly, studies among US adults have reported that the prevalence of metabolic syndrome is higher among Hispanics (31.9%) and lower among black adults (21.6%) than among white adults (23.8%) [31].

Paradoxically, although the prevalence of obesity among black and non-Hispanic black adolescents in the USA is also high (21%), they tend to have a lower prevalence of the syndrome [25, 32, 33] when a definition similar to that used by the NCEP Adult Treatment Panel III is applied. Some have hypothesized that this paradox may result from the fact that black youth (like adults) have lower triglycerides and higher HDL cholesterol levels than do their white counterparts, even though they have higher blood pressure [32]. These findings suggest that the impact of obesity on the components of metabolic syndrome may vary by ethnic group. Indeed, a recent

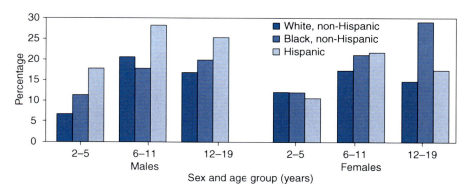

Fig. 2.3 Prevalence of obesity among children and adolescents by sex, age group, and race/ethnicity, United States, 2007–2008 (Reprinted from Centers for Disease Control and Prevention [6])

American Heart Association scientific statement calls for research to determine whether there are racial and ethnic differences in the overall prevalence, mechanisms, and pathways to metabolic syndrome in children and adolescents [16].

Relationship Between Socioeconomic Status and Pediatric Metabolic Syndrome

Limited research has resulted in conflicting views on the association between socioeconomic status and adolescent metabolic syndrome. Initially, childhood overweight, and thus the metabolic syndrome, was considered an issue most heavily concentrated in high-income populations; however, in 2010, over 80% of obese children under 5 were living in developing countries [34] (Fig. 2.4).

One analysis of NHANES 1999–2002 found no correlation between the two [36]. On the other hand, several studies have found an inverse relationship between adolescent SES and adulthood metabolic syndrome in women, even independent of

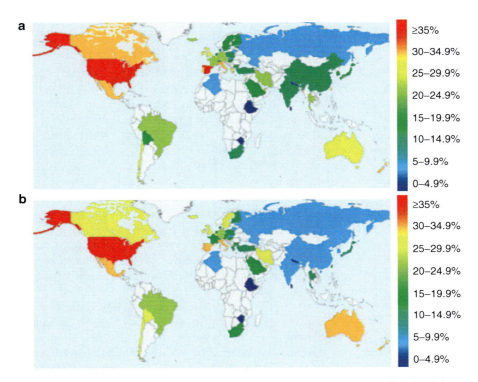

Fig. 2.4 Percent of overweight (**a**) female and (**b**) male children by country (Reprinted from Spruijt-Metz [35]. With permission from John Wiley & Sons, Inc.)

adolescent BMI and blood pressure levels [37]. Women from the lowest childhood social classes are at over twice the risk of having low HDL cholesterol and high waist circumference than from the highest social classes [38]. One reason for this difference is that the social pressure against obesity is stronger amongst those with higher socioeconomic positions, a trend that continues through adolescents [39]. A study of female adolescents in England found that adolescents with a higher SES were more aware of social ideals of "slimness" and used a lower body mass index to define "fat" [40]. Additional tests could reveal that such factors indeed demonstrate an association between SES and pediatric metabolic syndrome.

Another social indicator showing a correlation with adult metabolic syndrome is food security. A study conducted by Parker using data from the NHANES Surveys 1999–2006 found that households with low food security are also more likely to have adults with metabolic syndrome [41]. Interestingly, this same study did not observe an association between pediatric metabolic syndrome and food security. Various reasons were cited, such as potential nutritious food sources at school or parents sacrificing their healthier food for the children.

Population-Based Prevalence Estimates of Pediatric Metabolic Syndrome

The National Health and Nutrition Examination Survey (NHANES) is the primary data source for monitoring the prevalence of overweight and obesity in the USA, as well as all components of metabolic syndrome in those aged 12 and older. Also, since 1960, NHANES anthropometry data has been used to determine obesity levels in the USA [42]. NHANES surveys used a stratified, multistage probability design to capture a representative sample of the civilian non-institutionalized US population. The major objectives of NHANES are: (1) to estimate the number and percent of persons in the US population and designated subgroups with selected diseases and risk factors; (2) to monitor trends in the prevalence, awareness, treatment, and control of selected diseases; (3) to monitor trends in risk behaviors and environmental exposures; (4) to analyze risk factors for selected diseases; (5) to study the relationship between diet, nutrition and health; (6) to explore emerging public health issues and new technologies; (7) to establish a national probability sample of genetic material for future genetic research; and (8) to establish and maintain a national probability sample of baseline information on health and nutritional status.

Although the NHANES III (1988–1994) survey was designed to be nationally representative for either 3 or 6 years of data collection, since 1999 the survey has been conducted bi-annually and since 2007 annually, and is designed to identify annually a nationally representative sample. The NHANES data include demographic, survey, and laboratory information. Demographic and survey information are collected in a home interview, and all laboratory and physical examination data are collected at a medical visit scheduled at a separate time.

One of the unique advantages to using the NHANES data to generate prevalence estimates is the sampling weights created by the National Center for Health Statistics. The purpose of weighting the NHANES sample data is to permit the analysis of estimates that would have been obtained if the entire sampling frame had been surveyed; in this case, every single child in the USA. Weighting takes into account several features of the surveys: the specific probabilities of selection for the individual domains that were over-sampled (in both the 1999–2000 and 2001–2002 surveys, Mexican Americans and blacks were over-sampled), as well as non-response and differences between the sample and the total population.

NHANES III Prevalence Estimates

The first attempts to estimate the prevalence of metabolic syndrome at a population-based level used the NHANES III data [25]. One group of authors defined metabolic syndrome threshold criteria based on the National Cholesterol Education Program's (NCEP) Adult Treatment Panel III adult definition because these criteria had never before been formally defined or applied in children or adolescents [25]. The authors state that in developing a definition for metabolic syndrome in adolescents [43], they considered reference values from the NCEP Pediatric Panel report [44], the American Diabetes Association's statement on type 2 diabetes in children and adolescents [45], and the updated Task Force report on the diagnosis and management of hypertension in childhood [43], as well as on Adult Treatment Panel III [26].

Youth with a waist circumference at or above the 90th percentile value for age and sex were defined as having abdominal obesity. Elevated systolic or diastolic blood pressures were defined as a value at or above the 90th percentile for age, sex, and height, as defined by the National High Blood Pressure Education Program [43]. The NCEP *Report of the Expert Panel on Blood Cholesterol Levels in Children and Adolescents* [44] was used to establish the criteria for cholesterol level abnormalities. The range of 35–45 mg/dL (0.91–1.16 mmol/L) was given for borderline low HDL cholesterol levels for all sexes and ages. In children aged 10–19 years, a borderline high range for triglyceride levels was given as 90–129 mg/dL (1.02–1.46 mmol/L). Therefore, the midpoint value for HDL cholesterol [≤40 mg/dL (≤1.03 mmol/L)] was used as a 10th percentile value, and the midpoint value for triglycerides [≥110 mg/dL (≥1.24 mmol/L)] was taken as the 90th percentile value for age. The reference value for elevated fasting glucose was taken from the American Diabetes Association guideline of 110 mg/dL or higher (≥6.1 mmol/L) [45].

On the basis of these threshold criteria, these authors estimated that nearly 1 million adolescents aged 12–19 in the USA during the late 1980s and the first half of the 1990s, or about 4% of the population of that age, have signs and symptoms of metabolic syndrome [25]. They also found three or more components of the syndrome in 29% of children classified as overweight by the Centers for Disease Control percentile definition (≥95th percentile), in 7% of at-risk adolescents (between the 85th and 95th percentile of body mass index), and in 0.1% of children with a body mass index (BMI) below the 85th percentile. The prevalence of one and two components of the syndrome was 41% and 14%, respectively. The most common abnormalities were high triglycerides and low high-density lipoprotein (HDL) cholesterol levels. In contrast, the prevalence of high fasting glucose was relatively low at 1.5%.

A second analysis of the same data set (NHANES III) among the same age group also extrapolated the threshold definition from adult criteria, but it differed slightly. Triglyceride and HDL thresholds were taken from equivalent pediatric percentiles [46]. This analysis also defined hyperglycemia using the Adult Treatment Panel III threshold but used a different criterion for waist circumference based on the adult threshold of the 70th percentile [47]. As in the previous analysis, the National Heart, Lung, and Blood Institute's National High Blood Pressure Education Program recommended threshold of the 90th percentile for age, sex, and height was used to define elevated systolic or diastolic blood pressure.

This second analysis showed that low HDL, hypertriglyceridemia, and central obesity were common but that elevated blood pressure and glucose were not. The authors reported that 10% of all US children aged 12–19 years and almost one-third of overweight and obese children had metabolic syndrome. Moreover, two-thirds of all adolescents had at least one metabolic component.

The metabolic syndrome definition implemented by the first group used more restrictive lipid and abdominal waist circumference thresholds, which ultimately lead to the lower prevalence estimates in adolescents (4%). Translating their definition into pediatric percentiles, an HDL level of 40 mg/dL represents the 10th to the 25th percentile in boys and the 10th to the 15th percentile in girls, lower than the adult 40th percentile. The higher triglyceride threshold of 110 mg/dL represents the 85th to the 95th pediatric percentile, also higher than the adult 75th to 85th percentile used by the second group. Additionally, the first group used an abdominal circumference threshold of the 90th percentile, whereas the second group used the 75th percentile.

Regardless of their discrepancies in defining metabolic syndrome, these two analyses were the first population-based attempts to identify metabolic syndrome risk in youth. Each analysis indicated that a substantial percentage of US adolescents may be at substantially heightened risk for metabolic syndrome in adulthood and the subsequent risks for type 2 diabetes and premature coronary artery disease, and they ultimately laid the foundation for future NHANES analyses, particularly in light of the obesity epidemic of the last 20–30 years.

Later NHANES Prevalence Estimates

In the time between the publication of the first NHANES III national prevalence estimates and later NHANES samples, namely 1999 and beyond, several smaller clinical studies estimated the prevalence of metabolic syndrome among specific groups of children, such as children in ethnic groups or those who were obese. For example, Cruz et al. [15] showed that 30% of overweight Hispanic youth had metabolic syndrome, Weiss et al. [27] reported that 39% of moderately obese and 50% of severely obese youth had metabolic syndrome, and Goodman et al. [48], using the adult NCEP criteria, and found that 4.2% of adolescents met these criteria.

Analysis of the NHANES 1999–2002 combined data showed that the prevalence of metabolic syndrome among all US 12-to-19-year-olds ranged from 2.0% to 9.4%, depending on the definition used. Among obese adolescents, the prevalence varied from 12.4% to 44.2%. In the group of obese teens, applying the definition by Cruz et al. [15] produced a prevalence of 12.4%, whereas applying a different definition by Caprio [49] produced a rate of 14.1%. None of the normal weight or overweight teens met either definition. Applying the definition by Cook [25] produced a prevalence rate of 7.8% in overweight teens and 44% in obese teens. The adult definition of metabolic syndrome produced a prevalence rate of 16% in overweight teens and 26% in obese teens.

More recently, an analysis of the NHANES 1999–2006 combined data estimating the prevalence of metabolic syndrome among 12-to-19-year-olds [50] used a definition by Ford et al. [51] that included having three or more of the following five characteristics: a waist circumference above the 90th percentile for age and sex according to the 1988–1994 NHANES III data [52]; either a systolic or a diastolic blood pressure in the 90th percentile for height, age, and sex [53]; a triglyceride concentration of 110 mg/dL or greater (to convert to millimoles per liter, multiply by 0.0113); an HDL-cholesterol concentration of 40 mg/dL or less; and a glucose concentration of 100 mg/dL or greater (to convert to millimoles per liter, multiply by 0.0555). The authors reported that 8.6% of the sample had metabolic syndrome, and approximately half of the participants had at least 1 component. Prevalence was higher in boys (10.8%) than in girls (6.1%), and in Hispanic (11.2%) and non-Hispanic white (8.9%) adolescents than in non-Hispanic black adolescents (4.0%). In non-Hispanic black girls, the prevalence of a large waist circumference was high (23.3%), but no one individual component dominated its diagnosis in non-Hispanic blacks of either sex. Elevated waist circumference, abnormal (high) fasting triglyceride levels, and low HDL serum cholesterol concentrations were the most prevalent components in Hispanic and white adolescents of both sexes, whereas elevated glucose concentrations were prominent among Hispanic and non-Hispanic white boys.

Given the ensuing obesity epidemic among increasingly younger children, we analyzed the 1999–2004 NHANES dataset for 8-to-14-year-olds [1]. We compared in our analysis: (1) a crude profile similar to that used in the NHANES III analysis [25] that included single, non-adjusted threshold points to define elevated blood lipids, waist circumference, and blood glucose, and (2) an age-, sex-, and ethnicity-adjusted profile. All individual component threshold values were based on national standardized norms and were similar to those reported by others [54, 55]. We found that the prevalence of metabolic syndrome among children as young as 8 years old ranged from 2% to 9%, using two age-, sex-, and ethnicity-adjusted definitions [1]. Using a similar (crude) profile for comparison purposes, we found at least three metabolic syndrome components in 9% of 12-to-14-year-olds (about twice the 4% reported by Cook et al. [25]) and in 44% of those who are overweight (again, about twice the 29% reported by Cook). This relative doubling of the prevalence of obesity and overweight in the past 10 years has been reported elsewhere [56–58], yet few have reported associated cardiovascular disease risk factors, particularly in large numbers of 8-to-11-year-olds. Regrettably, our data showed that the prevalence of overweight in the younger children was similar to that of the older children.

Our higher prevalence rates may be the result of classification differences; namely, our use of the 75th percentile as a threshold for waist circumference for the adjusted profile rather than the 90th percentile as used in other studies [25]. Interestingly, the authors [52] who generated the standardized waist circumference threshold values for the US pediatric population that we used stated "Based on these values, the careful attention to children and adolescents with waist circumference values that fall on the 75th and 90th percentile, according to their ethnic classification and sex, becomes important in the identification—and prevention—of children at risk for various comorbidities, including cardiovascular disease, hyperinsulinemia, and type 2 diabetes [59]." On the basis of their recommendations, on previous authors' [27] use of the 75th percentile as a threshold for waist circumference, and on the probability that these current 75th percentile values are similar to those of the 90th percentile only 20 years ago as a result of the current obesity epidemic, our goal with this work was to help move the field forward by presenting an analysis that differed from previous studies yet still addressed the lack of a consensus for a definition of metabolic syndrome in children.

Other Regional-Based Sample Estimates

As stated above, describing the smaller clinic-based prevalence estimates of metabolic syndrome in children and adolescents is beyond the scope of this chapter. This issue becomes more complicated given the large number of definitions of the syndrome[60]. A recent exhaustive literature review on the pediatric definitions of the syndrome found at least 27 articles with 46 definitions of the syndrome, most of them unique [49, 60]. The following section summarizes a few of the better-known and larger cohort studies in the USA.

The Bogalusa Heart Study [32], a regional, longitudinal study of cardiovascular disease risk factors in black and white children ages 5–17 years old, defined metabolic syndrome as having four components greater than the 75th percentile for age and sex derived from their own population data. Based on this definition, the prevalence of metabolic syndrome was 4% among white children and 3% among black children [33].

Similarly, the Cardiovascular Risk in Young Finns Study [61], another large multicenter study of risk factors for heart disease in children and young adults, found the prevalence to be 4% among children aged 6–18 years old.

Goodman et al. [48] determined the prevalence of metabolic syndrome among adolescents by using definitions from the NCEP's Adult Treatment Panel III and World Health Organization (WHO) guidelines. The WHO definition requires either insulin resistance, hyperglycemia, or known diabetes. In addition to this requirement for WHO-defined metabolic syndrome, two of three other risk factors had to be present: hypertension, dyslipidemia (hypertriglyceridemia or low HDL cholesterol), and central obesity (a high waist circumference, or a BMI≥30). In contrast, to have NCEP-defined metabolic syndrome, three of five possible risk factors had to be present, including hypertension, low HDL cholesterol, hypertriglyceridemia, hyperglycemia, or high waist circumference. Risk-factor thresholds were those used for adults, except in relation to obesity, which was defined by the established and widely used epidemiologic definition in adolescence of a BMI at or above the 95th percentile. The study analyzed a school-based, cross-sectional sample of 1,513 black, white, and Hispanic teenagers who had a fasting morning blood sample drawn and a physical examination. The prevalence of metabolic syndrome was 4.2% by the NCEP definition and 8.4% by the WHO definition. The syndrome was found almost exclusively among obese teens, for whom the prevalence was 20% by the NCEP definition and 39% by the WHO definition.

International Pediatric Metabolic Syndrome Prevalence Estimates

There has been an increased volume of studies focused on adolescent metabolic syndrome internationally, paralleling the global obesity epidemic. According to these studies, prevalence rates for children in Asia remain below those in the USA. Using De Ferranti's definition of pediatric MetS, while 10% of children in the USA suffer from metabolic syndrome, the rate is 6.6% for their Chinese counterparts [62]. Additionally, 2.5% of Korean adolescents between the ages of 12 and 19 suffer from the IDF-defined metabolic syndrome, in contrast to USA's rate of 5.5% [63].

A study conducted in Guangzhou, China suggests that Asian adults generally have a higher body fat percentage than adults in the USA and therefore calls for race-specific percentile cut points [62]. The BIG study, which included samples of children and adolescents in Brazil, Iran, and Germany, identified a variety in the prevalence of the individual components based on respective ethnicities. These findings therefore called for an examination of the role of genetics [64]. Research should eventually help guide pediatric clinical practice by clarifying the predictive value of using an ethnic-specific definition or a "one-definition–fits-all" approach to metabolic syndrome.

Secular Trends in Metabolic Syndrome Throughout the Lifespan

Secular trends and longitudinal studies have shown that cardiometabolic disease risk factors that are present in childhood predict adult disease. The Princeton Lipid Research Clinics Follow-up study showed that over 30 years, the risk for cardiovascular disease was 9 times as high, and that for type 2 diabetes mellitus was 4 times as high, in children with metabolic syndrome than in children without the syndrome, after adjusting for age, sex, ethnicity, and family history [65]. This same study reported that differences between adults with and without metabolic syndrome first occurred at ages 8 and 13 for BMI and at ages 6 and 13 for waist circumference in boys and girls, respectively [2]. The authors concluded that children with BMI and waist circumference values exceeding the established criterion values are at increased risk for the adult metabolic syndrome.

In the Cardiovascular Risk in Young Finns Study, one of the first studies to explore childhood predictors of metabolic syndrome, fasting insulin at baseline was related to the development of the syndrome after a 6-year follow-up of 1,865 children and adolescents 6–18 years old. Baseline insulin concentration was higher in children who subsequently developed metabolic syndrome, lending support to the theory that insulin resistance precedes the development of the syndrome in childhood [52].

More recently, the Bogalusa Heart Study explored the relationship of childhood obesity (as measured by BMI) and insulin resistance (as measured by fasting insulin levels) on the risk of developing metabolic syndrome as an adult [66]. Researchers followed 718 children ages 8–17 at baseline for an average of 11.6 years. They defined metabolic syndrome as having four of the following: a BMI, fasting insulin, systolic or mean arterial blood pressure, and a triglycerides/HDL ratio in the highest quartile for age, sex, ethnicity, and study year. The highest childhood BMI and insulin quartiles were significantly related to the incidence of risk-factor clustering in adulthood. More specifically, children in the top quartile for BMI and insulin versus those in the bottom quartile were 11.7 and 3.6 times, respectively, more likely to develop the clustering of factors that defines metabolic syndrome as adults. A high childhood BMI was significantly associated with adult onset of the syndrome, even after adjusting for childhood insulin levels, suggesting that childhood-onset obesity can predict the development of metabolic syndrome in adulthood.

Despite differences in the definition of metabolic syndrome in the studies reviewed above, overall findings suggest that both obesity and insulin resistance contribute to the development of the syndrome during childhood.

The current epidemic of obesity and increased prevalence of type 2 diabetes mellitus in adolescents with its attendant consequences is a clinical and public health priority because interventions that target cardiometabolic risk in youth are more easily instituted than are those to modify behaviors later, when deleterious health habits are established [44]. However, given the current prevalence of childhood and adolescent obesity, it is unlikely that this major public health problem can be managed solely in clinical settings. Rather, public health strategies must be integrated into home and family, school, and community-based settings. Currently, the USA allocates substantially more resources to the adult obesity epidemic than to preventive strategies among children and adolescents. Clearly, prevention strategies for both age groups must take into account the causal factors of obesity that begin in childhood.

Future Projections

For the first time in decades, the life expectancy of Americans is projected to *decrease* as a consequence of obesity alone [67]. Furthermore, given the current obesity epidemic among adolescents, it is most likely that in a decade, the country will be dealing with a young adult population facing potential chronic disease. Yet, we do not know the potential lifelong consequences of being obese and having metabolic syndrome as a child. Learning more about how eating and physical activity patterns develop through infancy, childhood, and adolescence and how they track into adulthood should improve the effectiveness of obesity prevention strategies and interventions.

Clearly, the current adolescent obesity epidemic, if left to continue on into adulthood, will indirectly affect all Americans because it undoubtedly will take a heavy toll on the health-care system. For example, a December 2004 report from Feinberg School of Medicine at Northwestern University in Chicago found that for men, the total average annual Medicare charges for those not overweight were $7,205, for the overweight $8,390, for the obese $10,128, and for the severely obese $13,674. The total average annual charges for women in the same four categories were, respectively, $6,224, $7,653, $9,612, and $12,342. The annual average Medicare charges for severely obese men were $6,469 *more* than for non-overweight men, and for severely obese women, annual average charges were $5,618 *more* than for women not overweight [68].

Conclusions

The possibility of becoming obese is greater than ever for US children and adolescents. If current prevalence trends continue, our children will grow up to be the most obese generation of adults in US history, faced at increasingly younger ages with the onset of chronic conditions, such as metabolic syndrome, which in turn will lead to chronic and costly outcomes, such as diabetes and cardiovascular disease. However, even more troubling is that before reaching adulthood, as we have clearly shown here, large proportions of overweight and obese children are already experiencing substantial medical effects related to their overweight in the form of metabolic syndrome.

Acknowledgments We are very thankful for the editorial and research assistance of Ms. Cristina Vega.

References

1. Messiah SE, Arheart K, Luke B, Lipshultz SE, Miller TL. Relationship between body mass index and metabolic syndrome risk factors among US 8 to 14 year olds, 1999–2002. J Pediatr. 2008;153(2):215–21.
2. Morrison JA, Friedman LA, Gray-McGuire C. Metabolic syndrome in childhood predicts adult cardiovascular disease 25 years later: the Princeton lipid research clinics follow-up study. Pediatrics. 2007;120(2):340–5.

3. Morrison J, Friedman L, Wang P, Glueck C. Metabolic syndrome in childhood predicts adult metabolic syndrome and type 2 diabetes mellitus 25 to 30 years later. J Pediatr. 2007;152(2): 201–6.
4. Sun SS, Liang R, Huang TT-K, et al. Childhood obesity predicts adult metabolic syndrome: the Fels Longitudinal study. J Pediatr. 2008;152(2):191–200. Epub 2007 Oct 3.
5. Ogden CL, Carroll MD, Flegal KM. High body mass index for age among US children and adolescents, 2003–2006. JAMA. 2008;299(20):2401–5.
6. Centers for Disease Control and Prevention. CDC grand rounds: childhood obesity in the United States. MMWR. 2011;60:42–6.
7. Whitaker R, Wright J, Pepe M, Seidel K, Dietz W. Predicting obesity in young adulthood from childhood and parental obesity. N Engl J Med. 1997;337(13):869–73.
8. Newman III WP, Freedman DS, Voors AW, et al. Relation of serum lipoprotein levels and systolic blood pressure to early atherosclerosis: the Bogalusa heart study. N Engl J Med. 1986;314(3):138–44.
9. Baker J, Olsen L, Sorenson T. Childhood body-mass index and the risk of coronary heart disease in adulthood. N Engl J Med. 2007;357(23):2329–37.
10. Bibbins-Domingo K, Coxson P, Pletcher M, Lightwood J, Goldman L. Adolescent overweight and future coronary heart disease. N Engl J Med. 2007;357(23):2371–9.
11. Duncan GE, Li SM, Zhou XH. Prevalence and trends of a metabolic syndrome phenotype among U.S. Adolescents, 1999–2000. Diabetes Care. 2004;27(10):2438–43.
12. Berenson GS, Srinivasan SR, Bao W, Newman III WP, Tracy RE, Wattigney WA, Bogalusa Heart Study. Association between multiple cardiovascular risk factors and the early development of atherosclerosis. N Engl J Med. 1998;338(23):1650–6.
13. McGill Jr HC, McMahan CA, Zieske AW, Malcom GT, Tracy RE, Strong JP, Pathobiological Determinants of Atherosclerosis in Youth (PDAY) Research Group. Effect of nonlipid risk factors on atherosclerosis in youth with favorable lipoprotein profile. Circulation. 2001; 103(11):1546–50.
14. McGill Jr HC, McMahan CA, Malcolm GT, Oalmann MC, Strong JP. Effects of serum lipoproteins and smoking on atherosclerosis in young men and women. The PDAY Research Group. Pathobiological determinants of atherosclerosis in youth. Arterioscler Thromb Vasc Biol. 1997;17(1):95–106.
15. Cruz ML, Weigensberg MJ, Huang TT, Ball G, Shaibi GQ, Goran MI. The metabolic syndrome in overweight Hispanic youth and the role of insulin sensitivity. J Clin Endocrinol Metab. 2004;89:108–13.
16. Steinberger J, Daniels SR, Eckel RH, et al. Progress and challenges in metabolic syndrome in children and adolescents. A Scientific Statement from the American Heart Association Atherosclerosis, Hypertension, and Obesity in the Young Committee of the Council on Cardiovascular Disease in the Young; Council on Cardiovascular Nursing; and Council on Nutrition, Physical Activity, and Metabolism. Circulation. 2009;119(4):628–47. Epub 2009 Jan 12.
17. Reaven GM. Relationship between insulin resistance and hypertension. Diabetes Care. 1991;14 Suppl 4:33–8.
18. Reaven GM. Dietary therapy for non-insulin-dependent diabetes mellitus. N Engl J Med. 1998;319(13):862–4.
19. Sinaiko AR, Jacobs Jr DR, Steinberger J, et al. Insulin resistance syndrome in childhood: associations of the euglycemic insulin clamp and fasting insulin with fatness and other risk factors. J Pediatr. 2001;139(5):700–7.
20. Food and Drug Administration. Draft guidance for industry developing products for weight management. Washington, D.C.: U.S. Department of Health and Human Services; 2007.
21. Kassi E, Pervanidou P, Kaltsas G, Crousos G. Metabolic syndrome: definitions and controversies. BMC Med. 2011;9:48.
22. Zimmet P, Alberti KGMM, Kaufman F, Tajima N, Silink M, Arslanian S, Wong G, Bennett P, Shaw J, Caprio S, IDF Consensus Group. The metabolic syndrome in children and adolescents – an IDF consensus report. Pediatric Diabetes. 2007;8(5):299–306.

23. Gorter PM, Olijhoeck JK, van der Graf Y, Algra A, Rabelink TJ, Visseren FLJ, SMART Study Group. Prevalence of the metabolic syndrome in patients with coronary heart disease, cerebrovascular disease, peripheral arterial disease or abdominal aortic aneurysm. Atherosclerosis. 2004;173:363–9.
24. Isomaa B, Almgren P, Tuomi T, et al. Cardiovascular morbidity and mortality associated with the metabolic syndrome. Diabetes Care. 2001;24(4):683–9.
25. Cook S, Weitzman M, Auinger P, Nguyen M, Dietz WH. Prevalence of a metabolic syndrome phenotype in adolescents: findings from the third national health and nutrition examination survey, 1988–1994. Arch Pediatr Adolesc Med. 2003;157:821–7.
26. National Institutes of Health. The Third Report of the National Cholesterol Education Program Expert Panel on Detection, Evaluation, and Treatment of High Blood Cholesterol in Adults (Adult Treatment Panel III), NIH Publication 01–3670. Bethesda: National Institutes of Health; 2001.
27. de Ferranti SD, Gauvreau K, Ludwig DS, Neufeld EJ, Newburger JW, Rifai N. Prevalence of the metabolic syndrome in American adolescents: findings from the third national health and nutrition examination survey. Circulation. 2004;110:2494–7.
28. Weiss R, Dziura J, Burgert T, et al. Obesity and the metabolic syndrome in children and adolescents. N Engl J Med. 2004;350:2362–74.
29. Rodriguez-Moran M, Salazar-Vazquez B, Violante R, Guerrero-Romero F. Metabolic syndrome among children and adolescents aged 10–18 years. Diabetes Care. 2004;27:2516–7.
30. Cossrow N, Falkner B. Race/ethnic issues in obesity and obesity-related comorbidities. J Clin Endocrinol Metab. 2004;89(6):2590–4. Review.
31. Ford ES, Giles WH, Dietz WH. Prevalence of the metabolic syndrome among US adults: findings from the third national health and nutrition examination survey. JAMA. 2002;287(3): 356–9.
32. Chen W, Bao W, Begum S, Elkasabany A, Srinivasan SR, Berenson GS. Age-related patterns of the clustering of cardiovascular risk variables of syndrome X from childhood to young adulthood in a population made up of black and white subjects: the Bogalusa Heart Study. Diabetes. 2000;49(6):1042–8.
33. Chen W, Srinivasan SR, Elkasabany A, Berenson GS. Cardiovascular risk factors clustering features of insulin resistance syndrome (syndrome X) in a biracial (black-white) population of children, adolescents, and young adults: the Bogalusa Heart Study. Am J Epidemiol. 1999;150:667–74.
34. World Health Organization. Obesity and overweight. World Health Organization. http://www.who.int/mediacentre/factsheets/fs311/en/index.html. Updated March 2011. Accessed 14 June 2011.
35. Spruijt-Metz D. Etiology, treatment, and prevention of obesity in childhood and adolescence: a decade in review. J Res Adolesc. 2011;21(1):129–52.
36. Loucks EB, Magnusson KT, Cook S, Rehkopf DH, Ford ES, Berkman LF. Socioeconomic position and the metabolic syndrome in early, middle, and late life: evidence from NHANES 1999–2002. Ann Epidemiol. 2007;17(10):782–90.
37. Gustafsson PE, Persson M, Hammarstrom A. Life course origins of the metabolic syndrome in middle-aged women and men: the role of socioeconomic status and metabolic risk factors in adolescence and early adulthood. Ann Epidemiol. 2010;21(2):103–10.
38. Langenberg C, Kuh D, Wadsworth MEJ, Brunner E, Hardy R. Social circumstances and education: life course origins of social inequalities in metabolic risk in a prospective national birth cohort. Am J Public Health. 2006;96(12):2216–21.
39. Senese LC, Almeida ND, Fath AK, Smith BT, Loucks EB. Associations between childhood socioeconomic position and adulthood obesity. Epidemiol Rev. 2009;31:21–51.
40. Wardle J, Robb KA, Johnson F, Griffith J, Power C, Brummer E, et al. Socioeconomic variation in attitudes to eating and weight in female adolescents. Health Psychol. 2004;23(3): 275–82.
41. Parker ED, Widome R, Nettleton JA, Pereira MA. Food security and metabolic syndrome in U.S. Adults and adolescents: findings from the national health and nutrition examination survey, 1999–2006. Ann Epidemiol. 2010;20(5):364–70.

42. Flegal KM, Carroll MD, Ogden CL, Johnson CL. Prevalence and trends in obesity among US adults, 1999–2000. JAMA. 2002;288(14):1723–7.
43. National High Blood Pressure Education Program Working Group on Hypertension Control in Children and Adolescents. Update on the 1987 task force report on high blood pressure in children and adolescents: a working group report from the National High Blood Pressure Education Program. Pediatrics. 1996;98(4 pt 1):649–58.
44. National Cholesterol Education Panel. Report of the expert panel on blood cholesterol levels in children and adolescents, NIH Publication No. 91-2732. Bethesda: National Institutes of Health; 1991.
45. American Diabetes Association. Type 2 diabetes in children and adolescents. Diabetes Care. 2000;23:381–9. doi:10.2337.
46. The Lipid Research Clinics Program Epidemiology Committee. Plasma lipid distributions in selected North Am populations: the Lipid Research Clinics Program Prevalence Study. Circulation. 1979;60:427–39.
47. Zhu S, Wang Z, Heshka S, et al. Waist circumference and obesity-associated risk factors among whites in the third National Health and Nutrition Examination Survey: clinical action thresholds. Am J Clin Nutr. 2002;76:743–9.
48. Goodman E, Daniels SR, Morrison J, Huang B, Dolan LM. Contrasting prevalence of and demographic disparities in the World Health Organization and National Cholesterol Education Program Adult Treatment Panel III definitions of metabolic syndrome among adolescents. J Pediatr. 2004;145:445–51.
49. Caprio S. Definitions and pathophysiology of the metabolic syndrome in obese children and adolescents. Int J Obes (Lond). 2005;29 Suppl 2:S24–5.
50. Johnson WD, Kroon JJ, Greenway FL, Bouchard C, Ryan D, Katzmarzyk PT. Prevalence of risk factors for metabolic syndrome in adolescents: National Health and Nutrition Examination Survey (NHANES), 2001–2006. Arch Pediatr Adolesc Med. 2009;163(4):371–7.
51. Ford ES, Li C, Cook S, Choi HK. Serum concentrations of uric acid and the metabolic syndrome among US children and adolescents. Circulation. 2007;115(19):2526–32.
52. Fernandez JR, Redden DT, Pietrobelli A, Allison DB. Waist circumference percentiles in nationally representative samples of African-American, European-American, and Mexican-American children and adolescents. J Pediatr. 2004;145:439–44.
53. National High Blood Pressure Education Program Working Group on High Blood Pressure in Children and Adolescents. The fourth report on the diagnosis, evaluation, and treatment of high blood pressure in children and adolescents. Pediatrics. 2004;114:555–76.
54. Chi CH, Wang Y, Wilson DM, Robinson TN. Definition of metabolic syndrome in preadolescent girls. J Pediatr. 2006;148:788–92. e2.
55. Freedman DS, Mei Z, Srinivasan SR, Berenson GS, Dietz WH. Cardiovascular risk factors and excess adiposity among overweight children and adolescents: the Bogalusa Heart Study. J Pediatr. 2007;150:12–7. e2.
56. Institute of Medicine. Preventing childhood obesity. Health in the balance. Washington, DC: National Academy Press; 2004.
57. Ogden CL, Carroll MD, Curtin LR, McDowell MA, Tabak CJ, Flegal KM. Prevalence of overweight and obesity in the United States, 1999–2004. JAMA. 2006;295:1549–55.
58. Office of the Surgeon General. The Surgeon General's call to action to prevent and decrease overweight and obesity. Rockville: Public Health Service, Office of the Surgeon General; 2001. Available from: U.S. GPO, Washington.
59. American Diabetes Association. Clinical practice recommendations 2002. Diabetes Care. 2002;25:S1–147.
60. Ford ES, Chaoyang L. Defining the MS in children and adolescents: will the real definition please stand up? J Pediatr. 2008;152(2):160–4.
61. Raitakari OT, Porkka KV, Ronnemaa T, et al. The role of insulin in clustering of serum lipids and blood pressure in children and adolescents. The cardiovascular risk in young Finns study. Diabetologia. 1995;38:1042–50.

62. Liu W, Lin R, Liu A, Du L, Chen Q. Prevalence and association between obesity and metabolic syndrome among Chinese elementary school children: a school-based survey. BMC Public Health. 2010;10:780.
63. Park J, Hilmers DC, Medoza JA, Stuff JE, Liu Y, Nicklas TA. Prevalence of metabolic syndrome and obesity in adolescents aged 12 to 19 years: comparison between the United States and Korea. J Korean Med Sci. 2010;25(1):75–82.
64. Schwandt P, Kelishadi R, Ribeiro RQ, Haas GM, Poursafa P. A three-country study on the components of the metabolic syndrome in youths: the BIG study. Int J Pediatr Obes. 2010;5(4):334–41.
65. Hickman TB, Briefel RR, Carroll MD, Rifkind BM, Cleeman JI, Maurer KR, et al. Distributions and trends of serum lipid levels among United States children and adolescents ages 4–19 years: data from the third national health and nutrition examination survey. Prev Med. 1998;27:879–90.
66. Srinivasan SR, Myers L, Berenson GS. Predictability of childhood adiposity and insulin for developing insulin resistance syndrome (syndrome X) in young adulthood: the Bogalusa heart study. Diabetes. 2002;51(1):204–9.
67. Olshansky SJ, Passaro DJ, Hershow RC, et al. A potential decline in life expectancy in the United States in the 21st century. N Engl J Med. 2005;352(11):1138–45.
68. Daviglus ML, Liu K, Yan LL, et al. Relation of body mass index in young adulthood and middle age to Medicare expenditures in older age. JAMA. 2004;292(22):2743–9.

Chapter 3
Perinatal Epidemiology of Metabolic Syndrome Risk Factors

Barbara Luke and Mary L. Hediger

Abstract The concept that events in the perinatal period have far-reaching effects throughout the life course has become increasingly accepted. An enlarging body of literature strongly suggests that exposure to altered maternal nutrition and maternal health status might not cause major malformations, yet can have far-reaching latency effects, such as restricted growth, hypertension, cardiovascular events, and altered renal function in adult life for the exposed offspring. The fetal origins literature also directs attention to intergenerational transmission via the translation of maternal experience from her own gestation and life course onwards into the in utero and child-rearing environments of her offspring. Constitutive of these environments are physiological (e.g., maternal metabolic regulation), psychobehavioral (e.g., stress or smoking), and ecological conditions (e.g., poverty or unstable food supply). In this literature, "programming" is understood as a "setting" of physiological function by conditions operating during a sensitive developmental period to produce long-term effects on function and thereby on health outcomes. This paradigm has particular implications for cardiometabolic disease and namely the metabolic syndrome.

Keywords Fetal growth • Birthweight • Adiposity • Maternal hyperglycemia • Inflammation • Maternal weight gain

B. Luke, ScD, MPH (✉)
Department of Obstetrics, Gynecology, and Reproductive Biology,
College of Human Medicine, Michigan State University,
A628 East Fee Hall, East Lansing, MI 48824, USA
e-mail: lukeb@msu.edu

M.L. Hediger, Ph.D.
Division of Epidemiology, Statistics and Prevention Research,
Eunice Kennedy Shriver National Institute of Child Health and Human Development,
National Institute of Health,
Rockville, MD, USA

Introduction

Studies in Britain two decades ago demonstrated that individuals who had been born with low birthweight (LBW, <2,500 g) or small for gestational age (SGA) were at increased risk for coronary heart disease and related disorders: stroke, non-insulin-dependent diabetes, raised blood pressure, and the metabolic syndrome [1–3]. Numerous studies since have confirmed these associations, providing evidence for the fetal origins of adult disease. Known as the Barker hypothesis [4], the fetal origins hypothesis, or metabolic programming [5], this concept suggests that fetal growth and development is reset to accommodate the intrauterine environment. Since the studies in the 1960s by McCance [6] on the long-term effects of early nutrition in rats, numerous animal studies have shown that nutrition in fetal life or infancy can induce lifetime effects on metabolism, growth, and neurodevelopment and on major disease processes such as hypertension, diabetes, atherosclerosis, and obesity [7–12].

More recent research has focused on the metabolic effect of fetal overnutrition, elevated birthweight, and excess adiposity at birth on long-term health. Large cohort studies have demonstrated strong associations between nutritional excess during pregnancy (as maternal pregravid overweight or obesity, maternal hyperglycemia and gestational diabetes, and high gestational weight gain) and later development of obesity and diabetes during adulthood [13–15]. Cohort studies have demonstrated a J-shaped relationship between birthweight and subsequent risk of obesity, with an increased risk among individuals born SGA but a much greater prevalence among those born LGA [16–19]. More recent studies suggest that maternal triglyceride levels may be a better correlate of excessive fetal growth, as well as the development of the metabolic syndrome in childhood (obesity, insulin resistance, glucose intolerance, hypertension, and dyslipidemia) [20–24]. This chapter summarizes our current understanding of fetal growth, adaptations to a suboptimal fetal environment, and the early childhood sequelae.

Assessing Fetal Growth

Fetal size and growth are important indicators of fetal health, and an understanding of normal growth is important for defining abnormalities, particularly intrauterine growth restriction, that may be associated with metabolic syndrome risk factors in children. However, properly defining normal fetal growth is a challenge because of the normal variation in fetal size and proportions with parental factors and environmental factors, such as maternal nutrition and weight gain. Fetal growth is commonly categorized at birth by the designations, "small for gestational age" (SGA) and "large for gestational age" (LGA), which categorizes the size of the fetus or neonate in reference to their relative percentile for gestational age. In the United States, the most common cutoff for SGA is the 10th percentile and LGA, the 90th. It should be noted that an SGA classification is not necessarily the same as "intrauterine growth restriction" (IUGR), since infants whose growth faltered late in pregnancy may be born above the 10th percentile, although their growth has been constrained by the time they are born. Likewise, an infant born LGA may be normal and large and not show signs and symptoms of having been exposed to gestational diabetes mellitus (GDM) or excessive maternal weight gain, both of which may increase birthweight.

Fetal imaging to evaluate growth is done primarily by ultrasonography. The gestational and yolk sacs can be seen as early as 4–6 weeks' gestation, and fetal crown-rump length (CRL) is measured in the first trimester to establish dates. Thereafter, a number of equations employ various combinations of measured fetal head circumference (HC), abdominal circumference (AC), biparietal diameter (BPD), and femur length (FL) measured by ultrasound to estimate fetal weight in relation to gestational age [25]. Not only are bony dimensions and ossification centers [26] visualized, but it is now also possible to visualize elements of fetal body composition, such as cross-sectional subcutaneous fat layers and muscle [27, 28]. Organ dimensions (e.g., kidney, liver) can be measured using two-dimensional (2D) ultrasonography and have been used for research purposes. Volumes can be obtained using three-dimensional (3D) ultrasound and are again beginning to be used for fetal body composition studies [29] and to study organ development.

Fetal Growth as an Outcome

Despite its limitations, weight at birth is still used as the primary indicator of neonatal status and reflects the outcome of fetal growth processes and complications. A number of cutoffs, indices, and ratios have been devised to relate birthweight to risk of mortality and morbidity. Low birthweight (LBW), an outcome defined as a birthweight below 2,500 g (5 lb, 8 oz), is by far the most common and is used worldwide in surveillance [30] and in epidemiological studies. Historically, it was the level below which neonatal mortality was seen to be significantly increased. About 67% of LBW infants are born preterm, and all term LBW infants are SGA. The problem with an LBW classification is that it is a mixture of both preterm deliveries and growth-restricted infants and, as such, is not very useful when the outcome, such as the metabolic syndrome, may be differentially related to preterm delivery or abnormal growth. Using an absolute cutoff for a high birthweight alone (e.g., ≥4,500 g) also underestimates the proportion of neonates whose mothers had gestational diabetes and delivered at a late-preterm (35–36 weeks) or early-term gestation to avoid delivery complications.

Factors Affecting Fetal Growth

Beginning in the second trimester and up to about 20–24 weeks' gestation, fetal size (weight) estimated using biometric parameters is still fairly closely associated with dates. After that point, however, the differences in fetal size associated with gender, ethnicity, and a number of other maternal factors, such as cigarette smoking and gestational weight gain, affect fetal growth rates and significantly bias estimates of gestational age based on size [31, 32]. For example, gender differences in fetal head dimensions (BPD, HC), with males having larger dimensions than female fetuses, are measureable on the average by 12–14 weeks' gestation and significant by 24 weeks [33, 34]. Also as early as the second trimester, the ethnic differences in body proportions that are evident in children and adults are already seen in the fetus, which can complicate estimates of fetal size and growth, depending on the reference used. Beginning in the second trimester (15–20 weeks), the femur lengths (FL) of non-Hispanic black fetuses are already longer than those of non-Hispanic white fetuses of the same gestational age [34, 35], while the FL of Asian fetuses are shorter than those of non-Hispanic whites [35], and these differences are magnified in the third trimester. Likewise for the arm, the humerus lengths (HL) of non-Hispanic black fetuses tend to be longer than those of non-Hispanic whites which are longer than those of Asians, in turn [36]. These are important considerations in the evaluation of fetal body proportions in relation to postnatal growth.

Measurement Approaches for Determining Abnormal Fetal Growth

Almost all estimated fetal weight for gestation and birthweight-for-gestational-age charts are considered "references" (not "standards") because they are descriptive, may include abnormal cases, and are population specific. Fetal growth references are created by measuring the birthweights of a relatively large number of live-born neonates at each gestational week and identifying birthweight cutoffs at the 10th and 90th percentiles. The problem with this approach is that it had been shown repeatedly that birthweights at preterm gestations are not representative of the concurrent intrauterine weights of fetuses that deliver at term [37–40]. Two references have been developed for twins [41] and triplets [42] which utilized both repeated in utero measures and birthweight, overcoming the limitations of using either measure alone.

Most fetal growth references are stratified by sex, providing separate SGA and LGA cutoffs for male and female fetuses [43, 44], although there are references available for the sexes combined [45]. Gardosi et al. [46, 47] extended this concept of stratifying by factors that affect fetal growth and proposed fetal growth "standards" that predict optimal growth and are simultaneously customized not only for fetal sex but also for maternal factors, i.e., maternal height, weight, parity, and ethnicity. Categorizations based on customized growth standards have been found to perform better than birthweight-for-gestational-age references in terms of predicting adverse perinatal outcomes [48–50] and may be useful in predicting postnatal patterns of growth that associated with child morbidity.

Causes of Poor and Excessive Fetal Growth

The causes of poor and excessive fetal growth are categorized into maternal, fetal, and placental factors [51, 52]. Maternal factors include maternal diseases and pregnancy complications, such as hypertensive disorders in pregnancy and preeclampsia. Maternal diseases that can lead to growth restriction include autoimmune diseases (such as antiphospholipid syndrome and systemic lupus erythematosus), diabetes, and renal and cardiac disease. Cigarette smoking is a common cause of poor fetal growth in industrialized countries with the birthweight among infants of smoking women averaging 150 g less than that of infants born to nonsmoking women [53].

The main maternal causes of excessive fetal growth are gestational diabetes mellitus (GDM) and maternal obesity [51, 52]. Uncontrolled maternal diabetes mellitus, either preexisting or GDM, leads to maternal hyperglycemia and consequently fetal hyperglycemia which in turn lead to a higher output of fetal insulin, excessive uptake of glucose by fetal tissues, and an increase in fetal growth dimensions, particularly subcutaneous fat.

Gestational Weight Gain

The World Health Organization Collaborative Study [54] found the anthropometric factors most strongly correlated with both length of gestation and birthweight to be maternal height, pregravid or early pregnancy body weight, maternal fat deposition, mid-upper-arm circumference (MUAC), and gestational weight gain. Although each factor independently influences birthweight and length of gestation, their effects are neither equal nor additive. The landmark studies in this area are from the Collaborative Perinatal Project, which was conducted from 1959 to 1964 [55–58]. Based on term singleton pregnancies, these studies demonstrated that: (1) a progressive increase in weight gain was paralleled by an increase in mean birthweight and a decline in the incidence of LBW; (2) increasing pregravid weight diminishes the effect of weight gain on birthweight; (3) an inverse relationship between weight gain and perinatal mortality, with gains up to 30 lb; and (4) higher gestational weight gains are related to higher birthweights and better growth and development during the first postnatal year.

Aside from cigarette smoking, the most important and potentially modifiable maternal factor associated with fetal growth, both poor and excessive, is gestational weight gain.

The major guidelines for maternal weight gain were first introduced in 1990 by the Institute of Medicine (IOM) [59] which recommended that appropriate weight gain during pregnancy should be encouraged (by dietary intervention and counseling), especially among high-risk groups, such as young adolescents (within 2 years of menarche), black women, women with low pregravid weight or short stature (<157 cm), and mothers of twins and higher-order multiples, to enhance fetal growth and to diminish the risk of LBW [59].

The unique feature of the IOM recommendations was that the target weight gain ranges were specific to maternal pregravid weight status, using the body mass index (BMI, kg/m^2) as the preferred index of maternal pregravid nutritional status and provisional cutoffs to define underweight, overweight, and obesity. The IOM showed that, in both developed and developing countries and for all racial/ethnic groups, the correlation between birthweight and total weight gain ranges between 0.20 and 0.30. In addition, maternal pregravid BMI (kg/m^2) and weight gain have independent and additive effects on birthweight outcome. The average magnitude of the effect on birthweight (in women with a normal BMI) is, assuming a base birthweight of about 3,000 g, approximately 20 g of birthweight for every 1 kg of total gain [60], and pregravid BMI is a strong effect modifier such that the impact of a given weight gain is greatest in thin women and least in the overweight and obese.

Low gestational weight gain is strongly associated with an increased risk for LBW and intrauterine growth restriction (IUGR). In original analyses of data from the 1980 National Natality Survey, Kleinman [61] demonstrated a greater than twofold risk of term LBW with a low total weight gain (≤10 kg) for both underweight women and normal-weight women, while the relationship was attenuated at this level of weight gain for overweight women. Although the recommendations did not address the issues of excessive weight gain, maternal obesity, and their relationship with LGA births; cesarean delivery; and maternal postpartum weight retention, these concerns were raised soon after [62, 63]. Many investigators have subsequently confirmed these associations, including the link between low prepregnancy weight and both prematurity and intrauterine growth retardation, with reported odds ratios ranging from 1.7 to 3.0, depending on the study population [64]. The population attributable risk for early preterm birth (<32 weeks) with low prepregnancy weight is as much as 31% among white women and 43% among black women [65]. Low maternal weight gain has also been significantly associated with both intrauterine growth retardation and preterm birth, with odds ratios of 2.1:4.3 [59, 66–70]. In addition, a significant joint effect has been shown between low pregravid weight and low weight gain on the risk of preterm birth (AOR, 5.63, 95% CI, 2.35–13.8) [68].

Since the original IOM report [59] was issued, there have been a number of studies that have directly evaluated various aspects of the weight gain recommendations and used the originally suggested BMI categories as part of the evaluative criteria [71]. The primary outcomes of interest have been SGA births or LBW which are increased with weight gain below the IOM recommended ranges and LGA births, cesarean delivery, and maternal postpartum weight retention which are increased with weight gain above or in excess of the IOM range. These results appeared to validate the IOM recommendations as reasonable targets for total weight gain or at least show that pregnancy weight gain within the recommended ranges is associated with the best outcomes [72].

The most recent set of IOM recommendations [73] assert that guidelines for weight gain and weight gain rates be adjusted to the definitions of BMI status currently used by the National Heart, Lung, and Blood Institute (1998). The IOM committee also suggested strongly that women be counseled to avoid excessive weight gain to minimize postpartum weight retention and set guidelines for weight gain in obese gravidas

(5.0–9.0 kg). Further, the report concluded that there was insufficient evidence to support modifications of the recommendations for women of short stature (<157 cm), adolescents (<20 years old), and different racial/ethnic groups. For the first time, the IOM also endorsed provisional weight gain guidelines for women carrying twins (reestimated from Luke et al. [74]) based on the newer BMI cutoffs and interquartile ranges for a series of twin pregnancies that delivered between 37 and 42 weeks' gestation and where the twins weighed 2,500 g or more on average: normal weight, 17–25 kg (37–54 lb); overweight, 14–23 kg (31–50 lb); and obese, 11–19 kg (25–42 lb).

The pattern of maternal weight gain has been shown to be as important as total weight gain in its effect on birthweight in both singleton and twin pregnancies. Although the increase in fetal weight is greatest during the third trimester (after 28 weeks), gains during mid-gestation (either second trimester or 20–28 weeks) have the strongest association with birthweight [68, 75–83]. In singletons, Abrams and Selvin [78] demonstrated that birthweight increased in each trimester by 18, 33, and 17 g, respectively, per kilogram per week of maternal weight gain. Scholl, Hediger, et al. [80] reported that weight gains to 20 weeks and to 28 weeks were most strongly related to birthweight, contributing 22–24 g to birthweight per kilogram per week of maternal weight gain. In addition, a low rate of weight gain or a poor pattern of weight gain is also associated with an increased risk of preterm birth [68, 83, 84].

A substantial portion of gestational weight gain is maternal body fat, which when measured as the triceps skinfold thickness or mid-upper-arm circumference (MUAC) increases in the first two trimesters and decreases in the third, reflecting the early accretion of maternal body fat and the subsequent utilization in late gestation to meet increasing energy needs. Prior studies of well-nourished women pregnant with singletons, based on deuterium oxide and underwater weighing [85–88], as well as anthropometric measures [89–91], have reported a pattern of small gains in maternal body fat early in pregnancy, rapid accumulation between 20 and 30 weeks' gestation, and a leveling off between 30 weeks and delivery. A consistent finding in studies with diverse ethnic and racial groups is the correlation between triceps skinfold or MUAC measures during the second trimester and birthweight, with the loss of upper arm fat or the failure to accrue maternal fat during the second trimester associated with poor fetal growth and subsequent lower birthweights [89–93]. Follow-up studies have reported that the combination of maternal triceps skinfold below the median (15 mm) at 18 weeks plus reduced pregnancy weight gain is associated with significantly higher blood pressure in their children at age 11 (systolic pressure increased by 11.3 mmHg, 95% CI, 2.2–20.4; diastolic pressure increased by 10.1 mmHg, 95% CI, 3.2–17.1 for every kg/week decrease in weight gain) [94].

Fetal Undernutrition

Fetal nutrition is determined by a combination of the mother's dietary intake and nutrient stores, and transfer capabilities of the placenta. In response to undernutrition, the fetus makes physiological, metabolic, and hormonal adaptations that influence fetal growth, including reducing metabolic dependence on glucose and increasing oxidation of other nutritional substrates, including amino acids and lactate. These endocrine changes, combined with reduced nutrient supply, divert amino acids from protein synthesis and tissue growth, resulting in impaired growth of the kidneys, liver, and heart: the developing organs with the highest rates of cellular turnover [95–100]. Insufficient maternal dietary protein can result from a deficit in the absolute amount of protein, intake of low-quality protein, inadequate calories (with protein diverted to meet energy needs), or a combination of these factors. Regardless of the cause, the potential consequences of an inadequate supply of protein to the developing fetus are both immediate and long term.

The availability of amino acids from the maternal supply is an important factor for fetal growth, with lower maternal levels reported in pregnancies complicated by growth restriction [101, 102] and maternal smoking [103, 104]. Reduced maternal substrate availability has an adverse effect on placental size, compounding the deficit in the maternal supply. When placental growth is restricted, the supply of amino acids may become limiting to fetal growth by restricting protein synthesis. With both hypoxemia and altered substrate supply (hypoglycemia and/or inadequate amino acids), there is an increase in uteroplacental production and accumulation of lactate as a means of sequestering available carbohydrate in the fetoplacental circulation for use by fetal tissues [105]. Reduction in fetal growth sufficient to cause growth restriction reverses the uptake of many amino acids by the fetus, resulting in a release (predominately of nonessential amino acids) back to the placenta. As a consequence of this reversed flux of amino acids from the fetus, uteroplacental consumption of amino acids is greatly increased, substituting for glucose to sustain placental oxidative metabolism and increased placental production of lactate. In most animal models, prolonged undernutrition results in intrauterine growth restriction and large decreases in the fractional rates of protein synthesis in the fetal liver, kidneys, and heart. Reduced umbilical plasma concentrations may reflect impaired fetal activity of specific enzymes essential for the biosynthesis pathways, as reported with key hepatic enzymes involved with glucose metabolism [106]. With fetal hypoxemia, the ratios of nonessential to essential amino acids are increased, which is similar to findings in children with kwashiorkor (protein-calorie malnutrition), indicating that intrauterine starvation occurs with growth restriction [101, 102].

Fetal adaptations to undernutrition also manifest as changes in lipid metabolism and liver function. In comparing small-for-gestational-age (SGA) versus appropriate-for-gestational-age (AGA) infants, Jones et al. [107] reported markedly diminished fetal liver-derived apolipoprotein A-I levels, decreased total lipid levels, lowered free fatty acids, and elevated triglycerides, signifying an inability to hydrolyze circulating triglycerides and leading to diminished peripheral adipose deposition. Decreased liver-derived apolipoprotein A-I levels reflects impaired hepatic synthesis, consistent with reports of the limited ability of SGA infants to metabolize very-low-density lipoproteins and to clear intravenous lipids during the early neonatal period [108]. Fetal growth restriction is also associated with higher umbilical plasma concentrations of apolipoprotein B and a higher ratio of apolipoprotein B to A-I, which have been linked to elevated apolipoprotein B levels in adulthood and a higher risk for atherosclerosis in later life [109]. Ultrasound measurements of the abdominal circumference correlate with umbilical plasma concentrations of glucose, total bilirubin, lactic dehydrogenase, and triglyceride in the growth-restricted neonate [98]. Reduced abdominal circumference at birth is positively associated with plasma concentrations of fibrinogen [110], serum cholesterol, and serum apolipoprotein B in adult life [111], as well as death from coronary heart disease [4]; all associations are stronger in men than in women and are independent of length of gestation. In animal studies, fetal growth restriction also results in permanent changes in key hepatic enzymes of glycolysis and gluconeogenesis, as well as reductions in hepatic insulin and glucagon sensitivity [112]. Reduced abdominal circumference at birth in guinea pigs results in altered cholesterol metabolism [113]. These associations help explain the altered fat metabolism and susceptibility to excess body fat gain in nutritionally stunted children [114, 115].

Fetal growth restriction has also been shown to adversely affect renal morphology and function in both animal and human studies [97, 100, 106, 116–118]. Maximal nephrogenic development occurs during the third trimester, a critical period when the final nephron endowment is set [96, 116]. Research has demonstrated a significant inverse correlation between fetal kidney anteroposterior and transverse diameters and umbilical vein active renin levels at birth [96]. Thinner neonates have smaller kidneys relative to their body size, suggesting that the ponderal index (a measure of weight for length) may provide information about relative kidney size in mid- to late gestation [100]. Inadequate renal growth before birth may be linked to the development of hypertension in later life (Chap. 6 contains in-depth information in this particular area).

Chronic placental inflammation may underlie fetal growth restriction. Chronic placental inflammation is more common among preterm births, and the associations stronger between markers of fetal growth restriction and inflammation in these births. Williams et al. [119] reported symmetric fetal growth restriction to be more strongly correlated with inflammation at 28–32 weeks' gestation (AOR 11.0, 95% CI, 3.5–36), whereas asymmetric fetal growth restriction was correlated with inflammation at term (after 36 weeks' gestation) (AOR 1.6, 95% CI, 1.04–2.4). These associations have also been reported by Hediger et al. [38], suggesting that infants delivered before term, after preterm rupture of membranes, exhibited evidence of more chronic stress (symmetric fetal growth restriction), whereas infants delivered for medical or obstetrical indications had increased rates of asymmetric fetal growth restriction, indicating a more recent onset of growth abnormalities. Data strongly suggest that maternal undernutrition and micronutrient deficiencies are factors that abrogate control of the inflammatory response [120, 121]. In animal studies, the combination of mildly hyperglycemic and amino-acid-depleted maternal diet during the preimplantation period results in irreversible programming of slower fetal growth [122].

Fetal Overnutrition

Overweight and obese women have neonates who are heavier than lean or average-weight women because of increased adiposity [123], even when the mother had normal glucose tolerance levels. Conversely, nonobese mothers with abnormal oral glucose challenge test results and without gestational diabetes also have neonates with significantly increased adiposity [27]. In a longitudinal study evaluating perinatal risk factors, maternal pregravid BMI, independent of maternal glucose status or birthweight, was the strongest predictor of childhood obesity at age 9 years [124]. In another longitudinal study, children born LGA to diabetic mothers were at greatest risk of developing the metabolic syndrome during childhood (follow-up to ages 6, 7, 9, and 11 years) [20]. These studies suggest that maternal pregravid weight and the presence of maternal diabetes may each independently affect the risk of adolescent obesity in the child.

Obesity and Inflammation

There is a growing body of literature suggesting that in adults, insulin resistance is an indicator of inflammation driven by interleukin-1β (IL-1β), interleukin-6 (IL-6), and tumor necrosis factor-α [125, 126]. Stress (from infection, inflammation, trauma, or psychological distress) raises plasma glucose concentrations by increasing the contrainsulin hormones (e.g., cortisol and placental growth hormone). Scholl et al. [127] suggests that high maternal glucose concentrations may be a risk factor or a risk marker for the subclinical infection that gives rise to chorioamnionitis. Subclinical infection associated with very preterm delivery is manifested as a systemic inflammatory response that is otherwise asymptomatic. In his analysis of data from the Collaborative Perinatal Project, Naeye [128] reported that an increased risk of very preterm delivery was associated with acute chorioamnionitis among obese gravidas. Scholl et al. [127] suggests that higher but seemingly normal maternal plasma glucose concentrations are associated with very preterm delivery by predisposing to or acting as a marker for placental inflammation and subclinical infection and that insulin resistance might be an underlying cause of very preterm delivery.

Adipose tissue expresses and releases the proinflammatory cytokine IL-6, potentially inducing low-grade systemic inflammation in overweight and obese individuals. The acute-phase C-reactive protein (CRP) is a sensitive marker for systemic inflammation. In a recent analysis of the Third National Health and Nutrition Examination Survey, Visser et al. [129] reported BMI to be associated with raised CRP levels in women, particularly those with a higher waist-to-hip ratio, because abdominal adipose tissue releases more IL-6 than subcutaneous adipose tissue [130]. These findings suggest that a state of low-grade systemic inflammation is present in overweight and obese individuals. CRP concentrations are independent of pregnancy and gestational age and do not cross the placenta. Elevated CRP levels are more often found in patients who are refractory to tocolysis, suggesting an underlying infectious morbidity. A positive association has also been reported between elevated CRP levels and histological evidence of placental infection [131].

Elevated plasma glucose concentrations during pregnancy have also been linked to the development of preeclampsia. Hsu et al. [132] reported that among pregnant women with insulin-dependent diabetes mellitus, those with elevated hemoglobin A_{1c} values (>8%) between 16 and 20 weeks' gestation had significantly higher incidence of preeclampsia compared to those whose mean hemoglobin A_{1c} level was normalized during this stage of gestation (46% vs. 26%). Although the mechanisms mediating the effect of glycosylated hemoglobin on the development of preeclampsia remain unknown, it has been suggested that generation of advanced glycosylated end products may be involved, impairing vascular responses. Hyperglycemia-induced inflammation may be part of the causal pathway through which obesity predisposes to preeclampsia.

Effect of Maternal Smoking

Prenatal exposure to maternal smoking is associated with impaired linear growth and overweight by early childhood (age 4 years), and significantly greater subcutaneous and intra-abdominal fat by late puberty (26% and 33%, respectively), as well as a 50% greater risk for overweight [133–135]. Prenatal exposure to maternal smoking increases both the risk for early-onset type 2 diabetes and nondiabetic obesity [136]. This association amplifies the accelerated weight gain that normally occurs during late puberty, increases intra-abdominal adiposity, strengthens with age, and is largely independent of known confounders. Cohort studies that have tracked the offspring of smokers to adulthood report a more adverse cardiovascular risk profile as well as higher BMI and central adiposity [137].

Body Proportions at Birth and Subsequent Disease Risks

Four birth phenotypes associated with later disease have been identified [138, 139]. The first occurs when overall growth is downregulated early in pregnancy. This type of growth is associated with a higher risk of preterm labor and preterm birth [38, 39, 140, 141] and results in a *symmetrically small newborn*. During infancy, growth continues to be slow, with reduced weight and all measurements still lagging behind by 1 year of age. In terms of metabolic programming, this type of fetal growth is associated with an increased risk for hypertension during adult life.

The second phenotype occurs when growth is downregulated during the second trimester. This pattern is also associated with preterm labor and preterm birth and results in a reduction in birthweight, but head circumference and birth length are normal: a *thin newborn*. During infancy, growth catches up, resulting in normal weight by 1 year of age. Babies that are thin tend to be insulin resistant as children and adults and are therefore more liable to develop the insulin resistance syndrome [142].

The third phenotype includes babies that are *short in relation to their head circumference* and have a *reduced abdominal circumference*. Individuals with these growth parameters at birth tend to have persisting abnormalities of liver function, including raised serum low-density lipoprotein (LDL) cholesterol and plasma fibrinogen concentrations [110, 111]. This type of growth can result from brain-sparing circulatory adaptations by which cardiac output is diverted to the brain at the expense of the trunk. This last pattern of growth is associated with an increased risk of asthma during childhood [143] and the most risks during adult life, including hypertension, non-insulin-dependent diabetes, elevated cholesterol, and cardiovascular disease. The thymus, which is vital to regulating the body's immune response, is one of the organs which may suffer with this pattern of impaired growth, resulting in an increased susceptibility to infection during childhood and adult life [143–145].

The fourth phenotype includes babies that are born *short and fat*. As adults, these individuals tend to become insulin deficient and have higher rates of non-insulin-dependent diabetes [146]. This is consistent with findings in Pima Indians and with observations in Sheffield, UK, that showed a U-shaped association between abdominal circumference at birth and death from coronary heart disease [4, 147]. Babies that are short and fat are thought to be the result of maternal hyperglycemia, with consequent imbalance in the supply of glucose and other nutrients to the fetus.

Gender Effects

It has also been shown that the effects of impaired fetal growth and subsequent disease risks vary by gender. For example, although both men and women who had low birth weight are at increased risk for coronary heart disease, unlike men, low rates of growth during infancy were not linked to coronary heart disease in women. Forsèn et al. [148] found that the highest risks for coronary heart disease were among women who were stunted at birth (reduced birth lengths) and among men who were thin at birth (normal birth length but reduced birth weights); these associations were stronger than those of birthweight alone. Stunting and thinness may represent different responses to fetal malnutrition, and each may differ in long-term consequences. While both have been found to be associated with raised blood pressure in later life [110, 149], stunting is associated with persistent changes in liver function, including raised serum cholesterol concentration [111] and plasma fibrinogen [110], while thinness is associated with features of the insulin resistance syndrome including impaired glucose tolerance and dyslipidemia [150].

Modulating Effect of Childhood Factors

Path of Growth

The path of growth throughout childhood modifies the risk of disease associated with size at birth [151]. Recent studies from Helsinki have reported the highest death rates from coronary heart disease among men who were thin at birth and women who were short at birth but had accelerated weight gain during childhood [148, 151]. It is not known whether this association is because of the pathological effects of a higher proportion of body fat persisting into adult life, deleterious effects of catch-up growth, or the intrauterine resetting of endocrine axes that control growth. In an editorial, Barker [139] wrote "that while the primary prevention of coronary heart disease and non-insulin dependent diabetes may ultimately depend on changing the body composition and diets of young women, more immediate benefit may come from preventing imbalances between prenatal and postnatal growth among children."

Diet During Infancy

Factors present during infancy may modify prenatal factors. For example, nutrition after birth may also have an important influence on subsequent disease risk. Studies in primates have shown that infant nutrition programmed later obesity and atherosclerosis [152, 153]. Human epidemiological studies also indicate the importance of postnatal factors such as the relation between the duration of breastfeeding and later ischemic heart disease [154], with breastfeeding for more than 1 year associated with an increased risk of cardiovascular disease (elevated serum low-density lipoprotein concentrations) in men but not in women [154]. The possible mechanism, derived from observations in baboons, could be that thyroid hormones present in breast milk may downregulate the infant's thyroid function in later life, thereby influencing cholesterol metabolism [155]. The absence or reduced length of breastfeeding is also a well-established risk factor for obesity [156–158].

Factors During Childhood

Risks of Central Body Fat

Children with impaired fetal growth tend to have less muscle and relatively more fat at the same weight as children who had been well grown at birth [159, 160]. In addition, these children, as well as earlier-maturing girls (menarche before age 12), tend to put on fat in the trunk and abdominal areas, independent of overall fatness, a pattern which is strongly associated with an increase in blood pressure, dyslipidemia, and risks of diabetes and coronary heart disease [161–166]. This tendency to put fat on centrally is stronger in girls than in boys, particularly with excessive weight gain during late adolescence (ages 14–16), and is further exaggerated among adolescents who smoke [163, 167–171]. Studies of stunted (height-for-age z-scores < −1.5) versus more normally grown (height-for-age z-scores > −1.5) prepubertal children ages 8–11 years showed that the former group had significantly higher respiratory quotient and fasting fat oxidation [115]. These findings suggest that childhood nutritional stunting is associated with impaired fat oxidation, a factor that may predict obesity in other at-risk populations.

While some studies have suggested that poor growth before birth, particularly late in pregnancy when the liver is growing rapidly, may be related to raised fibrinogen levels (a risk factor for cardiovascular disease) in adult life [110, 149], other studies have shown a stronger relationship to level of body fat and physical activity before puberty [172]. The effect of excess body fat during childhood is much stronger than that of low birthweight: one standard deviation increase in the ponderal index during childhood raised the serum fibrinogen level by 13.7 mg/dl, whereas one standard deviation fall in birthweight increased childhood fibrinogen levels by 1.6 mg/dl [172]. In a study of children in New York City, Shea et al. [173] also found that central obesity, as assessed by the subscapular-to-triceps skinfold ratio, was independently associated with plasma fibrinogen level, after adjustment for body mass index. Level of body fat, particularly an increase in central body fat (as a rise in subscapular to triceps skinfold ratio) during puberty and at older ages (13–27 years), is significantly associated with an increase in systolic blood pressure in males and females and a decrease in high-density lipoprotein cholesterol in males [164, 174].

Evidence of Accelerated Aging

Impaired fetal growth to insure survival may be at the expense of longevity, in addition to higher mortality from chronic diseases. In rats, the combination of prenatal undernutrition with retarded fetal growth and good postnatal nutrition with accelerated growth leads to striking reductions in life span [175]. Girls who are born short at birth, either symmetrically small (slowed growth from the first trimester onwards) or short but of normal birthweight (slowed growth during the third trimester), have an earlier menarche (perhaps because of a higher percent of body fat) and an earlier menopause [164, 176–179]. Follow-up studies of children born with very low birthweight (<1,500 g) [180] or extremely low birthweight (<1,000 g) [181] have documented advanced bone age at 12–18 years of age. Postmenarcheal girls who had been born small for gestational age have significantly higher values of insulin and androstenedione and twofold higher concentrations of DHEAS (dehydroepiandrosterone sulfate) compared to those who had been born appropriate for gestational age, suggesting exaggerated adrenarche [182].

In a longitudinal study of dietary intake and body size to menarche and adolescent growth in girls from birth through adolescence, Berkey et al. [183] concluded that age at menarche, age at peak height growth velocity, and peak height growth velocity were all associated with diet and body size much earlier in childhood. Menarche occurred earlier in girls who were taller and who consumed more animal protein and less vegetable protein as early as ages 3–5 years. For all ages before menarche, the same three factors emerged as being most important: more calories, more animal protein, and lower body mass indices were consistently associated with higher peak growth velocity.

Among overweight children, blood pressure was found to be higher in those that had been low birthweight as newborns compared to other children. In addition, the beneficial effects of maternal calcium supplementation during pregnancy on subsequent childhood blood pressure have been shown to be strongest among overweight children [184].

Importance of Changes in Z-Scores or Centile Crossing

It has been suggested that the relationship between disease risk and early body size should be interpreted only in the context of later body size [185]. The critical point is that early size adjusted for later size is a measure of change in size between earlier and later measurements, as changes in z-scores or centile crossing. Evidence for this concept has come from many studies in which the relationship between size at birth and current risk factors is significant only after adjustment for later size [146, 162, 166, 186–190]. Catch-up growth raises a further difficulty. Small babies tend to show greater upward centile crossing than larger babies, and this regression towards the mean results in an inherent correlation between birthweight and centile crossing, each being a proxy for the other. Adjusting for both early and later size allows the two effects to be disentangled and identifies which (low birthweight or centile crossing) is more relevant to later outcomes.

Potential mechanisms have been suggested regarding the detrimental effects of catch-up growth during childhood after impaired fetal growth on chronic disease risks [151]. Because fetal growth restriction leads to reduced cell numbers, subsequent catch-up growth is achieved by overgrowth of a limited cell mass. Alternatively, both catch-up growth and chronic disease may share a common pathway, reflecting persisting changes in the secretion of growth hormones and factors which were established in utero in response to undernutrition and which both influence childhood growth and the development of chronic disease.

Socioeconomic Effects

Some studies have accounted for the current (childhood or adult) or prior (pregnancy/fetal) socioeconomic status [189–192], but the majority have not. The conditions during pregnancy and childhood may be important modifiers of the association between fetal growth and adult risks for disease, as shown in the studies of pregnancies during World War II. For populations that had been chronically malnourished, followed by improved nutrition, mothers who had been short and light become fatter and may increase the risk of coronary heart disease for their children [193]. With continued improvements in nutrition, women become taller and heavier, their babies are adequately nourished, and maternal fatness no longer increases the risk of coronary heart disease for their children.

Intergenerational Effects

Several studies have suggested an intergenerational effect on fetal growth. Reduced uterine and ovarian size has been reported among girls born small for gestational age [179, 194]. Other studies have linked small size at birth with subsequent development of gestational diabetes [195, 196].

Future Research: Epigenetic Studies

The newest area of research in metabolic programming is that of epigenetics, covalent modifications to DNA and chromatin that alter gene expression independent of gene sequence [197–199]. One example is excess fetal lipid exposure regulating genes involved with lipid sensing and metabolism, since lipids act as both transcriptional activators and signaling molecules. A substantial component of metabolic disease risk has a prenatal developmental basis.

Conclusions

Recognition of the fetal origins of adult health has heightened attention to gestational processes, particularly the nature of the fetal impacts responsible for observed postnatal effects on function and health, and the gestational conditions that exert these impacts. There is increasing epidemiological evidence suggesting that certain metabolic disorders in adults, such as insulin resistance and type 2 diabetes, might originate from in utero exposures. Longitudinal case–control studies on large cohorts of children from birth to adolescence will continue to quantify the metabolic risk, identify the critical time windows, and determine the effects of other risk factors, such as obesity or genetic predisposition.

References

1. Barker DJP, Osmond C, Winter PD, Margetts B, Simmonds SJ. Weight in infancy and death from ischaemic heart disease. Lancet. 1989;ii:577–80.
2. Barker DJP, Fall C, Osmond C, et al. Fetal and infant growth and impaired glucose tolerance. Br Med J. 1991;303:1474–5.
3. Law CM, Shiell AW. Is blood pressure inversely related to birth weight? The strength of evidence from a systematic review of the literature. J Hypertens. 1996;14:935–41.
4. Barker DJP, Martyn CN, Osmond C, Wield GA. Abnormal liver growth in utero and death from coronary heart disease. Br Med J. 1995;310:703–4.
5. Waterland RA, Garza C. Potential mechanisms of metabolic imprinting that lead to chronic disease. Am J Clin Nutr. 1999;69:179–97.
6. McCance RA. Growth, food, and time. Lancet. 1962;ii:271–2.
7. Hahn P. Effect of litter size on plasma cholesterol and insulin and some liver and adipose tissue enzymes in adult rodents. J Nutr. 1984;114:1231–4.
8. Pitts GC. Cellular aspects of growth and catch-up growth in the rat: a reevaluation. Growth. 1986;50:419–36.
9. Dahri S, Snoeck A, Reusens-Billen B, Remacle C, Hoet JJ. Islet function in offspring of mothers on low-protein diet during gestation. Diabetes. 1991;20 Suppl 2:115–20.
10. Langley SC, Jackson AA. Increased systolic blood pressure in adult rats induced by exposure to maternal low protein diets. Clin Sci. 1994;86:217–22.
11. Lucas A. Programming by early nutrition: an experimental approach. J Nutr. 1998;128 Suppl 2:401–6S.
12. Woodall SM, Johnston BM, Breier BH, Gluckman PD. Chronic maternal undernutrition in the rat leads to delayed postnatal growth and elevated blood pressure of offspring. Pediatr Res. 1996;40:438–43.
13. Dabelea D, Hanson RL, Lindsay RS, Pettitt DJ, Imperatore G, Gabir MM, Roumain J, Bennett PH, Knowler WC. Intrauterine exposure to diabetes conveys risks for type 2 diabetes and obesity: a study of discordant sibships. Diabetes. 2000;49:2208–11.
14. Metzger BE, Lowe LP, Dyer AR, Trimble ER, Chaovarindr U, Coustan DR, Hadden DR, McCance DR, Hod M, McIntyre HD, Oats JJ, Persson B, Rogers MS, Sacks DA. Hyperglycemia and adverse pregnancy outcomes. N Engl J Med. 2008;358:1991–2002.
15. Lawlor DA, Lichtenstein P, Långström N. Association of maternal diabetes mellitus in pregnancy with offspring adiposity into early adulthood. Circulation. 2011;123:258–65.
16. Curhan GC, Cherton GM, Willett WC, Spiegelman D, Colditz GA, Manson JE, et al. Birth weight and adult hypertension and obesity in women. Circulation. 1996;94:1310–5.
17. Curhan GC, Willett WC, Rimm EB, Spiegelman D, Ascherio AL, Stampfer MJ. Birth weight and adult hypertension, diabetes mellitus and obesity in US men. Circulation. 1996;94:3246–50.
18. Martorell R, Stein AD, Schroeder DG. Early nutrition and adiposity. J Nutr. 2001;131:874S–80S.
19. Oken E, Gillman MW. Fetal origins of obesity. Obes Res. 2003;11:496–506.
20. Boney CM, Verma A, Tucker R, Vohr BR. Metabolic syndrome in childhood: association with birth weight, maternal obesity, and gestational diabetes mellitus. Pediatrics. 2005;115:e290–6.
21. Di CG, Miccoli R, Volpe L, Lencioni C, Ghio A, Giovannitti MG, Cuccuru I, Pellegrini G, Chatzianagnostou K, Boldrini A, Del PS. Maternal triglyceride levels and newborn weight in pregnant women with normal glucose tolerance. Diabet Med. 2005;22:21–5.
22. Kelishadi R, Badiee Z, Adeli K. Cord blood lipid profile and associated factors: baseline data of a birth cohort study. Paediatr Perinat Epidemiol. 2007;21:518–24.

23. Khan NA. Role of lipids and fatty acids in macrosomic offspring of diabetic pregnancy. Cell Biochem Biophys. 2007;48:79–88.
24. Schaefer-Graf UM, Graf K, Kulbacka I, Kjos SL, Dudenhausen J, Vetter K, Herrera E. Maternal lipids as strong determinants of fetal environment and growth in pregnancies with gestational diabetes mellitus. Diabetes Care. 2008;31:1858–63.
25. Anderson NG, Jolly IJ, Wells JE. Sonographic estimation of fetal weight: comparison of bias, precision and consistency using 12 different formulae. Ultrasound Obstet Gynecol. 2007;30:173–9.
26. Gottlieb AG, Galan HL. Nontraditional sonographic pearls in estimating gestational age. Semin Perinatol. 2008;32:154–60.
27. Parretti E, Carignani L, Cioni R, Bartoli E, Borri P, La Torre P, Mecacci F, Martini E, Scarselli G, Mello G. Sonographic evaluation of fetal growth and body composition in women with different degrees of normal glucose metabolism. Diabetes Care. 2003;26:2741–8.
28. Larciprete G, Valensise H, Vasapollo B, Novelli GP, Parretti E, Altomare F, Di Pierro G, Menghini S, Barbati G, Mello G, Arduini D. Fetal subcutaneous tissue thickness (SCTT) in healthy and gestational diabetic pregnancies. Ultrasound Obstet Gynecol. 2003;22:591–7.
29. Lee W, Balasubramaniam M, Deter RL, Hassan SS, Gotsch F, Kusanovic JP, Gonçalves LF, Romero R. Fetal growth parameters and birth weight: their relationship to neonatal body composition. Ultrasound Obstet Gynecol. 2009;33(4):441–6. doi:10.1002/uog.6317.
30. UNICEF. The State of the World's Children 2008: child survival. New York: The United Nations Children's Fund (UNICEF); 2007.
31. Henriksen TB, Wilcox AJ, Hedegaard M, Secher NJ. Bias in studies of preterm and postterm delivery due to ultrasound assessment of gestational age. Epidemiology. 1995;6:533–7.
32. Dietz PM, England LJ, Callaghan WM, Pearl M, Wier ML, Kharrazi M. A comparison of LMP-based and ultrasound-based estimates of gestational age using linked California livebirth and prenatal screening records. Paediatr Perinat Epidemiol. 2007;21 Suppl 2:62–71.
33. Parker AJ, Davies P, Mayho AM, Newton JR. The ultrasound estimation of sex-related variations of intrauterine growth. Am J Obstet Gynecol. 1984;149:665–9.
34. Davis RO, Cutter GR, Goldenberg RL, Hoffman HJ, Cliver SP, Brumfield CG. Fetal biparietal diameter, head circumference, abdominal circumference and femur length. A comparison by race and sex. J Reprod Med. 1993;38:201–6.
35. Shipp TD, Bromley B, Mascola M, Benacerraf B. Variation in fetal femur length with respect to maternal race. J Ultrasound Med. 2001;20:141–4.
36. Mastrobattista JM, Pschirrer ER, Hamrick MA, Glaser AM, Schumacher V, Shirkey BA, Wicklund CA, Hollier LM. Humerus length evaluation in different ethnic groups. J Ultrasound Med. 2004;23:227–31.
37. Goldenberg RL, Nelson KG, Koski JF, Cutter GR. Low birth weight, intrauterine growth retardation, and preterm delivery. Am J Obstet Gynecol. 1985;152:980–4.
38. Ott WJ. Intrauterine growth retardation and preterm delivery. Am J Obstet Gynecol. 1993;168 (6 Pt 1):1710–5; discussion 1715–7.
39. Hediger ML, Scholl TO, Schall JI, Miller LW, Fischer RL. Fetal growth and the etiology of preterm delivery. Obstet Gynecol. 1995;85:175–82.
40. Smith-Bindman R, Chu PW, Ecker JL, Feldstein VA, Filly RA, Bacchetti P. US evaluation of fetal growth: prediction of neonatal outcomes. Radiology. 2002;223:153–61.
41. Min S-J, Luke B, Gillespie B, Min L, Newman RB, Mauldin JG, Witter FR, Salman FA, O'Sullivan MJ. Birth weight references for twins. Am J Obstet Gynecol. 2000;182:1250–7.
42. Min S-J, Luke B, Misiunas R, Anderson E, Nugent C, van de Ven C, Martin D, O'Sullivan MJ, Eardley S, Witter FR, Mauldin JG, Newman RB. Birthweight references for triplets. Am J Obstet Gynecol. 2002;187:S82.
43. Zhang J, Bowes Jr WA. Birth-weight-for-gestational-age patterns by race, sex, and parity in the United State population. Obstet Gynecol. 1995;86:200–8.
44. Kramer MS, Platt RW, Wen SW, Joseph KS, Allen A, Abrahamowicz M, Bréart G, for the Fetal/Infant Health Study Group of the Canadian Perinatal Surveillance System. A new and improved population-based Canadian reference for birth weight for gestational age. Pediatrics. 2001;108:e35.

45. Alexander GR, Himes JH, Kaufman RB, Mor R, Kogan M. A United States national reference for fetal growth. Obstet Gynecol. 1996;87:163–8.
46. Gardosi J, Chang A, Kalyan B, Sahota D, Symonds E. Customised antenatal growth charts. Lancet. 1992;339:283–7.
47. Gardosi J, Mongelli M, Wilcox M, Chang A. An adjustable fetal weight standard. Ultrasound Obstet Gynecol. 1995;6:168–74.
48. Clausson B, Gardosi J, Francis A, Cnattingius S. Perinatal outcome in SGA births defined by customised versus population-based birthweight standards. BJOG. 2001;108:830–4.
49. McCowan L, Harding J, Stewart AW. Customised birthweight centiles predict SGA pregnancies with perinatal morbidity. BJOG. 2005;112:1026–33.
50. Ego A, Subtil D, Grange G, Thiebaugeorges O, Senat MV, Vayssiere C, Zeitlin J. Customized versus population-based birth weight standards for identifying growth restricted infants: a French multicenter study. Am J Obstet Gynecol. 2006;194:1042–9.
51. Das UG, Sysyn GD. Abnormal fetal growth: intrauterine growth retardation, small for gestational age, large for gestational age. Pediatr Clin North Am. 2004;51:639–54.
52. Maulik D. Fetal growth restriction: the etiology. Clin Obstet Gynecol. 2006;49:228–35.
53. Kramer MS. Determinants of low birth weight: methodological assessment and meta-analysis. Bull World Health Organ. 1987;65:663–737.
54. World Health Organization. Maternal anthropometry and pregnancy outcomes: a WHO collaborative project. Bull World Health Organ. 1995;73(Suppl):1–6.
55. Niswander K, Jackson E. Physical characteristics of the gravida and their association with birth weight and perinatal death. Am J Obstet Gynecol. 1974;119:306–13.
56. Niswander KR, Singer J, Westphal M, Weiss W. Weight gain during pregnancy and prepregnancy weight: association with birth weight of term gestations. Obstet Gynecol. 1969;33:482–91.
57. Eastman NJ, Jackson E. Weight relationships in pregnancy: the bearing of maternal weight gain and pre-pregnancy weight on birthweight in full term pregnancies. Obstet Gynecol Surv. 1968;23:1003–25.
58. Singer JE, Westphal M, Niswander K. Relationship of weight gain during pregnancy to birth weight and infant growth and development in the first year of life. Obstet Gynecol. 1968;31:417–23.
59. Institute of Medicine. Nutrition during pregnancy. Washington, DC: National Academy Press; 1990.
60. Abrams BF, Laros RK. Prepregnancy weight, weight gain, and birth weight. Am J Obstet Gynecol. 1986;154:503–9.
61. Kleinman JC. Maternal weight gain during pregnancy: determinants and consequences. NCHS Working Paper Series No. 33. Hyattsville: National Center for Health Statistics, Public Health Service, U.S. Department of Health and Human Services; 1990.
62. Johnson JWC, Longmate JA, Frentzen B. Excessive maternal weight and pregnancy outcome. Am J Obstet Gynecol. 1992;167:353–72.
63. Johnson JWC, Yancey MK. A critique of the new recommendations for weight gain in pregnancy. Am J Obstet Gynecol. 1996;174:254–8.
64. World Health Organization. Physical status: the use and interpretation of anthropometry. WHO Technical Report Series 854. Geneva, Switzerland, 1995.
65. Goldenberg RL, Iams JD, Mercer BM, et al. The preterm prediction study: the value of new vs standard risk factors in predicting early and spontaneous preterm births. Am J Public Health. 1998;88:233–8.
66. Abrams B, Newman V, Key T, Parker J. Maternal weight gain and preterm delivery. Obstet Gynecol. 1989;74:577–83.
67. Abrams B, Newman V. Small-for-gestational-age birth: maternal predictors and comparison with risk factors of spontaneous preterm delivery in the same cohort. Am J Obstet Gynecol. 1991;164:785–90.
68. Spinillo A, Capuzzo E, Piazzi G, Ferrari A, Morales V, Di Mario M. Risk for spontaneous preterm delivery by combined body mass index and gestational weight gain patterns. Acta Obstet Gynecol Scand. 1998;77:32–6.

69. Virji SK, Cottington E. Risk factors associated with preterm deliveries among racial groups in a national sample of married mothers. Am J Perinatol. 1991;8:347–53.
70. Berkowitz GS. Clinical and obstetric risk factors for preterm delivery. Mt Sinai J Med. 1985;52:239–47.
71. Siega-Riz AM, Viswanathan M, Moos M-K, Deierlein A, Mumford S, Knaack J, Thieda P, Lux LJ, Lohr KN. A systematic review of outcomes of maternal weight gain according to the Institute of Medicine recommendations: birthweight, fetal growth, and postpartum weight retention. Am J Obstet Gynecol. 2009;201:339.e1–14.
72. Abrams B, Altman SL, Pickett KE. Pregnancy weight gain: still controversial. Am J Clin Nutr. 2000;71(5 Suppl):1233S–41.
73. Institute of Medicine, Committee to Reexamine IOM Pregnancy Weight Guidelines. In: Rasmussen KM, Yaktine AL, editors. Weight gain during pregnancy: reexamining the guidelines. Washington, DC: National Academy Press; 2009.
74. Luke B, Hediger ML, Nugent C, Newman RB, Mauldin JG, Witter FR, O'Sullivan MJ. Body mass index-specific weight gains associated with optimal birth weight in twin pregnancies. J Reprod Med. 2003;48:217–24.
75. Hediger ML, Scholl TO, Salmon RW. Early weight gain in pregnant adolescents and fetal outcome. Am J Hum Biol. 1989;1:665–72.
76. Hediger ML, Scholl TO, Belsky DH, Ances IG, Salmon RW. Patterns of weight gain in adolescent pregnancy: effects on birth weight and preterm delivery. Obstet Gynecol. 1989;74:6–12.
77. Hickey CA, Cliver SP, Goldenberg RL, Kohatsu J, Hoffman HJ. Prenatal weight gain patterns and birth weight among nonobese black and white women. Obstet Gynecol. 1996;88:490–6.
78. Abrams B, Selvin S. Maternal weight gain pattern and birth weight. Obstet Gynecol. 1995;86:163–9.
79. Abrams B, Carmichael S, Selvin S. Factors associated with the pattern of maternal weight gain during pregnancy. Obstet Gynecol. 1995;86:170–6.
80. Scholl TO, Hediger ML, Ances IG, Belsky DH, Salmon RW. Weight gain during pregnancy in adolescents: predictive ability of early weight gain. Obstet Gynecol. 1990;75:948–53.
81. Strauss RS, Dietz WH. Low maternal weight gain in the second or third trimester increases the risk for intrauterine growth retardation. J Nutr. 1999;129:988–93.
82. Li R, Haas JD, Habicht J-P. Timing of the influence of maternal nutritional status during pregnancy on fetal growth. Am J Hum Biol. 1998;10:529–39.
83. Carmichael S, Abrams B, Selvin S. The association of pattern of maternal weight gain with length of gestation and risk of spontaneous preterm delivery. Paediatr Perinat Epidemiol. 1997;11:392–406.
84. Kramer MS, Coates AL, Michoud M-C, Dagenais S, Hamilton EF, Papageorgiou A. Maternal anthropometry and idiopathic preterm labor. Obstet Gynecol. 1995;86:744–8.
85. Pipe NGG, Smith T, Halliday D, et al. Changes in fat, fat-free mass and body water in human normal pregnancy. Br J Obstet Gynaecol. 1979;86:929–40.
86. Hytten FE, Thomson AM, Taggart N. Total body water in normal pregnancy. J Obstet Gynaecol Br Commonw. 1966;73:553–61.
87. Seitchik J, Alper C, Szutka A. Changes in body composition during pregnancy. Ann N Y Acad Sci. 1963;110:821–9.
88. Van Raaij JMA, Schonk CM, Vermaat-Miedema SH, Peek M, Hautvast J. Body fat mass and basal metabolic rate in Dutch women before, during, and after pregnancy: a reappraisal of energy cost of pregnancy. Am J Clin Nutr. 1989;49:765–72.
89. Villar J, Cogswell M, Kestler E, Castillo P, Menendez R, Repke JT. Effect of fat and fat-free mass deposition during pregnancy on birthweight. Am J Obstet Gynecol. 1992;167:1344–52.
90. Viegas OAC, Cole TJ, Wharton BA. Impaired fat deposition in pregnancy: an indicator for nutritional intervention. Am J Clin Nutr. 1987;45:23–8.
91. Neggers Y, Goldenberg RL, Cliver SP, Hoffman HJ, Cutter GR. Usefulness of various maternal skinfold measurements for predicting newborn birth weight. J Am Diet Assoc. 1992;92:1393–4.

92. Bissenden JG, Scott PH, King J, Hallum J, Mansfield HN, Wharton BA. Anthropometric and biochemical changes during pregnancy in Asian and European mothers having well grown babies. Br J Obstet Gynaecol. 1981;88:992–8.
93. Bissenden JG, Scott PH, King J, Hallum J, Mansfield HN, Wharton BA. Anthropometric and biochemical changes during pregnancy in Asian and European mothers having light for gestational age babies. Br J Obstet Gynaecol. 1981;88:999–1008.
94. Clark PM, Atton C, Law CM, Shiell A, Godfrey K, Barker DJP. Weight gain in pregnancy, triceps skinfold thickness, and blood pressure in offspring. Obstet Gynecol. 1998;91:103–7.
95. Veille JC, Hanson R, Sivakoff M, Hoen H, Ben-Ami M. Fetal cardiac size in normal, intrauterine growth retarded, and diabetic pregnancies. Am J Perinatol. 1993;10:275–9.
96. Konje JC, Bell SC, Morton JJ, de Chazal R, Taylor DJ. Human fetal kidney morphometry during gestation and the relationship between weight, kidney morphometry and plasma active rennin concentration at birth. Clin Sci. 1996;91:169–75.
97. Konje JC, Okaro CI, Bell SC, de Chazal R, Taylor DJ. A cross-sectional study of changes in fetal renal size with gestation in appropriate- and small-for-gestational-age fetuses. Ultrasound Obstet Gynecol. 1997;9:22–6.
98. Roberts AB, Mitchell JM, McCowan LM, Barker S. Ultrasonographic measurement of liver length in the small-for-gestational-age fetus. Am J Obstet Gynecol. 1999;180:634–8.
99. Blake KV, Gurrin LC, Beilin LJ, Stanley FJ, Kendall GE, Landau LI, Newnham JP. Prenatal ultrasound biometry related to subsequent blood pressure in childhood. J Epidemiol Community Health. 2002;56:713–8.
100. Lampl M, Kuzawa CW, Jeanty P. Infants thinner at birth exhibit smaller kidneys for their size in late gestation in a sample of fetuses with appropriate growth. Am J Hum Biol. 2002;14:398–406.
101. Economides DL, Nicolaides KH, Gahl WA, Evans MI. Plasma amino acids in appropriate- and small-for-gestational-age fetuses. Am J Obstet Gynecol. 1989;161:1219–27.
102. Bajoria R, Sooranna SR, Ward S, D'Souza S, Hancock M. Placental transport rather than maternal concentration of amino acids regulates fetal growth in monochorionic twins: implications for fetal origin hypothesis. Am J Obstet Gynecol. 2001;185:1239–46.
103. Jauniaux E, Gulbis B, Acharya G, Gerlo E. Fetal amino acid and enzyme levels with maternal smoking. Obstet Gynecol. 1999;93:680–3.
104. Jauniaux E, Biernaux V, Gerlo E, Gulbis B. Chronic maternal smoking and cord blood amino acid and enzyme levels at term. Obstet Gynecol. 2001;97:57–61.
105. Liechty EA, Denne SC. Regulation of fetal amino acid metabolism: substrate or hormonal regulation? J Nutr. 1998;128:342S–6S.
106. Desai M, Crowther NJ, Lucas A, Hales CN. Organ-selective growth in the offspring of protein-restricted mothers. Br J Nutr. 1996;76:591–603.
107. Jones NJ, Gercel-Taylor C, Taylor DD. Altered cord serum lipid levels associated with small for gestational age infants. Obstet Gynecol. 1999;93:527–31.
108. Munoz A, Uberos J, Molina A, Valenzuela A, Cano D, Ruiz C, Molina Font JA. Relationship of blood rheology to lipoprotein profile during normal pregnancies and those with intrauterine growth retardation. J Clin Pathol. 1995;48:571–4.
109. Radunovic N, Kuczynski E, Rosen T, Dukanac J, Petkovic S, Lockwood CJ. Plasma apoprotein A-I and B concentrations in growth-retarded fetuses: a link between low birth weight and adult atherosclerosis. J Clin Endocrinol Metab. 2000;85:85–8.
110. Martyn CN, Barker DJP, Jespersen S, Greenwald S, Osmond C, Berry C. Growth in utero, adult blood pressure, and arterial compliance. Br Heart J. 1995;73:116–21.
111. Barker DJP, Martyn CN, Osmond C, Hales CN, Fall CHD. Growth in utero and serum cholesterol concentrations in adult life. Br Med J. 1993;307:1524–7.
112. Hales CN. Fetal and infant growth and impaired glucose tolerance in adulthood: the "thrifty phenotype" hypothesis revisited. Acta Paediatr Suppl. 1997;422:73–7.
113. Kind KL, Clifton PM, Katsman AI, Tsiounis M, Robinson JS, Owens JA. Restricted fetal growth and the response to dietary cholesterol in the guinea pig. Am J Physiol. 1999;277:R1675–82.

114. Sawaya AL, Grillo LP, Verreschi I, da Silva AC, Roberts SB. Mild stunting is associated with higher susceptibility to the effects of high fat diets: studies in a shantytown population in São Paulo, Brazil. J Nutr. 1998;128:415S–20S.
115. Hoffman DJ, Sawaya AL, Verreschi I, Tucker KL, Roberts SB. Why are nutritionally stunted children at increased risk of obesity? Studies of metabolic rate and fat oxidation in shantytown children from São Paulo, Brazil. Am J Clin Nutr. 2000;72:702–7.
116. Hinchliffe SA, Lynch MRJ, Sargent PH, Howard CV, Vanvelzen D. The effect of intrauterine growth retardation on the development of renal nephrons. Br J Obstet Gynaecol. 1992;99: 296–301.
117. Hoet JJ, Ozanne S, Reusens B. Influences of pre- and postnatal nutritional exposures on vascular/endocrine systems in animals. Environ Health Perspect. 2000;108:563–8.
118. Eriksson J, Forsen T, Tuomilehto J, Osmond C, Barker D. Fetal and childhood growth and hypertension in adult life. Hypertension. 2000;36:790–4.
119. Williams MC, O'Brien WF, Nelson RN, Spellacy WN. Histologic chorioamnionitis is associated with fetal growth restriction in term and preterm infants. Am J Obstet Gynecol. 2000; 183:1094–9.
120. Faggioni R, Feingold KR, Grunfeld C. Leptin regulation of the immune response and the immunodeficiency of malnutrition. FASEB J. 2001;15(14):2565–71.
121. Stephensen CB, Vitamin A. Infection, and immune function. Annu Rev Nutr. 2001;21: 167–92.
122. Kwong WY, Wild AE, Roberts P, Willis AC, Fleming TP. Maternal undernutrition during the preimplantation period of rat development causes blastocyst abnormalities and programming of postnatal hypertension. Development. 2000;127:4195–202.
123. Sewell MF, Huston-Presley L, Super DM, Caqtalano P. Increased neonatal fat mass, not lean body mass, is associated with maternal obesity. Am J Obstet Gynecol. 2006;195:1100–3.
124. Catalano PM, Farrell K, Thomas A, Huston-Presley L, Mencin P, de Mouzon SH, Amini SB. Perinatal risk factors for childhood obesity and metabolic dysregulation. Am J Clin Nutr. 2009;90:1303–13.
125. Hak AE, Stehouwer CDA, Bots ML, et al. Associations of C-reactive protein with measures of obesity, insulin resistance, and subclinical atherosclerosis in healthy, middle-aged women. Arterioscler Thromb Vasc Biol. 1999;19:1986–91.
126. Pickup JC, Mattock MB, Chusney GD, et al. NIDDM as a disease of the innate immune system: association of acute-phase reactants and interleukin-6 with metabolic syndrome X. Diabetologia. 1997;40:1286–92.
127. Scholl TO, Sowers MF, Chen X, Lenders C. Maternal glucose concentration influences fetal growth, gestation, and pregnancy complications. Am J Epidemiol. 2001;154:514–20.
128. Naeye RL. Maternal body weight and pregnancy outcome. Am J Clin Nutr. 1990;52:273–9.
129. Visser M, Bouter LM, McQuillan GM, Wener MH, Harris TB. Elevated C-reactive protein levels in overweight and obese adults. JAMA. 1999;282:2131–5.
130. Fried SK, Bunkin DA, Greenberg AS. Omental and subcutaneous adipose tissues of obese subjects release interleukin-6. J Clin Endocrinol Metab. 1998;83:847–50.
131. Cammu H, Goossens A, Derde MP, Temmerman M, Foulon W, Amy JJ. C-reactive protein in preterm labour: association with outcome of tocolysis and placental histology. Br J Obstet Gynaecol. 1989;96:314–9.
132. Hsu C-D, Hong S-F, Nickless NA, Copel JA. Glycosylated hemoglobin in insulin-dependent diabetes mellitus related to preeclampsia. Am J Perinatol. 1998;15:199–202.
133. Oken E, Levitan EB, Gillman MW. Maternal smoking during pregnancy and child overweight: systematic review and meta-analysis. Int J Obes. 2008;32:201–10.
134. Syme C, Abrahamowicz M, Mahboubi A, Leonard GT, Perron M, Richer L, Veillette S, Gaudet D, Paus T, Pausova Z. Prenatal exposure to maternal cigarette smoking and accumulation of intra-abdominal fat during adolescence. Obesity. 2010;18:1021–5.
135. Matijasevich A, Brion M-J, Menezes AM, Barros AJD, Santos IS, Barros FC. Maternal smoking during pregnancy and offspring growth in childhood: 1993 and 2004 Pelotas cohort studies. Arch Dis Child. 2011;96:519–25.

136. Montgomery SM, Ekbom A. Smoking during pregnancy and diabetes mellitus in a British longitudinal birth cohort. BMJ. 2002;324:26–7.
137. Power C, Atherton K, Thomas C. Maternal smoking in pregnancy, adult adiposity and other risk factors for cardiovascular disease. Atherosclerosis. 2010;211:643–8.
138. Barker DJP. Mothers, babies and health in later life. Edinburgh: Churchill Livingstone; 1998.
139. Barker DJP. Early growth and cardiovascular disease. Arch Dis Child. 1999;80:305–10.
140. MacGregor SN, Sabbagha RE, Tamura RK, Pielet BW, Feigenbaum SL. Differing fetal growth patterns in pregnancies complicated by preterm labor. Obstet Gynecol. 1988;72: 834–7.
141. Weiner CP, Sabbagha RE, Vaisrub N, Depp R. A hypothetical model suggesting suboptimal intrauterine growth in infants delivered preterm. Obstet Gynecol. 1985;65:323–6.
142. Phillips DIW, Barker DJP, Hales CN, Hirst S, Osmond C. Thinness at birth and insulin resistance in adult life. Diabetologia. 1994;37:150–4.
143. Fergusson DM, Crane J, Beasley R, Horwood LJ. Perinatal factors and atopic disease in childhood. Clin Exp Allergy. 1997;27:1377–9.
144. Phillips DIW, Barker DJP, Osmond C. Infant feeding, fetal growth and adult thyroid function. Acta Endocrinol. 1993;129:134–8.
145. Godfrey KM, Barker DJP, Osmond C. Disproportionate fetal growth and raised IgE concentration in adult life. Clin Exp Allergy. 1994;24:641–8.
146. Fall CHD, Stein CE, Kumaran K, et al. Size at birth, maternal weight, and non-insulin dependent diabetes in South India. Diabet Med. 1998;15:220–7.
147. McCance DR, Pettitt DJ, Hanson RL, Jacobsson LTH, Knowler WC, Bennett PH. Birth weight and non-insulin dependent diabetes: thrifty genotype, thrifty phenotype, or surviving small baby genotype? Br Med J. 1994;308:942–5.
148. Forsèn T, Eriksson JG, Tuomilehto J, Osmond C, Barker DJP. Growth in utero and during childhood among women who develop coronary heart disease: longitudinal study. Br Med J. 1999;319:1403–7.
149. Barker DJP, Godfrey KM, Osmond C, Bull A. The relation of fetal length, ponderal index and head circumference to blood pressure and the risk of hypertension in adult life. Paediatr Perinat Epidemiol. 1992;6:35–44.
150. Lithell HO, McKeigue PM, Berglund L, Mohsen R, Lithell UB, Leon DA. Relation of size at birth to non-insulin dependent diabetes and insulin concentrations in men aged 50–60 years. Br Med J. 1996;312:406–10.
151. Eriksson JG, Forsèn T, Tuomilehto J, Winter PD, Osmond C, Barker DJP. Catch-up growth in childhood and death from coronary heart disease: longitudinal study. Br Med J. 1999;318:427–31.
152. Lewis DS, Bertrand HA, McMahan CA, McGill Jr HC, Carey KD, Masoro EJ. Preweaning food intake influences the adiposity of young adult baboons. J Clin Invest. 1986;78: 899–905.
153. Lewis DS, Mott GE, McMahan CA, Masoro EJ, Carey KD, McGill Jr HC. Deferred effects of preweaning diet on atherosclerosis in adolescent baboons. Arteriosclerosis. 1988;8: 274–80.
154. Fall CHD, Barker DJP, Osmond C, Winter PD, Clark PMS, Hales CN. Relation of infant feeding to adult serum cholesterol concentration and death from ischaemic heart disease. Br Med J. 1992;304:801–5.
155. Phillips DIW, Cooper C, Fall C, Prentice L, Osmond C, Barker DJP, Rees Smith B. Fetal growth and autoimmune thyroid disease. Q J Med. 1993;86:247–53.
156. Ravelli GP, Stein ZA, Susser MW. Obesity in young men after famine exposure in utero and early infancy. N Engl J Med. 1976;1976:349–53.
157. Parsons TJ, Power C, Logan S, Summerbell CD. Childhood predictors of adult obesity: a systematic review. Int J Obes. 1999;23:S1–107.
158. Parsons TJ, Power C, Manor O. Fetal and early life growth and body mass index from birth to early adulthood in 1958 British cohort: longitudinal study. Br Med J. 2001;323:1331–5.

159. Hediger ML, Overpeck MD, Kuczmarski RJ, McGlynn A, Maurer KR, Davis WW. Muscularity and fatness of infants and young children born small- or large-for-gestational age. Pediatrics. 1998;102:e60.
160. Yau K-IT, Chang M-H. Growth and body composition of preterm, small-for-gestational-age infants at a postmenstrual age of 37–40 weeks. Early Hum Dev. 1993;33:117–31.
161. Larsson B, Svardsudd K, Welin L, Wilhelmsen L, Bjorntorp P, Tibblin G. Abdominal adipose tissue distribution, obesity, and risk of cardiovascular disease and death: 13 year follow up of participants in the study of men born in 1913. Br Med J. 1984;288:1401–4.
162. Law CM, Barker DJP, Osmond C, Fall CHD, Simmonds SJ. Early growth and abdominal fatness in adult life. J Epidemiol Community Health. 1992;46:184–6.
163. Hediger ML, Scholl TO, Schall JI, Cronk CE. One-year changes in weight and fatness in girls during late adolescence. Pediatrics. 1995;96:253–8.
164. Van Lenthe FJ, Kemper HCG, van Mechelen W, et al. Biological maturation and the distribution of subcutaneous fat from adolescence into adulthood: the Amsterdam growth and health study. Int J Obes. 1996;20:121–9.
165. Ravelli ACJ, van der Meulen JHP, Osmond C, Barker DJP, Bleker OP. Obesity at the age of 50 y in men and women exposed to famine prenatally. Am J Clin Nutr. 1999;70:811–6.
166. Ong KK, Ahmed ML, Emmett PM, Preece MA, Dunger DB. Association between postnatal catch-up growth and obesity in childhood: prospective cohort study. Br Med J. 2000;320: 967–71, 320:1244.
167. Haffner SM, Stern MP, Hazuda HP, et al. Upper body and centralized adiposity in Mexican Americans and non-Hispanic whites: relationship to body mass index and other behavioral and demographic variables. Int J Obes. 1986;10:493–502.
168. Shimokata H, Muller DC, Andres R. Studies in the distribution of body fat. III. Effects of cigarette smoking. JAMA. 1989;261:1169–73.
169. Valdez R, Athens MA, Thompson GH, Bradshaw BS, Stern MP. Birthweight and adult health outcomes in a biethnic population in the USA. Diabetologia. 1994;37:624–31.
170. Malina RM, Katzmarzyk PT, Beunen G. Birth weight and its relationship to size attained and relative fat distribution at 7 to 12 years of age. Obes Res. 1996;4:385–90.
171. Barker M, Robinson S, Osmond C, Barker DJP. Birth weight and body fat distribution in adolescent girls. Arch Dis Child. 1997;77:381–3.
172. Cook DG, Whincup PH, Miller G, Carey I, Adshead FJ, Papacosta O, Walker M, Howarth D. Fibrinogen and factor VII levels are related to adiposity but not fetal growth or social class in children aged 10–11 years. Am J Epidemiol. 1999;150:727–36.
173. Shea S, Isai CR, Couch S, Starc TJ, Tracy RP, Deckelbaum R, Talmud P, Berglund L, Humphries SE. Relations of plasma fibrinogen level in children to measures of obesity, the (G-455→A) mutation in the ß-fibrinogen promoter gene, and family history of ischemic heart disease. The Columbia University BioMarkers Study. Am J Epidemiol. 1999;150:737–46.
174. Van Lenthe FJ, van Mechelen W, Kemper HCG, Twisk JWR. Association of a central pattern of body fat with blood pressure and lipoproteins from adolescence into adulthood. Am J Epidemiol. 1998;147:686–93.
175. Hales CN, Desai M, Ozanne SE, Crowther NJ. Fishing in the stream of diabetes: from measuring insulin to the control of fetal organogenesis. Biochem Soc Trans. 1996;24:341–50.
176. Cresswell JL, Egger P, Fall CHD, Osmond C, Fraser RB, Barker DJP. Is the age of menopause determined in utero? Early Hum Dev. 1997;49:143–8.
177. Francois I, de Zegher F. Adrenarche and fetal growth. Pediatr Res. 1997;41:440–2.
178. Persson I, Ahlsson F, Ewald U, et al. Influence of perinatal factors on the onset of puberty in boys and girls: implications for interpretation of link with risk of long term diseases. Am J Epidemiol. 1999;150:747–55.
179. Ibáñez L, Potau N, Enriquez G, de Zegher F. Reduced uterine and ovarian size in adolescent girls born small for gestational age. Pediatr Res. 2000;47:575–7.
180. Powls A, Botting N, Cooke RWI, Pilling D, Marlow N. Growth impairment in very low birthweight children at 12 years of age: correlation with perinatal and outcome variables. Arch Dis Child. 1996;75:F152–7.

181. Peralta-Carrcelen M, Jackson DAS, Goran MI, Royal SA, Mayo MS, Nelson KG. Growth of adolescents who were born at extremely low birth weight without major disability. J Pediatr. 2000;136:633–40.
182. Ibáñez L, Potau N, Marcos MV, de Zegher F. Exaggerated adrenarche and hyperinsulinemia in adolescent girls born small for gestational age. J Clin Endocrinol Metab. 1998;24: 4739–41.
183. Berkey CS, Gardner JD, Frazier AL, Colditz GA. Relation of childhood diet and body size to menarche and adolescent growth in girls. Am J Epidemiol. 2000;152:446–52.
184. Belizán JM, Villar J, Bergel E, del Pino A, Di Fulvio S, Galliano SV, Kattan C. Long term effect of calcium supplementation during pregnancy on blood pressure of offspring: follow up of a randomized controlled trial. Br Med J. 1997;315:281–5.
185. Lucas A, Fewtrell MS, Cole TJ. Fetal origins of adult disease—the hypothesis revisited. BMJ. 1999;319:245–9.
186. Forrester TE, Wilks RJ, Bennett FI, Simeon D, Osmond C, Allen M, et al. Fetal growth and cardiovascular risk factors in Jamaican schoolchildren. Br Med J. 1996;312:56–60.
187. Taylor SJ, Whincup PH, Cook DG, Papacosta O, Walker M. Size at birth and blood pressure: cross sectional study in 8–11 year old children. Br Med J. 1997;314:475–80.
188. Fall CHD, Paudit AN, Law CM, Yajnik CS, Clark PM, Breier B, et al. Size at birth and plasma insulin-like growth factor-1 concentrations. Arch Dis Child. 1995;73:287–93.
189. Frankel S, Smith GD, Gunnell D. Childhood socioeconomic position and adult cardiovascular mortality: the Boyd Orr cohort. Am J Epidemiol. 1999;150:1081–4.
190. Whincup PH, Cook DG, Adshead F, Taylor SJC, Walker M, Papacosta O, et al. Childhood size is more strongly related than size at birth to glucose and insulin levels in 10–11-year-old children. Diabetologia. 1997;40:319–26.
191. Whincup PH, Bredow M, Fiona Payne, Sadler S, Golding J, the ALSPAC Study Team. Size at birth and blood pressure at 3 years of age. Am J Epidemiol. 1999;149:730–9.
192. Leon DA, Lithell HO, Vargero D, et al. Reduced fetal growth rate and increased risk of death from ischaemic heart disease: Cohort study of 15,000 Swedish men and women born 1915–29. Br Med J. 1998;317:241–5.
193. Forsèn T, Eriksson JG, Tuomilehto J, Osmond C, Barker DJP. Mother's weight in pregnancy and coronary heart disease in a cohort of Finnish men: follow up study. Br Med J. 1997; 315:837–40.
194. de Bruin JP, Dorland M, Bruinse HW, Spliet W, Nikkels PGJ, Te Velde ER. Fetal growth retardation as a cause of impaired ovarian development. Early Hum Dev. 1998;51:39–46.
195. Plante LA. Small size at birth and later diabetic pregnancy. Obstet Gynecol. 1998;92:781–4.
196. Williams MA, Emanuel I, Kimpo C, Leisenring WM, Hale CB. A population-based cohort study of the relation between maternal birthweight and risk of gestational diabetes in four racial/ethnic groups. Paediatr Perinat Epidemiol. 1999;13:452–65.
197. Godfrey KM, Sheppard A, Gluckman PD, Lillycrop KA, Burdge GC, McLean C, et al. Epigenetic gene promoter methylation at birth is associated with child's later adiposity. Diabetes. 2011;60:1528–34.
198. Blumberg B. Obesogens, stem cells and the maternal programming of obesity. J Dev Orig Health Dis. 2011;2:3–8.
199. Heerwagen MJR, Miller MR, Barbour LA, Friedman JE. Maternal obesity and fetal metabolic programming: a fertile epigenetic soil. Am J Physiol Regul Integr Comp Physiol. 2010;299:R711–22.

Chapter 4
Metabolic Syndrome in Childhood as a Risk Factor for Type 2 Diabetes

Nicola Santoro, Cosimo Giannini, and Sonia Caprio

Abstract The worldwide epidemic of childhood obesity in the last decades is responsible for the occurrence in pediatrics of disorders once mainly found in adults, such as the metabolic syndrome and type 2 diabetes. A key factor in their pathogenesis is insulin resistance, a phenomenon occurring mainly in obese subjects with a general resistance to the insulin effect only on carbohydrates metabolism. Given that the metabolic syndrome and type 2 diabetes in youths are driven by obesity, the prevalence of the latter will strongly influence their prevalence. Although obesity is the most frequent cause of insulin resistance in youths, it should be taken into consideration that a transient physiological insulin-resistant state occurs in children during puberty, maybe due to the increase in growth hormone and sex steroids, and that this state may worsen the insulin resistance present in obese children accelerating the progression to metabolic syndrome and type 2 diabetes. Thus, the key points to understand the progression leading to the occurrence of metabolic syndrome and type 2 diabetes are (1) when and how insulin resistance occurs in obese children and adolescents and (2) what are the underlying putative defects leading to glucose dysregulation.

Keywords Obesity • Insulin resistance • Insulin secretion • Type 2 diabetes • Youths

N. Santoro, M.D., Ph.D. • C. Giannini, M.D., Ph.D. • S. Caprio, M.D.(✉)
Department of Pediatrics, Yale University,
330 Cedar Street, New Haven, CT 06511, USA
e-mail: sonia.caprio@yale.edu

Introduction

Many of the metabolic and cardiovascular complications of obesity are already present during childhood probably as a consequence of insulin resistance, which is the most common abnormality of obesity and the most important pathogenetic determinant of its metabolic complications [1]. The clustering of some complications occurring in obese patients (such as dyslipidemia and hypertension) defines the metabolic syndrome (METS). The common denominator of all these features is represented by insulin resistance, whose increase parallels the increase of the risk of metabolic abnormalities [1]. Although obesity is the most frequent cause of insulin resistance in youth, it should be taken into consideration that a transient physiological insulin-resistant state occurs in children during puberty, maybe due to the increase in growth hormone and sex steroids [2], and that this state may worsen the insulin resistance present in obese children accelerating the progression to METS and type 2 diabetes. Thus, the key points to understand the progression leading to the occurrence of the metabolic complications seen in obese youth, including type 2 diabetes, are (1) when and how insulin resistance occurs in obese youths and (2) what are the underlying putative defects leading to glucose dysregulation.

Insulin Resistance and Ectopic Fat Deposition in the Obese Child

Recent studies have shown that patterns of lipid partitioning are a major determinant of the metabolic profile and not just the obesity per se. Total body fat is not the sole source of the adverse health complications of obesity; rather, fat distribution or the relative proportion of lipids in key insulin-sensitive tissues and organs is what determines the metabolic risk of the individual. The increase in intramyocellular lipid content also in obese children and adolescents has been found to be strongly related to insulin resistance [3]. Fat accumulation in skeletal muscle tissue and liver has been shown, in fact, to increase the amount of diacylglycerol (DAG) which can alter insulin signaling [4]. DAG-induced insulin resistance in muscle and liver can be explained in most forms of obesity, in which increased delivery of fatty acids overwhelms the capacity of the cells to oxidize fat or convert DAG to triacylglycerols [4]. In this context, the role of adiponectin in the development of insulin resistance seems important. Indeed, plasma adiponectin levels are positively related to insulin sensitivity, whereas they are strongly inversely related to triglyceride levels, intramyocellular lipid content (IMCL) content, and fasting insulin levels [5]. The relationship between adiponectin and IMCL is stronger in obese subjects [5], suggesting that the relationship is more prominent above a certain threshold of IMCL content, typical of obese children, and has a minor significance in children with lower IMCL content. The close association between adiponectin and IMCL lipid content is interesting and consistent with data, indicating that adiponectin acts primarily on skeletal muscle tissue to increase influx and combustion of FFAs, thereby reducing muscle triglyceride content in mouse models of obesity [6]. Although initial studies in elderly suggested that insulin resistance might be a consequence of the aging [7], studies in children and adolescents have shown that intramyocellular and extramyocellular accumulation of triglycerides occur early in the natural course of obesity thus suggesting that insulin resistance in youth might develop throughout different and still poorly known mechanisms [3].

Another important determinant of insulin resistance is the ectopic fat deposition into the liver, which represents the hallmark of the hepatic steatosis. Although it remains unclear whether hepatic steatosis is an important marker of multiorgan insulin resistance [8] and is considered itself a component of the METS. The intrahepatic fat accumulation, in fact, causes the development of nonalcoholic fatty liver disease (NAFLD) that is a pathological condition of emerging importance in obese children [9]. NAFLD encompasses the entire spectrum of liver conditions, ranging from asymptomatic steatosis with elevated or normal aminotransferases to steatohepatitis (nonalcoholic steatohepatitis, NASH) and advanced fibrosis with cirrhosis [10, 11].

The association between NAFLD and a metabolic derangement has been clearly demonstrated by Burgert et al. [9]. In this study, as surrogate of liver injury, alanine aminotransferase (ALT) levels were measured in 392 obese adolescents. Elevated ALT (>35 U/l) levels were found in 14% of participants, with a predominance of White/Hispanic. After adjusting for potential confounders, rising ALT levels were associated with deterioration in insulin sensitivity and glucose tolerance as well as increasing FFA and triglyceride levels. Furthermore, increased hepatic fat accumulation (assessed using fast magnetic resonance imaging) was found in 32% of obese adolescents and was associated with decreased insulin sensitivity and adiponectin levels and with increased triglycerides and visceral fat [9]. These results demonstrate that in obese childhood and adolescence, hepatic fat accumulation is associated with the components of METS, such as insulin resistance, dyslipidemia, and altered glucose metabolism.

Recent studies have shown that patterns of fat partitioning are probably one major link between insulin resistance and NAFLD in obese youth [12]. In a multi-ethnic cohort study, 118 obese adolescents were stratified into tertiles based on the proportion of abdominal fat in the visceral depot. Abdominal fat and intramyocellular lipid (IMCL) were respectively measured by magnetic resonance imaging and by proton magnetic resonance spectroscopy. A higher proportion of visceral fat was associated with higher IMCL, hepatic steatosis, insulin resistance, high triglycerides, and low HDL and adiponectin levels. As the proportion of visceral fat increased across tertiles, percentage subcutaneous fat decreased. Notably, the risk for the METS was five times greater in the adolescence with this particular fat partitioning profile compared with those with lower visceral accumulation [13]. That is why it has been suggested that obese adolescents with a high proportion of visceral fat and relatively low subcutaneous fat have a phenotype reminiscent of partial lipodystrophy. Those who fit this profile are not necessarily the most severe obese, yet they suffer from severe metabolic complications of obesity and are at high risk of having

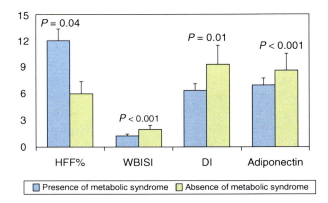

Fig. 4.1 Metabolic patterns according to the presence or absence of the MS in 1,589 obese children and adolescents (mean age 13.2 ± 3.0; mean z-score BMI 2.30 ± 058). MS (32% of the cohort), defined according to Weiss et al. [14], clearly shows a higher hepatic fat content (*HFF%*), a lower insulin sensitivity as evaluated by the whole-body insulin sensitivity index (*WBISI*), a lower insulin secretion as evaluated by the disposition index (*DI*), and lower levels of adiponectin (Based on personal data)

METS [12, 13]. In Fig. 4.1, we show our personal data on 1,589 obese children and adolescents (mean age 13.2 ± 3.0; mean z-score BMI 2.30 ± 058). The 513 (32%) subjects with the features of the METS clearly show a higher hepatic fat content (HFF%), a lower insulin sensitivity as evaluated by the whole body insulin sensitivity index (WBISI), a lower insulin secretion as evaluated by the disposition index (DI), and lower levels of adiponectin (Fig. 4.1).

In summary, the co-occurrence of ectopic fat distribution and alterations in insulin-stimulated glucose metabolism seen in some obese adolescents are key to the development of insulin resistance and the most fearful complication of childhood obesity: type 2 diabetes.

How this scenario will lead to glucose homeostasis derangement? Is insulin resistance enough to develop prediabetes or type 2 diabetes?

Metabolic Staging of Type 2 Diabetes in Youth: the Long Trip Through Prediabetes

For many years insulin resistance has dominated the scene as the main cause of type 2 diabetes. Recently, however, the attention has been more on the beta-cell dysfunction indicating its important and early role in the development of type 2 diabetes. It is now well established that the decline of beta-cell function starts much earlier than the development of overt diabetes. Previous work using the glucose clamp techniques revealed that while there is a strong overlap in insulin resistance between many normal glucose tolerance (NGT) and impaired glucose tolerance (IGT) obese

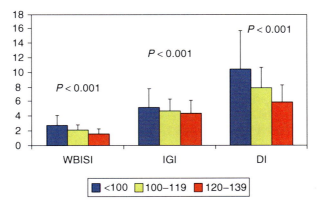

Fig. 4.2 This figure is based on our personal data on 1,371 obese children and adolescents and shows the relationship between β-cell function expressed as insulinogenic index (*IGI*) as well as disposition index (*DI*) and insulin sensitivity (*WBISI*) as a function of 2-h glucose. In particular, the population was divided into three groups according to the 2-h glucose levels: less than 100 (267 subjects), between 100 and 119 (582 subjects), and between 120 and 139 (522 subjects). Data are expressed as means and standard deviations

children and adolescents [15], the major distinguishing feature between the severely insulin-resistant IGT and NGT youth is the failure of the ß-cell in the IGT group to increase the early insulin response to the glucose load. Similarly, the loss of ß-cell compensation has been shown in the progression from the NGT to the prediabetic state in adults [3, 16]. In a study involving obese children and adolescents with 2-h glucose lower than 140 mg/dl, at first glance, the 2-h glucose category data suggest that worsening insulin resistance may contribute to early deterioration in glucose tolerance [17]. On further analysis, however, insulin secretion, as reflected by the insulinogenic index (IGI; the ratio of insulin to glucose, a measure of the effect of meals on prediabetics), appeared to have a stronger impact on glucose tolerance (albeit still normal), irrespective of insulin sensitivity. As illustrated in Fig. 4.2 at any level of insulin sensitivity (WBISI), the IGI was lowest in the group with the highest 2-h glucose level. These data provide support for the notion that even obese youths with NGT, who are the most insulin sensitive, can have a perturbed β-cell response to a normal physiological stimulus (glucose ingestion). Moreover, recent published data in obese children and adolescent clearly show that a decline in beta-cell function can be observed also with fasting glucose levels lower than 100 mg/dl [18]. These data clearly indicate that impaired insulin secretion is present long before the full blown occurrence of type 2 diabetes. Thus, prior to the diagnosis of diabetes, most if not all obese youths go though some intermediates metabolic states of glucose intolerance globally defined as prediabetes [19]. The duration and natural evolution or regression of prediabetes in youth is not well understood. What is, however, clear that both insulin resistance together with beta-cell dysfunction are fully manifested. Hence, prediabetes in obese youth is a major risk for future development of diabetes (T2D) in the obese adolescents [20].

Type 2 Diabetes in Youth: The Fall in Insulin Secretion

What happens to the beta-cell in the progression from the normal glucose tolerance to type 2 diabetes? Type 2 diabetes is progressive because of the continued decline in β-cell function [21]. Several studies [21] have demonstrated that diabetes and prediabetes do not develop until the β-cell fails to compensate appropriately to the peripheral insulin resistance state. The ability of the β-cell to secrete sufficient insulin to adequately respond to the peripheral insulin resistance state depends on multiple factors, including β-cell mass [21] and secretory capacity [21], influenced by genetic [22] and environmental factors [22]. In fact, although the progressive loss of β-cell function could be due to different metabolic derangements (insulin resistance, lipotoxicity), several studies have suggested that β-cell dysfunction depends also on a preexisting and perhaps genetically determined risk, which is crucial for β-cell dysfunction to occur [21, 22].

In a normal individual, on stimulation, the β-cell responds with a prompt but short-lived (0–10 min) release of insulin (first phase) followed by a steady and longer-lasting increase in plasma insulin concentration (second phase) [16]. From prediabetes through the course of type 2 diabetes, abnormalities in the biphasic nature of insulin release have been found in adults [15, 23]. Indeed, an altered acute-phase insulin release in response to glucose marks the early stages of decline in β-cell function [16]. Recent studies reported that in obese adolescents, the hallmark of IGT is insulin resistance, with no apparent decline in first-phase insulin release [3, 24]. However, in obese adolescents with type 2 diabetes, impaired β-cell function was clearly evident [25]. Our previous published data demonstrate that in the passage from NGT to IGT to type 2 diabetes, the obese adolescent experiences a fall in first-phase insulin secretion [17]. For each change in glucose tolerance, the decrement of first-phase sensitivity to glucose was approximately the same or one-third of the average value in the obese adolescent with NGT. Since there were no significant differences in insulin sensitivity among the studied groups, the best correlate of glucose tolerance class was first-phase insulin secretion, in close agreement with a wealth of data obtained in adults [26]. Since second-phase secretion is still normal in IGT, the defect of the second phase seen in the adolescents with type 2 diabetes is impairment specific to this age range. This does not mean that the defect of the first phase is less influential than the defect of the second phase in causing hyperglycemia, yet simply recognizes that the decline of the first phase accompanies the increase in ambient glucose levels across the whole range of glycemia, whereas the defect in the second phase is required for the development of type 2 diabetes. Importantly, the relationship between second-phase secretion and insulin sensitivity, although still detectable in the children with diabetes, is clearly shifted to the left (Fig. 4.3). Thus, it is reasonable to think that loss of the capability of β-cell second-phase secretion to compensate for insulin resistance is a pathophysiological fingerprint of type 2 diabetes in childhood. In a nutshell, the defect of the first phase is the most sensitive index of both nondiabetic and diabetic hyperglycemia, but the disruption of the second phase is a specific hallmark of type 2 diabetes [27].

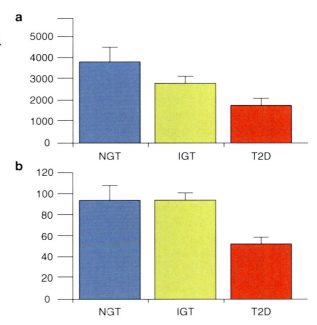

Fig. 4.3 Glucose sensitivity of the first- and second-phase insulin response in NGT, IGT, and diabetic subjects. (**a**) Glucose sensitivity of β-cell first-phase secretion in adolescents with NGT (*blue*), IGT (*yellow*), and type 2 diabetes (T2DM) (*red*). (**b**) Glucose sensitivity of β-cell second-phase secretion in adolescents with NGT (*blue*), IGT (*yellow*), and type 2 diabetes (*red*). *P*<0.01 for IGT versus NGT; *P*<0.02 for type 2 diabetes versus IGT (Modified from Weiss et al. [27]). With permission from the American Diabetes Association)

Undoubtedly, different genetic predisposition plays an important role in the development of type 2 diabetes. This idea is supported both by genome-wide association studies (GWAS) [22] and by clinical studies clearly showing that subjects, who develop IGT or type 2 diabetes, have a compromising insulin secretion even before developing IGT or type 2 diabetes. When estimating insulin secretion in the context of the "resistant milieu" of the IGT subjects, and thus using the disposition index (DI; a quantitative measure that describes the relationship between β-cell sensitivity and insulin sensitivity), it has been found that IGT subjects had a significantly lower DI than the NGT group. The lower DI indicates that the secretion of insulin is not able to compensate for the increased resistance, resulting in a marked decrease in insulin-stimulated glucose metabolism in the IGT subjects [28]. More recently, Cali et al. showed that obese adolescents with normal glucose tolerance who progress to IGT manifest a primary defect in beta-cell function [29]. These data are in agreement with those reported by Lyssenko et al. in the Botnia studies in adults showing that impaired insulin secretion and action, particularly insulin secretion adjusted for insulin resistance (disposition index), are strong predictors of future diabetes [22]. Interestingly, the progression to type 2 diabetes in obese youth seems to be faster than in adults [25]. An accurate case report by Gungor et al., in fact, suggested that the deterioration in β-cell function in youth with type 2 diabetes may be much more accelerated (~15% per year) than that observed in adults [25].

Future Perspectives

A better understanding of the mechanisms underlying the pathogenesis of type 2 diabetes in youth is needed. While environmental factors associated with obesity development are playing a role, it is also important to note that genetic factors may be critical. In the last few years, genetic studies, mainly GWAS, have identified several novel loci associated with population-based type 2 diabetes [30]. Interestingly, although the majority of them seem to be linked to the beta-cell function, the mechanisms by which they can lead to type 2 diabetes seem to be diverse and sometimes involve also genes implicated in the lipid metabolism [30]. As for example, the rs1290629 variant located in the *GCKR* gene confers a higher risk to develop hypertriglyceridemia as well as hyperglycemia [30], and more recently, it has been associated with hepatic fat accumulation (Santoro N, October 10, 2010, TOS, personal communication). Thus, the possibility exists that some of these variants may lead to type 2 diabetes through pathways other than those related to the beta-cell dysfunction, being good candidate as genes clustering for the features defining the METS.

References

1. Cali AM, Caprio S. Obesity in children and adolescents. J Clin Endocrinol Metab. 2008;93:S31–6.
2. Kamagate A, Dong HH. FoxO1 integrates insulin signaling to VLDL production. Cell Cycle. 2008;7:3162–70.
3. Weiss R, Dufour S, Taksali SE, Tamborlane WV, Petersen KF, Bonadonna RC, Boselli L, Barbetta G, Allen K, Rife F, Savoye M, Dziura J, Sherwin R, Shulman GI, Caprio S. Prediabetes in obese youth: a syndrome of impaired glucose tolerance, severe insulin resistance, and altered myocellular and abdominal fat partitioning. Lancet. 2003;362:951–7.
4. Samuel VT, Petersen KF, Shulman GI. Lipid-induced insulin resistance: unravelling the mechanism. Lancet. 2010;375:2267–77.
5. Weiss R, Dufour S, Groszmann A, Petersen K, Dziura J, Taksali SE, Shulman G, Caprio S. Low adiponectin levels in adolescent obesity: a marker of increased intramyocellular lipid accumulation. J Clin Endocrinol Metab. 2003;88:2014–8.
6. Yamauchi T, Kamon J, Waki H, Terauchi Y, Kubota N, Hara K, Mori Y, Ide T, Murakami K, Tsuboyama-Kasaoka N, Ezaki O, Akanuma Y, Gavrilova O, Vinson C, Reitman ML, Kagechika H, Shudo K, Yoda M, Nakano Y, Tobe K, Nagai R, Kimura S, Tomita M, Froguel P, Kadowaki T. The fat-derived hormone adiponectin reverses insulin resistance associated with both lipoatrophy and obesity. Nat Med. 2001;7:941–6.
7. Petersen KF, Dufour S, Befroy D, Garcia R, Shulman GI. Impaired mitochondrial activity in the insulin-resistant offspring of patients with type 2 diabetes. N Engl J Med. 2004;350:664–71.
8. Fabbrini E, Sullivan S, Klein S. Obesity and nonalcoholic fatty liver disease: biochemical, metabolic, and clinical implications. Hepatology. 2010;51:679–89.
9. Burgert TS, Taksali SE, Dziura J, Goodman TR, Yeckel CW, Papademetris X, Constable RT, Weiss R, Tamborlane WV, Savoye M, Seyal AA, Caprio S. Alanine aminotransferase levels and fatty liver in childhood obesity: associations with insulin resistance, adiponectin, and visceral fat. J Clin Endocrinol Metab. 2006;91:4287–94.
10. Manco M, Marcellini M, Devito R, Comparcola D, Sartorelli MR, Nobili V. MS and liver histology in paediatric non-alcoholic steatohepatitis. Int J Obes (Lond). 2008;32:381–7.

11. Angulo P. Nonalcoholic fatty liver disease. N Engl J Med. 2002;346:1221–31.
12. Taksali SE, Caprio S, Dziura J, Dufour S, Cali AM, Goodman TR, Papademetris X, Burgert TS, Pierpont BM, Savoye M, Shaw M, Seyal AA, Weiss R. High visceral and low abdominal subcutaneous fat stores in the obese adolescent: a determinant of an adverse metabolic phenotype. Diabetes. 2008;57:367–71.
13. Cali AM, Caprio S. Ectopic fat deposition and the MS in obese children and adolescents. Horm Res. 2009;71 Suppl 1:2–7.
14. Weiss R, Dziura J, Burgert TS, Tamborlane WV, Taksali SE, Yeckel CW, Allen K, Lopes M, Savoye M, Morrison J, Sherwin RS, Caprio S. Obesity and the MS in children and adolescents. N Engl J Med. 2004;350:2362–74.
15. Weyer C, Bogardus C, Pratley RE. Metabolic characteristics of individuals with impaired fasting glucose and/or impaired glucose tolerance. Diabetes. 1999;48:2197–203.
16. Del Prato S, Marchetti P, Bonadonna RC. Phasic insulin release and metabolic regulation in type 2 diabetes. Diabetes. 2002;51 Suppl 1:S109–16.
17. Yeckel CW, Taksali SE, Dziura J, Weiss R, Burgert TS, Sherwin RS, Tamborlane WV, Caprio S. The normal glucose tolerance continuum in obese youth: evidence for impairment in beta-cell function independent of insulin resistance. J Clin Endocrinol Metab. 2005;90:747–54.
18. O'Malley G, Santoro N, Northrup V, D'Adamo E, Shaw M, Eldrich S, Caprio S. High normal fasting glucose level in obese youth: a marker for insulin resistance and beta cell dysregulation. Diabetologia. 2010;53:1199–209.
19. American Diabetes Association. Standards of medical care in diabetes—2011. Diabetes Care. 2011;34 Suppl 1:S11–61.
20. Cali AM, Bonadonna RC, Trombetta M, Weiss R, Caprio S. Metabolic abnormalities underlying the different prediabetic phenotypes in obese adolescents. J Clin Endocrinol Metab. 2008;93:1767–73.
21. Defronzo RA. Banting lecture. From the triumvirate to the ominous octet: a new paradigm for the treatment of type 2 diabetes mellitus. Diabetes. 2009;58:773–95.
22. Lyssenko V, Jonsson A, Almgren P, Pulizzi N, Isomaa B, Tuomi T, Berglund G, Altshuler D, Nilsson P, Groop L. Clinical risk factors, DNA variants, and the development of type 2 diabetes. N Engl J Med. 2008;359:2220–32.
23. Gerich JE. Metabolic abnormalities in impaired glucose tolerance. Metabolism. 1997;46:40–3.
24. Goran MI, Bergman RN, Avila Q, Watkins M, Ball GD, Shaibi GQ, Weigensberg MJ, Cruz ML. Impaired glucose tolerance and reduced beta-cell function in overweight Latino children with a positive family history for type 2 diabetes. J Clin Endocrinol Metab. 2004;89:207–12.
25. Gungor N, Arslanian S. Progressive beta cell failure in type 2 diabetes mellitus of youth. J Pediatr. 2004;144:656–9.
26. Bonadonna RC, Stumvoll M, Fritsche A, Muggeo M, Haring H, Bonora E, van Haeften TW. Altered homeostatic adaptation of first- and second-phase beta-cell secretion in the offspring of patients with type 2 diabetes: studies with a minimal model to assess beta-cell function. Diabetes. 2003;52:470–80.
27. Weiss R, Caprio S, Trombetta M, Taksali SE, Tamborlane WV, Bonadonna R. Beta-cell function across the spectrum of glucose tolerance in obese youth. Diabetes. 2005;54:1735–43.
28. Weiss R, Caprio S. The metabolic consequences of childhood obesity. Best Pract Res Clin Endocrinol Metab. 2005;19:405–19.
29. Cali AM, Man CD, Cobelli C, Dziura J, Seyal A, Shaw M, Allen K, Chen S, Caprio S. Primary defects in beta-cell function further exacerbated by worsening of insulin resistance mark the development of impaired glucose tolerance in obese adolescents. Diabetes Care. 2009;32:456–61.
30. Billings LK, Florez JC. The genetics of type 2 diabetes: what have we learned from GWAS? Ann N Y Acad Sci. 2010;1212:59–77.

Chapter 5
Effects of Metabolic Syndrome on Atherosclerosis in Childhood

Muhammad Yasir Qureshi, Sarah E. Messiah, Tracie L. Miller, and Steven E. Lipshultz

Abstract Atherosclerosis is a chronic disease of the arterial wall that starts in childhood but does not usually manifest clinically until adulthood. Its progression depends on several risk factors, most of which are components of metabolic syndrome. In this chapter, we summarize the evidence of pediatric onset of atherosclerosis and discuss its pathogenesis. We also review the effects of various components of metabolic syndrome on the development of atherosclerosis and the strategies for stratifying and reducing the risk of atherosclerosis. A substantial amount of data confirms the early initiation of atherosclerosis. Therefore, earlier efforts to identify, prevent, and treat metabolic syndrome may improve the quality and length of life.

Keywords Atherosclerosis • Cardiovascular risk factors • Pediatrics • Adolescents • Metabolic syndrome

M.Y. Qureshi, M.D.
Division of Pediatric Cardiology, Department of Pediatrics,
University of Miami/Jackson Memorial Hospital,
Miami, FL, USA

S.E. Messiah, M.D.
Division of Pediatric Clinical Research, Department of Pediatrics,
University of Miami Miller School of Medicine,
Miami, FL, USA

T.L. Miller, M.D.
Division of Pediatric Clinical Research, Department of Pediatrics,
University of Miami Miller School of Medicine,
Batchelor Children's Research Institute,
Miami, FL, USA

S.E. Lipshultz, M.D. (✉)
Department of Pediatrics, University of Miami Miller School of Medicine,
1601 NW 12th Avenue, 9th Floor, Miami, FL 33136, USA
e-mail: slipshultz@med.miami.edu

Introduction

Atherosclerosis is a disease of the arterial intima characterized by lipid deposition with a fibrous cap along the vessel wall, which progressively narrows the arterial lumen and eventually causes ischemia in end organs. Involving either the coronary or cerebral arteries, atherosclerosis is the leading cause of death and morbidity in the world [1]. Although the clinical effects of atherosclerosis, such as myocardial infarction, stroke, and peripheral vascular disease, usually do not appear until later in adulthood, they start developing early in childhood [2, 3] and even before birth [4].

Metabolic syndrome is a constellation of medical conditions—increased waist circumference, insulin resistance, dyslipidemia, and hypertension—that increase the risk of developing cardiovascular disease and diabetes. The prevalence of the metabolic syndrome in childhood is increasing [5]. The components of metabolic syndrome are also risk factors of atherosclerosis [6, 7]. As a result, the metabolic syndrome increases the risk that atherosclerosis will develop earlier and more extensively [8–11]. Furthermore, the conditions comprising the metabolic syndrome in childhood tend to persist into adulthood [12, 13], where they continue to increase the threat of rapid progression of atherosclerosis. Some risk factors of atherosclerosis are not modifiable, such as advancing age, male sex, and family history. However, most of the modifiable risk factors of atherosclerosis, except smoking, are an integral part of the metabolic syndrome. Hence, identifying and preventing metabolic syndrome in childhood can have a great and beneficial effect on cardiovascular health in adulthood.

The Epidemiology of Atherosclerosis

A historic study of soldiers killed in the Korean War found that the incidence of coronary atherosclerosis in asymptomatic American men with an average age of 22 years was 77%. The severity of disease ranged from minimal eccentric thickening to complete occlusion of one or more of the major coronary arteries [14, 15]. Large population-based prospective studies, such as the Framingham Heart Study [6] and the Atherosclerosis Risk in Communities Study [7], have identified the risk factors for atherosclerosis in adults. In addition, the childhood onset of atherosclerosis long before the development of clinical cardiovascular disease has been documented in classic autopsy studies such as the Bogalusa Study [12, 16–31] and the Pathobiological Determinants of Atherosclerosis in Youth (PDAY) study [32–41]. These studies identified modifiable risk factors, such as dyslipidemia, that affect the development of atherosclerosis proportionately. Other studies have documented the persistence of dyslipidemia in childhood into adulthood [16, 17, 31]. Fatty streaks, which are an accumulation of lipid-filled macrophages in the arterial wall, begin to appear at a young age [42] and increase in prevalence and extent in the second to fourth decade of life [43, 44].

The progression of atherosclerosis is associated with a number of cardiovascular risk factors, such as higher body-mass index, high blood pressure, and dyslipidemia [23, 29, 30, 45]. The Cardiovascular Risk in Young Finns study reported an association between the cardiovascular risk profile of children and the thickness of their carotid intima media (a marker of subclinical atherosclerosis) as adults [46].

The Pathogenesis of Atherosclerosis

The pathogenesis of atherosclerosis [47] has been thoroughly reviewed in the literature [48–54] and involves all the established risk factors (Fig. 5.1). During pathogenesis, the initial fatty streak progresses into an atheromatous plaque [55, 56]. The initial atherosclerotic event is endothelial damage caused by hemodynamic stress [57]

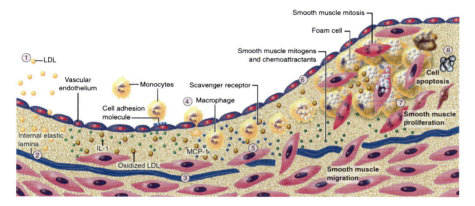

Fig. 5.1 Schematic of the evolution of the atherosclerotic plaque [47]. *1*: Accumulation of lipoprotein particles in the intima. The modification of these lipoproteins is depicted by the darker color. Modifications include oxidation and glycation. *2*: Oxidative stress, including products found in modified lipoproteins, can induce local cytokine elaboration. *3*: The cytokines, thus induced, increase expression of adhesion molecules for leukocytes that cause their attachment and chemoattractant molecules that direct their migration into the intima. *4*: Blood monocytes, on entering the artery wall in response to chemoattractant cytokines such as monocyte chemoattractant protein 1 (*MCP-1*), encounter stimuli such as macrophage colony-stimulating factor that can augment their expression of scavenger receptors. *5*: Scavenger receptors mediate the uptake of modified lipoprotein particles and promote the development of foam cells. Macrophage foam cells are a source of mediators, such as further cytokines and effector molecules like hypochlorous acid, superoxide anion, and matrix metalloproteinases. *6*: Smooth muscle cells migrate into the intima from the media. *7*: Smooth muscle cells can then divide and elaborate extracellular matrix, promoting extracellular matrix accumulation in the growing atherosclerotic plaque. In this manner, the fatty streak can evolve into a fibrofatty lesion. *8*: In later stages, calcification can occur (not depicted) and fibrosis continues, sometimes accompanied by smooth muscle cell death (including apoptosis), yielding a relatively acellular fibrous capsule surrounding a lipid-rich core that may also contain dying or dead cells and their debris. *Abbreviations*: *IL-1* interleukin-1, *LDL* low-density lipoprotein, *MCP-1* monocyte chemo-attractant protein 1 (Reprinted from Libby [47])

or inflammation [48–50]. This damage increases endothelial permeability, which allows lipids to accumulate in the vascular wall. Leukocytes adhere to the damaged site and smooth muscle proliferates adding to the inflammation. Smooth muscle cells synthesize extracellular matrix and create a "fibrous cap" that covers the surface of the plaque, whose core is comprised of lipid-laden cells and fatty remains. The plaque begins to protrude into the vessel lumen, causing turbulence in blood flow, damaging the vessel wall further, and progressively narrowing the lumen even more. Disruption of the fibrous cap can cause acute vascular occlusion that, in turn, can lead to end-organ necrosis. Dyslipidemia hastens plaque development by quickly increasing the lipid content of atheromatous plaques, whereas hypertension causes increased and chronic wall stress and may be responsible for the initial endothelial damage.

Components of Metabolic Syndrome and Their Effect on Atherosclerosis

Obesity

Obesity is a major independent risk factor of cardiovascular disease in adults [6, 58, 59]. Obesity-related endothelial dysfunction is what contributes to the development of atherosclerosis [50, 60]. Obese adults (those with a body-mass index above 30 kg/m^2) are four times as likely to experience cardiovascular disease than are individuals of normal weight [61, 62]. Among overweight adolescents, the risk of death from cardiovascular disease was 2.3 times as great as that of normal-weight adolescents 55 years later [63]. This risk was independent of their adult weight.

Obese adolescents and young adult men are at a higher cardiovascular risk than are obese women [34, 64]. Also, several studies have shown that obese children tend to become obese adults [65–67]. Moreover, obesity is associated with the clustering of other cardiovascular risk factors, such as hypertension, dyslipidemia, and insulin resistance, in both adults [68] and children [22, 69–71]. This clustering of risk factors is proportional to the degree of adiposity [66]. Obesity also promotes a sedentary life style: obese individuals are less likely to exercise. This lack of exercise worsens obesity and increases the accumulation of other cardiovascular risk factors.

Body-mass index and waist circumference, as measures of central obesity, may identify children at risk for cardiovascular disease later in life [72]. Obesity increases peripheral vascular resistance [73, 74] in children and contributes to the development of another risk factor, hypertension [74]. Obesity is common in survivors of childhood cancer [75] and may be a factor in increasing their risk of cardiovascular disease [76].

Environmental factors, such as diet and lifestyle, are important in the development of obesity. For example, mean body-mass index among children immigrating from Haiti to the USA increases 3.7% for each year of US residency, a difference attributed to changes in diet and lifestyle [77]. On the other hand, weight loss improves cardiovascular risk by decreasing blood pressure and insulin resistance [78, 79].

Atherogenic Dyslipidemia

Hypercholesterolemia is usually equated with atherosclerosis and has thus been a primary target of prevention strategies [80, 81]. The National Cholesterol Education Program's Adult Treatment Panel III report (ATP III) [82], the World Health Organization (WHO) [83], the American Association of Clinical Endocrinologists (AACE) [84], the American Heart Association (AHA) [85], and the International Diabetes Federation (IDF) [86] have proposed various definitions and diagnostic criteria for hypercholesterolemia, but all include dyslipidemia as an essential component of the metabolic syndrome.

Total serum cholesterol includes low-density lipoprotein cholesterol (LDL-C), high-density lipoprotein cholesterol (HDL-C), and very-low-density lipoprotein cholesterol (VLDL-C). Whereas LDL-C is the "bad cholesterol" and is atherogenic, HDL-C is the "good cholesterol" and protects against atherosclerosis [87]. Non-HDL-C is a combined measure of all atherogenic lipids: LDL-C, VLDL-C, intermediate-density lipoprotein cholesterol (IDL-C), and lipoprotein (a) [82]. Non-HDL-C concentrations are strongly associated with the metabolic syndrome in adolescents [88]. Atherosclerotic lesions are more commonly found in autopsies of children and adolescents with elevated serum cholesterol, especially LDL-C and non-HDL-C [23, 35–37, 39, 89]. Adolescents with high LDL cholesterol concentrations are likely to have at least subclinical atherosclerosis as they mature into adulthood [20, 46]. In addition, children with dyslipidemia are likely to become adults with dyslipidemia [17, 25, 27, 90, 91], carrying the increased risk of atherosclerosis into adulthood. In the Bogalusa Heart Study, about half the children with elevated total cholesterol or LDL cholesterol concentrations at baseline had elevated concentrations 12 years later [27].

Familial hypercholesterolemia is a genetic disorder characterized by defects in the LDL receptors that occurs in about 1 of every 500 individuals [92]. These individuals are especially at high risk for atherosclerosis and its complications [93]. Between 75% and 85% of men with familial hypercholesterolemia will have a myocardial infarction by age 60.

The metabolic syndrome is a common cause of hypertriglyceridemia [88, 94]. The triglycerides are transported from liver to the peripheral tissues in blood in the form of very-low-density lipoproteins (VLDL) and intermediate lipoproteins. There is a strong correlation of coronary artery disease with VLDL and tryglyceride concentration [95, 96]. Hypertriglyceridemia has a central role in the pathophysiology of dyslipidemia in insulin resistance and type 2 diabetes [97]. Although the LDL-C is the main focus of attention for atherosclerosis, triglyceride-rich lipoproteins are known to mimic LDL-C [98]. Both of these are present in the atherosclerotic lesions [99] and are involved in monocyte chemoattractant protein-1 expression [100] and monocyte adhesion [101]. Both of these have a role in foam cell formation [102], endothelial dysfunction [103–105], inflammation, and thrombogenesis [106–109]. Individuals with high LDL-C/HDL-C ratio and elevated triglycerides benefit from reduction of triglycerides by gemfibrozil. In such individuals, there is 70% reduction of coronary artery disease risk [110].

High Blood Pressure

High blood pressure promotes atherosclerosis by causing hemodynamic stress on the vascular wall and is strongly associated with atherosclerosis in the coronary arteries [38, 41]. Blood pressure norms vary by age, sex, and height [111]. Adjusting for these norms, several studies have shown that childhood blood pressure is associated with blood pressure in later life [112–115]. Hypertension is an established predictor of atherosclerosis in adults [6, 116] and is a recognized pediatric illness, the incidence of which is rising primarily because of the increasing prevalence of the metabolic syndrome [117]. Hypertension that persists from childhood to adulthood may have greater adverse effects and may be responsible for earlier or more widespread atherosclerosis [12, 18, 20, 23].

Insulin Resistance

Insulin resistance, another component of the metabolic syndrome, is strongly associated with extensive atherosclerosis of the aorta and coronary arteries [40]. It contributes to undesirable changes in lipoprotein concentrations, leading to high LDL-C and low HDL-C concentrations [118], which promote atherosclerosis. It also causes endothelial dysfunction [119] and increases oxidative stress [120]. Obese children tend to have both atherogenic dyslipidemia and hyperinsulinism [22]. Insulin resistance also clusters with other cardiovascular risk factors [121], worsening the overall risk profile for cardiovascular disease.

Proinflammatory and Prothrombotic States

Inflammation is essential to the pathogenesis of atherosclerosis [48, 50]. Chronic inflammatory states, such as systemic lupus erythematosus and rheumatoid arthritis, put affected individuals at a higher risk for accelerated development of atherosclerotic cardiovascular disease [122–124]. Prothrombotic states associated with these chronic inflammatory diseases, such as the presence of antiphospholipid antibodies and elevated lipoprotein (a), can increase the risk of vascular thrombosis [125–127].

Serum markers of inflammation, such as C-reactive protein and tumor necrosis factor-α, mediate atherosclerotic development [128–130]. Several other biomarkers related to inflammation and oxidative stress have been explored and may be a target of interventions in the future [131]. Adiponectin, a marker of inflammation and a cytokine produced in adipocytes, is anti-inflammatory. In obese individuals, its secretion is paradoxically decreased, which increases the concentrations of inflammatory proteins [132], decreases the concentration of HDL cholesterol [132–135], and increases triglyceride concentrations [133]. Decreased adiponectin concentrations are associated with premature atherosclerosis in children and adolescents [133, 136]. Leptin is an appetite-suppressant factor produced in adipocytes and is believed to regulate fat storage in tissues such as myocardium [137]. Patients with congenital deficiency of leptin have insatiable appetite, which leads to obesity due to increased food intake [138]. Exogenous administration of leptin in these patients can reinstate normal appetite and decreased fat mass [138]. However, most of the obese individuals have paradoxically high levels of leptin, likely due to leptin resistance [139]. This leads to exaggerated appetite in these children.

Other Factors Influencing Atherogenesis

Smoking, active or passive, is another well-established contributor to cardiovascular disease [39, 140, 141] that is associated with microscopic and macroscopic atherosclerotic lesions in the aorta and coronary arteries [33, 36]. Smoking adversely alters the lipid profile and increases platelet aggregation. It also decreases exercise capacity and promotes obesity and a sedentary lifestyle, which are other predictors of cardiovascular disease.

Risk factors that are not modifiable are advanced age, male sex, and a family history of cardiovascular disease or dyslipidemia. Certain prenatal factors have also been associated with unfavorable cardiovascular risk profiles. Prenatal cocaine exposure, advanced maternal age, and high maternal blood pressure can lead to hypertension in childhood [112, 142]. On the other hand, maternal calcium intake during pregnancy is associated with lower blood pressure in infancy [143].

Cumulative Effects of Multiple Risk Factors

Most people have more than one risk factor for cardiovascular disease. To predict cumulative risk in this case, the PDAY risk score was developed (Table 5.1) [89]. Scores were derived from the prevalence of atherosclerotic lesions in the aorta and coronary arteries found in autopsies of individuals aged 15–34 years. Scores help identify individuals in the above age range who are at risk for advanced atherosclerosis in the aorta and coronary arteries. The risk scores were normalized so that a 1-unit increase was equivalent to a 1-year increase in age. For coronary artery disease, the odds ratio of having atherosclerosis increases by 1.18 (95% confidence interval, 1.14–1.22) for each 1-unit increase in the score.

Table 5.1 Risk scores for predicting target lesions in the coronary arteries

Risk factor	Score
Age, years	
15–19	0
20–24	5
25–29	10
30–34	15
Sex	
Male	0
Female	−1
Non-HDL cholesterol, mg/dL	
<130	0
130–159	2
160–189	4
190–219	6
≥220	8
HDL cholesterol, mg/dL	
<40	1
40–59	0
≥60	−1
Smoking	
Nonsmoker	0
Smoker	1
Blood pressure	
Normotensive	0
Hypertensive	4
Obesity (BMI, kg/m^2)	
Men	
≤30	0
>30	6
Women	
≤30	0
>30	0
Hyperglycemia (glycohemoglobin, %)	
<8	0
≥8	5

Modified from McMahan et al. [89]. © 2005 American Medical Association. All rights reserved
BMI body-mass index, *HDL* high-density lipoprotein

Cardiovascular Risk Stratification and Reduction in Children

In 1992, National Cholesterol Education Program (NCEP) published the first guidelines for preventing heart disease in children [144]. In 2006, the AHA issued a scientific statement [145] regarding cardiovascular risk reduction in children that was based on risk stratification. The American Academy of Pediatrics (AAP) endorsed this statement [146].

Cholesterol Screening

Despite the fact that screening for hypercholesterolemia solely because of family history would fail to detect a significant number of children with hypercholesterolemia [147], universal screening with serum cholesterol concentrations of all children is currently not recommended by the AHA or the AAP until recently. The NCEP devised two approaches to lower blood cholesterol in children: the population approach and the individualized approach [144]. The population approach is aimed at reducing the average blood cholesterol in children by modifying dietary habits in general. A healthy diet is the essence of the population approach. The recommended diet includes calories adequate for growth and development, lower total and saturated fats, and lower dietary cholesterol. The individualized approach is aimed at identifying children who are at high risk of developing coronary heart disease. The recent NHLBI guidelines continue to recommend similar approach [148]. These guidelines recommend universal lipid screening between age 9 and 11 with non-fasting non-HDL or fasting lipid profile. Another evaluation is recommended between 18 and 21 years of age. For proper evaluation, the fasting lipid profile should be checked twice with at least 2 weeks interval but within 3 months. The average of the two measurements should be considered for any decision or intervention. The NHLBI also recommends lipid screening in any child (> 2 year of age) with risk factors or with a moderate- or high-risk condition (see Risk Stratification). The risk factors are as follows:

- Positive family history: myocardial infarction, angina, coronary artery bypass graft/stent/angioplasty, sudden cardiac death in parent, grandparent, aunt, or uncle at < 55 years for males, < 65 y for females
- High-level risk factors:
  - Hypertension that requires drug therapy (BP ≥ 99th percentile + 5 mm Hg)
  - Current cigarette smoker
  - BMI at the ≥ 97th percentile
  - Presence of high-risk conditions (see Risk Stratification)
- Moderate-level risk factors:
  - Hypertension that does not require drug therapy
  - BMI at the ≥ 95th percentile but < 97th percentile
  - HDL cholesterol < 40 mg/dL
  - Presence of moderate-risk conditions (see Risk Stratification)

The NCEP [149] and NHLBI [148] acknowledge hypertriglyceridemia as an independent risk factor for coronary artery disease and classifies serum triglycerides as follows:

- Normal triglycerides: <150 mg/dL
- Borderline-high triglycerides: 150–199 mg/dL
- High triglycerides: 200–499 mg/dL
- Very high triglycerides: ≥500 mg/dL

Serum lipoprotein analysis can help in diagnosing primary hypertriglyceridemias.

Risk Stratification

The AHA/AAP statement [145, 146] identifies eight pediatric diseases which are considered at high risk of developing early adult cardiovascular disease. The risk posed by each disease was stratified into one of three tiers:

- Tier I: pathological or clinical evidence of manifesting coronary artery disease before age 30 years. The diseases are homozygous familial hypercholesterolemia, type 1 diabetes mellitus, chronic kidney disease [150], postorthotopic heart transplantation [151], and Kawasaki disease with current coronary aneurysms [152]
- Tier II: pathophysiologic evidence for arterial dysfunction indicating accelerated atherosclerosis before age 30 years. The diseases are heterozygous familial hypercholesterolemia, Kawasaki disease with regressed coronary aneurysms [152], type 2 diabetes mellitus [153], and chronic inflammatory diseases
- Tier III: increased cardiovascular risk factors with epidemiologic evidence of manifesting coronary artery disease after age 30 years. The diseases are congenital heart disease, Kawasaki disease without detected coronary involvement [152], and cancer survivors

The recent NHLBI guidelines reduced these to two risk categories:

- High-risk—Tier I: clinical evidence of manifesting coronary artery disease before age 30 years. The diseases are type 1 or type 2 diabetes mellitus, chronic kidney disease/end stage renal disease/post-renal transplant, post-orthotopic heart transplantation, and Kawasaki disease with current coronary aneurysms.
- Moderate-risk—Tier II: pathophysiologic evidence of accelerated atherosclerosis. The diseases are Kawasaki disease with regressed coronary aneurysms, chronic inflammatory diseases (systemic lupus erythematosus, juvenile rheumatoid arthritis), HIV infection and nephritic syndrome.

Predominantly because of the presence of diabetes, children with the metabolic syndrome will fall into one of the above tiers. Moreover, the presence of the metabolic syndrome in these diseases adds to their overall risk and can upgrade their risk category. Individuals are classified into a higher-risk tier based on presence of two or more additional risk factors, such as dyslipidemia, smoking, a family history of early onset of coronary artery disease, hypertension, obesity, insulin resistance, and a lack of physical activity (step 2, Fig. 5.2). Most of these factors are components of the metabolic syndrome.

Fig. 5.2 Risk stratification and treatment algorithm for high-risk pediatric populations [145] *Directions*: *Step 1*: Risk stratification by disease process. *Step 2*: Assess all cardiovascular risk factors. If there are two or more comorbidities, assign patient to the next higher risk tier for subsequent management. *Step 3*: Tier-specific treatment goals and intervention cut points are defined. *Step 4*: Initial therapy: For tier I, initial management is therapeutic lifestyle change (Table 5.2) PLUS disease-specific management (Table 5.3). For tiers II and III, initial management is therapeutic lifestyle change (Table 5.2). *Step 5*: For tiers II and III, if goals are not met, consider medication as outlined in Table 5.2. *Abbreviations*: *%ile* percentile, *BMI* body-mass index, *BP* blood pressure, *CAD* coronary artery disease, *CV* cardiovascular, *ESRD* end-stage renal disease, *FG* fasting glucose, *FH* familial hypercholesterolemia, *HgbA1c* hemoglobin A1c, *ht%ile* height percentile, *LDL* low-density lipoprotein, *TLC* therapeutic lifestyle change (Reprinted from Kavey et al. [145]. With permission from Lippincott Williams & Wilkins)

5 Effects of Metabolic Syndrome on Atherosclerosis in Childhood

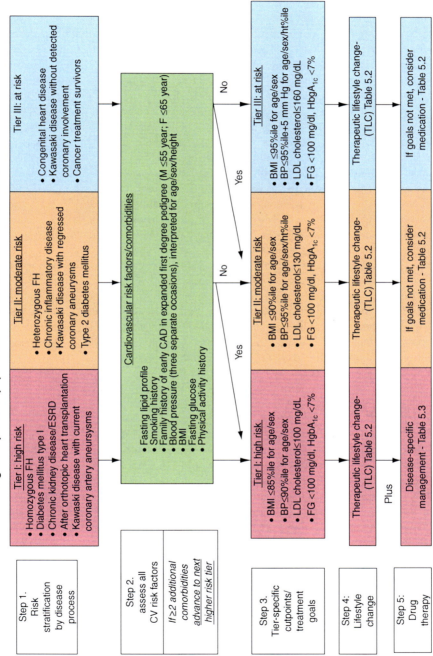

Cardiometabolic abnormalities occur in individuals with human immunodeficiency virus (HIV) infection. Antiretroviral therapy also increases their cardiovascular risk [154, 155]. The unfavorable lipid profiles, insulin resistance, cardiovascular inflammation, and vascular stiffness predispose HIV-infected individuals to accelerated cardiovascular disease [156–159]. Children with HIV infection in particular are at high risk for cardiovascular disease because many of them have been exposed to both HIV and antiretroviral therapies for a long time, often even before birth [155–157].

Several biomarkers of vascular dysfunction are elevated in HIV-infected children [160]. The arteriopathy, as seen on autopsy, in children with HIV infection includes microscopic coronary disease as well as vasa vasorum involvement of the large vessels, such as the aorta and the pulmonary arteries [161]. Because the left ventricular mass is increased in children with HIV [162], minor changes in coronary blood supply may become significant as tissue demands increase.

With advancements in cancer therapies, the number of childhood cancer survivors is increasing. These children are at high risk for cardiovascular disease as a result of treatment-related myocardial damage [163], as well as having a high prevalence of an unfavorable cardiovascular risk profile [76]. The myocardial damage may or may not be related to anthracycline or cardiac radiation exposures [164–166].

Kawasaki disease is a vasculitis of unknown etiology. Children with coronary aneurysms are at greatest risk for cardiovascular disease, but those with regressed aneurysms and those without aneurysms are still at risk. Coronary artery calcifications, as detected by electron beam computed tomography, may help in risk stratification of patients with Kawasaki disease [167].

Risk Reduction

Lifestyle modifications and treatment of comorbid conditions are the mainstays of cardiovascular disease risk reduction. The AHA/AAP statement not only summarizes the risk-reduction strategies for the abovementioned high-risk diseases, but Table 5.2 from this statement also provides general guidance to reduce cardiovascular risk in anyone, including children with metabolic syndrome. Step 3 in Fig. 5.2 gives the therapeutic goals of interventions, whereas steps 4 and 5 give the therapeutic strategies, which are elaborated in Tables 5.2 and 5.3.

Treatment of Dyslipidemia

For hypercholesterolemia and hypertriglyceridemia, the NHLBI [148] recommends treatment strategy based on the severity. Lifestyle modifications, including dietary alterations, weight reduction and increasing physical activity, are the essence of

Table 5.2 Tiers I, II, and III: treatment recommendations

Growth/diet

  Nutritionist evaluation, diet education for all: total fat <30% of calories, saturated fat <10% of calories, cholesterol <300 mg/day, avoid *trans* fats; adequate calories for growth

  Calculate BMI percentile for gender/height[a]

    If initial BMI >95th percentile:

      Step 1:

        Age-appropriate reduced-calorie training for child and family

        Specific diet/weight F/U every 2–4 weeks for 6 months; repeat BMI calculation at 6 months

        Activity counseling (see below)

        If F/U BMI >85th percentile for tier I, >90th percentile for tier II, or >95th percentile for tier III:

      Step 2:

        Weight-loss program referral plus exercise training program appropriate for cardiac status

Blood pressure (tiers I, II, and III)

  BP measurement/interpretation for age/gender/height

      If SBP and/or DBP = 90–95th percentile or BP >120/80 mmHg (three separate occasions within 1 month):

    Step 1: decreased calorie intake, increased activity for 6 months

      If initial SBP and/or DBP >95th percentile (confirmed within 1 week) *OR* 6-month F/U SBP and/or DBP >95th percentile:

    Step 2: initiate pharmacological therapy per Fourth Task Force recommendations

Lipids

  LDL-C (tiers II and III)

    See Table 5.3 for recommendations for LDL-C for tier I

    If initial LDL-C ≥130 mg/dL (tier II) or ≥160 mg/dL (tier III):

      Step 1: nutritionist training for diet with <30% of calories from fat, <7% of calories from saturated fat, cholesterol <200 mg/day, avoidance of *trans* fats for 6 months

    If repeat LDL-C >130 mg/dL in tier II or >160 mg/dL in tier III and child >10 years old:

      Step 2: initiate statin therapy with LDL goal of 130 mg/dL

  Triglycerides

    If initial TG = 150–400 mg/dL:

      Step 1:

        Nutritionist training for low simple carbohydrate, low-fat diet

        If elevated TGs are associated with excess weight, nutritionist referral for weight loss management: energy balance training plus activity recommendations (see below)

    If TG >700–1,000 mg/dL, initial or F/U:

      Step 2:

        Consider fibrate or niacin if >10 years old[b]

        Weight loss recommended when TG elevation is associated with overweight/obesity

Glucose (tiers I, II, and III, except for patients with diabetes mellitus)

  If fasting glucose = 100–126 mg/dL:

    Step 1: reduced-calorie diet, increased activity aimed at 5–10% decrease in weight over 6 months

  If repeat fasting glucose = 100–126 mg/dL:

(continued)

Table 5.2 (continued)

Step 2: insulin-sensitizing medication per endocrinologist
Casual glucose >200 mg/dL or fasting glucose >126 mg/dL=diabetes mellitus endocrine referral for evaluation and management
Maintain HbA$_{1C}$ <7%
Smoking (tiers I, II, and III)
Step 1: parental smoking history at every visit; child smoking history beginning at age 10. Active antismoking counseling for all; smoke-free home strongly recommended at each encounter
Step 2: smoking cessation referral for any history of cigarette smoking
Activity (tiers I, II and III)
For children in all tiers, participation in activity is at the discretion of the physician(s) directing care. For specific cardiac diagnoses such as Kawasaki disease and congenital heart disease, activity guidelines are referenced
Step 1: specific activity history for each child, focusing on time spent in active play and screen time (television + computer + video games). Goal is ≥1 h of active play per day; screen time limited to ≤2 h/day
Encourage activity at every encounter.
Step 2: after 6 months, if goals not met, consider referral for exercise testing, recommendations from exercise specialist

Reprinted from Kavey et al. [145]. With permission from Lippincott Williams & Wilkins
Specific treatment goals for each risk factor and each tier are given in the algorithm (Fig. 5.2)
F/U follow-up, *BP* blood pressure, *SBP* systolic blood pressure, *DBP* diastolic blood pressure, *LDL-C* LDL cholesterol, *TG* triglycerides
[a]Normal BMI values for age and sex are available at http://www.cdc.gov/growthcharts
[b]Elevation of triglycerides to ≥1,000 mg/dL is associated with significant risk for acute pancreatitis. A fasting TG of 700 mg/dL is likely to rise to >1,000 mg/dL postprandially. Treatment recommendation is congruent with guidelines for management of dyslipidemia in diabetic children

dyslipidemia management and are the initial steps in treatment. CHILD-1 and CHILD-2 are stepwise dietary recommendations aimed to decrease fat content and total cholesterol in the diet. Re-evaluation of lipid profile in 6 months after lifestyle modification guides further management. The statin therapy is not initiated if the LDL-C continues to be less than 130 mg/dL after lifestyle modifications. In the absence of other risk factors and family history, statin therapy is deferred unless the LDL-C is more than 190 mg/dL. Generally, the statin therapy is not recommended in children younger than 10 years unless they have high-risk conditions, multiple high-risk factors or high-risk family history. Intermittent monitoring of lipid profiles and liver enzymes is recommended. Lifestyle modifications, including dietary changes, attempts to reduce weight and increase physical activity, continue with the drug therapy.

Table 5.3 Tier I conditions: specific treatment recommendations

Rigorous age-appropriate education in diet, activity, and smoking cessation for all

Specific therapy as needed to achieve BP, LDL-C, glucose, and HbA1C goals as indicated for each tier, as outlined in algorithm; timing individualized for each patient and diagnosis. Step 1 and Step 2 therapy for all outlined in Table 5.2

Homozygous FH

    LDL management: scheduled apheresis every 1–2 weeks beginning at diagnosis to maximally lower LDL-C, plus statin and cholesterol absorption inhibitor

    Rx per cardiologist/lipid specialist (specific therapeutic goals for LDL-C are not meaningful with this diagnosis.)

    Assess BMI, BP, and FG: Step 1 management for 6 months

    If tier I goals not achieved, proceed to Step 2

Diabetes mellitus, type 1

    Intensive glucose management per endocrinologist, with frequent glucose monitoring/insulin titration to maintain PG <200 mg/dL, HbA1C <7%

    Assess BMI, fasting lipids: Step 1 management of weight, lipids for 6 months

    If goals not achieved, proceed to Step 2; statin Rx if >10 years old to achieve tier I treatment goals

    Initial BP >90th percentile: Step 1 management plus no added salt, increased activity for 6 months

    BP consistently >95th percentile for age/sex/height: initiate ACE inhibitor therapy with BP goal <90th percentile or <130/80 mmHg, whichever is lower

CKD/ESRD

    Optimization of renal failure management with dialysis/transplantation per nephrology

    Assess BMI, BP, lipids, FG: Step 1 management for 6 months

    If goals not achieved, proceed to Step 2; statin Rx if >10 years old to achieve tier I treatment goals

After heart transplantation

    Optimization of antirejection therapy, treatment for CMV, routine evaluation by angiography/perfusion imaging per transplant physician

    Assess BMI, BP, lipids, FG: initiate Step 2 therapy, including statins, immediately in all patients >1 year old to achieve tier I treatment goals

Kawasaki disease with coronary aneurysms

    Antithrombotic therapy, activity restriction, ongoing myocardial perfusion evaluation per cardiologist

    Assess BMI, BP, lipids, FG: Step 1 management for 6 months

    If goals not achieved, proceed to Step 2; statin Rx if >10 years old to achieve tier I treatment goals

Reprinted from Kavey et al. [145]. With permission from Lippincott Williams & Wilkins
BP blood pressure, *LDL-C* LDL cholesterol, *Rx* prescription/treatment, *FG* fasting glucose, *PG* plasma glucose, *ACE* angiotensin-converting enzyme, *CMV* cytomegalovirus

Conclusion

The progression of atherosclerosis depends on several risk factors. Most of these risk factors are integral components of the metabolic syndrome. A high cardiovascular risk profile in childhood predicts the accelerated development of atherosclerosis and predisposes them to early manifestation of its clinical effects. Interventions aimed at alleviating obesity and the metabolic syndrome may improve the length and the quality of life in these children. Simpler interventions early in life such as healthy diet, exercise, weight reduction, and smoking cessation may also prevent more invasive and expensive interventions during adulthood.

Addendum

While this book was in the final proof stage, the US National Heart, Lung, and Blood Institute published new recommendations for comprehensive cardiac risk assessment and risk reduction [149]. These include recommendations for universal cholesterol screening during childhood [149]. References to these new guidelines [149] and a critical review of them [168] are included below.

References

1. World Health Organization. The top 10 causes of death. http://www.who.int/mediacentre/factsheets/fs310/en/index.html. Updated June 2011. Accessed 17 Sept 2011.
2. Kannel WB, Dawber TR. Atherosclerosis as a pediatric problem. J Pediatr. 1972;80(4):544–54.
3. Holman RL. Atherosclerosis—a pediatric nutrition problem? Am J Clin Nutr. 1961;9:565–9.
4. Napoli C, Glass CK, Witztum JL, Deutsch R, D'Armiento FP, Palinski W. Influence of maternal hypercholesterolaemia during pregnancy on progression of early atherosclerotic lesions in childhood: fate of early lesions in children (FELIC) study. Lancet. 1999;354(9186):1234–41.
5. Messiah SE, Arheart KL, Lipshultz SE, Miller TL. Prevalence of the metabolic syndrome in US youth. In: Bagchi D, editor. Global perspectives on childhood obesity: current status, consequences and prevention. San Diego, CA: Academic Press, an Imprint of Elsevier; 2010.
6. Wilson PW, Castelli WP, Kannel WB. Coronary risk prediction in adults (the Framingham Heart Study). Am J Cardiol. 1987;59(14):91G–4.
7. Chambless LE, Folsom AR, Sharrett AR, et al. Coronary heart disease risk prediction in the atherosclerosis risk in communities (ARIC) study. J Clin Epidemiol. 2003;56(9):880–90.
8. Rodriguez-Colon SM, Mo J, Duan Y, et al. Metabolic syndrome clusters and the risk of incident stroke: the atherosclerosis risk in communities (ARIC) study. Stroke. 2009;40(1):200–5.
9. Kasai T, Miyauchi K, Kubota N, et al. The relationship between the metabolic syndrome defined by various criteria and the extent of coronary artery disease. Atherosclerosis. 2008;197(2):944–50.
10. Wang JJ, Li HB, Kinnunen L, et al. How well does the metabolic syndrome defined by five definitions predict incident diabetes and incident coronary heart disease in a Chinese population? Atherosclerosis. 2007;192(1):161–8.

11. Skilton MR, Moulin P, Serusclat A, Nony P, Bonnet F. A comparison of the NCEP-ATPIII, IDF and AHA/NHLBI metabolic syndrome definitions with relation to early carotid atherosclerosis in subjects with hypercholesterolemia or at risk of CVD: evidence for sex-specific differences. Atherosclerosis. 2007;190(2):416–22.
12. Magnussen CG, Koskinen J, Chen W, et al. Pediatric metabolic syndrome predicts adulthood metabolic syndrome, subclinical atherosclerosis, and type 2 diabetes mellitus but is no better than body mass index alone: the Bogalusa Heart Study and the Cardiovascular Risk in Young Finns Study. Circulation. 2010;122(16):1604–11.
13. Morrison JA, Friedman LA, Wang P, Glueck CJ. Metabolic syndrome in childhood predicts adult metabolic syndrome and type 2 diabetes mellitus 25 to 30 years later. J Pediatr. 2008;152(2):201–6.
14. Enos Jr WF, Beyer JC, Holmes RH. Pathogenesis of coronary disease in American soldiers killed in Korea. J Am Med Assoc. 1955;158(11):912–4.
15. Enos WF, Holmes RH, Beyer J. Coronary disease among United States soldiers killed in action in Korea; preliminary report. J Am Med Assoc. 1953;152(12):1090–3.
16. Magnussen CG, Venn A, Thomson R, et al. The association of pediatric low- and high-density lipoprotein cholesterol dyslipidemia classifications and change in dyslipidemia status with carotid intima-media thickness in adulthood evidence from the Cardiovascular Risk in Young Finns Study, the Bogalusa Heart Study, and the CDAH (Childhood Determinants of Adult Health) Study. J Am Coll Cardiol. 2009;53(10):860–9.
17. Magnussen CG, Raitakari OT, Thomson R, et al. Utility of currently recommended pediatric dyslipidemia classifications in predicting dyslipidemia in adulthood: evidence from the Childhood Determinants of Adult Health (CDAH) Study, Cardiovascular Risk in Young Finns Study, and Bogalusa Heart Study. Circulation. 2008;117(1):32–42.
18. Chen W, Srinivasan SR, Li S, Xu J, Berenson GS. Metabolic syndrome variables at low levels in childhood are beneficially associated with adulthood cardiovascular risk: the Bogalusa Heart Study. Diabetes Care. 2005;28(1):126–31.
19. Li X, Li S, Ulusoy E, Chen W, Srinivasan SR, Berenson GS. Childhood adiposity as a predictor of cardiac mass in adulthood: the Bogalusa Heart Study. Circulation. 2004;110(22):3488–92.
20. Li S, Chen W, Srinivasan SR, et al. Childhood cardiovascular risk factors and carotid vascular changes in adulthood: the Bogalusa Heart Study. JAMA. 2003;290(17):2271–6.
21. Nicklas TA, von Duvillard SP, Berenson GS. Tracking of serum lipids and lipoproteins from childhood to dyslipidemia in adults: the Bogalusa Heart Study. Int J Sports Med. 2002;23 Suppl 1:S39–43.
22. Freedman DS, Dietz WH, Srinivasan SR, Berenson GS. The relation of overweight to cardiovascular risk factors among children and adolescents: the Bogalusa Heart Study. Pediatrics. 1999;103(6 Pt 1):1175–82.
23. Berenson GS, Srinivasan SR, Bao W, Newman 3rd WP, Tracy RE, Wattigney WA. Association between multiple cardiovascular risk factors and atherosclerosis in children and young adults. The Bogalusa Heart Study. N Engl J Med. 1998;338(23):1650–6.
24. Berenson GS, Srinivasan SR, Bao W. Precursors of cardiovascular risk in young adults from a biracial (black-white) population: the Bogalusa Heart Study. Ann N Y Acad Sci. 1997;817: 189–98.
25. Bao W, Srinivasan SR, Wattigney WA, Bao W, Berenson GS. Usefulness of childhood low-density lipoprotein cholesterol level in predicting adult dyslipidemia and other cardiovascular risks. The Bogalusa Heart Study. Arch Intern Med. 1996;156(12):1315–20.
26. Urbina EM, Gidding SS, Bao W, Pickoff AS, Berdusis K, Berenson GS. Effect of body size, ponderosity, and blood pressure on left ventricular growth in children and young adults in the Bogalusa Heart Study. Circulation. 1995;91(9):2400–6.
27. Webber LS, Srinivasan SR, Wattigney WA, Berenson GS. Tracking of serum lipids and lipoproteins from childhood to adulthood. The Bogalusa Heart Study. Am J Epidemiol. 1991;133(9): 884–99.
28. Dennison BA, Kikuchi DA, Srinivasan SR, Webber LS, Berenson GS. Serum total cholesterol screening for the detection of elevated low-density lipoprotein in children and adolescents: the Bogalusa Heart Study. Pediatrics. 1990;85(4):472–9.

29. Berenson GS, Foster TA, Frank GC, et al. Cardiovascular disease risk factor variables at the preschool age. The Bogalusa Heart Study. Circulation. 1978;57(3):603–12.
30. Frerichs RR, Srinivasan SR, Webber LS, Berenson GR. Serum cholesterol and triglyceride levels in 3,446 children from a biracial community: the Bogalusa Heart Study. Circulation. 1976;54(2):302–9.
31. Juonala M, Magnussen CG, Venn A, et al. Influence of age on associations between childhood risk factors and carotid intima-media thickness in adulthood: the Cardiovascular Risk in Young Finns Study, the Childhood Determinants of Adult Health Study, the Bogalusa Heart Study, and the Muscatine Study for the International Childhood Cardiovascular Cohort (i3C) Consortium. Circulation. 2010;122(24):2514–20.
32. McGill Jr HC, McMahan CA, Gidding SS. Preventing heart disease in the 21st century: implications of the Pathobiological Determinants of Atherosclerosis in Youth (PDAY) study. Circulation. 2008;117(9):1216–27.
33. Zieske AW, McMahan CA, McGill Jr HC, et al. Smoking is associated with advanced coronary atherosclerosis in youth. Atherosclerosis. 2005;180(1):87–92.
34. McGill Jr HC, McMahan CA, Herderick EE, et al. Obesity accelerates the progression of coronary atherosclerosis in young men. Circulation. 2002;105(23):2712–8.
35. McGill Jr HC, McMahan CA, Zieske AW, Malcom GT, Tracy RE, Strong JP. Effects of non-lipid risk factors on atherosclerosis in youth with a favorable lipoprotein profile. Circulation. 2001;103(11):1546–50.
36. McGill Jr HC, McMahan CA, Herderick EE, et al. Effects of coronary heart disease risk factors on atherosclerosis of selected regions of the aorta and right coronary artery. PDAY Research Group. Pathobiological Determinants of Atherosclerosis in Youth. Arterioscler Thromb Vasc Biol. 2000;20(3):836–45.
37. Rainwater DL, McMahan CA, Malcom GT, et al. Lipid and apolipoprotein predictors of atherosclerosis in youth: apolipoprotein concentrations do not materially improve prediction of arterial lesions in PDAY subjects. The PDAY Research Group. Arterioscler Thromb Vasc Biol. 1999;19(3):753–61.
38. McGill Jr HC, McMahan CA, Tracy RE, et al. Relation of a postmortem renal index of hypertension to atherosclerosis and coronary artery size in young men and women. Pathobiological Determinants of Atherosclerosis in Youth (PDAY) Research Group. Arterioscler Thromb Vasc Biol. 1998;18(7):1108–18.
39. McGill Jr HC, McMahan CA, Malcom GT, Oalmann MC, Strong JP. Effects of serum lipoproteins and smoking on atherosclerosis in young men and women. The PDAY Research Group. Pathobiological Determinants of Atherosclerosis in Youth. Arterioscler Thromb Vasc Biol. 1997;17(1):95–106.
40. McGill Jr HC, McMahan CA, Malcom GT, Oalmann MC, Strong JP. Relation of glycohemoglobin and adiposity to atherosclerosis in youth. Pathobiological Determinants of Atherosclerosis in Youth (PDAY) Research Group. Arterioscler Thromb Vasc Biol. 1995;15(4):431–40.
41. McGill Jr HC, Strong JP, Tracy RE, McMahan CA, Oalmann MC. Relation of a postmortem renal index of hypertension to atherosclerosis in youth. The Pathobiological Determinants of Atherosclerosis in Youth (PDAY) Research Group. Arterioscler Thromb Vasc Biol. 1995;15(12):2222–8.
42. Klotz O. Fatty streaks in the intima of arteries. J Pathol Bacteriol. 1911;16(1):211–20.
43. Strong JP, Malcom GT, McMahan CA, et al. Prevalence and extent of atherosclerosis in adolescents and young adults: implications for prevention from the Pathobiological Determinants of Atherosclerosis in Youth Study. JAMA. 1999;281(8):727–35.
44. Holman RL, McGill Jr HC, Strong JP, Geer JC. The natural history of atherosclerosis: the early aortic lesions as seen in New Orleans in the middle of the 20th century. Am J Pathol. 1958;34(2):209–35.
45. Lauer RM, Connor WE, Leaverton PE, Reiter MA, Clarke WR. Coronary heart disease risk factors in school children: the Muscatine study. J Pediatr. 1975;86(5):697–706.

46. Raitakari OT, Juonala M, Kahonen M, et al. Cardiovascular risk factors in childhood and carotid artery intima-media thickness in adulthood: the Cardiovascular Risk in Young Finns Study. JAMA. 2003;290(17):2277–83.
47. Libby P. The vascular biology of atherosclerosis. In: Bonow RO, Mann DL, Zipes DP, Libby P, editors. Braunwald's heart disease—A textbook of cardiovascular medicine. Philadelphia, PA: Saunders Elsevier; 2011. p. 897.
48. Hansson GK, Robertson AK, Soderberg-Naucler C. Inflammation and atherosclerosis. Annu Rev Pathol. 2006;1:297–329.
49. Hansson GK. Inflammation, atherosclerosis, and coronary artery disease. N Engl J Med. 2005;352(16):1685–95.
50. Ross R. Atherosclerosis—an inflammatory disease. N Engl J Med. 1999;340(2):115–26.
51. Gau GT, Wright RS. Pathophysiology, diagnosis, and management of dyslipidemia. Curr Probl Cardiol. 2006;31(7):445–86.
52. Davies MJ. A macro and micro view of coronary vascular insult in ischemic heart disease. Circulation. 1990;82(3 Suppl):II38–46.
53. Libby P. Atherosclerosis: disease biology affecting the coronary vasculature. Am J Cardiol. 2006;98(12A):3Q–9.
54. Stary HC, Chandler AB, Dinsmore RE, et al. A definition of advanced types of atherosclerotic lesions and a histological classification of atherosclerosis. A report from the Committee on Vascular Lesions of the Council on Arteriosclerosis, American Heart Association. Arterioscler Thromb Vasc Biol. 1995;15(9):1512–31.
55. Robertson WB, Geer JC, Strong JP, McGill Jr HC. The fate of the fatty streak. Exp Mol Pathol. 1963;52 Suppl 1:28–39.
56. Stary HC. Evolution and progression of atherosclerotic lesions in coronary arteries of children and young adults. Arteriosclerosis. 1989;9(1 Suppl):I19–32.
57. Chatzizisis YS, Coskun AU, Jonas M, Edelman ER, Feldman CL, Stone PH. Role of endothelial shear stress in the natural history of coronary atherosclerosis and vascular remodeling: molecular, cellular, and vascular behavior. J Am Coll Cardiol. 2007;49(25):2379–93.
58. Hubert HB, Feinleib M, McNamara PM, Castelli WP. Obesity as an independent risk factor for cardiovascular disease: a 26-year follow-up of participants in the Framingham Heart Study. Circulation. 1983;67(5):968–77.
59. Manson JE, Colditz GA, Stampfer MJ, et al. A prospective study of obesity and risk of coronary heart disease in women. N Engl J Med. 1990;322(13):882–9.
60. Williams IL, Wheatcroft SB, Shah AM, Kearney MT. Obesity, atherosclerosis and the vascular endothelium: mechanisms of reduced nitric oxide bioavailability in obese humans. Int J Obes Relat Metab Disord. 2002;26(6):754–64.
61. Manson JE, Willett WC, Stampfer MJ, et al. Body weight and mortality among women. N Engl J Med. 1995;333(11):677–85.
62. Willett WC, Manson JE, Stampfer MJ, et al. Weight, weight change, and coronary heart disease in women. Risk within the 'normal' weight range. JAMA. 1995;273(6):461–5.
63. Must A, Jacques PF, Dallal GE, Bajema CJ, Dietz WH. Long-term morbidity and mortality of overweight adolescents. A follow-up of the Harvard Growth Study of 1922 to 1935. N Engl J Med. 1992;327(19):1350–5.
64. McGill Jr HC, McMahan CA, Zieske AW, et al. Association of coronary heart disease risk factors with microscopic qualities of coronary atherosclerosis in youth. Circulation. 2000;102(4):374–9.
65. The NS, Suchindran C, North KE, Popkin BM, Gordon-Larsen P. Association of adolescent obesity with risk of severe obesity in adulthood. JAMA. 2010;304(18):2042–7.
66. Steinberger J, Moran A, Hong CP, Jacobs Jr DR, Sinaiko AR. Adiposity in childhood predicts obesity and insulin resistance in young adulthood. J Pediatr. 2001;138(4):469–73.
67. Sun SS, Liang R, Huang TT, et al. Childhood obesity predicts adult metabolic syndrome: the Fels Longitudinal Study. J Pediatr. 2008;152(2):191–200.
68. Irace C, Scavelli F, Carallo C, Serra R, Cortese C, Gnasso A. Body mass index, metabolic syndrome and carotid atherosclerosis. Coron Artery Dis. 2009;20(2):94–9.

69. Shalitin S, Phillip M. Frequency of cardiovascular risk factors in obese children and adolescents referred to a tertiary care center in Israel. Horm Res. 2008;69(3):152–9.
70. Zhang CX, Tse LA, Deng XQ, Jiang ZQ. Cardiovascular risk factors in overweight and obese Chinese children: a comparison of weight-for-height index and BMI as the screening criterion. Eur J Nutr. 2008;47(5):244–50.
71. Messiah SE, Arheart KL, Luke B, Lipshultz SE, Miller TL. Relationship between body mass index and metabolic syndrome risk factors among US 8- to 14-year-olds, 1999 to 2002. J Pediatr. 2008;153(2):215–21.
72. Messiah SE, Arheart KL, Lipshultz SE, Miller TL. Body mass index, waist circumference, and cardiovascular risk factors in adolescents. J Pediatr. 2008;153(6):845–50.
73. Rocchini AP, Moorehead C, Katch V, Key J, Finta KM. Forearm resistance vessel abnormalities and insulin resistance in obese adolescents. Hypertension. 1992;19(6 Pt 2):615–20.
74. Virdis A, Ghiadoni L, Masi S, et al. Obesity in the childhood: a link to adult hypertension. Curr Pharm Des. 2009;15(10):1063–71.
75. Oeffinger KC, Mertens AC, Sklar CA, et al. Obesity in adult survivors of childhood acute lymphoblastic leukemia: a report from the Childhood Cancer Survivor Study. J Clin Oncol. 2003;21(7):1359–65.
76. Miller TL, Lipsitz SR, Lopez-Mitnik G, et al. Characteristics and determinants of adiposity in pediatric cancer survivors. Cancer Epidemiol Biomarkers Prev. 2010;19(8):2013–22.
77. Strickman-Stein N, Gervais MD, Ludwig DA, Messiah SE, Lipshultz SE, Miller TL. Body mass index as a function of length of United States residency among Haitian immigrant children. Ethn Dis. 2010;20(1):22–8.
78. Su HY, Sheu WH, Chin HM, Jeng CY, Chen YD, Reaven GM. Effect of weight loss on blood pressure and insulin resistance in normotensive and hypertensive obese individuals. Am J Hypertens. 1995;8(11):1067–71.
79. de la Cruz-Munoz N, Messiah SE, Arheart KL, Lopez-Mitnik G, Lipshultz SE, Livingstone A. Bariatric surgery significantly decreases the prevalence of type 2 diabetes mellitus and pre-diabetes among morbidly obese multiethnic adults: long-term results. J Am Coll Surg. 2011;212(4):505–11; discussion 512–3.
80. Alvarez JA, Miller TL, Messiah SE, Lipshultz SE. Chapter 32: Lipid abnormalities. In: McInerny TK, Adams HM, Campbell DE, Kamat DM, Kelleher KJ, editors. American academy of pediatrics textbook of pediatric care. 2nd ed. Oak Grove Village: American Academy of Pediatrics; 2009.
81. Alvarez JA, Miller TL, Starc TJ, McGrath K, Lipshultz SE. Chapter 32: Preventive cardiology. In: McInerny TK, Adams HM, Campbell DE, Kamat DM, Kelleher KJ, editors. American Academy of Pediatrics textbook of pediatric care. Oak Grove Village, IL: American Academy of Pediatrics; 2008. p. 2935.
82. National Cholesterol Education Program (NCEP) Expert Panel on Detection, Evaluation, and Treatment of High Blood Cholesterol in Adults (Adult Treatment Panel III). Third Report of the National Cholesterol Education Program (NCEP) Expert Panel on Detection, Evaluation, and Treatment of High Blood Cholesterol in Adults (Adult Treatment Panel III) final report. Circulation. 2002;106(25):3143–421.
83. Alberti KG, Zimmet PZ. Definition, diagnosis and classification of diabetes mellitus and its complications. Part 1: Diagnosis and classification of diabetes mellitus provisional report of a WHO consultation. Diabet Med. 1998;15(7):539–53.
84. Einhorn D, Reaven GM, Cobin RH, et al. American College of Endocrinology position statement on the insulin resistance syndrome. Endocr Pract. 2003;9(3):237–52.
85. Grundy SM, Brewer Jr HB, Cleeman JI, et al. Definition of metabolic syndrome: report of the National Heart, Lung, and Blood Institute/American Heart Association conference on scientific issues related to definition. Circulation. 2004;109(3):433–8.
86. Zimmet P, Alberti G, Kaufman F, et al. The metabolic syndrome in children and adolescents. Lancet. 2007;369(9579):2059–61.
87. Gordon DJ, Rifkind BM. High-density lipoprotein—the clinical implications of recent studies. N Engl J Med. 1989;321(19):1311–6.

88. Li C, Ford ES, McBride PE, Kwiterovich PO, McCrindle BW, Gidding SS. Non-high-density lipoprotein cholesterol concentration is associated with the metabolic syndrome among US youth aged 12–19 years. J Pediatr. 2011;158(2):201–7.
89. McMahan CA, Gidding SS, Fayad ZA, et al. Risk scores predict atherosclerotic lesions in young people. Arch Intern Med. 2005;165(8):883–90.
90. Friedman LA, Morrison JA, Daniels SR, McCarthy WF, Sprecher DL. Sensitivity and specificity of pediatric lipid determinations for adult lipid status: findings from the Princeton Lipid Research Clinics Prevalence Program Follow-up Study. Pediatrics. 2006;118(1):165–72.
91. Porkka KV, Viikari JS, Taimela S, Dahl M, Akerblom HK. Tracking and predictiveness of serum lipid and lipoprotein measurements in childhood: a 12-year follow-up. The Cardiovascular Risk in Young Finns Study. Am J Epidemiol. 1994;140(12):1096–110.
92. Brown MS, Goldstein JL. A receptor-mediated pathway for cholesterol homeostasis. Science. 1986;232(4746):34–47.
93. Scientific Steering Committee on behalf of the Simon Broome Register Group. Mortality in treated heterozygous familial hypercholesterolaemia: implications for clinical management. Atherosclerosis. 1999;142(1):105–12.
94. Kolovou GD, Anagnostopoulou KK, Kostakou PM, Bilianou H, Mikhailidis DP. Primary and secondary hypertriglyceridaemia. Curr Drug Targets. 2009;10(4):336–43.
95. Castelli WP. Epidemiology of triglycerides: a view from Framingham. Am J Cardiol. 1992;70(19):3H–9.
96. Patsch JR, Miesenbock G, Hopferwieser T, et al. Relation of triglyceride metabolism and coronary artery disease. Studies in the postprandial state. Arterioscler Thromb. 1992;12(11):1336–45.
97. Taskinen MR. Diabetic dyslipidaemia: from basic research to clinical practice. Diabetologia. 2003;46(6):733–49.
98. Le NA, Walter MF. The role of hypertriglyceridemia in atherosclerosis. Curr Atheroscler Rep. 2007;9(2):110–5.
99. Rapp JH, Lespine A, Hamilton RL, et al. Triglyceride-rich lipoproteins isolated by selected-affinity anti-apolipoprotein B immunosorption from human atherosclerotic plaque. Arterioscler Thromb. 1994;14(11):1767–74.
100. Shin HK, Kim YK, Kim KY, Lee JH, Hong KW. Remnant lipoprotein particles induce apoptosis in endothelial cells by NAD(P)H oxidase-mediated production of superoxide and cytokines via lectin-like oxidized low-density lipoprotein receptor-1 activation: prevention by cilostazol. Circulation. 2004;109(8):1022–8.
101. Kawakami A, Tanaka A, Nakajima K, Shimokado K, Yoshida M. Atorvastatin attenuates remnant lipoprotein-induced monocyte adhesion to vascular endothelium under flow conditions. Circ Res. 2002;91(3):263–71.
102. Kawakami A, Tani M, Chiba T, et al. Pitavastatin inhibits remnant lipoprotein-induced macrophage foam cell formation through ApoB48 receptor-dependent mechanism. Arterioscler Thromb Vasc Biol. 2005;25(2):424–9.
103. Playford DA, Watts GF, Best JD, Burke V. Effect of fenofibrate on brachial artery flow-mediated dilatation in type 2 diabetes mellitus. Am J Cardiol. 2002;90(11):1254–7.
104. Zhao SP, Liu L, Gao M, Zhou QC, Li YL, Xia B. Impairment of endothelial function after a high-fat meal in patients with coronary artery disease. Coron Artery Dis. 2001;12(7):561–5.
105. Vogel RA, Corretti MC, Plotnick GD. Effect of a single high-fat meal on endothelial function in healthy subjects. Am J Cardiol. 1997;79(3):350–4.
106. Meade TW, Mellows S, Brozovic M, et al. Haemostatic function and ischaemic heart disease: principal results of the Northwick park heart study. Lancet. 1986;2(8506):533–7.
107. Simpson HC, Mann JI, Meade TW, Chakrabarti R, Stirling Y, Woolf L. Hypertriglyceridaemia and hypercoagulability. Lancet. 1983;1(8328):786–90.
108. Avellone G. Fibrinolysis in hypertriglyceridaemic subjects in response to venous occlusion. Blood Coagul Fibrinolysis. 1993;4(3):429–33.
109. de Man FH, Nieuwland R, van der Laarse A, et al. Activated platelets in patients with severe hypertriglyceridemia: effects of triglyceride-lowering therapy. Atherosclerosis. 2000;152(2):407–14.

110. Manninen V, Tenkanen L, Koskinen P, et al. Joint effects of serum triglyceride and LDL cholesterol and HDL cholesterol concentrations on coronary heart disease risk in the Helsinki Heart Study. Implications for treatment. Circulation. 1992;85(1):37–45.
111. National High Blood Pressure Education Program Working Group on High Blood Pressure in Children and Adolescents. The fourth report on the diagnosis, evaluation, and treatment of high blood pressure in children and adolescents. Pediatrics. 2004;114(2 Suppl 4th Report):555–76.
112. Gillman MW, Rich-Edwards JW, Rifas-Shiman SL, Lieberman ES, Kleinman KP, Lipshultz SE. Maternal age and other predictors of newborn blood pressure. J Pediatr. 2004;144(2):240–5.
113. Chen X, Wang Y. Tracking of blood pressure from childhood to adulthood: a systematic review and meta-regression analysis. Circulation. 2008;117(25):3171–80.
114. Cook NR, Gillman MW, Rosner BA, Taylor JO, Hennekens CH. Combining annual blood pressure measurements in childhood to improve prediction of young adult blood pressure. Stat Med. 2000;19(19):2625–40.
115. Zinner SH, Rosner B, Oh W, Kass EH. Significance of blood pressure in infancy. Familial aggregation and predictive effect on later blood pressure. Hypertension. 1985;7(3 Pt 1):411–6.
116. Oyama N, Gona P, Salton CJ, et al. Differential impact of age, sex, and hypertension on aortic atherosclerosis: the Framingham Heart Study. Arterioscler Thromb Vasc Biol. 2008;28(1):155–9.
117. Sokol KC, Messiah SE, Buzzard CJ, Lipshultz SE. Chapter 191: High blood pressure in infants, children, and adolescents. In: McInerny TK, Adams HM, Campbell DE, Kamat DM, Kelleher KJ, editors. American Academy of Pediatrics textbook of pediatric care. Oak Grove Village, IL: American Academy of Pediatrics; 2008.
118. Stalder M, Pometta D, Suenram A. Relationship between plasma insulin levels and high density lipoprotein cholesterol levels in healthy men. Diabetologia. 1981;21(6):544–8.
119. Enderle MD, Benda N, Schmuelling RM, Haering HU, Pfohl M. Preserved endothelial function in IDDM patients, but not in NIDDM patients, compared with healthy subjects. Diabetes Care. 1998;21(2):271–7.
120. Rudich A, Tirosh A, Potashnik R, Hemi R, Kanety H, Bashan N. Prolonged oxidative stress impairs insulin-induced GLUT4 translocation in 3 T3-L1 adipocytes. Diabetes. 1998;47(10):1562–9.
121. Sinaiko AR, Jacobs Jr DR, Steinberger J, et al. Insulin resistance syndrome in childhood: associations of the euglycemic insulin clamp and fasting insulin with fatness and other risk factors. J Pediatr. 2001;139(5):700–7.
122. Manzi S, Meilahn EN, Rairie JE, et al. Age-specific incidence rates of myocardial infarction and angina in women with systemic lupus erythematosus: comparison with the Framingham Study. Am J Epidemiol. 1997;145(5):408–15.
123. Gazarian M, Feldman BM, Benson LN, Gilday DL, Laxer RM, Silverman ED. Assessment of myocardial perfusion and function in childhood systemic lupus erythematosus. J Pediatr. 1998;132(1):109–16.
124. Kumeda Y, Inaba M, Goto H, et al. Increased thickness of the arterial intima-media detected by ultrasonography in patients with rheumatoid arthritis. Arthritis Rheum. 2002;46(6):1489–97.
125. Park KW. The antiphospholipid syndrome. Int Anesthesiol Clin. 2004;42(3):45–57.
126. McEntegart A, Capell HA, Creran D, Rumley A, Woodward M, Lowe GD. Cardiovascular risk factors, including thrombotic variables, in a population with rheumatoid arthritis. Rheumatology (Oxford). 2001;40(6):640–4.
127. Borba EF, Santos RD, Bonfa E, et al. Lipoprotein(a) levels in systemic lupus erythematosus. J Rheumatol. 1994;21(2):220–3.
128. Smith SC, Jr Anderson JL, Cannon RO, et al. CDC/AHA workshop on markers of inflammation and cardiovascular disease: application to clinical and public health practice: report from the Clinical Practice Discussion Group. Circulation. 2004;110(25):e550–3.
129. Ridker PM, Hennekens CH, Buring JE, Rifai N. C-reactive protein and other markers of inflammation in the prediction of cardiovascular disease in women. N Engl J Med. 2000;342(12):836–43.

130. Mangge H, Hubmann H, Pilz S, Schauenstein K, Renner W, Marz W. Beyond cholesterol–inflammatory cytokines, the key mediators in atherosclerosis. Clin Chem Lab Med. 2004;42(5):467–74.
131. Balagopal PB, de Ferranti SD, Cook S, et al. Nontraditional risk factors and biomarkers for cardiovascular disease: mechanistic, research, and clinical considerations for youth: a scientific statement from the American Heart Association. Circulation. 2011;123(23): 2749–69.
132. Winer JC, Zern TL, Taksali SE, et al. Adiponectin in childhood and adolescent obesity and its association with inflammatory markers and components of the metabolic syndrome. J Clin Endocrinol Metab. 2006;91(11):4415–23.
133. Pilz S, Horejsi R, Moller R, et al. Early atherosclerosis in obese juveniles is associated with low serum levels of adiponectin. J Clin Endocrinol Metab. 2005;90(8):4792–6.
134. Arnaiz P, Acevedo M, Barja S, et al. Adiponectin levels, cardiometabolic risk factors and markers of subclinical atherosclerosis in children. Int J Cardiol. 2010;138(2):138–44.
135. Chu NF, Shen MH, Wu DM, Lai CJ. Relationship between plasma adiponectin levels and metabolic risk profiles in Taiwanese children. Obes Res. 2005;13(11):2014–20.
136. Beauloye V, Zech F, Tran HT, Clapuyt P, Maes M, Brichard SM. Determinants of early atherosclerosis in obese children and adolescents. J Clin Endocrinol Metab. 2007; 92(8):3025–32.
137. Zhang Y, Proenca R, Maffei M, Barone M, Leopold L, Friedman JM. Positional cloning of the mouse obese gene and its human homologue. Nature. 1994;372(6505):425–32.
138. Farooqi IS, Jebb SA, Langmack G, et al. Effects of recombinant leptin therapy in a child with congenital leptin deficiency. N Engl J Med. 1999;341(12):879–84.
139. Balagopal PB, Gidding SS, Buckloh LM, et al. Changes in circulating satiety hormones in obese children: a randomized controlled physical activity-based intervention study. Obesity (Silver Spring). 2010;18(9):1747–53.
140. Feldman J, Shenker IR, Etzel RA, et al. Passive smoking alters lipid profiles in adolescents. Pediatrics. 1991;88(2):259–64.
141. Neufeld EJ, Mietus-Snyder M, Beiser AS, Baker AL, Newburger JW. Passive cigarette smoking and reduced HDL cholesterol levels in children with high-risk lipid profiles. Circulation. 1997;96(5):1403–7.
142. Messiah SE, Miller TL, Lipshultz SE, Bandstra ES. Potential latent effects of prenatal cocaine exposure on growth and the risk of cardiovascular and metabolic disease in childhood. Prog Pediatr Cardiol. 2011;31(1):59–65.
143. Gillman MW, Rifas-Shiman SL, Kleinman KP, Rich-Edwards JW, Lipshultz SE. Maternal calcium intake and offspring blood pressure. Circulation. 2004;110(14):1990–5.
144. American Academy of Pediatrics. National Cholesterol Education Program: Report of the Expert Panel on Blood Cholesterol Levels in Children and Adolescents. Pediatrics. 1992; 89(3 Pt 2):525–84.
145. Kavey RE, Allada V, Daniels SR, et al. Cardiovascular risk reduction in high-risk pediatric patients: a scientific statement from the American Heart Association Expert Panel on Population and Prevention Science; the Councils on Cardiovascular Disease in the Young, Epidemiology and Prevention, Nutrition, Physical Activity and Metabolism, High Blood Pressure Research, Cardiovascular Nursing, and the Kidney in Heart Disease; and the Interdisciplinary Working Group on Quality of Care and Outcomes Research: endorsed by the American Academy of Pediatrics. Circulation. 2006;114(24):2710–38.
146. American Academy of Pediatrics. Cardiovascular risk reduction in high-risk pediatric populations. Pediatrics. 2007;119(3):618–21.
147. Dennison BA, Kikuchi DA, Srinivasan SR, Webber LS, Berenson GS. Parental history of cardiovascular disease as an indication for screening for lipoprotein abnormalities in children. J Pediatr. 1989;115(2):186–94.
148. Expert Panel on Detection, Evaluation, and Treatment of High Blood Cholesterol in Adults (2001) Executive Summary of the Third Report of the National Cholesterol Education Program (NCEP) Expert Panel on Detection, Evaluation, and Treatment of High Blood Cholesterol in Adults (Adult Treatment Panel III). JAMA 285(19):2486–97

149. National Heart, Lung, and Blood Institute. Expert panel on integrated guidelines for cardiovascular health and risk reduction in children and adolescents: summary report. Pediatrics 2011;128(Suppl 5):S213–56.
150. Lipshultz SE, Somers MJ, Lipsitz SR, Colan SD, Jabs K, Rifai N. Serum cardiac troponin and subclinical cardiac status in pediatric chronic renal failure. Pediatrics. 2003; 112(1 Pt 1):79–86.
151. Moran AM, Lipshultz SE, Rifai N, et al. Non-invasive assessment of rejection in pediatric transplant patients: serologic and echocardiographic prediction of biopsy-proven myocardial rejection. J Heart Lung Transplant. 2000;19(8):756–64.
152. Newburger JW, Harmon WG, Lipshultz SE. Kawasaki disease. In: Burg FD, Ingelfinger JR, Polin RA, Gershon AA, editors. Current pediatric therapy. 18th ed. Philadelphia: Saunders Elsevier; 2006. p. 497.
153. Bonow RO, Mitch WE, Nesto RW, et al. Prevention conference VI: diabetes and cardiovascular disease: Writing Group V: management of cardiovascular-renal complications. Circulation. 2002;105(18):e159–64.
154. Fisher SD, Miller TL, Lipshultz SE. Impact of HIV and highly active antiretroviral therapy on leukocyte adhesion molecules, arterial inflammation, dyslipidemia, and atherosclerosis. Atherosclerosis. 2006;185(1):1–11.
155. Fisher SD, Kanda BS, Miller TL, Lipshultz SE. Cardiovascular disease and therapeutic drug related cardiovascular consequences in HIV infected patients. Am J Cardiovasc Drugs. 2011;11(6):383–94.
156. Miller TL, Grant YT, Almeida DN, Sharma T, Lipshultz SE. Cardiometabolic disease in human immunodeficiency virus-infected children. J Cardiometab Syndr. 2008;3(2):98–105.
157. Sharma TS, Messiah S, Fisher S, Miller TL, Lipshultz SE. Accelerated cardiovascular disease and myocardial infarction risk in patients with the human immunodeficiency virus. J Cardiometab Syndr. 2008;3(2):93–7.
158. Miller TL, Orav EJ, Lipshultz SE, et al. Risk factors for cardiovascular disease in children infected with human immunodeficiency virus-1. J Pediatr. 2008;153(4):491–7.
159. Grinspoon SK, Grunfeld C, Kotler DP, et al. State of the science conference: initiative to decrease cardiovascular risk and increase quality of care for patients living with HIV/AIDS: executive summary. Circulation. 2008;118(2):198–210.
160. Miller TL, Somarriba G, Orav EJ, et al. Biomarkers of vascular dysfunction in children infected with human immunodeficiency virus-1. J Acquir Immune Defic Syndr. 2010;55(2): 182–8.
161. Perez-Atayde AR, Kearney DI, Bricker JT, et al. Cardiac, aortic, and pulmonary arteriopathy in HIV-infected children: the Prospective P2C2 HIV Multicenter Study. Pediatr Dev Pathol. 2004;7(1):61–70.
162. Dube MP, Lipshultz SE, Fichtenbaum CJ, et al. Effects of HIV infection and antiretroviral therapy on the heart and vasculature. Circulation. 2008;118(2):e36–40.
163. Lipshultz SE, Adams MJ. Cardiotoxicity after childhood cancer: beginning with the end in mind. J Clin Oncol. 2010;28(8):1276–81.
164. Landy DC, Miller TL, Mitnik GL, et al. LV structure, LV function, and serum NT-proBNP in childhood cancer survivors without anthracycline or cardiac radiation exposures. Prog Pediatr Cardiol. 2011;31(2):141–2.
165. Franco VI, Henkel JM, Miller TL, Lipshultz SE. Cardiovascular effects in childhood cancer survivors treated with anthracyclines. Cardiol Res Pract. 2011;2011:134679.
166. Trachtenberg BH, Landy DC, Franco VI, et al. Anthracycline-associated cardiotoxicity in survivors of childhood cancer. Pediatr Cardiol. 2011;32(3):342–53.
167. Dadlani GH, Gingell RL, Orie JD, et al. Coronary artery calcifications in the long-term follow-up of Kawasaki disease. Am Heart J. 2005;150(5):1016.
168. Lipshultz SE, Schaechter J, Carrillo A, Sanchez J, Qureshi MY, Messiah SE, Hershorin ER, Wilkinson JD, Miller TL. In debate: can the consequences of universal cholesterol screening during childhood prevent cardiovascular disease and thus reduce long-term health care costs? Pediatr Endocrin Rev. 2012 [in press].

Chapter 6
Metabolic Syndrome and Associated Kidney Disease

Carolyn L. Abitbol and Wacharee Seeherunvong

Abstract With the rise in the incidence of childhood obesity, it is increasingly evident that the burden of chronic kidney disease (CKD) has increased proportionately and has its origins in early life. This chapter will discuss the central role of the kidney in the mediation of elements of the metabolic syndrome (MetS) including glucose disposal, hyperinsulinemia, uric acid excretion, and the renin-angiotensin-aldosterone system (RAAS). There is evidence that an adverse fetal environment with accelerated postnatal growth may contribute to a low nephron "endowment" and predispose to MetS and CKD in later life. The focus will be on the primary end points of hypertension, proteinuria, hyperuricemia, urolithiasis, and CKD. We will provide recommended treatment strategies and discuss necessary future research projects related to the MetS and CKD in children and adolescents.

Keywords Fetal programming • Hyperuricemia • Obesity-related glomerulopathy (ORG) • Hypertension • Proteinuria

---

C.L. Abitbol M.D. (✉)
Department of Pediatric Nephrology,
University of Miami Miller School of Medicine, Holtz Children Hospital,
P.O. Box 016960 (M714) 1611 NW 12th Avenue, Institute-Annex 504,
Miami, FL 33101, USA
e-mail: cabitbol@med.miami.edu

W. Seeherunvong M.D.
Division of Pediatric Nephrology, Department of Pediatrics,
University of Miami Miller School of Medicine, Holtz Children Hospital,
Miami, FL, USA

Introduction

The marked increase in the incidence of childhood obesity in recent decades has led to the recognition that insulin resistance and the incipient features of the metabolic syndrome (MetS) begin as early as infancy. Since Gerald Reaven first described the constellation of metabolic disturbances as "Syndrome X" in the late 1980s, he considered the kidney an innocent bystander and the earliest end-organ target of disease [1]. The life-threatening consequences of the MetS rarely manifest in childhood, but the intermediary end points such as hypertension, endothelial dysfunction, proteinuria, and renal scarring are now recognized with increasing frequency in children [2]. In this chapter, we will outline the predisposing factors to cardiorenal disease in young individuals as they relate to components of the MetS *independent* of diabetes mellitus. Important aspects of this problem include a focus on the recognition of vulnerable populations and assessments for hypertension, cardiorenal disease, urolithiasis, and progressive kidney disease, all of which impact on adult health and are potentially modifiable in childhood. Finally, we will discuss the potential treatments and future directions in translational research.

The Role of the Kidney in the Metabolic Syndrome (MetS)

Reaven's initial description of "Syndrome X" in 1988 purported that insulin resistance is the common etiologic factor for the metabolic disturbances that we now call MetS consisting of hyperinsulinemia, impaired glucose tolerance, high levels of low-density lipoprotein and triglycerides, low levels of high-density lipoprotein cholesterol, and hypertension [1]. It is the direct effect of insulin on the kidney that contributes to the systemic and local pathology and justifies Reaven's characterization of the kidney as an early and primary end-organ target [1].

It is well known that insulin resistance often precedes the development of type 2 diabetes mellitus (T2DM) [2]. The process is usually one of many years and most often occurs in adulthood. However, the manifestations of insulin resistance and hyperinsulinemia on the kidney are now known to manifest early in childhood in some individuals. In fact, organs that do not manifest insulin resistance, such as the kidney and vascular bed, are subject to harmful consequences and contribute to the adverse components of the MetS. Specifically, the physiological properties of insulin that stimulate sympathetic nervous system activity and enhance renal sodium retention contribute directly to the development of hypertension [2]. It is during the early phase of hyperinsulinemia that there are subtle increases in renal perfusion leading to hyperfiltration and glomerular hypertrophy [3].

Evidence suggests that insulin influences renal function primarily at the tubular level with specific binding sites for insulin greatest at the thick ascending limb and distal tubules, although the exact points of insulin action in the tubules have not been fully elucidated [4]. Of great importance is that the sodium-retaining action of insulin remains active whether or not there is insulin resistance and, therefore, contributes to "salt-sensitive hypertension" in normal or insulin-resistant states such as kidney failure and obesity (Fig. 6.1).

6 Metabolic Syndrome and Associated Kidney Disease

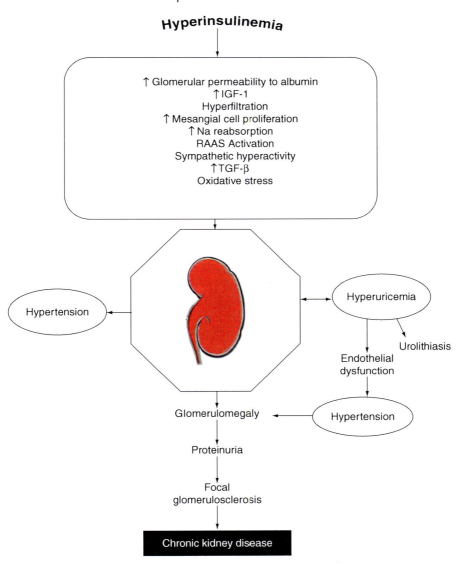

Fig. 6.1 Renal consequences of the metabolic syndrome: Hyperinsulinemia potentially causes salt sensitive hypertension driven by its diverse effects in altering glomerular permeability, causing hyperfiltration, increased sodium reabsorption, releasing growth factors, cytokines, activating RAAS, sympathetic hyperactivity as well as oxidative stress. Hyperuricemia further mediates endothelial dysfunction and could be the focus of urolithiasis. Hypertension aggravates glomerulomegaly and proteinuria, resulting in focal glomerulosclerosis and progressive loss of renal function culminating in chronic kidney disease. *IGF-1* insulin-like growth factor-1, *RAAS* renin-angiotensin-aldosterone system, *TGF-beta* transforming growth factor beta

Experiments on the direct effects of insulin on glomerular function have shown variable responses [4, 5]. However, it is postulated that insulin increases glomerular filtration rate (GFR) due to its antinatriuretic effect with increased proximal sodium reabsorption and reduced sodium chloride delivery to the macula densa, leading to activation of the renin-angiotensin-aldosterone system (RAAS), afferent arteriolar vasodilation, and resultant glomerular hyperfiltration [5, 6].

Insulin has long been recognized as a stimulus to cell growth and has been shown to stimulate the proliferation of vascular smooth muscle cells (VSMC) in a dose-dependent manner [6, 7]. We now know that the mitogenic actions of insulin are mediated through the stimulation of the VSMC and other cell types to produce insulin-like growth factor-1 (IGF-1), which has both autocrine and paracrine growth hormone activity. Since insulin and IGF-1 have close similarity in molecular structure, they have similar receptor affinity. Although the affinity of insulin for IGF-1 receptors is lower than that of IGF-1 per se, the elevated insulin levels in the MetS have a strong stimulatory effect on the IGF-1 receptors [7, 8]. Studies have further found that insulin-stimulated endothelial vascular proliferation is mediated through both the enhancement of IGF-1 production and the stimulation of its receptor [6–8].

Similar phenotypic changes in glomerular mesangial cell proliferation and extracellular matrix expansion are early important events in the genesis of focal glomerular sclerosis and diabetic nephropathy. Similar to the vascular endothelial cells, the glomerular mesangial cells respond to a high-insulin milieu with increased production of IGF-1 and its receptors [6, 8]. Moreover, the new mesangial phenotype endures and secretes abhorrent collagen resembling extracellular matrix collagens I and III, instead of collagen IV, and decreases matrix metalloproteinase-2 which is responsible for extracellular matrix degradation. This in turn leads to extracellular matrix expansion and, ultimately, renal fibrosis [7, 9].

Insulin may also contribute to the progression of kidney disease by its direct action or through its stimulation of IGF-1 via modulation of the production or action of other growth factors. For example, insulin increases the production of transforming growth factor beta (TGF-β) in mesangial and proximal tubule epithelial cells, which, in turn, leads to an increase in type IV collagen and its accumulation in the extracellular matrix [6, 7].

Evidence for a direct effect of high insulin levels on the systemic and intrarenal RAAS is limited. It is known that insulin has a stimulatory effect on angiotensinogen production from hepatic cells, but its effect on other cells is less clear [6, 10]. As for renal cells, in vitro studies show that insulin is necessary for the angiotensin II-induced contraction of mesangial cells in concert with an increase in TGF-β and collagen protein production. These studies support the upregulation of intrarenal RAAS by insulin as another mechanism of renal injury in the insulin-resistant state [10, 11].

Endothelin-1, a product of glomerular endothelial, mesangial, and tubular epithelial cells, has long been implicated in the pathogenesis of various diseases of the kidney. It causes severe vasoconstriction of the renal vasculature, mesangial cell contraction and proliferation, enhanced sodium and water retention, and proteinuria [12]. In turn, insulin has been shown to directly stimulate these actions through the insulin receptor, independent of IGF-1, and in a dose-dependent fashion [6, 12]. Hence, there is a strong association between insulin resistance and the progression of renal injury mediated through this link. It is further supported by experimental studies demonstrating the salutary effects of treatment with an endothelin receptor antagonist on renal injury and proteinuria [13].

The Nephron Endowment and "Obesity-Related Glomerulopathy"

The nephron endowment refers to the number of functioning nephrons that an individual has at birth. In the human fetus, renal development reaches completion at approximately 34–36 weeks of gestation [14]. Thereafter, there is only loss of nephron mass through natural aging or by disease, trauma, or surgical ablation [15, 16]. At term birth, the total number of nephrons per kidney averages 1 million, but this number is highly variable, ranging widely from approximately 300,000 to over 2 million per kidney [16]. Females have fewer nephrons than males, and certain ethnic populations are born with a relative nephron deficit (i.e., <5th percentile) [17, 18]. Infants born before completing 32 weeks' gestation and during active nephrogenesis will have a decrease in nephron number proportional to their abbreviated length of gestation [19]. No new nephrons are formed in the extrauterine environment. Individuals at the lower end of the normal distribution of the nephron endowment have been shown to be at increased risk of hypertension and the late development of cardiovascular and renal diseases [20–22].

In the context of pediatric kidney disease, reduced nephron mass and increased risk for end-stage kidney disease have been associated with individuals born small for gestational age as well as those born preterm and appropriate for gestational age [19, 23]. Epidemiologic studies indicate that low birth weight in conjunction with rapid postnatal growth imposes an increased risk for hypertension, insulin resistance, and T2DM in later life [24, 25]. Preterm infants fed fortified formulas in the newborn period are more likely to develop childhood and adult obesity than those preterm breast-fed infants [26, 27]. Our previous clinical observations suggest that early excessive weight gain contributes to progression of kidney disease in patients who have suffered acute kidney injury as a neonate [28]. It remains unclear whether these manifestations are the results of "perinatal programming" induced by adverse environmental events in utero or during the vulnerable periods in early postnatal life [29–32]. The population of surviving low-birth-weight individuals born preterm are the focus of much research since they offer some insight into the phenomenon of glucose sensitivity [24–27, 29], low nephron mass [19, 23], and cardiovascular disease risk [28, 30–32].

Based on clinical and laboratory observations related to mammalian hypertension and chronic kidney disease (CKD), Brenner and Mackenzie proposed the

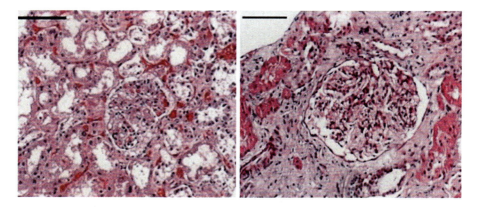

Fig. 6.2 Histopathologic findings of obesity-related glomerulopathy (*ORG*). The *left panel* illustrates glomerulomegaly in a child who was born preterm and who developed obesity-related glomerulopathy and proteinuria. Note that the glomerular tuft was significantly increased in size compared with the normal glomerular tuft on the *right panel* (Adapted from Abitbol et al. [37]. With permission from Springer)

"Hyperfiltration Theory" in 1996, which states that "early loss in nephron mass results in hyperfiltration of remaining nephrons, proteinuria and progressive kidney injury" [33]. Importantly, the pathologic confirmation of this hypothesis comes from the demonstrable change in the size of nephrons that undergo hyperfiltration. There is measurable increase in size of the glomerular tuft in association with podocyte disruption and clinical proteinuria [18, 34].

The additive risks of obesity and low nephron mass in humans gained recognition in the clinical observations of Praga et al. in Spain when they reported a large series of obese adults who developed proteinuria and progressive kidney failure after unilateral nephrectomy [35]. The onset of the proteinuria and renal insufficiency was over a prolonged period, usually greater than 10 years, and was characterized by few symptoms despite heavy proteinuria [35, 36]. The renal pathologic lesion included glomerulomegaly and focal glomerulosclerosis (FSGS) and was termed "obesity-related glomerulopathy" (ORG) in a large series of adults [34]. Soon thereafter, ORG was described in morbidly obese adolescents with renal biopsies showing FSGS (Fig. 6.2) [38]. Similar lesions have been reported in athletes with increased muscle mass [39] and adults and children of extremely low birth weight [37, 40] as well as cases of "late-onset oligomeganephronia" [41, 42]. These cases emphasize the likely "2-hit" phenomenon in the development of hyperfiltration injury (Fig. 6.3). That is, an individual with a primary nephron deficit, whether congenital or acquired, is more vulnerable to developing "hyperfiltration nephropathy" and progressive kidney disease [33, 43]. Moreover, subtle increments in body mass index and each component of the MetS are now recognized as a major contributor to the progression of primary kidney diseases as well as renal allograft dysfunction, particularly in those from certain ethnic populations [44–48].

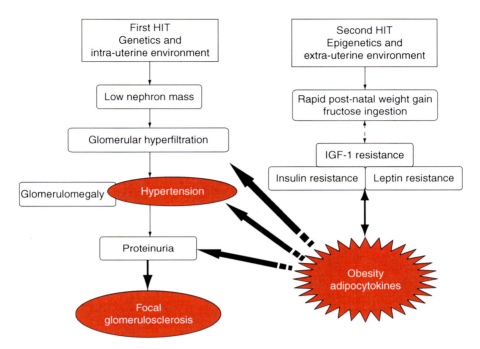

Fig. 6.3 Schematic proposing the evolution of kidney diseases in metabolic syndrome with a "two-hit hypothesis." Genetic and intrauterine environment determine the nephron endowment. Early loss in nephron mass results in hyperfiltration and glomerulomegaly. Epigenetic and postnatal events, especially fructose consumption, determine the development of obesity and the involvement of adipose tissue in the pathogenesis of hypertension and focal segmental glomerulosclerosis (*FSGS*)

Fructose, Hyperuricemia, and the Metabolic Syndrome

The genesis of the epidemic of obesity and insulin resistance may be nestled in the introduction of fructose, especially high-fructose corn syrup, as a component of processed foods and sweetened drinks in the Western diet since the 1970s [49]. There is a strong historical association of the parallel increase in cardiovascular disease with the increase in high dietary fructose which now makes up as much as 30% of the US diet [49, 50]. Although fructose is a simple sugar, it is distinct from glucose in that it is metabolized in the liver by fructokinase to fructose-1-phosphate, which depletes intracellular ATP, causing an abrupt increase in intracellular and systemic uric acid and triglyceride levels [50, 51]. Administration of fructose to humans and animals has been shown to induce features of the MetS and inflammatory markers that contribute to endothelial dysfunction, hypertension, and renal disease progression [52, 53]. It appears that the effects of fructose and uric acid co-stimulate endothelial inflammatory processes by upregulating intercellular adhesion molecule-1 (ICAM-1) and monocyte chemoattractant protein-1 (MCP-1) [53, 54].

The single most noxious product of the fructose cycle is uric acid, which is elevated [55]. It is an intracellular pro-oxidant, reduces levels of nitric oxide, stimulates the renin-angiotensin system, and induces renovascular lesions independent of blood pressure [55, 56]. Newly diagnosed hypertension in children has been associated with elevated uric acid levels [56, 57], and treatment with allopurinol has been effective in lowering blood pressure in hyperuricemic adolescents [58]. Clinical trials designed to show the renal and cardiovascular benefits of uric acid-lowering therapy have been challenging [59]. Allopurinol, a xanthine oxidase inhibitor, may decrease the progression of kidney disease and reduce the number of cardiovascular events in adults, but due to the high rate of adverse events associated with allopurinol, other less toxic drugs are being investigated [59]. Febuxostat, a selective xanthine oxidase inhibitor, is approved for the prevention of gout and has a higher safety profile than allopurinol, although more expensive. It has been shown to prevent progression of kidney disease in partially nephrectomized rats [60]. Interestingly, the use of low-fructose diets in a small group of patients with chronic kidney disease improved markers of inflammation, insulin resistance, and blood pressure [61].

Central Adiposity

There is an extensive body of literature that depicts adipose tissue as a functioning organ system that contributes to the vicious cycle of insulin resistance and inflammation in the MetS [62]. Central or visceral adiposity as measured by waist circumference is associated with the development of hypertension in children [63] as in adults [64]. Visceral adipose tissue, as opposed to subcutaneous or intramuscular fat, perpetuates hypertension and subclinical renal disease in children with the MetS [65, 66]. Accumulation of large, poorly differentiated adipocytes in visceral fat leads to the increased production of bioactive molecules including angiotensinogen, plasminogen activator inhibitor one (PAI-1), endothelin, and reactive oxygen species [62, 67]. Macrophages infiltrating the visceral fat mass also secrete pro-inflammatory mediators including tumor necrosis factor alpha (TNF-α), interleukin-6 (IL-6), monocyte chemoattractant protein 1 (MCP-1), and inducible nitric oxide synthase (iNOS) [62, 67, 68].

Hypertension: Multifactorial

Hypertension is likely the earliest and most subtle manifestation of the MetS in children, especially in the setting of obesity [69, 70]. It also forebodes the systemic and lifelong cardiovascular disease with "tracking" into adulthood [71, 72]. The insulin resistance and hyperinsulinemia characteristics of the MetS result in increased sodium reabsorption by the kidney, leading to volume expansion and "salt-sensitive" hypertension [2–4]. In addition, adipocytokines released by the central adipose tissue stimulate the sympathetic nervous system as well as RAAS [6, 7]. A constant state of oxidative stress and inflammation result in endothelial dysfunction with high levels of endothelin which also contributes to systemic and intrarenal hypertension [12, 13, 56, 57, 73–75]. This multifactorial pathologic mix requires a comprehensive approach to assessment and treatment, especially in children [76].

Blood pressure (BP) can be assessed in a number of ways, including traditional methods obtained by manual sphygmomanometer with auscultation of the brachial artery or by using oscillometric devices in the outpatient setting or at home. These measurements are called "casual" BPs. An ambulatory BP (ABP) can also be obtained by using a small portable device programmed to monitor BP regularly throughout the day and night. Blood pressure measurements in children are known to vary by age, gender, and stature. It is essential to use standardized techniques and tools to obtain accurate BP readings. Selection of an appropriate cuff size with an inflatable bladder width that is at least 40% of the right mid-arm circumference is essential for accurate measurement of BP. Measurements are overestimated to a greater degree with a cuff that is too small than underestimated by a cuff that is too large. If the cuff is too small, the next largest cuff should be used, even if it is appears large. The details of good technique and normative data of office BPs in children and adolescents have been published and revised in the 4th report of the National Task Force on High BP in Children [77]. Systolic (SBP) and diastolic (DBP) blood pressure percentiles according to gender, age, and height serve as the basis of defining "normal" BP, "prehypertension," and "hypertension" in children and adolescents as defined below [77].

Normal	SBP and/or DBP <90th percentile
Prehypertension	SBP and/or DBP ≥90th or <95th percentile
Hypertension	SBP and/or DBP ≥95th percentile or ≥140/90 mmHg for >3 occasions

Ambulatory blood pressure has recently been evaluated to provide more information than casual blood pressure measurements with respect to end-organ damage in children. It helps in identifying "white coat hypertension" or "masked hypertension" that could be missed by casual BPs [78]. In addition, it is important to note that in healthy individuals, BP normally has a diurnal variation with a "dip" of at least 10–20% during sleep called the "dipping phenomenon" [79]. It increases during the day and peaks during late afternoon [79]. The ABP monitoring has an advantage over casual BP in that it allows additional information, including pattern of nocturnal dipping, the absence of which signals a pathologic pattern of hypertension associated with increased cardiovascular risk and mortality in adults [79–81]. ABP monitoring is an essential diagnostic tool to identify this pattern [78–82]. Moreover, current recommendations suggest that echocardiography to examine for left ventricular hypertrophy (LVH) should be included in the initial evaluation of obese patients due to the lack of predictive value from either casual or ABP monitoring in children [82].

Proteinuria: The Common Denominator for Chronic Kidney Disease

Proteinuria, the hallmark of endovascular dysfunction and an independent predictor of cardiovascular mortality in adults, is linked to hyperinsulinemia and the MetS [83]. Proteinuria and microalbuminuria are predictive markers of progressive CKD in adults and children [84–87]. The modulation of proteinuria has become a primary focus of early treatment toward prevention of progression of CKD regardless of underlying etiology [88, 89]. The role of insulin on the renal excretion of albumin and other proteins remains poorly understood. A few studies suggest that hyperinsulinemia directly and selectively increases urinary excretion of albumin in T2DM without affecting systemic albumin permeability [90].

In children, proteinuria needs to be differentiated as to its origin since younger patients tend to have congenital tubular obstructive disease [84, 85]. Therefore, the proteinuria can be profiled into the *glomerular* component, which is primarily the *albumin* component, and *tubular* proteinuria, which is composed primarily of low molecular weight proteins such as β(beta)2-microglobulin or other microglobulins. We, therefore, fractionate the proteinuria by measuring the total protein and the albumin and determining the albumin and the non-albumin or tubular proteinuria [91]. The best urine sample is the first morning void, which can be sent for the total protein, creatinine, and microalbumin to determine the ratios [92].

A fivefold increase in the prevalence of CKD in adults in the USA has been shown to be associated with increasing components of the MetS [93, 94]. In children, features of insulin resistance in concert with the MetS have also been associated with progressive kidney disease [95]. This association is more pronounced in children with suspected nephron deficit such as those born preterm of low birth weight [95]. Glomerular hyperfiltration in apparently healthy young men with components of the MetS has recently been recognized as an early and silent risk factor for renal disease [96]. All these features merit close scrutiny in the assessment of children with obesity.

Urolithiasis

Urolithiasis is well recognized as an association with the MetS in adults but is probably overlooked in children [97]. Although hyperuricemia is a major component of the MetS and contributes to the components of inflammation, endothelial dysfunction, and hypertension, its role in urolithiasis is less straightforward [98]. Those with the MetS rarely have uricosuria [98]. Rather, it is believed that the uric acid serves as a nidus for calcium oxalate stones [99]. Moreover, it has been shown that urinary buffers and citrate excretion are low in the MetS, making it more likely that the urine will have an acid pH making it more lithogenic [97, 100].

Vitamin D Insufficiency: An Emerging Component of the MetS

Multiple large epidemiologic studies in both children and adults, including the recent Nutritional Health and Nutrition Examination Survey (NHANES) 2001–2006, have consistently documented that low serum vitamin D levels are independently associated with insulin resistance and cardio-metabolic risk factors regardless of obesity [101]. Vitamin D is now recognized as having pleiotropic roles beyond bone and mineral homeostasis, with the vitamin D receptors and metabolizing machinery identified in multiple tissues [102]. Vitamin D supplementation in patients with MetS may have positive effects on improving insulin sensitivity, decreasing proteinuria, and attenuating the progression of kidney disease [103]. Several translational research studies have demonstrated that vitamin D plays an important role in RAAS suppression, insulin sensitivity, and immunity [104]. Mice with knockout of the vitamin D receptor gene show upregulation of the RAAS and left ventricular hypertrophy [105]. Several ongoing multicenter randomized controlled trials have been implemented to evaluate whether intervention with vitamin D supplementation can improve insulin sensitivity and diminish inflammation and adipocyte-endocrine dysregulation [106, 107].

Evaluation and Treatment

Childhood obesity may be the most important modifiable risk factor in promoting the health of our future generations (Fig. 6.4). Addressing these issues is essential in altering the rising incidence of cardiovascular and renal disease morbidity and mortality experienced worldwide [108]. The escalation in the recognition of obesity-related MetS and renal disease in our children and young adults is representative of the growing obesity crisis, as well as genetic and environmental factors that continue to emerge and require further research for elucidation [93, 94].

Prevention remains the best resource for pediatricians in dealing with the potential long-term complications of the MetS in an effort to forestall the development of late cardiorenal disease [109]. The demographics that characterize an individual's risks are an important first step in assessing interventions (Table 6.1). The first encounter with a patient should include racial/ethnic origins, birth weight and length of gestation, history of the perinatal course, and family history of obesity and diabetes mellitus or renal disease. In infants, especially those born preterm and/or of low birth weight, the growth trajectory should be plotted with attention to weight/length ratios [24, 25]. Special hypercaloric formulas and carbohydrate supplements should be discouraged, and the rate of weight gain and "catch-up" growth modulated as much as possible [26, 27].

Nutritional therapy is indicated for all patients with the MetS, especially those with obesity, hypertension, hyperuricemia, and/or proteinuria. Counseling should

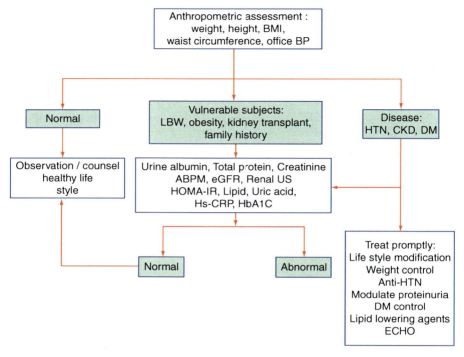

Fig 6.4 Assessment paradigm: This diagram outlines the evaluation and management of kidney disease in children and adolescents with metabolic syndrome

Table 6.1 Diagnosis and assessments

Assessment	Tools
Markers of metabolic syndrome	Body mass index (BMI) waist-to-hip ratio
	Fasting glucose and insulin, HOMA-IR
	Fasting lipid profile
	Microalbuminuria
	Uric acid, Hs-CRP
	Oral glucose tolerance test
	Serum adiponectin, leptin
	Serum 25-hydroxy vitamin D
Blood pressure and cardiovascular assessment	Office casual BP
	24-h ABP monitoring: nocturnal HTN, non-dipping pattern
	Echocardiogram for LVH and function
	Doppler US: carotid intima-media wall thickness (cIMT)
Markers of renal function	First morning urine: protein, microalbumin, creatinine
	eGFR by serum creatinine and/or cystatin C
Nephron mass	Ultrasound kidneys for renal size and volume
	Renal micro-histomorphology if available
Urolithiasis	24-h urine analysis for stone risk: volume, acid–base, solutes (uric acid, calcium, phosphate, oxalate, citrate, and electrolytes)

HOMA-IR homeostatic model assessment of insulin resistance, *Hs-CRP* high-sensitivity C-reactive protein, *ABP* ambulatory blood pressure, *HTN* hypertension, *LVH* left ventricular hypertrophy, *eGFR* estimated glomerular filtration rate include the limitation of fructose in the diet, including all drinks sweetened with high-fructose corn syrup such as sodas, sports drinks, and even some fruit juices [49–51]. Sodium should also be limited, especially in the hypertensive [4, 32].

The components of the metabolic syndrome including hypertension and insulin resistance are addressed primarily with a weight loss and exercise program [72–76]. Even short periods of exercise and small but sustained increments in weight reduction have important positive effects on the metabolic consequences imposed on the kidneys [76, 109]. Elevated blood pressures persistently ≥95th percentile for age, height and gender should be treated. This is especially true if there is a nocturnal "non-dipping pattern" by ABP monitoring [78–81]. The first-line drug categories should be angiotensin-converting enzyme inhibitors or angiotensin receptor blockers to decrease intraglomerular and systemic hypertension, counter insulin resistance, and decrease proteinuria if it is present [110–113]. In patients with CKD, these angiotensin antagonists can improve insulin resistance and preserve renal function, while other antihypertensive medications from classes including thiazide diuretics, calcium channel blockers, and beta blockers may not [76, 110–113]. There is some evidence that the development of T2DM may also be averted with angiotensin blockade [113].

Allopurinol has been shown to successfully treat adolescents with recent-onset hypertension associated with hyperuricemia [58]. However, this drug is associated with significant side effects. More recently, a clinical trial is ongoing to compare allopurinol with febuxostat versus a placebo in the treatment of uric acid-associated hypertension [59, 60].

The treatment of dyslipidemia in children associated with kidney disease and the MetS remains controversial [114, 115]. Although statins have been shown to decrease proteinuria and preserve renal function in the short term in adults [114], late treatment has not been shown to prevent progression to end-stage kidney disease [114, 115]. Currently, no recommendation can be made on the use of lipid-lowering therapies in children with the MetS and progressive kidney disease.

Vitamin D supplementation in patients with obesity and the MetS may have positive effects on decreasing proteinuria and slowing progression of kidney disease [103, 106, 107]. Supplementation with vitamin D analogues has also been shown to ameliorate the dyslipidemia associated with the insulin resistance of CKD in adolescents [116].

An estimation of renal function using either serum creatinine or cystatin C will allow the classification of current kidney function [117, 118] (Table 6.2). An elevated eGFR above 160 ml/min/1.73 m^2 may be the earliest sign of hyperfiltration and may warrant early intervention with medications that alter the postglomerular efferent arteriolar constriction including angiotensin blockers and nitric oxide enhancers [110, 111]. In obese individuals, medications that alter hyperfiltration and insulin resistance may provide long-term protection, especially in those with existing hypertension [112]. More advanced stages of CKD with eGFR <60 ml/min/1.73 m^2 will require closer surveillance and referral to a nephrologist.

Proteinuria is a consistent marker of progressive kidney disease. Its magnitude reflects severity of disease and may provide a useful assay for monitoring response to therapeutic regimens including weight loss and dosing of medications [91, 110]. Angiotensin, aldosterone, and endothelin inhibitors have been shown to have independent roles in improving proteinuria and slowing renal disease progression

Table 6.2 Summary of formula calculations

Markers Calculation	Calculation	Abnormal
HOMA-IR	[Fasting glucose (mmol/l) × fasting insulin (microunit/ml)] ÷ 22.5	≥3
Proteinuria (mg/mg Cr)	U protein(mg/dl) ÷ U creatinine (mg/dl)	≥0.2
Albuminuria (mg/g Cr)	[U microalbumin (mg/dl) × 1,000] ÷ [U creatinine (mg/dl)]	≥30
eGFR (Revised Schwartz) ml/min/1.73 m2	[0.413 × height (cm)] ÷ S creatinine (mg/dl)	<90 or
eGFR by cystatin C ml/min/1.73 m2	$75 \div (\text{serum cystatin C})^{1.33}$	>160

Formulae derived from references [91, 117–119]
HOMA-IR homeostatic model assessment of insulin resistance, *eGFR* estimated glomerular filtration rate, *U* urine concentration, *mg/dl* milligrams/deciliter, *mg/mg Cr* milligrams/milligram creatinine, *mg/g Cr* milligrams/grams creatinine

[110–113]. Combination drug regimens may complement the effects of single drugs but require careful monitoring for potential adverse effects [110–113]. Patients with obesity-related nephrotic syndrome and secondary FSGS should not be treated with corticosteroids since this aggravates the underlying renal pathology and promotes obesity. There is some evidence in experimental models of FSGS that immune modulation with mycophenolate mofetil alone or in combination with angiotensin blockers may be beneficial in controlling interstitial renal fibrosis, but this remains experimental [120, 121].

In some children who have reached sexual maturity, bariatric surgery for morbid obesity may be an option in an effort to avoid progression to end-stage renal disease [122–124].

Future Perspectives

If the current epidemic of obesity and the MetS is to be curtailed, education and the enlistment of communities in the effort must occur. Prevention of obesity and the early recognition of insulin resistance and renal disease should begin in infancy, and medical management should begin in early childhood. It is particularly important to study infants and children in an attempt to recognize critical windows during early life in which programming may occur. Ultimately, these may become the potential windows for therapeutic interventions aimed to prevent late onset of disease. Prospective investigations into the genetic and environmental origins of low nephron mass, insulin resistance, obesity, and focal glomerulosclerosis should begin in the perinatal period with tracking throughout childhood, especially in ethnic minority populations. Early clinical renal evaluations of high-risk infants and children should include tests to detect early hypertension, insulin resistance, hyperfiltration, and microalbuminuria.

References

1. Reaven GM. The kidney: an unwilling accomplice in syndrome X. Am J Kidney Dis. 1997;30:928–31.
2. Steinberger J, Daniels SR, Eckel RH, et al. Progress and challenges in metabolic syndrome in children and adolescents: a scientific statement from the American Heart Association Atherosclerosis, Hypertension, and Obesity in the Young Committee of the Council on Cardiovascular Disease in the Young; Council on Cardiovascular Nursing; and Council on Nutrition, Physical Activity, and Metabolism. Circulation. 2009;119(4):628–47.
3. Srivastava T. Nondiabetic consequences of obesity on kidney. Pediatr Nephrol. 2006;21:463–70.
4. Horita S, Seki G, Yamada H. Insulin resistance, obesity, hypertension, and renal sodium transport. Int J Hypertens. 2011;2011:8. doi:10.4061/2011/391762.
5. Savino A, Pelliccia P, Chiarelli F, Mohn A. Obesity-related renal injury in childhood. Horm Res Paediatr. 2010;73:303–11.
6. Sarafidis PA, Ruilopensulin LM. Insulin resistance, hyperinsulinemia, and renal injury: mechanisms and implications. Am J Nephrol. 2006;26:232–44.
7. Quinones-Galvan A, Ferrannini E. Renal effects of insulin in man. J Nephrol. 1997;10:188–91.
8. Weiss O, Anner H, Nephesh I, et al. Insulin-like growth factor-I (IGF-I) and IGF-I receptor gene expression in the kidney of the chronically hypoinsulinemic rat and hyperinsulinemic rat. Metabolism. 1995;44:982–6.
9. Baricos WH. Chronic renal disease: do metalloproteinase inhibitors have a demonstrable role in extracellular matrix accumulation? Curr Opin Nephrol Hypertens. 1995;4:365–8.
10. Zhang SL, Chen X, Filep JG, et al. Insulin inhibits angiotensinogen gene expression via the mitogen activated protein kinase pathway in rat kidney proximal tubular cells. Endocrinology. 1999;140:5285–92.
11. Chen X, Zhang SL, Pang L, et al. Characterization of a putative insulin-responsive element and its binding protein(s) in rat angiotensinogen gene promoter: regulation by glucose and insulin. Endocrinology. 2001;142:2577–85.
12. Sarafidis PA, Lasaridis AN. Insulin resistance and endothelin: another pathway for renal injury in patients with the cardiometabolic syndrome? J Cardiometab Syndr. 2008;3:183–7.
13. Kohan DE. Endothelin, hypertension and chronic kidney disease: new insights. Curr Opin Nephrol Hypertens. 2010;19(2):134–9.
14. Abitbol CL, Ingelfinger JR. Nephron mass and cardiovascular and renal disease risks. Semin Nephrol. 2009;29:445–54.
15. Anderson S, Brenner BM. Effects of aging on the renal glomerulus. Am J Med. 1986;80:435–42.
16. Merlet-Bénichou C, Gilbert T, Vilar J, et al. Nephron number: variability is the rule. Causes and consequences. Lab Invest. 1999;79:515–27.
17. Hershkovitz D, Burbea Z, Skorecki K, Brenner BM. Fetal programming of adult kidney disease: cellular and molecular mechanisms. Clin J Am Soc Nephrol. 2007;2:334–42.
18. Hoy WE, Douglas-Denton RN, Hughson M, et al. A stereological study of glomerular number and volume: preliminary findings in a multiracial study of kidneys at autopsy. Kidney Int. 2003;63:S31–7.
19. Rodríguez MM, Gómez AH, Abitbol CL, et al. Histomorphometric analysis of postnatal glomerulogenesis in extremely preterm infants. Pediatr Dev Pathol. 2004;7:17–25.
20. Hoy WE, Hughson MD, Douglas-Denton R, Amann K. Nephron number, hypertension, renal disease and renal failure. J Am Soc Nephrol. 2005;16:2557–64.
21. Keller G, Zimmer G, Mall G, Ritz E, Amann K. Nephron number in patients with primary hypertension. N Engl J Med. 2003;348:101–8.
22. Hoy WE, Hughson MD, Singh GR, et al. Reduced nephron number and glomerulomegaly in Australian Aborigines: a group at high risk for renal disease and hypertension. Kidney Int. 2006;70:104–10.

23. Mañalich R, Reyes L, Herrera M, et al. Relationship between weight at birth and the number and size of renal glomeruli in humans: a histomorphometric study. Kidney Int. 2000;58:770–3.
24. Regan FM, Cutfield WS, Jefferies C, et al. The impact of early nutrition in premature infants on later childhood insulin sensitivity and growth. Pediatrics. 2006;118(5):1943–9.
25. Jimenez-Chillaron JC, Patti ME. To catch up or not to catch up: is this the question? Lessons from animal models. Curr Opin Endocrinol Diabetes Obes. 2007;14(1):23–9.
26. Lucas A. Programming by early nutrition: an experimental approach. J Nutr. 1998;128:401S–6.
27. Singhal A, Farooqi IS, O'Rahilly S, Lucas A. Early nutrition and leptin concentrations in later life. Am J Clin Nutr. 2002;75:993–9.
28. Abitbol CL, Bauer CR, Montané B, et al. Long-term follow-up of extremely low birth weight infants with neonatal renal failure. Pediatr Nephrol. 2003;18:887–93.
29. Hovi P, Andersson S, Eriksson JG, et al. Glucose regulation in young adults with very low birth weight. N Engl J Med. 2007;356:2053–63.
30. Lackland DT, Bendal HE, Osmond C, et al. Low birth weight contributes to the high rates of early onset chronic renal failure on the Southeast United States. Arch Intern Med. 2000;160:1472–6.
31. Vikse BE, Irgens LM, Leivestad T, et al. Low birth weight increases risk for end stage renal disease. J Am Soc Nephrol. 2008;19:151–7.
32. Simonetti GD, Raio L, Surbek D, et al. Salt sensitivity of children with low birth weight. Hypertension. 2008;52:625–30.
33. Brenner BM, Lawler EV, Mackenzie HS. The hyperfiltration theory: a paradigm shift in nephrology. Kidney Int. 1996;49:1774–7.
34. Kambham N, Markowitz GS, Valeri AM, et al. Obesity-related glomerulopathy: an emerging epidemic. Kidney Int. 2001;59:1498–509.
35. Praga M, Hernández E, Herrero JC, et al. Influence of obesity on the appearance of proteinuria and renal insufficiency after unilateral nephrectomy. Kidney Int. 2000;58:2111–8.
36. Praga M, Hernández E, Morales E, et al. Clinical features and long-term outcome of obesity-associated focal segmental glomerulosclerosis. Nephrol Dial Transplant. 2001;16:1790–8.
37. Abitbol CL, Chandar J, Rodríguez MM, et al. Obesity and preterm birth: additive risks in the progression of kidney disease in children. Pediatr Nephrol. 2009;24:1363–70.
38. Adelman RD, Restaino JG, Alon US, Blowley DL. Proteinuria and focal segmental glomerulosclerosis in severely obese adolescents. J Pediatr. 2001;138:482–5.
39. Schwimmer JA, Markowitz GS, Valeri AM, et al. Secondary focal segmental glomerulosclerosis in non-obese patients with increased muscle mass. Clin Nephrol. 2003;60:233–41.
40. Hodgin JB, Rasoulpour M, Markowitz GS, D'Agati VD. Very low birth weight is a risk factor for secondary focal segmental glomerulosclerosis. Clin J Am Soc Nephrol. 2009;4:71–6.
41. Kawanishi K, Takei T, Kojima C, et al. Three cases of late-onset oligomeganephronia. NDT Plus. 2011;4:14–6.
42. Drukker A. Oligonephropathy: from a rare childhood disorder to a possible health problem in the adult. Isr Med Assoc J. 2002;4:191–5.
43. Brenner BM, Mackenzie HS. Nephron mass as a risk factor for progression of renal disease. Kidney Int Suppl. 1997;63:S124–7.
44. Hsu C, McCulloch CE, Iribarren C, et al. Body mass index and risk for end-stage renal disease. Ann Intern Med. 2006;144:21–8.
45. Bonnet F, Deprele C, Sassolas A, et al. Excessive body weight as a new independent risk factor for clinical and pathological progression in primary IgA nephritis. Am J Kidney Dis. 2001;37:720–7.
46. Meier-Kriesche HU, Arndorfer JA, Kaplan B. The impact of body mass index on renal transplant outcomes: a significant independent risk factor for graft failure and patient death. Transplantation. 2002;73:70–4.
47. Singh GR, Hoy WE. Kidney volume, blood pressure and albuminuria: findings in an Australian Aboriginal community. Am J Kidney Dis. 2004;43:254–9.

48. Narva AS. The spectrum of kidney disease in American Indians. Kidney Int Suppl. 2003; 83:53–7.
49. Neilson EG. The fructose nation. J Am Soc Nephrol. 2007;18:2619–21.
50. Johnson RJ, Sanchez-Lozada LG, Nakagawa T. The effect of fructose on renal biology and disease. J Am Soc Nephrol. 2010;21:2036–9.
51. Stanhope KL, Havel PJ. Fructose consumption: potential mechanisms for its effects to increase visceral adiposity and induce dyslipidemia and insulin resistance. Curr Opin Lipidol. 2008; 19:16–24.
52. Sanchez-Lozada LG, Tapia E, Jimenez A, et al. Fructose-induced metabolic syndrome is associated with glomerular hypertension and renal microvascular damage in rats. Am J Physiol Renal Physiol. 2007;292:F423–9.
53. Glushakova O, Kosugi T, Roncal C, et al. Fructose induces the inflammatory molecule ICAM-1 in endothelial cells. J Am Soc Nephrol. 2008;19:1712–20.
54. Cirillo P, Gersch MS, Mu W, et al. Ketohexokinase-dependent metabolism of fructose induces proinflammatory mediators in proximal tubular cells. J Am Soc Nephrol. 2009;20:545–55.
55. Feig DI, Kang DH, Johnson RJ. Uric acid and cardiovascular risk. N Engl J Med. 2008;359:1811–21.
56. Nguyen S, Choi HK, Lustig RH, Hsu CY. Sugar-sweetened beverages, serum uric acid, and blood pressure in adolescents. J Pediatr. 2009;154:807–13.
57. Feig DI, Johnson RJ. Hyperuricemia in childhood primary hypertension. Hypertension. 2003; 42(3):247–52.
58. Feig DI, Soletsky B, Johnson RJ. Effect of allopurinol on blood pressure of adolescents with newly diagnosed essential hypertension: a randomized trial. JAMA. 2008;300:924–32.
59. Badve SV, Brown F, Hawley CM, et al. Challenges of conducting a trial of uric-acid-lowering therapy in CKD. Nat Rev Nephrol. 2011;7:295–300.
60. Sánchez-Lozada LG, Tapia E, Soto V, et al. Effect of febuxostat on the progression of renal disease in 5/6 nephrectomy rats with and without hyperuricemia. Nephron Physiol. 2008;108:69–78.
61. Brymora A, Flisinski M, Johnson RJ, et al. Nephrol dial transplant.. 2011. doi:10.1093/ndt/gfr223.
62. Kershaw EE, Flier JS. Adipose tissue as an endocrine organ. J Clin Endocrinol Metab. 2004;89:2548–56.
63. Campagnolo PD, Hoffman DJ, Vitolo MR. Waist-to-height ratio as a screening tool for children with risk factors for cardiovascular disease. Ann Hum Biol. 2011;38:265–70.
64. Pinto-Sietsma SJ, Navis G, Janssen WMT, de Zeeuw D, Gans ROB, de Jong PE, for the PREVEND Study Group. A central body fat distribution is related to renal function impairment, even in lean subjects. Am J Kidney Dis. 2003;41:733–41.
65. Sanad M, Gharib A. Evaluation of microalbuminuria in obese children and its relation to metabolic syndrome. Pediatr Nephrol. 2011;26:2193–9. doi:10.1007/s00467–011–1931–9.
66. Savino A, Pelliccia P, Giannini C, et al. Implications for kidney disease in obese children and adolescents. Pediatr Nephrol. 2011;26:749–58.
67. DeMarco VG, Johnson MS, Whaley-Connell AT, Sowers JR. Cytokine abnormalities in the etiology of the cardiometabolic syndrome. Curr Hypertens Rep. 2010;12:93–8.
68. Wahba IM, Mak RH. Obesity and obesity-initiated metabolic syndrome: mechanistic links to chronic kidney disease. Clin J Am Soc Nephrol. 2007;2:550–62.
69. Flynn JT, Alderman MH. Characteristics of children with primary hypertension seen at a referral center. Pediatr Nephrol. 2005;20:961–6.
70. Bibbins-Domingo K, Coxson P, Pletcher MJ, et al. Adolescent overweight and future adult coronary heart disease. N Engl J Med. 2007;357:2371–9.
71. Li Z, Snieder H, Harshfield GA, et al. A 15-year longitudinal study on ambulatory blood pressure tracking from childhood to early adulthood. Hypertens Res. 2009;32:404–10.
72. Flynn JT. Metabolic syndrome as a predictor of cardiovascular risk in children and adolescents. Am J Hypertens. 2007;20(8):883.
73. Flynn JT, Falkner BE. Obesity hypertension in adolescents: epidemiology, evaluation, and management. J Clin Hypertens (Greenwich). 2011;13:323–31.

74. Litwin M, Sladowska J, Antoniewicz J. Metabolic abnormalities, insulin resistance, and metabolic syndrome in children with primary hypertension. Am J Hypertens. 2007;20:875–82.
75. Ostrow V, Wu S, Aguilar A, et al. Association between oxidative stress and masked hypertension in a multi-ethnic population of obese children and adolescents. J Pediatr. 2011;158:628–33.e1.
76. Puri M, Flynn JT. Management of hypertension in children and adolescents with the metabolic syndrome. J Cardiometab Syndr. 2006;1(4):259–68.
77. National High Blood Pressure Education Program Working Group on High Blood Pressure in Children and Adolescents. The fourth report on the diagnosis, evaluation, and treatment of high blood pressure in children and adolescents pediatrics. Pediatrics. 2004;114(Suppl):555–76.
78. Lurbe E, Torro I, Alvarez V, et al. Prevalence, persistence, and clinical significance of masked hypertension in youth. Hypertension. 2005;45:493–8.
79. Urbina E, Alpert B, Flynn J, et al. Ambulatory blood pressure monitoring in children and adolescents: recommendations for standard assessment: a scientific statement from the American Heart Association Atherosclerosis, Hypertension, and Obesity in Youth Committee of the council on cardiovascular disease in the young and the council for high blood pressure research. Hypertension. 2008;52:433–51.
80. Lurbe E, Torro I, Aguilar F, et al. Added impact of obesity and insulin resistance in nocturnal blood pressure elevation in children and adolescents. Hypertension. 2008;51:635–41.
81. Routledge FS, McFetridge-Durdle JA, Dean CR. Canadian Hypertension Society Night-time blood pressure patterns and target organ damage: a review. Can J Cardiol. 2007;23:132–8.
82. Brady TM, Fivush B, Flynn JT, Parekh R. Ability of blood pressure to predict left ventricular hypertrophy in children with primary hypertension. J Pediatr. 2008;152:73–8.
83. Tillin T, Forouhi N, McKeigue P, Chaturvedi N. Microalbuminuria and coronary heart disease risk in an ethnically diverse UK population: a prospective cohort study. J Am Soc Nephrol. 2005;16:3702–10.
84. Ardissino G, Testa S, Dacco V, et al. Proteinuria as a predictor of disease progression in children with hypodysplastic nephropathy. Data from the Ital Kid Project. Pediatr Nephrol. 2004;19:172–7.
85. Wong CS, Pierce CB, Cole SR, et al. Association of proteinuria with race, cause of chronic kidney disease, and glomerular filtration rate in the chronic kidney disease in children study. Clin J Am Soc Nephrol. 2009;4:812–9.
86. Peralta CA, Shlipak MG, Judd S, et al. Detection of chronic kidney disease with creatinine, cystatin C, and urine albumin-to-creatinine ratio and association with progression to end-stage renal disease and mortality. JAMA. 2011;305:1545–52.
87. Satoh-Asahara N, Suganami T, Majima T, et al. Urinary cystatin C as a potential risk marker for cardiovascular disease and chronic kidney disease in patients with obesity and metabolic syndrome. Clin J Am Soc Nephrol. 2011;6:265–73.
88. Wuhl E, Mehls O, Schaefer F, for the ESCAPE Trial Group, et al. Antihypertensive and antiproteinuric efficacy of ramipril in children with chronic renal failure. Kidney Int. 2004;6:768–76.
89. Schaefer F. Proteinuria: not a small problem in the little ones. Clin J Am Soc Nephrol. 2009;4:696–7.
90. Musso C, Javor E, Cochran E, et al. Spectrum of renal diseases associated with extreme forms of insulin resistance. Clin J Am Soc Nephrol. 2006;1:616–22.
91. Abitbol CL, Chandar J, Onder AM, et al. Profiling proteinuria in pediatric patients. Pediatr Nephrol. 2006;21:995–1002.
92. Lambers Heerspink HJ, Gansevoort RT, Brenner BM, et al. Comparison of different measures of urinary protein excretion for prediction of renal events. J Am Soc Nephrol. 2010;21:1355–60.
93. Lee S, Bacha F, Gungor N, Arslanian S. Comparisons of different definitions of pediatric metabolic syndrome: relation to abdominal obesity, insulin resistance, adiponectin, and inflammatory biomarkers. J Pediatr. 2008;152:177–84.

94. Zimmet P, Alberti K, George MM, for the IDF Consensus Group, et al. The metabolic syndrome in children and adolescents – an IDF consensus report. Pediatr Diabetes. 2007;8: 299–306.
95. Tomaszewski M, Charchar FJ, Maric C, et al. Glomerular hyperfiltration: a new marker of metabolic risk. Kidney Int. 2007;71:816–21.
96. Grundy SM, Cleeman JI, Merz CN, for the American Heart Association, et al. Implications of recent clinical trials for the National Cholesterol Education Program Adult Treatment Panel III guidelines. Circulation. 2004;110:227–39. Erratum in: Circulation. 2004;110:763.
97. Maalouf NM. Metabolic syndrome and the genesis of uric acid stones. J Ren Nutr. 2011; 21:128–31.
98. Sakhaee K, Adams-Huet B, Moe OW, et al. Pathophysiologic basis for normouricosuric uric acid nephrolithiasis. Kidney Int. 2002;62:971–9.
99. Coe FL, Strauss AL, Tembe V, et al. Uric acid saturation in calcium nephrolithiasis. Kidney Int. 1980;17:662–8.
100. Maalouf NM, Cameron MA, Moe OW, et al. Low urine pH: a novel feature of the metabolic syndrome. Clin J Am Soc Nephrol. 2007;2:883–8.
101. Ganji V, Zhang X, Shaikh N, Tangpricha V. Serum 25-hydroxyvitamin D concentrations are associated with prevalence of metabolic syndrome and various cardiometabolic risk factors in US children and adolescents based on assay-adjusted serum 25-hydroxyvitamin D data from NHANES 2001–2006. Am J Clin Nutr. 2011;94:225–33.
102. Holick MF. Sunlight and vitamin D for bone health and prevention of autoimmune diseases, cancers, and cardiovascular disease. Am J Clin Nutr. 2004;80:1678S–88.
103. Agarwal R, Vitamin D. Proteinuria, diabetic nephropathy, and progression of CKD. Clin J Am Soc Nephrol. 2009;4:1523–8.
104. Witham MD, Dove FJ, Dryburgh M, et al. The effect of different doses of vitamin D(3) on markers of vascular health in patients with type 2 diabetes: a randomised controlled trial. Diabetologia. 2010;53:2112–9.
105. Li YC, Kong J, Wei M, et al. 1,25-Dihydroxyvitamin D(3) is a negative endocrine regulator of the renin-angiotensin system. J Clin Invest. 2002;110:229–38.
106. Petchey WG, Hickman IJ, Duncan E, et al. The role of 25-hydroxyvitamin D deficiency in promoting insulin resistance and inflammation in patients with chronic kidney disease: a randomised controlled trial. BMC Nephrol. 2009;10:41. doi:10.1186/1471-2369-10-41.
107. Thiem U, Heinze G, Segel R, et al. VITA-D: cholecalciferol substitution in vitamin D deficient kidney transplant recipients: a randomized, placebo-controlled study to evaluate the post-transplant outcome. Trials. 2009;10:36. doi:10.1186/1745–6215–10–36.
108. Hossain P, Kawar B, El Nahas M. Obesity and diabetes in the developing world—a growing challenge. N Engl J Med. 2007;356:213–5.
109. Kelishadi R, Hashemi M, Mohammadifard N, et al. Association of changes in oxidative and proinflammatory states with changes in vascular function after a lifestyle modification trial among obese children. Clin Chem. 2008;54:147–53.
110. Chandar J, Abitbol C, Montané B, Zilleruelo G. Angiotensin blockade as sole treatment for proteinuric kidney disease in children. Nephrol Dial Transplant. 2007;22:1332–7.
111. de Paula RB, da Silva AA, Hall JE. Aldosterone antagonism attenuates obesity-induced hypertension and glomerular hyperfiltration. Hypertension. 2004;43:41–7.
112. Bosch J, Lonn E, Pogue J, for the HOPE/HOPE-TOO Study Investigators, et al. Long-term effects of ramipril on cardiovascular events and on diabetes: results of the HOPE study extension. Circulation. 2005;30:1339–46.
113. Mann JF, Schmieder RE, McQueen M, for the ONTARGET Investigators, et al. Renal outcomes with telmisartan, ramipril, or both, in people at high vascular risk (the ONTARGET study): a multicentre, randomised, double-blind, controlled trial. Lancet. 2008;372: 547–53.
114. Tullus K. Dyslipidemia in children with CKD: should we treat with statins? Pediatr Nephrol. 2011. doi:10.1007/s00467–011–1872–3.

115. de Ferranti S, Ludwig DS. Storm over statins—the controversy surrounding pharmacologic treatment of children. N Engl J Med. 2008;359:1309–12.
116. Mak RH. 1,25 vitamin D3 corrects insulin and lipid abnormalities in uremia. Kidney Int. 1998;53:1353–7.
117. Schwartz GJ, Muñoz A, Schneider MF, et al. New equations to estimate GFR in children with CKD. J Am Soc Nephrol. 2009;20:629–37.
118. Filler G, Lepage N. Should the Schwartz formula for estimation of GFR be replaced by cystatin C formula? Pediatr Nephrol. 2003;18:981–5.
119. Tresaco B, Bueno G, Pineda I, et al. Homeostatic model assessment (HOMA) index cut-off values to identify the metabolic syndrome in children. J Physiol Biochem. 2005;6:381–8.
120. Fujihara CK, Noronha IL, Malheiros DM, et al. Combined mycophenolate mofetil and losartan therapy arrests established injury in the remnant kidney. J Am Soc Nephrol. 2000;11:283–90.
121. Rodríguez-Iturbe B, Quiroz Y, Shahkarami A, et al. Mycophenolate mofetil ameliorates nephropathy in the obese Zucker rat. Kidney Int. 2005;68:1041–7.
122. Fowler SM, Kon V, Ma L, et al. Obesity-related focal and segmental glomerulosclerosis: normalization of proteinuria in an adolescent after bariatric surgery. Pediatr Nephrol. 2009;24:851–5.
123. Lawson ML, Kirk S, Mitchell T, for the Pediatric Bariatric Study Group, et al. One-year outcomes of Roux-en-Y gastric bypass for morbidly obese adolescents: a multicenter study from the Pediatric Bariatric Study Group. J Pediatr Surg. 2006;41:137–43.
124. Shield JPH, Crowne E, Morgan J. Is there a place for bariatric surgery in treating childhood obesity? Arch Dis Child. 2008;93:369–72.

Chapter 7
Metabolic Syndrome and Related Liver Diseases

Aymin Delgado-Borrego

Abstract The metabolic syndrome is often accompanied by liver disease, specifically nonalcoholic fatty liver disease (NAFLD). NAFLD is a clinicopathological entity characterized by accumulation of fat in the liver in the setting of minimal to no alcohol intake. It represents a spectrum of liver disease ranging from steatosis to advanced fibrosis or cirrhosis and can lead to hepatocellular carcinoma. The causes of NAFLD are multifactorial and include genetic predisposition and environmental factors including overnutrition. NAFLD is not a defining characteristic of the metabolic syndrome, but these conditions frequently coexist, especially in the setting of obesity. The prevalence of NAFLD in pediatrics has not been clearly determined, but this is considered the most common pediatric liver disease. An important challenge is that NAFLD is typically asymptomatic and is usually not diagnosed unless the clinician specifically evaluates the patient for it. The diagnosis of NAFLD is established through a liver biopsy. There are pathogenetic links between NAFLD and the metabolic syndrome, but the precise pathogeneses of these conditions remain to be fully elucidated. The effects of NAFLD on the natural history of the metabolic syndrome, and vice versa, are not known. However, it is possible that these conditions may exacerbate one another. Further research is needed to answer important questions regarding pediatric NAFLD and its relationship to the metabolic syndrome. What is clear is that given the high prevalence of overweight and obesity, clinicians need to be well informed about the risk of liver disease in the patient with metabolic syndrome.

Keywords Nonalcoholic fatty liver disease (NAFLD) • Nonalcoholic steatohepatitis (NASH) • Liver • Obesity • Steatosis • Fibrosis • Cirrhosis • Alanine aminotransferase (ALT) • Liver enzymes • Vitamin E

A. Delgado-Borrego, M.D., MPH
Division of Pediatrics/Gastroenterology, University of Miami,
1580 NW 10th Avenue, Room 523, 33136 Miami, FL, USA
e-mail: adelgado5@med.miami.edu

Introduction

The worldwide obesity epidemic has brought about an increase in associated pediatric liver disease. Although not traditionally included among its defining characteristics, the metabolic syndrome is often accompanied by hepatic abnormalities. Nonalcoholic fatty liver disease (NAFLD), widely considered to be a hepatic manifestation of this syndrome, is of great public health relevance as it has become the most common cause of chronic liver disease in children and adolescents in the USA and most of the Western world [1]. Unfortunately, clinicians often focused on a single organ system or abnormality and frequently fail to recognize common associations relevant to the metabolic syndrome. A global understanding of the multiple health threats faced by children with or at risk for this syndrome is a crucial first step in the prevention of significant morbidity and mortality.

This chapter reviews the association between the metabolic syndrome and liver disease in children, in particular pediatric NAFLD, focusing on epidemiological and pathophysiological considerations. Common histological findings are discussed, and issues pertaining to identification, management, and prevention are reviewed.

Nonalcoholic Fatty Liver Disease

The association between chronic liver disease and obesity was first reported in the late 1970s in obese pregnant women [2]. One year later, in 1980, Ludwig et al. introduced the term NASH (non-alcoholic steatohepatitis) to describe a pattern of liver disease resembling alcoholic hepatitis but in the absence of significant alcohol intake [3]. In 1983, this condition was recognized in children by Moran et al. [4]. More recently, a new term, nonalcoholic fatty liver disease, has gained acceptance in an effort to acknowledge a wider spectrum of disease. NAFLD is a clinicopathological entity defined as accumulation of fat in the liver in the setting of minimal to no alcohol intake. This condition represents a spectrum of liver disease ranging from asymptomatic hepatic fat accumulation (steatosis) to nonalcoholic steatohepatitis (NASH), a progressive form of liver disease that may lead to advanced fibrosis, cirrhosis, and hepatocellular carcinoma in a subset of affected individuals [5, 6]. The hallmarks of this condition are macrovesicular steatosis, ballooning degeneration, sometimes the presence of Mallory bodies, and lobular or portal inflammation with or without fibrosis [7]. The development and progression of NAFLD is determined by a combination of genetic and environmental factors including nutrition, which represents a modifiable risk.

As a result of evolving terminology and the intrinsic difficulties in establishing its diagnosis, the exact prevalence of pediatric NAFLD has not been determined. The reported prevalence of this condition has varied widely within the USA and throughout the world. Data from 2,450 children aged 12 to 18 based on the third National Health and Nutrition Examination Survey (NHANES) demonstrated elevated alanine aminotransferases (>30 U/L) in 3% of normal weight, in 6% of

Table 7.1 NAFLD summary

Chronic liver diseases associated with obesity was first reported in 1979
The term NASH was introduced in 1980
NAFLD was recognized in children in 1983
NAFLD is a clinicopathological entity defined as accumulation of fat in the liver in the setting of minimal alcohol intake
Exact prevalence of pediatric NAFLD is unknown but reported prevalence ranges from 10% to 77%
NAFLD represents a spectrum of liver disease ranging from asymptomatic hepatic fat accumulation (steatosis) to nonalcoholic steatohepatitis (NASH) which is a progressive form of liver disease
Histological hallmarks of NAFLD: macrovesicular steatosis, ballooning degeneration, sometimes Mallory bodies, lobular or portal inflammation with or without fibrosis
NAFLD is determined by a combination of genetics and environmental factors

overweight, and in 10% of obese adolescents [8], with a similar prevalence noted based on data derived from the Korean National Health and Nutrition Examination Survey from 1998 [9]. In a study conducted by Schwimmer et al., the autopsies of 742 children aged 2 to 19 years who died from sudden, unexpected deaths outside the hospital setting in San Diego County between 1993 and 2003 were evaluated revealing a prevalence of fatty liver adjusted for age, gender, race, and ethnicity of 9.6%. In this cohort, older age, male gender, overweight, and Hispanic ethnicity (mostly comprised of Mexican Americans) were independent predictors of fatty liver disease [10]. The prevalence of fatty liver disease among obese children in China, Italy, Japan, and the USA has been reported to be between 10% and 77% [8, 11–13] (Table 7.1).

An important challenge in diagnosing NAFLD is that it is typically asymptomatic. About 42–59% of patients report abdominal pain [14, 15], often localized to the right upper quadrant. Hepatomegaly is present in 40–50% of children with NAFLD [15, 16], although this may be difficult to appreciate on exam in the setting of abdominal obesity. Acanthosis nigricans, a velvety thickening and hyperpigmentation localized to the posterior neck, axillae, and other flexural areas of the skin in persons with hyperinsulinemia [17], may be observed in 30–50% of children with NAFLD [15, 16]. An abnormally elevated serum alanine aminotransferase (ALT) level is most commonly used to screen for NAFLD, but the sensitivity or specificity for any cutoff value for detection of fatty liver in children is unclear and it must be noted that NAFLD can occur in the setting of normal ALT levels [18]. Noninvasive radiologic imaging studies are important adjuncts in the diagnosis of pediatric NAFLD. Liver ultrasonography is the technique most used in the evaluation of hepatic fat as a result of its low cost and wide availability. However, it has important limitations. Ultrasonography is operator and machine dependent, limiting the reproducibility of its results. In addition, body habitus can influence the assessment of hyperechogenicity and signal attenuation [19], leading to a false positive diagnosis of fat deposition in overweight patients as a result of abdominal fat. Furthermore, coexisting hepatic involvement, such as fibrosis and inflammation, is not detectable on ultrasound but alters liver echogenicity [19–22]. Computed tomography (CT) is a more specific method than ultrasonography for the detection of fatty liver, in particular noncontrast

CT [23, 24], but exposure to radiation limits its use especially in children. Magnetic resonance imaging (MRI) or magnetic resonance spectroscopy (MRS) may be ideal in children. They have a high degree of accuracy given their ability to quantify intrahepatic lipid, are noninvasive in nature, and do not use ionizing radiation [25, 26]. Nevertheless, even MR techniques fail to detect fibrotic tissue. Elastography is another promising noninvasive technique that may be used in the assessment of liver fibrosis and can be either ultrasound or MR based. However, it has not yet received approval from the Federal Drug Administration for clinical use in the USA [27–29]. At present, the gold standard for establishing the diagnoses of NAFLD or NASH is liver biopsy, which allows for the evaluation of histology, in conjunction with clinical history since other causes of liver disease must be excluded.

The natural history of pediatric NAFLD is not clearly understood as a result of limited long-term prospective data. Fibrosis has been reported in 53–100% of children with NAFLD [14–16, 30]. Advanced fibrosis has been reported to develop in 5–10% of cases, and there have been multiple reports of NAFLD-associated cirrhosis in the young [16, 31, 32]. There have also been reports of adolescents in the USA undergoing liver transplantation for end-stage liver disease caused by NASH [32, 33], as well as cases of hepatocellular carcinoma associated with NASH in children [34, 35]. Feldstein et al. recently published a retrospective longitudinal study of 63 children with NAFLD followed for up to 20 years [1]. Four children with baseline normal fasting glucose developed type 2 diabetes 4–11 years after NAFLD diagnosis. There was progression of fibrosis stage in four of the five patients who underwent liver biopsies during the follow-up period. In addition, two children died and two underwent liver transplantation for decompensated cirrhosis. The observed survival period free of liver transplantation was significantly shorter in the NAFLD cohort as compared to the expected survival in the general US population of the same age and gender. NAFLD recurred in the allograft among transplanted cases, with one progressing to cirrhosis [1]. In addition to its effects on the liver itself, NAFLD has been associated with a number of important extrahepatic comorbidities. Most of the recognized comorbidities in adults as well as in children represent risk factors for cardiovascular disease including insulin resistance, dyslipidemia, and hypertension [36]. Furthermore, increased carotid artery intima-medial thickness (IMT) has been observed in obese children with fatty liver as compared to obese children with no steatosis [37, 38], demonstrating evidence of cardiovascular involvement early on in life. Other extrahepatic conditions associated with NAFLD include obstructive sleep apnea [39] and hypothyroidism [40]. NAFLD has been associated with increased risk of mortality (liver-related and all-cause mortality) among adults [41]. In the study by Feldstein et al. described above, the investigators observed that children with NAFLD had 13.6 higher odds of mortality or needing a liver transplant than age- and gender-matched controls [1].

What is the basis for an association between NAFLD and the metabolic syndrome? And what is the clinical relevance of NAFLD in the setting of the metabolic syndrome? What should clinicians do to identify, diagnose, and manage liver disease in the setting of the metabolic syndrome? The sections below will discuss the existent pertinent information in an effort to answer these important questions.

Basis for an Association Between the Metabolic Syndrome and NAFLD

Although NAFLD and the metabolic syndrome often coexist, NAFLD is not a defining feature of the metabolic syndrome. The obvious link between these two conditions in children as in adults is obesity. Obesity is a risk factor for the development of the metabolic syndrome as it is a risk factor for the development of NAFLD, and as such, there is clearly an overlap. But are these conditions more intrinsically linked than what may be expected from two independent comorbidities of a single condition such as obesity?

Epidemiological Considerations

A frequent finding of elevated liver enzymes in patients with metabolic syndrome has been reported by several investigators. Alanine aminotransferase (ALT) is the liver enzyme most closely associated with inflammation in the setting of hepatic steatosis [42], and as such, it is commonly used as a surrogate marker of NAFLD. In 2009, Di Bonito et al. evaluated the association between ALT levels and metabolic factors among 358 obese children and 206 nonobese controls [43]. The investigators found that 36% of obese boys and 55% of obese girls had elevated ALT. Obese boys with ALT > 30 IU/L had higher BMI, waist circumference, insulin resistance (homeostasis model assessment (HOMA-IR)), systolic and diastolic blood pressure, and maternal BMI than boys with normal ALT. When evaluated in multivariate linear regression analysis, waist circumference was an independent factor associated with ALT. Obese girls with higher ALT were younger and had higher triglyceride levels than those with normal ALT, and triglycerides were independently associated with ALT levels in multivariate regression. In 2010, Wei et al. evaluated 216 obese children and found that those with elevated ALT levels were more likely to fulfill criteria for metabolic syndrome and have elevated glucose levels during an oral glucose tolerance test (OGTT) [44]. A study of multiethnic children in the Netherlands demonstrated a strong association between ALT and the metabolic syndrome (odds ratio (OR) = 7.1), adjusted for age, gender, and body mass index (BMI) Z score, as well as insulin resistance. In a univariate analysis, 43.3% of children with elevated ALT (>30 IU/L) met criteria for the metabolic syndrome as compared with 22.7% of those with normal ALT [45]. Together, the above studies demonstrate a clear association between the metabolic syndrome and elevated ALT in the young. Moreover, the relevance of increased ALT levels with respect to the metabolic syndrome was underscored by a recently published study. Patel et al. reported that among 1,525 preadolescents (4–11 years) and 1,060 adolescents (12–18 years) within the Bogalusa Heart Study, the area under the curve (AUC) values to determine the ability of ALT to identify preadolescents and adolescents

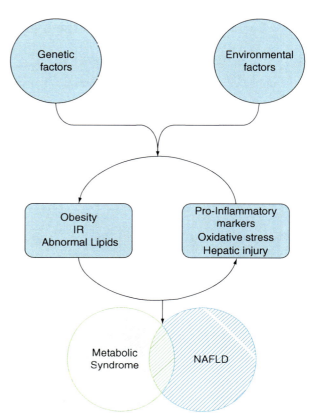

Fig. 7.1 A combination of certain genetic and environmental factors may predispose individuals to an adverse endocrine-metabolic milieu, characterized by obesity, insulin resistance and hyperlipedemia, with proinflammatory markers and oxidative stress playing a central role in its pathogenetic basis. This endocrine-metabolic milieu may be considered a vicious loop that exacerbates underlying clinical conditions (i.e., IR, hyperlipidemia) and that often leads to outcomes such as the metabolic syndrome or NAFLD in the setting of liver injury. Indirect evidence suggests that the overlap of the metabolic syndrome and NAFLD may be associated with worse clinical outcomes than each of these conditions alone

with clustering of adverse levels of all four metabolic syndrome variables were 0.67 and 0.82 respectively. They concluded that ALT may be useful as a biomarker of the presence of metabolic syndrome and related risk in the pediatric population, especially among adolescents [46].

The coexistence of NAFLD and the metabolic syndrome in adults has been reported by numerous investigators who have demonstrated a high prevalence of metabolic syndrome among various cohorts of adult patients with NAFLD as well as a correlation between the presence of this syndrome and progression of liver disease [47–50]. Similarly, metabolic syndrome has been found to predict the presence and severity of NAFLD in obese adolescents [51–54]. Children with the metabolic syndrome, as defined by Adult Treatment Panel III [55], have been found to be five times more likely to have NAFLD than overweight and obese children without the metabolic syndrome [36]. Another study of children with biopsy-proven NAFLD revealed that 66% had metabolic syndrome based also on the National Cholesterol Education Program (NCEP), Adult Treatment Panel III [56]. Moreover, the investigators also found an association between histological severity of disease and some components of the metabolic syndrome [56] (Fig. 7.1).

Table 7.2 Histopathological features of liver disease in metabolic syndrome

Type 1 NASH	Type 2 NASH
Macrovesicular steatosis	Steatosis
Lobular inflammation	Portal inflammation
Ballooning degeneration	Perisinusoidal fibrosis
Perisinusoidal fibrosis	Portal fibrosis
Present in 17% of pediatric NAFLD	Present in 51% of pediatric NAFLD
Typical adult pattern	Younger patients
	More severe obesity
	Boys
	More common in:
	Asians
	Native Americans
	Hispanics (Mexican Americans)

Histopathological Features of Liver Disease in Metabolic Syndrome

As discussed previously, liver disease often coexists with metabolic syndrome in adults as well as in children. The liver histopathology frequently observed in the setting of metabolic syndrome is that of NAFLD, which is considered by many the hepatic manifestation of this syndrome. The typical pattern of adult NAFLD/NASH includes macrovesicular steatosis, lobular inflammation and ballooning degeneration, and/or perisinusoidal fibrosis in the absence of portal changes. However, pediatric NAFLD/NASH differs from adults [57]. A study of 100 children with NAFLD by Schwimmer et al. identified two different types of steatohepatitis [31]. The pattern consistent with that observed in adults was labeled type 1 NASH. However, a second pattern (type 2 NASH) was also observed characterized by steatosis, portal inflammation, and/or portal fibrosis in the absence of ballooning degeneration and perisinusoidal fibrosis. Type 1 NASH was reported to be present in 17% of pediatric NAFLD, while type 2 NASH was present in 51%. Simple steatosis was noted in 16% of subjects, advanced fibrosis in 8%, and cirrhosis in 3%. Patients with advanced fibrosis tended to exhibit a pattern consistent with type 2 NASH. Children with type 2 NASH were younger and had more severe obesity than those with type 1 NASH. Boys were more likely to have type 2 NASH than girls. Type 2 NASH was more common in children of Asian, Native American, and Hispanic (mostly comprised of Mexican American) ethnicity [31]. The existence of these two different histological patterns of NASH has been confirmed by investigators from Italy [58] and Japan [57], although these cohorts demonstrated lower prevalence of type 1 and type 2 NASH and a higher percentage of a mixed type than those described in the US cohort possibly as a result of differences in the ethnic/racial distribution of study subjects (Table 7.2).

Although pediatric patients with metabolic syndrome may exhibit any or all of the histological features of NAFLD, certain specific associations have been noted. Hepatocellular ballooning and NAFLD pattern ("definite NASH" vs. "not NASH" pattern) are associated with metabolic syndrome based on a study of 254 children 6–17 years of age enrolled in the Nonalcoholic Steatohepatitis Clinical Research Network [59]. Children with grade 3 steatosis had 2.6 times greater risk of metabolic syndrome than those with grade 1 steatosis. Children with advanced fibrosis (stage 3/4) were 3.2 times more likely to have metabolic syndrome than those without fibrosis (stage 0). Furthermore, the mean NAFLD Activity Score (NAS) was greater among children with than those without metabolic syndrome [59]. In another investigation from a cohort of 120 Italian children, increasing stage of fibrosis was associated with the metabolic syndrome [56]. These associations suggest that the coexistence of NAFLD and metabolic syndrome likely leads to a more rapid progression of liver disease and/or that more severe hepatic involvement may increase metabolic risks. In any event, histopathological features of liver disease are highly relevant in children with or at risk for the metabolic syndrome.

Pathogenetic Link Between NAFLD and Metabolic Syndrome

The precise pathogenesis of NAFLD and that of the metabolic syndrome have not been fully elucidated. However, the overlap between these two conditions provides insight into their pathogenesis. In 1998, Day and James proposed a "two hit hypothesis" as the basis for NAFLD, and this notion was later replaced by the "multiple hits" hypothesis [60, 61] as it became clear that the pathogenesis of this disorder is highly complex. The initial step in the progression of NAFLD is hepatic steatosis, namely, the accumulation of fat in hepatocytes mostly in the form of triglycerides. Fatty acids are normally esterified into triglycerides within the hepatocytes, and some of these triglycerides are exported out of hepatocytes as very-low-density lipoproteins (VLDL). Steatosis results from an imbalance between the mechanisms responsible for uptake and synthesis and those responsible for oxidation and export of fatty acids [62]. This imbalance can occur as a result of excessive import of free fatty acids (FFA) from adipose tissue, from diminished hepatic export of FFA (secondary to reduced synthesis or secretion of VLDL), or from impaired beta-oxidation of FFA. A number of conditions may alter these mechanisms, and some are more likely to occur in the case of NAFLD/NASH. Obesity leads to excessive FFA import and, thus, increased hepatic triglycerides. In addition, excessive conversion of carbohydrates and proteins to triglycerides, as a result of overfeeding, can lead to steatosis. Impaired VLDL synthesis, and subsequent triglyceride accumulation, has been postulated to be the result of a defect in postprandial Apo B secretion in some patients with NASH [63]. Furthermore, it has also been noted that patients with obesity-related NASH may have a significant impairment in the ability to recover from hepatic ATP depletion, leading to decreased beta-oxidation of FFA's [64].

As FFA intake exceeds the storage and oxidative capacity of peripheral tissues, FFAs are diverted to metabolic pathways leading to intracellular accumulation of toxic lipid-derived metabolites. These events may induce insulin resistance and activate oxidative stress signaling as well as inflammatory pathways [61, 65]. Insulin resistance is tightly linked to the development of steatosis and is considered to be a critical factor in the pathogenesis of NAFLD in children and adolescents [56, 66, 67]. Insulin resistance enhances peripheral lipolysis, stimulates triglyceride synthesis, and increases hepatic uptake of fatty acids, thus contributing to the accumulation of triglycerides within the hepatocyte [68–73]. Increased uptake of fatty acids within hepatocytes induces cytochrome P-450 microsomal lipoxygenases, resulting in the production of free oxygen radicals that may be hepatotoxic through lipid peroxidation of hepatocyte membranes [62]. Furthermore, the accumulation of intrahepatic triglycerides induces a preferential shift from glucose oxidation to mitochondrial fatty acid beta-oxidation, which, in the setting of preexisting defects of mitochondrial oxidative phosphorylation, may increase free radical formation, hepatocellular injury, and fibrosis [69].

Thus, obesity and insulin resistance were traditionally considered the "first hits" in the development of NAFLD. Then, the vulnerable fatty liver may be exposed to "second hits" further accelerating the progression to NASH. Such insults may include further oxidative stress, mitochondrial dysfunction, and imbalance of adipocytokines [74]. Saturation of oxidative processes, as a result of intrahepatic fat accumulation, induces the release of reactive oxygen species that may exceed the defensive capacity of intracellular antioxidants [61]. This results in the activation of adipocytokines and hepatic stellate cells, stimulating an inflammatory response and inducing fibrogenesis [75, 76]. Notable among the adipocytokines involved in this process are tumor necrosis factor alpha (TNF-alpha) and adiponectin, which play important roles in the associations between obesity, insulin resistance, and development of hepatic steatosis [65, 76]. Children and adolescents with NAFLD have been noted to have decreased adiponectin and increased leptin levels, which are, in turn, associated with insulin resistance [77, 78]. Recently, the gut/liver hypothesis has been proposed. This hypothesis suggests a role for gut bacterial endotoxins and the innate immune response in the development of hepatic steatosis and subsequent inflammatory process leading to further progression of NAFLD/NASH [74, 79]. Thus, small intestinal bacterial overgrowth may be an additional environmental factor involved in the development and progression of NAFLD.

As important as they are in the pathogenesis of NAFLD, obesity and insulin resistance also play a crucial role in the development of metabolic syndrome in the young [5]. Excess of nutrients, as a result of increased food intake and decreased energy expenditure in the setting of sedentary lifestyles, is a well-accepted risk factor for metabolic syndrome. Furthermore, diets high in carbohydrates have been associated with increased risk of metabolic syndrome in children and adolescents [80, 81].

However, as in the case of NAFLD, it is clear that the etiology of metabolic syndrome is multifactorial. Adipose tissue is involved in the excessive release of free fatty acids as well as in the release of proinflammatory cytokines that lead to peripheral and hepatic insulin resistance [82]. Hepatic insulin resistance leads to gluconeogenesis, VLDL secretion, production of proinflammatory factors such as C-reactive protein (CRP), and increased production of thrombotic factors such as fibrinogen. Evidence suggests that oxidative stress may also play a role in the development of metabolic syndrome in children and adolescents [83–85]. Increased oxidative stress is associated with features of the metabolic syndrome including hyperglycemia, hyperinsulinemia, hypertriglyceridemia, as well as hypertension [83, 84]. In addition, adipocytokines including TNF-alpha and adiponectin, among others, are also important mediators in the association between obesity, insulin resistance, and inflammatory processes in children and adults [82, 86, 87].

Although the pathogenetic influences that lead to NAFLD and the metabolic syndrome discussed thus far likely increase throughout one's lifetime, risk factors for the development of these conditions appear to exert their influence since the earliest phases of life, in the prenatal period. The intrauterine environment plays a role in the development of insulin resistance, type 2 diabetes, and metabolic syndrome in adulthood [88–90]. The "thrifty phenotype hypothesis" establishes that in the setting of fetal undernutrition during critical periods of fetal development, adaptive mechanisms to preserve nutrients to vital organs lead to permanent in utero programming. Later, exposure to a different postnatal environment, one characterized by overnutrition, creates a mismatch that, in turn, predisposes the individual to insulin resistance and metabolic syndrome when exposed to environmental triggers later in life [91–93]. Similarly, intrauterine growth retardation has also been identified as an important risk factor for pediatric NAFLD [94].

Genetic Link Between NAFLD and Metabolic Syndrome

As noted above, NAFLD and the metabolic syndrome share most of the essential risk factors and pathophysiological mechanisms. Environmental factors such as overnutrition and sedentary lifestyle are key components in the development of both conditions. Insulin resistance, the activation of inflammatory processes through adipocytokines, and oxidative stress are further mediators of the progression of these disorders. However, an important question, then, is why some individuals develop both of these conditions while others do not. In other words, what is less understood may be the differences in risk factors or pathogenesis between these two conditions. An understanding of such differences would likely elucidate a great deal about both NAFLD as well as the metabolic syndrome and would lead to better identification and management of individuals at risk.

It is likely that genetic predisposition may explain why some individuals develop both NAFLD and metabolic syndrome, while others develop one and not the other condition. Although obesity is strongly associated with the development of NAFLD, steatohepatitis may also occur in the absence of obesity in a minority of individuals. This illustrates that there are multiple environmental as well as genetic factors determining the development and progression of NAFLD. NAFLD has been shown to cluster in families [95, 96]. In addition, studies comparing the prevalence of NAFLD among various ethnic groups have demonstrated important differences such as higher prevalence among Hispanics (Mexican Americans being most widely studied), lower prevalence among non-Hispanic Caucasians, and significantly lower prevalence in African Americans, and these differences could not always be explained by variations in body mass index [97]. Ethnic disparities with regard to NAFLD have also been reported in children, among whom Hispanics, Asians, and indigenous Americans demonstrated a predisposition for this condition [10]. These observations have sparked significant research interest in the genetic basis of NAFLD. Single-nucleotide polymorphisms (SNPs) in genes encoding various adipocytokines and apoE have been reported and could play a role in an individual's predisposition toward developing NAFLD [98]. Genome-wide association studies have identified the patatin-like phospholipase domain-containing protein-3 (PNPLA3 or adiponutrin) gene as conferring susceptibility to NAFLD; this is considered to be the first NAFLD gene [99]. Variations in PNPLA3 contribute to racial differences observed with regard to steatosis and influence susceptibility toward NAFLD. Interestingly, it has been noted that the hepatic expression of adiponutrin increases with Western-style diets that are rich in carbohydrates [100], illustrating an interaction between genetic and environmental influences that could be synergistic.

The genetic origin of NAFLD seems to be shared to a large extent with that of the metabolic syndrome. A number of gene polymorphisms predisposing to NAFLD also confer susceptibility to components of the metabolic syndrome [61]. Notable among these are SNPs in genes encoding for TNF-alpha and adiponectin, which predispose to NAFLD and have been associated with components or traits of the metabolic syndrome in adults as well as in children [101–104]. Polymorphisms in genes encoding microsomal triglyceride transfer protein, peroxisome proliferator-activated receptor alpha, leptin receptor, hepatic lipase, and apolipoprotein A5 are also associated both with NAFLD and with components of the metabolic syndrome [105–109]. On the other hand, certain polymorphisms identified in NAFLD do not appear to play a role in metabolic syndrome. The association between SNPs encoding peroxisome proliferator-activated receptor gamma coactivator 1 alpha and NAFLD has been noted but is controversial with regard to the metabolic syndrome [110]. SNPs in the gene encoding methylenetetrahydrofolate reductase and in the hemochromatosis (HFE) gene are associated with NAFLD, but no relevant association with the metabolic syndrome has been reported [61]. With regard to the "NAFLD gene," although the adiponutrin gene family plays a role in adult as well as childhood obesity [111], a possible association with the metabolic syndrome remains to be investigated. Interestingly, a cross-sectional evaluation of adolescents in the National Health and Nutrition Examination Survey (1999–2002) revealed significant gender and ethnic differences in the association of pediatric metabolic syndrome with elevated ALT, suggesting the existence of genetic modifiers that vary according to ethnicity [112]. Continued efforts will be needed to improve our current understanding of the genetic basis of both NAFLD and metabolic syndrome, and these are expected to reveal valuable information in the upcoming years.

Natural History of NAFLD in the Setting of Metabolic Syndrome

What happens to the natural history of NAFLD or the metabolic syndrome when these conditions coexist? The answer to this question is not known. At present, there is very limited information about the natural history of each of these conditions in children and no direct evidence to understand the impact of one over the other. However, indirect data raises concern about the possibility that such coexistence may have important adverse consequences likely associated with significant morbidity and early mortality.

Metabolic syndrome may accelerate the progression of liver disease among individuals with NAFLD or NASH. Studies of adult patients with NAFLD have identified predictors of advanced fibrosis and cirrhosis. It is established that insulin resistance and type 2 diabetes accelerate the progression of NAFLD and other liver disease [113–115] likely through the effect of insulin on inducing proliferation of hepatic stellate cells [116]. Other proposed predictors of fibrosis and cirrhosis among patients with NAFLD include hypertension, hypertriglyceridemia, and elevated ALT levels [113, 117, 118]. Since several of these predictors include components of the metabolic syndrome, it is reasonable to assume that patients with NAFLD and metabolic syndrome would likely face an accelerated progression of liver disease.

Possible effects of NAFLD on the natural history of metabolic syndrome are likely more complex. Although insulin resistance plays a role in the pathogenesis of NAFLD/NASH as discussed previously, evidence also supports the notion that NAFLD itself induces insulin resistance [119–122]. In addition, NAFLD appears to be an independent risk factor for cardiovascular disease. NAFLD markers such as elevated ALT have been shown to predict coronary heart disease events, independently of other traditional risk factors [123]. In addition, ALT has been associated with endothelial dysfunction, indicating that NAFLD might be involved in early atherogenesis [124]. Furthermore, cardiovascular disease is the most important cause of death among patients with NASH, and, as mentioned previously, patients with NAFLD/NASH have reduced survival as compared to the general population [125, 126]. Thus, indirect evidence suggests that NAFLD may induce or worsen insulin resistance and accelerate the development of cardiovascular disease among patients who have metabolic syndrome and might be already predisposed. Furthermore, it may be reasonable to assume that NAFLD may further increase mortality among patients with metabolic syndrome. On the other hand, assuming that NAFLD and what is typically considered the metabolic syndrome could simply be manifestations of the same underlying disorder, it is possible that their coexistence may not alter the underlying natural history of these disorders. In that case, then, it is possible that their coexistence could be a manifestation or marker of more severe disease.

There are many more questions than answers regarding the effect of NAFLD on the natural history of metabolic syndrome and vice versa. However, abundant evidence strongly suggests that children and adolescents suffering from both of these conditions need close medical attention. Most importantly in this regard, research is needed to address these questions and to prevent morbidity and mortality associated with these conditions.

Diagnosis of Liver Disease in Children with Metabolic Syndrome

The first step toward diagnosing liver disease in a child with metabolic syndrome is to consider the possibility of their coexistence in order to initiate proper evaluations. Good past medical and family history are key aspects of the evaluation in order to distinguish NAFLD from other liver diseases, which may present with similar histological features. A thorough medical exam must be performed, documenting the presence of signs of liver disease such as palmar erythema, spider angiomata, muscular wasting, jaundice, or encephalopathy. Such signs are rarely observed, but their presence would certainly guide the intensity of the evaluation as they would be associated with significant liver disease. Laboratory studies are then necessary to assess liver enzymes and to evaluate hepatic function. Specifically, ALT and aspartate aminotransferase (AST), alkaline phosphatase, gamma-glutamyl transpeptidase (GGT), and liver function tests such as albumin, bilirubin levels, prothrombin time (PT), partial thromboplastin time (PTT), or international normalized ratio (INR) may be ordered. Children with metabolic syndrome may also have biliary abnormalities, specifically cholelithiasis or choledocolithiasis, leading to cholestasis as evidenced by elevated bilirubin, alkaline phosphatase, and GGT [127]. All of the above tests should be obtained as part of a more comprehensive general laboratory evaluation for children with obesity and/or the metabolic syndrome, including assessment for the possibility of diabetes mellitus, lipid abnormalities, thyroid disorders, vitamin deficiencies, among others.

Children with an ALT elevation of greater than two times the normal (using updated normal values) that persist for greater than 3 months should undergo further evaluations for the presence of NAFLD and other chronic liver diseases. Ultrasonography may then be performed to confirm the presence of hepatic steatosis or fatty liver manifested by increased echogenicity. Although ultrasonography has low sensitivity and specificity for the diagnosis of NAFLD, it can also be useful to assess for features that may demand more intensive evaluations, such as splenomegaly, liver nodularity suggesting the possibility of advanced fibrosis or cirrhosis, and even to evaluate for the possibility of abnormal masses or tumors. Furthermore, ultrasonography is also useful in the patient with metabolic syndrome to evaluate the biliary system specifically to assess for the possibility of cholelithiasis. A comprehensive hepatologic evaluation should be performed to rule out other causes of liver disease in patients with persistent transaminitis (e.g., viral hepatitis, autoimmune hepatitis, Wilson disease, alpha-1-antitrypsin deficiency) [128]. It is important to understand, however, that neither the degree of transaminitis nor the presence of steatosis on imaging can determine the extent of hepatic involvement (i.e., inflammation or fibrosis) or establish the diagnosis of NAFLD. The indications for liver biopsy in the case of suspected NAFLD have not been established in children or adults. Because there is no established treatment for NAFLD, the risk and cost of performing a liver biopsy may not outweigh its possible benefits. A liver biopsy is frequently considered in the setting of persistent transaminitis for at least 6 months in order to confirm the diagnosis, exclude other potential causes of liver disease, and establish the extent of hepatic inflammation or fibrosis. Knowing the extent of liver

Table 7.3 Evaluation of liver disease in children with metabolic syndrome

Medical history	Family history
	Past medical history
Medical exam	Vital signs
	Weight, height, BMI
	BP
	General appearance
	Muscular wasting
	Cardiovascular
	Pulmonary
	Gastrointestinal
	Organomegaly
	Hemorrhoids
	Endocrine
	Tanner staging
	Extremities
	Clubbing
	Neurologic
	Encephalopathy
	Skin
	Jaundice
	Palmar erythema
	Spider angiomata
Laboratory studies	ALT
	AST
	Alkaline phosphatase
	GGT
	Albumin
	Bilirubin
	PT/ INR
	PTT
Additional evaluations	Ultrasonography
	Liver biopsy

disease may be particularly important for young patients, since advanced fibrosis is associated with a number of risks including death secondary to hepatocellular carcinoma [35, 117] (Table 7.3).

Management of Liver Disease in the Setting of Metabolic Syndrome

At present, there is no approved pharmacologic therapy for NAFLD. The overall goal in the management of the patient with NAFLD is to improve the individual's quality of life and reduce long-term cardiovascular and liver morbidity and mortality [6].

Given that most patients with metabolic syndrome and NAFLD are overweight, nutrition and exercise are important elements in the management of obesity which should help to control the burden of disease. The efficacy of weight loss in improving pediatric NAFLD is unknown. Based on studies in adult patients with NAFLD, greater than 5% weight loss was associated with significant histological improvement [129]. In addition, there is no information as to whether a specific type of diet may be more beneficial than others in the management of NAFLD. A low glycemic index diet has been proven superior to a low-fat diet in achieving weight loss in obese adolescents and adults, [130] but has not been tested in patients with pediatric NAFLD. A very low-carbohydrate diet has been associated with a reduction in liver fat content in adults [131]. Further studies are needed to evaluate the effects of specific diets in children with NAFLD.

The use of therapies such as metformin or vitamin E has recently been studied in children. The NASH Clinical Research Network performed the Treatment of NAFLD in Children (TONIC) trial. TONIC was a randomized, double-blind, double-dummy, placebo-controlled clinical trial conducted at ten academic centers in 173 patients 8–17 years of age with biopsy-confirmed NAFLD between 2005 and 2010, performed to investigate the use of insulin-sensitizing agents and vitamin E for the treatment of pediatric NAFLD and nonalcoholic steatohepatitis (NASH). The investigators found that sustained reduction in ALT level was similar to placebo in both the vitamin E and metformin treatment groups. However, there was a statistically significant difference in mean change in hepatocellular ballooning scores with the vitamin E group undergoing a greater reduction followed by metformin and the placebo undergoing a small increase. Similarly, the NAFLD activity score decreased more substantially in the vitamin E followed by metformin groups as compared to placebo. Furthermore, 58% of children in the vitamin E group had resolution of NASH, 41% had resolution in the metformin group, and only 28% had resolution of NASH in the placebo group. There were no other histological improvements noted in the therapy as opposed to the placebo arms. The authors concluded that neither vitamin E nor metformin was superior to placebo in attaining the primary outcome of sustained reduction in ALT level in patients with pediatric NAFLD, but the use of vitamin E did demonstrate histological improvements as compared to the control group [132].

Based on the available evidence thus far, the risk of liver biopsy may outweigh the benefits of therapy. Development of noninvasive markers for diagnosis and monitoring of NAFLD in children is highly necessary. The long-term effects of vitamin E in the management of children with biopsy-proven NAFLD remain to be established. Most importantly, further investigations are needed on therapies that may reverse or halt the progression of this condition in the young.

The treatment of NAFLD remains a challenge. Lifestyle modification, including a combination of healthy nutrition and increased physical activity or exercise, is warranted in all children with NAFLD and the metabolic syndrome. Given the paucity of effective interventions, prevention of obesity in early childhood combined with strong public messages about the importance of a healthy lifestyle and increasing awareness of liver disease and other consequences of obesity are the best methods to help control morbidity and reduce the burden of pediatric NAFLD.

Conclusion

NAFLD is a condition that frequently coexists with the metabolic syndrome. These two conditions share common features, but the details underlying the pathogenesis of this association, in particular with respect to cause and effect, are not completely understood. Nevertheless, it is imperative for clinicians to be aware of the risk of liver disease among patients with the metabolic syndrome. A number of clinical evaluations of patients at risk for NAFLD have been recommended in this chapter. However, the only way to establish the diagnosis of NAFLD at present is through a combination of clinical history and liver histology. Management of NAFLD starts with prevention in the patient at risk. Lifestyle modification is warranted in all patients with NAFLD. A number of pharmacological therapies have been evaluated, including vitamin E which was associated with some histological improvement in children with NAFLD, yet a positive clinical impact of pharmacological agents has yet to be demonstrated. Research remains to be done in order to better understand the pathophysiology, natural history, and most importantly, to find efficacious and effective methods to control the growing impact of nonalcoholic fatty liver disease in children as well as in adults.

References

1. Feldstein AE, et al. The natural history of non-alcoholic fatty liver disease in children: a follow-up study for up to 20 years. Gut. 2009;58(11):1538–44.
2. Adler M, Schaffner F. Fatty liver hepatitis and cirrhosis in obese patients. Am J Med. 1979;67(5):811–6.
3. Ludwig J, et al. Nonalcoholic steatohepatitis: Mayo Clinic experiences with a hitherto unnamed disease. Mayo Clin Proc. 1980;55(7):434–8.
4. Moran JR, et al. Steatohepatitis in obese children: a cause of chronic liver dysfunction. Am J Gastroenterol. 1983;78:374–7.
5. Alisi A, et al. Pediatric nonalcoholic fatty liver disease in 2009. J Pediatr. 2009;155(4): 469–74.
6. Loomba R, et al. Advances in pediatric nonalcoholic fatty liver disease. Hepatology. 2009; 50(4):1282–93.
7. Kleiner DE, et al. Design and validation of a histological scoring system for nonalcoholic fatty liver disease. Hepatology. 2005;41(6):1313–21.
8. Strauss RS, Barlow SE, Dietz WH. Prevalence of abnormal serum aminotransferase values in overweight and obese adolescents. J Pediatr. 2000;136(6):727–33.
9. Park HS, et al. Relation between elevated serum alanine aminotransferase and metabolic syndrome in Korean adolescents. Am J Clin Nutr. 2005;82(5):1046–51.
10. Schwimmer JB, et al. Prevalence of fatty liver in children and adolescents. Pediatrics. 2006;118(4):1388–93.
11. Franzese A, et al. Liver involvement in obese children. Ultrasonography and liver enzyme levels at diagnosis and during follow-up in an Italian population. Dig Dis Sci. 1997; 42(7):1428–32.
12. Chan DF, et al. Hepatic steatosis in obese Chinese children. Int J Obes Relat Metab Disord. 2004;28(10):1257–63.

13. Tazawa Y, et al. Serum alanine aminotransferase activity in obese children. Acta Paediatr. 1997;86(3):238–41.
14. Manton ND, et al. Non-alcoholic steatohepatitis in children and adolescents. Med J Aust. 2000;173(9):476–9.
15. Schwimmer JB, et al. Obesity, insulin resistance, and other clinicopathological correlates of pediatric nonalcoholic fatty liver disease. J Pediatr. 2003;143(4):500–5.
16. Rashid M, Roberts EA. Nonalcoholic steatohepatitis in children. J Pediatr Gastroenterol Nutr. 2000;30(1):48–53.
17. Nguyen TT, et al. Relation of acanthosis nigricans to hyperinsulinemia and insulin sensitivity in overweight African American and white children. J Pediatr. 2001;138(4):474–80.
18. Fishbein MH, et al. The spectrum of fatty liver in obese children and the relationship of serum aminotransferases to severity of steatosis. J Pediatr Gastroenterol Nutr. 2003;36(1):54–61.
19. Taylor KJ, et al. Ultrasonography of alcoholic liver disease with histological correlation. Radiology. 1981;141(1):157–61.
20. Needleman L, et al. Sonography of diffuse benign liver disease: accuracy of pattern recognition and grading. AJR Am J Roentgenol. 1986;146(5):1011–5.
21. Mathiesen UL, et al. Increased liver echogenicity at ultrasound examination reflects degree of steatosis but not of fibrosis in asymptomatic patients with mild/moderate abnormalities of liver transaminases. Dig Liver Dis. 2002;34(7):516–22.
22. Celle G, et al. Is hepatic ultrasonography a valid alternative tool to liver biopsy? Report on 507 cases studied with both techniques. Dig Dis Sci. 1988;33(4):467–71.
23. Bydder GM, et al. Computed tomography attenuation values in fatty liver. J Comput Tomogr. 1981;5(1):33–5.
24. Jacobs JE, et al. Diagnostic criteria for fatty infiltration of the liver on contrast-enhanced helical CT. AJR Am J Roentgenol. 1998;171(3):659–64.
25. Rinella ME, et al. Dual-echo, chemical shift gradient-echo magnetic resonance imaging to quantify hepatic steatosis: implications for living liver donation. Liver Transpl. 2003;9(8):851–6.
26. Fishbein MH, et al. Introduction of fast MR imaging in the assessment of hepatic steatosis. Magn Reson Imaging. 1997;15(3):287–93.
27. Nobili V, et al. Accuracy and reproducibility of transient elastography for the diagnosis of fibrosis in pediatric nonalcoholic steatohepatitis. Hepatology. 2008;48(2):442–8.
28. Yoneda M, et al. Noninvasive assessment of liver fibrosis by measurement of stiffness in patients with nonalcoholic fatty liver disease (NAFLD). Dig Liver Dis. 2008;40(5):371–8.
29. Huwart L, et al. Magnetic resonance elastography for the noninvasive staging of liver fibrosis. Gastroenterology. 2008;135(1):32–40.
30. Baldridge AD, et al. Idiopathic steatohepatitis in childhood: a multicenter retrospective study. J Pediatr. 1995;127(5):700–4.
31. Schwimmer JB, et al. Histopathology of pediatric nonalcoholic fatty liver disease. Hepatology. 2005;42(3):641–9.
32. Molleston JP, et al. Obese children with steatohepatitis can develop cirrhosis in childhood. Am J Gastroenterol. 2002;97(9):2460–2.
33. Jonas MM, et al. Rapid recurrence of nonalcoholic fatty liver disease after transplantation in a child with hypopituitarism and hepatopulmonary syndrome. Liver Transpl. 2005;11(1):108–10.
34. Adams LA, et al. Nonalcoholic fatty liver disease among patients with hypothalamic and pituitary dysfunction. Hepatology. 2004;39(4):909–14.
35. Cuadrado A, et al. Non-alcoholic steatohepatitis (NASH) and hepatocellular carcinoma. Obes Surg. 2005;15(3):442–6.
36. Schwimmer JB, et al. Cardiovascular risk factors and the metabolic syndrome in pediatric nonalcoholic fatty liver disease. Circulation. 2008;118(3):277–83.
37. Demircioglu F, et al. Intima-media thickness of carotid artery and susceptibility to atherosclerosis in obese children with nonalcoholic fatty liver disease. J Pediatr Gastroenterol Nutr. 2008;47(1):68–75.

38. Pacifico L, et al. Nonalcoholic fatty liver disease and carotid atherosclerosis in children. Pediatr Res. 2008;63(4):423–7.
39. Norman D, et al. Serum aminotransferase levels are associated with markers of hypoxia in patients with obstructive sleep apnea. Sleep. 2008;31(1):121–6.
40. Gardner CJ, et al. Hypothyroidism in a patient with non-alcoholic fatty liver disease. BMJ. 2011;342:c7199.
41. Lee TH, et al. Serum aminotransferase activity and mortality risk in a United States community. Hepatology. 2008;47(3):880–7.
42. Schindhelm RK, et al. Alanine aminotransferase as a marker of non-alcoholic fatty liver disease in relation to type 2 diabetes mellitus and cardiovascular disease. Diabetes Metab Res Rev. 2006;22(6):437–43.
43. Di Bonito P, et al. Association of elevated serum alanine aminotransferase with metabolic factors in obese children: sex-related analysis. Metabolism. 2009;58(3):368–72.
44. Wei C, et al. Abnormal liver function in children with metabolic syndrome from a UK-based obesity clinic. Arch Dis Child. 2011;96:1003–7. doi:10.1136/adc.2010.190975.
45. van Vliet M, et al. The association of elevated alanine aminotransferase and the metabolic syndrome in an overweight and obese pediatric population of multi-ethnic origin. Eur J Pediatr. 2009;168(5):585–91.
46. Patel DA, et al. Serum alanine aminotransferase and its association with metabolic syndrome in children: the bogalusa heart study. Metab Syndr Relat Disord. 2011;9(3):211–6.
47. Marchesini G, et al. Nonalcoholic fatty liver, steatohepatitis, and the metabolic syndrome. Hepatology. 2003;37(4):917–23.
48. Fan JG, et al. Fatty liver and the metabolic syndrome among Shanghai adults. J Gastroenterol Hepatol. 2005;20(12):1825–32.
49. Kim HC, et al. Severity of ultrasonographic liver steatosis and metabolic syndrome in Korean men and women. World J Gastroenterol. 2005;11(34):5314–21.
50. Hamaguchi M, et al. The metabolic syndrome as a predictor of nonalcoholic fatty liver disease. Ann Intern Med. 2005;143(10):722–8.
51. Love-Osborne KA, et al. Presence of the metabolic syndrome in obese adolescents predicts impaired glucose tolerance and nonalcoholic fatty liver disease. J Adolesc Health. 2008;42(6):543–8.
52. Tominaga K, et al. Prevalence of non-alcoholic fatty liver disease in children and relationship to metabolic syndrome, insulin resistance, and waist circumference. Environ Health Prev Med. 2009;14(2):142–9.
53. Kelishadi R, et al. Association of the components of the metabolic syndrome with non-alcoholic fatty liver disease among normal-weight, overweight and obese children and adolescents. Diabetol Metab Syndr. 2009;1:29.
54. Fu JF, et al. Non-alcoholic fatty liver disease: an early mediator predicting metabolic syndrome in obese children? World J Gastroenterol. 2011;17(6):735–42.
55. Executive Summary of The Third Report of The National Cholesterol Education Program (NCEP) Expert Panel on Detection, Evaluation, and Treatment of High Blood Cholesterol in Adults (Adult Treatment Panel III). JAMA. 2001;285(19):2486–97.
56. Manco M, et al. Metabolic syndrome and liver histology in paediatric non-alcoholic steatohepatitis. Int J Obes (Lond). 2008;32(2):381–7.
57. Takahashi Y, Fukusato T. Pediatric nonalcoholic fatty liver disease: overview with emphasis on histology. World J Gastroenterol. 2010;16(42):5280–5.
58. Nobili V, et al. NAFLD in children: a prospective clinical-pathological study and effect of lifestyle advice. Hepatology. 2006;44(2):458–65.
59. Patton HM, et al. Association between metabolic syndrome and liver histology among children with nonalcoholic fatty liver disease. Am J Gastroenterol. 2010;105(9):2093–102.
60. de Alwis NM, Day CP. Non-alcoholic fatty liver disease: the mist gradually clears. J Hepatol. 2008;48 Suppl 1:S104–12.
61. Alisi A, et al. Non-alcoholic fatty liver disease and metabolic syndrome in adolescents: pathogenetic role of genetic background and intrauterine environment. Ann Med. 2011. doi:10.3109/07853890.2010.547869.

62. Angulo P. Nonalcoholic fatty liver disease. N Engl J Med. 2002;346(16):1221–31.
63. Musso G, et al. Dietary habits and their relations to insulin resistance and postprandial lipemia in nonalcoholic steatohepatitis. Hepatology. 2003;37(4):909–16.
64. Cortez-Pinto H, et al. Alterations in liver ATP homeostasis in human nonalcoholic steatohepatitis: a pilot study. JAMA. 1999;282(17):1659–64.
65. Cusi K. Role of insulin resistance and lipotoxicity in non-alcoholic steatohepatitis. Clin Liver Dis. 2009;13(4):545–63.
66. Boden G, et al. Free fatty acids produce insulin resistance and activate the proinflammatory nuclear factor-kappaB pathway in rat liver. Diabetes. 2005;54(12):3458–65.
67. Park SH, et al. Insulin resistance and C-reactive protein as independent risk factors for non-alcoholic fatty liver disease in non-obese Asian men. J Gastroenterol Hepatol. 2004;19(6):694–8.
68. Kral JG, et al. Hepatic lipid metabolism in severe human obesity. Metabolism. 1977;26(9):1025–31.
69. Sanyal AJ, et al. Nonalcoholic steatohepatitis: association of insulin resistance and mitochondrial abnormalities. Gastroenterology. 2001;120(5):1183–92.
70. Sundaram SS, Zeitler P, Nadeau K. The metabolic syndrome and nonalcoholic fatty liver disease in children. Curr Opin Pediatr. 2009;21(4):529–35.
71. Saltiel AR, Kahn CR. Insulin signalling and the regulation of glucose and lipid metabolism. Nature. 2001;414(6865):799–806.
72. Fleischmann M, Iynedjian PB. Regulation of sterol regulatory-element binding protein 1 gene expression in liver: role of insulin and protein kinase B/cAkt. Biochem J. 2000;349(Pt 1):13–7.
73. Shimomura I, et al. Insulin selectively increases SREBP-1c mRNA in the livers of rats with streptozotocin-induced diabetes. Proc Natl Acad Sci U S A. 1999;96(24):13656–61.
74. Tilg H, Moschen AR. Insulin resistance, inflammation, and non-alcoholic fatty liver disease. Trends Endocrinol Metab. 2008;19(10):371–9.
75. Malaguarnera M, et al. Molecular mechanisms involved in NAFLD progression. J Mol Med. 2009;87(7):679–95.
76. Neuschwander-Tetri BA. Hepatic lipotoxicity and the pathogenesis of nonalcoholic steatohepatitis: the central role of nontriglyceride fatty acid metabolites. Hepatology. 2010;52(2):774–88.
77. Louthan MV, et al. Decreased serum adiponectin: an early event in pediatric nonalcoholic fatty liver disease. J Pediatr. 2005;147(6):835–8.
78. Nobili V, et al. Leptin, free leptin index, insulin resistance and liver fibrosis in children with non-alcoholic fatty liver disease. Eur J Endocrinol. 2006;155(5):735–43.
79. Baffy G. Kupffer cells in non-alcoholic fatty liver disease: the emerging view. J Hepatol. 2009;51(1):212–23.
80. O'Sullivan TA, et al. Dietary glycaemic carbohydrate in relation to the metabolic syndrome in adolescents: comparison of different metabolic syndrome definitions. Diabet Med. 2010;27(7):770–8.
81. Aeberli I, et al. Diet determines features of the metabolic syndrome in 6- to 14-year-old children. Int J Vitam Nutr Res. 2009;79(1):14–23.
82. Chu NF, Chang JB, Shieh SM. Plasma leptin, fatty acids, and tumor necrosis factor-receptor and insulin resistance in children. Obes Res. 2003;11(4):532–40.
83. Turi S, et al. Oxidative stress in juvenile essential hypertension. J Hypertens. 2003;21(1):145–52.
84. Sinaiko AR, et al. Relation of body mass index and insulin resistance to cardiovascular risk factors, inflammatory factors, and oxidative stress during adolescence. Circulation. 2005;111(15):1985–91.
85. Kelly AS, et al. Oxidative stress and adverse adipokine profile characterize the metabolic syndrome in children. J Cardiometab Syndr. 2006;1(4):248–52.
86. Korner A, et al. New predictors of the metabolic syndrome in children – role of adipocytokines. Pediatr Res. 2007;61(6):640–5.
87. Calcaterra V, et al. Adiponectin, IL-10 and metabolic syndrome in obese children and adolescents. Acta Biomed. 2009;80(2):117–23.

88. Hales CN, et al. Fetal and infant growth and impaired glucose tolerance at age 64. BMJ. 1991;303(6809):1019–22.
89. Geremia C, Cianfarani S. Insulin sensitivity in children born small for gestational age (SGA). Rev Diabet Stud. 2004;1(2):58–65.
90. Levy-Marchal C, Czernichow P. Small for gestational age and the metabolic syndrome: which mechanism is suggested by epidemiological and clinical studies? Horm Res. 2006;65 Suppl 3:123–30.
91. Hales CN, Barker DJ. The thrifty phenotype hypothesis. Br Med Bull. 2001;60:5–20.
92. Ross MG, Beall MH. Adult sequelae of intrauterine growth restriction. Semin Perinatol. 2008;32(3):213–8.
93. Godfrey KM, et al. Epigenetic mechanisms and the mismatch concept of the developmental origins of health and disease. Pediatr Res. 2007;61(5 Pt 2):5R–10.
94. Nobili V, et al. Intrauterine growth retardation, insulin resistance, and nonalcoholic fatty liver disease in children. Diabetes Care. 2007;30(10):2638–40.
95. Struben VM, Hespenheide EE, Caldwell SH. Nonalcoholic steatohepatitis and cryptogenic cirrhosis within kindreds. Am J Med. 2000;108(1):9–13.
96. Willner IR, et al. Ninety patients with nonalccholic steatohepatitis: insulin resistance, familial tendency, and severity of disease. Am J Gastroenterol. 2001;96(10):2957–61.
97. Browning JD, et al. Prevalence of hepatic steatosis in an urban population in the United States: impact of ethnicity. Hepatology. 2004;40(6):1387–95.
98. Moore JB. Non-alcoholic fatty liver disease: the hepatic consequence of obesity and the metabolic syndrome. Proc Nutr Soc. 2010;69(2):211–20.
99. Romeo S, et al. Genetic variation in PNPLA3 confers susceptibility to nonalcoholic fatty liver disease. Nat Genet. 2008;40(12):1461–5.
100. Hoekstra M, et al. The expression level of non-alcoholic fatty liver disease-related gene PNPLA3 in hepatocytes is highly influenced by hepatic lipid status. J Hepatol. 2010;52(2):244–51.
101. Sookoian SC, Gonzalez C, Pirola CJ. Meta-analysis on the G-308A tumor necrosis factor alpha gene variant and phenotypes associated with the metabolic syndrome. Obes Res. 2005;13(12):2122–31.
102. Sookoian S, et al. The G-308A promoter variant of the tumor necrosis factor-alpha gene is associated with hypertension in adolescents harboring the metabolic syndrome. Am J Hypertens. 2005;18(10):1271–5.
103. Vasseur F, Meyre D, Froguel P. Adiponectin, type 2 diabetes and the metabolic syndrome: lessons from human genetic studies. Expert Rev Mol Med. 2006;8(27):1–12.
104. Ferguson JF, et al. Gene-nutrient interactions in the metabolic syndrome: single nucleotide polymorphisms in ADIPOQ and ADIPOR1 interact with plasma saturated fatty acids to modulate insulin resistance. Am J Clin Nutr. 2010;91(3):794–801.
105. Zak A, et al. The influence of polymorphism of -493 G/T MTP gene promoter and metabolic syndrome on lipids, fatty acids and oxidative stress. J Nutr Biochem. 2008;19(9):634–41.
106. Robitaille J, et al. Association between the PPARalpha-L162V polymorphism and components of the metabolic syndrome. J Hum Genet. 2004;49(9):482–9.
107. Phillips CM, et al. Leptin receptor polymorphisms interact with polyunsaturated fatty acids to augment risk of insulin resistance and metabolic syndrome in adults. J Nutr. 2010;140(2):238–44.
108. Stancakova A, et al. Effect of gene polymorphisms on lipoprotein levels in patients with dyslipidemia of metabolic syndrome. Physiol Res. 2006;55(5):483–90.
109. Zhou YJ, et al. Influence of polygenetic polymorphisms on the susceptibility to non-alcoholic fatty liver disease of Chinese people. J Gastroenterol Hepatol. 2010;25(4):772–7.
110. Vimaleswaran KS, et al. Absence of association of metabolic syndrome with PPARGC1A, PPARG and UCP1 gene polymorphisms in Asian Indians. Metab Syndr Relat Disord. 2007;5(2):153–62.

111. Johansson LE, et al. Genetic variance in the adiponutrin gene family and childhood obesity. PLoS One. 2009;4(4):e5327.
112. Graham RC, Burke A, Stettler N. Ethnic and sex differences in the association between metabolic syndrome and suspected nonalcoholic fatty liver disease in a nationally representative sample of US adolescents. J Pediatr Gastroenterol Nutr. 2009;49(4):442–9.
113. Hossain N, et al. Independent predictors of fibrosis in patients with nonalcoholic fatty liver disease. Clin Gastroenterol Hepatol. 2009;7(11):1224–9, 1229 e1–2.
114. Angulo P, et al. Independent predictors of liver fibrosis in patients with nonalcoholic steatohepatitis. Hepatology. 1999;30(6):1356–62.
115. D'Souza R, Sabin CA, Foster GR. Insulin resistance plays a significant role in liver fibrosis in chronic hepatitis C and in the response to antiviral therapy. Am J Gastroenterol. 2005;100(7):1509–15.
116. Svegliati-Baroni G, et al. Insulin and insulin-like growth factor-1 stimulate proliferation and type I collagen accumulation by human hepatic stellate cells: differential effects on signal transduction pathways. Hepatology. 1999;29(6):1743–51.
117. McCullough AJ. The clinical features, diagnosis and natural history of nonalcoholic fatty liver disease. Clin Liver Dis. 2004;8(3):521–33, viii.
118. Hesham AKH. Nonalcoholic fatty liver disease in children living in the obeseogenic society. World J Pediatr. 2009;5(4):245–54.
119. Nielsen S, et al. Splanchnic lipolysis in human obesity. J Clin Invest. 2004;113(11):1582–8.
120. Donnelly KL, et al. Sources of fatty acids stored in liver and secreted via lipoproteins in patients with nonalcoholic fatty liver disease. J Clin Invest. 2005;115(5):1343–51.
121. Kelley DE, et al. Fatty liver in type 2 diabetes mellitus: relation to regional adiposity, fatty acids, and insulin resistance. Am J Physiol Endocrinol Metab. 2003;285(4): E906–16.
122. Uusitupa M, et al. Long-term improvement in insulin sensitivity by changing lifestyles of people with impaired glucose tolerance: 4-year results from the Finnish Diabetes Prevention Study. Diabetes. 2003;52(10):2532–8.
123. Schindhelm RK, et al. Alanine aminotransferase predicts coronary heart disease events: a 10-year follow-up of the Hoorn Study. Atherosclerosis. 2007;191(2):391–6.
124. Schindhelm RK, et al. Liver alanine aminotransferase, insulin resistance and endothelial dysfunction in normotriglyceridaemic subjects with type 2 diabetes mellitus. Eur J Clin Invest. 2005;35(6):369–74.
125. Ekstedt M, et al. Long-term follow-up of patients with NAFLD and elevated liver enzymes. Hepatology. 2006;44(4):865–73.
126. Montecucco F, Mach F. Does non-alcoholic fatty liver disease (NAFLD) increase cardiovascular risk? Endocr Metab Immune Disord Drug Targets. 2008;8(4):301–7.
127. Amaral JF, Thompson WR. Gallbladder disease in the morbidly obese. Am J Surg. 1985;149(4):551–7.
128. Baker S, et al. Overweight children and adolescents: a clinical report of the North American Society for Pediatric Gastroenterology, Hepatology and Nutrition. J Pediatr Gastroenterol Nutr. 2005;40(5):533–43.
129. Petersen KF, et al. Reversal of nonalcoholic hepatic steatosis, hepatic insulin resistance, and hyperglycemia by moderate weight reduction in patients with type 2 diabetes. Diabetes. 2005;54(3):603–8.
130. Ebbeling CB, et al. Effects of a low-glycemic load vs low-fat diet in obese young adults: a randomized trial. JAMA. 2007;297(19):2092–102.
131. Benjaminov O, et al. The effect of a low-carbohydrate diet on the nonalcoholic fatty liver in morbidly obese patients before bariatric surgery. Surg Endosc. 2007;21(8):1423–7.
132. Lavine JE, et al. Effect of vitamin E or metformin for treatment of nonalcoholic fatty liver disease in children and adolescents: the TONIC randomized controlled trial. JAMA. 2011;305(16):1659–68.

Chapter 8
The Relationship Between Asthma, Sleep Apnea, and Other Respiratory Disorders and Childhood Metabolic Syndrome

Erick Forno and Annabelle Quizon

Abstract *Introduction*: Obesity and the metabolic syndrome are associated with increased morbidity from chronic respiratory diseases such as asthma and sleep-disordered breathing, as well as increased risk of perioperative respiratory complications.

Asthma: Asthma is the most common chronic disease of childhood, and its prevalence has risen significantly in the last few decades, in parallel with the increase in childhood obesity and metabolic syndrome. There is ever-growing evidence of an association between both, and while our understanding of this relationship far from complete, several mechanisms have been proposed. These include mechanical changes on the airways and the lungs due to excess weight, alterations in the function of airway smooth muscle, a generalized inflammatory state that induces airway inflammation and hyperreactivity, several metabolic abnormalities such as decreased vitamin D or increased oxidative stress, alterations in insulin metabolism that promotes airway remodeling, hormonal differences, and shared genetic determinants between both illnesses.

Sleep-disordered breathing: This term encompasses upper airway resistance syndrome, obstructive sleep apnea (OSA), and obesity hypoventilation syndrome, all of which have been associated with obesity. Proposed mechanisms are in part similar to those mentioned for asthma, including mechanical effects of added weight in the upper airways, a systemic proinflammatory milieu, hormonal changes, and oxidative stress. As a result, these patients are also at higher risk of cardiovascular and other complications from both their obesity/metabolic syndrome and their sleep-disordered breathing.

E. Forno, M.D., MPH (✉) • A. Quizon, M.D.
Division of Pediatric Pulmonology,
University of Miami,
1580 NW 10th Avenue #123, Miami,
FL 33130, USA
e-mail: eforno@med.miami.edu

Other conditions: Patients with obesity/metabolic syndrome are also at higher risk of perioperative respiratory complications, and patients should be carefully assessed and monitored to minimize morbidity. While studies in children are lacking, obese adults are also at increased risk for acute lung injury and acute respiratory distress syndrome (ARDS), with increased length of stay and increased mortality.

Keywords Metabolic syndrome • Childhood obesity • Childhood asthma • Obstructive sleep syndrome • Asthma and obesity • Obesity and sleep

Introduction

Obesity is associated with increased risk of chronic respiratory diseases and impairment of quality of life. It is linked with abnormalities in pulmonary function as well as alterations in gas exchange, breathing mechanics, and physiology which play an important role in understanding symptoms and pathophysiology of chronic respiratory diseases. Over the last few decades, the prevalence of obesity and asthma, the most common chronic respiratory disease in children, have increased, and the prevalence of sleep-disordered breathing – specifically obstructive sleep apnea (OSA) – is increased among obese patients. In this chapter, we will discuss mechanisms that may putatively explain the relationship of obesity and metabolic syndrome with asthma and OSA, emphasizing that obesity/metabolic syndrome leads to a systemic proinflammatory state that underlies both of these conditions. This proinflammatory state leads to several metabolic and cardiovascular complications of obesity which further contribute to long-term adverse outcomes. Furthermore, we will discuss the perioperative risks associated with obesity and the metabolic syndrome as we anticipate an increased proportion of obese patients presenting for surgery likely indicated for complications from obesity. Related to this is a brief overview of obesity as a risk factor for acute lung injury or the acute respiratory distress syndrome.

Relationship Between Asthma, Obesity, and the Metabolic Syndrome

Epidemiology

Asthma is a chronic respiratory disease characterized by airway inflammation and hyperreactivity leading to episodes of bronchospasm. It affects over 300 million people in the world [1], and over 7 million children in the USA alone [2]. The prevalence of childhood asthma has risen dramatically over the last several decades, from approximately ~3.5% in 1980 to 9.6% in 2009 [2, 3]. Every year, there are over 700,000 urgent care visits and over 205,000 hospitalizations for childhood asthma in the USA [4], and the estimated direct costs of the asthma in children and adults exceed $16 billion per year, without even including the cost of medications or indirect costs [5, 6].

The increase in asthma prevalence has paralleled the increase in the prevalence of overweight and obesity in the USA over the last few decades, both in children and adults. There has been increasing epidemiological evidence of an association between both conditions. Several studies have shown that measures of obesity or increased adiposity in children are associated with subsequent, incident asthma [7–12]. A recent meta-analysis of 12 longitudinal studies found that children with high birth weight or with high BMI were at higher risk of developing asthma [13]. Today, there is little doubt of the association between obesity and asthma.

However, our understanding of this relationship is far from clear. Some studies in children have reported a stronger association among girls [14], while others have reported findings mainly or solely among boys [15]. Other studies have found an effect of obesity on asthma only among nonallergic children [16]. Overall, significant advances have been made in the study of this association, but many questions remain to be answered. In this section, we will review the proposed mechanisms that would explain the causal relationship of obesity and metabolic syndrome to childhood asthma (see Fig. 8.1).

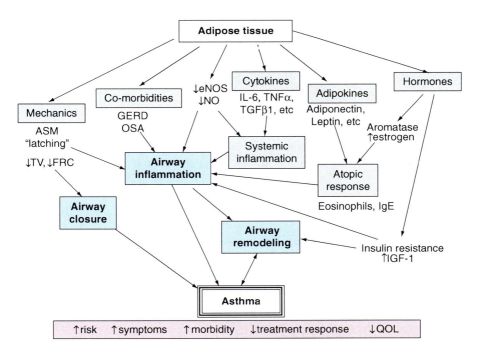

Fig. 8.1 Obesity and asthma. Schematization of several proposed biological mechanisms and pathways involved in the association between obesity/metabolic syndrome and asthma in children. Please refer to text for details and abbreviations

Effects of Obesity on Lung Mechanics and Physiology

Obesity leads to reduction in lung volumes, specifically expiratory reserve volume (ERV) and functional residual capacity (FRC) [17]; thus, patients tend to breathe more rapidly and at lower lung volumes. This restrictive deficit alone, observed in obese adults, could compose or worsen asthma symptoms. This is perhaps the most intuitive mechanism and the first one proposed: extra weight places extra burden on the chest, the airways, and the lung and makes it difficult for patients to take deep breaths, which in turn lowers the threshold for the sensation of dyspnea. However, several studies in obese asthmatic children have found an obstructive deficit (decreased air flow with relatively preserved lung volumes) [18, 19] rather than the restrictive deficit seen in adults, perhaps because in general, obesity in childhood is less pronounced than in adults.

Lung volume reduction that is not significant enough to produce clinical signs of restriction may result in reduced stretching of airway smooth muscle, which alters the actin-myosin bridges and produces "latching" of the muscle [20]. Furthermore, the protective effects of deep inspiration are reduced or lost in obesity [21]. When studying airway hyperreactivity (AHR) to methacholine challenge in asthmatic children, we found that obese and nonobese asthmatics have similar AHR (unpublished data); however, while the decrease in FEV_1 was similar, obese children had less obstruction (measured by the drop in FEV_1/FVC) and significantly more airway closure (measured by changes in FVC). As a result, obese children have lungs that are more prone to collapse, airways more prone to either obstruction or closure, and more pronounced airway smooth muscle contraction.

Asthma and Systemic Inflammation

Asthma is characterized by airway inflammation. Obesity and the metabolic syndrome, on the contrary, are characterized by increased systemic inflammation. Adipose tissue secretes several inflammatory substances, or adipokines, including interleukin-6 (IL-6), tumor necrosis factor alpha (TNF-α), eotaxin, leptin, and adiponectin, among others. Many of these have been implicated in asthma [22, 23]. Adipose tissue can also produce other proinflammatory molecules such as transforming growth factor beta-1 (TGF-β1), which has also been linked to asthma [24, 25].

Leptin is produced by adipocytes and is involved in neuron regulation of hunger/satiety and basal metabolic rate [26]. It has been shown to increase IgE and airway responsiveness following allergen challenge in murine models of asthma [27, 28]. Adiponectin, an adipokine with anti-inflammatory properties, is also the only adipokine that is reduced in obesity. In mice, exogenous adiponectin reduces or abolishes airway inflammation and responsiveness [29], and recently, it has been shown that higher levels of adiponectin is associated with decreased airway obstruction and decreased asthma symptoms and exacerbations in adolescents (similarly, this effect was limited to boys) [30].

While the details and mechanisms are still not completely understood, it is reasonable and biologically plausible to propose that systemic inflammation derived from excess adipose tissue may have an effect on the airways (as it does on other systems and organs) and therefore predisposes children with metabolic syndrome or obesity to asthma, or worsens existing disease.

Relationship of Asthma and Insulin Resistance

It is well known that in the metabolic syndrome and in obesity, increased insulin resistance can lead to increases in free insulin growth factor-1 (IGF-1). Recent studies in adults have shown that insulin resistance is associated with new-onset asthma and with asthma-like symptoms [31]. Among a host of other effects throughout the body, both insulin itself and IGF-1 can increase airway smooth muscle contraction, and inhaled insulin has been reported to produce acute declines in lung function [32]. Hyperglycemia, hyperinsulinemia, and increased IGF-1 may also lead to increased submucosal gland metaplasia, proliferation and differentiation of fibroblasts, and resultant airway collagen deposition and fibrosis [33]. All these mechanisms could constitute causal pathways in the relationship between metabolic syndrome/obesity and asthma. Furthermore, it suggests that in the presence of metabolic syndrome, asthmatics may be at higher risk of airway fibrosis, or the so-called airway remodeling.

Genetic Determinants

Both asthma and obesity (and the metabolic syndrome) have well-recognized, significant hereditary components. It is therefore reasonable to propose there may be shared genetic determinants underlying the effect of obesity on asthma incidence and morbidity. A recent study reported that single nucleotide polymorphisms (SNPs) of the *PRKCA* (protein kinase C alpha) gene were associated with both BMI and asthma [34]; this was the first time a genome-wide approach was used to identify novel genes associated with both diseases at the same time in a cohort of children. Also recently, a candidate-gene, case–control study reported an association between SNPs in the leptin gene and asthma in children [35]. *TNF-α* haplotypes have been shown to modify the association between asthma and obesity [36, 37]. The genes for the β2-adrenergic (ADRB2) and the glucocorticoid (NR3C1) receptors are located on chromosome 5q and have been implicated (in separate studies) in pathways related to both asthma and obesity. Similarly, polymorphisms of the fractalkine CX3CR1 receptor have been linked with asthma, atopy, and obesity in separate studies [38, 39].

While this work is still in its infancy, it is not unreasonable to think that many of the proposed mechanisms linking metabolic syndrome, obesity, and asthma may have shared genetic roots.

Comorbidities

It is well known that obesity predisposes to other comorbidities, and this extends to the metabolic syndrome as well. Obese subjects have a higher prevalence of gastroesophageal reflux disease (GERD), and GERD may in turn produce airway inflammation, predisposing to or exacerbating asthma symptoms [40]. In a recent birth cohort study from New Zealand, GERD symptoms such as heartburn and regurgitation were risk factors for cough, wheezing, and diagnosis of asthma [41]. Similarly, as we describe later in this chapter, obesity and the metabolic syndrome are associated with obstructive sleep apnea (OSA) [42]. OSA can lead to increased airway inflammation as measured by fractional exhaled nitric oxide (FeNO), and this could in turn lead to an increased risk of asthma or increased asthma symptoms [43]. Finally, overweight and obese people have a higher prevalence of depression, decreased medication compliance, and other factors [44], which could further complicate their asthma.

Vitamin D, Asthma, and Pulmonary Complications

Variants of the vitamin D receptor gene have been associated with asthma phenotypes; levels of vitamin D are implicated in airway smooth muscle function and correlate with measures of asthma severity in children [45]. At the same time, individuals with higher adiposity have higher risk of vitamin D deficiency [46]. In a recent study, we showed decreased serum levels of vitamin D among overweight/obese asthmatic children, and these levels were significantly associated with decreased FEV_1 [47]. Conversely, administration of vitamin D to cultures of CD4 T cells from steroid-resistant asthmatics has been shown to reverse such resistance; furthermore, in combination with fluticasone, vitamin D has been shown to modulate secretion of proinflammatory cytokines by airway smooth muscle cells [48]. Although the precise mechanisms are still unclear, given the importance of vitamin D in both diseases, it is likely that the vitamin will play an important role in clarifying their relationship.

Arginine and Nitric Oxide

In obesity and the metabolic syndrome, insulin resistance together with an increased protein turnover produces elevated levels of asymmetric dimethylarginine (ADMA) and other similar molecules [33]. ADMA is a competitive inhibitor of the enzyme endothelial nitric oxide synthase (eNOS); high levels of ADMA decrease the availability of arginine and its conversion by eNOS, which could lead to decreased production of nitric oxide (NO). NO is an important endogenous regulatory molecule and acts as in many biological processes, including endothelial and platelet function, interaction with reactive oxygen species, immune function, and bronchial tone and reactivity. Subcutaneous infusions of ADMA in mice have been shown to increase AHR and fibrosis [49]. Conversely, L-arginine supplementation has been shown to improve certain measures of asthma and of the metabolic syndrome [33]. Ongoing studies seem to show that increased methylation of genes related to the arginine-NO pathway is associated with increased exhaled nitric oxide (FeNO), a marker of airway inflammation [50]. Similarly, increased total genome Alu methylation seems to correlate with higher BMI and with allergic sensitization [51].

Hormonal Differences

Given the gender differences – albeit inconsistent – found in asthma/obesity studies, it is reasonable to propose that hormonal differences by obesity status and gender may play a role. Aromatase, an enzyme found in high concentrations in adipose tissue, converts androgens to estrogens and partly explains the increased levels of estrogens in obesity. Elevated estrogen levels have been found to be an independent risk factor for asthma in adult obese women [52]. Putatively, estrogen has been reported to enhance eosinophil adhesion and degranulation, whereas testosterone reduces their adhesion and viability [53]; furthermore, estrogen appears to induce secretion of IL-3 and IL-4 by monocytes.

Decreased Medication Response

A few studies in adults have shown a decreased response to inhaled corticosteroids – one of the mainstays of chronic asthma therapy – among obese adults, and we recently reported a similar decrease among obese asthmatic children compared to asthmatic children of normal weight [47]. On the other hand, the response to systemic asthma therapy such as leukotriene modifiers does not seem to be impaired in obesity [54]. This could be explained by the theory of systemic inflammation, which may be affected by systemic medications but not by inhaled therapies, whose effects would be confined to the airway. It could also mean there is an intrinsic steroid resistance in obese asthmatics. The glucocorticoid receptor has two isoforms, one of which is active (GRα) and the other inhibitory (GRβ). GRβ strongly inhibits the α-isoform by preventing activation of glucocorticoid-responsive genes, and it has been associated with steroid resistance in asthma [55]. Cytokines associated with obesity, such as TNF-α and IL-6, regulate GR expression with accumulation of

GRβ [56] and could therefore reduce the activity of the receptor, effectively rendering obese asthmatic patients steroid resistant.

Weight Loss Interventions

Few studies have looked at the effect of weight loss on asthma. A meta-analysis by Eneli et al. looked at 15 studies reporting weight loss and asthma-related measures and found that regardless of the type of intervention (medical vs. surgical), weight loss seemed to lead to an improvement in asthma measures [57]. However, asthma was the primary outcome in only five of those studies. Only one of the studies included pediatric patients which in fact included only one asthmatic adolescent, whose symptoms improved with weight reduction. Clearly, further studies are needed to address this question in children.

A Different Type of Childhood Asthma?

Obese children have a higher risk of developing asthma, have more frequent or significant symptoms, have higher risk of exacerbations, which tend to be longer, and seem to respond less to certain asthma medications. Furthermore, the association of obesity with asthma appears to be stronger in nonallergic children, varies with gender, and may lead to alterations in pulmonary function such as decreased airway hyperreactivity and increased airway closure. All these findings, put together, have led to the theory that asthma in the obese child may be a different disease than asthma in the child of normal weight. Whereas alterations in lung mechanics play an important role, this "obese asthma" would be the product of several shared genetic polymorphisms rather than just allergen sensitivities, of systemic rather than airway inflammation alone, of insulin resistance and arginine metabolism abnormalities, and of a distinct milieu of hormones and adipokines present in patients with obesity or metabolic syndrome. While thus far this is only a nascent theory, it certainly holds biological plausibility from several potential pathways, and it could have very important implications for two major public health problems on the rise.

Metabolic Syndrome and Sleep-Disordered Breathing

Epidemiology of Sleep-Disordered Breathing

The spectrum of sleep-disordered breathing (SDB) occurs in children of all ages and encompasses obstructive sleep apnea (OSA) and upper airway resistance syndrome. Obstructive sleep apnea (OSA) is a prevalent condition in pediatrics, affecting 2–3% of school-aged children [58, 59]. It is characterized by repetitive upper airway obstructions during sleep, resulting in intermittent hypoxia and sleep fragmentation caused by arousals. Upper airway resistance syndrome is a more frequent occurrence, affecting up to 27% of children and characterized by habitual snoring and increased respiratory effort during sleep without significant decrease in airflows or ventilatory abnormalities [59–62].

Definition of Obstructive Apnea

Obstructive apnea is defined as the absence of airflow with continued chest wall and abdominal movement over at least two breaths. Hypopnea is defined as a decrease in oronasal flow of at least 50% with a corresponding arousal or a decrease in oxygen saturation (SaO_2) of at least 3%. The obstructive apnea/hypopnea index (AHI) is the number of apneas and hypopneas per hour of total sleep time (TST). An obstructive AHI of at least 5/h of TST is considered significant, i.e., moderate to severe obstruction. OSA results from a number of factors and their interactions that play a role in upper airway collapsibility such as lymphoadenoid hyperplasia and anatomic and neurologic factors. Abnormal neuromotor function results in diminished upper airway tone specifically involving upper airway dilator muscles. Furthermore, children with OSA have been found to have absent or delayed arousal during an obstructive event, suggesting alteration in central chemosensitivity.

Obesity Hypoventilation Syndrome

Whereas the focus of this section is the pathophysiologic link between the MS and OSA, it is important to briefly discuss obesity hypoventilation syndrome (OHS), a more severe manifestation of ventilatory abnormalities related to morbid obesity. OHS represents the interaction between sleep-disordered breathing, diminished respiratory drive, and obesity-related respiratory impairment. Patients with OHS have daytime hypercapnia ($PaCO_2 > 45$ mmHg) and hypoxia ($PaO_2 < 70$ mmHg) and have BMI > 30 kg/m^2, all in the absence of significant pulmonary or neuromuscular disease [63, 64]. The reported prevalence in adult patients seen in outpatient sleep clinics is around 10–20%; the incidence of OHS increases as obesity increases [64, 65]. Several mechanisms have been invoked as to how morbid obesity leads to hypoventilation, including abnormal respiratory mechanics, impaired or blunted central responsiveness to hypercapnia and hypoxia, and sleep-disordered breathing [66–69]. Neurohormonal mechanisms have also been studied, including leptin resistance, which contributes to the development of awake hypoventilation; higher serum leptin concentrations are associated with reduced respiratory drive and reduced response to hypercapnia in morbidly obese individuals [70–72]. Whereas respiratory failure accounts for morbidity and mortality, patients with OHS also suffer from greater cardiovascular and metabolic complications compared to patients with a diagnosis solely of OSA or obesity, and these include hypertension, congestive heart failure, and *cor pulmonale*. Patients also have more severe insulin resistance, endothelial dysfunction, and high levels of inflammatory markers, all of which are associated with poor prognosis [67, 73].

Obstructive Sleep Apnea

The major determinants however of OSA are obesity and upper airway lymphoid tissue hyperplasia manifesting as adenoid and tonsillar hypertrophy. Fat deposition around the neck and submental area aggravates upper airway collapsibility in the supine position; moreover, obesity reduces lung volumes [74]. Obesity is a major risk factor for persistent OSA even after treatment (such as adenotonsillectomy) and results in increased severity of morbidities associated with OSA involving the neurocognitive, cardiovascular, and metabolic systems.

OSA and Cardiovascular Complications

OSA is associated with an increased prevalence of the metabolic syndrome and cardiovascular complications; constituents of the latter also comprise the metabolic syndrome such as hypertension. Hypertension can affect other target organs such as the heart, blood vessels, and kidneys and thus contributes to increased cardiovascular risks. Children with OSA may exhibit abnormal left ventricular geometry and ventricular hypertrophy [75] and prognosticate for cardiovascular disease in adulthood. The pathogenesis of hypertension and cardiovascular consequences in OSA is complex and is related to alterations in autonomic nervous system control that result in increased parasympathetic activity, decreased baroreceptor activity, neurohormonal mechanisms, and endothelial dysfunction [76]. Endothelial dysfunction resulting from induction of cellular adhesion molecules in response to inflammatory cytokines is contributory to cardiovascular morbidity; increased oxidant production related to endothelial dysfunction in the microcirculation of OSA patients has been reported [77, 78]. Moreover, increased levels of C-reactive protein (CRP) have been found in pediatric patients with OSA; CRP is a marker of inflammation, and its elevation is associated with severity and progression of coronary artery disease and atherosclerosis [79, 80]. It is important to mention that the intermittent hypoxemia that occurs in OSA may lead to increased pulmonary artery pressure and potentially to right ventricular dysfunction; indeed, *cor pulmonale* has been documented even in pediatric patients with OSA.

OSA and Oxidative Stress

In OSA, repeated episodes of hypoxia followed by reoxygenation result in elevation of proinflammatory cytokines and also induce oxidative stress of vascular endothelium

8 Asthma and Other Childhood Respiratory Disorders and the Metabolic Syndrome

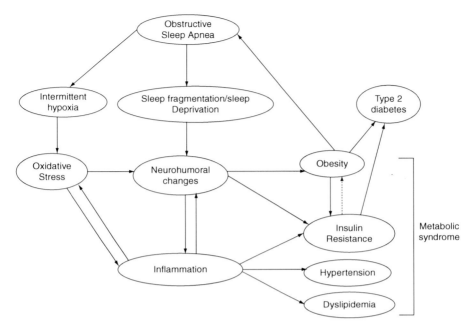

Fig. 8.2 Possible mechanistic links between obstructive sleep apnea, metabolic syndrome, and type 2 diabetes

and lead to a heightened state of systemic inflammation [81–83]. Thus, the putative mechanisms by which OSA exacerbates MS include the activation of cytokines by stress hypoxia and/or by increased adipokines and free fatty acids released by excess adipose tissue, the latter reinforcing that obesity is a determinant of OSA [74].

Intermittent hypoxia induces oxidative stress, which has been shown to adversely affect glucose homeostasis and increase the risk of type 2 diabetes [84–86]. The complex interplay of factors, such as increased sympathetic activation, dysregulation of the hypothalamus-pituitary axis, generation of reactive oxygen species, and activation of inflammatory pathways, leads to alteration in glucose metabolism in OSA [87]. Tasali and Ip elaborated on the mechanistic links between OSA, MS, and type 2 diabetes as shown in Fig. 8.2. This figure illustrates multiple feedback and the so-called feed-forward mechanisms perpetuating the metabolic aberrations.

OSA and Systemic Inflammation

Inflammation plays a key role in the linkage between OSA, MS, and obesity. In fact, these three conditions are regarded as proinflammatory states [74]. CRP is a systemic marker of inflammation and linked to risk of cardiovascular disease [82, 88]; it has been found to be elevated in a severity-dependent manner among pediatric patients with OSA even after correction for BMI. Adipose tissue is a rich source of cytokines such as TNF-a and IL-6, which have been implicated in the development of insulin resistance and are elevated in OSA [88–91]. Oxidative stress from chronic intermittent hypoxia and the stimulation of NF-κB in cardiovascular tissues operate in a bidirectional manner in the pathogenesis of cardiometabolic complications in MS [91]. Elevated NF-κB binding to circulating neutrophils and monocytes has been shown in patients with OSA [92]. The endothelial dysfunction that underlies vascular complications in MS results from induction of cellular adhesion molecules in response to inflammatory cytokines. Circulating monocytes in patients with OSA have been shown to have increased expression of adhesion molecules associated with increased intracellular reactive oxygen species [93]. O'Brien and coworkers however reported that elevations in adhesion molecules such as ICAM-1 were found to be primarily associated with obesity rather than with SDB in children; in contrast, the elevation of plasma levels of P-selectin, a marker of platelet activation that may contribute to accelerated risk for cardiovascular morbidity, was associated with SDB [77]. Platelet activation and elevation of fibrinogen and plasminogen activation inhibitor (PAI-1) have been demonstrated with MS. In patients with OSA, increased fibrinogen levels, exaggerated platelet activity, and reduced fibrinolytic capacity were found independent of obesity and contribute to cardiovascular complications [89, 94, 95].

The role of adipokines in OSA has also been studied with conflicting results. Patients with OSA exhibit higher leptin levels compared with BMI-matched controls and in some studies correlated with insulin levels [96–98]. Diurnal variation in leptin levels has also been associated with OSA such that evening levels were found to be higher in patients with OSA even after adjusting for obesity [99]. On the other hand, studies on the relationship of adiponectin and OSA have not shown any significant independent relationship [96, 100]; nonetheless, reduced levels of adiponectin in patients with OSA have been reported by other investigators [101, 102].

OSA and Interventional Studies

Interventional studies involving the use of continuous positive airway pressure (CPAP) in patients with OSA have reported decrease in proinflammatory activities of these cytokines thereby underscoring their putative mechanistic role in OSA and by inference, to MS [88, 92, 101, 103–106]. For that matter, elevated serum CRP concentrations as well as lipid profiles and apolipoprotein B in both obese and nonobese children with OSA normalized proportionately to the improvements in OSA after tonsillectomy and adenoidectomy [83, 107]. Rodent models further corroborate this statement. Chronic intermittent hypoxia simulates events in OSA in humans and has been associated with activation of NF-κB in cardiovascular tissues in mice [108]. Polotsky reported that leptin-deficient obese mice developed a time-dependent increase in fasting serum insulin levels and worsening glucose tolerance after a 12-week exposure to intermittent hypoxia, invoking the role of oxidative stress in OSA and MS [109].

OSA, Obesity, and Metabolic Syndrome: Interacting Pathophysiology

Indeed, there is a close association between OSA, obesity, and metabolic syndrome, with these entities sharing interacting pathophysiologies that may lead to long-term adverse outcomes [82]. Activation of the inflammatory cascade appears to be the final common pathway linking the overlapping entities of obesity, OSA, and MS [74]. Morbidities arising from this association are significant. Thus, increased awareness of this association should lead to clinically meaningful interventions to include public health measures that address the epidemic of obesity.

Obesity and Perioperative Adverse Events

With the increasing prevalence of obesity in the pediatric population, anesthesiologists and surgeons are likely to see a higher proportion of obese patients who present for surgery. Obese children have complications that require surgical intervention such as adenotonsillectomy for OSA and orthopedic repair of slipped capital femoral epiphysis. Cholelithiasis associated with hypercholesterolemia may require surgical intervention. Obese patients are also referred for bariatric surgery. Retrospective and prospective studies have been done to describe the prevalence of overweight and obese pediatric surgical patients. Whereas these studies had basic methodological differences and different age- and gender-specific standards for the definition of overweight and obesity, prevalence rates for overweight and obese were 14–16% and 17–20%, respectively [110–113].

Obese children present with a number of known significant comorbidities that include asthma and obstructive sleep apnea. Obesity is a component of the metabolic syndrome, which also includes hypertension, hyperlipidemia, and hyperinsulinemia. These preexisting metabolic abnormalities are known predictors of adverse events in patients undergoing elective surgery [114]. In 2002, the American Academy of Pediatrics released a clinical practice guideline for OSA; the report stated that the risk of postoperative respiratory compromise in patients undergoing adenotonsillectomy was highest in patients younger than 3 years of age, those with associated medical problems, and those with severe polysomnogram findings [115, 116]. In 2006, the American Society of Anesthesiologists published their practice guideline for perioperative management of patients with OSA; they cited obesity as a pediatric risk factor and increased perioperative risk associated with adenotonsillectomy in children younger than 3 years [117]. In recent years, Tait and coworkers conducted a prospective study that identified obesity and a history of OSA as independent predictors of perioperative adverse respiratory events in children [111]. Schewengel et al. cited clinical features that predict respiratory compromise after adenotonsillectomy and persistent OSA that included morbid obesity, severe OSA, hypertension, and age less than 3 years, among others [115].

Anesthesia and surgery result in a metabolic stress response characterized by increase secretion of catabolic hormones such as catecholamines, cortisol, and glucagon, which may further aggravate the metabolic derangements in the obese patient. Excessive adipose tissue in the upper airway and soft tissue around the neck lead to upper airway narrowing and pose problems with regard to intubation and respiratory problems postextubation; this is further aggravated by relaxation of pharyngeal muscles under general anesthesia [113]. Physiological derangements in lung mechanics such as reduction in functional residual capacity (FRC), decreased chest wall compliance, and upward displacement of the diaphragm in the supine position impact on intraoperative ventilation and airway management [115]. Nafiu et al. reported that obese children had greater frequency of difficult mask ventilation, difficult laryngoscopy, and postoperative airway obstruction [118]. Greater risk of intraoperative desaturation and bronchospasm is encountered with greater frequency in obese patients [111]. Gastroesophageal reflux and delayed gastric emptying time have also been reported which contribute to adverse respiratory outcomes [119–121].

Preoperative CPAP has been implemented for children with very severe OSA and at risk for persistent OSA and those with cardiovascular complications; preoperative regimen can also be used in the postoperative care [115, 122]. In reference to intraoperative management, short-acting anesthetics are preferred, given the risk for depression of ventilation; if sedatives are used, patients should be monitored closely postoperatively until recovery is demonstrated. General anesthesia with the use of volatile anesthetics may aggravate airway collapse from relaxation of upper airway muscles, which further increase the risk of airway obstruction. Postoperative opioid administration increases the risk of depression of ventilation especially in obese patients with OSA such that there is a need for close monitoring [123]. Challenges with regard to anesthetic drug dosing regimens for obese patients, specific recommendations on anesthetics, and details regarding choice of technique for airway management (e.g., endotracheal intubation, laryngeal mask, mask ventilation) are beyond the scope of this section.

Adenotonsillectomy in the obese and morbidly obese child postoperative outcomes require special mention. Persistent respiratory abnormalities may be seen in obese children, especially those with severe OSA [124, 125]. Immediate postoperative complications may include pulmonary edema, laryngospasm, bronchospasm, apnea, and hypertensive crisis [126, 127]. Overnight inpatient monitoring is recommended for high-risk children in a setting that ensures monitoring and intervention for signs of airway depression and airway obstruction [116, 128]. As mentioned earlier, children who are given opioids for pain control require close monitoring. Pediatric intensive care unit (PICU) admission is reserved for patients with very severe OSA that is usually based on preoperative polysomnographic data, very young children, and those with comorbidities that cannot be managed in regular floors or hospital settings other than the intensive area unit [115]. On the other hand, there are studies that showed that postoperative care of obese patients does not require ICU admission. In a retrospective study on postoperative admissions to the ICU, Spector reported that routine PICU admission was not warranted for most morbidly obese pediatric patients, although several required supplemental oxygen and BIPAP; only 1 of 14 patients required prolonged intubation beyond the first 24 h postsurgery [129]. The same conclusion was corroborated by Shine et al. with the caveat that special consideration must be given to the postoperative nursing environment to ensure regular positional and suctioning intervention as well as monitoring [130].

Thus, obese patients who present for anesthesia and surgery are at risk for perioperative adverse respiratory complications. Cognizance and anticipation of risk factors associated with obesity can help mitigate and treat complications and optimize anesthetic and surgical outcomes.

Obesity and Acute Lung Injury/Acute Respiratory Distress Syndrome

Acute lung injury (ALI) describes the pulmonary response to a broad range of insults occurring directly or indirectly to the lung or resulting from injury or inflammation at other sites of the body. Acute respiratory distress syndrome (ARDS) represents the more severe presentation of ALI. ALI/ARDS is associated with a significantly high mortality rate depending on the age group and inciting cause [131, 132]. Clinically, ALI/ARDS is defined by acute onset, bilateral radiographic infiltrates, and gas exchange abnormalities that occur shortly after a predisposing injury in the absence of left atrial hypertension. In terms of pathophysiology, increase in alveolocapillary permeability from endothelial cell injury resulting in pulmonary edema is a basic underlying abnormality in both ARDS and ALI, although it is more severe in the former. Complex interactions between inflammatory cells and between these cells and the endothelium generate a variety of inflammatory mediators that promote inflammation and drive lung injury [133].

Many risk factors for the development of ARDS and related mortality have been studied. In children, increased mortality and prolonged mechanical ventilation were associated with the initial severity of oxygenation defect, the presence of central nervous system (CNS) dysfunction, and the presence of nonpulmonary, non-CNS organ dysfunction [134]. As the prevalence of obesity increases in the population, a higher proportion of obese patients will present with acute respiratory failure. There has been a paucity of studies with regard to obesity as a risk factor, given the lower prevalence of ALI/ARDS in children compared to adults [135–137]. In a study by Gong and coworkers, increased BMI was shown to be associated with increased risk of ARDS and with increased length of stay but not with mortality in adults. In this study, increasing weight was associated with younger age, diabetes, higher blood glucose, lower prevalence of direct pulmonary injury, and later development of ARDS [138]. Gajic et al. conducted a multicenter cohort study evaluating a lung injury prediction score; obesity was reported as one of the risk modifiers predicting higher risk for ALI in the scoring system [139]. Critically ill obese patients who suffered blunt trauma suffered more complications and required longer hospital stays including longer duration of mechanical ventilation; obesity was independently associated with mortality in this group of patients [140].

Physiologic alterations in lung and chest wall mechanics and lung volumes in obese patients contribute to the duration of mechanical ventilation need for higher airway pressures and oxygen requirements [138, 141]. Altered drug pharmacokinetics in the obese patient may impact on the extended effect of sedatives used during mechanical ventilation and weaning regimen [141]. Aside from these, the effect of comorbidities, difficulty in postinjury care, and the underlying inflammatory and thromboembolic states of obese patients predispose these patients to increased morbidity and mortality during acute critical illness [140].

Conclusions

Obesity is associated with the metabolic syndrome, and taken together they result in significant respiratory morbidity. With the increase in prevalence of childhood obesity, we have seen a corresponding increase in the prevalence of asthma and sleep-disordered breathing. Obesity and the metabolic disorder are associated with a generalized proinflammatory state, which appears to be one of the common pathways for these respiratory conditions. Moreover, obesity contributes to increased upper airway collapsibility and is associated with abnormalities in lung function and the mechanics of breathing. Obesity and the metabolic syndrome confer greater perioperative risk for respiratory morbidity, and both are considered risk factors for the development of acute lung injury and the acute respiratory distress syndrome. Thus, strategies to curb the rising trend in obesity and the metabolic syndrome, which are of utmost importance, will also impact the morbidity and health care utilization associated with these respiratory diseases.

References

1. Taussig L, Landau LI. Pediatric respiratory medicine. 2nd ed. Philadelphia: Elsevier Health Sciences; 2008.
2. Akinbami LJ. The state of childhood asthma, United States, 1980–2005. National Center for Health Statistics, Hyatsville; 2006. Report no.: 24.
3. CDC. Vital signs: asthma prevalence, disease characteristics, and self-management education - United States, 2001–2009. MMWR Morb Mortal Wkly Rep. 2011;60(17):547–52.
4. Moorman JE, Rudd RA, Johnson CA, King M, Minor P, Bailey C, et al. National surveillance for asthma – United States, 1980–2004. Morb Mortal Wkly Rep Surveill Summ. 2007;56(8):18–54.
5. Ramsey F, Ussery-Hall A, Garcia D, McDonald GJ, Easton A, Kambon M, et al. Prevalence of selected risk behaviors and chronic diseases – behavioral risk factor surveillance system (BRFSS), 39 steps communities, United States, 2005. MMWR Morb Mortal Wkly Rep [Internet] 2008 [cited 8/4/2010]; 57(SS11):8/04/2010.
6. Dilley JA, Pizacani BP, Macdonald SM, Bardin J. The burden of asthma in Washington state. Washington State Department of Health, Olympia; 2005. Report no.: DOH Pub No. 345-201.
7. Garcia-Marcos L, Valverde-Molina J, Ortega ML, Sanchez-Solis M, Martinez-Torres AE, Castro-Rodriguez JA. Percent body fat, skinfold thickness or body mass index for defining

obesity or overweight, as a risk factor for asthma in schoolchildren: Which one to use in epidemiological studies? Matern Child Nutr. 2008;4(4):304–10.
8. Taveras EM, Rifas-Shiman S, Camargo Jr CA, Gold DR, Litonjua AA, Oken E, et al. Higher adiposity in infancy associated with recurrent wheeze in a prospective cohort of children. J Allergy Clin Immunol. 2008;121(5):1161–6.
9. Michelson PH, Williams LW, Benjamin DK, Barnato AE. Obesity, inflammation, and asthma severity in childhood: data from the national health and nutrition examination survey 2001–2004. Ann Allergy Asthma Immunol. 2009;103(5):381–5.
10. Reichman NE, Nepomnyaschy L. Maternal pre-pregnancy obesity and diagnosis of asthma in offspring at age 3 years. Matern Child Health J. 2008;12(6):725–33.
11. Ronmark E, Andersson C, Nystrom L, Forsberg B, Jarvholm B, Lundback B. Obesity increases the risk of incident asthma among adults. Eur Respir J. 2005;25(2):282–8.
12. Ma J, Xiao L, Knowles SB. Obesity, insulin resistance and the prevalence of atopy and asthma in US adults. Allergy. 2010;65(11):1455–63. doi:10.1111/j.1398-9995.2010.02402.x.
13. Flaherman V, Rutherford GW. A meta-analysis of the effect of high weight on asthma. Arch Dis Child. 2006;91(4):334–9.
14. Guerra S, Wright AL, Morgan WJ, Sherrill DL, Holberg CJ, Martinez FD. Persistence of asthma symptoms during adolescence: role of obesity and age at the onset of puberty. Am J Respir Crit Care Med. 2004;170(1):78–85.
15. Mannino DM, Mott J, Ferdinands JM, Camargo CA, Friedman M, Greves HM, et al. Boys with high body masses have an increased risk of developing asthma: findings from the national longitudinal survey of youth (NLSY). Int J Obes (Lond). 2006;30(1):6–13.
16. Gold DR, Damokosh AI, Dockery DW, Berkey CS. Body-mass index as a predictor of incident asthma in a prospective cohort of children. Pediatr Pulmonol. 2003;36(6):514–21.
17. Collins LC, Hoberty PD, Walker JF, Fletcher EC, Peiris AN. The effect of body fat distribution on pulmonary function tests. Chest. 1995;107(5):1298–302.
18. Al Dabal L, Bahammam AS. Obesity hypoventilation syndrome. Ann Thorac Med. 2009;4(2):41–9.
19. Tantisira KG, Litonjua AA, Weiss ST, Fuhlbrigge AL, Childhood Asthma Management Program Research Group. Association of body mass with pulmonary function in the childhood asthma management program (CAMP). Thorax. 2003;58(12):1036–41.
20. Fredberg JJ, Inouye D, Miller B, Nathan M, Jafari S, Raboudi SH, et al. Airway smooth muscle, tidal stretches, and dynamically determined contractile states. Am J Respir Crit Care Med. 1997;156(6):1752–9.
21. Boulet LP, Turcotte H, Boulet G, Simard B, Robichaud P. Deep inspiration avoidance and airway response to methacholine: influence of body mass index. Can Respir J. 2005;12(7):371–6.
22. Canoz M, Erdenen F, Uzun H, Muderrisoglu C, Aydin S. The relationship of inflammatory cytokines with asthma and obesity. Clin Invest Med. 2008;31(6):E373–9.
23. Matricardi PM, Gruber C, Wahn U, Lau S. The asthma-obesity link in childhood: open questions, complex evidence, a few answers only. Clin Exp Allergy. 2007;37(4):476–84.
24. Alessi MC, Bastelica D, Morange P, Berthet B, Leduc I, Verdier M, et al. Plasminogen activator inhibitor 1, transforming growth factor-beta1, and BMI are closely associated in human adipose tissue during morbid obesity. Diabetes. 2000;49(8):1374–80.
25. Sharma S, Raby BA, Hunninghake GM, Soto-Quiros M, Avila L, Murphy AJ, et al. Variants in TGFB1, dust mite exposure, and disease severity in children with asthma. Am J Respir Crit Care Med. 2009;179(5):356–62.
26. Weiss ST. Obesity: insight into the origins of asthma. Nat Immunol. 2005;6(6):537–9.
27. Johnston RA, Zhu M, Rivera-Sanchez YM, Lu FL, Theman TA, Flynt L, et al. Allergic airway responses in obese mice. Am J Respir Crit Care Med. 2007;176(7):650–8.
28. Shore SA. Obesity and asthma: lessons from animal models. J Appl Physiol. 2007;102(2):516–28.
29. Shore SA, Terry RD, Flynt L, Xu A, Hug C. Adiponectin attenuates allergen-induced airway inflammation and hyperresponsiveness in mice. J Allergy Clin Immunol. 2006;118(2):389–95.

30. Kattan M, Kumar R, Bloomberg GR, Mitchell HE, Calatroni A, Gergen PJ, et al. Asthma control, adiposity, and adipokines among inner-city adolescents. J Allergy Clin Immunol. 2010;125(3):584–92.
31. Thuesen BH, Husemoen LL, Hersoug LG, Pisinger C, Linneberg A. Insulin resistance as a predictor of incident asthma-like symptoms in adults. Clin Exp Allergy. 2009;39(5):700–7.
32. Dekkers BG, Schaafsma D, Tran T, Zaagsma J, Meurs H. Insulin-induced laminin expression promotes a hypercontractile airway smooth muscle phenotype. Am J Respir Cell Mol Biol. 2009;41(4):494–504.
33. Agrawal A, Mabalirajan U, Ahmad T, Ghosh B. Emerging interface between metabolic syndrome and asthma. Am J Respir Cell Mol Biol. 2011;44(3):270–5.
34. Murphy A, Tantisira KG, Soto-Quiros ME, Avila L, Klanderman BJ, Lake S, et al. PRKCA: a positional candidate gene for body mass index and asthma. Am J Hum Genet. 2009;85(1):87–96.
35. Szczepankiewicz A, Breborowicz A, Sobkowiak P, Popiel A. Are genes associated with energy metabolism important in asthma and BMI? J Asthma. 2009;46(1):53.
36. Castro-Giner F, Kogevinas M, Imboden M, de Cid R, Jarvis D, Machler M, et al. Joint effect of obesity and TNFA variability on asthma: two international cohort studies. Eur Respir J. 2009;33(5):1003–9.
37. Choi IW, Sun-Kim KYS, Ko HM, Im SY, Kim JH, et al. TNF-alpha induces the late-phase airway hyperresponsiveness and airway inflammation through cytosolic phospholipase A(2) activation. J Allergy Clin Immunol. 2005;116(3):537–43.
38. Tremblay K, Lemire M, Provost V, Pastinen T, Renaud Y, Sandford AJ, et al. Association study between the CX3CR1 gene and asthma. Genes Immun. 2006;7(8):632–9.
39. Sirois-Gagnon D, Chamberland A, Perron S, Brisson D, Gaudet D, Laprise C. Association of common polymorphisms in the fractalkine receptor (CX3CR1) with obesity. Obesity (Silver Spring). 2011;19(1):222–7. Epub 2010 Jun 3.
40. Pashankar DS, Corbin Z, Shah SK, Caprio S. Increased prevalence of gastroesophageal reflux symptoms in obese children evaluated in an academic medical center. J Clin Gastroenterol. 2009;43(5):410–3.
41. Hancox RJ, Poulton R, Taylor DR, Greene JM, McLachlan CR, Cowan JO, et al. Associations between respiratory symptoms, lung function and gastro-oesophageal reflux symptoms in a population-based birth cohort. Respir Res. 2006;7:142.
42. Sulit LG, Storfer-Isser A, Rosen CL, Kirchner HL, Redline S. Associations of obesity, sleep-disordered breathing, and wheezing in children. Am J Respir Crit Care Med. 2005;171(6):659–64.
43. Verhulst SL, Aerts L, Jacobs S, Schrauwen N, Haentjens D, Claes R, et al. Sleep-disordered breathing, obesity, and airway inflammation in children and adolescents. Chest. 2008;134(6):1169–75.
44. Strine TW, Mokdad AH, Balluz LS, Gonzalez O, Crider R, Berry JT, et al. Depression and anxiety in the United States: findings from the 2006 behavioral risk factor surveillance system. Psychiatr Serv. 2008;59(12):1383–90.
45. Brehm JM, Celedón JC, Soto-Quiros ME, Avila L, Hunninghake GM, Forno E, et al. Serum vitamin D levels and markers of severity of childhood asthma in Costa Rica. Am J Respir Crit Care Med. 2009;179(9):765–71.
46. Alemzadeh R, Kichler J, Babar G, Calhoun M. Hypovitaminosis D in obese children and adolescents: relationship with adiposity, insulin sensitivity, ethnicity, and season. Metabolism. 2008;57(2):183–91.
47. Forno E, Lescher R, Strunk R, Weiss S, Fuhlbrigge A, Celedón JC. Decreased response to inhaled steroids in overweight and obese asthmatic children. J Allergy Clin Immunol. 2011;127(3):741–9.
48. Litonjua AA. Childhood asthma may be a consequence of vitamin D deficiency. Curr Opin Allergy Clin Immunol. 2009;9(3):202–7.
49. Wells SM, Buford MC, Migliaccio CT, Holian A. Elevated asymmetric dimethylarginine alters lung function and induces collagen deposition in mice. Am J Respir Cell Mol Biol. 2009;40(2):179–88.

50. Breton CV, Byun HM, Wang X, Salam MT, Siegmund K, Gilliland FD. DNA methylation in the arginase-nitric oxide synthase pathway is associated with exhaled nitric oxide in children with asthma. Am J Respir Crit Care Med. 2011;184(2):191–7.
51. Sordillo JE, Lange NE, Tarantini L, Bollati V, Zanobetti A, Sparrow D, et al. Global DNA methylation, BMI, wheeze, and allergic sensitization in older men. Am J Respir Crit Care Med. 2011;183:A5679.
52. Troisi RJ, Speizer FE, Willett WC, Trichopoulos D, Rosner B. Menopause, postmenopausal estrogen preparations, and the risk of adult-onset asthma. A prospective cohort study. Am J Respir Crit Care Med. 1995;152(4 Pt 1):1183–8.
53. Hamano N, Terada N, Maesako K, Numata T, Konno A. Effect of sex hormones on eosinophilic inflammation in nasal mucosa. Allergy Asthma Proc. 1998;19(5):263–9.
54. Peters-Golden M, Swern A, Bird SS, Hustad CM, Grant E, Edelman JM. Influence of body mass index on the response to asthma controller agents. Eur Respir J. 2006;27(3):495–503.
55. Sousa AR, Lane SJ, Cidlowski JA, Staynov DZ, Lee TH. Glucocorticoid resistance in asthma is associated with elevated in vivo expression of the glucocorticoid receptor beta-isoform. J Allergy Clin Immunol. 2000;105(5):943–50.
56. Webster JC, Oakley RH, Jewell CM, Cidlowski JA. Proinflammatory cytokines regulate human glucocorticoid receptor gene expression and lead to the accumulation of the dominant negative beta isoform: a mechanism for the generation of glucocorticoid resistance. Proc Natl Acad Sci USA. 2001;98(12):6865–70.
57. Eneli IU, Skybo T, Camargo Jr CA. Weight loss and asthma: a systematic review. Thorax. 2008;63(8):671–6.
58. Beck LA, Leung DYM. Allergen sensitization through the skin induces systemic allergic responses. J Allergy Clin Immunol. 2000;106(5, Part 2):258–63.
59. Kalliomaki M, Kirjavainen P, Eerola E, Kero P, Salminen S, Isolauri E. Distinct patterns of neonatal gut microflora in infants in whom atopy was and was not developing. J Allergy Clin Immunol. 2001;107(1):129–34.
60. Bottcher MF, Nordin EK, Sandin A, Midtvedt T, Bjorksten B. Microflora-associated characteristics in faeces from allergic and nonallergic infants. Clin Exp Allergy. 2000;30(11):1590–6.
61. Bjorksten B, Naaber P, Sepp E, Mikelsaar M. The intestinal microflora in allergic Estonian and Swedish 2-year-old children. Clin Exp Allergy. 1999;29(3):342–6.
62. Sepp E, Julge K, Vasar M, Naaber P, Bjorksten B, Mikelsaar M. Intestinal microflora of Estonian and Swedish infants. Acta Paediatr. 1997;86(9):956–61.
63. Gronlund MM, Lehtonen OP, Eerola E, Kero P. Fecal microflora in healthy infants born by different methods of delivery: permanent changes in intestinal flora after cesarean delivery. J Pediatr Gastroenterol Nutr. 1999;28(1):19–25.
64. Weiner HL. Current issues in the treatment of human diseases by mucosal tolerance. Ann N Y Acad Sci. 2004;1029:211–24.
65. Umetsu DT, Akbari O, Dekruyff RH. Regulatory T cells control the development of allergic disease and asthma. J Allergy Clin Immunol. 2003;112(3):480–7.
66. Strauch UG, Obermeier F, Grunwald N, Guerster S, Dunger N, Schultz M, et al. Influence of intestinal bacteria on induction of regulatory T-cells: lessons from a transfer model of colitis. Gut. 2005;54(11):1546–52. Epub 2005 Jun 29.
67. Cooper PJ, Chico ME, Rodrigues LC, Strachan DP, Anderson HR, Rodriguez EA, et al. Risk factors for atopy among school children in a rural area of Latin America. Clin Exp Allergy. 2004;34(6):845–52.
68. Robinson DS, Larche M, Durham SR. Tregs and allergic disease. J Clin Invest. 2004;114(10):1389–97.
69. Guarner F, Malagelada JR. Gut flora in health and disease. Lancet. 2003;361(9356):512–9.
70. Sudo N, Sawamura S, Tanaka K, Aiba Y, Kubo C, Koga Y. The requirement of intestinal bacterial flora for the development of an IgE production system fully susceptible to oral tolerance induction. J Immunol. 1997;159(4):1739–45.
71. Moreau MC, Corthier G. Effect of the gastrointestinal microflora on induction and maintenance of oral tolerance to ovalbumin in C3H/HeJ mice. Infect Immun. 1988;56(10):2766–8.

72. Moreau MC, Gaboriau-Routhiau V. The absence of gut flora, the doses of antigen ingested and aging affect the long-term peripheral tolerance induced by ovalbumin feeding in mice. Respir Immunol. 1996;147:49–59.
73. Rask C, Evertsson S, Telemo E, Wold AE. A full flora, but not monocolonization by Escherichia coli or lactobacilli, supports tolerogenic processing of a fed antigen. Scand J Immunol. 2005; 61(6):529–35.
74. Mah KW, Bjorksten B, Lee BW, van Bever HP, Shek LP, Tan TN, et al. Distinct pattern of commensal gut microbiota in toddlers with eczema. Int Arch Allergy Immunol. 2006;140(2): 157–63.
75. Romagnani S. Immunologic influences on allergy and the TH1/TH2 balance. J Allergy Clin Immunol. 2004;113(3):395–400.
76. Dransfield MT, Garver RI, Weill D. Standardized guidelines for surveillance bronchoscopy reduce complications in lung transplant recipients. J Heart Lung Transplant. 2004;23(1): 110–4.
77. Janson C, Asbjornsdottir H, Birgisdottir A, Sigurjonsdottir RB, Gunnbjornsdottir M, Gislason D, et al. The effect of infectious burden on the prevalence of atopy and respiratory allergies in Iceland, Estonia, and Sweden. J Allergy Clin Immunol. 2007;120(3):673–9.
78. Benden C, Ranasinghe AS, Harpur-Sinclair O, Aurora P. 20: the role of surveillance bronchoscopy in pediatric lung transplant recipients. J Heart Lung Transpl. 2006;25((2, Suppl 1)): 50–1.
79. Kalliomaki M, Salminen S, Poussa T, Arvilommi H, Isolauri E. Probiotics and prevention of atopic disease: 4-year follow-up of a randomised placebo-controlled trial. Lancet. 2003; 361(9372):1869–71.
80. Li Y, Saxena D, Barnes VM, Trivedi HM, Ge Y, Xu T. Polymerase chain reaction-based denaturing gradient gel electrophoresis in the evaluation of oral microbiota. Oral Microbiol Immunol. 2006;21(5):333–9.
81. Fujimoto C, Maeda H, Kokeguchi S, Takashiba S, Nishimura F, Arai H, et al. Application of denaturing gradient gel electrophoresis (DGGE) to the analysis of microbial communities of subgingival plaque. J Periodontal Res. 2003;38(4):440–5.
82. Osman M, Hansell AL, Simpson CR, Hollowell J, Helms PJ. Gender-specific presentations for asthma, allergic rhinitis and eczema in primary care. Prim Care Respir J. 2007;16(2): 28–35.
83. Ramsey CD, Celedón JC. The hygiene hypothesis and asthma. Curr Opin Pulm Med. 2005;11(1):14–20.
84. Thomsen SF, Ulrik CS, Kyvik KO, JvB H, Skadhauge LR, Steffensen I, et al. Importance of genetic factors in the etiology of atopic dermatitis: a twin study. Allergy Asthma Proc. 2007;28:535–9.
85. Mannino DM, Homa DM, Akinbami LJ, Moorman JE, Gwynn C, Redd SC. Surveillance for asthma – United States, 1980–1999. Morb Mortal Wkly Rep Surveill Summ. 2002;51(1):1–13.
86. Coca AF, Cooke RA. On the classification of the phenomena of hypersensitiveness. J Immunol. 1922;8:163–82.
87. Penders J, Thijs C, van den Brandt PA, Kummeling I, Snijders B, Stelma F, et al. Gut microbiota composition and development of atopic manifestations in infancy: the KOALA birth cohort study. Gut. 2007;56(5):661–7.
88. Bjorksten B. The intrauterine and postnatal environments. J Allergy Clin Immunol. 1999; 104(6):1119–27.
89. CDC. Asthma – United States, 1982–1992. MMWR. 1995;43:952–5.
90. Harris JM, Williams HC, White C, Moffat S, Mills P, Newman Taylor AJ, et al. Early allergen exposure and atopic eczema. Br J Dermatol. 2007;156(4):698–704.
91. Schabereiter-Gurtner C, Maca S, Rolleke S, Nigl K, Lukas J, Hirschl A, et al. 16S rDNA-based identification of bacteria from conjunctival swabs by PCR and DGGE fingerprinting. Invest Ophthalmol Vis Sci. 2001;42(6):1164–71.
92. Kalliomaki M, Salminen S, Arvilommi H, Kero P, Koskinen P, Isolauri E. Probiotics in primary prevention of atopic disease: a randomised placebo-controlled trial. Lancet. 2001; 357(9262):1076–9.

93. Pearce N, Pekkanen J, Beasley R. How much asthma is really attributable to atopy. Thorax. 1999;54(3):268–72.
94. Sheffer A. In: A global initiative for asthma. NHLBI/WHO workshop report: National heart, lung, and blood institute publication #96–3659A; Bethesda; 1995.
95. Ninan TK, Russell G. Respiratory symptoms and atopy in Aberdeen schoolchildren: evidence from two surveys 25 years apart. BMJ. 1992;304:873–5.
96. Robertson CF, Heycock E, Bishop J, Nolan T, Olinsky A, Phelan PD. Prevalence of asthma in Melbourne schoolchildren: changes over 26 years. BMJ. 1991;302(6785):1116–8.
97. Eckburg PB, Bik EM, Bernstein CN, Purdom E, Dethlefsen L, Sargent M, et al. Diversity of the human intestinal microbial flora. Science. 2005;308(5728):1635–8.
98. Miyake Y, Ohya Y, Tanaka K, Yokoyama T, Sasaki S, Fukushima W, et al. Home environment and suspected atopic eczema in Japanese infants: the Osaka maternal and child health study. Pediatr Allergy Immunol. 2007;18(5):425–32.
99. Weston S, Halbert AR, Richmond P, Prescott SL. Effects of probiotics on atopic dermatitis: a randomised controlled trial. Arch Dis Child. 2005;90(9):892–7. Epub 2005 Apr 29.
100. Peat JK, Haby M, Spijker J, Berry G, Woolcock AJ. Prevalence of asthma in adults in Busselton, Western Australia. BMJ. 1992;305(6865):1326–9.
101. Hopper JL, Jenkins MA, Carlin JB, Giles GG. Increase in the self-reported prevalence of asthma and hay fever in adults over the last generation: a matched parent-offspring study. Aust J Public Health. 1995;19(2):120–4.
102. Gillespie KM, Bain SC, Barnett AH, Bingley PJ, Christie MR, Gill GV, et al. The rising incidence of childhood type 1 diabetes and reduced contribution of high-risk HLA haplotypes. Lancet. 2004;364(9446):1645–7.
103. Strachan DP. Family size, infection and atopy: the first decade of the "hygiene hypothesis". Thorax. 2000;55 Suppl 1:S2–10.
104. Wegmann TG, Lin H, Guilbert L, Mosmann TR. Bidirectional cytokine interactions in the maternal-fetal relationship: Is successful pregnancy a TH2 phenomenon? Immunol Today. 1993;14(7):353–6.
105. Prescott SL, Macaubas C, Holt BJ, Smallacombe TB, Loh R, Sly PD, et al. Transplacental priming of the human immune system to environmental allergens: universal skewing of initial T cell responses toward the Th2 cytokine profile. J Immunol. 1998;160(10):4730–7.
106. Lotz M, Gutle D, Walther S, Menard S, Bogdan C, Hornef MW. Postnatal acquisition of endotoxin tolerance in intestinal epithelial cells. J Exp Med. 2006;203(4):973–84.
107. Romagnani S. The increased prevalence of allergy and the hygiene hypothesis: missing immune deviation, reduced immune suppression, or both? Immunology. 2004;112(3):352–63.
108. Cooper PJ, Chico ME, Rodrigues LC, Ordonez M, Strachan D, Griffin GE, et al. Reduced risk of atopy among school-age children infected with geohelminth parasites in a rural area of the tropics. J Allergy Clin Immunol. 2003;111(5):995–1000.
109. Mohrenschlager M, Schafer T, Huss-Marp J, Eberlein-Konig B, Weidinger S, Ring J, et al. The course of eczema in children aged 5–7 years and its relation to atopy: differences between boys and girls. Br J Dermatol. 2006;154(3):505–13.
110. Asher MI, Montefort S, Bjorksten B, Lai CK, Strachan DP, Weiland SK, et al. Worldwide time trends in the prevalence of symptoms of asthma, allergic rhinoconjunctivitis, and eczema in childhood: ISAAC phases one and three repeat multicountry cross-sectional surveys. Lancet. 2006;368(9537):733–43.
111. Pearce N, Ait-Khaled N, Beasley R, Mallol J, Keil U, Mitchell E, et al. Worldwide trends in the prevalence of asthma symptoms: phase III of the international study of asthma and allergies in childhood (ISAAC). Thorax. 2007;62(9):757–65.
112. Tantisira KG, Weiss ST. Complex interactions in complex traits: obesity and asthma. Thorax. 2001;56 Suppl 2:ii64–73.
113. Sporik R, Platts-Mills TA. Allergen exposure and the development of asthma. Thorax. 2001;56 Suppl 2:ii58–63.
114. Diaz-Sanchez D, Proietti L, Polosa R. Diesel fumes and the rising prevalence of atopy: An urban legend? Curr Allergy Asthma Rep. 2003;3(2):146–52.

115. Ball TM, Castro-Rodriguez JA, Griffith KA, Holberg CJ, Martinez FD, Wright AL. Siblings, day-care attendance, and the risk of asthma and wheezing during childhood. N Engl J Med. 2000;343(8):538–43.
116. McKeever TM, Britton J. Pulmonary perspective: diet and asthma. Am J Respir Crit Care Med. 2004;15(170):725–9.
117. Karmaus W, Botezan C. Does a higher number of siblings protect against the development of allergy and asthma? A review. J Epidemiol Community Health. 2002;56(3):209–17.
118. Celedón JC, Wright RJ, Litonjua AA, Sredl D, Ryan L, Weiss ST, et al. Day care attendance in early life, maternal history of asthma, and asthma at age 6 years. Am J Respir Crit Care Med. 2003;167(9):1239–43.
119. McKeever TM, Lewis SA, Smith C, Hubbard R. Vaccination and allergic disease: a birth cohort study. Am J Public Health. 2004;94(6):985–9.
120. Matricardi PM, Yazdanbakhsh M. Mycobacteria and atopy, 6 years later: a fascinating, still unfinished, business. Clin Exp Allergy. 2003;33(6):717–20.
121. Maitra A, Sherriff A, Griffiths M, Henderson J. Pertussis vaccination in infancy and asthma or allergy in later childhood: birth cohort study. BMJ. 2004;328(7445):925–6.
122. Krause TG, Hviid A, Koch A, Friborg J, Hjuler T, Wohlfahrt J, et al. BCG vaccination and risk of atopy. JAMA. 2003;289(8):1012–5.
123. Bager P, Rostgaard K, Nielsen NM, Melbye M, Westergaard T. Age at bacille calmette-guerin vaccination and risk of allergy and asthma. Clin Exp Allergy. 2003;33(11):1512–7.
124. Ota MO, van der Sande MA, Walraven GE, Jeffries D, Nyan OA, Marchant A, et al. Absence of association between delayed type hypersensitivity to tuberculin and atopy in children in the Gambia. Clin Exp Allergy. 2003;33(6):731–6.
125. Illi S, von Mutius E, Lau S, Bergmann R, Niggemann B, Sommerfeld C, et al. Early childhood infectious diseases and the development of asthma up to school age: a birth cohort study. BMJ. 2001;322(7283):390–5.
126. Matricardi PM, Rosmini F, Riondino S, Fortini M, Ferrigno L, Rapicetta M, et al. Exposure to foodborne and orofecal microbes versus airborne viruses in relation to atopy and allergic asthma: epidemiological study. BMJ. 2000;320(7232):412–7.
127. Matricardi PM, Rosmini F, Panetta V, Ferrigno L, Bonini S. Hay fever and asthma in relation to markers of infection in the United States. J Allergy Clin Immunol. 2002;110(3):381–7.
128. Ponsonby AL, Couper D, Dwyer T, Carmichael A, Kemp A. Relationship between early life respiratory illness, family size over time, and the development of asthma and hay fever: a seven year follow up study [in process citation]. Thorax. 1999;54(8):664–9.
129. Cullinan P, Harris JM, Newman Taylor AJ, Jones M, Taylor P, Dave JR, et al. Can early infection explain the sibling effect in adult atopy? Eur Respir J. 2003;22(6):956–61.
130. Uter W, Stock C, Pfahlberg A, Guillen-Grima F, Aguinaga-Ontoso I, Brun-Sandiumenge C, et al. Association between infections and signs and symptoms of 'atopic' hypersensitivity–results of a cross-sectional survey among first-year university students in Germany and Spain. Allergy. 2003;58(7):580–4.
131. Yunginger JW, Reed CE, O'Connell EJ, Melton 3rd LJ, O'Fallon WM, Silverstein MD. A community-based study of the epidemiology of asthma, incidence rates, 1964–1983. Am Rev Respir Dis. 1992;146(4):888–94.
132. Vargas PA, Simpson PM, Gary Wheeler J, Goel R, Feild CR, Tilford JM, et al. Characteristics of children with asthma who are enrolled in a head start program. J Allergy Clin Immunol. 2004;114(3):499–504.
133. Linneberg A, Ostergaard C, Tvede M, Andersen LP, Nielsen NH, Madsen F, et al. IgG antibodies against microorganisms and atopic disease in Danish adults: the Copenhagen allergy study. J Allergy Clin Immunol. 2003;111(4):847–53.
134. Lara M, Rosenbaum S, Rachelefsky G, Nicholas W, Morton SC, Emont S, et al. Improving childhood asthma outcomes in the United States: a blueprint for policy action. Pediatrics. 2002;109(5):919–30.
135. Morgan WJ, Crain EF, Gruchalla RS, O'Connor GT, Kattan M, Evans 3rd R, et al. Results of a home-based environmental intervention among urban children with asthma. N Engl J Med. 2004;351(11):1068–80.

136. Burrows B, Martinez FD, Halonen M, Barbee RA, Cline MG. Association of asthma with serum IgE levels and skin-test reactivity to allergens. N Engl J Med. 1989;320(5):271–7.
137. Sunyer J, Anto JM, Tobias A, Burney P. Generational increase of self-reported first attack of asthma in fifteen industrialized countries. European Community Respiratory Health Study (ECRHS). Eur Respir J. 1999;14(4):885–91.
138. Schernhammer ES, Vutuc C, Waldhor T, Haidinger G. Time trends of the prevalence of asthma and allergic disease in Austrian children. Pediatr Allergy Immunol. 2007;19(2):125–31.
139. Ramsey CD, Gold DR, Litonjua AA, Sredl DL, Ryan L, Celedón JC. Respiratory illnesses in early life and asthma and atopy in childhood. J Allergy Clin Immunol. 2007;119(1):150–6.
140. Braun-Fahrlander C, Gassner M, Grize L, Takken-Sahli K, Neu U, Stricker T, et al. No further increase in asthma, hay fever and atopic sensitisation in adolescents living in Switzerland. Eur Respir J. 2004;23(3):407–13.
141. Beasley R, Crane J, Lai CK, Pearce N. Prevalence and etiology of asthma. J Allergy Clin Immunol. 2000;105(2 Pt 2):S466–72.

Chapter 9
The Relationship Between Components of the Metabolic Syndrome and Bone Health

Zeina M. Nabhan and Linda A. DiMeglio

Abstract Childhood obesity has become a global epidemic in the past decade. It is now estimated that more than 17% of the US children and adolescents are obese. The effects of childhood obesity on overall health are multiple and involve various organ systems including the musculoskeletal system. Increased fat mass is associated with increased bone mineral density in adults; however, studies regarding obesity's effects on bone mass in children have been conflicting. Some pediatric studies have demonstrated increased bone mass in overweight children compared to healthy weight peers, while others have shown that overweight youth have decreased bone mass relative to bone size and body weight and thus are at increased risk for fracture. Childhood obesity is associated with high fracture rates due to a combination of biologic and biomechanical factors. Childhood obesity has also been linked to multiple orthopedic complications. Reports indicate increased prevalence of musculoskeletal pain, lower extremity malalignment, slipped capital femoral epiphysis, genu valgum, Blount's disease, and foot structure abnormalities in obese children compared to normal-weight counterparts. Increased physical activity is a cornerstone for treatment of childhood obesity; however, obese children often lead a more sedentary lifestyle than normal-weight peers, which in part results from musculoskeletal pain in the back, knees, and feet. In conclusion, while the full impact of obesity on the overall function and development of the growing child has not been studied completely, it is well established that obesity adversely affects the musculoskeletal system. More research is needed to better understand the full impact of obesity on bone accrual, fracture rates, and physical function in children.

Keywords Musculoskeletal pain • Slipped capital femoral epiphysis • Blount's disease • Fracture • Childhood obesity

Z.M. Nabhan, M.D., M.S. • L.A. DiMeglio, M.D., MPH (✉)
Section of Pediatric Endocrinology and Diabetology, Department of Pediatrics,
Riley Hospital for Children, Indiana University School of Medicine,
705 Riley Hospital Drive, Rm 5960, Indianapolis, IN 46202, USA
e-mail: dimeglio@iupui.edu

Introduction

Obesity is a global epidemic. One in 10 children worldwide is overweight (BMI>85%), and up to 30–45 million are obese (BMI>95%) [1]. In the USA, the prevalence of childhood obesity has more than doubled since 1980. It is estimated that overall 17% of US children and adolescents are clinically obese [2]. Childhood obesity affects multiple organ systems including the musculoskeletal system. Obesity has been linked to an increased risk of fracture in children. It also has been reported to result in multiple orthopedic problems such as musculoskeletal discomfort, impaired mobility, and joint malalignment. This chapter provides a detailed review of the recent literature regarding the effects of childhood obesity on aspects of bone health.

Fat and Bone in Children

Bone Physiology

Bone is a dynamic organ. A careful balance between the activity of osteoblasts (which build bone) and osteoclasts (which resorb bone) results in bone which is matched in structure and strength to the necessary physiologic demands on the skeleton. A third cell type found in bone is the osteocyte. Osteocytes are derived from osteoblasts and are also involved with bone remodeling and may play a role in the sensing of mechanical stimuli.

As children grow, they increase body weight, gain lean body mass, and increase muscle strength. Skeletal strength increases primarily as an adaptation to the strains of applied mechanical loads [3] and is optimized to resist mechanical failure under normal physiologic loading. Nearly 80% of bone strength is determined by the amount of bone [4]. Bone mass is both highly heritable and related to the amount of muscle mass. Total body bone mineral content is more strongly associated with lean mass than with either total mass or fat mass [5]. Osteocytes and osteoblasts are mechanoresponsive cells, adapting in vivo to changes in strain as well as strain-generated changes in surrounding fluid. Continued mechanical strains are important for bone accrual during childhood. Matching of bone capacity to the perceived mechanical needs continues in adulthood.

The most commonly used quantitative assessment of the amount of bone is bone mineral density (BMD), usually assessed by dual x-ray absorptiometry (DXA). DXA uses two different photon absorption energies to calculate projected amounts of bone mineral, soft tissue, and fat. DXA provides measurements of BMD and body composition at multiple sites, including total body (often assessed with subtraction of the head), lumbar spine, and proximal femur. DXA assessments generate standard deviation scores. In children, these should be analyzed and reported as Z-scores (standardized comparisons to age- and sex-matched populations).

Decreases in bone mineralization may result in osteoporosis. The World Health Organization has defined osteoporosis as a "systemic skeletal disease characterized by low bone mass and microarchitectural deterioration of bone tissue, with a consequent increase in bone fragility and susceptibility to fracture" [6]. In adults, osteoporosis is defined by T-score comparisons to young adult normative data. T-score reports are not useful in children. The diagnosis of osteoporosis in children instead requires both a low Z-score and a significant fracture history [7]. Osteoporosis can also be accompanied by defective mineralization of newly formed osteoid, a condition known as osteomalacia. Both osteoporosis and osteomalacia lower BMD.

Relationship Between Fat Mass and Bone Density

Body fat is positively correlated with increased bone mineral density (BMD) in both men and women throughout life [8]. Prepubertal children with more fat mass accrue more bone mass, although this effect may be attenuated or even reversed in adolescents [9, 10]. Conversely lower amounts of body fat are associated with lower BMDs. There are a variety of mechanisms proposed to explain the positive relationship between fat and bone including increased mechanical load from high body weight triggering the skeletal mechanostat and increasing bone formation [11], adipokine effects, and influences of other hormonal mediators such as beta cell hormones and gut hormones.

Adipose-Derived Hormones and Bones

Adipose tissue exerts important influences on the maintenance and development of bone. Some of this is mediated through mechanical loading of bone, and some is mediated through the adipose-derived hormones. The most studied adipose-derived hormone with effects on bone is leptin. Its predominant action appears to be anti-osteogenic. Leptin is the product of the *Lep* gene and the ligand for the leptin receptor coded for by *Lepr*. It is secreted by white adipose tissue in proportion to the total body adipocyte mass. Leptin's primary function seems to be to inhibit appetite at the level of the hypothalamus. Leptin also has complex effects on bone. It has hypothalamically mediated anti-osteogenic effects and yet can also promote osteogenesis via direct effects on osteoblasts and osteoclasts [12].

The centrally mediated anti-osteogenic effects of leptin are orchestrated by the sympathetic nervous system, in particular by leptin's effects on serotonin. Serotonin works centrally to stimulate bone mass accrual by binding to HTR2C receptors on neurons in the ventromedial hypothalamus. Serotonin then travels to the hypothalamus. Efferent outputs from hypothalamic sympathetic nerves target β_2 adrenergic receptors on osteoblasts and regulate their proliferation and differentiation [13]. These targeted osteoblasts increase RANK-ligand (RANK-L) expression. RANK-L signals through the receptor activator of NF-κB (RANK) receptor on monocytic osteoclast precursors and stimulates them to fuse, forming new osteoclasts and enhancing bone resorption. Leptin also works at the level of the brainstem to decrease serotonin synthesis. Both leptin-deficient *ob/ob* mice (which have inactivating *Lep* mutations) and *db/db* mice which have inactivating *Lepr* mutations have obesity and sterility. The hypogonadism and high serum cortisol levels seen in these mutant mice should adversely affect bone mass, yet both strains of mice have massively increased bone mass. The high bone mass is not simply due to obesity, as it is present in young, lean *ob/ob* mice and in *ob/ob* who are kept on low fat diets and do not become massively obese.

Under physiologic conditions, the effect of leptin is most likely osteogenic and mediated through direct effects of leptin on bone cells. Systemic leptin administration in intact, ovarectomized, and *ob/ob* mice has been shown to have a variety of osteogenic effects, including increased bone formation and decreased skeletal fragility. Leptin decreases bone resorption through modulation of the cocaine- and amphetamine-related transcript (CART) pathway [14]. CART is a neuropeptide precursor protein involved in regulation of food intake and energy expenditure. CART knockout mice have high bone resorption due to higher levels of RANK-L and subsequent osteoporosis. High leptin decreases CART expression. Leptin also directly signals through a leptin receptor on osteoblasts, promoting osteoblast proliferation and differentiation and inhibiting osteoclastogenesis by increasing OPG expression and reducing RANK expression [12, 15].

Adiponectin, like leptin, is produced by adipocytes. It is also produced at low levels by osteoblasts [16]. Osteoblasts have adiponectin receptors, suggesting that adiponectin has paracrine and/or endocrine actions in bone. Adiponectin is structurally similar to tumor necrosis factor alpha (TNFα) family members, including RANK-L and osteoprotegerin. Unlike leptin, plasma adiponectin levels are inversely related to visceral fat mass and BMI, and therefore low in obese individuals. Recent in vitro data suggest that adiponectin has a role in the regulation of bone mass. Like leptin, adiponectin has complex osteogenic and anti-osteogenic actions, although it seems that physiologically it functions primarily as an anti-osteogenic hormone. Studies are conflicting, with some reporting that adiponectin has osteogenic effects including stimulating growth of osteoblastic cells [16] and inhibiting in vitro osteoclastogenesis [17]. However, in other studies, adiponectin reduced osteoblast growth [18]. RANK-L and osteoprotegerin are important for osteoclastogenesis. Since it is structurally similar to TNFα, adiponectin may regulate induced nuclear transcription factor (NF)-κB activation. Adiponectin's role may be more limited than that of leptin since transgenic mice that overexpress or are deficient in adiponectin do not have a bone phenotype at 8 weeks of age [18], but by 14 weeks, adiponectin-deficient mice have high bone mass [19]. There is evidence that adiponectin may affect bone mass in humans, as higher adiponectin levels are associated with lower bone mass in children due to decreases in cortical thickness of bone [20].

Resistin is also adipocyte-derived. It is named "resistin" because mice injected with resistin became insulin resistant; however, its primary biological function is unknown. Serum resistin levels increase with obesity. Resistin is expressed in mesenchymal bone marrow stem cells, osteoblasts, and osteoclasts [21]. It appears to stimulate osteoblast proliferation and osteoclast differentiation. Higher resistin levels may result in higher bone turnover. An inverse correlation has been seen in adult men between human serum resistin levels and lumbar spine BMD [22].

Adipose tissue also produces estrogens by aromatization of androgens to estrogens. Obese individuals have more adipose tissue and therefore have higher rates of aromatization of androgen to estrogen. However, estrogen is not felt to be a major pathway by which fat mass influences BMD [23]. Adipose-bone "crosstalk" is not limited to fat-derived hormones. Recent data suggest roles of a variety of neuropeptide systems, including neuromedin U (which appears to work downstream of leptin to regulate bone formation) and neuropeptide Y.

Beta Cell Hormones and Bones

Beta cells produce insulin, which has a wide variety of physiologic effects, including controlling blood glucose levels by increasing glycogen synthesis. Increased insulin secretion in association with insulin resistance is a characteristic finding in obese children and adults. Despite its negative metabolic effects, hyperinsulinemia has both direct and indirect positive effects on bone mass [24]. Insulin directly stimulates osteoblast growth [25, 26]. Insulin also indirectly increases bone mass in several ways. Hyperinsulinemia is associated with increased levels of circulating free fatty acids which are known to directly inhibit osteoclastogenesis [27]. Hyperinsulinemia also results in increased circulating levels of free androgens and estrogens due to inhibition of sex hormone-binding globulin production in the liver. Higher levels of free circulating sex hormones directly augment bone formation as seen in women with polycystic ovarian syndrome [28].

While clinical studies in children regarding the effects of insulin per se on bone mass are lacking, several studies in men and postmenopausal women have shown that the positive effects of insulin resistance on bone mass are partly independent of adiposity. In a study of 96 men, Abrahamsen et al. [29] showed that insulin sensitivity as measured by intravenous glucose tolerance test was inversely related to bone density independent of BMI. In addition, this study showed that the dependence of bone density on fat mass was lost when insulin sensitivity was entered into a multiple regression analysis, suggesting that this relationship was mediated by insulin sensitivity. The San Antonio Heart Study showed comparable findings in women [30]. More recently, insulin resistance has been associated with a nearly 50% decrease in fracture risk in adults with the greatest insulin resistance [31].

Beta cells also produce amylin, which is cosecreted with insulin and works synergistically with insulin to inhibit the rate of appearance of ingested nutrients in plasma. Amylin also has anabolic effects on bone. It not only directly stimulates osteoblast growth [32] but exhibits calcitonin-like effects, resulting in decreased osteoclastic bone resorption [33].

Gut Hormones and Bones

Several gut peptides have been shown to have an impact on bone metabolism including gastric inhibitory peptide (GIP), glucagon-like peptide (GLP-1), and ghrelin. GIP is a 42-amino acid protein secreted by the K-cells of the duodenum. It induces secretion of insulin and glucagon from the pancreas and has been shown to stimulate osteoblast proliferation [34]. GIP acts directly on bone; its receptor is expressed on chondrocytes, osteoblasts, osteocytes, and osteoclasts [34]. Transgenic mice that overexpress GIP demonstrate increased bone formation, decreased bone resorption, and increased bone mass [35], whereas mice lacking the GIP receptor have increased numbers of mature osteoclasts and reduced bone mass [36].

GLP-1 and 2 are hormones expressed by the intestinal L-cells. Their main function is to increase insulin secretion postmeals. While GLP-1 has no direct effect on osteoblasts and osteoclasts, GLP-2 is expressed on osteoclasts and has been shown in clinical studies to result in decreased bone resorption as measured by a reduction in circulating bone turnover markers [37, 38].

Ghrelin is a 28-amino acid peptide secreted by the A-like cells of the stomach in response to fasting. It is an orexigenic hormone and thus acts as an appetite stimulant. Ghrelin receptors are expressed on osteoblasts [39]; however, clinical studies regarding its effects on BMD have been contradictory. In a study of 21 healthy adolescent girls, ghrelin secretion strongly correlated with BMD irrespective of body composition [40]; however, no consistent relationship has been seen between ghrelin levels and BMD in older men and women [41].

Musculoskeletal Effects of Obesity and Metabolic Syndrome

Although childhood obesity is an established risk factor for various metabolic abnormalities such as insulin resistance, type 2 diabetes, hypertension, and dyslipidemia, studies regarding its effects on the growing skeleton have been very inconsistent. In adults, most data support a positive relationship between fat mass and bone mass [42, 43]. However, some pediatric studies have demonstrated increased bone mass in overweight children compared to healthy weight peers [44, 45], while others have shown that overweight youth have decreased bone mass relative to bone size and body weight and thus are at increased risk for skeletal fractures [46, 47]. One explanation for this inconsistency is that the majority of these pediatric studies did not investigate the effects of the various components of the metabolic syndrome on bone development. Afghani et al. [48] were the first to show a trend between impaired glucose tolerance and lower total body bone mineral content (BMC) in a cohort of 184 overweight Latino adolescents. In this study, an inverse relationship between BMC and fasting and 2-h insulin levels was also noted. In a more recent study of 140 prepubertal overweight children [47], Pollock et al. showed that total body BMC was 4% lower in overweight children with prediabetes than in those without prediabetes, suggesting that abnormal glucose regulation may have negative effects on the growing skeleton. Moreover, Pollock and colleagues were able to show that both total and central adiposity have significant but opposing relationships with bone mass. While total body fat mass has a positive association with total body bone mass, central adiposity measures such visceral and subcutaneous abdominal adipose tissue have a negative association with bone mass and bone structure [31, 47, 48]. To date, no associations have been found between bone mass and total cholesterol, HDL, LDL, and triglycerides in overweight children; however, 2-h insulin, insulin area under the curve (AUC), and CRP are reported to be inversely related to total body BMC in children with prediabetes [48].

Obesity and Fracture Risk

Childhood fractures are quite common, with approximately 50% of boys and 40% of girls having at least one fracture by the age of 18 [49]. Two-thirds of all fractures during growth are sustained by children who have more than one fracture during childhood, suggesting that some children have a greater predisposition to fracture than others. Distal forearm fractures are the most common site of fracture during childhood (~30% of all fractures). Fractures in children are associated with a variety of risk factors, including family history of fracture, low bone mineral density for age and sex, smaller bone size than peers, poor calcium intake, and both low and high BMI.

Although the data are at times conflicting, most data suggest that obesity is associated with a higher risk of fracture in childhood. Overweight or obese children are more likely to sustain forearm fracture [50, 51] and recurrent fracture [52] than normal-weight peers. The majority of these fractures may be in persons with normal BMD. Adult data also demonstrate that obese and morbidly obese persons are likely to sustain low-trauma fractures even with normal hip BMD assessed by DXA [53].

At first, the positive association between BMI and fracture risk in obese children may seem paradoxical, since low-weight individuals are also known to be at high risk of fracture and the higher BMD for age and sex seen in most overweight individuals is typically regarded as protective for fracture [11, 54]. It appears, however, that the increased risk of fracture is mediated by biomechanical, behavioral, and biologic factors. Overweight children's bones must support a higher force at impact relative to bone strength in the event of a fall, since they have a higher ratio of body weight to bone mass and bone area [55]. The force exerted when they fall, therefore, may exceed the relative protection afforded by the higher BMD induced by the obesity [54, 56]. Obese children also have region-specific deficits in muscle mass relative to fat mass. They also have lower bone mass with narrower bones than expected for weight. Body size-adjusted bone mass appears to be particularly compromised in obese children with prior fractures [57]. In a study of 52 obese children with a history of fracture compared to nonobese controls without a history of fracture, the obese children had less bone mineral relative to lean mass and had a

0.8–1.2 SD decrease in total body BMD and a 2.0–3.0 SD decrease in volumetric L2-L4 BMAD. In this sample, 18% of the obese children met the International Society of Clinical Densitometry criteria for pediatric osteoporosis [7, 57].

Physical activity mechanically stresses bone with impacts and increases lean body mass. Physical activity patterns during adolescence account for as much as 22% of the variability of adult BMD [58]. Elite athletes who engage in intensive, weight-bearing activities during childhood have significantly greater volumetric BMD than normal controls. Short-term, controlled activity intervention trials also demonstrate gains in bone mineral accrual rates if the activity is intense in nature [59]. Yet physical activity may put obese children at higher risk for fracture, since they may have poorer balance and lower competence for sports. Overweight male adolescents have been shown to have poorer balance than normal-weight adolescents [60]. This raises their risk for fracture both by increasing their risk for falling as well as by limiting their ability to stop once they start to fall. Overweight children also have lower perceived and actual competence in physical activities [61], likely leading to them having less time engaged in weight-bearing exercise that is essential for building bone mass. It is not known either what the best forms of exercise for osteogenesis may be or if the demonstrated increases in BMC/BMD translate into increases in bone strength or are maintained after the training regimen attenuates. There are no data on the best exercises for bone health in obese children.

Obesity and Orthopedic Complications

The impact of obesity on the growing musculoskeletal system is still not completely understood; however, recent data suggest that obesity affects the child's locomotor system both functionally and structurally and can lead to significant impairment in the overall function of the child. In the first published cohort to examine the musculoskeletal consequences of obesity, Taylor et al. [62] found increased prevalence of musculoskeletal pain and impairment in mobility in an overweight group compared to normal-weight counterparts. In addition, the overweight cohort had greater prevalence of abnormal lower extremity alignment. Others have shown that the detrimental effect of pediatric obesity on the lower extremity is not only limited to malalignment but also negative effects on the function of hips, knees, and feet [63, 64].

At the hip, obesity creates an increased load on the cartilaginous growth plate of the femoral head that increases the duration and the magnitude of both shear and compressive forces on the growth plate [65, 66]. This increase in mechanical shear forces in addition to the increased body weight can result in slipped capital femoral epiphysis (SCFE). SCFE is a debilitating condition caused by nontraumatic displacement of the proximal femoral epiphysis from the metaphysis. SCFE usually occurs during the adolescent growth spurt and is often seen between 12 and 15 years of age. However, the age of SCFE diagnosis has been shown to decrease with increasing obesity [67], making this condition a significant health risk for overweight children [68]. In a series of 1,337 children assessed for SCFE, 51.5% had a body weight greater than the 90th percentile and 11.7% had a body weight greater than the 95th percentile for their age and gender, respectively [67]. Other studies have reported the prevalence of obesity in SCFE patients to be as high as 81% [69]. Moreover, Bhatia et al. [68] were able to show that children with bilateral SCFE tend to have higher BMIs compared to those with unilateral slips.

At the level of the knee, measurements of the metaphyseal-diaphyseal angle in the tibia as well as intermalleolar distance measurements show a significantly higher prevalence of valgus alignment in overweight children when compared with normal-weight counterparts [62]. This association between valgus deformity and obesity has been supported by other studies [70, 71]. de Sa Pinto et al. [70] found increased prevalence of genu valgum in a population of 49 obese children. Similarly, Stevens et al. [71] identified valgus abnormalities in 37.5% of another population of obese children. Genu valgum can result in knee discomfort, pain, and abnormal knee kinetics and kinematics, leading to increased knee valgus, hip abduction, and frontal knee moments [71]. Moreover genu valgum has been associated with greater step width due to tarsus distortion [72]. Greater step width can increase the risk of falls.

In addition to valgus deformity of the knee, overweight children are also predisposed to varus alignment resulting in genu varum or Blount's disease. Blount's disease is a skeletal disorder that affects the medial portion of the tibial physis [73]. Overweight children with physiologic genu varum often exert abnormal weight-bearing forces on the medial aspect of the knee, inhibiting the growth of the medial aspect of the tibial physis [74, 75]. This abnormal growth results in a three-dimensional deformity manifesting as nonphysiologic varus deformity of the tibia, internal tibial torsion, and procurvatum [76]. The association between Blount's disease and obesity has been established by multiple studies [76–78]. In a group of 69 young children referred for idiopathic genu varum, Scott et al. found significantly increased BMIs in those who were diagnosed with infantile Blount's disease compared to those who had physiologic bowing [78]. Similarly, Pirpiris et al. reported a clear association between BMI and infantile and late-onset Blount's disease in a group of children referred for surgery to correct this deformity [77]. Other studies have found that that the magnitude of the deformity strongly correlated with BMI, particularly in extremely obese children (BMI > 40 kg/m^2) [76].

Excess fat mass can affect the foot structure at an age as early as 3–5 years [79]. Foot dimensions including breadth and circumference have been reported to be larger in overweight children compared to normal-weight children [79, 80]. In addition, several studies have reported lower longitudinal medial arch and mean arch height in obese children which is associated with a decrease in the integrity of the foot as a weight-bearing structure [81–83]. Excess body weight can also cause structural dysfunction at the level of the foot, leading to the collapse of the longitudinal arch [81]. These structural changes often result in increased pressure within the foot, particularly in the midfoot and the second through the fifth metatarsal heads, increasing the risk for development of stress fractures or skin ulceration in the feet of overweight children [81–83].

Musculoskeletal Function and Gait

Although data regarding the overall effects of obesity on the function of the musculoskeletal system in children are limited, obese children are often described to have normal to enhanced upper extremity strength and yet lag behind their peers in weight-bearing and endurance activities. Greater upper limb push and pull strength was noted in a study of 43 obese children when compared to their nonobese peers; however, lower limb function was significantly impaired, which was attributed to moving a greater body mass against gravity [82]. Similarly, in a much larger study, Deforche et al. reported that the obese children had inferior performances on all tests requiring lifting of body mass (standing broad jump, sit-ups, bent-arm hang, speed shuttle run, and endurance shuttle run) when compared with their nonobese counterparts; however, they had a greater strength in handgrip [84]. Others have shown that obese children perform worse with running activity, fine motor performance, and postural balance [85, 86].

Alterations in normal gait have also been described in obese children. As a result of excess fat mass, overweight children tend to have a slower and a more tentative walking pattern [87]. Normally, as the individual matures, single-limb support time and step length and velocity increase during normal walking, while cadence and double-limb support time decreases. On the contrary, overweight children have been shown to have decreased step velocity along with an increase in the time duration of a gait cycle which results in spending more time in double-limb support stance [87–89]. Moreover, increase in step width has consistently been reported in overweight children during various walking speeds [88]. Additional gait abnormalities associated with obesity include a more rigid posture during walking due to impaired knee and hip flexion and a flatter foot during heel strike due to a quicker plantar flexion during the swing phase [87].

Musculoskeletal Pain

Musculoskeletal pain is a common complaint in obese children. Several studies are currently available that describe a positive association between BMI and musculoskeletal pain in children [90]. In a study of 135 obese children [91], back pain was reported to be the most common, occurring in 39% of the children, followed by foot pain (26%) and knee pain (24%). In another study, however, lower extremity pain was the most common, occurring in 45%, followed by back pain (30%) [70]. Taylor et al. [62] also evaluated their patient population and found a higher incidence of musculoskeletal pain in their obese children compared to their age-matched non-overweight counterparts, with knee pain being the most common, affecting 21% of the population. While these studies clearly show a link between obesity and musculoskeletal pain, additional studies are needed to better understand this relationship and its long-term consequences on the function of the obese child.

Arthritis

Arthritis is rare in children; however, obesity has been consistently identified as a risk factor for development and progression of osteoarthritis in adults, particularly at the knee [92]. Since this chapter is focused on the effects of obesity on the bones and joints of the growing child, we will not discuss this topic further but will note that since obese children have twice the risk of developing obesity in adulthood than their nonobese peers, persistence of obesity from childhood to adulthood can certainly result in the development of osteoarthritis in the weight-bearing joints at younger ages.

Bariatric Surgery and Bones

Bariatric surgery as a treatment option for obesity will be discussed in detail in Chap. 15. We provide here a brief discussion of the effects of bariatric surgery on bone heath in children. In children and adolescents, lifestyle changes, behavioral modifications, and medications have not been able to result in significant long-term improvement in body weight [93]. As a result, increasing numbers of adolescents are electing to have bariatric surgery, particularly Roux-en-Y gastric bypass (RYGB), to treat obesity [94]. While dramatic weight loss has been reported with RYGB [95, 96], the long-term consequences of this procedure at such a young age are still not well understood. In adults, several studies have found an increase in markers of bone resorption and bone loss in subjects following RYGB or adjustable silicone gastric banding for weight loss [97–101]. Bone mineral losses have also been reported in adult patients undergoing other operations for obesity, such as vertical banded gastroplasty [102] or jejunoileal bypass [103, 104]. However, studies investigating bone mass changes following bariatric surgery in adolescents who may be having surgeries at the same time as they are accruing bone mass are scarce. Recently, Kaulfers et al. [105] reported a 7.4% decline by 2 years in BMC in a retrospective study of 61 adolescents who had total body BMC and BMD assessments done at various time points up to 2 years following RGYB surgery. BMD Z-scores decreased from 1.5 to 0.1. Weight loss accounted for 14% of the decrease in BMC in the first year after surgery. However, this study followed patients for a mean of 14 months only; therefore, long-term outcome studies are needed to determine whether bone mass continues to decrease or stabilizes. Studies in adults suggest that weight loss after bariatric surgery is accompanied by long-term increases in serum markers that indicate increased bone resorption, which persist up to 18 months after surgery [106].

The potential mechanisms for loss of bone after bariatric surgery are multiple and include changes in both lean and fat mass with weight loss leading to differences in the mechanostat signals that maintain and build bone, alterations in nutrient intakes and absorption (particularly calcium and vitamin D), and hormonal perturbations including decreases in IGF-1, leptin, and ghrelin and increases in adiponectin [105].

Conclusion

As the prevalence of childhood obesity continues to increase, so will the likelihood of associated medical comorbidities. Although the full impact of obesity on the overall function and development of the growing child has not been studied completely, it is well established that obesity adversely affects the bones and the musculoskeletal system in children. There is a clear association between obesity and increased risk of fracture, SCFE, and development of Blount's disease. Currently, more studies are emerging that show a link between obesity and various musculoskeletal symptoms such as pain, decrease in function, and development of structural deformity. Increased physical activity is the cornerstone for treatment of childhood obesity; however, obese children often lead a more sedentary lifestyle which is believed to be related to musculoskeletal pain in the back, knees, and feet. More research is needed to better understand the full impact of obesity on the physical function in children.

References

1. Lobstein T, Baur L, Uauy R. Obesity in children and young people: a crisis in public health. Obes Rev. 2004;5 Suppl 1:4–104.
2. August GP, Caprio S, Fennoy I, et al. Prevention and treatment of pediatric obesity: an endocrine society clinical practice guideline based on expert opinion. J Clin Endocrinol Metab. 2008;93(12):4576–99.
3. Frost HM. Bone "mass" and the "mechanostat": a proposal. Anat Rec. 1987;219(1):1–9.
4. Smith CB, Smith DA. Relations between age, mineral density and mechanical properties of human femoral compacta. Acta Orthop Scand. 1976;47(5):496–502.
5. Kohrt WM, Barry DW, Schwartz RS. Muscle forces or gravity: what predominates mechanical loading on bone? Med Sci Sports Exerc. 2009;41(11):2050–5.
6. World Health Organization. Assessment of fracture risk and its application to screening for postmenopausal osteoporosis. 1994. WHO, Geneva. Technical Report Series.
7. Rauch F, Plotkin H, DiMeglio L, et al. Fracture prediction and the definition of osteoporosis in children and adolescents: the ISCD 2007 Pediatric Official Positions. J Clin Densitom. 2008;11(1):22–8.
8. Reid IR. Relationships among body mass, its components, and bone. Bone. 2002;31(5): 547–55.
9. Clark EM, Ness AR, Bishop NJ, Tobias JH. Association between bone mass and fractures in children: a prospective cohort study. J Bone Miner Res. 2006;21(9):1489–95.
10. Nagasaki K, Kikuchi T, Hiura M, Uchiyama M. Obese Japanese children have low bone mineral density after puberty. J Bone Miner Metab. 2004;22(4):376–81.
11. Fischer S, Milinarsky A, Giadrosich V, Dib G, Arriagada M, Arinoviche R. X-ray absorptiometry of bone in obese and eutrophic children from Valparaiso, Chile. J Rheumatol. 2000;27(5):1294–6.
12. Holloway WR, Collier FM, Aitken CJ, et al. Leptin inhibits osteoclast generation. J Bone Miner Res. 2002;17(2):200–9.
13. Takeda S, Elefteriou F, Levasseur R, et al. Leptin regulates bone formation via the sympathetic nervous system. Cell. 2002;111(3):305–17.
14. Elefteriou F, Ahn JD, Takeda S, et al. Leptin regulation of bone resorption by the sympathetic nervous system and CART. Nature. 2005;434(7032):514–20.

15. Cornish J, Callon KE, Bava U, et al. Leptin directly regulates bone cell function in vitro and reduces bone fragility in vivo. J Endocrinol. 2002;175(2):405–15.
16. Berner HS, Lyngstadaas SP, Spahr A, et al. Adiponectin and its receptors are expressed in bone-forming cells. Bone. 2004;35(4):842–9.
17. Yamaguchi N, Kukita T, Li YJ, et al. Adiponectin inhibits osteoclast formation stimulated by lipopolysaccharide from Actinobacillus actinomycetemcomitans. FEMS Immunol Med Microbiol. 2007;49(1):28–34.
18. Shinoda Y, Yamaguchi M, Ogata N, et al. Regulation of bone formation by adiponectin through autocrine/paracrine and endocrine pathways. J Cell Biochem. 2006;99(1):196–208.
19. Williams GA, Wang Y, Callon KE, et al. In vitro and in vivo effects of adiponectin on bone. Endocrinology. 2009;150(8):3603–10.
20. Sayers A, Timpson NJ, Sattar N, et al. Adiponectin and its association with bone mass accrual in childhood. J Bone Miner Res. 2010;25(10):2212–20.
21. Thommesein L, Stunes AK, Monjo M, et al. Expression and regulation of resistin in osteoblasts and osteoclasts indicate a role in bone metabolism. J Cell Biochem. 2006;99(3):824–34.
22. Oh KW, Lee WY, Rhee EJ, et al. The relationship between serum resistin, leptin, adiponectin, ghrelin levels and bone mineral density in middle-aged men. Clin Endocrinol (Oxf). 2005;63(2):131–8.
23. Reid IR, Ames R, Evans MC, et al. Determinants of total body and regional bone mineral density in normal postmenopausal women – a key role for fat mass. J Clin Endocrinol Metab. 1992;75(1):45–51.
24. Reid IR. Fat and bone. Arch Biochem Biophys. 2010;503(1):20–7.
25. Hickman J, McElduff A. Insulin promotes growth of the cultured rat osteosarcoma cell line UMR-106-01: an osteoblast-like cell. Endocrinology. 1989;124(2):701–6.
26. Cornish J, Callon KE, Reid IR. Insulin increases histomorphometric indices of bone formation in vivo. Calcif Tissue Int. 1996;59(6):492–5.
27. Cornish J, MacGibbon A, Lin JM, et al. Modulation of osteoclastogenesis by fatty acids. Endocrinology. 2008;149(11):5688–95.
28. Dagogo-Jack S, al-Ali N, Qurttom M. Augmentation of bone mineral density in hirsute women. J Clin Endocrinol Metab. 1997;82(9):2821–5.
29. Abrahamsen B, Rohold A, Henriksen JE, Beck-Nielsen H. Correlations between insulin sensitivity and bone mineral density in non-diabetic men. Diabet Med. 2000;17(2):124–9.
30. Haffner SM, Bauer RL. The association of obesity and glucose and insulin concentrations with bone density in premenopausal and postmenopausal women. Metabolism. 1993;42(6):735–8.
31. Gilsanz V, Chalfant J, Mo AO, Lee DC, Dorey FJ, Mittelman SD. Reciprocal relations of subcutaneous and visceral fat to bone structure and strength. J Clin Endocrinol Metab. 2009;94(9):3387–93.
32. Cornish J, Callon KE, Cooper GJ, Reid IR. Amylin stimulates osteoblast proliferation and increases mineralized bone volume in adult mice. Biochem Biophys Res Commun. 1995;207(1):133–9.
33. Cornish J, Callon KE, Bava U, Kamona SA, Cooper GJ, Reid IR. Effects of calcitonin, amylin, and calcitonin gene-related peptide on osteoclast development. Bone. 2001;29(2):162–8.
34. Bollag RJ, Zhong Q, Phillips P, et al. Osteoblast-derived cells express functional glucose-dependent insulinotropic peptide receptors. Endocrinology. 2000;141(3):1228–35.
35. Xie D, Zhong Q, Ding KH, et al. Glucose-dependent insulinotropic peptide-overexpressing transgenic mice have increased bone mass. Bone. 2007;40(5):1352–60.
36. Xie D, Cheng H, Hamrick M, et al. Glucose-dependent insulinotropic polypeptide receptor knockout mice have altered bone turnover. Bone. 2005;37(6):759–69.
37. Haderslev KV, Jeppesen PB, Hartmann B, et al. Short-term administration of glucagon-like peptide-2. Effects on bone mineral density and markers of bone turnover in short-bowel patients with no colon. Scand J Gastroenterol. 2002;37(4):392–8.
38. Henriksen DB, Alexandersen P, Bjarnason NH, et al. Role of gastrointestinal hormones in postprandial reduction of bone resorption. J Bone Miner Res. 2003;18(12):2180–9.

39. Fukushima N, Hanada R, Teranishi H, et al. Ghrelin directly regulates bone formation. J Bone Miner Res. 2005;20(5):790–8.
40. Misra M, Miller KK, Stewart V, et al. Ghrelin and bone metabolism in adolescent girls with anorexia nervosa and healthy adolescents. J Clin Endocrinol Metab. 2005;90(9):5082–7.
41. Weiss LA, Langenberg C, Barrett-Connor E. Ghrelin and bone: is there an association in older adults?: the Rancho Bernardo study. J Bone Miner Res. 2006;21(5):752–7.
42. Reid IR, Plank LD, Evans MC. Fat mass is an important determinant of whole body bone density in premenopausal women but not in men. J Clin Endocrinol Metab. 1992;75(3): 779–82.
43. Reid IR, Evans MC, Ames RW. Volumetric bone density of the lumbar spine is related to fat mass but not lean mass in normal postmenopausal women. Osteoporos Int. 1994;4(6):362–7.
44. Clark EM, Ness AR, Tobias JH. Adipose tissue stimulates bone growth in prepubertal children. J Clin Endocrinol Metab. 2006;91(7):2534–41.
45. Ducher G, Bass SL, Naughton GA, Eser P, Telford RD, Daly RM. Overweight children have a greater proportion of fat mass relative to muscle mass in the upper limbs than in the lower limbs: implications for bone strength at the distal forearm. Am J Clin Nutr. 2009;90(4): 1104–11.
46. Janicka A, Wren TA, Sanchez MM, et al. Fat mass is not beneficial to bone in adolescents and young adults. J Clin Endocrinol Metab. 2007;92(1):143–7.
47. Pollock NK, Bernard PJ, Wenger K, et al. Lower bone mass in prepubertal overweight children with prediabetes. J Bone Miner Res. 2010;25(12):2760–9.
48. Afghani A, Goran MI. The interrelationships between abdominal adiposity, leptin and bone mineral content in overweight Latino children. Horm Res. 2009;72(2):82–7.
49. Jones IE, Williams SM, Dow N, Goulding A. How many children remain fracture-free during growth? A longitudinal study of children and adolescents participating in the Dunedin Multidisciplinary Health and Development Study. Osteoporos Int. 2002;13(12):990–5.
50. Goulding A, Jones IE, Taylor RW, Williams SM, Manning PJ. Bone mineral density and body composition in boys with distal forearm fractures: a dual-energy x-ray absorptiometry study. J Pediatr. 2001;139(4):509–15.
51. Goulding A, Cannan R, Williams SM, Gold EJ, Taylor RW, Lewis-Barned NJ. Bone mineral density in girls with forearm fractures. J Bone Miner Res. 1998;13(1):143–8.
52. Manias K, McCabe D, Bishop N. Fractures and recurrent fractures in children; varying effects of environmental factors as well as bone size and mass. Bone. 2006;39(3):652–7.
53. Premaor MO, Pilbrow L, Tonkin C, Parker RA, Compston J. Obesity and fractures in postmenopausal women. J Bone Miner Res. 2010;25(2):292–7.
54. Leonard MB, Shults J, Wilson BA, Tershakovec AM, Zemel BS. Obesity during childhood and adolescence augments bone mass and bone dimensions. Am J Clin Nutr. 2004;80(2):514–23.
55. Goulding A, Taylor RW, Jones IE, McAuley KA, Manning PJ, Williams SM. Overweight and obese children have low bone mass and area for their weight. Int J Obes Relat Metab Disord. 2000;24(5):627–32.
56. Davidson PL, Goulding A, Chalmers DJ. Biomechanical analysis of arm fracture in obese boys. J Paediatr Child Health. 2003;39(9):657–64.
57. Dimitri P, Wales JK, Bishop N. Fat and bone in children: differential effects of obesity on bone size and mass according to fracture history. J Bone Miner Res. 2010;25(3):527–36.
58. Lloyd T, Beck TJ, Lin HM, et al. Modifiable determinants of bone status in young women. Bone. 2002;30(2):416–21.
59. Bachrach LK. Acquisition of optimal bone mass in childhood and adolescence. Trends Endocrinol Metab. 2001;12(1):22–8.
60. Goulding A, Jones IE, Taylor RW, Piggot JM, Taylor D. Dynamic and static tests of balance and postural sway in boys: effects of previous wrist bone fractures and high adiposity. Gait Posture. 2003;17(2):136–41.
61. Jones RA, Okely AD, Caputi P, Cliff DP. Perceived and actual competence among overweight and non-overweight children. J Sci Med Sport. 2010;13(6):589–96.
62. Taylor ED, Theim KR, Mirch MC, et al. Orthopedic complications of overweight in children and adolescents. Pediatrics. 2006;117(6):2167–74.

63. Doak CM, Visscher TL, Renders CM, Seidell JC. The prevention of overweight and obesity in children and adolescents: a review of interventions and programmes. Obes Rev. 2006;7(1): 111–36.
64. Kiess W, Galler A, Reich A, et al. Clinical aspects of obesity in childhood and adolescence. Obes Rev. 2001;2(1):29–36.
65. Galbraith RT, Gelberman RH, Hajek PC, et al. Obesity and decreased femoral anteversion in adolescence. J Orthop Res. 1987;5(4):523–8.
66. Pritchett JW, Perdue KD. Mechanical factors in slipped capital femoral epiphysis. J Pediatr Orthop. 1988;8(4):385–8.
67. Loder RT. The demographics of slipped capital femoral epiphysis. An International Multicenter Study. Clin Orthop Relat Res. 1996;322:8–27.
68. Bhatia NN, Pirpiris M, Otsuka NY. Body mass index in patients with slipped capital femoral epiphysis. J Pediatr Orthop. 2006;26(2):197–9.
69. Manoff EM, Banffy MB, Winell JJ. Relationship between Body Mass Index and slipped capital femoral epiphysis. J Pediatr Orthop. 2005;25(6):744–6.
70. de Sa Pinto AL, de Barros Holanda PM, de Barros Holanda PM, Radu AS, Villares SM, Lima FR. Musculoskeletal findings in obese children. J Paediatr Child Health. 2006;42(6):341–4.
71. Stevens PM, MacWilliams B, Mohr RA. Gait analysis of stapling for genu valgum. J Pediatr Orthop. 2004;24(1):70–4.
72. Pretkiewicz-Abacjew E. Knock knee and the gait of six-year-old children. J Sports Med Phys Fitness. 2003;43(2):156–64.
73. Dietz Jr WH, Gross WL, Kirkpatrick Jr JA. Blount disease (tibia vara): another skeletal disorder associated with childhood obesity. J Pediatr. 1982;101(5):735–7.
74. Bradway JK, Klassen RA, Peterson HA. Blount disease: a review of the English literature. J Pediatr Orthop. 1987;7(4):472–80.
75. Wills M. Orthopedic complications of childhood obesity. Pediatr Phys Ther. 2004;16(4):230–5.
76. Sabharwal S, Lee Jr J, Zhao C. Multiplanar deformity analysis of untreated Blount disease. J Pediatr Orthop. 2007;27(3):260–5.
77. Pirpiris M, Jackson KR, Farng E, Bowen RE, Otsuka NY. Body mass index and Blount disease. J Pediatr Orthop. 2006;26(5):659–63.
78. Scott AC, Kelly CH, Sullivan E. Body mass index as a prognostic factor in development of infantile Blount disease. J Pediatr Orthop. 2007;27(8):921–5.
79. Mickle KJ, Steele JR, Munro BJ. The feet of overweight and obese young children: are they flat or fat? Obesity (Silver Spring). 2006;14(11):1949–53.
80. Wearing SC, Hennig EM, Byrne NM, Steele JR, Hills AP. The impact of childhood obesity on musculoskeletal form. Obes Rev. 2006;7(2):209–18.
81. Hills AP, Hennig EM, Byrne NM, Steele JR. The biomechanics of adiposity – structural and functional limitations of obesity and implications for movement. Obes Rev. 2002;3(1):35–43.
82. Riddiford-Harland DL, Steele JR, Storlien LH. Does obesity influence foot structure in prepubescent children? Int J Obes Relat Metab Disord. 2000;24(5):541–4.
83. Dowling AM, Steele JR, Baur LA. Does obesity influence foot structure and plantar pressure patterns in prepubescent children? Int J Obes Relat Metab Disord. 2001;25(6):845–52.
84. Deforche B, Lefevre J, De Bourdeaudhuij I, Hills AP, Duquet W, Bouckaert J. Physical fitness and physical activity in obese and nonobese Flemish youth. Obes Res. 2003;11(3):434–41.
85. Haerens L, Deforche B, Maes L, Cardon G, De Bourdeaudhuij I. Physical activity and endurance in normal weight versus overweight boys and girls. J Sports Med Phys Fitness. 2007;47(3):344–50.
86. D'Hondt E, Deforche B, De Bourdeaudhuij I, Lenoir M. Childhood obesity affects fine motor skill performance under different postural constraints. Neurosci Lett. 2008;440(1):72–5.
87. Hills AP, Parker AW. Gait characteristics of obese children. Arch Phys Med Rehabil. 1991;72(6):403–7.
88. Hills AP, Parker AW. Locomotor characteristics of obese children. Child Care Health Dev. 1992;18(1):29–34.
89. Gushue DL, Houck J, Lerner AL. Effects of childhood obesity on three-dimensional knee joint biomechanics during walking. J Pediatr Orthop. 2005;25(6):763–8.

90. Bell LM, Byrne S, Thompson A, et al. Increasing body mass index z-score is continuously associated with complications of overweight in children, even in the healthy weight range. J Clin Endocrinol Metab. 2007;92(2):517–22.
91. Stovitz SD, Pardee PE, Vazquez G, Duval S, Schwimmer JB. Musculoskeletal pain in obese children and adolescents. Acta Paediatr. 2008;97(4):489–93.
92. Lohmander LS, Felson D. Can we identify a 'high risk' patient profile to determine who will experience rapid progression of osteoarthritis? Osteoarthr Cartilage. 2004;12(Suppl A):S49–52.
93. Whitlock EA, O'Connor EP, Williams SB, Beil TL, Lutz KW. Effectiveness of weight management programs in children and adolescents. Evid Rep Technol Assess (Full Rep). 2008;(170):1–308.
94. Tsai WS, Inge TH, Burd RS. Bariatric surgery in adolescents: recent national trends in use and in-hospital outcome. Arch Pediatr Adolesc Med. 2007;161(3):217–21.
95. Inge T, Wilson KA, Gamm K, Kirk S, Garcia VF, Daniels SR. Preferential loss of central (trunk) adiposity in adolescents and young adults after laparoscopic gastric bypass. Surg Obes Relat Dis. 2007;3(2):153–8.
96. Collins J, Mattar S, Qureshi F, et al. Initial outcomes of laparoscopic Roux-en-Y gastric bypass in morbidly obese adolescents. Surg Obes Relat Dis. 2007;3(2):147–52.
97. Coates PS, Fernstrom JD, Fernstrom MH, Schauer PR, Greenspan SL. Gastric bypass surgery for morbid obesity leads to an increase in bone turnover and a decrease in bone mass. J Clin Endocrinol Metab. 2004;89(3):1061–5.
98. von Mach MA, Stoeckli R, Bilz S, Kraenzlin M, Langer I, Keller U. Changes in bone mineral content after surgical treatment of morbid obesity. Metabolism. 2004;53(7):918–21.
99. Fleischer J, Stein EM, Bessler M, et al. The decline in hip bone density after gastric bypass surgery is associated with extent of weight loss. J Clin Endocrinol Metab. 2008;93(10):3735–40.
100. Johnson JM, Maher JW, Samuel I, Heitshusen D, Doherty C, Downs RW. Effects of gastric bypass procedures on bone mineral density, calcium, parathyroid hormone, and vitamin D. J Gastrointest Surg. 2005;9(8):1106–10.
101. Carrasco F, Ruz M, Rojas P, et al. Changes in bone mineral density, body composition and adiponectin levels in morbidly obese patients after bariatric surgery. Obes Surg. 2009;19(1):41–6.
102. Cundy T, Evans MC, Kay RG, Dowman M, Wattie D, Reid IR. Effects of vertical-banded gastroplasty on bone and mineral metabolism in obese patients. Br J Surg. 1996;83(10):1468–72.
103. Compston JE, Vedi S, Gianetta E, Watson G, Civalleri D, Scopinaro N. Bone histomorphometry and vitamin D status after biliopancreatic bypass for obesity. Gastroenterology. 1984;87(2):350–6.
104. Bano G, Rodin DA, Pazianas M, Nussey SS. Reduced bone mineral density after surgical treatment for obesity. Int J Obes Relat Metab Disord. 1999;23(4):361–5.
105. Kaulfers AM, Bean JA, Inge TH, Dolan LM, Kalkwarf HJ. Bone loss in adolescents after bariatric surgery. Pediatrics. 2011;127(4):e956–61.
106. Bruno C, Fulford AD, Potts JR, et al. Serum markers of bone turnover are increased at six and 18 months after Roux-en-Y bariatric surgery: correlation with the reduction in leptin. J Clin Endocrinol Metab. 2010;95(1):159–66.

Chapter 10
The Relationship of Childhood Obesity with Cardiomyopathy and Heart Failure

Muhammad Yasir Qureshi, James D. Wilkinson, and Steven E. Lipshultz

Abstract Obesity causes structural and functional changes in the hearts of children, in addition to increasing cardiometabolic risk and predisposition to early coronary artery disease. In this chapter, we summarize the evidence of obesity-related cardiomyopathy and discuss the pathophysiology of its development. We also describe the current practices in its diagnosis and treatment in children. The evidence shows that obesity-related cardiac changes in childhood can eventually worsen cardiac function and increase the risk of heart failure in early adulthood. Thus, efforts to improve the diagnosis, prevention, and treatment of obesity-related cardiomyopathy could improve not only length and quality of life for obese children but also produce substantial savings in future care.

Keywords Obesity • Cardiomyopathy • Heart failure • Pediatric • Adolescents

---

M.Y. Qureshi, M.D. (✉)
Division of Pediatric Cardiology, Department of Pediatrics,
University of Miami/Jackson Memorial Hospital,
P.O. Box 016960 (R-76) North Wing, Room 109, Miami, FL 33101, USA
e-mail: mqureshi@med.miami.edu

J.D. Wilkinson, M.D., MPH
Department of Pediatrics and Epidemiology, University of Miami Miller School of Medicine,
Miami, FL, USA

S.E. Lipshultz, M.D.
Department of Pediatrics, University of Miami Miller School of Medicine,
Miami, FL, USA

Introduction

A definition of obesity-related cardiomyopathy comes from Wong et al. [1] who define it as "myocardial disease in obese individuals that cannot be explained by diabetes mellitus, hypertension, coronary artery disease or other etiologies." Heart failure in morbidly obese adults was identified several decades ago. However, the cause of heart failure was initially attributed solely to comorbid conditions, such as coronary artery disease, hypertension, diabetes mellitus, and obstructive sleep apnea. Recently, evidence supports the notion that obesity directly causes myocardial dysfunction.

The term "cardiomyopathy of obesity" was first used by J. Alexander in 1985 to describe heart failure in obese adults in the absence of other comorbidities [2]. Since then, whether "cardiomyopathy of obesity" exists, has been debated. Recent studies have identified obesity as an independent predictor of heart failure [3]. Because obese children tend to grow into obese adults [4], identifying the early changes in cardiac structure and function in obese and overweight children has become of interest. In fact, the duration of obesity is one of the most significant predictors of the cardiac structural and functional changes [5, 6] that may predispose obese children to heart failure in early adulthood.

Other than the direct cardiotoxic effect of obesity, a substantial number of overweight adolescents are at high risk of metabolic syndrome [7], which may also increase their risk of early-onset cardiovascular disease. Obesity is a major independent risk factor for heart failure in adults [8, 9]. This risk is incremental and is directly related to body mass index [10]. Idiopathic dilated cardiomyopathy is more common in obese individuals [11]. Moreover, type 2 diabetes mellitus, which is common in obese individuals, causes structural and functional changes in the heart in both adults and adolescents [12, 13]. In adults, sudden cardiac death has also been associated with obesity [14].

Evidence of Obesity-Related Cardiomyopathy

The initial evidence of obesity-related cardiomyopathy came from Smith and Willius' 1933 description of four obese patients who died of heart failure without other confounding factors. In 1984, results from the Framingham Heart Study [9] identified obesity as one of the major risk factors of heart failure in adults. As mentioned above, the duration of morbid obesity is the strongest predictor of heart failure [5, 15]. For every year of morbid obesity, the odds of heart failure increase by 1.5 which translates into a 66% probability of heart failure after 20 years of obesity and a 93% probability of heart failure after 25 years of obesity [15].

The degree and type of obesity are other risk factors for heart failure. In particular, incremental changes in body mass index carry a graded risk for developing heart failure [10]. Android obesity, with predominantly visceral fat in the upper torso, may be another risk factor for heart failure [16]. There are structural and functional changes in the heart associated with obesity, which provide evidence in favor of the existence of obesity-related cardiomyopathy.

Obesity-Related Anatomical Changes in the Heart

Wall Thickness and Chamber Dimensions

Obesity-related geometric changes in cardiac chambers have been identified in autopsies and cardiac imaging of live individuals. Echocardiography can evaluate these cardiac structural changes long before heart failure symptoms appear. The geometric changes seen in obesity are increased left and right ventricular mass and volume. Left atrial enlargement has also been described [17] and may be explained by impaired left ventricular diastolic function [18].

Increased left ventricular mass may be the earliest and most important structural change that can be measured in children and adolescents. Increased left ventricular mass, left ventricular regional wall hypertrophy, and left ventricular dilation in obese adults have been described in several studies [6, 15, 19–23]. Increased left ventricular mass independently predicts cardiovascular disease and death in adults [24, 25], whereas left ventricular dilation is one of the early signs of heart failure. Increased left ventricular mass and left ventricular hypertrophy are present in children and adolescents with high body mass indices [26–30] and can be found in children as young as 6 years old [31]. Increased left ventricular mass may progress to left ventricular dilation with increasing body mass index [26].

Both the duration and severity of obesity are associated with increased left ventricular mass and left ventricular dilation [5, 20, 32–34]. In addition, obese children who do not have increased left ventricular mass during childhood can have it develop in early adulthood [35]. If diabetes coexists with obesity in children, hypertrophy of the left ventricle can be exaggerated [13, 36]. Left ventricular hypertrophy in obesity is often eccentric [20, 22, 29], whereas that in chronic hypertension is concentric. This difference indicates that the pathology of left ventricular hypertrophy in obesity differs from that of hypertension. The early cardiac changes in obesity are generally reversible by weight loss [37].

Adipose Tissue Distribution

Endomyocardial biopsy and autopsy specimens show that microscopic and gross changes in the distribution of cardiac adipose tissue are associated with obesity. In the normal heart, adipose tissue is distributed in the atrioventricular and interventricular grooves around the blood vessels [38]. In obese individuals, the amount of epicardial adipose tissue is increased around the coronary arteries, in the atrioventricular and interventricular grooves, and at the apex [39]. There may also be fatty infiltration of the myocardium [40]. Fatty infiltration surrounded by fibrosis has been described specifically in obese individuals with coronary artery disease [40]. However, the effect of myocardial fatty infiltration and increased epicardial adipose tissue on myocardial function is unclear. Fatty infiltration around the cardiac conduction system has also been noted in autopsies of obese children and young adults who experienced sudden death [41].

Obesity-Related Myocardial Functional Changes

Diastolic Function

Diastolic dysfunction implies abnormal relaxation of the myocardium and may be an early change in asymptomatic left ventricular dysfunction secondary to cardiomyopathy. Increased left ventricular mass, as seen in some obese individuals, can by itself cause abnormal diastolic function. Cardiac hemodynamic parameters measured during cardiac catheterization can show elevated end-diastolic left ventricular pressures or elevated pulmonary capillary wedge pressures in obese individuals [42], which suggests abnormal myocardial relaxation. End-diastolic pressures can get even higher when the heart is stressed during exercise [43, 44]. With left ventricular diastolic dysfunction, the left atrium has to exert a greater force to pump blood into the left ventricle. With persistent pressure overload, the left atrium can progressively dilate. Therefore, left atrial dilation, as measured by two-dimensional echocardiography, is another measure of left ventricular diastolic dysfunction and has been reported in obese children [17]. Doppler mapping of abnormal blood flow across the mitral valve also indicates left ventricular diastolic dysfunction and has been reported in obese children [45] and adults [21, 46]. Left ventricular diastolic dysfunction has been documented in obese and diabetic individuals using tissue Doppler measurements as well [46]. It is common in patients with newly diagnosed [47] and poorly controlled [13, 48] type 2 diabetes mellitus, which may [47] or may not [49] be reversible with good glycemic control. Left ventricular diastolic dysfunction has been reported in both obese adolescents and in those with type 2 diabetes [36]. Diabetic patients, who have normal Doppler patterns at rest, may show exercise-induced left ventricular diastolic dysfunction [50].

Systolic Function

Obese individuals initially have enhanced systolic function [30, 51] that declines over time [5]. Systolic dysfunction, which typically appears only after a long period of obesity [5, 52], is probably the reason that obesity-related symptomatic heart failure is uncommon in children [53].

Diastolic dysfunction is seen in all types of cardiomyopathy and may eventually progress to systolic heart failure. As in obesity, increased myocardial performance has been described in children with type 1 diabetes [54]. Decreased systolic function is well known in adults with type 2 diabetes [55–57], but an initial increase in systolic function has not been observed [30]. The right-sided heart failure seen in obese individuals has mostly been attributed to coexisting obstructive sleep apnea. However, increasing body mass index has also been associated with worsening right ventricular dysfunction in the absence of obstructive sleep apnea [58].

Pathophysiology

Obesity-Related Metabolic Changes and Lipotoxicity

Insulin resistance, which is common in obesity, may disturb myocardial metabolism, which, in turn, may be partly responsible for the development of cardiomyopathy. Myocardial fatty acid delivery and oxidation are increased in obesity and insulin resistance [59–62] before the cardiac functional changes are observed [59]. The increased myocardial oxygen consumption seen in obese individuals is also associated with decreased cardiac efficiency [62]. In obese individuals with insulin resistance, plasma fatty acid levels are commonly elevated, which in turn can upregulate uncoupling proteins. This uncoupling may lead to decreased efficiency of oxidative metabolism and may be the reason for increased myocardial oxygen consumption [63].

Myocardial fatty acid storage and triglyceride content may also be increased in obese individuals with insulin resistance [64–66]. Increased myocardial fatty acid metabolism [64] may lead to the accumulation of toxic metabolites, such as long-chain nonesterified fatty acids, diacylglycerols, and ceramides [67], which may result in myocardial tissue injury. Increased fatty acid storage may lead to programmed cell death: "lipoapoptosis" or "lipotoxicity" [68]. Leptin is a protein, believed to regulate fat storage. Depletion of leptin increases myocardial fat storage [69], which may induce apoptosis of myocytes [68]. In insulin resistance, blood flow and glucose metabolism are mismatched as well [70]. Energy metabolism is also impaired due to altered leptin-dependent compensatory oxidation with a lower phosphocreatine-to-ATP ratio in type 2 diabetes [71]. Insulin-like growth factor may contribute to myocardial dysfunction [66]; however, its exact function is unclear. All these factors may contribute to the development of cardiomyopathy.

Adiponectin and Inflammation

Adiponectin is a cytokine produced by adipocytes. It is anti-inflammatory and is thought to have a protective effect on the myocardium by inhibiting insulin-mediated myocardial hypertrophy [72]. Paradoxical to the fact that it is secreted from adipose tissue, its level is decreased in obese individuals [73–75]. Lower levels of adiponectin are associated with increased inflammatory proteins [76], decreased high-density-lipoprotein cholesterol [75–78], and increased triglyceride levels [77]. Lower levels of adiponectin have also been associated with premature atherosclerosis in children and adolescents [77, 79]. The level of adiponectin is inversely proportional to the degree of insulinemia [78]. A sex-specific difference in the relationship between levels of adiponectin and those of N-terminal probrain natriuretic peptide, a cardiac biomarker of neuroendocrine activation in heart failure, was found in adolescent girls and varies by the degree of obesity [80]. Inflamed adipose tissue can secrete adipokines and several inflammatory mediators [81] that may contribute to the development of cardiomyopathy in obese individuals. It has also been postulated that chronic inflammatory disease initiated in adipose tissue may contribute to obesity-related insulin resistance [82].

Systemic Response and Hemodynamic Changes

The pathophysiology and hemodynamic alterations in obesity-related cardiomyopathy are well described by Alpert [83] (Fig. 10.1). With excess adipose tissue, circulating blood volume is increased [84], and systemic vascular resistance is lower [85]. Heart rate does not change, so the stroke volume has to increase to maintain cardiac output. However, to perfuse all the surplus adipose tissue, the total cardiac output is augmented [44, 84, 85]. This persistent high cardiac output eventually dilates the left ventricle and increases left ventricular wall stress. In response to the additional left ventricular wall stress, the heart becomes hypertrophic. However, in obesity, this hypertrophy tends to be eccentric [27, 29], not concentric. The ventricular hypertrophy is, at least in part, responsible for diastolic dysfunction. When the ventricular wall can no longer compensate for the increased stress, overt ventricular failure with systolic and diastolic dysfunction results. The left-sided heart failure also contributes to right ventricular failure by increasing pulmonary vascular pressures [42, 44, 86, 87]. The major factors in the development of right ventricular failure are probably obstructive sleep apnea and alveolar hypoventilation. However, right ventricular changes in obese individuals, in the absence of obstructive sleep apnea, have also been reported [58].

In addition to hemodynamic alterations, the renin-angiotensin-aldosterone system may contribute to myocardial dysfunction. This system is highly active in obese individuals [88, 89], owing to insulin resistance [89] and increased insulin levels [90]. Subcutaneous adipose tissue itself is a source of angiotensin II [90] and may be one reason hypertension is seen in obesity. Increased left ventricular afterload related to hypertension in an overstressed left ventricle increases myocardial dysfunction. Angiotensin II is also known to cause myocardial hypertrophy and fibrosis [91] and therefore, may contribute to the development of increased left ventricular mass and diastolic dysfunction. The sympathetic nervous system may also be overactive in obese individuals [92] as a result of insulin resistance [93] or activation of the renin-angiotensin-aldosterone system. Myocardial dysfunction itself triggers the activation

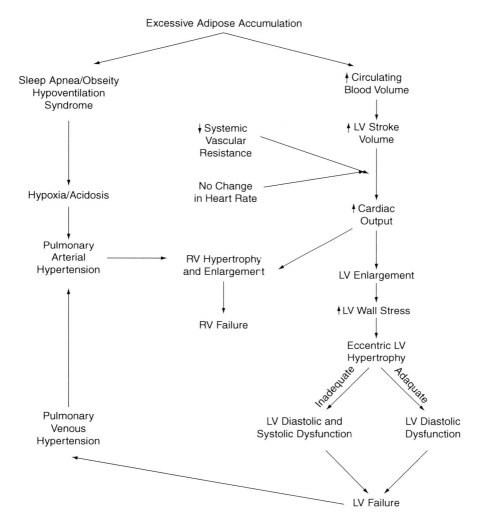

Fig. 10.1 Pathophysiology of obesity-associated cardiomyopathy. *LV* left ventricle, *RV* right ventricle (Reprinted from Alpert [83], with permission from Lippincott Williams & Wilkins)

of the sympathetic nervous system to maintain cardiac output. This response, in turn, activates several neurohormonal cascades [92], whose direct detrimental effects on cardiac myocytes may further decrease myocardial performance.

Small vessel disease of the myocardium may also contribute to myocardial dysfunction. Microvascular vasoreactivity is abnormal in obese individuals [94, 95] and is worse in the presence of type 2 diabetes [94]. Normally, insulin enhances myocardial blood flow, but this effect is blunted in obese individuals [95]. These conditions may be early signs of coronary artery disease in obese and diabetic individuals, but they may also be responsible for the development of obesity-related cardiomyopathy.

Diagnosis

Clinical Presentation

Clinical features of heart failure vary depending on the stage of myocardial dysfunction. Most obese children are asymptomatic unless they have right heart failure secondary to obstructive sleep apnea. However, subtle signs of diastolic dysfunction, such as a gallop rhythm, may be present. Diastolic dysfunction of the left ventricle increases pressure in the left atrium, leading to pulmonary vascular congestion. In obese adults, atrial arrhythmias caused by left atrial dilation from persistent pressure overload have been reported [96–98]. Pulmonary vascular congestion may cause symptoms of dyspnea, orthopnea, or paroxysmal nocturnal dyspnea. Pulmonary crackles may be audible on auscultation. Right heart failure has more notable signs on examination. Jugular venous distension, hepatomegaly, ascites, and pedal edema can be seen with right ventricular dysfunction. Adults with obesity-associated cardiomyopathy can die of either progressive heart failure leading to pump failure [39] or sudden cardiac death [14, 41, 99, 100].

Electrocardiography

In obese individuals, subcutaneous adipose tissue partially insulates the heart from the electrodes used in electrocardiography, resulting in low QRS voltages [101, 102]. This reduced voltage can obscure the voltage criteria of left ventricular hypertrophy [103] which is solely based on amplitudes of the QRS complexes in the precordial leads. T-wave flattening, representing abnormal repolarization, is common [102] and may represent diastolic dysfunction. The P, QRS and T waves axes may shift to the left [101]. The voltage criteria of left ventricular hypertrophy and left atrial enlargement can also be found [101].

Echocardiography

Cardiac imaging with echocardiography has revealed the natural progression of heart failure from early geometric changes and diastolic dysfunction to systolic dysfunction. Echocardiography is the main modality used to detect early indicators of the development of cardiomyopathy in children. However, in obese individuals, the echocardiographic windows are poor, and a comprehensive echocardiographic assessment is difficult to complete [104]. Two-dimensional echocardiography can reveal internal dimensions of the left ventricle and assess ventricular dilation. Ventricular wall and interventricular septal thickness can be measured echocardiograms to assess ventricular hypertrophy. Measurements of left atrial volume can predict left ventricular diastolic dysfunction [18]. Diastolic function can also be assessed by Doppler mapping of blood flow across the mitral valve, as well as with tissue Doppler imaging. Tissue Doppler imaging measures the velocity of myocardial excursion and can directly measure the degree of relaxation of the heart muscle. Isovolumic relaxation time is another measure of diastolic function that is abnormal in obese individuals [105]. Assessing systolic function usually consists of measuring left ventricular fractional shortening by M-mode echocardiography and left ventricular ejection fraction by two-dimensional echocardiography. Exercise echocardiography may detect myocardial dysfunction that is absent at rest [50].

Myocardial strain imaging is another new and advanced echocardiographic technique used to assess myocardial tissue characterization. Several points in the myocardium are tracked over a cardiac cycle to assess myocardial deformity between those points during systole and diastole. It is a linear measure of tissue deformation. This helps to evaluate regional myocardial function. Myocardial strain measurements vary with body mass index [46]. Very early myocardial functional changes can be diagnosed with this technique in obese individuals, even when conventional two-dimensional echocardiogram shows normal ejection fraction [106, 107].

Other Types of Cardiac Imaging

In addition to echocardiography, radionuclide imaging has also detected impaired systolic and diastolic function in asymptomatic obese individuals in the absence of other comorbid conditions [108]. However, it may have the same technical limitations as echocardiography as a result of body habitus [109]. Advanced imaging with computed tomography and magnetic resonance cardiac imaging can be utilized. However, these are currently rarely utilized in asymptomatic patients. Computed tomography can accurately measure ventricular mass and dimensions [110] and can also be used to assess coronary artery disease and systolic function. Magnetic resonance imaging, in addition to assessing ventricular systolic and diastolic function [111], can also detect myocardial fibrosis and adiposity, which may predispose to atherosclerotic coronary artery disease [112].

Laboratory Tests

Serum brain natriuretic peptide and N-terminal probrain natriuretic peptide are routinely used in managing heart failure [113]. However, in obesity, the interpretation of these biomarker levels may be challenging. The levels of these biomarkers are inversely proportional to body mass index, and therefore their levels may not be appropriately elevated in patients with obesity, even when left ventricular wall stress and diastolic dysfunction are present [114–116].

Treatment

Weight Control

Weight control is the primary intervention to prevent or ameliorate obesity-related cardiomyopathy. Because the duration of obesity is a major predictor of heart failure [15], every effort must be made to control weight in childhood to prevent premature heart failure in adulthood. In adults, weight loss improves myocardial function and glucose metabolism [21, 117]. Weight loss improves lipid metabolism and insulin signaling [118] as well as favorably alters the renin-angiotensin-aldosterone system by decreasing aldosterone levels [119]. Weight loss can usually be achieved by dietary control, exercise, drugs, surgery, or some combination of these treatments. Dietary modification and exercise alone can improve left ventricular structure [120, 121]. Although not commonly used in adolescents, bariatric surgery has resulted in improved cardiometabolic risk factors in obese adults [122], as well as in adolescents [123]. Bariatric surgery substantially reduces weight in obese adolescents and has improved left ventricular mass, hypertrophy, and diastolic function [37].

Pharmacotherapy

Certain drugs can induce weight loss in adults [124], but their cardiovascular effects are unknown. Although their use seemed promising, these are not routinely used in children and adolescents with obesity. Sertraline, a selective serotonin reuptake inhibitor, is used in adolescents with obsessive-compulsive disorder and depression. It is also used to treat certain eating disorders, such as binge eating disorder [125] and night eating syndrome [126]. Sertraline use has been associated with a decreased left ventricular mass and blood pressure with reduced weight in obese individuals [127]. Rimonabant, a cannabinoid-1 receptor blocker, is used for weight loss in several European countries. It has been associated with a reduction in cardiometabolic disease risk factors by improving lipid profile and glucose metabolism and by increasing serum levels of adiponectin [128]. On the other hand, sibutramine is an appetite suppressant that induces weight loss in adolescents but does not affect myocardial structure and function [129]. Fenfluramine and dexfenfluramine are also serotonergic appetite suppressant drugs which were withdrawn from the market due to severe adverse effects of valvular heart disease [130]. The adverse effects have been linked to activation of 5-HT2B receptors which is known to induce mitogenesis in fibroblasts causing valve dysfunction [131]. About 20% of all those who have been exposed to fenfluramine or dexfenfluramine show aortic or mitral valve regurgitation [132]. The newer serotonergic drugs in development, like lorcaserin [133], are targeting 5-HT2C receptors rather than 5-HT2B receptors to avoid valvular heart disease. Beloranib (ZGN-433) is an experimental drug, which, by inhibiting methionine aminopeptidase 2, has shown weight reduction in severely obese individuals by metabolizing body fat [134]. The cardiovascular effects of this drug are unknown. Melanin-concentrating hormone receptor 1 antagonists reduce food intake and have shown weight loss in animal models [135]. The cardiovascular effects of these agents are not known.

Obesity-related heart failure requiring medical therapy is not common in children without right heart failure resulting from obstructive sleep apnea. In general, heart failure is treated with beta-blockers, angiotensin-converting enzyme inhibitors, angiotensin receptor blockers, and diuretics. Beta-blockers improve cardiac function and symptoms and are well tolerated by children with heart failure [136]. However, they induce weight gain [137] and must be used judiciously.

Thiazolidinediones and metformin are oral hypoglycemic agents routinely used to treat type 2 diabetes. These drugs may benefit the myocardium by decreasing insulin resistance and improving cardiometabolic risk [138]. Metformin is used in adolescents with type 2 diabetes, whereas pediatric use of thiazolidinediones has not been approved.

Conclusion

Childhood obesity is not only a major risk factor for early coronary artery disease, it is also a risk factor for generalized myocardial dysfunction. The pathophysiological pathways resulting in pediatric cardiac damage need to be better characterized. Effective interventions aimed at reducing obesity in children and adolescents could potentially decrease the risk of premature-onset cardiomyopathy and heart failure as well as decrease lifetime global cardiovascular risk.

References

1. Wong C, Marwick TH. Obesity cardiomyopathy: pathogenesis and pathophysiology. Nat Clin Pract Cardiovasc Med. 2007;4(8):436–43.
2. Alexander JK. The cardiomyopathy of obesity. Prog Cardiovasc Dis. 1985;27(5):325–34.
3. Poirier P, Giles TD, Bray GA, et al. Obesity and cardiovascular disease: pathophysiology, evaluation, and effect of weight loss: an update of the 1997 American Heart Association Scientific Statement on Obesity and Heart Disease from the Obesity Committee of the Council on Nutrition, Physical Activity, and Metabolism. Circulation. 2006;113(6):898–918.
4. The NS, Suchindran C, North KE, Popkin BM, Gordon-Larsen P. Association of adolescent obesity with risk of severe obesity in adulthood. JAMA. 2010;304(18):2042–7.
5. Alpert MA, Lambert CR, Panayiotou H, et al. Relation of duration of morbid obesity to left ventricular mass, systolic function, and diastolic filling, and effect of weight loss. Am J Cardiol. 1995;76(16):1194–7.
6. Nakajima T, Fujioka S, Tokunaga K, Hirobe K, Matsuzawa Y, Tarui S. Noninvasive study of left ventricular performance in obese patients: influence of duration of obesity. Circulation. 1985;71(3):481–6.

7. Messiah SE, Arheart KL, Luke B, Lipshultz SE, Miller TL. Relationship between body mass index and metabolic syndrome risk factors among US 8- to 14-year-olds, 1999 to 2002. J Pediatr. 2008;153(2):215–21.
8. He J, Ogden LG, Bazzano LA, Vupputuri S, Loria C, Whelton PK. Risk factors for congestive heart failure in US men and women: NHANES I epidemiologic follow-up study. Arch Intern Med. 2001;161(7):996–1002.
9. Hubert HB, Feinleib M, McNamara PM, Castelli WP. Obesity as an independent risk factor for cardiovascular disease: a 26-year follow-up of participants in the Framingham Heart Study. Circulation. 1983;67(5):968–77.
10. Kenchaiah S, Evans JC, Levy D, et al. Obesity and the risk of heart failure. N Engl J Med. 2002;347(5):305–13.
11. Kasper EK, Hruban RH, Baughman KL. Cardiomyopathy of obesity: a clinicopathologic evaluation of 43 obese patients with heart failure. Am J Cardiol. 1992;70(9):921–4.
12. Factor SM, Minase T, Sonnenblick EH. Clinical and morphological features of human hypertensive-diabetic cardiomyopathy. Am Heart J. 1980;99(4):446–58.
13. Whalley GA, Gusso S, Hofman P, et al. Structural and functional cardiac abnormalities in adolescent girls with poorly controlled type 2 diabetes. Diabetes Care. 2009;32(5):883–8.
14. Duflou J, Virmani R, Rabin I, Burke A, Farb A, Smialek J. Sudden death as a result of heart disease in morbid obesity. Am Heart J. 1995;130(2):306–13.
15. Alpert MA, Terry BE, Mulekar M, et al. Cardiac morphology and left ventricular function in normotensive morbidly obese patients with and without congestive heart failure, and effect of weight loss. Am J Cardiol. 1997;80(6):736–40.
16. Malavazos AE, Ermetici F, Coman C, Corsi MM, Morricone L, Ambrosi B. Influence of epicardial adipose tissue and adipocytokine levels on cardiac abnormalities in visceral obesity. Int J Cardiol. 2007;121(1):132–4.
17. Daniels SR, Witt SA, Glascock B, Khoury PR, Kimball TR. Left atrial size in children with hypertension: the influence of obesity, blood pressure, and left ventricular mass. J Pediatr. 2002;141(2):186–90.
18. Pritchett AM, Mahoney DW, Jacobsen SJ, Rodeheffer RJ, Karon BL, Redfield MM. Diastolic dysfunction and left atrial volume: a population-based study. J Am Coll Cardiol. 2005;45(1):87–92.
19. Amad KH, Brennan JC, Alexander JK. The cardiac pathology of chronic exogenous obesity. Circulation. 1965;32(5):740–5.
20. Lauer MS, Anderson KM, Levy D. Separate and joint influences of obesity and mild hypertension on left ventricular mass and geometry: the Framingham Heart Study. J Am Coll Cardiol. 1992;19(1):130–4.
21. Karason K, Wallentin I, Larsson B, Sjostrom L. Effects of obesity and weight loss on cardiac function and valvular performance. Obes Res. 1998;6(6):422–9.
22. Messerli FH, Sundgaard-Riise K, Reisin ED, et al. Dimorphic cardiac adaptation to obesity and arterial hypertension. Ann Intern Med. 1983;99(6):757–61.
23. Wikstrand J, Pettersson P, Bjorntorp P. Body fat distribution and left ventricular morphology and function in obese females. J Hypertens. 1993;11(11):1259–66.
24. Levy D, Garrison RJ, Savage DD, Kannel WB, Castelli WP. Prognostic implications of echocardiographically determined left ventricular mass in the Framingham Heart Study. N Engl J Med. 1990;322(22):1561–6.
25. Brown DW, Giles WH, Croft JB. Left ventricular hypertrophy as a predictor of coronary heart disease mortality and the effect of hypertension. Am Heart J. 2000;140(6):848–56.
26. Chinali M, de Simone G, Roman MJ, et al. Impact of obesity on cardiac geometry and function in a population of adolescents: the Strong Heart Study. J Am Coll Cardiol. 2006;47(11):2267–73.
27. Crowley DI, Khoury PR, Urbina EM, Ippisch HM, Kimball TR. Cardiovascular impact of the pediatric obesity epidemic: higher left ventricular mass is related to higher body mass index. J Pediatr. 2011;158(5):709–14.
28. Urbina EM, Gidding SS, Bao W, Pickoff AS, Berdusis K, Berenson GS. Effect of body size, ponderosity, and blood pressure on left ventricular growth in children and young adults in the Bogalusa Heart Study. Circulation. 1995;91(9):2400–6.

29. Yoshinaga M, Yuasa Y, Hatano H, et al. Effect of total adipose weight and systemic hypertension on left ventricular mass in children. Am J Cardiol. 1995;76(11):785–7.
30. Berry C, Sattar N. Stressed hearts in children with obesity and diabetes: a cause for concern? Diabetologia. 2011;54(4):715–8.
31. Kono Y, Yoshinaga M, Oku S, Nomura Y, Nakamura M, Aihoshi S. Effect of obesity on echocardiographic parameters in children. Int J Cardiol. 1994;46(1):7–13.
32. Alpert MA, Lambert CR, Terry BE, et al. Interrelationship of left ventricular mass, systolic function and diastolic filling in normotensive morbidly obese patients. Int J Obes Relat Metab Disord. 1995;19(8):550–7.
33. Rasooly Y, Sasson Z, Gupta R. Relation between body fat distribution and left ventricular mass in men without structural heart disease or systemic hypertension. Am J Cardiol. 1993;71(16):1477–9.
34. de la Maza MP, Estevez A, Bunout D, Klenner C, Oyonarte M, Hirsch S. Ventricular mass in hypertensive and normotensive obese subjects. Int J Obes Relat Metab Disord. 1994;18(4):193–7.
35. Li X, Li S, Ulusoy E, Chen W, Srinivasan SR, Berenson GS. Childhood adiposity as a predictor of cardiac mass in adulthood: the Bogalusa Heart Study. Circulation. 2004;110(22):3488–92.
36. Shah AS, Khoury PR, Dolan LM, et al. The effects of obesity and type 2 diabetes mellitus on cardiac structure and function in adolescents and young adults. Diabetologia. 2011;54(4):722–30.
37. Ippisch HM, Inge TH, Daniels SR, et al. Reversibility of cardiac abnormalities in morbidly obese adolescents. J Am Coll Cardiol. 2008;51(14):1342–8.
38. Sons HU, Hoffmann V. Epicardial fat cell size, fat distribution and fat infiltration of the right and left ventricle of the heart. Anat Anz. 1986;161(5):355–73.
39. Smith HL, Willius FA. Adiposity of the heart: a clinical and pathologic study of one hundred and thirty-six obese patients. Arch Intern Med. 1933;52:911–31.
40. Carpenter HM. Myocardial fat infiltration. Am Heart J. 1962;63:491–6.
41. Bharati S, Lev M. Cardiac conduction system involvement in sudden death of obese young people. Am Heart J. 1995;129(2):273–81.
42. Alexander JK. Obesity and cardiac performance. Am J Cardiol. 1964;14:860–5.
43. Backman L, Freyschuss U, Hallberg D, Melcher A. Cardiovascular function in extreme obesity. Acta Med Scand. 1973;193(5):437–46.
44. Kaltman AJ, Goldring RM. Role of circulatory congestion in the cardiorespiratory failure of obesity. Am J Med. 1976;60(5):645–53.
45. Sharpe J. Impact of obesity on diastolic function in subjects < or = 16 years of age. Am J Cardiol. 2006;98(5):691–3.
46. Wong CY, O'Moore-Sullivan T, Leano R, Byrne N, Beller E, Marwick TH. Alterations of left ventricular myocardial characteristics associated with obesity. Circulation. 2004;110(19):3081–7.
47. Beljic T, Miric M. Improved metabolic control does not reverse left ventricular filling abnormalities in newly diagnosed non-insulin-dependent diabetes patients. Acta Diabetol. 1994;31(3):147–50.
48. Poirier P, Bogaty P, Garneau C, Marois L, Dumesnil JG. Diastolic dysfunction in normotensive men with well-controlled type 2 diabetes: importance of maneuvers in echocardiographic screening for preclinical diabetic cardiomyopathy. Diabetes Care. 2001;24(1):5–10.
49. Vanninen E, Mustonen J, Vainio P, Lansimies E, Uusitupa M. Left ventricular function and dimensions in newly diagnosed non-insulin-dependent diabetes mellitus. Am J Cardiol. 1992;70(3):371–8.
50. Tarumi N, Iwasaka T, Takahashi N, et al. Left ventricular diastolic filling properties in diabetic patients during isometric exercise. Cardiology. 1993;83(5–6):316–23.
51. Pascual M, Pascual DA, Soria F, et al. Effects of isolated obesity on systolic and diastolic left ventricular function. Heart. 2003;89(10):1152–6.
52. Alpert MA, Terry BE, Lambert CR, et al. Factors influencing left ventricular systolic function in nonhypertensive morbidly obese patients, and effect of weight loss induced by gastroplasty. Am J Cardiol. 1993;71(8):733–7.

53. Koehler B, Malecka-Tendera E, Drzewiecka B, et al. Evaluation of the cardiovascular system in children with simple obesity. Part II. Echocardiographic assessment. Mater Med Pol. 1989;21(2):131–3.
54. Kimball TR, Daniels SR, Khoury PR, Magnotti RA, Turner AM, Dolan LM. Cardiovascular status in young patients with insulin-dependent diabetes mellitus. Circulation. 1994;90(1): 357–61.
55. Uusitupa M, Siitonen O, Pyorala K, Lansimies E. Left ventricular function in newly diagnosed non-insulin-dependent (type 2) diabetics evaluated by systolic time intervals and echocardiography. Acta Med Scand. 1985;217(4):379–88.
56. Palmieri V, Bella JN, Arnett DK, et al. Effect of type 2 diabetes mellitus on left ventricular geometry and systolic function in hypertensive subjects: Hypertension Genetic Epidemiology Network (HyperGEN) study. Circulation. 2001;103(1):102–7.
57. Mustonen JN, Uusitupa MI, Tahvanainen K, et al. Impaired left ventricular systolic function during exercise in middle-aged insulin-dependent and noninsulin-dependent diabetic subjects without clinically evident cardiovascular disease. Am J Cardiol. 1988;62(17):1273–9.
58. Wong CY, O'Moore-Sullivan T, Leano R, Hukins C, Jenkins C, Marwick TH. Association of subclinical right ventricular dysfunction with obesity. J Am Coll Cardiol. 2006;47(3):611–6.
59. Aasum E, Hafstad AD, Severson DL, Larsen TS. Age-dependent changes in metabolism, contractile function, and ischemic sensitivity in hearts from db/db mice. Diabetes. 2003;52(2):434–41.
60. Mazumder PK, O'Neill BT, Roberts MW, et al. Impaired cardiac efficiency and increased fatty acid oxidation in insulin-resistant ob/ob mouse hearts. Diabetes. 2004;53(9):2366–74.
61. Buchanan J, Mazumder PK, Hu P, et al. Reduced cardiac efficiency and altered substrate metabolism precedes the onset of hyperglycemia and contractile dysfunction in two mouse models of insulin resistance and obesity. Endocrinology. 2005;146(12):5341–9.
62. Peterson LR, Herrero P, Schechtman KB, et al. Effect of obesity and insulin resistance on myocardial substrate metabolism and efficiency in young women. Circulation. 2004;109(18): 2191–6.
63. Murray AJ, Anderson RE, Watson GC, Radda GK, Clarke K. Uncoupling proteins in human heart. Lancet. 2004;364(9447):1786–8.
64. Zhou YT, Grayburn P, Karim A, et al. Lipotoxic heart disease in obese rats: implications for human obesity. Proc Natl Acad Sci USA. 2000;97(4):1784–9.
65. Szczepaniak LS, Dobbins RL, Metzger GJ, et al. Myocardial triglycerides and systolic function in humans: in vivo evaluation by localized proton spectroscopy and cardiac imaging. Magn Reson Med. 2003;49(3):417–23.
66. McGavock JM, Victor RG, Unger RH, Szczepaniak LS. American College of Physicians and the American Physiological Society. Adiposity of the heart, revisited. Ann Intern Med. 2006;144(7):517–24.
67. Listenberger LL, Schaffer JE. Mechanisms of lipoapoptosis: implications for human heart disease. Trends Cardiovasc Med. 2002;12(3):134–8.
68. Unger R. Lipotoxic diseases. Annu Rev Med. 2002;53:319–36.
69. Minhas KM, Khan SA, Raju SV, et al. Leptin repletion restores depressed {beta}-adrenergic contractility in ob/ob mice independently of cardiac hypertrophy. J Physiol. 2005;565(Pt 2):463–74.
70. Iozzo P, Chareonthaitawee P, Rimoldi O, Betteridge DJ, Camici PG, Ferrannini E. Mismatch between insulin-mediated glucose uptake and blood flow in the heart of patients with Type II diabetes. Diabetologia. 2002;45(10):1404–9.
71. Scheuermann-Freestone M, Madsen PL, Manners D, et al. Abnormal cardiac and skeletal muscle energy metabolism in patients with type 2 diabetes. Circulation. 2003;107(24):3040–6.
72. Shibata R, Ouchi N, Ito M, et al. Adiponectin-mediated modulation of hypertrophic signals in the heart. Nat Med. 2004;10(12):1384–9.
73. Valle M, Martos R, Gascon F, Canete R, Zafra MA, Morales R. Low-grade systemic inflammation, hypoadiponectinemia and a high concentration of leptin are present in very young obese children, and correlate with metabolic syndrome. Diabetes Metab. 2005;31(1):55–62.

74. Arita Y, Kihara S, Ouchi N, et al. Paradoxical decrease of an adipose-specific protein, adiponectin, in obesity. Biochem Biophys Res Commun. 1999;257(1):79–83.
75. Arnaiz P, Acevedo M, Barja S, et al. Adiponectin levels, cardiometabolic risk factors and markers of subclinical atherosclerosis in children. Int J Cardiol. 2010;138(2):138–44.
76. Winer JC, Zern TL, Taksali SE, et al. Adiponectin in childhood and adolescent obesity and its association with inflammatory markers and components of the metabolic syndrome. J Clin Endocrinol Metab. 2006;91(11):4415–23.
77. Pilz S, Horejsi R, Moller R, et al. Early atherosclerosis in obese juveniles is associated with low serum levels of adiponectin. J Clin Endocrinol Metab. 2005;90(8):4792–6.
78. Chu NF, Shen MH, Wu DM, Lai CJ. Relationship between plasma adiponectin levels and metabolic risk profiles in Taiwanese children. Obes Res. 2005;13(11):2014–20.
79. Beauloye V, Zech F, Tran HT, Clapuyt P, Maes M, Brichard SM. Determinants of early atherosclerosis in obese children and adolescents. J Clin Endocrinol Metab. 2007;92(8):3025–32.
80. Pervanidou P. Associations between circulating N-terminal pro-Brain Natriuretic Peptide (NT-proBNP) and adiponectin concentrations depend on obesity level in female adolescents: gender dimorphic findings. Horm Metab Res. 2009;41(11):829–33.
81. Rasouli N, Kern PA. Adipocytokines and the metabolic complications of obesity. J Clin Endocrinol Metab. 2008;93(11 Suppl 1):S64–73.
82. Xu H, Barnes GT, Yang Q, et al. Chronic inflammation in fat plays a crucial role in the development of obesity-related insulin resistance. J Clin Invest. 2003;112(12):1821–30.
83. Alpert MA. Obesity cardiomyopathy: pathophysiology and evolution of the clinical syndrome. Am J Med Sci. 2001;321(4):225–36.
84. Alexander JK, Dennis EW, Smith WG, Amad KH, Duncan WC, Austin RC. Blood volume, cardiac output, and distribution of systemic blood flow in extreme obesity. Cardiovasc Res Cent Bull. 1962;1:39–44.
85. Messerli FH, Christie B, DeCarvalho JG, et al. Obesity and essential hypertension. Hemodynamics, intravascular volume, sodium excretion, and plasma renin activity. Arch Intern Med. 1981;141(1):81–5.
86. de Divitiis O, Fazio S, Petitto M, Maddalena G, Contaldo F, Mancini M. Obesity and cardiac function. Circulation. 1981;64(3):477–82.
87. Agarwal N, Shibutani K, SanFilippo JA, Del Guercio LR. Hemodynamic and respiratory changes in surgery of the morbidly obese. Surgery. 1982;92(2):226–34.
88. Giacchetti G, Faloia E, Mariniello B, et al. Overexpression of the renin-angiotensin system in human visceral adipose tissue in normal and overweight subjects. Am J Hypertens. 2002;15(5):381–8.
89. Goodfriend TL, Kelley DE, Goodpaster BH, Winters SJ. Visceral obesity and insulin resistance are associated with plasma aldosterone levels in women. Obes Res. 1999;7(4):355–62.
90. Harte A, McTernan P, Chetty R, et al. Insulin-mediated upregulation of the renin angiotensin system in human subcutaneous adipocytes is reduced by rosiglitazone. Circulation. 2005;111(15):1954–61.
91. Brilla CG, Matsubara LS, Weber KT. Anti-aldosterone treatment and the prevention of myocardial fibrosis in primary and secondary hyperaldosteronism. J Mol Cell Cardiol. 1993;25(5):563–75.
92. Corry DB, Tuck ML. Obesity, hypertension, and sympathetic nervous system activity. Curr Hypertens Rep. 1999;1(2):119–26.
93. Festa A, D'Agostino Jr R, Hales CN, Mykkanen L, Haffner SM. Heart rate in relation to insulin sensitivity and insulin secretion in nondiabetic subjects. Diabetes Care. 2000;23(5):624–8.
94. Sivitz WI, Wayson SM, Bayless ML, Sinkey CA, Haynes WG. Obesity impairs vascular relaxation in human subjects: hyperglycemia exaggerates adrenergic vasoconstriction arterial dysfunction in obesity and diabetes. J Diabetes Complications. 2007;21(3):149–57.
95. Sundell J, Laine H, Luotolahti M, et al. Obesity affects myocardial vasoreactivity and coronary flow response to insulin. Obes Res. 2002;10(7):617–24.
96. Wang T. Obesity and the Risk of New-Onset Atrial Fibrillation. JAMA. 2004;292(20):2471–7.

97. Dublin S, French B, Glazer NL, et al. Risk of new-onset atrial fibrillation in relation to body mass index. Arch Intern Med. 2006;166(21):2322–8.
98. Zacharias A, Schwann TA, Riordan CJ, Durham SJ, Shah AS, Habib RH. Obesity and risk of new-onset atrial fibrillation after cardiac surgery. Circulation. 2005;112(21):3247–55.
99. Drenick EJ, Fisler JS. Sudden cardiac arrest in morbidly obese surgical patients unexplained after autopsy. Am J Surg. 1988;155(6):720–6.
100. Messerli FH, Nunez BD, Ventura HO, Snyder DW. Overweight and sudden death. Increased ventricular ectopy in cardiomyopathy of obesity. Arch Intern Med. 1987;147(10):1725–8.
101. Alpert MA, Terry BE, Cohen MV, Fan TM, Painter JA, Massey CV. The electrocardiogram in morbid obesity. Am J Cardiol. 2000;85(7):908–10. A10.
102. Eisenstein I, Edelstein J, Sarma R, Sanmarco M, Selvester RH. The electrocardiogram in obesity. J Electrocardiol. 1982;15(2):115–8.
103. Okin PM, Roman MJ, Devereux RB, Kligfield P. ECG identification of left ventricular hypertrophy Relationship of test performance to body habitus. J Electrocardiol. 1996;29(Suppl):256–61.
104. Alpert MA. Value and limitations of echocardiography in the assessment of obese patients. Echocardiography. 1986;3(3):261–72.
105. Stoddard MF, Tseuda K, Thomas M, Dillon S, Kupersmith J. The influence of obesity on left ventricular filling and systolic function. Am Heart J. 1992;124(3):694–9.
106. Leong DP, De Pasquale CG, Selvanayagam JB. Heart failure with normal ejection fraction: the complementary roles of echocardiography and CMR imaging. JACC Cardiovasc Imaging. 2010;3(4):409–20.
107. Hoit BD. Strain and strain rate echocardiography and coronary artery disease. Circ Cardiovasc Imaging. 2011;4(2):179–90.
108. Ferraro S, Perrone-Filardi P, Desiderio A, et al. Left ventricular systolic and diastolic function in severe obesity: a radionuclide study. Cardiology. 1996;87(4):347–53.
109. Abidov A, Hachamovitch R, Berman DS. Modern nuclear cardiac imaging in diagnosis and clinical management of patients with left ventricular dysfunction. Minerva Cardioangiol. 2004;52(6):505–19.
110. Orakzai SH, Orakzai RH, Nasir K, Budoff MJ. Assessment of cardiac function using multidetector row computed tomography. J Comput Assist Tomogr. 2006;30(4):555–63.
111. Epstein FH. MRI of left ventricular function. J Nucl Cardiol. 2007;14(5):729–44.
112. Iacobellis GG. Cardiac adiposity and cardiovascular risk: potential role of epicardial adipose tissue. Curr Cardiol Rev. 2007;3(1):11–4.
113. Lainscak M, von Haehling S, Anker SD. Natriuretic peptides and other biomarkers in chronic heart failure: from BNP, NT-proBNP, and MR-proANP to routine biochemical markers. Int J Cardiol. 2009;132(3):303–11.
114. Iwanaga Y, Kihara Y, Niizuma S, et al. BNP in overweight and obese patients with heart failure: an analysis based on the BNP-LV diastolic wall stress relationship. J Card Fail. 2007;13(8):663–7.
115. Taylor JA, Christenson RH, Rao K, Jorge M, Gottlieb SS. B-type natriuretic peptide and N-terminal pro B-type natriuretic peptide are depressed in obesity despite higher left ventricular end diastolic pressures. Am Heart J. 2006;152(6):1071–6.
116. Wang TJ, Larson MG, Levy D, et al. Impact of obesity on plasma natriuretic peptide levels. Circulation. 2004;109(5):594–600.
117. Tuomilehto J, Lindstrom J, Eriksson JG, et al. Prevention of type 2 diabetes mellitus by changes in lifestyle among subjects with impaired glucose tolerance. N Engl J Med. 2001;344(18):1343–50.
118. Verreth W, De Keyzer D, Pelat M, et al. Weight-loss-associated induction of peroxisome proliferator-activated receptor-alpha and peroxisome proliferator-activated receptor-gamma correlate with reduced atherosclerosis and improved cardiovascular function in obese insulin-resistant mice. Circulation. 2004;110(20):3259–69.
119. Tuck ML, Sowers J, Dornfeld L, Kledzik G, Maxwell M. The effect of weight reduction on blood pressure, plasma renin activity, and plasma aldosterone levels in obese patients. N Engl J Med. 1981;304(16):930–3.

120. Hinderliter A, Sherwood A, Gullette EC, et al. Reduction of left ventricular hypertrophy after exercise and weight loss in overweight patients with mild hypertension. Arch Intern Med. 2002;162(12):1333–9.
121. Wirth A, Kroger H. Improvement of left ventricular morphology and function in obese subjects following a diet and exercise program. Int J Obes Relat Metab Disord. 1995;19(1):61–6.
122. de la Cruz-Munoz N, Messiah SE, Arheart KL, Lopez-Mitnik G, Lipshultz SE, Livingstone A. Bariatric surgery significantly decreases the prevalence of type 2 diabetes mellitus and pre-diabetes among morbidly obese multiethnic adults: long-term results. J Am Coll Surg. 2011;212(4):505–11, discussion 512–3.
123. Inge TH, Miyano G, Bean J, et al. Reversal of type 2 diabetes mellitus and improvements in cardiovascular risk factors after surgical weight loss in adolescents. Pediatrics. 2009;123(1):214–22.
124. Bray GA, Ryan DH. Drug treatment of the overweight patient. Gastroenterology. 2007;132(6):2239–52.
125. Leombruni P, Piero A, Lavagnino L, Brustolin A, Campisi S, Fassino S. A randomized, double-blind trial comparing sertraline and fluoxetine 6-month treatment in obese patients with Binge Eating Disorder. Prog Neuropsychopharmacol Biol Psychiatry. 2008;32(6):1599–605.
126. Stunkard AJ, Allison KC, Lundgren JD, et al. A paradigm for facilitating pharmacotherapy at a distance: sertraline treatment of the night eating syndrome. J Clin Psychiatry. 2006;67(10):1568–72.
127. Jordan J, Messerli FH, Lavie CJ, Aepfelbacher FC, Soria F. Reduction of weight and left ventricular mass with serotonin uptake inhibition in obese patients with systemic hypertension. Am J Cardiol. 1995;75(10):743–4.
128. Aronne LJ, Isoldi KK. Cannabinoid-1 receptor blockade in cardiometabolic risk reduction: efficacy. Am J Cardiol. 2007;100(12A):18P–26.
129. Godoy-Matos A, Carraro L, Vieira A, et al. Treatment of obese adolescents with sibutramine: a randomized, double-blind, controlled study. J Clin Endocrinol Metab. 2005;90(3):1460–5.
130. Connolly HM, McGoon MD. Obesity drugs and the heart. Curr Probl Cardiol. 1999;24(12):745–92.
131. Rothman RB, Baumann MH. Appetite suppressants, cardiac valve disease and combination pharmacotherapy. Am J Ther. 2009;16(4):354–64.
132. Dahl CF, Allen MR, Urie PM, Hopkins PN. Valvular regurgitation and surgery associated with fenfluramine use: an analysis of 5743 individuals. BMC Med. 2008;6:34.
133. Bays HE. Lorcaserin: drug profile and illustrative model of the regulatory challenges of weight-loss drug development. Expert Rev Cardiovasc Ther. 2011;9(3):265–77.
134. Hughes TE, Vath JE, Marjason J, Proietto J. ZGN-433 is well-tolerated, reduces body weight rapidly and improves cardiovascular risk markers in obese subjects: The ZAF-001 proof of concept trial. Diabetes. 2011;60(Suppl 1A):LB15.
135. Luthin DR. Anti-obesity effects of small molecule melanin-concentrating hormone receptor 1 (MCHR1) antagonists. Life Sci. 2007;81(6):423–40.
136. Rusconi P, Gomez-Marin O, Rossique-Gonzalez M, et al. Carvedilol in children with cardiomyopathy: 3-year experience at a single institution. J Heart Lung Transplant. 2004;23(7):832–8.
137. Rossner S, Taylor CL, Byington RP, Furberg CD. Long term propranolol treatment and changes in body weight after myocardial infarction. BMJ. 1990;300(6729):902–3.
138. Raji A, Seely EW, Bekins SA, Williams GH, Simonson DC. Rosiglitazone improves insulin sensitivity and lowers blood pressure in hypertensive patients. Diabetes Care. 2003;26(1):172–8.

Chapter 11
Childhood Metabolic Syndrome and Cancer Risk

Stefanie R. Brown and Steven E. Lipshultz

Abstract Metabolic syndrome in children age 10 years and older, as defined by consensus among experts through the International Diabetes Federation, is a cluster of six risk factors for cardiovascular disease: obesity (defined by waist circumference or central obesity), elevated triglyceride concentrations, low high-density lipoprotein concentrations, elevated blood pressure, and elevated fasting glucose concentrations or type 2 diabetes. Of these risk factors, obesity in adults is the second leading cause of preventable death in the USA and is also a risk factor for cancer in adults. Obesity has been associated with increased risks of postmenopausal breast, colon, endometrial, esophageal, and kidney cancers, and it probably also increases the risk of gallbladder, ovarian, pancreatic, thyroid, and prostate cancers. In this chapter, we review the epidemiology of obesity and cancer, the effect of obesity on cancer morbidity and mortality, and the biochemical factors associated with obesity in association with increased cancer risk. We also explore the rates of obesity and its consequences in long-term survivors of childhood cancers.

Keywords Child • Adolescent • Metabolic syndrome • Obesity • Cancer

S.R. Brown, M.D., FAAP (✉)
Department of Pediatrics (R-131), University of Miami Miller School of Medicine,
1611 NW 12th Avenue C600D (R-131) Miami, FL 33136, USA
e-mail: sbrown5@med.miami.edu

S.E. Lipshultz, M.D.
Department of Pediatrics, University of Miami Miller School of Medicine,
Miami, FL, USA

Introduction

The two most common definitions of metabolic syndrome are those of The National Cholesterol Education Program and the International Diabetes Federation (IDF) [1, 2]. In adults, the definition consists of the presence of at least three of the following: abdominal obesity, high triglycerides, low high-density lipoprotein (HDL), high blood pressure, or established diabetes or raised fasting plasma glucose. The International Diabetes Federation developed by consensus a similar, but age-based, definition of metabolic syndrome in children (Table 11.1) [1].

One criterion for metabolic syndrome in children—obesity—is a risk factor for malignancy in adults. Obesity in adults is the second leading cause of preventable premature death in the USA [3]. In a recent study of 1.46 million adults, overweight and obesity were associated with increased all-cause mortality [4]. With the increasing incidence of obesity in children and its persistence into adulthood, even small increases in the risk of cancer can have marked effects on public health. In this chapter, we review the epidemiology of obesity and cancer, the effect of obesity on morbidity and mortality in patients with cancer, the biochemical factors associated with obesity and its increased cancer risk, and the rates of obesity and its consequences in long-term survivors of childhood cancers.

The Epidemiology of Obesity's Association with Cancer

Obesity has long been a known risk factor for cancer in adults. As early as the 1950s, Tannenbaum and Silverstone [5] found evidence in life insurance statistics that body weight might be associated with an increased risk of cancer. In 1976, in an observational study, Blitzer et al. found an association between obesity in adolescence and increases in the subsequent incidence of endometrial cancer in women belonging to a national weight-loss group [6].

The American Cancer Society guidelines on nutrition and physical activity for cancer prevention state that being overweight as an adult is linked to an increased risk of breast (postmenopausal), colon, endometrial, esophageal, and kidney cancers and that it also likely increases the risk of cervical, gallbladder, Hodgkin lymphoma, multiple myeloma, ovarian, pancreatic, thyroid, and aggressive forms of prostate cancer [7–9].

In 2001, approximately 35% of cancer-related deaths worldwide were attributable to nine potentially modifiable risk factors, including overweight or obesity. In high-income countries, such as the USA, obesity contributes to 14% of deaths from colon and rectal cancer, 13% of deaths from breast cancer, and 43% of deaths from uterine cancer (noncervical) [10]. Overall, 69,000 cancer-related deaths in 2001 were attributed to overweight or obesity. Calle et al. prospectively followed 900,000 cancer-free patients for 16 years (from 1982 to 1998) and found that higher body mass index (BMI) was significantly associated with higher rates of death from esophageal, colorectal, liver, gallbladder, pancreatic, and renal cancer [11].

Table 11.1 Consensus definitions of metabolic syndrome in children and adolescents issued by the International Diabetes Federation

Age group, year	Obesity (waist circumference for central obesity)	Triglycerides, mg/dL	HDL-C, mg/dL	Blood pressure, mm Hg	Glucose (mmol/L) or known type 2 diabetes
6 to <10	>90th percentile	Metabolic syndrome cannot be diagnosed, but further measurements should be taken if there is a family history of metabolic syndrome or its components			
10 to <16	≥90th percentile for sex and age or adult cutoff percentile if lower	>150	<40	Systolic >130; diastolic >85	Fasting plasma glucose >100 mg/dL or previously diagnosed type 2 diabetes
16+	Central obesity (ratio of waist circumference and height >102 cm for males and >88 cm for females)	>150	<40	Systolic >130; diastolic >85 (or treatment of previously diagnosed hypertension)	Fasting plasma glucose >100 mg/dL (or previously diagnosed type 2 diabetes)

Modified from Ref. [1], with permission from The International Diabetes Federation
HDL-C high-density lipoprotein cholesterol

Table 11.2 Relative risk estimates of obesity-related cancer by sites in men

Cancer type and site	Number of studies	Relative risk
Esophageal adenocarcinoma	5	1.52 (1.33–1.74)
Thyroid	4	1.33 (1.04–1.70)
Colon	22	1.24 (1.20–1.28)
Kidney	11	1.24 (1.15–1.34)
Liver	4	1.24 (0.95–1.62)
Malignant melanoma	6	1.17 (1.05–1.30)
Multiple myeloma	7	1.11 (1.05–1.18)
Rectum	18	1.09 (1.06–1.12)
Gallbladder	4	1.09 (0.99–1.21)

Based on data from Ref. [16]

The literature on obesity as a long-term risk factor for cancer in children is both newer and scarcer than that in adults. In 1989, one of the first of these studies noted an earlier incidence of cancer in 500 obese Swedish children. More recently, two observational studies of long-term follow-up data from growth studies begun before World War II reported a similar association [12–14].

The Epidemiology of Cancer's Association with Obesity

Several studies note the increased risk and mortality of cancer in obese people. In the study by Calle et al. mentioned above, adult patients with a BMI of 40 or higher had death rates from all cancers that were 52% higher in men and 62% higher for women than they were in controls of normal weight. This relationship was direct and linear with respect to increasing BMI [11]. This relationship is not limited to cancer developing in obese adults. In a 50-year follow-up of the Boyd Orr Study from prewar Britain (1937–1939), the risk of cancer in adulthood increased by 9% for each standard deviation increase in BMI measured during childhood [14]. This association was stronger in children measured at age 8 years or older.

The Million Women Study in the UK found that a 10-unit increase in BMI was associated with statistically significant increases in the relative risk (RR) of endometrial cancer (2.89), esophageal cancer (2.38), colorectal cancer in postmenopausal women (1.61), kidney cancer (1.53), leukemia (1.50), postmenopausal breast cancer (1.40), multiple myeloma (1.31), and pancreatic cancer (1.24) [15].

In a 2008 meta-analysis of 221 datasets extracted from prospective observational studies with a pooled sample size of 57,866,501 patients including men and women, an increase of BMI by 5 was strongly associated in men with an increased risk of esophageal adenocarcinoma, as well as thyroid, colon, and kidney cancers, and, in women, of endometrial, gallbladder, and esophageal adenocarcinomas, and kidney cancer (see Tables 11.2 and 11.3). There was an increased risk of postmenopausal breast cancer but a decreased risk of premenopausal breast cancer (RR: 0.92) [16].

Table 11.3 Relative risk estimates of obesity-related cancer by sites in women

Cancer type and site	Number of studies	Relative risk
Endometrium	19	1.59 (1.50–1.68)
Gallbladder	2	1.59 (1.02–2.47)
Esophageal adenocarcinoma	3	1.51 (1.31–1.74)
Kidney	12	1.34 (1.25–1.43)
Leukemia	7	1.17 (1.04–1.32)
Postmenopausal breast	31	1.12 (1.08–1.16)
Pancreas	11	1.12 (1.02–1.22)
Multiple myeloma	6	1.11 (1.07–1.15)
Colon	19	1.09 (1.05–1.13)

Based on data from Ref. [16]

Colorectal Cancer

Obesity has been consistently associated with a higher risk of colorectal cancer. Multiple studies have observed a direct association in adults, and additionally a few studies show an association with childhood, adolescent, and early adult obesity. In a follow-up of the Harvard Growth Study of 1922–1935, in men who were overweight during adolescence, there was an adjusted RR of colorectal cancer of 5.6 (95% CI 0.6 – 57.5) and an RR of mortality from colorectal cancer of 9.1 (95% CI 1.1 – 77.5) [13].

In a retrospective cohort study conducted in 2010, 15,322 University of Glasgow students were followed for a median of 49 years. A positive relationship was found between BMI in early adulthood and colorectal cancer incidence and mortality [17].

In 2007, 2 meta-analyses observed an increased risk of colorectal cancer with obesity [18, 19]. In one of these studies, Larrson et al. found that a 5-unit increase in BMI was associated with an RR for colon cancer of 1.3 in men and of 1.2 in women and an RR for rectal cancer of 1.12 in men [18]. In the other study, Moghaddam et al. reported that obesity was associated with an RR for colorectal cancer of 1.41 in men and 1.08 in women [19]. In 2008, Rapp et al., in a cohort study of 65,000 Austrian adults, observed an inverse association between weight loss of more than 0.10 kg/m^2/year over a 5- to 9-year period and the incidence of colon cancer (hazard ratio 0.50) [20].

Obesity raises the risk of colon cancer in both men and women, but the link seems to be stronger in men [7]. Studies have evaluated whether this risk is the result of central adiposity (in contrast to general adiposity), most commonly measured as the waist-to-hip ratio, which is more common in men. However, studies measuring both BMI and waist-to-hip ratio measures in women found no association with the risk of colorectal cancer [21].

Breast Cancer

Breast cancer is the most common cancer in women and the second leading cause of cancer death in women. Overweight and obese women have higher rates of incidence, recurrence, and mortality in breast cancer. Studies documenting the association between obesity and breast cancer appear as early as the 1970s [6, 22]. Obesity, central adiposity, and adult weight gain all increase the rates of postmenopausal breast cancer [21]. A 1992 meta-analysis estimated that being overweight (BMI ≥ 25 to 29 kg/m^2) was also associated with a 78–91% increased risk of breast cancer recurrence [23].

Studies of breast cancer mortality and survival also show an association with poorer survival in obese women than in nonobese women [24]. In the 2001 American Cancer Society's Cancer Prevention Study, breast cancer mortality in very obese women (BMI ≥ 40) was three times higher than that in lean women (BMI ≤ 20.5), suggesting that 30–50% of breast cancer deaths are caused by obesity [25]. In a more recent meta-analysis of 43 studies with sample sizes of 100–424,168, the hazard ratio of survival in obese women compared with nonobese women was 1.33 [24].

Several theories have been proposed about how obesity might increase cancer risk, but no human studies have revealed a causal mechanism. Studies evaluating patterns of weight loss and weight gain often observe that consistent weight gain in young adult women over time (between 18 years and menopause) is associated with higher rates of breast cancer than those in women who lost weight over time (between 18 and 30 years old in the first study and from 30 years old to age of menopause in the second) [26, 27]. Molecular theories of causation include increased exposure of estrogen receptor-positive cancers to circulating estrogen in obese women and the possibility that IGF-1 may be involved because it is associated with mammary gland hyperplasia and mammary cancer in animals [21].

Endometrial Cancer

Endometrial cancer is the fourth most common cancer in women. In 2008, the lifetime risk of this cancer was 2.6%. The most important risk factors for endometrial cancer are unopposed estrogen, a sedentary lifestyle, and obesity [28]. In fact, the evidence for a link between obesity and endometrial cancer is strong [7]. The RR for endometrial cancer is 3.0 in women 21–50 lb overweight and 10.0 in women more than 50 lb overweight [29]. Several biological factors in the molecular pathway of obesity and endometrial cancer are discussed below.

Perhaps 70–90% of women with endometrial cancer are obese, and because many have comorbidities, their perioperative risk of morbidity is substantial.

Kidney Cancer

Obesity is definitely related to kidney cancer [7]. The risk of kidney cancer worldwide is 1.5- to 2.5-fold higher in overweight and obese persons, and the risk is linearly related to BMI [11].

Table 11.4 Biochemical markers as related to obesity and risk of malignancy

Biochemical marker	Obesity[a]	Breast cancer	Endometrial cancer	Colorectal cancer	Prostate cancer	Esophageal cancer	Pancreatic cancer
Vitamin D	↓[b]	↑	↑	↑	↑	↑	↑
Adiponectin	↓	↑[c]	↑	↑	↓[d]		
Leptin	↑	↑	↑	↑	↑		[e]
Estrogen	↑	↑	↑				
IGF-1	↑	↑	↑				

Based on data from Refs. [31, 33–37]
[a]Arrows indicate levels of biochemical marker in obesity and indicate increase or decrease of risk in type of cancer
[b]Decreased bioavailability of active forms of vitamin D occurs in obesity
[c]Postmenopausal women only
[d]Correlation is not consistent across studies, but the trend is toward decreased risk. In vitro, adiponectin inhibits growth and proliferation in metastatic prostate cancer cell lines
[e]More than 1 study shows lower levels of leptin, but it is unclear if this is secondary to the weight loss usually associated with pancreatic cancer

Esophageal Cancer

Esophageal adenocarcinoma has been rapidly increasing in Western countries, and the rate parallels the increased prevalence of gastroesophageal reflux, which is a main causal factor. Obesity increases the risk for cancer in the lower esophagus and at the junction of the esophagus and stomach [7, 30].

Pancreatic Cancer

Some studies have linked obesity, physical inactivity (factors strongly linked to diabetes and prediabetes), and diets high in processed and red meats with an increased risk of pancreatic cancer [7]. However, in a meta-analysis of 14 observational studies, the RR of pancreatic cancer in obese patients, compared to that of patients with normal body weight, was 1.19, indicating an association [31].

Biochemical Factors in Obesity and Cancer

Body weight, obesity, and diabetes or impaired glucose tolerance affect some biochemical and molecular factors that can alter cancer risk, in particular, peptides and steroid hormones and their binding factors, such as insulin-like growth factor-1 (IGF-1), estradiol, vitamin D, leptin, and adiponectin. Macrophages in adipose tissue also release TNFα, nitric oxide synthetase, and other inflammatory factors [32]. Many of these biochemical factors are associated with an increased risk of cancer (Table 11.4).

Insulin-Like Growth Factor-1

The protein IGF-1 stimulates cell proliferation, inhibits apoptosis, and induces mitosis in many cancer cell lines. In vitro studies show that IGF-1 promotes the growth of both colonic carcinoma and breast cancer cells and has been associated with an increased risk of endometrial cancer [21, 33, 38]. Several possible mechanisms for these effects of IGF-1 have been proposed, including chronic hyperinsulinemia, insulin resistance (through insulin growth factor), and decreased levels of adipokines [34, 38].

Vitamin D

Obesity is associated with lower serum vitamin D concentrations. In a study of 127 obese children and adolescents, 74% had low (serum 25[OH] vitamin D concentration <75 nmol/L) serum vitamin D concentrations [7, 35]. Circulating concentrations of vitamin D are inversely correlated with several components of metabolic syndrome, including insulin sensitivity, type 2 diabetes, and obesity in both adults and adolescents [7]. Low levels of vitamin D increase the risk or mortality from 13 different cancers in the USA [36, 37].

Adiponectin

Adiponectin is a peptide expressed exclusively in adipocytes. Adipocytes are downregulated by factors that are increased in obesity, such as TNFα, IL-6, and IL-18. They have anti-inflammatory and anti-atherogenic effects and increase insulin sensitization, as well as help to maintain the balance of vascularization in adipose tissue. In vitro studies have shown that they also regulate neovascularization in tumors [37].

Enzymatic activity in adipose tissue may increase the rate at which precursors convert to estrogen, a process that can be implicated in endometrial cancer, among other conditions.

Leptin

Leptin is an adipokine produced mainly by white adipose tissue. Its levels are positively correlated with leptin and increased adipose tissue. Leptin increased the growth, migration, and invasiveness of tumor cells in vitro [37, 39].

Long-Term Survivors of Childhood Cancer and Metabolic Syndrome

More than 75% of children with cancer now survive into adulthood, but increasing evidence indicates that survivors have a higher incidence of chronic disease, including a higher risk of morbidity and mortality from cardiovascular disease, than that of the general population [40, 41]. Cardiovascular risk factors are associated with different types of malignancies and therapies. Obesity is most commonly associated with leukemia and central nervous system tumors. Dyslipidemia is associated with adult survivors of childhood cancers treated with platinum agents, and hypertension has been associated with renal damage caused by some treatments. In a comparison of 8,599 survivors more than 5 years after the end of treatment with 2,936 sibling controls, the odds ratios (OR; 95% confidence interval) of survivors for the presence of three or more cardiovascular risk factors (surrogate criteria for metabolic syndrome) were 1.9 (1.6–2.2) for hypertension, 1.6 (1.3–2.0) for dyslipidemia, and 1.7 (1.2–2.3) for impaired glucose metabolism. Factors associated with having cardiovascular risk factors were older age at the time of the study (OR, 4.4), exposure to total body irradiation (8.2), or radiation to the chest and abdomen (2.3) [40].

Obesity Therapy and Cancer Prevention

Several studies have shown an association between weight loss, increased activity levels, and a decreased risk of breast and colon cancer. Harvie et al., in a prospective cohort study of 33,600 women between the ages 18–30 and ages 30 to menopause, found that breast cancer rates were lowest in women who maintained baseline weight or lost weight before menopause, after menopause, or both [26]. Greater lifetime physical activity was associated with a decreased risk of breast cancer [42], and in one study, recreational activity, especially in late adolescence and early adulthood, was protective [7].

Some studies report a lower risk of colon cancer among people who are moderately but regularly active. More vigorous activity may reduce the risk of colon cancer even further [7].

In one study of 9,949 patients after gastric bypass surgery, mortality from cancer decreased by 60% over a 7.1-year follow-up compared to controls [43]. However, in a more recent cohort study, gastric bypass surgery was not associated with an overall decrease in standardized incidence ratios for obesity-related cancers [44].

Summary

In the USA, obesity is epidemic and is the second leading cause of preventable death. Obesity is also associated with increased risk of the most common cancers. Primary prevention through lifestyle and environmental interventions has been suggested as the best approach for addressing cancer worldwide [38]. However, few studies have examined the relationship between weight loss during childhood and decreased cancer risk in adulthood. Clinical guidelines for assessing and managing obesity in children and adults should nevertheless be implemented.

As shown in National Health and Nutrition Examination Survey data, obesity in childhood persists into adulthood. The probability that overweight school children will become obese adults is estimated to be 50%, whereas the probability that obese adolescents will become obese adults is between 70% and 80% [45]. Increases in the risk of cancer among obese people range from 9% to 60%. Given that these increases are accompanied by high rates of childhood obesity that persist into adulthood, the implications for public health are severe.

References

1. The International Diabetes Federation consensus definition of the metabolic syndrome in children and adolescents. http://www.idf.org/webdata/docs/Mets_definition_children.pdf. Accessed 4 May, 2011.
2. Alberti KG, et al. Harmonizing the Metabolic Syndrome: a joint interim statement of the International Diabetes Federation Task Force on Epidemiology and Prevention; National Heart, Lung and Blood Institute; American Heart Association; World Heart Federation; International Atherosclerosis Society; and International Association for the Study of Obesity. Circulation. 2009;120:1640–5.
3. Mokdad AH, Marks JS, Stroup DF, Gerberding JL. Actual causes of death in the United States, 2000. JAMA. 2004;291:1238–45.
4. Berrinton de Gonzalez A, Hartge P, Cerhan JR, et al. Body-mass index and mortality among 1.46 million white adults. N Engl J Med. 2010;363:2211–9.
5. Tannenbaum A, Silverstone H. Nutritional relation to cancer. Adv Cancer Res. 1953;1:451–501.
6. Blitzer PH, Blitzer EC, Rimm AA. Association between teenage obesity and cancer. Prev Med. 1976;5:20–31.
7. Biro FM, Wien M. Childhood obesity and adult morbidities. Am J Clin Nutr. 2010;91:1499S–505.
8. Bianchini F, Kaaks R, Vainio H. Overweight, obesity and cancer risk. Lancet Oncol. 2002;3:565–74.
9. American Cancer Society guidelines on nutrition and physical activity for cancer prevention. http://www.cancer.org/acs/groups/cid/documents/webcontent/002577-pdf.pdf. Accessed 1 May 2011.
10. Danaei G, Hoorn SV, Lopez AD, et al. Causes of cancer in the world: comparative risk assessment of nine behavioural and environmental risk factors. Lancet. 2005;366:1784–93.
11. Calle EE, Rodriguez C, Walker-Thurmond AK, Thun MJ. Overweight, obesity, and mortality from cancer in a prospectively studied cohort of U.S. adults. N Engl J Med. 2003;348:1625–38.

12. Mossberg HO. 40-year follow-up of overweight children. Lancet. 1989;2(8661):491–3.
13. Must A, Jacques PF, Dallal GE, Bajema CJ, Dietz WH. Long-term morbidity and mortality of overweight adolescents. A follow-up of the Harvard Growth Study of 1922 to 1935. N Engl J Med. 1992;327:1350–5. PMID: 1406836.
14. Jeffreys M, Smith GD, Martin RM, et al. Childhood body mass index and later cancer risk: a 50-year follow-up of the Boyd Orr Study. Int J Cancer. 2004;112:348–51.
15. Reeves GK, Pirie K, Beral V, et al. Cancer incidence and mortality in relation to body mass index in the Million Women Study: cohort study. BMJ. 2007;335:1134–45.
16. Renehan AG, Tyson M, Egger M, Heller RF, Zwahlen M. Body-mass index and incidence of cancer: a systematic review and meta-analysis of prospective observational studies. Lancet. 2008;371:569–78.
17. Burton A, Martin R, Galogardes B, et al. Young adulthood body mass index and risk of cancer in later adulthood: historical cohort study. Cancer Causes Control. 2010;21:2069–77.
18. Larsson SC, Wolk A. Obesity and colon and rectal cancer risk: a meta-analysis of prospective studies. Am J Clin Nutr. 2007;86:556–65.
19. Moghaddam AA, Woodward M, Huxley R. Obesity and risk of colorectal cancer: a meta-analysis of 31 studies with 70,000 events. Cancer Epidemiol Biomarkers Prev. 2007;16:2533–47.
20. Rapp K, Klenk J, Ulmer H, et al. Weight change and cancer risk in a cohort of more than 65,000 adults in Austria. Ann Oncol. 2008;19:641–8.
21. Calle EE, Thun MJ. Obesity and cancer. Oncogene. 2004;23:6365–78.
22. De Waard F, Baanders-Van Halewijn EA. A prospective study in general practice on breast-cancer risk in postmenopausal women. Int J Cancer. 1974;14:153–60.
23. McTiernan A, Irwin M, VonGruenigen V. Weight, physical activity, diet, and prognosis in breast and gynecologic cancers. J Clin Oncol. 2010;28:4074–80.
24. Protani M, Coory M, Martin JH. Effect of obesity on survival of women with breast cancer: systematic review and meta-analysis. Breast Cancer Res Treat. 2010;123:627–35.
25. Petrelli J, Calle E, Rodriguez C, Thun M. Body mass index, height, and postmenopausal breast cancer mortality in a prospective cohort of US women. Cancer Causes Control. 2002;13:325–32.
26. Harvie M, Howell A, Vierkant RA, et al. Association of gain and loss of weight before and after menopause with risk of postmenopausal breast cancer in the Iowa women's health study. Cancer Epidemiol Biomarkers Prev. 2005;14:656–61.
27. Coates RJ, Uhler RJ, Hall HI, et al. Risk of breast cancer in young women in relation to body size and weight gain in adolescence and early adulthood. Br J Cancer. 1999;81:167–74.
28. Schouten LJ, Goldbohm RA, van den Brandt PA. Anthropometry, physical activity, and endometrial cancer risk: results from the Netherlands Cohort Study. J Natl Cancer Inst. 2004;96:1635–8.
29. Smith RA, von Eschenbach AC, Wender R, et al. American Cancer Society guidelines for early endometrial cancer detection: Update 2001. http://caonline.amcancersoc.org/cgi/content/full/51/1/38. Accessed 18 Apr 2011.
30. Hongo M, Nagasaki Y, Shoji T. Epidemiology of esophageal cancer: orient to occident. Effects of chronology, geography and ethnicity. J Gastroenterol Hepatol. 2009;24:729–35.
31. Berrington de Gonalez A, Sweeland S, Spencer E. A meta-analysis of obesity and the risk of pancreatic cancer. Br J Cancer. 2003;89:519–23.
32. Nathan C. Epidemic inflammation: pondering obesity. Mol Med. 2008;13:485–92.
33. Fader AN, Arriba LN, Frasure JE, VonGruenigen VE. Endometrial cancer and obesity: epidemiology, biomarkers, prevention and survivorship. Gynecol Oncol. 2009;114:121–7.
34. Kaklamani VG, Wisinski KB, Sadim M, et al. Variants of the adiponectiv (ADIPOQ) and adiponectin receptor 1 (ADIPOR1) genes and colorectal cancer risk. JAMA. 2008;300:1523–31.
35. Alemzadeh R, Kichler J, Babar G, Calhoun M. Hypovitaminosis D in obese children and adolescents: relationship with adiposity, insulin sensitivity, ethnicity, and season. Metabolism. 2008;57:183–91.

36. Grant WB, Mohr SB. Ecological studies of ultraviolet B, vitamin D and cancer since 2000. Ann Epidemiol. 2009;19:446–54.
37. Paz-Filho G, Lim EL, Wong ML, Licinio J. Associations between adipokines and obesity-related cancers. Front Biosci. 2011;16:1634–50.
38. Brawer R, Brisbon N, Plumb J. Obesity and cancer. Prim Care. 2009;36:509–31. PMID: 19616153.
39. Catalano S, Marsico S, Giordano C, et al. Leptin enhances, via AP-1, expression of aromatase in the MCF-7 cell line. J Biol Chem. 2003;278:28668–76.
40. Meacham LR, Chow EJ, Ness KK, et al. Cardiovascular risk factors in adult survivors of pediatric cancer – a report from the childhood cancer survivor study. Cancer Epidemiol Biomarkers Prev. 2010;19:170–81.
41. Miller TL, Lipsitz SR, Lopez-Mitnik G, et al. Characteristics and determinants of adiposity in pediatric cancer survivors. Cancer Epidemiol Biomarkers Prev. 2010;19:2013–22.
42. Bianchini F, Kaaks R, Vainio H. Weight control and physical activity in cancer prevention. Obes Rev. 2002;3:5–8.
43. Adams TD, Gress RE, Smith SC, et al. Long term mortality after gastric bypass surgery. N Engl J Med. 2007;357:753–61.
44. Ostlund MP, Lu Y, Lagergren J. Risk of obesity-related cancer after obesity surgery in a population-based cohort study. Ann Surg. 2010;252:972–6.
45. Childhood obesity – Advancing effective prevention and treatment: An overview for professionals. NIHCM. http://www.nihcm.org/pdf/ChildObesityOverview.pdf. Accessed 18 May 2011.

Chapter 12
Neurocognitive and Psychological Correlates of Metabolic Syndrome in Childhood

Anna Maria Patino-Fernandez, Amber Daigre, and Alan M. Delamater

Abstract The purpose of this chapter is to review findings related to psychosocial and neurocognitive functioning in children identified as having metabolic syndrome. While many studies have focused on the definitions, prevalence, and predictors of metabolic syndrome in childhood, few have examined neurocognitive and psychological factors among youth with metabolic syndrome. This chapter therefore addresses these factors within each of the components of the metabolic syndrome. We first examine studies focusing on neurocognitive correlates in youth who are diagnosed as having high cholesterol or dyslipidemia, being overweight or obese, having high blood pressure, or having insulin resistance. The next section considers the few studies found that examine the relationship of psychological factors and metabolic syndrome, followed by a review of research examining psychological correlates of youth who have high cholesterol or dyslipidemia, are overweight, have high blood pressure, or are insulin resistant. The final section of the chapter provides a summary of the findings and discussion of future research needs.

Keywords Children • Adolescents • Metabolic syndrome • Neurocognitive functioning • Psychological functioning

A considerable amount of research has been conducted in recent years concerning metabolic syndrome in children and adolescents. Even though many studies have found that components of the metabolic syndrome cluster in children and adolescents [1–3], few have examined the role of psychosocial and neurocognitive factors in risk factor clustering. The purpose of this chapter is to review findings related to psychosocial and neurocognitive functioning in children identified as having metabolic syndrome.

Review of the literature indicated that while considerable studies have focused on the definitions, prevalence, and predictors of metabolic syndrome in childhood,

---

A.M. Patino-Fernandez, Ph.D. • A. Daigre, Ph.D. • A.M. Delamater, Ph.D. (✉)
Department of Pediatrics, University of Miami Miller School of Medicine,
1601 NW 12th Avenue, Miami, FL 33136, USA
e-mail: adelamater@med.miami.edu

there is a dearth of research that has examined neurocognitive and psychological factors among youth with metabolic syndrome. Therefore, the current review addresses these factors within each of the components of the metabolic syndrome. Most of these studies are correlational, with few studies using prospective designs. Future research must address the role of psychological and neurocognitive factors among children and adolescents with metabolic syndrome over time, so that the effects of metabolic syndrome on psychological and neurocognitive functioning can be determined.

We first examine studies focusing on neurocognitive correlates in youth who are diagnosed as having high cholesterol or dyslipidemia, being overweight or obese, having high blood pressure, or having insulin resistance. The next section considers the few studies found that examine the relationship of psychological factors and metabolic syndrome, followed by a review of research examining psychological correlates of youth who have high cholesterol or dyslipidemia, are overweight, have high blood pressure, or are insulin resistant. The final section of the chapter provides a summary of the findings and discussion of future research needs.

Neurocognitive Correlates of Metabolic Syndrome

Neuropsychological assessment can detect alterations in central nervous system (CNS) dysfunction. These assessments typically evaluate specific cognitive functions, such as perception, memory, attention, reasoning, visuospatial skills, psychomotor speed, mental flexibility, and general intelligence. In the adult literature, evidence has emerged regarding the detrimental impact of metabolic syndrome and its component features (obesity, cholesterol/dyslipidemia, hypertension, and impaired glucose tolerance) on cognitive functions [4]. Most studies examine these component features rather than the metabolic syndrome per se.

To our knowledge, no published studies to date have examined the neurocognitive consequences of the metabolic syndrome's multiple risk factors in a multivariate context, making it difficult to draw conclusions regarding the relationship between metabolic syndrome and cognitive functioning in youth. Thus, this section focuses on the component features of the metabolic syndrome and their relationship to neurocognitive abilities in adolescents. Nevertheless, one must consider the potential increase in risk for neurocognitive difficulty with increasing metabolic risk factors.

Cholesterol and Neurocognitive Functioning

Research investigating the relationship between cholesterol level and neurocognitive abilities in healthy youth has found that certain abilities are inversely associated with serum cholesterol while others are not. In an early study of male high school students, small but statistically significant relationships were found between serum cholesterol and intelligence (IQ), school grades, and performance on word generation tasks, suggesting lower levels were related to better performance [5]. Although these findings suggest that higher cholesterol levels are associated with worse performance on cognitive tasks, this study did not adjust for or take into account confounding variables such as socioeconomic status that could potentially influence the results. More recently, results of a study including a wider age range of children (ages 6–16) revealed that neither serum total cholesterol, high-density lipoprotein (HDL) cholesterol, nor non-HDL cholesterol were related to cognitive ability after controlling for potentially confounding variables [6].

It is well accepted that variation in serum cholesterol affects and alters the brain's composition and cellular activity through numerous biological pathways [7]. This supports the concept that high cholesterol or dyslipidemia may have adverse effects on neurocognitive functioning. However, more sophisticated studies of HDL cholesterol, LDL cholesterol, and triglycerides are needed in youth before conclusions can be drawn as to the role of serum cholesterol on the neurodevelopment of children. Furthermore, longer observation and follow-up periods are necessary to improve the sensitivity of findings, as the subtle effects of minor differences in serum cholesterol may become more evident in adulthood [6].

Overweight and Neurocognitive Functioning

Although historically this metabolic syndrome component has been largely ignored as a risk factor in investigations of neurocognitive functioning, it is now being recognized as an independent risk for decline in cognitive performance in adults. Its relationship with hypertension and cholesterol, its direct effect on neuronal degradation [8], and its association with subclinical inflammatory status [9] make obesity a prime variable for further research in youth. Another potential explanation for the relationship between obesity and cognitive decline is related to the effects of sleep apnea. In fact, studies have demonstrated that increased BMI is related to an increased risk of obstructive sleep apnea in youth [10].

Few well-controlled studies have been conducted examining obesity and neurocognitive functioning. A meta-analysis conducted in 2009 that included one study of adolescents found that in pubertal Chinese children (12–18 years of age), obesity, measured as a ratio of weight/ideal weight (W/IW), and intelligence, measured by Full Scale IQ (FSIQ), were inversely related [11]. This review confirmed previous findings of an inverse relationship between childhood FSIQ and obesity (measured either by BMI or W/IW) but also found that once educational attainment was controlled for the association was no longer significant. The authors speculate whether educational attainment is perhaps a mediator between intelligence and obesity. In studies of Chinese and Thai children, intelligence and school performance were found to be related to body weight, with lower IQ and lower academic grade point average (GPA) related to overweight status and higher body mass index [12, 13].

In contrast, among American children, one study found that after controlling for parent education and home environment, the relationship between obesity and academic performance was no longer significant [14]. In a more recent investigation examining both cognitive functioning and academic performance among a nationally representative sample of children in the USA, results revealed a trend for scores on measures of visuospatial organization (block design), attention and concentration (digit span), and global functioning to decrease as weight (BMI percentile) increased even after adjustments for potential confounding variables [15]. Furthermore, scores on block design, a measure of visuospatial organization, demonstrated a strong and significant association with weight status.

High Blood Pressure/Hypertension and Neurocognitive Functioning

With few exceptions, the results of numerous studies have found that hypertension has a negative impact on cognitive functioning at all ages. Furthermore, there appears to be a dose-dependent relationship between blood pressure (BP) and cognitive functioning. In children and adolescents, even mild to moderate BP elevations have been found to be related to lower cognitive functioning. For example, in one study of 6–16-year-olds, systolic BP (≥90th percentile) was related to significantly lower scores on digit span, a neuropsychological measure of attention and concentration, after controlling for potentially confounding variables [16]. This study also determined that the decrease in digit span scores was greater for youth with systolic BP ≥95th percentile compared to those at the ≥90th percentile. Findings from a study examining the clustering of cardiovascular risk factors in adolescents, including high BP (≥75th percentile) and overweight (based on BMI), revealed that the extent of clustering was greater, but not statistically significant, in youth from lower income families and those with lower cognitive function, as measured by academic achievement and nonverbal reasoning [17]. Unfortunately, this study did not control for socioeconomic status, and thus the unique effect of high BP on cognitive function is unclear.

A number of underlying biological mechanisms have been proposed in the relationship between hypertension and cognitive functions [18]. Waldstein and Kazdel illustrate a working model that takes into account not only hypertension, but also genetics and environment, stress-induced physiological reactivity, neuroanatomy, neurophysiology, and metabolic syndrome [18].

Given that the origins of cardiovascular disease and primary hypertension are early in life, that hypertensive end-organ damage may occur at a young age, and that neurocognitive deficits are associated with elevated systolic BP, there is evidence to support early treatment of systolic hypertension in youth [16, 19, 20].

Insulin Resistance and Neurocognitive Functioning

There is some evidence in the adult literature that impaired glucose tolerance is associated with neurocognitive deficits [21]. However, in human models, the effects of obesity and insulin resistance independent of each other have not been reported.

In a rat model, where the influence of obesity and insulin resistance can be separated, findings support a negative influence on cognitive function even in the absence of obesity [22]. Studies addressing this issue with youth are not available in the extant research literature.

Psychological Correlates of Metabolic Syndrome

Though often thought of in medical and physiological terms, it is also important to consider the psychological factors that are related to metabolic syndrome. Several studies with adult and adolescent populations have investigated the relationship between psychological symptoms and metabolic syndrome. Among children and teenagers, research has shown hostility to be a predictor of metabolic syndrome factors [23]. Similar findings have been reported in adult populations where greater severity of depressive symptoms, higher levels of hostility, and a propensity to express anger were significantly associated with higher levels of fasting insulin as well as higher blood glucose and greater HOMA-insulin resistance [24]. Psychological factors such as stressful life events [25] as well as psychological distress (e.g., depression and anxiety) [24, 26] and hostility [23] have also been identified as precursors to the development of metabolic syndrome in adult populations. However, the majority of the studies are cross-sectional, and thus it is not possible to make causal inferences on the relationship among these variables. Therefore, the findings of these studies warrant discussion as we consider the psychological correlates of metabolic syndrome and its component parts in children and adolescents.

Investigations with adult subjects have found significant relationships between psychosocial stress-related factors and metabolic syndrome [27–30], as well as relationships between the metabolic syndrome components and depression and anxiety [31]. Specifically, psychosocial stress including anger, hostility, and impatience has shown significant associations with components of metabolic syndrome (i.e., elevated systolic blood pressure, cholesterol, and triglycerides) [27] as well as findings that metabolic syndrome predicts increases in anger and anxiety in women [28]. Anger and hostility often comprise a specific personality type that places a person at risk for elevated blood pressure, an important component of metabolic syndrome [32, 33]. Additionally, a "graded relationship" has been described between increasing number of components of metabolic syndrome and depression [29]. The findings of these studies seem to suggest a causal relationship whereby depression may be a precursor to metabolic syndrome.

Increased rates of psychiatric diagnoses among adolescents with metabolic syndrome have also been shown. Given the important ramifications that psychiatric diagnoses can have on physical activity, medical regimen adherence, and dietary habits [34, 35], these findings provide insight into the associations between psychological factors and metabolic syndrome. A recent study found that the rate of internalizing and externalizing psychiatric diagnoses for children with metabolic syndrome was significantly higher than that of children in the chronic illness comparison groups (i.e., asthma, cystic fibrosis, JRA, and sickle cell disease) [36]. In looking at the components of metabolic syndrome, rates of these psychiatric diagnoses were significantly higher for children with dyslipidemia than those in the chronic illness comparison group.

Although these studies mainly involved adults, the results suggest significant relationships among metabolic syndrome and symptoms of psychological distress. However, further longitudinal research is needed to determine the direction of the relationship between depressive symptoms and other components of metabolic syndrome (e.g., high cholesterol and triglycerides), especially in youth. To date, the child and adolescent literature in this area is sparse, and thus to further our understanding of the psychological correlates of metabolic syndrome, it is important to consider the individual components of metabolic syndrome and their relationships to psychological functioning among youth.

Cholesterol and Psychosocial Functioning

Research on the relationship between cholesterol and psychological health is varied. A 1990 meta-analysis revealed increased mortality due to suicide among adult patients involved in cholesterol lowering interventions [7]. In a study of adolescent psychiatric inpatients, research has shown an association between higher cholesterol levels and increased suicide attempts [37]. However, in another study of youth hospitalized for psychiatric disorders, a relationship among lower cholesterol, high triglycerides, and suicidal tendencies was reported [38].

The topic of anxiety and cholesterol has received attention as high rates of circulatory system complications have been observed in adult patients with panic disorder [39, 40]. The mechanism for this relationship is attributed to high cholesterol levels associated with sympathetic nervous system arousal [41]. These studies provide some interesting initial findings about the association between psychological functioning and the lipid component of metabolic syndrome, specifically cholesterol. Studies of psychological functioning among youth with dyslipidemia are needed.

Overweight and Psychosocial Functioning

The most studied component of metabolic syndrome as it relates to psychological functioning is overweight status. The psychological and psychosocial struggles of overweight children and adolescents are well documented [42], and while the physiological ramifications of obesity are important, the psychological consequences are clearly significant as well [43]. Obese children and adolescents are at risk for psychological and social adjustment problems, such as lower perceived competence in the areas of social and athletic abilities as well as overall self-worth and low quality of life [43, 44]. Furthermore, overweight children are more likely to be the recipients or the perpetrator of peer victimization [34, 45, 46]. Research on peer victimization shows direct associations with increased levels of depression and anxiety and decreased self-worth [47]. For example, in a study of Swedish school-aged children, obese children reported more shaming experiences (i.e., being degraded or ridiculed by others) than normal-weight or overweight children. Additionally, when compared to normal-weight and overweight children, obese youth reported significantly more depressive symptoms. However, associations between BMI and depressive symptoms were no longer significant once demographic variables and shame were accounted for. A number of other studies have reported similar results, including associations between the degree of overweight and greater depressed mood, lower self-esteem, and greater peer victimization [48].

In addition to the direct associations with overweight and obesity, peer victimization of overweight children represents a potential pathway by which psychological difficulties arise. For example, in a study of female adults, researchers found that a childhood history of weight-related teasing was positively correlated with depression and poor self-esteem [49, 50]. Additionally, research with child and adolescent populations reveals that weight-related teasing was positively correlated with suicidal ideation and suicide attempts [51]. These findings persisted even after actual body weight was accounted for. This latter finding suggests that peer victimization is an important mediator in the relationship between childhood overweight/obesity and psychological distress.

Blood Pressure and Psychosocial Functioning

Depressed mood has been associated with higher blood pressure levels in adult study samples [52–54]. Research generally attributes this relationship to depression as a risk factor for the development of hypertension [54]. Unfortunately, this relationship has not been examined in child and adolescent samples; thus, additional research is needed to better understand the role of depression and other psychological factors and blood pressure in youth.

Insulin Resistance and Psychosocial Functioning

Shomaker and colleagues studied a sample of 136 healthy adolescents of varied body weight [55]. Results indicated that greater depressive symptoms were associated with decreased insulin sensitivity and higher fasting insulin. Similar results have also been shown among adult populations [27].

Summary and Future Research Needs

The research to date has contributed to our understanding of the neurocognitive and psychological correlates of metabolic syndrome in youth. This is an area with a promising future, as much more research is needed to reach a consensus regarding the exact nature of the relationship between metabolic syndrome and neurocognitive and psychological functioning. The temporal sequence of this relationship as well as the directionality is yet unclear.

The literature on neurocognitive functioning in adolescents with metabolic syndrome is limited to examining the components of metabolic syndrome, rather than the multiple risk factors that comprise it. Studies have revealed that in youth, neither total cholesterol, HDL, nor LDL cholesterol are related to cognitive ability after controlling for potentially confounding variables [6]. In contrast, obesity and intelligence have been shown to be inversely related across Asian samples [13, 28]. Inconsistent findings have been reported, however, for children in the USA, with one study reporting no relationship [14] and another finding lower visuospatial organization, attention and concentration, and global functioning as weight increased [15]. In children and adolescents, even mild to moderate BP elevations have been found to be related to lower attention and concentration skills [16].

In the few studies of adolescents with metabolic syndrome, there is some evidence that the rate of internalizing and externalizing psychiatric diagnoses is significantly higher in youth with metabolic syndrome than in those in chronic illness comparison groups [36] and that hostility predicts metabolic syndrome [23]. Similarly, when considering the components of metabolic syndrome, the published findings are sparse, with a few studies finding relationships between cholesterol and distress [37, 38], and insulin sensitivity and depression [55]. With such a limited research base, conclusions are limited.

One exception is the research in the area of child obesity, however, where there is a strong literature with child and adolescent populations. In fact, numerous psychological consequences related to overweight and obesity have been identified, including low self-worth and depression [43, 44]. Many of the findings implicate peer victimization as playing a large role, as this is related to self-esteem, suicidal ideation, and externalizing disorders [47, 48]. Furthermore, the relationship between obesity and psychosocial functioning in childhood seems to have long-standing effects, such that a childhood history of weight-related teasing is related to adulthood depression and poor self-esteem [49, 50].

Several limitations compromise our ability to fully interpret the results of the aforementioned studies. Most significantly, the use of cross-sectional designs preclude temporal inferences. While we are able to recognize the correlation between variables, we cannot use these results to state whether neurocognitive and psychological factors contribute to the development of metabolic syndrome or its components, or whether metabolic syndrome causes these neurocognitive and psychological difficulties. Furthermore, many of the studies discussed are based on adult samples, and while informative, there is a need to extend these findings to child and adolescent populations. Given the growing prevalence of obesity and metabolic syndrome among children and adolescents, such studies would undoubtedly provide meaningful results not only to the medical community but also to patients and their parents.

It is difficult to draw conclusions from investigations with such diverse ways of conceptualizing neurocognitive functioning, with studies measuring any combination of abstract reasoning, visuospatial skills, attention and memory, and academic achievement. More comprehensive evaluations of intelligence and academic performance are needed. Most studies to date have utilized several subtests of cognitive and neuropsychological functioning, but few have looked at global functioning. A more comprehensive evaluation may yield novel findings that could assist in the design and implementation of interventions. Further studies are needed that examine all the components of metabolic syndrome as well as the clustering of the components in individuals with varying cognitive abilities in order to better determine which abilities are associated with or affected by the clustering of these health risk factors. Because the direction of the relationships between intelligence and components of the metabolic syndrome remains unclear, longitudinal studies are needed to further expand the knowledge base, allowing causation to be determined. Further mediators of the relationship between intelligence and metabolic syndrome should be examined, as factors such as educational attainment could better explain the associations.

Future research should focus on understanding the psychological consequences of being diagnosed with metabolic syndrome, as well as its components. Furthermore, interventions examining the effects of reductions in psychological distress on the development of metabolic syndrome are also warranted, as there is some evidence that psychological distress may increase risk for metabolic syndrome.

In conclusion, given the high prevalence of overweight in childhood, its persistence, and its relationship to metabolic syndrome, understanding the neurocognitive and psychological factors related to it is an important research issue of high public health significance. Further research is needed to understand how neurocognitive and psychological factors relate to metabolic syndrome in large samples of diverse children and adolescents, as well as how these factors may change over time as a consequence of having metabolic syndrome. Given the potential adverse effects of metabolic syndrome on neurocognitive and psychological functioning in youth, research is also needed to address the prevention of such sequelae.

References

1. Andersen LB, Wedderkopp N, Hansen HS, Cooper AR, Froberg K. Biological cardiovascular risk factors cluster in Danish children and adolescents: the European Youth Heart Study. Prev Med. 2003;37:363–7.
2. Myers L, Coughlin SS, Webber LS, Srinivasan SR, Berenson GS. Prediction of adult cardiovascular multifactoral risk status from childhood risk factor levels: the Bogalusa Heart Study. Am J Epidemiol. 1995;142:918–24.

3. Raitakari OT, Porkka KV, Rasanen L, Ronnemaa T, Viikari JS. Clustering and six year cluster-tracking of serum total cholesterol, HDL-cholesterol and diastolic blood pressure in children and young adults: the cardiovascular Risk in Young Finns study. J Clin Epidemiol. 1994;47:1084–93.
4. Taylor VH, MacQueen GM. Cognitive dysfunction associated with metabolic syndrome. Int J Obes Relat Metab Disord. 2007;8:409–18.
5. Kasl SV, Brooks GW, Roger WL. Serum uric acid and cholesterol in achievement behavior and motivation. JAMA. 1970;213:1158–64.
6. Perry LA, Sigger CB, Ainsworth BE, Zhang Jian. No association between cognitive achievements, academic performance and serum cholesterol concentrations among school-aged children. Nutr Neurosci. 2009;12:160–6.
7. Muldoon MF, Manuck SB, Mathews KA. Lowering cholesterol concentrations and mortality: a quantitative review of primary prevention trials. Br Med J. 1990;301:309–14.
8. Whitmer RA, Gunderson EP, Barrett-Connor E, Quesenberry CP, Yaffe K. Obesity in middle age and future risk of dementia: a 27 year longitudinal population based study. BMJ. 2005;330:1360.
9. Yaffe K, Kanaya A, Lindquist K, Simonsick EM, Harris T, Shorr Ri, Tylavsky FA, Newman AB. The metabolic syndrome, inflammation, and the risk of cognitive decline. JAMA. 2004;292:2237–42.
10. Amin RS, Kimball TR, Bean JA, et al. Left ventricular hypertrophy and abnormal ventricular geometry in children and adolescents with obstructive sleep apnea. Am J Respir Crit Care Med. 2002;165:1395–9.
11. Yu ZB, Han SP, Cao XG, Guo XR. Intelligence in relation to obesity: a systematic review and meta-analysis. Obesity. 2010;11:656–70.
12. Li X. A study of intelligence and personality in children with simple obesity. Int J Obes Relat Metab Disord. 1999;23:272–7.
13. Mo-suwan L, Lebel L, Puetpaiboon A, Junjana C. School performance and weight status of children and young adolescents in a transitional society on Thailand. Int J Obes Relat Metab Disord. 1999;23:272–7.
14. Datar A, Sturm R, Magnabosco JL. Childhood overweight and academic performance: national study of kindergartners and first–graders. Obes Res. 2004;12:58–68.
15. Li Y, Dai Q, Jackson JC, Zhang J. Overweight is associated with decreased cognitive functioning among school-age children and adolescents. Obesity. 2008;16(8):1809–15.
16. Lande MB, Kaczorowski JM, Auinger P, Schwartz GJ, Weitzman M. Elevated blood pressure and decreased cognitive function among school-age children and adolescents in the United States. J Pediatr. 2003;143(6):720–4.
17. Lawlor DA, O'Callaghan MJ, Mamun AA, Williams GM, Bor W, Najman JM. Socioeconomic position, cognitive function, and clustering of cardiovascular risk factors in adolescence: findings from the Mater University Study of Pregnancy and its Outcomes. Psychosom Med. 2005; 67:862–8.
18. Waldstein SR, Kadzel LI. In: Waldstein SR and Elias MF, editors. Neuropsychology of Cardiovascular Disease. Mahwah: Lawrence Erlbaum Associates; 2001. p. 15–36.
19. Sorof JM, Portman RJ. Ambulatory blood pressure monitoring in the pediatric patient. J Pediatr. 2000;136:578–86.
20. Belsha CW. Ambulatory blood pressure monitoring and hypertensive target-organ damage in children. Blood Press Monit. 1999;4:161–4.
21. Elias MF, Elias PK, Sullivan LM, Wolf PA, D'Agostino RB. Obesity, diabetes and cognitive deficit: the Framingham Heart Study. Neurobiol Aging. 2005;26:11–6.
22. McNay EC, Ong CT, McCrimmon RJ, Cresswell J, Bogan JS, Shewin RS. Hippocampal memory processes are modulated by insulin and high-fat-induced insulin resistance. Neurobiol Learn Mem. 2010;93:546–53.
23. Raikkonen K, Matthews K, Salomon K. Hostility predicts metabolic syndrome risk factors in children and adolescents. Health Psychol. 2003;33(3):279–86.
24. Suarez EC. Sex differences in the relation of depressive symptoms, hostility, and anger expression to indices of glucose metabolism in nondiabetic adults. Health Psychol. 2006;25(4):484–92.

25. Raikkonen K, Matthews KA, Kuller LH. Depressive symptoms and stressful life events predict metabolic syndrome among middle-aged women. Diabetes Care. 2007;30(4):872–7.
26. Cohen BE, Panguluri P, Na B, Whooley MA. Psychological risk factors and the metabolic syndrome in patients with coronary heart disease: findings from the Heart and Soul Study. Psychiatry Res. 2010;175(1–2):133–7.
27. Raikkonen K, Keltikangas-Jarvinen L. Adlercreutz, Hautanen A. Psychosocial stress and the insulin resistance syndrome. Metabolism. 1996;45(12):1533–8.
28. Raikkonen K, Matthews KA, Kuller LH. The relationship between psychological risk attributes and the metabolic syndrome in healthy women: antecedent or consequence? Metabolism. 2002;51(12):1573–7.
29. Dunbar JA, Reddy P, Davis-Lameloise N, Philpot B, et al. Depression: an important comorbidity with metabolic syndrome in general population. Diabetes Care. 2008;31(12):2368–73.
30. Skilton MR, Moulin P, Terra JL, Bonnet F. Associations between anxiety, depression, and the metabolic syndrome. Biol Psychiatry. 2007;62(11):1251–7.
31. Herva A, Rasanen P, Miettunen J, et al. Co-occurrence of metabolic syndrome with depression and anxiety in young adults: the Northern Finland 1966 British Cohort Study. Psychosom Med. 2006;68:213–6.
32. Jorgensen R, Johnson B, Kolodziej M, et al. Elevated blood pressure and personality: a meta-analytic review. Prev Med. 1996;120:293–320.
33. Marmot M. Psychosocial factors and blood pressure. Prev Med. 1985;14:451–65.
34. Storch EA, Milsom VA, DeBraganza N, Lewin AB, Geffken GR. Peer victimization, psychosocial adjustment, and physical activity in overweight and at-risk-for-overweight youth. J Pediatr Psychol. 2007;32(1):80–9.
35. Sallis J, Prochaska J, Taylor C. A review of correlates of physical activity of children and adolescents. Med Sci Sports Exerc. 2000;32:963–75.
36. Janicke DM, Harman JS, Kelleher KJ, et al. Psychiatric diagnosis in children and adolescents with obesity-related health conditions. J Dev Behav Pediatr. 2008;29(4):276–84.
37. Apter A, Laufer N, Bar-Sever M, et al. Serum cholesterol, suicidal tendencies, impulsivity, aggression, and depression in adolescent psychiatric inpatients. Biol Psychiatry. 1999;46(4): 532–41.
38. Glueck CJ, Kutler FE, Hamer T, et al. Hypocholesterolemia, hypertriglyceridemia, suicide and suicide ideation in children hospitalized for psychiatric diseases. Pediatr Res. 1994;35:602–10.
39. Agargun MY, Algun E, Sekero lu R, Kara H, Tarakcio M. Low cholesterol level in patients with panic disorder: the association with major depression. J Affect Disord. 1998;50(1): 29–32.
40. Bajwa WK, Asnis GM, Sanderson WC, et al. High cholesterol levels in patients with panic disorder. Am J Psychiatry. 1992;149(3):376–8.
41. Hayward C, Taylor CB, Roth WT, King R. Plasma lipid levels in patients with panic disorder or agoraphobia. Am J Psychiatry. 1989;146(7):917–9.
42. Jonides L, Buschbacher V, Barlow S. Management of child and adolescent obesity: psychological, emotional and behavioral assessment. Pediatrics. 2002;110:215–21.
43. Schwimmer JB, Burwinkle TM, Varni JW. Health-related quality of life of severely obese children and adolescents. JAMA. 2003;306(2):1813–9.
44. Banis HT, Varni JW, Wallander JL, et al. Psychological and social adjustment of obese children and their families. Child Care Health Dev. 1988;14(3):157–73.
45. Sjoeberg RL, Nilsson KW, Leppert J. Obesity, shame, and depression in school-aged children: a population-based study. Pediatrics. 2005;113(3):e389–92.
46. Janssen I, Craig W, Boyce W, Pickett W. Associations between overweight and obesity with bullying behaviors in school-aged children. Pediatrics. 2004;113(5):1187–94.
47. Hawker DS, Boulton MJ. Twenty years' research on peer victimization and psychosocial adjustment: a meta-analytic review of cross-sectional studies. J Child Psychol Psychiatry. 2000;41:441–55.
48. Sweeting H, Wright C, Minnis H. Psychosocial correlates of adolescent obesity, 'slimming down' and 'becoming obese'. J Adolesc Health. 2005;37(5):409.

49. Jackson TD, Grilo CM, Masheb RM. Teasing history, onset of obesity, current eating disorder psychopathology, body dissatisfaction, and psychological functioning in binge eating disorder. Obes Res. 2000;8:451–8.
50. Young-Hyman D, Schlundt DG, Herman-Wenderoth L, Bozlinski K. Obesity, appearance, and psychosocial adaptation in young African-American children. J Pediatr Psychol. 2003;28: 463–72.
51. Eisenberg ME, Neumark-Sztainer D, Story M. Associations of weight-based teasing and emotional well bring among adolescents. Arch Pediatr Adolesc Med. 2003;157:733–8.
52. Hughes JW, Stoney CM. Depressed mood is related to high-frequency heart rate variability during stressors. Psychosom Med. 2000;62(6):796–803.
53. Jonas BS, Lando JF. Negative affect as a prospective risk factors for hypertension. Psychosom Med. 2000;62(2):188–96.
54. Player M, King D, Mainous A, Geesy M. Psychosocial factors and progression from prehypertension to hypertension or coronary heart disease. Ann Fam Med. 2007;5:403–11.
55. Shomaker L, Tanofsky-Kraff M, Young-Hyman D, et al. Psychological symptoms and insulin sensitivity in adolescents. Pediatr Diabetes. 2010;11:417–23.

Chapter 13
Genomics of Pediatric Metabolic Syndrome

Evadnie Rampersaud and Maria A. Ciliberti

Abstract The genetics of the metabolic syndrome (MetS) and its components have been studied extensively in adults; however, in pediatric populations, the genetic contribution to MetS has not been as closely examined. Gene-mapping strategies to study MetS have evolved over time and are dependent on the prevalence of the disease, the underlying hypothesized genetic model, and the anticipated influence of environmental factors. While MetS in general is thought to be multifactorial and to result from the interaction of genetic and environmental factors, monogenic forms (i.e., congenital leptin deficiency, maturity onset diabetes of the young (MODY), and Liddle's syndrome) in children have been identified which have proved easier to map. Variants in six genes (*AGTR1*, *GHR*, *PLIN4*, *ENNP1*, *PA1–1*, and *3-BAR*) have been associated with common nonmonogenic forms of MetS in pediatric populations. Genetic investigations of endophenotypes of MetS (i.e., abdominal obesity, familial hypercholesterolemia, and dyslipidemia) in children have also been conducted, primarily as replication efforts of candidate genes such as *FTO*, *ADIPOQ*, and *INSIG2* which were originally identified in adult populations. With the availability of novel genome technologies such as next-generation sequencing and with better understanding of epigenetic mechanisms that may also play a role, it is becoming increasingly possible to more comprehensively study the full compendium of genetic variation that causes MetS.

Keywords Genomic associations • Gene environment interactions • Epigenetics • Genomic modeling and analysis • Rare mutations

E. Rampersaud, Ph.D. (✉)
John T. MacDonald Department of Human Genetics,
University of Miami Miller School of Medicine,
1501 NW 10th Avenue, BRB-318, Miami, FL 33129, USA
e-mail: erampersaud@med.miami.edu

M.A. Ciliberti, M.P.H.
John T. MacDonald Department of Human Genetics,
University of Miami Miller School of Medicine,
Miami, FL, USA

Introduction

Metabolic syndrome (MetS) is defined as a cluster of anthropomorphic, physiological, and biochemical abnormalities that predisposes an individual to development of diabetes and cardiovascular disease [1]. While various definitions of MetS have been used in studies of children and adolescents, no single standard operational definition currently exists [1, 2]. Hence, this review will primarily focus on each of the following components of MetS: (1) abdominal obesity, (2) atherogenic dyslipidemia, (3) elevated blood pressure, and (4) insulin resistance. The genetics of MetS and its components have been studied extensively in adults [3]; however, in pediatric populations, the genetic contribution to MetS has not been as closely examined. This review will summarize discoveries of genetic mutations and polymorphisms that are linked to pediatric MetS and its clinical components. Syndromic forms of pediatric MetS are also reviewed. The goal is to provide an overview of the most studied MetS candidate genes and to discuss the limitations of current methodology and potential novel approaches for identifying relevant MetS genes.

Heritability of Metabolic Syndrome

As is the case with many other common disorders, MetS and each of its individual components can cluster in families, suggesting a genetic etiology. Estimates of heritability from family studies provide a means of gauging the degree to which a genetic component exists for a particular disease. Heritability is defined as the proportion of the variation in a trait in a population that is due to genetic variation between individuals in that population. The heritability of components of MetS in adults ranges from 20% for type 2 diabetes [4] to 70% for abdominal obesity [5]. In other words, 20–70% of the variability in type 2 diabetes and obesity is due to genetic factors. Disorders with earlier onset are expected to have a stronger genetic basis; thus, extrapolation to childhood forms of MetS likely has even higher unexplained heritability that is due to genetics.

Gene-Mapping Strategies

The approaches for gene mapping have evolved over time and are dependent on the prevalence of the disease, the underlying hypothesized genetic model, and the anticipated influence of environmental factors. Figure 13.1 provides basic terminology and key concepts that will aid readers unfamiliar with genetics. For traits which demonstrate Mendelian genetic inheritance patterns (i.e., autosomal dominant, recessive, or x-linked), traditional gene-mapping strategies have focused on transmission of regions of the genome in families in order to correlate a given gene and

13 Genomics of Pediatric Metabolic Syndrome

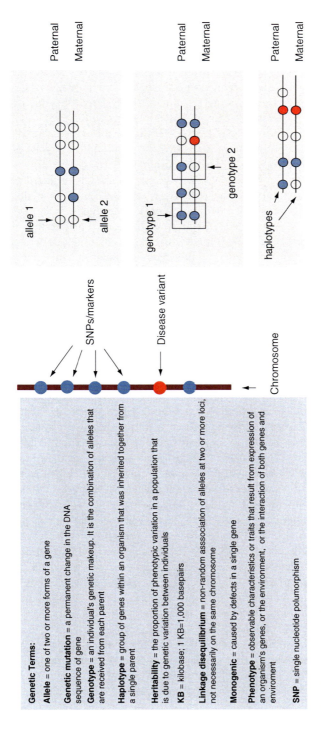

Fig. 13.1 Basic genetic terms and concepts

a disease phenotype. Typically, this involves genome-wide linkage screens or candidate genes studies. With a genome-wide linkage screen, affected relatives are examined at individual genetic markers across the genome to determine whether they inherited the same ancestral region which might harbor a disease gene. With candidate gene studies, individual coding and noncoding polymorphisms are examined for evidence of excess sharing among affected relatives beyond that expected by chance simply based on their familial relationships within the pedigree.

Ultimately, the identified gene is expected to harbor one or a small number of causative mutations that fundamentally alter the function of the gene or its protein product. This would suggest a monogenic rare disease model, usually with high penetrance (i.e., the probability of expressing a disease given that a person has a certain genetic mutation). While pediatric MetS and its components have been observed in subsets of families with a demonstrated genetic mode of inheritance, the majority of cases occur in isolation in sporadic cases, a pattern that mirrors what is observed for many complex common disorders including Alzheimer's, autism, and cardiovascular diseases, where both gene and environmental interactions are expected to influence the onset of disease. These disorders do not have a recognizable Mendelian genetic inheritance pattern.

The complex genetic architecture of pediatric MetS has led to the development of family and population-based gene-mapping approaches that take clinical (i.e., different subtypes of a disease) and genetic heterogeneity (i.e., different genes or alleles that cause a disease) into account. For example, it is expected that different genes (genetic heterogeneity) or different alleles within the same gene (allelic heterogeneity) can, in combination with each other or with environmental risk factors, increase the susceptibility to MetS. This complexity can cause difficulties for gene mapping in families. In contrast, population-based association gene-mapping approaches have been developed to compare the frequency of genetic variants in populations with the disease to those without the disease. Traditionally, this case–control approach was limited to candidate genes selected for their biological relevance until 2005 when the construction of the HapMap, a catalog of common human genetic variation in populations of different ancestries, along with the development of genomic technologies for high-throughput genotyping revolutionized the method in which gene mapping was conducted. Instead of focusing on selected candidate genes, researchers were able to explore genetic variation on a larger scale by looking at single nucleotide polymorphisms (SNPs) that spanned the entire genome. The genome-wide association study, or GWAS approach, was based on the "common disease, common variant" hypothesis, which hypothesized that common diseases are caused by common genetic variations (frequency >1% in the population). Under this hypothesis and with sufficiently large cohorts of cases and controls, this mapping strategy in theory should be able to identify causal variants or those SNPs that are in linkage disequilibrium (LD) with the true causal variant. The functional effects of these common disease variants differ from those that underlie rare monogenic diseases. Each genetic polymorphism or mutation associated with common diseases that have non-Mendelian inheritance is only expected to have a small effect on disease risk. Under the multifactorial liability threshold model of genetic

Fig. 13.2 Multifactorial liability threshold model of genetic inheritance. There is a liability toward the trait that consists of a combination of genetic and nongenetic factors and is normally distributed in the population. The trait is expressed only in individuals whose liability exceeds a threshold

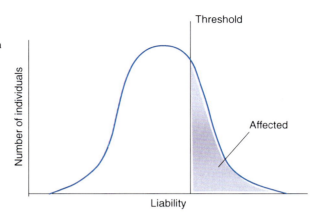

inheritance, it is hypothesized that the accumulation of many polymorphisms, each with small genetic risk, or in conjunction with environmental risk, would need to be exceeded for the disease to manifest. Figure 13.2 illustrates the concept of the multifactorial liability threshold disease-risk model underlying common, complex disorders. An alternative hypothesis is that common diseases are caused by rare genetic variations with moderate effect sizes. Under this model, multiple rare variants in one or multiple genes and gene networks can act synergistically to cause disease. Emerging technologies such as whole-exome and whole-genome sequencing can enable the identification of such rare variants in an unbiased manner.

For many decades, gene identification approaches have tended to focus on sequence defects at the level of deoxyribonucleic acid (DNA), the nucleic acid that is often called the genetic blueprint of life. These defects were expected, solely or in conjunction with the environment, to lead to altered protein function. However, it is becoming increasingly clear that the genomic milieu of disease is even more complicated than once envisioned. Epigenetics, or changes in trait or gene expression which can be caused by modifications that are independent of DNA level alterations, can also modulate the onset of disease. Known epigenetic mechanisms include methylation of DNA and histone modifications. With DNA methylation, a methyl group is added to the 5 position of the cytosine pyrimidine ring or the number 6 nitrogen of the adenine purine ring. DNA methylation can affect gene transcription, a process which ultimately leads to protein formation, in two ways – either hindering the binding of transcriptional proteins to the gene or by binding to proteins and recruiting additional proteins that limit the activation of chromatin. Histone modifications are posttranslational modifications of the core histone proteins that constitute the nucleosome, the fundamental unit of DNA packaging in the chromosomes. Some evidence suggests, although not conclusively, that these modifications are used to program genes for activation during specific steps in cellular differentiation. It has been postulated that epigenetic alterations in early stages of life can lead to biological programming that ultimately influences risk of diabetes, cardiovascular disease, and metabolic syndrome. A key example of this work comes from animal studies in mice. Mice with agouti yellow alleles (Avy) fed a maternal diet enriched with methyl donors caused hypermethylation which resulted in silencing of the Avy gene. As a result, the offspring of these mice were leaner and no longer hyperinsulinemic [6]. Other examples of epigenetics in humans occur through genomic imprinting that leads to Prader-Willi, Angelman, and Beckwith-Wiedemann syndromes and Albright's hereditary osteodystrophy, Russell-Silver syndrome, and transient neonatal diabetes mellitus (TNDM). We will use TNDM as an example to further illustrate the concept of imprinting as an epigenetic process. TNDM is a rare condition (affecting ~ 1/400,000 live births) that occurs in growth retarded infants in the first few weeks of life. The condition generally resolves within one year, although there is an elevated risk of insulin-requiring diabetes recurring later in life [7]. Involvement of imprinting in TNDM was first suspected in a 1995 case study when, in a search for the parental and chromosomal origin of a supernumerary marker chromosome in a child with TNDM, intrauterine growth retardation, and a large tongue, the child was found to have chromosome 6 microsatellite data consistent with two paternal copies (paternal uniparental disomy (UPD)) of chromosome 6 and no maternal copies other than the region contained in the marker chromosome [8]. Testing two unrelated patients with TNDM for UPD yielded one who also had UPD for chromosome 6, and these data combined with a patient reported in the literature with paternal UPD, methylmalonic acidemia (a rare recessive condition caused by mutations in a gene on chromosome 6) [9], strongly suggested an imprinting mechanism for TNDM. Subsequently, an association was found between TNDM and paternal, but not maternal, duplications of chromosome 6q24 [10], including all familial cases. The critical overlapping duplicated region was found to comprise 440 kb [11] and contains two imprinted genes, *ZAC* and *HYMAI* [12]. Most recently, it has been estimated based on 55 cases that 85% of individuals with TNDM have one of the following abnormalities of chromosome 6q24: paternal UPD6, paternal duplication of 6q24, or an isolated methylation defect of 6q24 [13].

Monogenic Forms of Pediatric Metabolic Syndrome

While MetS in general is thought to be multifactorial and to result from the interaction of genetic *and* environmental factors, monogenic forms in children have been identified which have proved easier to map. Table 13.1 summarizes what is known of these disorders. In general, monogenic inborn errors of metabolism can lead to early-onset obesity and tend to involve hormones or neurotransmitters and their hypothalamic receptors [14]. For example, congenital leptin and leptin-receptor deficiencies are rare disorders characterized by severe early-onset obesity and intense hyperphagia, a condition associated with an abnormally increased appetite for and consumption of food. Children with this disorder are homozygous for a frameshift mutation in the *OB* gene (ΔG133), which results in a truncated protein that is subsequently not secreted. Daily subcutaneous injections of leptin can have dramatic beneficial effects on appetite and weight loss [15]. Homozygosity or

13 Genomics of Pediatric Metabolic Syndrome

Table 13.1 Monogenic forms of metabolic syndrome components in pediatric and adolescent populations

Disorder	Affected gene
Abdominal obesity	
Congenital leptin and leptin receptor deficiency	*Ob(Lep)*
POMC deficiency	*POMC*
MC4R deficiency	*MC4R*
Atherogenic dyslipidemia	
Causes increased LDL-cholesterol	
Homozygous familial hypercholesterolemia (HoFH)	*LDLR*
Heterozygous familial hypercholesterolemia (HeFH)	*LDLR*
Familial defective apolipoprotein B (FDB)	*APOB*
PCKS9 gain-of-function	*PCSK9*
Autosomal recessive hypercholesterolemia (ARH)	*ARH*
Wolman disease	*LIPA*
Phytosterolemia	*ABCG5; ABCG8*
Causes decreased HDL-cholesterol	
A-beta-lipoproteinemia (ABL)	*MTP*
Familial hypobetalipoproteinemia (FHBL)	*APOB*
Primary bile acid malabsorption	*SLC10A2*
PCSK9 deficiency (loss-of-function)	*PCSK9*
Other monogenic dyslipidemias	
Tangier disease (TD)	*ABCA1*
Hyperchylomicronemia	*LPL;APOC2*
Elevated blood pressure	
Autosomal recessive mineralocorticoid excess	11β-hydroxysteroid dehydrogenase (HSD) type 2 enzyme
Glucocorticoid remediable aldosteronism/ Autosomal dominant hyperaldosteronism type I	*CYP11B1*
Congenital adrenal hyperplasia	11β-hydroxylase; 17α-hydroxylase
Liddle's syndrome	*SCNN1B*
Gordon's syndrome/Autosomal dominant hyperaldosteronism type II	*WNK1;WNK4*
Insulin resistance	
Maturity onset diabetes of the young (MODY1)	*HNF-4 α*
Maturity onset diabetes of the young (MODY2)	*GCK*
Maturity onset diabetes of the young (MODY3)	*HNF-1 α*

compound heterozygosity for mutations in the pro-opiomelanocortin (*POMC*) gene results in POMC deficiency which is also characterized by early-onset obesity and hyperphagia due to loss of melanocortin signaling at the melanocortin 4 receptor (*MC4R*). Dominantly inherited heterozygous mutations in *MC4R* also result in hyperphagia starting as early as the first year of life. Mutations in ~12 genes (see Table 13.2) have been found in children and adolescents with

Table 13.2 Gene mutations and polymorphisms associated with PMS and its components

Trait	Age range (years)	Study N	Gene	Mutation(s)	Ethnic population	Familial/sporadic	References
Abdominal obesity							
Obesity	6–18	3,503	*FTO*	rs9939609 A allele carriers	Chinese	Sporadic	[25]
	14–20	697 (adults included)	*FTO*	rs9939609 A allele carriers	German	Sporadic	[26]
	0–14	11,797	*FTO*	rs9939609 Homozygous A allele carriers	European White	Familial/sporadic	[27]
	4–17	344	*MC4R*	Obesity-associated (127 L) missense substitution (c.380 C>T; S127L)	Polish	Sporadic	[28]
	0–17	101	*FTO*	rs9939609 A allele carriers	Dutch Caucasian	Sporadic	[29]
	8–16	250	*MC4R*	(See below for individual-specific mutations) Val103Ile polymorphism Glu42Lys polymorphism	Turkish	Familial/sporadic	[30]
Obesity and dyslipidemia	3–6	470	*LPL*	(See below for individual-specific mutations) +495T>G polymorphism (heterozygous genotype) PvuII T>C polymorphism (heterozygous genotype)	Chinese	Sporadic	[31]
Atherogenic dyslipidemia							
Familial hypercholes-terolemia (ADH)	4–18	269	*LDLR*	77 different types of functional mutations found	Dutch (Netherlands)	Familial	[37]
	10–13	31	*LDLR*	Trp66>Gly mutation in exon 3	French Canadian	Familial	[34]
	12	5	*LDLR*	W165X (G>A substitution) of codon 165	Chinese	Familial	[35]
	11–16	53	*LDLR*	−27C>T nucleotide transition in the promoter sequence	Czech	Familial	[36]

Dyslipidemia	7–9	APOE	Epsilon 4 (E4) allele carriers	Vietnamese	Sporadic	[46]
	2–19	APOA5	rs 662799 (APOA5–1131T>C) C allele carriers	Brazil	Sporadic	[38]
	2–14	APOE	Epsilon 2 (E2) allele carriers	French	Sporadic	[48]
	6–8	APOA5	S19W polymorphism C allele carriers	Caucasian (Spain)	Sporadic	[39]
	9–17	FABP2, PON, APOC3, APOE	(See below for individual-specific mutations)	Aboriginal Canadians	Sporadic	[47]
		FABP2	T allele carriers			
		PON	192Q allele carriers			
		APOC3	455C allele carriers			
		APOE	Epsilon 4 (E4) carriers			
Elevated TC/HDL ratio	11–12	PPARG2	(See below for individual-specific mutations) Pro-allele heterozygotes	Greek	Sporadic	[41]
Hypertriglyceridemia	5–7	NPY	Leu7Pro polymorphism	Finnish	Sporadic	[42]
HDL deficiency	6–15	ABCA1	R230 C allele carriers	Mexican Mestizo	Sporadic	[43]
	3–18	WWOX	rs2548861 T allele carriers	Finnish	Sporadic	[44]
Hypertriglyceridemia and HDL deficiency	6–8	APOA5	−1131T>C polymorphism C allele carriers	Caucasian (Spain)	Sporadic	[39]
	9–13	APOA5	(See below for individual-specific mutations) SNP3; T/C genotype	Japanese	Sporadic	[40]
			SNP3; C/C genotype	Japanese	Sporadic	[40]

(continued)

Table 13.2 (continued)

Trait	Age range (years)	Study N	Gene	Mutation(s)	Ethnic population	Familial/sporadic	References
Triglyceride-induced insulin resistant DM	15–18	5	*LPL*	Silent mutations in exons 4 (GAG to GAA) and 8 (ACC to ACA); compound heterozygotes	White	Familial	[45]
Elevated blood pressure							
HUPRA syndrome: hyperuricemia, pulmonary hypertension, renal failure in infancy, and alkalosis	4–7 months	3	*SARS2*	Homozygous mutation (c.1169A>G) resulting in p.Asp390Gly in exon 13	Palestinian	Familial	[49]
Liddle's syndrome/familial hypertension	9–76	12 (Adults included in study N)	*[Beta]ENaC*	Missense mutation P616L; C>T transition of codon 616	Chinese	Familial	[50]
	11–76	10 (Adults included in study N)	*[Beta]ENaC*	De novo missense mutation; Pro>Leu mutation at codon 616	African American	Familial	[51]

13 Genomics of Pediatric Metabolic Syndrome   251

Primary pulmonary hypertension	1.0–18.8	21	5HTT	Homozygosity for the long variant of 5HTT	Caucasian	Sporadic	[53]
	2–14	147	BMPR2	(See below for individual-specific mutations)	Multiethnic: White, African American, Hispanic, and Asian	Sporadic	[54]
	2			Frameshift mutation (c. large deletion) in exon 2,3			
	5			Splice mutation (c.-5-248delTATAGGinsAC) in exon 3			
	9			Missense mutation (c.1471C>T) in exon 11			
	11			Frameshift mutation (c.2410–2413delGTCA) in exon 12			
	11			Missense mutation (c.1471C>T) in exon 11			
	12			Missense mutation (c.1156G>A) in exon 9			
	12			Splice mutation (c.247+1delG-CAAGTG) in exon 2			
	14			Missense mutation (c.295T>C) in exon 3			

(continued)

Table 13.2 (continued)

Trait	Age range (years)	Study N	Gene	Mutation(s)	Ethnic population	Familial/sporadic	References
Pulmonary arterial hypertension	2–14	21	ALK1, BMPR2	(See below for individual-specific mutations)	Japanese	Sporadic	[55]
	2		ALK1	R484Q (1451G A) exon 10			
	4		BMPR2	Q403X (1207C T) exon 9			
	7		ALK1	P424T (1270C A) exon 9			
	7		ALK1	R479Q (1436G A) in exon 10			
	9		BMPR2	C123R (367T C) in exon 3			
	9		ALK1	L381P (1142T C) exon 8			
	9		BMPR2	Y113X (339C G) exon 3			
	14		ALK1	H312Q (936C G) exon 7			
	14		BMPR2	Q42X (124C T) exon 2			
Insulin resistance							
Insulin resistance	7–15	32	FABP2	Thr/Thr54 genotype	Japanese	Sporadic	[56]
	12	3	INSR	Nonsense mutation (R331X)	Japanese	Familial	[57]
	16	5	IR	Heterozygous missense mutation of R1174W (nt3601C T) on exon 20	Asian	Familial	[58]
Insulin resistance in obese children	5–7	309	FABP4	rs16909233 polymorphism obese A allele carriers	Caucasian and African American	Sporadic	[59]
Abnormalities in glucose metabolism	17–27	1,295 (Adults included in study N)	INSIG2	rs7566605 polymorphism CC genotype	Sardinian	Sporadic	[60]
Insulin resistance and other MetS complications	8–13	131	ADIPOQ	SNP 276G>T	Italian	Sporadic	[61]

13 Genomics of Pediatric Metabolic Syndrome

Higher fasting insulin levels and HOMA-IR index	8–12	270	*ADIPOQ*	-11,391G>A GG genotype	Italian	Sporadic [62]
Higher fasting glucose, higher fasting insulin levels and HOMA-IR index and triglyceride levels	8–12	270	*ADIPOQ*	-11,377C>G G allele carriers	Italian	Sporadic [62]
Elevated FABP4 levels	5–7	309	*FABP4*	rs1054135 polymorphism A allele carriers	Caucasian and African American	Sporadic [59]
Metabolic syndrome						
Decreased MetS risk	15–17	350	*AGTR1*	AT1R/1166C allele carriers	Iranian	Sporadic [63]
MetS risk: elevated insulin secretion, disposition index, and hypertriglyceridemia	8–16	142	*GHR*	GHRd3 allele carriers	Caucasian (German)	Sporadic [64]
MetS risk: hypertriglyceridemia, HDL deficiency, and elevated IR concentrations	7–14	234	*PLIN4*	PLIN4 11482G>A minor A allele carriers	Brazilian	Sporadic [65]
MetS risk and IGT in obese children	2–16	809	*ENPP1*	rs997509 T allele carriers	Caucasian (Italian)	Sporadic [66]

(continued)

Table 13.2 (continued)

Trait	Age range (years)	Study N	Gene	Mutation(s)	Ethnic population	Familial/sporadic	References
MetS risk: dyslipidemia, insulin resistance, and obesity,	7–14	77	PAI-1 (Serpine)	4G/4G polymorphism	Turkish	Sporadic	[67]
MetS risk: obesity, hypertension, and insulin resistance	10–14	442	3-BAR	(See below for individual-specific mutations)	Hungarian	Sporadic	[68]
				Arg64 allele carriers (Arg64Arg homozygotes)			
				Arg64 allele carriers (Trp64Arg heterozygotes)			

ABCA1 ATP-binding cassette, subfamily A (ABC1), member 1; *ACE-1* angiotensin 1-converting enzyme (peptidyl-dipeptidase A) 1; *ADIPOQ* adiponectin gene; *AGT* angiotensinogen (serpin peptidase inhibitor, clade A, member 8); *AGTR1* angiotensin II type 1 receptor gene; *ALK1* activin receptor-like kinase 1; *APOA5* apolipoprotein A-V; *APOB* apolipoprotein B (including Ag(x) antigen); *APOC3* apolipoprotein C-III; *APOE* apolipoprotein E; *[Beta]ENaC* Beta subunit of the epithelial sodium channel; *BMPR2* bone morphogenetic protein receptor type II; *CYP1A1* cytochrome P450, family 1, subfamily A, polypeptide 1; *3-BAR* Beta3-adrenergic receptor; *5HTT* serotonin transporter; *ENPP1* ectonucleotide pyrophosphatase/phosphodiesterase 1; *FABP2* fatty-acid-binding protein 2, intestinal; *FABP4* fatty-acid-binding protein 4, adipocyte; *FTO* fat mass and obesity associated; *GHR* growth hormone receptor; *INSIG2* insulin-induced gene 2; *INSR* insulin receptor; *IR* insulin resistance; *LDLR* low-density lipoprotein receptor; *LPL* lipoprotein lipase; *MC4R* melanocortin 4 receptor; *NPY* neuropeptide Y; *PAI-1 (SERPINE)* serpin peptidase inhibitor, clade E (nexin, plasminogen activator inhibitor type 1), member 11; *PLIN4* perilipin 4; *PNPLA3* patatin-like phospholipase domain containing 3; *PON* paraoxonase; *PPARgamma2* peroxisome proliferator-activated receptor gamma; *UCP3* human uncoupling protein 3; *UGT1A1* UDP glucuronosyltransferase 1 family, polypeptide A1; *WWOX* WW-domain-containing oxidoreductase

dyslipidemias occurring early in life and usually demonstrating Mendelian inheritance. Rahalkar et al. provide a comprehensive review of monogenetic causes of dyslipidemia in pediatric groups [16]. Overall, loss-of-function and gain-of-function mutations in these genes can lead to unusually high or low levels of plasma cholesterol and/or triglycerides during infancy, childhood, and adolescence. Mutations causing defects in ~7 genes (*11β-hydroxysteroid dehydrogenase (HSD) type 2 enzyme*; *CYP11B1*; *11β-hydroxylase*; *17α-hydroxylase*; *SCNN1B*; *WNK1*; *WNK4*) lead to hypertension early in life [16, 17]. Monogenic forms of hypertension result in volume expansion and are associated with suppression of the renin-angiotensin system leading to low levels of plasma renin activity. Mutations responsible for several monogenic forms of nonautoimmune diabetes including maturity onset diabetes of the young MODY1, MODY2, and MODY3 [18, 19] were identified using linkage-mapping approaches in families. MODY is an autosomal dominant, genetically heterogeneous form of early-onset diabetes. Eight MODY genes have been described to date [20–22], with mutations in two of these genes, glucokinase (*GCK*; MODY2) and hepatic nuclear factor 1-alpha (*HNF-1α*; MODY 3) accounting for the majority of cases. Glucokinase, encoded by the MODY2 gene, is an enzyme catalyzing the phosphorylation of glucose in pancreatic beta cells, signaling the cells to release insulin; thus, defects in *GCK* cause a delayed insulin response to glucose. MODY2 is generally considered a disorder of glucose sensing. MODY2 generally causes mild hyperglycemia and is associated with a low rate of complications. Approximately 50% of *GCK* mutation carriers are estimated to develop gestational diabetes mellitus (GDM). Women with GDM are at increased risk of giving birth to babies with macrosomia, or increased birth weight. However, it has been shown in a study of 58 offspring of couples with one parent carrying a *GCK* mutation that a *fetal GCK* mutation is associated with *decreased* birth weight [23]. In this study, babies who did not have *GCK* mutations, but were born to women with *GCK* mutations, were, on average, of high birth weight (86th percentile adjusted for sex, birth order, and gestational age) as would be expected if the mothers had GDM. In contrast, babies with *GCK* mutations not inherited from their mothers were small (24th percentile). Finally, in cases in which both mother and fetus had a *GCK* mutation, birth weight was in the average range (53rd percentile). The mechanism appears to be as follows: Women with *GCK* mutations experience a hyperglycemic in utero environment, leading the fetus to increase insulin production to utilize the excess glucose, leading to a high birth weight. On the other hand, a fetus with a *GCK* mutation is unable to produce adequate insulin in response to normal amounts of blood glucose, leading to low glucose utilization and a low birth weight. It is believed that this is a direct result of the poor glucose sensing in the pancreas of the fetus, which in turn causes low insulin secretion and poor development. In mutation-concordant mother-infant pairs, it appears that the maternal hyperglycemia compensates for the poor glucose sensing in the fetus. A case report in which a woman was treated for GDM with diet and insulin gave birth to a baby in the lowest 1st percentile for weight showed that the baby was found to have a *GCK* mutation inherited from his mother; his younger brother who did not carry the mutation was of normal birth weight [24].

Several of the monogenic forms of Pediatric Metabolic Syndrome (PMS) and associated genes are discussed in more detail in the following section and in Table 13.2.

Genomic Risk to Pediatric Metabolic Syndrome and Its Clinical Components

Table 13.2 summarizes studies of genetic mutations and polymorphisms that have been conducted in pediatric and adolescent populations for associations with abdominal obesity, dyslipidemia, hypertension, insulin resistance, and MetS. Investigations in both familial and sporadic cases are reported for MetS and each of its individual components.

Abdominal Obesity

Genetic investigations of obesity and related phenotypes in children have been conducted, primarily as candidate gene replication efforts. Several ethnic groups have been studied including Chinese [25], European white [26–29], and Turkish [30]. Studies include both sporadic and familial cases of obese children. The genetic variants most consistently associated with obesity in children are in the fat mass and obesity-associated protein (*FTO*) gene which is located on chromosome 16. Across four studies, significant associations have been found for rs9939609. Two studies examined the melanocortin receptor 4 (*MC4R*) gene, which is localized in the central nervous system in areas known to regulate energy intake. Rare mutations in *MC4R* have been found for monogenic obesity whereas two *MC4R* variants are known to be negatively correlated with the risk of obesity. In a study of 243 Polish obese children where the entire coding sequence of the *MC4R* gene was examined, six nonsynonymous variants were identified along with two novel substitutions (K73R and M215L). A second study of Turkish obese children found that the frequency of *MC4R* Val103Ile, the most commonly associated with obesity in adults, was 2.4% and that of Glu42Lys was 5.6% in obese children but was absent among controls. Two polymorphisms found in the gene encoding for lipoprotein lipase (*LPL*), a water-soluble enzyme that hydrolyzes triglycerides in lipoproteins, were associated with obesity in Chinese children [31]. The function of *FTO* and *MC4R* are still unknown. *FTO* gene expression has been found to be significantly upregulated in the hypothalamus of rats that are deprived of food [32] and appears to be associated with regulation of energy intake [33]. *MC4R* is a downstream receptor of the leptin signaling pathway. Leptin is one of the most important adipose-derived hormones. It circulates in proportion to body adiposity and triggers neuropeptide responses in the brain, which modulate appetite and possibly energy expenditure.

Cholesterol and Trigylcerides

Familial Hypercholesterolemia

Several studies have identified rare mutations and common single nucleotide polymorphisms (SNPs) that are associated with high cholesterol and triglyceride levels in children. Four studies [34–37] screened for mutations in children with familial hypercholesterolemia in the low-density lipoprotein (*LDLR*) receptor gene. Familial hypercholesterolemia is a disorder that is transmitted in an autosomal dominant inheritance pattern (ADH) and clinically characterized by severely elevated low lipoprotein cholesterol (LDL-C) levels from birth and premature cardiovascular events. Early diagnosis and treatment with lipid-lowering medications can greatly reduce risk of such events. Defects in *LDLR* result in impaired uptake of LDL cholesterol (LDL-C) by the LDL receptor, which can lead to elevated levels of LDL in the circulation which is associated with premature clinical symptoms of coronary heart disease. Mutations in *LDLR* account for the majority of ADH; however, a small subset of ADH patients harbor mutations in the gene-encoding apolipoprotein B (*APOB*), the structural protein of the LDL particle that is the ligand to LDLR, and proprotein convertase subtilisin/kexin type 9 (*PCSK9*), a protein that promotes LDLR degradation. In a study of 269 Dutch pediatric individuals with LDL-C levels above 95th percentile for age and gender and from families demonstrating an autosomal dominant inheritance pattern of hypercholesterolemia, 95% carried one of 77 functional mutations in *LDLR* [37]. Novel mutations in *LDLR* have been found in Chinese (W165X (G>A substitution) of codon 165) [35] and Czech (−27C>T nucleotide transition in the promoter sequence) [36] families. Variable expressivity of familial hypercholesterolemia has been observed in a French-Canadian family where the same mutation was shared between affected brothers which suggests polygenic inheritance, i.e., multiple possibly interacting gene defects [34]. Other genes for which associations have been found in sporadic cases affected by dyslipidemia include: *APOE, APOA5* [38–40], *PPARG2* [41], *NPY* [42], *ABCA1* [43], *WWOX* [44], and *LPL* [45]. Although the majority of individuals with ADH have mutations in *LDLR* and to a lesser extent *APOB* and *PCSK9*, there are still genes that remain to be identified. Knowledge of the complete set of mutations or genes for which to screen family members of individuals with ADH can greatly aid in diagnosis and clinical care to reduce the risk of premature cardiovascular events.

Dyslipidemia

Dyslipidemias are characterized by elevated cholesterol and triglyceride levels and have been linked to atherosclerotic cardiovascular disease. While the role of genetics is better established for monogenic disorders like ADH, the underlying genetic model that explains variation in plasma lipoprotein in children and adolescents is likely to be more complex, with possible gene-environment interactions. Genetic mutations and polymorphisms in apolipoprotein A5 (*APOA5*) and apolipoprotein E (*APOE*), genes known to regulate cholesterol and triglyceride metabolism, have been associated with dyslipidemia in children. The *APOE* E4 allele has been consistently found to be associated with higher plasma concentrations of LDL-C, while the E2 allele has been associated with lower levels of LDL-C.

The risk association with the E4 and E2 alleles has been found in children of Vietnamese [46], aboriginal Canadian [47], and French [48] ancestry.

Elevated Blood Pressure

Studies in children of genetic causes of hypertension have focused on the following syndromes and conditions – HUPRA and Liddle's syndromes, primary pulmonary hypertension, and pulmonary arterial hypertension. One study investigated three infants of Palestinian descent who were diagnosed with HUPRA syndrome, which is characterized by multiorgan disease including kidney involvement, manifesting with hyperuricemia, hypochloremic metabolic alkalosis, progressive renal failure, and primary pulmonary hypertension [49]. The clinical features of HUPRA presented in the pedigrees of affected patients in an autosomal recessive manner. Mutation analysis identified a homozygous founder mutation in *SARS2*, which represents the mitochondrial seryl-tRNA synthetase and provides serine aminoacylation in two mitochondrial tRNAs. This mutation has a frequency of 1/15 in a Palestinian isolated village. Two studies [50, 51] screened for coding mutations in *ENaC* (epithelial sodium channel) in Chinese and African-American families with children diagnosed with Liddle's syndrome, an autosomal dominant disorder characterized by severe hypertension, hypokalemia, suppressed plasma renin activity (PRA), and low aldosterone secretion rates. In both families, a missense mutation (P616L) at codon 616 changes a proline to a leucine. Mutations in ENaC may lead to the accumulation of ENaC at the cell surface and thus increased renal sodium reabsorption in patients with Liddle's syndrome [52]. Associations with *5HTT* [53], *BMPR2* [[54], [55], and *ALK1* [55] have also been found for primary pulmonary hypertension and pulmonary arterial hypertension.

Insulin Resistance

A handful of candidate gene studies have been conducted to examine whether polymorphisms previously associated with insulin resistance in adults are also associated in younger individuals [56–62]. An alanine-for-threonine substitution at codon 54 (A54T) in the fatty-acid-binding protein 2 (*FABP2*) gene was found to be associated with long-chain-polyunsaturated fatty acid (LCPUFA) profile in Japanese children [56]. Carriers of the A allele in rs16909233 and rs1054135 in the fatty-acid-binding protein 4 (*FABP4*) were associated with insulin resistance in an obese cohort of Caucasian and African-American children [59]. An observed discrepancy in serum levels of insulin, glucose, and fatty acid composition in the early phases of obesity suggests a possible mechanism for insulin resistance wherein *FABP2* and *FABP4* may play a role. Zavattari et al. [60] found that rs7566605, a polymorphism located 10 kb upstream of the transcription start site of the insulin-induced gene *INSIG2*, was associated with serum glucose concentration in a cohort of 747 Sardinian obese children and adolescents. Two studies have examined polymorphisms in the adiponectin (*ADIPOQ*) gene that has been extensively studied for its role in modulating insulin sensitivity in Italian pediatric cohorts [61, 62]. Polymorphisms at two loci (−11,391G>A; −11,377C>G) in *ADIPOQ* were associated with higher-fasting insulin levels and the homeostasis model assessment insulin resistance model (HOMA-IR) [62].

A heterozygous nonsense mutation which causes a premature termination at amino acid 331 in the α subunit of the insulin receptor (*INSR*) gene (R331X) was identified in a 12-year-old Japanese girl with type A insulin resistance [57], and screening of other family members with impaired glucose intolerance and type 2 diabetes identified the same mutation. Little is known about the frequency of this mutation in non-Japanese patients.

Metabolic Syndrome

Variants in six genes (*AGTR1* [63], *GHR* [64], *PLIN4* [65], *ENNP1* [66], *PAI-1* [67], and *3-BAR* [68]) have been associated with MetS in pediatric populations. All studies have been conducted in sporadic cases of MetS. The angiotensin II type I receptor (*AGTR1*) gene interacts with angiotensin II, a hormone that is involved in the control of blood pressure and volume in the cardiovascular system. The frequency of the 1166C allele of *AGTR1* was less frequent among 350 Iranian girls with MetS compared to 249 controls, suggesting it may be associated with reduced risk of MetS [63]. *PLIN4* is a member of the set of genes encoding perilipins, proteins that localize to the surface of the lipid droplet in adipocytes and play important roles in cellular regulation of triglyceride. Among 234 obese Brazilian children and adolescents, the *PLIN4* 11482G>A allele was associated with higher risk of MetS [65]. In a cohort of Hungarian children, the Trp64Arg polymorphism of $β_3$-adrenergic (*3-BAR*) has been associated with several components of MetS [68]. *3-BAR* is the primary receptor mediating catecholamine-stimulated thermogenesis in brown adipose tissue but is also present in subcutaneous and abdominal white adipose tissue. Overexpression of the plasma membrane enzyme ectonucleotide pyrophosphatase inhibits tyrosine kinase activity in peripheral tissues including liver, muscle, and fat. The rs997509T polymorphisms in *ENPP1* has been shown to be associated with MetS in a study of 409 obese and 400 lean Italian children [66], suggesting that this variant may modulate the association that has been reported with the *ENPP1* 121Q allele and insulin resistance. Other genes that have been associated with MetS in German and Turkish pediatric cohorts include growth hormone receptor gene (*GHR*) [64] and *PAI-1* [67].

Genetics of Fitness and Physical Activity Responsiveness and Implications for Intervention Studies of Metabolic Syndrome in Pediatric Populations

An emerging area of research is focused on identifying underlying genomic factors that determine fitness responsiveness (i.e., changes in MetS components) to exercise. Increased physical activity is an established low-cost and proven prescription for reducing risk of risk and related disorders (i.e., obesity, hypertension) [69]. Cardiovascular disease (CVD) risk has been shown to decrease by ~35% among physically active individuals [70]. Importantly, the inverse relationship between high exercise capacity (i.e., cardiorespiratory fitness VO_2max) and low cardiovascular and all-cause mortality is strong even after adjustments for other confounding factors [71–73]. However, although it is clear that exercise promotes cardiovascular health, the cellular and molecular mechanisms that are responsible for this "cardioprotection" remain to be fully understood. Furthermore, accumulating evidence suggests that there is considerable interindividual variation in cardiovascular responsiveness to exercise (i.e., improvements in cardiorespiratory fitness or lipids) and that this variability may have a genetic basis [74]. In one of the largest and most rigorous studies to date, the HERITAGE family study, individuals participating in exercise of the same duration and intensity did not all experience equal cardiovascular fitness benefits [75, 76]. As an example, for HDL-cholesterol, some individuals falling in the upper quartile of % change in HDL had an 18% *increase* in HDL-C, whereas those falling in the lower quartile had a 9.3% *decrease* following exercise [77]. Additionally, improvements in VO_2max, considered the best indicator of cardiovascular fitness, varied considerably among individuals participating in the same standardized exercise program [78–81]. Altogether, approximately 40–70% of the variation in the exercise-induced responsiveness of CVD risk has been attributed to genetics [82–86]. Thus, while exercise prescription remains a primary clinical prevention tool for reducing CVD risk, a one-size-fits-all approach is unlikely to be effective. By understanding the genomic mechanisms that regulate exercise responsiveness, personalized tailoring of exercise prescriptions may be possible. This approach could prove more effective for combating CVD risk at the individual level. Studies of the effectiveness of exercise interventions in children that consider integrating knowledge of genetic variation in fitness-associated genes may be better able to understand the interactive role of gene-environment interactions in causing MetS. Similarly, the field of nutrigenomics aims to better understand how genes regulate absorption and metabolism of nutrients from food. Genomic approaches to studying PMS should aim to move beyond standard association and single-gene testing to larger unbiased sequencing and epigenetic studies and furthermore to more fully examine the interactions of diet and exercise with genetics.

Conclusions

MetS in pediatric and adolescent populations in large reflects the complex interactions between genetic and environmental risk factors. Disorders with early onset in life tend to have higher genetic predispositions. Indeed, there are examples of monogenic and familial forms of MetS and its components where single or a few genes explain the bulk of the disorder. However, for the majority of cases, further investigations are needed to understand the polygenic inheritance of the disorder and to explain the missing heritability. While many population-based studies have focused on MetS and its components in adults, including several large genome-wide association studies, very little is known about the genetics of common forms of MetS in children and adolescents. With the availability of novel genome technologies such as next generation sequencing and with increased understanding of epigenetic mechanisms that may also play a role, it is now possible to more comprehensively study the full compendium of genetic variation. Furthermore, emerging fields such as fitness genetics and nutrigenomics lend promise to the investigation of gene-environment interactions that underly MetS. Although substantial progress has already been achieved in understanding the genetics of MetS, there is still an enormous gap in our knowledge that remains to be filled.

References

1. Ford ES, Li C. Defining the metabolic syndrome in children and adolescents: will the real definition please stand up? J Pediatr. 2008;2:160–4.
2. Huang TT. Finding thresholds of risk for components of the pediatric metabolic syndrome. J Pediatr. 2008;2:158–9.
3. Monda KL, North KE, Hunt SC, Rao DC, Province MA, Kraja AT. The genetics of obesity and the metabolic syndrome. Endocr Metab Immune Disord Drug Targets. 2010;2:86–108.
4. Groop L, Forsblom C, Lehtovirta M, Tuomi T, Karanko S, Nissen M, Ehrnstrom BO, Forsen B, Isomaa B, Snickars B, et al. Metabolic consequences of a family history of NIDDM (the Botnia study): evidence for sex-specific parental effects. Diabetes. 1996;11:1585–93.
5. Carey DG, Nguyen TV, Campbell LV, Chisholm DJ, Kelly P. Genetic influences on central abdominal fat: a twin study. Int J Obes Relat Metab Disord. 1996;8:722–6.
6. Dolinoy DC, Weidman JR, Waterland RA, Jirtle RL. Maternal genistein alters coat color and protects Avy mouse offspring from obesity by modifying the fetal epigenome. Environ Health Perspect. 2006;4:567–72.
7. Temple IK, Shield JP. Transient neonatal diabetes, a disorder of imprinting. J Med Genet. 2002;12:872–5.
8. Temple IK, James RS, Crolla JA, Sitch FL, Jacobs PA, Howell WM, Betts P, Baum JD, Shield JP. An imprinted gene(s) for diabetes? Nat Genet. 1995;2:110–2.
9. Abramowicz MJ, Andrien M, Dupont E, Dorchy H, Parma J, Duprez L, Ledley FD, Courtens W, Vamos E. Isodisomy of chromosome 6 in a newborn with methylmalonic acidemia and agenesis of pancreatic beta cells causing diabetes mellitus. J Clin Invest. 1994;1:418–21.

10. Cave H, Polak M, Drunat S, Denamur E, Czernichow P. Refinement of the 6q chromosomal region implicated in transient neonatal diabetes. Diabetes. 2000;1:108–13.
11. Gardner RJ, Mackay DJ, Mungall AJ, Polychronakos C, Siebert R, Shield JP, Temple IK, Robinson DO. An imprinted locus associated with transient neonatal diabetes mellitus. Hum Mol Genet. 2000;4:589–96.
12. Arima T, Drewell RA, Oshimura M, Wake N, Surani MA. A novel imprinted gene, HYMAI, is located within an imprinted domain on human chromosome 6 containing ZAC. Genomics. 2000;3:248–55.
13. Mackay DJ, Temple IK, Shield JP, Robinson DO. Bisulphite sequencing of the transient neonatal diabetes mellitus DMR facilitates a novel diagnostic test but reveals no methylation anomalies in patients of unknown aetiology. Hum Genet. 2005;4:255–61.
14. Mitchell GA. Genetics, physiology and perinatal influences in childhood obesity: view from the chair. Int J Obes (Lond). 2009;S41–7.
15. Farooqi IS, Matarese G, Lord GM, Keogh JM, Lawrence E, Agwu C, Sanna V, Jebb SA, Perna F, Fontana S, et al. Beneficial effects of leptin on obesity, T cell hyporesponsiveness, and neuroendocrine/metabolic dysfunction of human congenital leptin deficiency. J Clin Invest. 2002;8:1093–103.
16. Rahalkar AR, Hegele RA. Monogenic pediatric dyslipidemias: classification, genetics and clinical spectrum. Mol Genet Metab. 2008;3:282–94.
17. Simonetti GD, Mohaupt MG, Bianchetti MG. Monogenic forms of hypertension. Eur J Pediatr 2011 [Epub ahead of print].
18. Travers ME, McCarthy MI. Type 2 diabetes and obesity: genomics and the clinic. Hum Genet 2011 [Epub ahead of print].
19. Rosenbloom AL, Joe JR, Young RS, Winter WE. Emerging epidemic of type 2 diabetes in youth. Diabetes Care. 1999;2:345–54.
20. Fajans SS, Bell GI, Polonsky KS. Molecular mechanisms and clinical pathophysiology of maturity-onset diabetes of the young. N Engl J Med. 2001;13:971–80.
21. Neve B, Fernandez-Zapico ME, Ashkenazi-Katalan V, Dina C, Hamid YH, Joly E, Vaillant E, Benmezroua Y, Durand E, Bakaher N, et al. Role of transcription factor KLF11 and its diabetes-associated gene variants in pancreatic beta cell function. Proc Natl Acad Sci U S A. 2005;3:4807–12.
22. Raeder H, Bjorkhaug L, Johansson S, Mangseth K, Sagen JV, Hunting A, Folling I, Johansen O, Bjorgaas M, Paus PN, et al. A hepatocyte nuclear factor-4 alpha gene (HNF4A) P2 promoter haplotype linked with late-onset diabetes: studies of HNF4A variants in the Norwegian MODY registry. Diabetes. 2006;6:1899–903.
23. Hattersley AT, Beards F, Ballantyne E, Appleton M, Harvey R, Ellard S. Mutations in the glucokinase gene of the fetus result in reduced birth weight. Nat Genet. 1998;3:268–70.
24. Spyer G, Hattersley AT, Sykes JE, Sturley RH, MacLeod KM. Influence of maternal and fetal glucokinase mutations in gestational diabetes. Am J Obstet Gynecol. 2001;1:240–1.
25. Xi B, Shen Y, Zhang M, Liu X, Zhao X, Wu L, Cheng H, Hou D, Lindpaintner K, Liu L, et al. The common rs9939609 variant of the fat mass and obesity-associated gene is associated with obesity risk in children and adolescents of Beijing, China. BMC Med Genet. 2010;11:107.
26. Muller TD, Hinney A, Scherag A, Nguyen TT, Schreiner F, Schafer H, Hebebrand J, Roth CL, Reinehr T. 'Fat mass and obesity associated' gene (FTO): no significant association of variant rs9939609 with weight loss in a lifestyle intervention and lipid metabolism markers in German obese children and adolescents. BMC Med Genet. 2008;9:85.
27. Frayling TM, Timpson NJ, Weedon MN, Zeggini E, Freathy RM, Lindgren CM, Perry JR, Elliott KS, Lango H, Rayner NW, et al. A common variant in the FTO gene is associated with body mass index and predisposes to childhood and adult obesity. Science. 2007;5826:889–94.
28. Nowacka-Woszuk J, Cieslak J, Skowronska B, Majewska KA, Stankiewicz W, Fichna P, Switonski M. Missense mutations and polymorphisms of the MC4R gene in Polish obese children and adolescents in relation to the relative body mass index. J Appl Genet. 2011 [Epub ahead of print].

29. Rutters F, Nieuwenhuizen AG, Bouwman F, Mariman E, Westerterp-Plantenga MS. Associations between a single nucleotide polymorphism of the FTO gene (rs9939609) and obesity-related characteristics over time during puberty in a Dutch children cohort. J Clin Endocrinol Metab. 2011;6:E939–42.
30. Demiralp DO, Berberoglu M, Akar N. Melanocortin-4 receptor polymorphisms in Turkish pediatric obese patients. Clin Appl Thromb Hemost. 2011;1:70–4.
31. Wang LN, Yu Q, Xiong Y, Liu LF, Zhang Z, Zhang XN, Cheng H, Wang B. Lipoprotein lipase gene polymorphisms and risks of childhood obesity in Chinese preschool children. Eur J Pediatr. 2011 [Epub ahead of print].
32. Fredriksson R, Hagglund M, Olszewski PK, Stephansson O, Jacobsson JA, Olszewska AM, Levine AS, Lindblom J, Schioth HB. The obesity gene, FTO, is of ancient origin, up-regulated during food deprivation and expressed in neurons of feeding-related nuclei of the brain. Endocrinology. 2008;5:2062–71.
33. Olszewski PK, Fredriksson R, Olszewska AM, Stephansson O, Alsio J, Radomska KJ, Levine AS, Schioth HB. Hypothalamic FTO is associated with the regulation of energy intake not feeding reward. BMC Neurosci. 2009;10:129.
34. Levy E, Minnich A, Cacan SL, Thibault L, Giroux LM, Davignon J, Lambert M. Association of an exon 3 mutation (Trp66–>Gly) of the LDL receptor with variable expression of familial hypercholesterolemia in a French Canadian family. Biochem Mol Med. 1997;1:59–69.
35. Xie L, Gong QH, Xie ZG, Liang ZM, Hu ZM, Xia K, Xia JH, Yang YF. Two novel mutations of the LDL receptor gene associated with familial hypercholesterolemia in a Chinese family. Chin Med J (Engl). 2007;19:1694–9.
36. Francova H, Trbusek M, Zapletalova P, Kuhrova V. New promoter mutations in the low-0density lipoprotein receptor gene which induce familial hypercholesterolaemia phenotype: molecular and functional analysis. J Inherit Metab Dis. 2004;4:523–8.
37. van der Graaf A, Avis HJ, Kusters DM, Vissers MN, Hutten BA, Defesche JC, Huijgen R, Fouchier SW, Wijburg FA, Kastelein JJ, et al. Molecular basis of autosomal dominant hypercholesterolemia: assessment in a large cohort of hypercholesterolemic children. Circulation. 2011;11:1167–73.
38. Brito DD, Fernandes AP, Gomes KB, Coelho FF, Cruz NG, Sabino AP, Cardoso JE, Figueiredo-Filho PP, Diamante R, Norton CR, et al. Apolipoprotein A5–1131T>C polymorphism, but not APOE genotypes, increases susceptibility for dyslipidemia in children and adolescents. Mol Biol Rep. 2010 [Epub ahead of print].
39. Guardiola M, Ribalta J, Gomez-Coronado D, Lasuncion MA, de Oya M, Garces C. The apolipoprotein A5 (APOA5) gene predisposes Caucasian children to elevated triglycerides and vitamin E (Four Provinces Study). Atherosclerosis. 2010;2:543–7.
40. Endo K, Yanagi H, Araki J, Hirano C, Yamakawa-Kobayashi K, Tomura S. Association found between the promoter region polymorphism in the apolipoprotein A-V gene and the serum triglyceride level in Japanese schoolchildren. Hum Genet. 2002;6:570–2.
41. Dedoussis GV, Theodoraki EV, Manios Y, Yiannakouris N, Panagiotakos D, Papoutsakis C, Skenderi K, Zampelas A. The Pro12Ala polymorphism in PPARgamma2 gene affects lipid parameters in Greek primary school children: a case of gene-to-gender interaction. Am J Med Sci. 2007;1:10–5.
42. Karvonen MK, Koulu M, Pesonen U, Uusitupa MI, Tammi A, Viikari J, Simell O, Ronnemaa T. Leucine 7 to proline 7 polymorphism in the preproneuropeptide Y is associated with birth weight and serum triglyceride concentration in preschool aged children. J Clin Endocrinol Metab. 2000;4:1455–60.
43. Flores-Dorantes T, Arellano-Campos O, Posadas-Sanchez R, Villarreal-Molina T, Medina-Urrutia A, Romero-Hidalgo S, Yescas-Gomez P, Perez-Mendez O, Jorge-Galarza E, Tusie-Luna T, et al. Association of R230C ABCA1 gene variant with low HDL-C levels and abnormal HDL subclass distribution in Mexican school-aged children. Clin Chim Acta. 2010;17–18:1214–7.
44. Lee JC, Weissglas-Volkov D, Kyttala M, Dastani Z, Cantor RM, Sobel EM, Plaisier CL, Engert JC, van Greevenbroek MM, Kane JP, et al. WW-domain-containing oxidoreductase is associated with low plasma HDL-C levels. Am J Hum Genet. 2008;2:180–92.

45. Mingrone G, Henriksen FL, Greco AV, Krogh LN, Capristo E, Gastaldelli A, Castagneto M, Ferrannini E, Gasbarrini G, Beck-Nielsen H. Triglyceride-induced diabetes associated with familial lipoprotein lipase deficiency. Diabetes. 1999;6:1258–63.
46. Nghiem NT, Ta TT, Ohmori R, Kuroki M, Nguyen VC, Nguyen TK, Kawakami M, Kondo K. Apolipoprotein E polymorphism in Vietnamese children and its relationship to plasma lipid and lipoprotein levels. Metabolism. 2004;12:1517–21.
47. Hegele RA, Connelly PW, Hanley AJ, Sun F, Harris SB, Zinman B. Common genomic variants associated with variation in plasma lipoproteins in young aboriginal Canadians. Arterioscler Thromb Vasc Biol. 1997;6:1060–6.
48. Parlier G, Thomas G, Bereziat G, Fontaine JL, Girardet JP. Relation of apolipoprotein E polymorphism to lipid metabolism in obese children. Pediatr Res. 1997;5:682–5.
49. Belostotsky R, Ben-Shalom E, Rinat C, Becker-Cohen R, Feinstein S, Zeligson S, Segel R, Elpeleg O, Nassar S, Frishberg Y. Mutations in the mitochondrial seryl-tRNA synthetase cause hyperuricemia, pulmonary hypertension, renal failure in infancy and alkalosis, HUPRA syndrome. Am J Hum Genet. 2011;2:193–200.
50. Gao PJ, Zhang KX, Zhu DL, He X, Han ZY, Zhan YM, Yang LW. Diagnosis of Liddle syndrome by genetic analysis of beta and gamma subunits of epithelial sodium channel–a report of five affected family members. J Hypertens. 2001;5:885–9.
51. Hansson JH, Schild L, Lu Y, Wilson TA, Gautschi I, Shimkets R, Nelson-Williams C, Rossier BC, Lifton RP. A de novo missense mutation of the beta subunit of the epithelial sodium channel causes hypertension and Liddle syndrome, identifying a proline-rich segment critical for regulation of channel activity. Proc Natl Acad Sci U S A. 1995;25:11495–9.
52. Goulet CC, Volk KA, Adams CM, Prince LS, Stokes JB, Snyder PM. Inhibition of the epithelial Na+ channel by interaction of Nedd4 with a PY motif deleted in Liddle's syndrome. J Biol Chem. 1998;45:30012–7.
53. Vachharajani A, Saunders S. Allelic variation in the serotonin transporter (5HTT) gene contributes to idiopathic pulmonary hypertension in children. Biochem Biophys Res Commun. 2005;2:376–9.
54. Rosenzweig EB, Morse JH, Knowles JA, Chada KK, Khan AM, Roberts KE, McElroy JJ, Juskiw NK, Mallory NC, Rich S, et al. Clinical implications of determining BMPR2 mutation status in a large cohort of children and adults with pulmonary arterial hypertension. J Heart Lung Transplant. 2008;6:668–74.
55. Fujiwara M, Yagi H, Matsuoka R, Akimoto K, Furutani M, Imamura S, Uehara R, Nakayama T, Takao A, Nakazawa M, et al. Implications of mutations of activin receptor-like kinase 1 gene (ALK1) in addition to bone morphogenetic protein receptor II gene (BMPR2) in children with pulmonary arterial hypertension. Circ J. 2008;1:127–33.
56. Okada T, Sato NF, Kuromori Y, Miyashita M, Iwata F, Hara M, Harada K, Hattori H. Thr-encoding allele homozygosity at codon 54 of FABP 2 gene may be associated with impaired delta 6 desaturase activity and reduced plasma arachidonic acid in obese children. J Atheroscler Thromb. 2006;4:192–6.
57. Takahashi I, Yamada Y, Kadowaki H, Horikoshi M, Kadowaki T, Narita T, Tsuchida S, Noguchi A, Koizumi A, Takahashi T. Phenotypical variety of insulin resistance in a family with a novel mutation of the insulin receptor gene. Endocr J. 2010;6:509–16.
58. Huang Z, Li Y, Tang T, Xu W, Liao Z, Yao B, Hu G, Weng J. Hyperinsulinaemic hypoglycaemia associated with a heterozygous missense mutation of R1174W in the insulin receptor (IR) gene. Clin Endocrinol (Oxf). 2009;5:659–65.
59. Khalyfa A, Bhushan B, Hegazi M, Kim J, Kheirandish-Gozal L, Bhattacharjee R, Capdevila OS, Gozal D. Fatty-acid binding protein 4 gene variants and childhood obesity: potential implications for insulin sensitivity and CRP levels. Lipids Health Dis. 2010;9:18.
60. Zavattari P, Loche A, Civolani P, Pilia S, Moi L, Casini MR, Minerba L, Loche S. An INSIG2 polymorphism affects glucose homeostasis in Sardinian obese children and adolescents. Ann Hum Genet. 2010;5:381–6.

61. Verduci E, Scaglioni S, Agostoni C, Radaelli G, Biondi M, Manso AS, Riva E, Giovannini M. The relationship of insulin resistance with SNP 276G>T at adiponectin gene and plasma long-chain polyunsaturated fatty acids in obese children. Pediatr Res. 2009;3:346–9.
62. Petrone A, Zavarella S, Caiazzo A, Leto G, Spoletini M, Potenziani S, Osborn J, Vania A, Buzzetti R. The promoter region of the adiponectin gene is a determinant in modulating insulin sensitivity in childhood obesity. Obesity (Silver Spring). 2006;9:1498–504.
63. Alavi-Shahri J, Behravan J, Hassany M, Tatari F, Kasaian J, Ganjali R, Tavallaie S, Sabouri S, Sahebkar A, Oladi M, et al. Association between angiotensin II type 1 receptor gene polymorphism and metabolic syndrome in a young female Iranian population. Arch Med Res. 2010;5:343–9.
64. Sorensen K, Aksglaede L, Munch-Andersen T, Aachmann-Andersen NJ, Leffers H, Helge JW, Hilsted L, Juul A. Impact of the growth hormone receptor exon 3 deletion gene polymorphism on glucose metabolism, lipids, and insulin-like growth factor-I levels during puberty. J Clin Endocrinol Metab. 2009;8:2966–9.
65. Deram S, Nicolau CY, Perez-Martinez P, Guazzelli I, Halpern A, Wajchenberg BL, Ordovas JM, Villares SM. Effects of perilipin (PLIN) gene variation on metabolic syndrome risk and weight loss in obese children and adolescents. J Clin Endocrinol Metab. 2008;12:4933–40.
66. Santoro N, Cirillo G, Lepore MG, Palma A, Amato A, Savarese P, Marzuillo P, Grandone A, Perrone L, Del Giudice EM. Effect of the rs997509 polymorphism on the association between ectonucleotide pyrophosphatase phosphodiesterase 1 and metabolic syndrome and impaired glucose tolerance in childhood obesity. J Clin Endocrinol Metab. 2009;1:300–5.
67. Kinik ST, Ozbek N, Yuce M, Yazici AC, Verdi H, Atac FB. PAI-1 gene 4G/5G polymorphism, cytokine levels and their relations with metabolic parameters in obese children. Thromb Haemost. 2008;2:352–6.
68. Erhardt E, Czako M, Csernus K, Molnar D, Kosztolanyi G. The frequency of Trp64Arg polymorphism of the beta3-adrenergic receptor gene in healthy and obese Hungarian children and its association with cardiovascular risk factors. Eur J Clin Nutr. 2005;8:955–9.
69. WRITING GROUP MEMBERS, Lloyd-Jones D, Adams RJ, Brown TM, Carnethon M, Dai S, De Simone G, Ferguson TB, Ford E, Furie K, et al. Heart disease and stroke statistics—2010 update: a report from the American Heart Association. Circulation. 2010;7:e46–215.
70. Nocon M, Hiemann T, Muller-Riemenschneider F, Thalau F, Roll S, Willich SN. Association of physical activity with all-cause and cardiovascular mortality: a systematic review and meta-analysis. Eur J Cardiovasc Prev Rehabil. 2008;3:239–46.
71. Kokkinos P, Myers J. Exercise and physical activity: clinical outcomes and applications. Circulation. 2010;16:1637–48.
72. Kokkinos P, Myers J, Faselis C, Panagiotakos DB, Doumas M, Pittaras A, Manolis A, Kokkinos JP, Karasik P, Greenberg M, et al. Exercise capacity and mortality in older men: a 20-year follow-up study. Circulation. 2010;8:790–7.
73. Myers J, Prakash M, Froelicher V, Do D, Partington S, Atwood JE. Exercise capacity and mortality among men referred for exercise testing. N Engl J Med. 2002;11:793–801.
74. Bouchard C, An P, Rice T, Skinner JS, Wilmore JH, Gagnon J, Perusse L, Leon AS, Rao DC. Familial aggregation of VO(2max) response to exercise training: results from the HERITAGE Family Study. J Appl Physiol. 1999;3:1003–8.
75. Bouchard C, Rankinen T. Individual differences in response to regular physical activity. Med Sci Sports Exerc. 2001;6 Suppl, S446–51, discussion S452–3.
76. Mori M, Higuchi K, Sakurai A, Tabara Y, Miki T, Nose H. Genetic basis of inter-individual variability in the effects of exercise on the alleviation of lifestyle-related diseases. J Physiol. 2009;Pt 23, 5577–84.
77. Leon AS, Togashi K, Rankinen T, Despres JP, Rao DC, Skinner JS, Wilmore JH, Bouchard C. Association of apolipoprotein E polymorphism with blood lipids and maximal oxygen uptake in the sedentary state and after exercise training in the HERITAGE family study. Metabolism. 2004;1:108–16.

78. Timmons JA, Knudsen S, Rankinen T, Koch LG, Sarzynski MA, Jensen T, Keller P, Scheele C, Vollaard NB, Nielsen S, et al. Using molecular classification to predict gains in maximal aerobic capacity following endurance exercise training in humans. J Appl Physiol. 2010 [Epub ahead of print].
79. Vollaard NB, Constantin-Teodosiu D, Fredriksson K, Rooyackers O, Jansson E, Greenhaff PL, Timmons JA, Sundberg CJ. Systematic analysis of adaptations in aerobic capacity and submaximal energy metabolism provides a unique insight into determinants of human aerobic performance. J Appl Physiol. 2009;5:1479–86.
80. An P, Perusse L, Rankinen T, Borecki IB, Gagnon J, Leon AS, Skinner JS, Wilmore JH, Bouchard C, Rao DC. Familial aggregation of exercise heart rate and blood pressure in response to 20 weeks of endurance training: the HERITAGE family study. Int J Sports Med. 2003;1:57–62.
81. Rice T, An P, Gagnon J, Leon AS, Skinner JS, Wilmore JH, Bouchard C, Rao DC. Heritability of HR and BP response to exercise training in the HERITAGE Family Study. Med Sci Sports Exerc. 2002;6:972–9.
82. Hopkins N, Stratton G, Maia J, Tinken TM, Graves LE, Cable TN, Green DJ. Heritability of arterial function, fitness, and physical activity in youth: a study of monozygotic and dizygotic twins. J Pediatr. 2010;6:943–8.
83. Gaskill SE, Rice T, Bouchard C, Gagnon J, Rao DC, Skinner JS, Wilmore JH, Leon AS. Familial resemblance in ventilatory threshold: the HERITAGE Family Study. Med Sci Sports Exerc. 2001;11:1832–40.
84. Bouchard C, Daw EW, Rice T, Perusse L, Gagnon J, Province MA, Leon AS, Rao DC, Skinner JS, Wilmore JH. Familial resemblance for VO2max in the sedentary state: the HERITAGE family study. Med Sci Sports Exerc. 1998;2:252–8.
85. Fagard R, Bielen E, Amery A. Heritability of aerobic power and anaerobic energy generation during exercise. J Appl Physiol. 1991;1:357–62.
86. Maes HH, Beunen GP, Vlietinck RF, Neale MC, Thomis M, Vanden Eynde B, Lysens R, Simons J, Derom C, Derom R. Inheritance of physical fitness in 10-yr-old twins and their parents. Med Sci Sports Exerc. 1996;12:1479–91.

Chapter 14
Physical Activity Assessment and Intervention

Gabriel Somarriba

Abstract Physical activity is the most common, everyday stress placed on the body, and may be used as a diagnostic and therapeutic tool in evaluating and treating children with many different medical conditions. Physical activity at recommended levels may reduce insulin resistance, dyslipidemia, and hypertension, among other factors, and for children with metabolic syndrome, physical activity may be as efficient and effective as pharmaceutical treatment. Metabolic syndrome in children has been linked to poor cardiovascular fitness. Children have also demonstrated beneficial effects, such as weight loss, increases in cardiorespiratory fitness, and strength, when participating in a structured physical activity intervention. Physical activity has many components, and it is important to address each when designing an exercise program or intervention for children with metabolic syndrome. Baseline assessments of the current level of fitness are necessary before prescribing any exercise program for children with metabolic syndrome. The tests may be repeated throughout the program to assess progress and set realistic goals for the program. There is no consensus on the best type of intervention to address the constellation of cardiovascular risk factors in metabolic syndrome, and future studies are needed to substantiate the effects of physical activity in children and adolescents with metabolic syndrome and to standardize the specific duration, intensity, and type of activity that yield positive results.

Keywords Physical activity • Aerobic exercise • Fitness • Exercise • Children

G. Somarriba, DPT
Division of Clinical Research, Department of Pediatrics, University of Miami,
Miller School of Medicine,
1580 NW 10th Avenue, Miami, FL 33136, USA
e-mail: gsomarriba2@med.miami.edu

Introduction

Exercise capacity may be the single most important aspect of a child's health because physical activity is the most common, everyday stress placed on the body. Exercise requires coordinated and proper responses from multiple systems of the body to maintain higher levels of activity over time. Despite numerous medical advances in diagnosis and treatment, exercise testing remains a vital diagnostic tool in evaluating children with many different medical conditions.

In recent years, interest has grown in assessing and restoring exercise capacity in children with chronic medical conditions. In particular, concerns about the rising incidence and prevalence of childhood obesity and metabolic syndrome [1] have intensified the need to prevent and manage these conditions in at-risk children. Studies establishing the beneficial effects of physical activity in adults [2] have stimulated research to determine whether physical activity would also provide these benefits in children. Guidelines for exercise testing now include specific recommendations for children [3–5], in hope of increasing awareness and to set minimum standards for the type and amount of regular physical activity required by children.

The Physiologic Basis of Exercise

To move from rest to exertion, several body systems need to respond and coordinate to sustain the new level of activity. It is this regular and sustained intensity that is credited with the beneficial outcomes of physical activity. The positive effects of exercise are appreciated throughout the body (Fig. 14.1). Metabolic syndrome is loosely defined as a constellation of several cardiometabolic—but modifiable—risk factors, all of which may respond to increased physical activity. Physical activity at recommended levels may reduce insulin resistance, dyslipidemia, and hypertension, among other factors, and for children with metabolic syndrome, physical activity may be as efficient and effective as pharmaceutical treatment [6].

Components of Fitness Assessments

Baseline assessments of the current level of fitness are necessary before prescribing any exercise program for children with metabolic syndrome. One of the purposes of assessing physical fitness at a baseline is to provide children and parents with information about how their current level of fitness compares with others of similar age and sex. The results of the tests will also help tailor a program that addresses all aspects of physical activity. The tests may be repeated throughout the program to assess progress. The results also allow measurable and realistic goals to be prescribed for the participant. Lastly, fitness assessments may be used to stratify risk factors, such as those related to cardiovascular disease and metabolic syndrome [4].

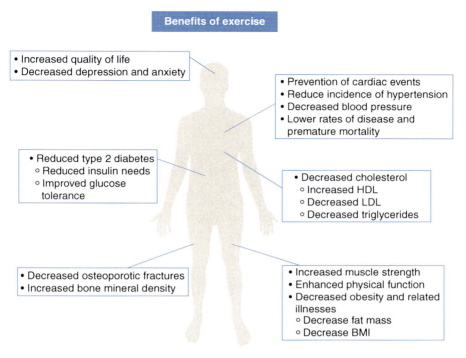

Fig. 14.1 Systemic benefits from regular physical activity and exercise (Based on data from Medicine ACoS [4])

The following series of physical fitness assessments are most suitable for children, with or at risk for metabolic syndrome.

Body Composition

Numerous studies have documented that higher percentages of body fat are associated with several medical conditions, including hypertension, diabetes, and hyperlipidemia [7, 8]. The percentage of body fat can easily be estimated roughly by calculating the body mass index (BMI), which is the ratio of weight to height-squared (kg/m^2). The BMI growth curves for children developed by the Center for Disease Control and Prevention identify the percentiles corrected for age and sex [9]. Central body fat distribution can also be estimated with waist-to-hip ratio, or the circumference of the waist divided by the circumference of the hips [10]. Body fat percentage may also be determined by several other methods, including skinfold measures, bioelectrical impedance, dual-energy X-ray absorptiometry, and the reference standard, hydrostatic weighing. For children, the recommended methods include the skinfold test if performed by a trained clinician or the more expensive but more reliable method of absorptiometry [11]. Although the cutoff values for body fat have not been standardized, body fat percentiles for normal, overweight, and obese categories have been suggested [12]. Finally, in addition to their more diagnostic value, body fat measures may also be used to compare baseline to post-treatment measures to assess outcomes of interventions.

Blood Pressure

High blood pressure is an independent risk factor for metabolic syndrome. Measuring resting blood pressure is important not only to diagnose hypertension but also to monitor changes during or after physical activity. However, the proper protocol must be used [13] and, in children, the results must be adjusted for age and sex [14].

Metabolic Laboratory Values

A standard fasting metabolic laboratory workup is recommended for children at baseline to determine current levels of cholesterol, including high- and low-density lipoprotein, as well as triglycerides, insulin, and hemoglobin A1C. Additional laboratory work-up should be assessed by the physician upon physical evaluation and medical history of the patient. The results may also be used to determine exercise-related changes.

Cardiorespiratory Fitness

Cardiorespiratory fitness, also known as aerobic capacity, is related to the volume of oxygen used by the muscles during an activity. Cardiorespiratory tests measure fitness in terms of maximal oxygen consumption (VO_2 max). Essentially, the higher the aerobic demand of an activity, the higher the VO_2 value. Maximum VO_2 is used to assess respiratory, cardiovascular, and musculoskeletal function.

Cardiorespiratory fitness is the most important exercise-specific measure because higher levels of VO_2 max are associated with higher levels of physical activity, which in turn is related to numerous health benefits [2]. Improvements in VO_2 max through physical activity reduce the risk of all-cause mortality. Low VO_2 max values are associated with a markedly increased risk of premature death from all causes but primarily from cardiovascular disease [2].

Research on how to administer and interpret these tests has been extensive. Most research has focused on adults, but more recent studies have used VO_2 max as the main outcome measure for the effectiveness of aerobic intervention studies in children.

Many protocols have been developed to measure cardiorespiratory fitness in adults and in children. From the equipment used, such as treadmills, bicycles, or arm ergometers, to the degree of testing, either to maximal or submaximal limits, the options are numerous. Children are usually tested on treadmills because the cycle ergometer can fatigue the underdeveloped knee extensors and end the exam prematurely [4]. Additionally, walking or running is an activity more common to children, and the larger muscle groups involved increase the demand on the cardiorespiratory system.

The specific protocol should allow children to achieve maximal effort. The most common protocols include the Bruce [15], Balke [16], and James [17]. In general, the goal of this exercise test is to reach VO_2 max in 8–12 min. Longer tests may result in local muscle fatigue, which can reduce the validity of the test.

Most children can exercise to maximum levels if the test is explained to them and if they are encouraged to put forth maximum effort during the test. Alternatively, submaximal tests usually are stopped when the heart rate reaches a set percentage of the predicted maximum (220-age), but most of such studies have not been validated in children.

Maximum effort in children needs to be defined by specific criteria. In adults, maximum effort is achieved when oxygen consumption plateaus with increasing exercise intensity, but only about 50% of children reach this plateau [18]. Proposed criteria to define maximum effort in children include reaching a heart rate of 200 beats/min on a treadmill [19], a respiratory exchange ratio of 1.05 [19], and the appearance of maximum effort as determined by the physiologist [20]. One of these criteria should be used when testing children for VO_2 max.

Exercise test results are expressed in terms of oxygen uptake per minute (L/min). More commonly, however, the results are reported relative to body weight as mL/kg/min. Values for VO_2 max also vary by age and sex. They increase throughout childhood and adolescence and plateau around 25 years of age before decreasing in adulthood. Normative VO_2 max values have been established for different age groups and males (Fig. 14.2) and females (Fig. 14.3) [21]. Poor or very poor results suggest sedentary lifestyles and may be associated with an increased risk of death from all causes [2].

Muscular Strength and Endurance

Strength and endurance measurements are important components of any physical activity program. Strength is the degree of force that can be exerted by a muscle or group of muscles, whereas endurance is the muscle's ability to repeat or sustain the application of force [22]. The health benefits of adequate muscular strength include increases in bone mass, increases in lean body mass, and muscle and tendon integrity, which lowers the risk of injury [4].

Peak force is the maximum voluntary contraction a muscle can exert. The most widely accepted measure of strength is the 1-repetition maximum test (1-RM) in which strength is the maximum resistance that can be moved through a full range of motion one time [4]. To interpret the results, the weight of the maximum resistance must be adjusted for body weight with a weight ratio (weight lifted/body weight).

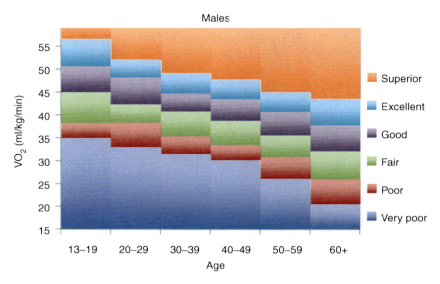

Fig. 14.2 VO$_2$ reference scale for males (Based on data from The Cooper Institute for Aerobics Research, Dallas, TX, revised 1997 printed in Heyward VH. Advance fitness assessment and exercise prescription, 3rd ed. Champaign, IL: Human Kinetics; 1998, p. 48)

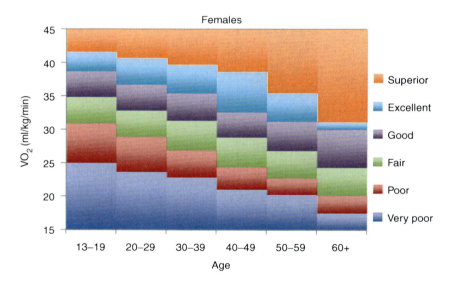

Fig. 14.3 VO$_2$ Reference scale for females (Based on data from The Cooper Institute for Aerobics Research, Dallas, TX, revised 1997 printed in Heyward VH. Advance fitness assessment and exercise prescription, 3rd ed. Champaign, IL: Human Kinetics; 1998, p. 48)

Endurance is measured by the amount of time an action can be sustained or repeated, that is, how long the muscles can work until they fatigue and can no longer perform the repetition. The endurance test most commonly used is the sit-up test [22]. The number of sit-ups in a set time is then compared to normative values established by the President's Council on Physical Activity [22].

Flexibility

Flexibility is the range of motion through which a joint can move. Flexibility is important to carrying out activities of daily living. The President's Council recommends assessing flexibility in children with the sit-and-reach test. This test assesses the flexibility of the hamstrings and low back by having children sit with their legs out and reach for their toes. The measure is the length of the reach relative to the child's foot or to another landmark. Normative values have been established [22].

Principles of Physical Activity

Physical activity has many components, any one of which may be used to describe the activity. Physical activity is most commonly thought of as aerobic training, but strength training and flexibility are also essential components. To ascertain the effectiveness of interventions for children and adolescents, it is important to have a clear understating of the components that make up the activity.

Physical activity is described by its frequency, intensity, time, and the type of activity, also known as the FITT principle. With the many different components of physical activity, it is important to address each when designing an exercise program or intervention for children with the metabolic syndrome.

Frequency generally refers to the number of sessions of exercise per week. According to the American Heart Association (AHA) and the American College of Sports Medicine (ACSM), children should participate in structured physical activity 3–5 days a week and in recreational activities most days of the week. With sedentary children, the frequency of exercise should begin low and then increased gradually to allow time to adapt to the new physical requirements. Initially, a day of rest between sessions is commonly suggested. Generally, the greatest overload occurs in the first few weeks and may increase the risk for injury, soreness, and fatigue.

Intervention studies in children and adolescents have varied in the prescribed frequency of exercise sessions per week. Protocols requiring five exercise sessions per week have had favorable results [23]. More recently, Miller et al. reported similar outcomes in children who participated in structured physical activity twice a week [24]. Intervention studies in children and adolescents with metabolic syndrome have generally varied between 1 and 5 sessions of physical activity per week for as few as 12 weeks [23, 25, 26]. These studies support the belief that 30–60 min of physical activity a day, 3–7 days a week reduces both central body fat and total body fat in children and adolescents [27, 28].

Intensity is the degree of effort generated during an activity (ACSM) [4]. As the intensity of an activity increases, greater demand is placed on the child's body. For regular physical activity, moderate intensity is recommended [4, 5]. Moderate intensity is reached by achieving 60–75% of VO_2 max (as determined by cardiorespiratory stress testing) or, more commonly, 60–75% of the age-adjusted maximum heart rate. Studies in children generally report that exercise of moderate intensity is sufficient to achieve positive outcomes [24, 27, 29, 30].

The duration of physical activity also influences the outcomes of physical activity. Current recommendations are that moderate-intensity physical activity should be sustained for about 30 min [4, 5]. Sedentary children may begin with shorter session with breaks and work up to the longer, continuous sessions. Exercise intervention studies in children generally use 20–30 min of aerobic activity and 15 min of 6–8 resistance exercises. Studies with these characteristics have shown promising beneficial results [24, 30, 31].

The type of activity can be modified for individual children to increase their adherence to the activity and still produce favorable results. The activities generally need to be interesting and varied enough to keep children engaged.

Physical Activity Interventions

The effects of physical activity on adults have been studied extensively. The increasing incidence and prevalence of obesity in children and adolescents have resulted in extending these studies to determine whether physical activity has similar beneficial results in children. Many studies with children have looked at single effects, such as weight loss [25, 32], cardiorespiratory fitness [24], or strength [24, 30], as the main outcome, but metabolic syndrome has raised new issues. To address the constellation of cardiovascular risk factors in metabolic syndrome, studies have begun to determine the effectiveness of physical activity on several risk factors [25]. The use of multiple endpoints has raised new challenges and has peaked interests into designing programs specifically for children with metabolic syndrome.

Physical Activity and Weight Management

A suspected cause of the increased prevalence of childhood obesity is the reduction in daily physical activity over the past years [33]. Physical activity has long been prescribed to prevent and manage obesity. However, the results of studies assessing the effectiveness of physical activity in managing weight, body fat, or central adiposity have been conflicting, partly because of the challenges in measuring the quantity and quality of physical activity. Many studies use questionnaires with self-reported answers to measure physical activity [34, 35]. In efforts to more accurately assess physical activity, accelerometers have been used. Accelerometers are small sensors, typically worn at the waist, that measure the intensity and cumulative time spent each day in activity, from which caloric expenditure can be calculated. Accelerometer studies indicate that waist circumference is negatively associated with physical activity [36].

Physical Activity and Blood Pressure

High blood pressure in childhood or adolescence tends to continue into adulthood [37, 38]. In children, obesity and hypertension are associated with low levels of physical activity [39, 40].

During aerobic activities, systolic blood pressure and heart rate increase as exercise intensity increases, whereas diastolic blood pressure remains fairly constant [13]. During the 2 h after aerobic physical activity, systolic blood pressure falls below the pre-exercise level [41], perhaps because of muscle relaxation and vasodilation of the blood vessels in the legs and organs [42]. Vasodilation is a primary effect after aerobic exercise, possibly as a result of thermal activity; chemical production, such as lactic acid and nitric oxide production; and decreased baroreceptor nerve activity [41, 42]. Decreased blood pressure as a result of chronic physical activity may be attributed to hemodynamic, humeral, and neural influences shown in Fig. 14.4 [43]. In adults, regular aerobic activity lowers blood pressure by an average of 6–10 mmHg, which is sustained over longer periods [44]. The effects of physical activity on blood pressure in children are conflicting. In a meta-analysis, reductions in blood pressure as a result of physical activity interventions in children resulted only in a 1% drop in systolic and a 3% drop in diastolic blood pressure, and neither reduction was statistically significant [45]. However, individual studies have reported that exercise markedly reduces blood pressure [40].

Physical Activity and Insulin Resistance

During childhood and adolescence, insulin sensitivity changes [46]. Increased body fat may accelerate the release of fatty acids from the abdominal adipose tissue that may then inhibit glucose transport and/or phosphorylation and reduce rates of glucose oxidation and muscle glycogen synthesis and cause insulin resistance [47]. Regular exercise and greater muscular strength have been associated with decreased insulin resistance [48, 49].

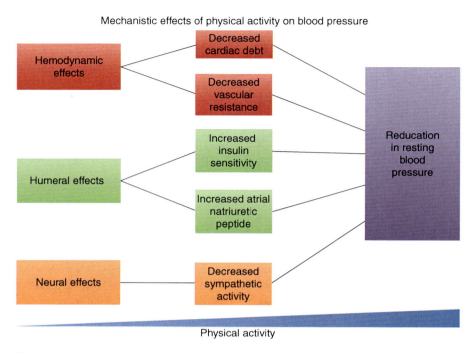

Fig. 14.4 Mechanisms driving decreased blood pressure in response to regular physical activity (Based on data from de Fatima Monteiro and Sobral Filho [43])

Physical Activity and Hyperlipidemia

Abnormal lipid levels (low-density lipoprotein, triglycerides, high-density lipoprotein) increase the risk of cardiovascular disease. Physical activity may improve these levels in most children and adolescents, which in turn may lower their risks of cardiovascular disease [50]. Weight loss can also greatly improve lipid levels [51]. Thus, exercise and weight loss are primary reasons for prescribing an exercise program. However, in children and adolescents, the effects of physical activity on lipid levels have been inconsistent [52, 53].

Exercise Interventions for Children with Metabolic Syndrome

The literature on the effectiveness of exercise in children and adolescents with metabolic syndrome is limited. However, with the increases in prevalence of obesity and metabolic comorbidities, interest in interventions for metabolic syndrome has also increased. Given the high probability that obese children will become obese adults, it appears that these interventions must begin earlier in life.

Current studies on metabolic syndrome in children have focused on identifying links between metabolic values and physical fitness levels, and some studies have linked poor cardiovascular fitness to metabolic syndrome [54]. However, many of these interventions have been directed to change overall lifestyles and have not isolated the results of physical activity. Reinehr et al. [25] developed a lifestyle intervention consisting of psychotherapy, nutrition, and exercise to determine whether it would reduce the prevalence of metabolic syndrome in children [25]. The study indicated that this lifestyle intervention program led to an improvement in the components of metabolic syndrome, particularly a decrease in BMI and improvement of waist circumference, blood pressure, and glucose values [25]. A study by Pedrosa et al. found that lifestyle intervention comprised of nutrition and physical activity reduced the prevalence of metabolic syndrome from 16.4% to 14.8% after 1 year [32].

The physical activity component for many of the above studies was mostly assessed with questionnaires. Future interventions need to use more objective outcome measures and focus on the effectiveness of structured physical activity, as recommended by the AHA at the recommended intensities.

Designing an Exercise Program for Children with Metabolic Syndrome

Exercise programs for children with metabolic syndrome need to be individualized to each child's physical abilities and goals while improving endurance, strength, and flexibility. Before beginning any exercise program, all children should be properly screened and then tested at baseline for the values as described in the assessment section of this chapter. After testing, the child should be told about the expectations of each exercise session. The optimal structured exercise session will last about an hour and will consist of 5–10 min of warm-up and flexibility exercises, 30–40 min of cardiovascular and resistance training, and 5–10 min of cool-down activities.

The purpose of the warm-up activities is generally to prepare the body for activity by increasing heart rate from rest. Static stretches should increase the mobility of all major muscle groups to reduce the risk of injuries. The exercise routine should allow the child to stay within the "safe range" of heart rate, the rate of perceived exertion (self-reported intensity of exercise), and without onset of symptoms.

Aerobic training is a major component of the exercise program. The goal of aerobic exercise is to increase and sustain the heart rate at 60–75% of the maximum heart rate (as measured with a cardiorespiratory stress test) for 30 min. The duration of aerobic exercise should be increased as the child's fitness improves.

The strength-training component requires equipment suitable for training all major muscle groups. Equipment is also based on physical location of the activities. Interventions completed at a rehabilitation center that provide greater supervision may use resistance machines, while thera-bands and free weights are more appropriate in the home-based setting. Protocols with a higher number of repetitions, rather than greater weight, are more effective for children during the first stages of strength training [30]. The results of the baseline 1-RM test should be used to determine the appropriate resistance for isotonic exercises. All children should be monitored during the beginning phases of training to make sure that their technique is appropriate, to decrease the risk of injury.

An exercise program for children with metabolic syndrome should include game-like and child-friendly activities and not rely solely on the traditional adult gym equipment (treadmills, stationary bicycles, etc.) [55]. For example, an activity-promoting video game, in which children must keep up with prescribed dance movements, can increase energy expenditure more than walking on a treadmill [56].

Conclusion

Although there is convincing evidence on the benefits of physical activity in children, there are limited data relating to the effects of physical activity for children and adolescents with metabolic syndrome. Regular physical activity is an important part of a healthy lifestyle and has positive effects on the components of the metabolic syndrome. Future research is needed to substantiate the effects of physical activity in children and adolescents with metabolic syndrome and to standardize the specific duration, intensity, and type of activity that yield positive results.

References

1. Messiah SE, Carrillo-Iregui A, Garibay-Nieto N, Lopez-Mitnik G, Cossio S, Arheart KL. Prevalence of metabolic syndrome in US-born Latin and Caribbean youth. J Immigr Minor Health. 2009;11(5):366–71.
2. Blair SN, Kohl 3rd HW, Barlow CE, Paffenbarger Jr RS, Gibbons LW, Macera CA. Changes in physical fitness and all-cause mortality. A prospective study of healthy and unhealthy men. JAMA. 1995;273(14):1093–8.
3. Haskell WL, Lee IM, Pate RR, et al. Physical activity and public health: updated recommendation for adults from the American College of Sports Medicine and the American Heart Association. Circulation. 2007;116(9):1081–93.
4. Medicine ACoS. ACSM's guidelines for exercise testing and prescription. Baltimore: Lippincott Williams & Wilkins; 2006.
5. Position AHAS: Physical activity and children. http://www.heart.org/HEARTORG/GettingHealthy/Physical-Activity-and-Children_UCM_304053_Article.jsp. Accessed 16 June 2011.
6. Guinhouya BC, Hubert H. Insight into physical activity in combating the infantile metabolic syndrome. Environ Health Prev Med. 2011;16(3):144–7.
7. NIH. Health implications of obesity. Ann Intern Med. 1985;163:1073–7.
8. Steinberger J, Daniels SR. Obesity, insulin resistance, diabetes, and cardiovascular risk in children: an American Heart Association scientific statement from the Atherosclerosis, Hypertension, and Obesity in the Young Committee (Council on Cardiovascular Disease in the Young) and the Diabetes Committee (Council on Nutrition, Physical Activity, and Metabolism). Circulation. 2003;107(10):1448–53.

9. Control CfD: CDC table for calculated body mass index values for selected heights and weights for ages 2–20 years. http://www.cdc.gov/nccdphp/dnpa/healthyweight/assessing/bmi/00binaries/bmi-tables.pdf. Accessed 4 June 2011.
10. Agirbasli M, Agaoglu NB, Ergonul O, et al. Comparison of anthropometric indices in predicting metabolic syndrome components in children. Metab Syndr Relat Disord. 2011;9(6):453–9 [Epub ahead of print].
11. Margulies L, Horlick M, Thornton JC, Wang J, Ioannidou E, Heymsfield SB. Reproducibility of pediatric whole body bone and body composition measures by dual-energy X-ray absorptiometry using the GE Lunar Prodigy. J Clin Densitom. 2005;8(3):298–304.
12. Freedman DS, Wang J, Thornton JC, et al. Classification of body fatness by body mass index-for-age categories among children. Arch Pediatr Adolesc Med. 2009;163(9):805–11.
13. Neiman D. Exercise testing and prescription: a health-related approach. 4th ed. Mountain View: Mayfield Publishing Company; 1999.
14. National Heart, Lung, and Blood Institute. Blood pressure tables for children and adolescents from the fourth report on the diagnosis, evaluation, and treatment of high blood pressure in children and adolescents. 2004. http://www.nhlbi.nih.gov/health/prof/heart/hbp/hbp_ped.pdf. Accessed 7 June, 2011.
15. Bruce RA, Kusumi F, Hosmer D. Maximal oxygen intake and nomographic assessment of functional aerobic impairment in cardiovascular disease. Am Heart J. 1973;85(4):546–62.
16. Balke B, Ware RW. An experimental study of physical fitness of Air Force personnel. US Armed Forces Med J. 1959;10(6):675–88.
17. James FW, Kaplan S, Glueck CJ, Tsay JY, Knight MJ, Sarwar CJ. Responses of normal children and young adults to controlled bicycle exercise. Circulation. 1980;61(5):902–12.
18. Rowland TW, Cunningham LN. Oxygen uptake plateau during maximal treadmill exercise in children. Chest. 1992;101(2):485–9.
19. Rowland TW. Aerobic exercise testing protocols. In: Rowland TW, editor. Pediatric laboratory exercise testing: clinical guidelines. Champaign: Human Kinetics; 1993.
20. Armstrong N, Welsman JR. Assessment and interpretation of aerobic fitness in children and adolescents. Exerc Sport Sci Rev. 1994;22:435–75.
21. Heyward V. The physical fitness specialist certification manual. 3rd ed. Dallas: The Cooper Institute for Aerobics Research; 1998 (Revised 1997 printed in Heyward VH. Advance fitness assessment and exercise prescription, 3rd ed. Champaign: Human Kinetics; 1998).
22. US Department of Health and Human Services PHS, Office of the Assistant Secretary for Health, editors. 1985 national school population fitness survey. Washington, DC;1986
23. Gutin B, Owens S. Role of exercise intervention in improving body fat distribution and risk profile in children. Am J Hum Biol. 1999;11(2):237–47.
24. Miller TL, Somarriba G, Kinnamon DD, Weinberg GA, Friedman LB, Scott GB. The effect of a structured exercise program on nutrition and fitness outcomes in human immunodeficiency virus-infected children. AIDS Res Hum Retroviruses. 2010;26(3):313–9.
25. Reinehr T, Kleber M, Toschke AM. Lifestyle intervention in obese children is associated with a decrease of the metabolic syndrome prevalence. Atherosclerosis. 2009;207(1):174–80.
26. Nassis GP, Papantakou K, Skenderi K, et al. Aerobic exercise training improves insulin sensitivity without changes in body weight, body fat, adiponectin, and inflammatory markers in overweight and obese girls. Metabolism. 2005;54(11):1472–9.
27. Barbeau P, Johnson MH, Howe CA, et al. Ten months of exercise improves general and visceral adiposity, bone, and fitness in black girls. Obesity (Silver Spring). 2007;15(8):2077–85.
28. Klijn PH, van der Baan-Slootweg OH, van Stel HF. Aerobic exercise in adolescents with obesity: preliminary evaluation of a modular training program and the modified shuttle test. BMC Pediatr. 2007;7:19.
29. Aouadi R, Khalifa R, Aouidet A, et al. Aerobic training programs and glycemic control in diabetic children in relation to exercise frequency. J Sports Med Phys Fitness. 2011;51(3):393–400.
30. Faigenbaum AD, Loud RL, O'Connell J, Glover S, Westcott WL. Effects of different resistance training protocols on upper-body strength and endurance development in children. J Strength Cond Res. 2001;15(4):459–65.

31. Somarriba G, Extein J, Miller TL. Exercise rehabilitation in pediatric cardiomyopathy. Prog Pediatr Cardiol. 2008;25(1):91–102.
32. Pedrosa C, Oliveira BM, Albuquerque I, Simoes-Pereira C, Vaz-de-Almeida MD, Correia F. Markers of metabolic syndrome in obese children before and after 1-year lifestyle intervention program. Eur J Nutr. 2011;50(6):391–400.
33. Tremblay MS, Willms JD. Is the Canadian childhood obesity epidemic related to physical inactivity? Int J Obes Relat Metab Disord. 2003;27(9):1100–5.
34. Gidding SS, Barton BA, Dorgan JA, et al. Higher self-reported physical activity is associated with lower systolic blood pressure: the Dietary Intervention Study in Childhood (DISC). Pediatrics. 2006;118(6):2388–93.
35. Ortega FB, Tresaco B, Ruiz JR, et al. Cardiorespiratory fitness and sedentary activities are associated with adiposity in adolescents. Obesity (Silver Spring). 2007;15(6):1589–99.
36. Dencker M, Thorsson O, Karlsson MK, Linden C, Wollmer P, Andersen LB. Daily physical activity related to aerobic fitness and body fat in an urban sample of children. Scand J Med Sci Sports. 2008;18(6):728–35.
37. Lauer RM, Clarke WR, Mahoney LT, Witt J. Childhood predictors for high adult blood pressure. The Muscatine Study. Pediatr Clin North Am. 1993;40(1):23–40.
38. Myers L, Coughlin SS, Webber LS, Srinivasan SR, Berenson GS. Prediction of adult cardiovascular multifactorial risk status from childhood risk factor levels. The Bogalusa Heart Study. Am J Epidemiol. 1995;142(9):918–24.
39. Despres JP, Bouchard C, Malina RM. Physical activity and coronary heart disease risk factors during childhood and adolescence. Exerc Sport Sci Rev. 1990;18:243–61.
40. McMurray RG, Harrell JS, Bangdiwala SI, Bradley CB, Deng S, Levine A. A school-based intervention can reduce body fat and blood pressure in young adolescents. J Adolesc Health. 2002;31(2):125–32.
41. Rueckert PA, Slane PR, Lillis DL, Hanson P. Hemodynamic patterns and duration of post-dynamic exercise hypotension in hypertensive humans. Med Sci Sports Exerc. 1996;28(1):24–32.
42. Brown SP, Li H, Chitwood LF, Anderson ER, Boatwright D. Blood pressure, hemodynamic, and thermal responses after cycling exercise. J Appl Physiol. 1993;75(1):240–5.
43. de Fatima Monteiro M, Sobral Filho D. Physical exercise and blood pressure control. Rev Bras Esporte. 2004;10(6):517–9.
44. Kelley G. Dynamic resistance exercise and resting blood pressure in adults: a meta-analysis. J Appl Physiol. 1997;82(5):1559–65.
45. Kelley GA, Kelley KS, Tran ZV. The effects of exercise on resting blood pressure in children and adolescents: a meta-analysis of randomized controlled trials. Prev Cardiol. 2003;6(1):8–16.
46. Cruz ML, Shaibi GQ, Weigensberg MJ, Spruijt-Metz D, Ball GD, Goran MI. Pediatric obesity and insulin resistance: chronic disease risk and implications for treatment and prevention beyond body weight modification. Annu Rev Nutr. 2005;25:435–68.
47. Roden M, Price TB, Perseghin G, et al. Mechanism of free fatty acid-induced insulin resistance in humans. J Clin Invest. 1996;97(12):2859–65.
48. Benson AC, Torode ME, Singh MA. Muscular strength and cardiorespiratory fitness is associated with higher insulin sensitivity in children and adolescents. Int J Pediatr Obes. 2006;1(4):222–31.
49. Sardinha LB, Andersen LB, Anderssen SA, et al. Objectively measured time spent sedentary is associated with insulin resistance independent of overall and central body fat in 9- to 10-year-old Portuguese children. Diabetes Care. 2008;31(3):569–75.
50. American Academy of Pediatrics, Committee on Nutrition. Cholesterol in childhood. Pediatrics. 1998;101(1 Pt 1):141–7.
51. Katzel LI, Bleecker ER, Colman EG, Rogus EM, Sorkin JD, Goldberg AP. Effects of weight loss vs aerobic exercise training on risk factors for coronary disease in healthy, obese, middle-aged and older men. A randomized controlled trial. JAMA. 1995;274(24):1915–21.

52. Kelley GA, Kelley KS. Effects of aerobic exercise on non-high-density lipoprotein cholesterol in children and adolescents: a meta-analysis of randomized controlled trials. Prog Cardiovasc Nurs. 2008;23(3):128–32.
53. Shalitin S, Ashkenazi-Hoffnung L, Yackobovitch-Gavan M, et al. Effects of a twelve-week randomized intervention of exercise and/or diet on weight loss and weight maintenance, and other metabolic parameters in obese preadolescent children. Horm Res. 2009;72(5):287–301.
54. Brufani C, Grossi A, Fintini D, et al. Cardiovascular fitness, insulin resistance and metabolic syndrome in severely obese prepubertal Italian children. Horm Res. 2008;70(6):349–56.
55. Tomassoni TL. Role of exercise in the management of cardiovascular disease in children and youth. Med Sci Sports Exerc. 1996;28(4):406–13.
56. Lanningham-Foster L, Jensen TB, Foster RC, et al. Energy expenditure of sedentary screen time compared with active screen time for children. Pediatrics. 2006;118(6):e1831–5.

Chapter 15
Nutritional Evaluation and Intervention

Runa Diwadkar Watkins, Daniela Neri, and Tracie L. Miller

Abstract Nutritional surveillance is central to the care of all children because of the national propensity for childhood obesity and metabolic complications. Sound nutritional advice should be given at the earliest times in life, even prenatally, as healthy nutritional practices instituted at an early age are likely to be the most sustainable over the life course. The assessment of body mass index should be a routine part of clinical care and other body composition methods, such as waist circumference and regional skinfolds, and should be employed to ascertain compartmentalization of body fat with a focus on central adiposity. A critical assessment of dietary intake is necessary to identify eating patterns and choices that are amenable to change. The 24-h, multiple-pass food recall method is the most reliable, but all methods are fraught with technical flaws. Biochemical indicators including cardiometabolic risk profile, inflammatory biomarkers, and micronutrient levels, including vitamins D, E, and iron, should be routinely measured. Treatment is aimed primarily at lifestyle modifications that advocate sound nutritional practices with weight loss or weight maintenance in the growing child kept in mind. However, nutritional interventions are unlikely to be effective when instituted in isolation. A multidisciplinary management strategy that addresses nutritional, lifestyle,

R.D. Watkins, M.D.
Division of Pediatric Gastroenterology, Department of Pediatrics,
University of Miami, Miami, FL, USA

D. Neri, M.S.
Division of Pediatric Clinical Research, Department of Pediatrics,
University of Miami Miller School of Medicine,
Miami, FL, USA

T.L. Miller, M.D. (✉)
Division of Pediatric Clinical Research, Department of Pediatrics,
Miller School of Medicine at the University of Miami,
Batchelor Children's Research Institute,
P.O. Box 016820, Miami, FL 33101, USA
e-mail: tracie.miller@miami.edu

psychological, and pharmacological approaches is essential to promote the most optimal nutrition to prevent and treat the metabolic syndrome in childhood.

Keywords Nutrition • Metabolic syndrome • Child • Body composition • Diet • Nutritional intervention • Nutritional evaluation

Introduction

Metabolic syndrome, also referred to as the dysmetabolic syndrome, syndrome X, or the insulin resistance syndrome, is a group of related risk factors associated with obesity and type 2 diabetes. It is defined as a series of clinical and laboratory abnormalities including hypertriglyceridemia, low levels of high-density lipoprotein cholesterol (HDL), hypertension, hyperglycemia, and central adiposity. The vast majority of studies on the metabolic syndrome have been conducted in adults, and it has been suggested that the main factors contributing to the syndrome are insulin resistance and central adiposity. This is now a topic of great consequence in the pediatric population, as the obesity epidemic is widely prevalent resulting in more children and adolescents developing the metabolic syndrome [1, 2]. This definition is further complicated by the anthropometric differences observed among ethnic minorities [3]. The metabolic syndrome in childhood results in tremendous health-care costs due to the onset of type 2 diabetes and cardiovascular disease at a younger age. Thus, prevention and treatment in childhood is critical. Treatment is aimed primarily at lifestyle modification with weight loss [1]. Pharmacotherapy can also be used if these lifestyle modifications do not provide significant improvements [1].

This chapter will detail the nutritional assessment of children with the metabolic syndrome through biochemical, anthropometric, and dietary evaluations. Furthermore, nutritional interventions including specific diets will be discussed.

Nutritional Evaluation: Anthropometry and Body Composition Measurements

The metabolic syndrome is not well defined in the pediatric population [3]. However, obesity is the strongest predictor of developing the metabolic syndrome in adulthood, and adult obesity often originates in childhood [4]. Because of the increased prevalence of obesity in childhood and its risk to track into adulthood, anthropometrics should be assessed during routine well-child care [5]. This is particularly important as often parents or children do not recognize that they are overweight or obese [6].

One of the main components of the metabolic syndrome is central adiposity. Anthropometric measurements change with age, and puberty normally changes fat distribution, which makes defining absolute thresholds for abnormalities difficult in this group. However, these measurements can assess obesity and growth both cross-sectionally and longitudinally [7].

A majority of the older studies assessed obesity by measuring body mass index (BMI), which is related to a person's weight and height [8]. Refinements of regional anthropometry, thought to reflect more specific body composition, lean and fat mass, allow for the assessment of the quality of growth, such as the extent of energy, fat, and protein deposition, as well as the potential for increased metabolic and cardiovascular risk in children and adolescents. This compartmentalization may be performed using a variety of techniques, such as skinfold thickness, waist and hip circumference, bioelectrical impedance analysis (BIA), computed tomography (CT) scans, dual-energy X-ray absorptiometry (DXA) scans, or magnetic resonance imaging (MRI).

Body Mass Index (BMI)

Body mass index (BMI) generally reflects body fat content and is widely used in pediatrics to screen for obesity. It is calculated by dividing the weight in kilograms by the height in meters squared. For children 2 to 20 years of age, BMI changes with age and sex; thus, it is generally presented in percentiles or z-scores (standard deviations from a normal population). For children under 2 years of age, weight-for-height percentiles or z-scores are used to track obesity [9]. It is important to minimize measurement error for both weight and height; thus, appropriate training and adherence to specified methods and procedures are key steps to obtain accurate measures. The interpretation of BMI can be limited because although it is an indicator of relative weight, it does not differentiate between lean body mass, fat mass, or extracellular water. This assessment, therefore, does not always provide the best estimate for the risk of the metabolic syndrome [5]. However, tracking BMI-for-age over time ensures early identification of abnormal growth. A BMI ≥85th percentile but less than the 95th percentile for age and sex indicates an individual who is overweight, while obesity is defined as a BMI ≥95th percentile when using the CDC growth charts [10] (Table 15.1).

Table 15.1 Weight classifications from the Expert Panel recommendations

Classification	BMI percentile for age
Underweight	<5th
Healthy weight	5th to 84th
Overweight	85th to 94th
Obesity	≥95th

Based on data from Barlow [10]

Waist and Hip Circumference

Waist circumference measurements have been incorporated into research studies to help predict the risk of the metabolic syndrome in children [8]. Waist circumference is an independent predictor of insulin resistance and intra-abdominal fat (visceral) in adults (risk factors for cardiometabolic disease) [2], and its utility in children is emerging [2]. It is a better indicator of central (visceral) adiposity than BMI and is not dependent on height [5]. It is also linked to hypertension and hypertriglyceridemia [3]. The Bogalusa Heart Study, an ongoing longitudinal study of children to determine cardiac risk factors in childhood, showed that increased waist circumference was associated with hypertriglyceridemia, high low-density lipoprotein (LDL) cholesterol, and insulin resistance [5].

The waist to hip ratio also measures central adiposity. One disadvantage of using either hip or waist circumference alone is there may be a reduction in both measurements as weight loss occurs. However, the waist to hip ratio may be preserved. Unfortunately, these values have shown a limited prognostic value in the pediatric population [11]. Although the waist to hip ratio correlates with intra-abdominal fat, higher correlations are found with waist circumference [12].

To measure waist circumference, the tape measure is applied horizontally at the level of the umbilicus, at the end of gentle expiration [13]. Age- and sex-adjusted percentiles for waist circumference for children aged 2–19 years have been released by NHANES III [14]. To measure hip circumference, a measuring tape should be placed around the point with the maximum circumference over the buttocks after the individual has removed all clothing, except for undergarments. The individual should stand with their feet close together and should breathe in a normal pattern. It is during the end of gentle exhalation that the measurement should be taken [13].

Skinfold Thickness

Skinfold thickness (SFT) is an established method for determining body fat. Because the thickness of subcutaneous fat is very specific to adipose tissue and can be measured noninvasively, SFT remains an important and valid anthropometric indicator of regional and total body fat, especially in research settings [15]. For older children, adolescents, and adults, SFT measurements correlate with body fat assessed by more direct measures, including dual-energy X-ray absorptiometry (DXA) [16]. The four principal regions where SFT measurements are taken are at the biceps, triceps, suprailiac, and subscapular areas. Each region provides a measurement of the skinfold at their respective area of the body. It is the sum of all the skinfolds that provides an estimate of body fat percentage. Thigh skinfolds have also been used. These measurements provide an estimate of an individual's body fat. The interpretation of SFT can be limited because the assumption that the subcutaneous fat in the various regions represents the total amount of fat in the body may not always be the case.

To assess body composition using SFT, prediction equations at two sites [17], four sites [18], or five sites [19] have been published, but they still need refinement in the pediatric population and cross validation to determine suitability to different populations. In routine clinical care, individuals need to be carefully trained to obtain accurate SFT measurements as imprecision is very common in anthropometry. In certain individuals, these measurements may be difficult to obtain, especially in those who are morbidly obese. All measurements should be taken on the same side of the body. Triplicate measurements should be taken and the mean of those measurements used [20]. The calipers are applied 1 cm below and at right angles to the pinch, and a reading in millimeters is taken. A full description of standard methods and procedures to obtain accurate measurements should be followed according to the NHANES manual [13].

Dual-Energy X-Ray Absorptiometry

Dual-energy X-ray absorptiometry (DXA) also measures body composition and regionalization of lean and fat mass using a three-compartment model (lean, fat, bone). DXA has been available since the late 1980s. It was originally developed to evaluate bone mineral density to diagnose and monitor osteoporosis in postmenopausal women. The fundamental principle of DXA is to measure the transmission of X-rays through the body at high and low energies, which allows for the discrimination between soft tissue and bone [21]. This technique has gained popularity for measuring body composition from infancy through adulthood [21]. This technique is quick, simple, and noninvasive, yet requires a designated clinical or research program to perform the scan, and this may not be widely available to all clinicians. The scan provides an estimate of absolute and percent lean and fat mass, as well as its regionalization (arm, leg, trunk). Figure 15.1 shows the typical DXA body composition report that is produced for an individual patient.

To assess whole-body bone mineral content (BMC) and bone mineral density (BMD), DXA scans can be performed on the whole body and on other specific areas including the femur and the lumbar spine (L1–L4). A BMC or BMD z-score is used as an indicator of bone mineral status. The T-score (comparison of patient's current BMD with the ideal peak adult BMD for same sex and ethnicity) is used to interpret DXA results in adults but should not be used to interpret results in children. Instead, a z-score, adjusted for age and sex [23], should be used. At the National Institutes of Health [24] Consensus Conference in 2000, a score defined as above −1.0 is considered normal. A low bone mass is between −1.0 and −2.5, and a score less than −2.5 is defined as osteoporosis. However, the diagnosis of osteoporosis should not be made on DXA results alone but should take into account other patient factors, including pubertal maturation and history of bone fractures. Figure 15.2 shows a typical report for BMD evaluations with DXA.

Obesity has historically been correlated with better bone mineral density [25]. However, recent studies have shown that components of the metabolic syndrome,

Fig. 15.1 Normal levels of body fat by age and sex (Based on data from Freedman et al. [22])

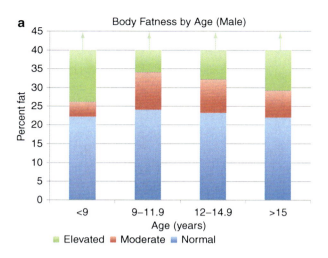

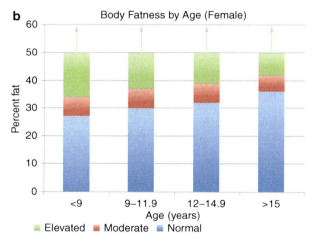

including hypertension, hypertriglyceridemia, and low HDL cholesterol, can be associated with decreased bone mineral density [26]. Systemic inflammation that often accompanies adiposity may be associated with increased bone turnover rate and bone mass. Lee et al. found an inverse correlation between hs-CRP levels and BMD, while there was a positive association with lean body mass [26].

Other Methods

Other methods used to evaluate an individual's body composition include bioelectrical impedance analysis (BIA), computed tomography (CT), and magnetic resonance imaging (MRI). BIA, a two-compartment model, became commercially

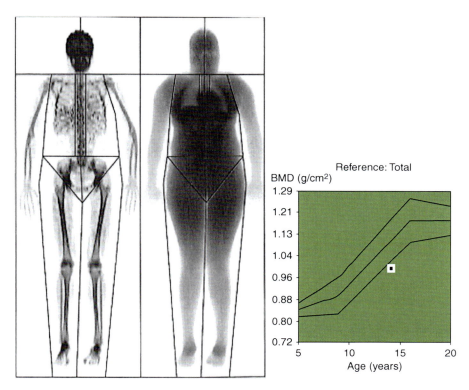

Fig. 15.2 Dual-energy X-ray absorptiometry analysis for bone mineral density in a 13-year-old obese girl. Raw bone mineral density data on total body scan is plotted on accepted norms specific for age and sex (NHANES). This scan shows that this child's bone mineral density is below normal for age and sex

available in the mid-1980s. It measures the resistance to an electrical current through body tissues, which, in turn, is used to calculate an estimation of a person's total body water. The amount of total body water can then be used to estimate the amount of fat-free mass (FFM) (typically well correlated with lean mass). The difference between total body weight and FFM will determine the body fat. Though this is a less accurate way to measure percent body fat, this method is still favorable, as it is widely available, inexpensive, and does not require high-level operator training [27]. However, the results can be skewed in the unfasted subject, those with abnormal body water based on an underlying illness (congestive heart failure, lung and renal disease, etc.), and those who have recently exercised, since hydration is an important source of error to estimate lean body mass. Regionalization of body fat can be accomplished using the quadripolar BIA [27].

Intra-abdominal fat can also be assessed by CT (Fig. 15.3). While anthropometry cannot differentiate between visceral and subcutaneous fat deposits, CT scans can. The advantage of CT scans is that they provide thin, cross-sectional, radiographic images that can be taken at any level in the body. Fat is easily visualized on these

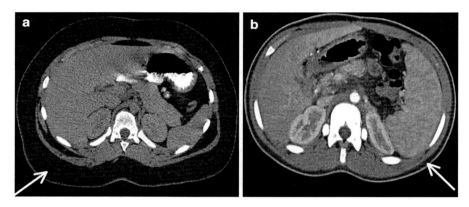

Fig. 15.3 Single-slice CT scan through the abdomen showing increased subcutaneous fat (**a**; *arrow*) compared to normal scan with minimal subcutaneous fat (**b**; *arrow*). Visceral adiposity can also be quantitated through single-slice CT imaging

images due to its low attenuation. CT scans allow for the precise calculation of the cross-sectional areas where visceral fat and subcutaneous fat are located, as the measurements include retroperitoneal mesenteric and omental fat [28]. While the CT provides reliable and valid data, the main disadvantage of this study is the amount of radiation an individual is exposed to, especially if repeated scans are needed. Similar to the single-slice CT scan, the MRI provides comparable results but exposes the subject to less radiation. Providing the same anatomic detail as the CT, it uses a magnetic field to capture the images [29]. It is a reliable method for assessing total and regional fat in an individual, and it can be repeated to assess the impact of intervention without radiation exposure. The main disadvantage of this study is cost. These tests are typically performed in the research setting.

Nutritional Evaluation: Dietary Intake

Dietary intake is directly related to the metabolic syndrome and its individual components including abdominal adiposity, hyperglycemia, dyslipidemia, and insulin resistance. When evaluating those who have or are at risk for the metabolic syndrome, it is important to obtain an accurate evaluation of dietary intake. It is important for the family/child to understand that there are no right or wrong answers. Assessment of specific dietary patterns and psychological behaviors is fundamental. The responses allow the observer to determine good and poor dietary habits and choices, which will help with further goal setting to change behavior.

The multiple-pass nonconsecutive 24-h dietary recall [30] is the gold standard in dietary recall methodology. Other methods include multiple-day food records, food frequency questionnaires, and "usual day" intakes. While all of these methods provide adequate information, they are subject to recall bias, as they rely on a patient's memory and personal preferences in reporting their diet [31]. Dietary intakes also vary by time of week (weekday versus weekend) and season (seasonal food availability) [31]. Furthermore, the knowledge that a dietary intake will be performed may alter the individual's eating pattern as they know the diet will be recorded. Obese individuals typically underreport intake [32].

A 24-h recall requires standard procedures to produce accurate results [33]. Obtaining a quick food list, probing for details, and reviewing for foods forgotten are steps that help the family/child remember and yield the most valid data. First, a list of all foods and beverages consumed should be listed. To improve accuracy, the patient should be probed to report timing and activity related to the consumption of the food item. Visual aids help the patient recall food and amounts. The cooking method and additions to food should be ascertained and also contribute more complete data. It is important to reassure the family and child that they will not be "judged" on their diet. Unfortunately, the correlation between "good" and "bad" foods may lead to bias, as these individuals do not want to be criticized for eating the "wrong" type of food.

A multiple-day food record is a written log of everything that is consumed in nonconsecutive days, usually obtained in real time. Two weekdays and one weekend day are thought to represent the most accurate picture of the entire week. It is important to emphasize that the diet record should be as detailed as possible (accurate amounts, preparation methods, use of condiments, etc.), as this provides the observer with more information than just a list of foods consumed. It is also important for the individual to be honest and not change his or her eating habits during this period. This method usually works for highly motivated patients.

Food frequency questionnaires (FFQ) are another accepted method of obtaining a quantitative assessment of an individual's usual nutrient intake. This method is a practical and economical way to obtain comprehensive dietary data. Individuals report their usual consumption of each food from a specific list of foods for a certain time period [34] when completing the FFQ. When providing information about an individual's dietary habits, there are no right or wrong answers, as the information is designed to log one's usual dietary intake. These responses will allow the observer to identify those habits that are good and those that should be changed. Unfortunately, when compared to 24-h diet recalls, FFQs generally collect less detail in regard to consumed foods, cooking methods, and portion sizes [34]. The Block and Willett FFQ are often used for epidemiological research in childhood [34].

A baseline nutrient analysis of child's dietary intake (Fig. 15.4) allows assessment of energy intake, percentage of estimated energy need, and percentage of energy from fat and carbohydrate, as well as micronutrients intake. However, evaluating dietary patterns or overall food combinations chosen by individuals rather than focusing on individual nutrients or foods help examine the effects of the global diet [35]. Dietary patterns represent a broader picture of food and nutrient consumption and may therefore be more predictive of eating behavior or disease risk. Among dietary factors that should be carefully monitored during a dietary assessment and may have a role in the development of overweight and obesity are increased total dietary fat intake and increased intake of calorically sweetened beverages. Increased fruits and vegetables intake may be associated with a decrease in risk [36].

NDSR 2010 Recommended Dietary Allowances/Adequate Intake Report

Project Abbreviation: INTAKE
Participant ID: JOHN PATIENT 10   Date of Intake: 08/10/2011
Life Stage Group: Males, Age 9-13 y

Nutrient	Amount Reported	RDA	%RDA	AI
Vitamin A	3212 mcg RAE	600 mcg RAE	535%	
Vitamin C	18.036 mg	45 mg	40%	
Vitamin D	12.111 mcg			5 mcg
Vitamin E	14.658 mg	11 mg	133%	
Vitamin K	2064.792 mcg			60 mcg
Thiamin	1.315 mg	0.9 mg	146%	
Riboflavin	3.046 mg	0.9 mg	338%	
Niacin	64.032 mg NE	12 mg NE	534%	
Vitamin B6	2.515 mg	1.0 mg	252%	
Folate	659 mcg DFE	300 mcg DFE	220%	
Vitamin B12	4.564 mcg	1.8 mcg	254%	
Pantothenic Acid	7.386 mg			4 mg
Choline	477.432 mg			375 mg
Calcium	2360 mg			1300 mg
Copper	1325 mcg	700 mcg	189%	
Iron	17.784 mg	8 mcg	222%	
Mangnesium	652 mg	240 mcg	272%	
Manganese	5.958 mg			1.9 mg
Phosphorus	2156 mg	1250 mcg	173%	
Selenium	155.119 mcg	40 mcg	388%	
Zinc	13.651 mg	8 mcg	171%	
Potassium	4 g			4.5 g
Sodium	4 g			1.5 g

RDA/AI values based on the Dietary Reference Intakes provided by National Academy of Sciences, Institute of Medicine, Food and Nutrition Board (1997-2005).

Additional Recommendations

Nutrient	Amount Reported	% of Energy	Recommended Intake
Energy	1717kcal		
Fat	46.319 g	23.781 %	25-35 %[1]
Carbohydrate	189.332 g	43.845 %	
Protein	139.178 g	32.444 %	
Alcohol	0.000 g	0.000 %	
Cholesterol	264 mg		<300 mg[1]
Saturated Fatty Acids	19.238 g	9.888 %	<10%[1]
Trans-Fatty Acids	1.336 g	0.690 %	
Monounsaturated Fatty Acids	14.667 g	7.573 %	10%[2]
Polyunsaturated Fatty Acids	7.833 g	3.993 %	10%[2]
Dietary Fiber	24.804 g		20-30 g[3]

Note: DSAM nutrients are not included in these totals. Nutrient totals may not equal the sum of their parts. (Refer to the NDSR User Manual.)
[1] Dietary Guidelines for Americans, 2005
[2] National Cholesterol Education Program, 1990
[3] National Cancer Institute Dietary Guidelines, 1998

Fig. 15.4 Typical one-day dietary analysis from data obtained by performing a multiple-pass 24-h recall. Total energy intake, macronutrient, and vitamin and mineral intake can be ascertained and expressed as norms for age and sex

The nutrition assessment should also consider other behaviors including the degree of physical activity, video game use, television viewing, parental restriction of highly palatable foods, meals consumed outside the home, increased portion sizes, and skipping breakfast.

Food Insecurity

Two commonly used definitions of food security come from the UN's Food and Agriculture Organization (FAO) [37] and the United States Department of Agriculture (USDA) [38, 39]. The first definition states food security exists when all people, at all times, have physical, social, and economic access to sufficient, safe, and nutritious food to meet their dietary needs and food preferences for an active and healthy life. The second definition states food security for a household means access by all members at all times to enough food for an active, healthy life. Food security includes the ready availability of nutritionally adequate and safe foods and an assured ability to acquire acceptable foods in socially acceptable ways [38]. It may be counterintuitive that food-insecure children have a propensity for obesity [40]. Early case reports identified food insecurity as a risk factor [40]. This case report spawned additional studies that evaluated the relationship between food insecurity and obesity [40]. A meta-analysis conducted by Dinour [41] showed the studies published from 1999 to 2006 had conflicting associations between obesity and food insecurity in children [41]. However, majority of studies do find a positive correlation between obesity and food insecurity, especially for those children living in poverty [42].

Nutritional Evaluation: Biochemical Nutrition Indicators

The most common biochemical indicators used in the evaluation of the metabolic syndrome are lipids, glucose, insulin, and glycosylated hemoglobin (HgbA$_1$C). These should be measured biannually in those at risk [10]. Lipids (total cholesterol, HDL cholesterol, LDL cholesterol, non-HDL cholesterol, and triglycerides) should be evaluated in the context of norms relative to age and sex [43]. Insulin and glucose levels can be used to determine the homeostatic model assessment of insulin resistance (HOMA-IR) [44] that is a quick reference for possible insulin resistance. Though HgbA$_1$C provides an assessment of long-term glycemic control in diabetic patients, it is unclear if it is of any clinical significance in diagnosing the metabolic syndrome as standardized values for this marker have not been well established in the pediatric population [45].

There is widespread evidence that obesity is associated with a state of chronic inflammation that correlates with markers of oxidative stress [46] (Table 15.2). High levels of free fatty acids impair glucose and lipid metabolism, which lead to the

Table 15.2 Biochemical indicators in the metabolic syndrome

Biochemical indicators	Action	Relation in metabolic syndrome
Adiponectin	Anti-inflammatory	Decreased
C-reactive protein (CRP)	Proinflammatory	Increased
Interleukin-6 (IL-6)	Proinflammatory	Increased
Plasminogen activator inhibitor-1 (PAI-1)	Prothrombotic	Increased
Fibrinogen	Prothrombotic	Increased
Leptin	Antiobesogenic	Increased (leptin resistance)

increased expression of the proinflammatory cytokines in adipocytes [46]. C-reactive protein (CRP) and IL-6, to a lesser extent, are tracked to monitor cardiovascular disease risk and are associated with obesity. IL-6 is a proinflammatory cytokine, which stimulates the production of CRP in the liver. Elevated levels of CRP are associated with obesity [47]. There are also anti-inflammatory markers involved, and the most common marker involved is adiponectin. Adiponectin is secreted exclusively by adipocytes [47]. The concentration of this cytokine decreases with increases in body fat, insulin resistance and is associated with inflammation [47]. Hypoadiponectinemia is considered a risk factor for the metabolic syndrome, especially in African-American children and Hispanic obese children [48]. Insulin resistance is also associated with proinflammatory cytokines [49].

Other acute-phase proteins that are associated with the metabolic syndrome, diabetes, and cardiovascular risk include plasminogen activator inhibitor 1 (PAI-1), fibrinogen, and leptin [49]. PAI-1 is also responsible for improper fibrinolysis, which can lead directly to vascular injury. It is believed that hypertriglyceridemia stimulates the visceral adipocytes to release increased amounts of PAI-1 into the circulation. These proteins seem to exert a suppressive effect on the regulatory T cells resulting in an altered immune response with obesity and the metabolic syndrome [50]. Most of these laboratory markers are performed in a research setting.

Vitamin and Mineral Deficiencies

Certain vitamin and mineral deficiencies are associated with the metabolic syndrome. Vitamin E is a natural antioxidant that is effective in reducing oxidative stress. Vitamin E also provides protection against bone loss that is associated with inflammatory cytokines. Vitamin E levels can be low in those with the metabolic syndrome [51], and vitamin E supplementation has been associated with a lowered risk of cardiovascular disease by decreasing LDL [52]. Vitamin D deficiency has been linked to obesity, insulin resistance, diabetes, and cardiovascular disease [43] and is prevalent in the metabolic syndrome [43]. Vitamin D may play a major role in influencing the secretion of insulin from the pancreas via the vitamin D receptors [43] and maintaining adequate concentrations of apolipoprotein, the main component of HDL [53].

Iron deficiency is one of the most common nutritional deficiencies seen in developed countries, and it has been linked to obesity in children [54]. Iron deficiency may result from increased hepcidin expression in the obese patient. Hepcidin is a peptide that is the main regulator of systemic iron homeostasis. It restricts intestinal iron absorption and macrophage iron release [55]. Amati, et al. [50] showed a lower hepcidin concentration with weight loss and decreased BMI in obese children, which resulted in an improvement in iron absorption [50]. These findings should be considered when managing an obese individual who also has poor iron status.

Interventions

Lifestyle interventions represent an attractive means of addressing metabolic syndrome, and weight loss is the most direct approach to decreasing the obesity epidemic and reducing obesity-related health risks (Fig. 15.5). Often, parents and families do not recognize that the child is overweight or obese [6]. Increased family awareness is critical to institute change. Adherence to healthful lifestyle practices has been found to be associated with an 83% reduction in the rate of coronary disease [56], a 91% reduction in diabetes [57] in women, and a 71% reduction in colon cancer in men [58]. The percentage of weight loss in obese individuals was found to be the main predictive factor for reducing the risk of the metabolic syndrome [59]. Moderate weight loss (5–10% of initial body weight) in combination with increased

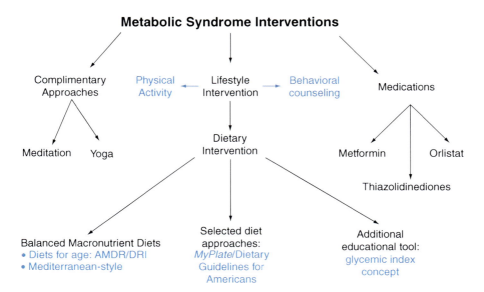

Fig. 15.5 Nutritional and lifestyle interventions for children with the metabolic syndrome

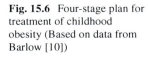

Fig. 15.6 Four-stage plan for treatment of childhood obesity (Based on data from Barlow [10])

activity can improve insulin sensitivity and glycemic control in individuals with type 2 diabetes and prevent the development of type 2 diabetes in those at high risk [60].

The Expert Committee recommendations on child and adolescent overweight and obesity [10] propose a staged treatment approach to the treatment of pediatric overweight and obesity based on body mass index (BMI) percentile and health risk. The Expert Committee recommends that primary care providers address the issue of weight with all children at least once each year. Practitioners are urged to assess key dietary habits (e.g., consumption of sweetened beverages), physical activity habits, readiness to change lifestyle habits, and family history of obesity and obesity-related illnesses. Laboratory testing recommendations are tailored to the degree of obesity and comorbid illnesses. The four-stage plan for treatment of childhood obesity is described in Fig. 15.6. This comprehensive approach to weight management includes prevention, structured weight management, comprehensive multidisciplinary intervention, and tertiary care intervention.

The components of interventions for pediatric weight management have been described as follows [61, 62]:

- Dietary counseling/nutrition education—dietary counseling should include the prescription of a specified caloric and/or nutrient content per day; nutrition education should involve provision of more general information on foods, shopping, and nutrition to promote healthful eating.
- Physical activity counseling/education—physical activity counseling should include the prescription of a specified amount and/or type of physical activity; physical activity education should involve provision of more general information on how to incorporate physical activity into child's daily routine.
- Behavioral counseling—involves counseling on self-monitoring of diet and physical activity, cue elimination, stimulus control, goal setting, action planning, modeling, limit setting, and other behavior modification strategies.

- Family counseling—specific to family-based interventions, involves behavioral counseling in which one or more family members accompanies the patient;
- Parent training—for family-based interventions, involves behavioral counseling targeted at parents to improve their parenting skills, including limit setting, role modeling, and positive reinforcement; parents should be provided with information on healthful diet and activity behaviors for their families.

Dietary Interventions for Pediatric Weight Management

The Academy of Nutrition and Dietetics (formerly the American Dietetic Association) distinguishes between balanced macronutrient dietary approaches and altered macronutrient dietary approaches. The first one includes balanced macronutrients diets for age according to Dietary Reference Intakes ranges (DRI) from the Institute of Medicine (IOM) and selected diet approaches such as general nutrition recommendations from Federal Government resources such as *MyPlate*. Among altered macronutrient diet approaches, low-fat, altered carbohydrate, and altered protein diets have been studied.

Balanced Macronutrients Diets

A balanced macronutrient diet for children is defined by the DRI in terms of percentages of daily energy intake. The Acceptable Macronutrient Distribution Ranges (AMDR) from IOM take into accounts both chronic disease risk reduction and intake of essential nutrients. AMDR for children are similar to those for adults (45–65% of their calories from carbohydrates, 20–35% from fat, and 10–35% from protein), except that infants and younger children need a slightly higher proportion of fat (25–40%).

According to the Academy of Nutrition and Dietetics' evidence-based pediatric weight management nutrition practice guideline [63], use of a balanced macronutrient diet that contains no fewer than 900 kcal/day for children aged 6–12 years and 1,200 kcal/day for adolescents aged 13–18 years is recommended to improve weight status within a multicomponent pediatric weight management program in which patients are medically monitored. Studies have shown that balanced macronutrient diets at 900–1,200 kcal/day are associated with short-term and longer-term (longer than 1 year) improved weight status and body composition in the pediatric population [64].

Dietary Guidelines for Americans and USDA Food Guide MyPlate

These are Federal Government resources that provide reliable, scientifically based information on nutrition and physical activity, as well as an evolving array of tools to facilitate Americans' adoption of healthy choices. The dietary and physical activity recommendations described in the Dietary Guidelines for Americans 2010 [65] may help people attain and maintain a healthy weight, reduce the risk of chronic disease, and promote overall health. These recommendations are intended to accommodate the varied food preferences, cultural traditions, and customs of the many and diverse groups living in the United States. A basic premise of the dietary guidelines is that nutrient needs should be met primarily through consuming foods.

In June 2011, the USDA food guide MyPlate replaced MyPyramid. MyPlate is a visual cue that identifies the five basic food groups from which consumers can choose healthy foods to build a healthy plate at mealtimes. Available on www.ChooseMyPlate.gov, this icon serves as a reminder for healthy eating, but it is not intended to provide specific messages.

Mediterranean-Style Diet

The Mediterranean-style diet (MSD) was described in the 1960s by Angel Keys when he observed food habits of some populations in the Mediterranean region. Subsequently, adherence to the MSD was associated with decreased CVD and improved survival [66]. The MSD pattern emphasizes consumption of fat (between 30% and 40% of daily energy intake) primarily from foods high in monounsaturated fatty acids and encourages consumption of fruits, vegetables, tree nuts, legumes, whole grains, and fish [67] and relatively low consumption of red meat [68] and full-fat milk and milk products (Dietary Guidelines for Americans 2010). These diets are considered the "gold standard" as they emphasize the high consumption of nutrient-dense foods and limit the consumption of refined and processed products that are high in sugar and saturated fats. In addition, this diet promotes the use and of olive oil and other healthy fats that have been associated with positive health outcomes. Some studies suggest that MSD have cardioprotective properties and decrease obesity [67, 69–71]. In a meta-analysis of randomized controlled trials, the MSD was helpful in reducing body weight, especially when combined with a physical activity program and energy restriction, despite the high content of fat [67, 71]. Although the MSD is known for its impact on cardiovascular health [72], epidemiological evidence shows a positive effect on diabetes and adiposity [73]. BMI was inversely related to MSD adherence [74] and waist-to-hip ratios [75, 76]. The mechanism by which the MSD exerts its positive and protective cardiometabolic effects is under avid investigation, but it is clear that the effect of the combination of foods is far greater than any single dietary component [35, 77]. Many have speculated that the overall diet has greater anti-inflammatory nutritional properties with less proinflammatory properties [78]. Lower levels of biomarkers associated with vascular inflammation have been associated with the MSD [79]. The MSD can also decrease biomarkers associated with oxidative stress. A one-unit increase in the MSD score was associated with a 7% increase in GSH/GSSG ratios [72]. The MSD has also shown cardiometabolic protection in some populations, regardless of weight loss [80], and the diet does not promote weight gain [71], metabolic syndrome, and related disorders. A number of studies have also shown that the MSD has its largest impact on weight reduction and improved cardiometabolic risk when administered in the context of energy restriction [81, 82]. A recent systematic review and meta-analysis showed that adherence with a Mediterranean diet reduced the risk of developing the metabolic syndrome by 31% and had beneficial effects on its individual components including decreased waist circumference, increased HDL cholesterol, decreased triglycerides, decreased blood pressure, and decreased glucose [83]. Although much of the research is convincing in the adult literature, there have been few studies among children with the metabolic syndrome.

Altered Macronutrient Dietary Approaches

Popular diet approaches including altered protein diet (sometimes called "protein-sparing modified fast" diets) and low-carbohydrate (e.g., ketogenic) diets have been associated to increased thermogenesis and increased satiety [84–86]. However, strong evidence shows that there is no optimal proportion of macronutrients that can facilitate weight loss or assist with maintaining weight loss. Although diets with a wide range of macronutrient proportions have been documented to promote weight loss and prevent weight regain after loss, evidence shows that the critical issue is not the relative proportion of macronutrients in the diet but whether or not the eating pattern is reduced in calories and the individual is able to maintain a reduced calorie intake over time. Therefore, for weight loss and maintenance of the loss, the Dietary Guidelines for Americans 2010 recommend individuals to select eating patterns that maintain appropriate calorie intake and have macronutrient proportions that are within the AMDR ranges recommended in the DRI.

Although total calorie intake is ultimately what affects calorie balance, some foods and beverages can be easily overconsumed, which results in a higher total calorie intake. Ideally, best advice is to monitor dietary intake and replace foods higher in calories with nutrient-dense foods and beverages relatively low in calories. The following guidance may help individuals control their total calorie intake and manage body weight:

- Increase intake of whole grains, vegetables, and fruits.
- Reduce intake of sugar-sweetened beverages and monitor intake of 100% fruit juice for children and adolescents [87].

Specific Nutrient Effects in Metabolic Syndrome

Calcium

In addition to being a high-quality protein source, milk and dairy products represent important sources of calcium, vitamin D (when milk is fortified), iodine, riboflavin, and B12. A potential role for calcium in body-weight regulation came from observations that a high-calcium diet attenuated adipocyte lipid accretion and weight gain, during periods of overconsumption of an energy-dense diet in animal models [87–93]. In the few randomized intervention trials of weight loss, increased intake of dairy products led to increased weight loss and decreased fat mass and waist circumference [91, 93, 94]. A longitudinal study done by Carruth et al. [95] studied children aged 2–96 months and showed that a higher intake of calcium with dairy products was associated with lower amounts of body fat [95]. These studies have identified calcium as a principal bioactive component with a proposed effect on adipocyte lipid metabolism, lipogenesis and lipolysis, fat oxidation, and fat absorption.

Studies have suggested that dairy constituents such as lactose, protein (in particular whey proteins), and their peptide derivatives may have an effect on body weight through the regulation of food intake and appetite [96]. Milk supplementation provided to women with very low milk intake during an energy-restricted diet intervention attenuated the weight loss-related increase in appetite, and it was attributed to the suppression of appetite caused by calcium supplementation and the increase in dairy protein intake [97]. According to this calcium-specific appetite control theory, fluctuations in calcium intake and/or stores might influence appetite sensations and food intake [97].

Dietary calcium has also been known to act at the level of the gastrointestinal tract to increase energy loss, through increased fecal fat [98]. Soares et al. [98] suggested that there was consistent evidence to support the stimulation of fat oxidation, following calcium alone or in combination with vitamin D [98]. However, an increased thermogenesis and greater lipolysis were not always observed. Evidence derived from intervention studies without energy restriction does not predict any effect of dairy products on either weight loss or weight gain. During energy restriction, although the results are still inconsistent, there are indications of a possible beneficial effect of dairy products in weight loss treatments while maintaining lean tissue in an overweight population. Therefore, the association of dairy products with body weight is still controversial.

Vitamin D

Vitamin D increases calcium absorption. It is obtained by sun exposure, from food (mainly fish liver oils, fatty fish, and eggs), fortified foods (such as milk, yogurt, margarine, oil spreads, and breakfast cereal), and supplements. Calcitriol [1,25(OH)2D3] is the active form of vitamin D found in the body, and calcidiol [25(OH)D3] is the form measured in the blood to assess vitamin D status.

There is an active interest regarding the role of vitamin D in chronic disease. The active metabolite, 1,25 (OH)2D3, independent of PTH, seems to modulate adipogenesis [99]. Cross-sectional studies consistently link low vitamin D to obesity. Reduced vitamin D stores have the potential to cause excess differentiation of preadipocytes to adipocytes. Animal studies convincingly indicate a role for vitamin D in energy regulation [100]. However, there is mixed evidence in humans to support a role in energy expenditure and fat oxidation [90, 101]. Currently, randomized clinical trials do not consistently provide evidence for the role of calcium and vitamin D supplementation [98] in weight loss program.

Omega-3 Fatty Acids

Omega-3 long-chain polyunsaturated fatty acids (ω3 LC-PUFA) are increasingly being used in the prevention and management of cardiovascular risk. Dietary supplementation with omega-3 fatty acids can lead to improvements in cardiometabolic health parameters [102]. Moore showed a diet supplemented with omega-3 fatty acids (two servings of fish per week) decreased triglyceride levels [102]. Omega-3 fatty acids also show favorable shifts in HDL and LDL cholesterol, providing a mechanism for potential antiatherogenic effects [103]. A main advantage of adding this supplement to the diet is that it does not interact adversely to common drug therapies used in the management and treatment of hypertension, dyslipidemia, type 2 diabetes, and obesity/metabolic syndrome, but in some instances works synergistically [104].

Fiber

Dietary fiber is an edible component of all plants and is resistant to digestion and absorption in the human gut. Examples of foods high in fiber include vegetables, fruits, legumes, and whole grains. Overweight and obese individuals consume a lower amount of high-fiber foods [105]. Studies have also shown a correlation between high-fiber intakes with lower body weight, lower BMI, improved plasma profiles, and improved glycemic control [106]. Fiber has clearly been associated with benefits and risk reduction for the components of the metabolic syndrome.

Dietary Educational Tool: The Glycemic Index

The concept of glycemic index (GI) was introduced in early 1981 as a method for classifying food carbohydrates according to their effect on postprandial glycemia [107]. The major contributors of carbohydrate intake include white breads, pasta, rice, and breakfast cereals. The GI is defined as the blood glucose response of a 50-g (or 25-g) carbohydrate portion of food, expressed as a percentage of the same amount of carbohydrate from a reference food—either glucose or white bread [108]. Although the GI predicts the potential of a food's carbohydrate to raise blood glucose levels, the overall blood glucose response to a food or meal is determined by both the quantity and quality (GI) of the carbohydrate consumed [109].

The concept of glycemic load (GL)—defined as the GI multiplied by the amount of carbohydrate per serving of food in grams—was introduced as a measure of the overall effect of a food on blood glucose and insulin levels. Dietary GL can be reduced in two ways: either by lowering the GI of the carbohydrate or by reducing the total carbohydrate in the diet. However, the metabolic effects of these changes are likely to be different [110]. The American Diabetes Association (ADA) recommendations state that the use of GI and GL may provide a modest additional benefit over that observed when total carbohydrate is considered alone.

A low-GI diet is consistent with healthy eating recommendations aimed at weight control and reducing chronic disease risk and easily meets all of the goals of medical nutrition therapy recommended for people with diabetes [111]. A Cochrane systematic review incorporating the findings of 11 randomized controlled trials (RCTs) for 4 weeks or longer found that a low-GI diet can improve glycemic control in diabetes while reducing the risk of hypoglycemic events [112]. In addition to reducing postprandial glycemia, a low-GI diet can improve insulin sensitivity after 3–4 weeks [113]. Although longer-term studies are needed, a low-GI meal can reduce postprandial glucose excursions in children with type 1 diabetes treated with both intensive multiple daily injection of insulin or insulin pump therapy [114, 115].

Diets with a lower GI or GL may also assist in weight management by influencing appetite and fuel partitioning. A meta-analysis of six RCTs found that overweight or obese individuals lost more weight and had greater improvement in lipid profiles on a low GI compared with a control diet [116]. Another randomized controlled study in obese adolescents showed that a reduced GL is more effective than a low-fat diet in achieving weight loss [117]. These results suggested that a decrease in this dietary load would be associated with a decreased reduction of the components of the metabolic syndrome, especially with obesity. However, there is limited evidence regarding the effectiveness of a low-glycemic diet for weight loss in children [118], although it may be effective for longer-term weight loss in adolescents [119].

Psychological Interventions

While the medical components of the metabolic syndrome are generally agreed upon, psychological components are not as well defined. A more complete discussion is addressed in Chap. 10. Depression, hostility, anger, and anxiety may also be related to the risk for developing the metabolic syndrome. Dysregulation of the hypothalamic pituitary adrenal axis may contribute to both the psychological and metabolic abnormalities [120]. Higher cortisol levels may produce both depression and changes in glucose regulation [120]. There is likely a bidirectional relationship between the metabolic syndrome and its psychological components. It is hypothesized that this psychological distress can lead to a decline in an individual's positive health behaviors resulting in poor dietary lifestyle choices and poor compliance.

Other Interventions

Other forms of intervention for the metabolic syndrome include motivational interviewing with a complimentary and integrative approach with participation in mind-body therapies of yoga and meditation, as well as pharmacologic interventions. While all of these individual therapies result in improvement, it is the balance of using these interventions together that make prevention and treatment of the metabolic syndrome more effective. Gastric bypass is a treatment option for morbidly obese adolescents for whom other comprehensive dietary and behavioral approaches to weight loss have been unsuccessful and is discussed in Chap. 15.

Conclusion

The pediatric metabolic syndrome does not have a uniform definition. The syndrome can develop in early childhood and is highly prevalent among overweight children and adolescents. Obesity is one of its principal components. Obese children develop into obese adults. Nutrition and nutritional assessment are critical in the management of the pediatric metabolic syndrome. Therefore, it is imperative that the child's weight and body composition be monitored closely. Proactive nutritional counseling for all children and families, regardless of obesity, is recommended. Diets high in sugars (fruit juice) and low in vegetable and fruit intake can lead to obesity [121]. It is important for health providers to help families understand the importance of family meals and active lifestyles. A multidisciplinary management strategy that addresses nutritional, lifestyle, psychological, and pharmacological approaches is essential to promote the most optimal nutrition. A comprehensive approach with nutrition as a key component will have the greatest likelihood of altering the current nutritional trajectory of the next generation.

References

1. Cruz ML, Goran MI. The metabolic syndrome in children and adolescents. Curr Diab Rep. 2004;4(1):53–62.
2. Messiah SE, Arheart KL, Luke B, Lipshultz SE, Miller TL. Relationship between body mass index and metabolic syndrome risk factors among US 8- to 14-year-olds, 1999 to 2002. J Pediatr. 2008;153(2):215–21.
3. Weiss R. Childhood metabolic syndrome: must we define it to deal with it? Diabetes Care. 2011;34 Suppl 2:S171–6.
4. Ford ES, Li C. Defining the metabolic syndrome in children and adolescents: will the real definition please stand up? J Pediatr. 2008;152(2):160–4.
5. Hirschler V, Maccallini G, Calcagno M, Aranda C, Jadzinsky M. Waist circumference identifies primary school children with metabolic syndrome abnormalities. Diabetes Technol Ther. 2007;9(2):149–57.

6. He M, Evans A. Are parents aware that their children are overweight or obese? Do they care? Can Fam Phys. 2007;53(9):1493–9.
7. Kleinman R. Pediatric nutrition handbook; 2009.
8. Garnett SP, Baur LA, Srinivasan S, Lee JW, Cowell CT. Body mass index and waist circumference in midchildhood and adverse cardiovascular disease risk clustering in adolescence. Am J Clin Nutr. 2007;86(3):549–55.
9. Kuczmarski RJ, Ogden CL, Grummer-Strawn LM, Flegal KM, Guo SS, Wei R, et al. CDC growth charts: United States. Adv Data. 2000;314:1–27.
10. Barlow SE. Expert committee recommendations regarding the prevention, assessment, and treatment of child and adolescent overweight and obesity: summary report. Pediatrics. 2007;120 Suppl 4:S164–92.
11. Freedman DS, Serdula MK, Srinivasan SR, Berenson GS. Relation of circumferences and skinfold thicknesses to lipid and insulin concentrations in children and adolescents: the Bogalusa Heart Study. Am J Clin Nutr. 1999;69(2):308–17.
12. Fredriks AM, van Buuren S, Fekkes M, Verloove-Vanhorick SP, Wit JM. Are age references for waist circumference, hip circumference and waist-hip ratio in Dutch children useful in clinical practice? Eur J Pediatr. 2005;164(4):216–22.
13. CDC. NHANES: Anthropometry procedures manual. In: NHANES, editor; 2002.
14. McDowell MA, Fryar CD, Ogden CL. Anthropometric reference data for children and adults: United States, 1988–1994. Vital and health statistics. Series 11, Data from the national health survey 2009(249):1–68.
15. Bedogni G, Iughetti L, Ferrari M, Malavolti M, Poli M, Bernasconi S, et al. Sensitivity and specificity of body mass index and skinfold thicknesses in detecting excess adiposity in children aged 8–12 years. Ann Hum Biol. 2003;30(2):132–9.
16. Goran MI. Measurement issues related to studies of childhood obesity: assessment of body composition, body fat distribution, physical activity, and food intake. Pediatrics. 1998;101(3 Pt 2):505–18.
17. Slaughter MH, Lohman TG, Boileau RA, Horswill CA, Stillman RJ, Van Loan MD, et al. Skinfold equations for estimation of body fatness in children and youth. Hum Biol. 1988;60(5):709–23.
18. Durnin JV, Lonergan ME, Good J, Ewan A. A cross-sectional nutritional and anthropometric study, with an interval of 7 years, on 611 young adolescent schoolchildren. Br J Nutr. 1974;32(1):169–79.
19. Wickramasinghe VP, Lamabadusuriay SP, Cleghorn GJ, Davies PS. Use of skin-fold thickness in Sri Lankan children: comparison of several prediction equations. Indian J Pediatr. 2008;75(12):1237–42.
20. Skinfolds. In: International Standards for Anthropometric Assessment. Undrdale, Australia: The International Society for the Advancement of Kinanthropometry (ISAK); 2001.
21. Ward KA, Ashby RL, Roberts SA, Adams JE, Zulf Mughal M. UK reference data for the Hologic QDR Discovery dual-energy x ray absorptiometry scanner in healthy children and young adults aged 6–17 years. Arch Dis Child. 2007;92(1):53–9.
22. Freedman DS, et al. Classification of body fatness by body mass index for age categories among children. Arch Pediatric Adolesc Med. 2009;163:805–11.
23. Gordon CM, Bachrach LK, Carpenter TO, Crabtree N, El-Hajj Fuleihan G, Kutilek S, et al. Dual energy X-ray absorptiometry interpretation and reporting in children and adolescents: the 2007 ISCD Pediatric Official Positions. J Clin Densit. 2008;11(1):43–58.
24. Klibanski A, Adams-Campbell L, Bassford T, Blair S, Boden SD, Dickersin K, Gifford DR, Glasse L, Goldring SR, Hruska K, Johnson SR, McCauley LK, Russell WE. Osteoporosis prevention, diagnosis, and therapy. JAMA. 2001;285(6):785–95.
25. Migliaccio S, Greco EA, Fornari R, Donini LM, Lenzi A. Is obesity in women protective against osteoporosis? Diab Metab Synd Obes. 2011;4:273–82.
26. Lee Y, Kim M, Choi K, Kim J, Bae W, Kim S, et al. Relationship between inflammation biomarkers, antioxidant vitamins, and bone mineral density in patients with metabolic syndrome. Nutr Res Pract. 2011;5(2):150–6.

27. Leahy S, O'Neill C, Sohun R, Jakeman P. A comparison of dual energy X-ray absorptiometry and bioelectrical impedance analysis to measure total and segmental body composition in healthy young adults. Eur J Appl Physiol. 2012 Feb;112(2):589–95.
28. Ashwell M, Cole TJ, Dixon AK. Obesity: new insight into the anthropometric classification of fat distribution shown by computed tomography. Br Med J. 1985;290(6483):1692–4.
29. Ross R, Leger L, Morris D, de Guise J, Guardo R. Quantification of adipose tissue by MRI: relationship with anthropometric variables. J Appl Physiol. 1992;72(2):787–95.
30. USDA. Automated multiple pass method. In: Service AR, editor; 2005.
31. McPherson RS, Feaganes JR, Siegler IC. Measurement of dietary intake in the UNC Alumni Heart Study. University of North Carolina. Prev Med. 2000;31(1):56–67.
32. Maffeis C, Provera S, Filippi L, Sidoti G, Schena S, Pinelli L, et al. Distribution of food intake as a risk factor for childhood obesity. Int J Obes Relat Metab Disord. 2000;24(1):75–80.
33. Doucet E, St-Pierre S, Almeras N, Tremblay A. Relation between appetite ratings before and after a standard meal and estimates of daily energy intake in obese and reduced obese individuals. Appetite. 2003;40(2):137–43.
34. Subar AF, Thompson FE, Kipnis V, Midthune D, Hurwitz P, McNutt S, et al. Comparative validation of the Block, Willett, and National Cancer Institute food frequency questionnaires: the Eating at America's Table Study. Am J Epidemiol. 2001;154(12):1089–99.
35. Newby PK, Muller D, Hallfrisch J, Andres R, Tucker KL. Food patterns measured by factor analysis and anthropometric changes in adults. Am J Clin Nutr. 2004;80(2):504–13.
36. Ledoux TA, Hingle MD, Baranowski T. Relationship of fruit and vegetable intake with adiposity: a systematic review. Obes Rev. 2011;12(5):e143–50.
37. FAO. Food security. 2006.
38. Nord M, Andrews, M, Carlson S. Food security in the United States: measuring household food security: USDA; 2008.
39. Nord M, Coleman-Jensen A, Andrews M, Carlson S. Household food security in the United States, 2009; 2010.
40. Dietz WH. Does hunger cause obesity? Pediatrics. 1995;95(5):766–7.
41. Dinour LM, Bergen D, Yeh MC. The food insecurity-obesity paradox: a review of the literature and the role food stamps may play. J Am Diet Assoc. 2007;107(11):1952–61.
42. Eisenmann JC, Gundersen C, Lohman BJ, Garasky S, Stewart SD. Is food insecurity related to overweight and obesity in children and adolescents? A summary of studies, 1995–2009. Obes Rev. 2011;12(5):e73–83.
43. Reis JP, von Muhlen D, Miller 3rd ER, Michos ED, Appel LJ. Vitamin D status and cardiometabolic risk factors in the United States adolescent population. Pediatrics. 2009;124(3):e371–9.
44. Matthews DR, Hosker JP, Rudenski AS, Naylor BA, Treacher DF, Turner RC. Homeostasis model assessment: insulin resistance and beta-cell function from fasting plasma glucose and insulin concentrations in man. Diabetologia. 1985;28(7):412–9.
45. Saaddine JB, Fagot-Campagna A, Rolka D, Narayan KM, Geiss L, Eberhardt M, et al. Distribution of HbA(1c) levels for children and young adults in the U.S.: third National Health and Nutrition Examination Survey. Diabetes Care. 2002;25(8):1326–30.
46. Zimmermann MB, Aeberli I. Dietary determinants of subclinical inflammation, dyslipidemia and components of the metabolic syndrome in overweight children: a review. Int J Obes. 2008;32 Suppl 6:S11–8.
47. Winer JC, Zern TL, Taksali SE, Dziura J, Cali AM, Wollschlager M, et al. Adiponectin in childhood and adolescent obesity and its association with inflammatory markers and components of the metabolic syndrome. J Clin Endocrinol Metab. 2006;91(11):4415–23.
48. Bush NC, Darnell BE, Oster RA, Goran MI, Gower BA. Adiponectin is lower among African Americans and is independently related to insulin sensitivity in children and adolescents. Diabetes. 2005;54(9):2772–8.
49. Valle M, Martos R, Gascon F, Canete R, Zafra MA, Morales R. Low-grade systemic inflammation, hypoadiponectinemia and a high concentration of leptin are present in very young obese children, and correlate with metabolic syndrome. Diabetes Metab. 2005;31(1):55–62.

50. Amati L, Marzulli G, Martulli M, Chiloiro M, Jirillo E. Effects of a hypocaloric diet on obesity biomarkers: prevention of low-grade inflammation since childhood. Curr Pharm Des. 2010;16(7):893–7.
51. Palmieri VO, Grattagliano I, Portincasa P, Palasciano G. Systemic oxidative alterations are associated with visceral adiposity and liver steatosis in patients with metabolic syndrome. J Nutr. 2006;136(12):3022–6.
52. Nunez-Cordoba JM, Martinez-Gonzalez MA. Antioxidant vitamins and cardiovascular disease. Curr Top Med Chem. 2011;11(14):1861–9.
53. Botella-Carretero JI, Alvarez-Blasco F, Villafruela JJ, Balsa JA, Vazquez C, Escobar-Morreale HF. Vitamin D deficiency is associated with the metabolic syndrome in morbid obesity. Clin Nutr. 2007;26(5):573–80.
54. Nead KG, Halterman JS, Kaczorowski JM, Auinger P, Weitzman M. Overweight children and adolescents: a risk group for iron deficiency. Pediatrics. 2004;114(1):104–8.
55. Andrews NC. Forging a field: the golden age of iron biology. Blood. 2008;112(2):219–30.
56. Stampfer MJ, Hu FB, Manson JE, Rimm EB, Willett WC. Primary prevention of coronary heart disease in women through diet and lifestyle. N Engl J Med. 2000;343(1):16–22.
57. Hu FB, Manson JE, Stampfer MJ, Colditz G, Liu S, Solomon CG, et al. Diet, lifestyle, and the risk of type 2 diabetes mellitus in women. N Engl J Med. 2001;345(11):790–7.
58. Platz EA, Willett WC, Colditz GA, Rimm EB, Spiegelman D, Giovannucci E. Proportion of colon cancer risk that might be preventable in a cohort of middle-aged US men. Cancer Causes Control. 2000;11(7):579–88.
59. Reinehr T, Kleber M, Toschke AM. Lifestyle intervention in obese children is associated with a decrease of the metabolic syndrome prevalence. Atherosclerosis. 2009;207(1):174–80.
60. Klein S, Sheard NF, Pi-Sunyer X, Daly A, Wylie-Rosett J, Kulkarni K, et al. Weight management through lifestyle modification for the prevention and management of type 2 diabetes: rationale and strategies. A statement of the American Diabetes Association, the North American Association for the Study of Obesity, and the American Society for Clinical Nutrition. Am J Clin Nutr. 2004;80(2):257–63.
61. Krebs NF, Jacobson MS. Prevention of pediatric overweight and obesity. Pediatrics. 2003;112(2):424–30.
62. Position of the American Dietetic Association. Individual-, family-, school-, and community-based interventions for pediatric overweight. J Am Diet Assoc. 2006;106(6):925–45.
63. American Dietetic Association. Childhood overweight evidence analysis project: updated 2006.
64. Spear BA, Barlow SE, Ervin C, Ludwig DS, Saelens BE, Schetzina KE, et al. Recommendations for treatment of child and adolescent overweight and obesity. Pediatrics. 2007;120 Suppl 4:S254–88.
65. Benjamin RM. Dietary guidelines for Americans, 2010: the cornerstone of nutrition policy. Public Health Rep. 2011;126(3):310–1.
66. Trichopoulou A, Bamia C, Trichopoulos D. Mediterranean diet and survival among patients with coronary heart disease in Greece. Arch Intern Med. 2005;165(8):929–35.
67. Willett WC, Sacks F, Trichopoulou A, Drescher G, Ferro-Luzzi A, Helsing E, et al. Mediterranean diet pyramid: a cultural model for healthy eating. Am J Clin Nutr. 1995;61(6 Suppl):1402S–6.
68. Giugliano D, Esposito K. Mediterranean diet and metabolic diseases. Curr Opin Lipidol. 2008;19(1):63–8.
69. Esposito K, Ciotola M, Giugliano D. Mediterranean diet and the metabolic syndrome. Mol Nutr Food Res. 2007;51(10):1268–74.
70. Esposito K, Giugliano D. Which Mediterranean diet in the management of metabolic syndrome? Archiv Int Med. 2009;169(11):1076. author reply 1077.
71. Esposito K, Kastorini CM, Panagiotakos DB, Giugliano D. Mediterranean diet and weight loss: meta-analysis of randomized controlled trials. Metab Syndr Relat Disord. 2011;9(1):1–12.
72. Giugliano D, Esposito K. Mediterranean diet and cardiovascular health. Ann N Y Acad Sci. 2005;1056:253–60.

73. Heidemann C, Hoffmann K, Spranger J, Klipstein-Grobusch K, Mohlig M, Pfeiffer AF, et al. A dietary pattern protective against type 2 diabetes in the European Prospective Investigation into Cancer and Nutrition (EPIC)–Potsdam Study cohort. Diabetologia. 2005;48(6):1126–34.
74. Sanchez-Villegas A, Bes-Rastrollo M, Martinez-Gonzalez MA, Serra-Majem L. Adherence to a Mediterranean dietary pattern and weight gain in a follow-up study: the SUN cohort. Int J Obes. 2006;30(2):350–8.
75. Panagiotakos DB, Arapi S, Pitsavos C, Antonoulas A, Mantas Y, Zombolos S, et al. The relationship between adherence to the Mediterranean diet and the severity and short-term prognosis of acute coronary syndromes (ACS): The Greek Study of ACS (The GREECS). Nutrition. 2006;22(7–8):722–30.
76. Panagiotakos DB, Chrysohoou C, Pitsavos C, Stefanadis C. Association between the prevalence of obesity and adherence to the Mediterranean diet: the ATTICA study. Nutrition. 2006;22(5):449–56.
77. Newby PK, Tucker KL. Empirically derived eating patterns using factor or cluster analysis: a review. Nutr Rev. 2004;62(5):177–203.
78. Esposito K, Giugliano D. The metabolic syndrome and inflammation: association or causation? Nutr Metab Cardiovasc Dis. 2004;14(5):228–32.
79. Salas-Salvado J, Garcia-Arellano A, Estruch R, Marquez-Sandoval F, Corella D, Fiol M, et al. Components of the Mediterranean-type food pattern and serum inflammatory markers among patients at high risk for cardiovascular disease. Eur J Clin Nutr. 2008;62(5):651–9.
80. Gaesser GA, Angadi SS, Sawyer BJ. Exercise and diet, independent of weight loss, improve cardiometabolic risk profile in overweight and obese individuals. Physician Sportsmed. 2011;39(2):87–97.
81. Esposito K, Marfella R, Ciotola M, Di Palo C, Giugliano F, Giugliano G, et al. Effect of a mediterranean-style diet on endothelial dysfunction and markers of vascular inflammation in the metabolic syndrome: a randomized trial. JAMA. 2004;292(12):1440–6.
82. McManus K, Antinoro L, Sacks F. A randomized controlled trial of a moderate-fat, low-energy diet compared with a low fat, low-energy diet for weight loss in overweight adults. Int J Obes Relat Metab Disord. 2001;25(10):1503–11.
83. Kastorini CM, Milionis HJ, Esposito K, Giugliano D, Goudevenos JA, Panagiotakos DB. The effect of Mediterranean diet on metabolic syndrome and its components: a meta-analysis of 50 studies and 534,906 individuals. J Am Coll Cardiol. 2011;57(11):1299–313.
84. Weigle DS, Breen PA, Matthys CC, Callahan HS, Meeuws KE, Burden VR, et al. A high-protein diet induces sustained reductions in appetite, ad libitum caloric intake, and body weight despite compensatory changes in diurnal plasma leptin and ghrelin concentrations. Am J Clin Nutr. 2005;82(1):41–8.
85. Johnstone AM, Horgan GW, Murison SD, Bremner DM, Lobley GE. Effects of a high-protein ketogenic diet on hunger, appetite, and weight loss in obese men feeding ad libitum. Am J Clin Nutr. 2008;87(1):44–55.
86. Stadler DD, Burden V, Connor W, et al. Impact of 42-day atkins diet and energy-matched low-fat diet on weight and anthropometric indices. Abstract of the 12th annual FASEB meeting on experimental biology. San Diego; 2003;17:4–5.
87. Ranjit N, Evans MH, Byrd-Williams C, Evans AE, Hoelscher DM. Dietary and activity correlates of sugar-sweetened beverage consumption among adolescents. Pediatrics. 2010;126(4):e754–61.
88. Shi H, Norman AW, Okamura WH, Sen A, Zemel MB. 1alpha,25-Dihydroxyvitamin D3 modulates human adipocyte metabolism via nongenomic action. FASEB J. 2001;15(14):2751–3.
89. Teegarden D. The influence of dairy product consumption on body composition. J Nutr. 2005;135(12):2749–52.
90. Teegarden D, Gunther CW. Can the controversial relationship between dietary calcium and body weight be mechanistically explained by alterations in appetite and food intake? Nutr Rev. 2008;66(10):601–5.
91. Zemel MB, Teegarden D, Van Loan M, et al. Role of dietary products in modulating weight and fat loss: a multi-center trial. FASEB J. 2004;18:566.5 (abstr).
92. Zemel MB, Shi H, Greer B, Dirienzo D, Zemel PC. Regulation of adiposity by dietary calcium. FASEB J. 2000;14(9):1132–8.

93. Zemel MB, Thompson W, Milstead A, Morris K, Campbell P. Calcium and dairy acceleration of weight and fat loss during energy restriction in obese adults. Obes Res. 2004;12(4): 582–90.
94. Shahar DR, Abel R, Elhayany A, Vardi H, Fraser D. Does dairy calcium intake enhance weight loss among overweight diabetic patients? Diabetes Care. 2007;30(3):485–9.
95. Carruth BR, Skinner JD. The role of dietary calcium and other nutrients in moderating body fat in preschool children. Int J Obes Relat Metab Disord. 2001;25(4):559–66.
96. Dougkas A, Reynolds CK, Givens ID, Elwcod PC, Minihane AM. Associations between dairy consumption and body weight: a review of the evidence and underlying mechanisms. Nutr Res Rev. 2011;1–24 [Epub ahead of print].
97. Gilbert JA, Joanisse DR, Chaput JP, Miegueu P, Cianflone K, Almeras N, et al. Milk supplementation facilitates appetite control in obese women during weight loss: a randomised, single-blind, placebo-controlled trial. Br J Nutr. 2011;105(1):133–43.
98. Soares MJ, Chan She Ping-Delfos W, Ghanbari MH. Calcium and vitamin D for obesity: a review of randomized controlled trials. Eur J Clin Nutr. 2011;65(9):994–1004.
99. Duque G, Macoritto M, Kremer R. 1,25(OH)2D3 inhibits bone marrow adipogenesis in senescence accelerated mice (SAM-P/6) by decreasing the expression of peroxisome proliferator-activated receptor gamma 2 (PPARgamma2). Exp Gerontol. 2004;39(3):333–8.
100. Wong KE, Szeto FL, Zhang W, Ye H, Kong J, Zhang Z, et al. Involvement of the vitamin D receptor in energy metabolism: regulation of uncoupling proteins. Am J Physiol Endocrinol Metab. 2009;296(4):E820–8.
101. Boon N, Hul GB, Sicard A, Kole E, Van Den Berg ER, Viguerie N, et al. The effects of increasing serum calcitriol on energy and fat metabolism and gene expression. Obesity. 2006;14(10):1739–46.
102. Moore CS, Bryant SP, Mishra GD, Krebs JD, Browning LM, Miller GJ, et al. Oily fish reduces plasma triacylglycerols: a primary prevention study in overweight men and women. Nutrition. 2006;22(10):1012–24.
103. Mori TA, Burke V, Puddey IB, Watts GF, O'Neal DN, Best JD, et al. Purified eicosapentaenoic and docosahexaenoic acids have differential effects on serum lipids and lipoproteins, LDL particle size, glucose, and insulin in mildly hyperlipidemic men. Am J Clin Nutr. 2000;71(5):1085–94.
104. Abeywardena MY, Patten GS. Role of omega3 longchain polyunsaturated fatty acids in reducing cardio-metabolic risk factors. Endocr Metab Immune Disord Drug Targets. 2011;11(3):232–46.
105. Slavin JL. Dietary fiber and body weight. Nutrition. 2005;21(3):411–8.
106. Rossi M, Bosetti C, Talamini R, Lagiou P, Negri E, Franceschi S, et al. Glycemic index and glycemic load in relation to body mass index and waist to hip ratio. Eur J Nutr. 2010;49(8):459–64.
107. Jenkins DJ, Wolever TM, Taylor RH, Barker H, Fielden H, Baldwin JM, et al. Glycemic index of foods: a physiological basis for carbohydrate exchange. Am J Clin Nutr. 1981;34(3):362–6.
108. Wolever TM, Jenkins DJ, Jenkins AL, Josse RG. The glycemic index: methodology and clinical implications. Am J Clin Nutr. 1991;54(5):846–54.
109. Brand-Miller JC, Petocz P, Colagiuri S. Meta-analysis of low-glycemic index diets in the management of diabetes: response to Franz. Diabetes Care. 2003;26(12):3363–4. author reply 3364–5.
110. Wolever TM, Mehling C. High-carbohydrate-low-glycaemic index dietary advice improves glucose disposition index in subjects with impaired glucose tolerance. Br J Nutr. 2002;87(5):477–87.
111. Marsh K, Barclay A, Colagiuri S, Brand-Miller J. Glycemic index and glycemic load of carbohydrates in the diabetes diet. Curr Diab Rep. 2011;11(2):120–7.
112. Thomas D, Elliott EJ. Low glycaemic index, or low glycaemic load, diets for diabetes mellitus. Cochrane Syst Rev Database. 2009(1):CD006296.

113. Frost G, Leeds A, Trew G, Margara R, Dornhorst A. Insulin sensitivity in women at risk of coronary heart disease and the effect of a low glycemic diet. Metabolism. 1998;47(10):1245–51.
114. O'Connell MA, Gilbertson HR, Donath SM, Cameron FJ. Optimizing postprandial glycemia in pediatric patients with type 1 diabetes using insulin pump therapy: impact of glycemic index and prandial bolus type. Diabetes Care. 2008;31(8):1491–5.
115. Ryan RL, King BR, Anderson DG, Attia JR, Collins CE, Smart CE. Influence of and optimal insulin therapy for a low-glycemic index meal in children with type 1 diabetes receiving intensive insulin therapy. Diabetes Care. 2008;31(8):1485–90.
116. Thomas DE, Elliott EJ, Baur L. Low glycaemic index or low glycaemic load diets for overweight and obesity. Cochrane Syst Rev Database. 2007(3):CD005105.
117. Kelishadi R, Zemel MB, Hashemipour M, Hosseini M, Mohammadifard N, Poursafa P. Can a dairy-rich diet be effective in long-term weight control of young children? J Am Coll Nutr. 2009;28(5):601–10.
118. Young PC, West SA, Ortiz K, Carlson J. A pilot study to determine the feasibility of the low glycemic index diet as a treatment for overweight children in primary care practice. Ambulatory Pediatr. 2004;4(1):28–33.
119. Ebbeling CB, Leidig MM, Sinclair KB, Hangen JP, Ludwig DS. A reduced-glycemic load diet in the treatment of adolescent obesity. Arch Pediatr Adolesc Med. 2003;157(8):773–9.
120. Goldbacher EM, Matthews KA. Are psychological characteristics related to risk of the metabolic syndrome? A review of the literature. Ann Behav Med. 2007;34(3):240–52.
121. Rolls BJ, Ello-Martin JA, Tohill BC. What can intervention studies tell us about the relationship between fruit and vegetable consumption and weight management? Nutr Rev. 2004;62(1):1–17.

Chapter 16
Pharmacological Therapies of Metabolic Syndrome

Adriana Carrillo-Iregui and Carley Gomez-Meade

Abstract Metabolic syndrome in children and adolescents correlates with increased cardiovascular risk in adulthood. This cardiometabolic risk may be modified by treatment of insulin resistance, obesity, and dyslipidemia. Lifestyle modification is the most effective treatment of metabolic syndrome. However, in children and adolescents who continue to have significant comorbidities despite intensive lifestyle treatment, pharmacological therapy may be added to lifestyle management. Metformin is approved for the treatment of type 2 diabetes and may lead to weight loss and improved insulin sensitivity in patients with metabolic syndrome. Orlistat is the only weight loss medication approved for the pediatric age group. In adults, bupropion, exenatide, and pramlintide in addition to others are currently under investigation for the treatment of obesity and may be available for children and adolescents in the future. Lipid-lowering medications targeting hypertriglyceridemia and low serum HDL in metabolic syndrome may be effective when lifestyle modification has failed. However, lipid-lowering agents in children and adolescents are not currently approved for the treatment of dyslipidemia in metabolic syndrome. The addition of drug therapy to lifestyle management in metabolic syndrome should be initiated and carefully monitored by medical team familiar with expected outcomes and possible side effects.

Keywords Obesity • Lipid • Metformin • Orlistat

A. Carrillo-Iregui, M.D.(✉)
Division of Pediatric Endocrinology, Department of Pediatrics,
Miller School of Medicine, University of Miami,
1601 NW 12th Avenue Suite 3044 A, Miami, FL, 33141, USA
e-mail: acarrillo@med.miami.edu

C. Gomez-Meade, D.O.
Division of Pediatric Endocrinology, Department of Pediatrics,
Jackson Memorial Hospital/Miller School of Medicine, University of Miami,
Miami, FL, USA

Introduction

Metabolic syndrome is a constellation of cardiometabolic risk factors characterized by central obesity, hypertension, insulin resistance with or without impaired fasting glucose, and an atherogenic lipid profile including elevated triglycerides with a low HDL. In children, metabolic syndrome is largely a complication of obesity. The prevalence among children and adolescents varies according to diagnostic criteria but appears to be related to severity of obesity, ethnicity, sex, and age. Using modified APT III and WHO criteria, up to 30% of adolescents who have BMI >95th percentile meet criteria for metabolic syndrome, but prevalence in pediatrics may be as high as 50% in severely obese patients [1, 2]. Overall prevalence of metabolic syndrome in the pediatric population is higher in males (6.1%) than females (2.1%) and higher in Mexican American (5.6%) and whites (4.8%) than in African American (2%) [1]. In children and adolescents, obesity is the main cause of insulin resistance which in turn increases risk for cardiovascular disease and type 2 diabetes mellitus. Insulin resistance is related to defects in insulin receptor signaling and results in hyperinsulinemia, abnormal glucose disposal, and increased endogenous glucose production. Insulin resistance is also associated with lipotoxicity through increase in ApoCIII that normally inhibits lipoprotein lipase, increase in VLDL production, and de novo synthesis of triglycerides. Insulin resistance causes hypertension in various ways such as increase in adrenergic activity, activation of renin-angiotensin system, increased levels of nonesterified fatty acids, and subsequent endothelial dysfunction. Hence, treatment of metabolic syndrome must be designed to decrease weight and increase insulin sensitivity as weight and insulin sensitivity are independent predictors of CVD and type 2 DM. Treatment of metabolic syndrome is a particular challenge. Lifestyle modification is mandatory but, in many cases, is not sufficient [3]. Pharmacotherapy for treatment of obesity and insulin resistance among children and adolescents is an area of debate and ongoing research. Specific pharmacotherapy must be tailored to address the complications of metabolic syndrome for children such as hyperlipidemia, impaired glucose tolerance, polycystic ovarian syndrome, and nonalcoholic fatty liver disease. In this chapter, we will review pharmacotherapy for insulin resistance, obesity, and dyslipidemia (Table 16.1).

Agents Targeting Insulin Resistance

Metformin

Metformin is a biguanide that has been available since 1995 for the treatment of type 2 diabetes in adults [4]. It is approved for treatment of type 2 diabetes in children over 10 years of age. However, metformin has not been approved as therapy for obesity, or for insulin resistance and prediabetes. Metformin lowers blood glucose

16 Pharmacological Therapies of Metabolic Syndrome

Table 16.1 Pharmacological agents for the treatment of metabolic syndrome

Agents targeting insulin resistance
Metformin
Rosiglitazone
Agents used for treatment of obesity
Orlistat
Sibutramine
Bupropion
Leptin
Exenatide
Albiglutide
Topiramate
Agents used for treatment of dyslipidemia
Fibric acid
Nicotinic acid
Omega-3 fatty acids
Statins
Bile acid sequestrants
Ezetimibe

by 25–30% through decreased hepatic glucose production, improved insulin sensitivity in skeletal muscle and adipose tissue, and increased peripheral glucose uptake. Metformin also decreases cardiovascular risk in patients with type 2 diabetes by decreasing plasma free fatty acids.

Mechanism of Action

The primary site of action of metformin is thought to be mitochondrial complex I [5]. Complex I is responsible for maintenance of the proton gradient of the mitochondria through ATP production (Fig. 16.1). Metformin inhibits complex I activity, resulting in increased AMP/ATP ratio. As a consequence, dephosphorylation of AMP-activated protein kinase (AMPK) is inhibited and AMPK activity is increased. Metformin may also activate AMPK by inhibition of AMP deaminase and indirectly by activation of LKB1, an upstream kinase mediating activation of AMPK. Metformin activates AMPK in hepatocytes, skeletal muscle, and adipose tissue. AMPK influences energy balance. Activation of AMPK normally occurs in states of energy deprivation or in accelerated energy consumption. Physiological stimuli of AMPK include exercise, glucose deprivation, hypoxia, and oxidative stress. Activated AMPK phosphorylates downstream substrates and thereby inhibits energy-consuming anabolic pathways and stimulates catabolic pathways.

Increased AMP/ATP ratio and AMPK activity both result in decreased hepatic gluconeogenesis. Changes in energy status are paralleled by decrease expression of genes for gluconeogenic proteins. As hepatic glucose synthesis is an anabolic process that requires ATP, diminished levels of ATP induce a shift to oxidation of fatty

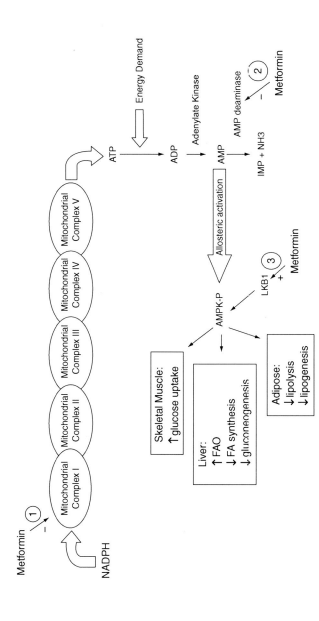

Fig. 16.1 Metformin has been shown to increase activation of AMPK. Possible mechanisms include: (1) inhibition of mitochondrial complex I decreases ATP production; (2) inhibition of AMP deaminase decreases AMP degradation; (3) activation of LKB1 activates AMPK

acids and suppression of fatty acid synthesis. The latter process lowers plasma fatty acids and triglycerides both acutely and in the long term. AMPK directly prevents activation of hormone-sensitive lipase in adipose tissue, limiting lipolysis [6, 7]. Various studies in vitro using cell lines also provide information of metformin action. Metformin-mediated AMPK stimulation increases GLUT-4 mRNA expression, GLUT-4 translocation to plasma membrane, and glucose uptake in adipose tissue [8]. In skeletal muscle, metformin stimulates glucose uptake by translocation of GLUT-4 glucose transporters to the cell surface independently of insulin [6]. In beta cell lines, metformin induced activation of AMPK and attenuated insulin secretion in response to glucose. Metformin may prevent atherosclerotic plaque formation through decreased intracellular lipid accumulation in macrophages. In bovine aortic endothelial cells, metformin stimulated nitric oxide in an AMPK-dependent manner (see Fig. 16.1). Metformin is also transported by organic cation transporter 1 (OCT-1) into intestinal cells and hepatocytes. Polymorphisms in OCT-1 may affect metformin effect on gluconeogenesis and lactic acidosis.

Efficacy of Therapy

Studies indicated in adults that metformin is an effective therapy for the treatment of metabolic syndrome and for the reduction of diabetes. The Diabetes Prevention Trial which included 3,234 patients indicated a 2.5% reduction in body weight versus placebo over a 2.8-year period and 31% reduction in the incidence of diabetes when patients with prediabetes were treated. The reduction in diabetes was most prevalent among patients <45 years of age and with a BMI> 35 kg/m^2. However, metformin is less effective than lifestyle intervention alone, the latter resulting in a 58% reduction in the incidence of diabetes. Metformin also decreased the incidence of new onset metabolic syndrome by 17% and reversed metabolic syndrome in 23% [9, 10].

In pediatric subjects as young as 6 years of age, several randomized controlled trials (RCTs) indicated efficacy of metformin in modest weight reduction. In these studies, there was also a decrease in fasting glucose and HOMA-IR [11–19] (Table 16.2). Metformin was studied recently in 100 children 6–12 years old who had insulin resistance and BMI≥95th percentile. The placebo-controlled phase lasted for 6 months and indicated significantly decreased BMI (−1.09 kg/m^2, CI −1.87 to 0.31, $P = 0.006$) and body weight (3.38 kg, CI −5.2 to −1.57, $P<0.001$) in the metformin-treated group. Curiously, in the next 6 months, open-label phase indicated decreased BMI Z score in the same placebo group, but not in the metformin-treated group. Although HOMA-IR improved more in the metformin-treated group, there was no significant difference on the first-phase insulin secretion or in the clamp insulin sensitivity. Side effects occurred in about 17% of the subjects and were dose-related. Younger children (8.8±1.9 year) received less the full dose of metformin (2,000 mg) due to side effects [19].

A multicenter, double-blind study investigated obese adolescents aged 13–18 years treated with metformin extended release medication for 12 months and then monitored for almost a year afterward. The study indicated a decrease in BMI of

Table 16.2 Randomized control trials of metformin in pediatric ages

Type of study	Patient age (years)	Intervention (number of patients)	Duration of intervention	BMI (kg/m^2)	Fasting insulin (μU/mL)	HOMA-IR	Triglycerides (mg/dL)	HDL (mg/dL)
Randomized, double-blind, placebo-controlled [19]	6–12	Metformin 1,000 mg twice daily (53) vs. placebo (47)	6 months	−0.78 vs. 0.32 ($P = .006$)	3.24 vs. 9.0 ($P = 0.02$)	0.68 vs. 2.23 ($P = 0.006$)	7.7 vs. 3.79 ($P = 0.72$)	0.12 vs. −0.27 ($P = 0.79$)
Randomized, double-blind, placebo-controlled [18]	13–18	Metformin XR 2,000 mg once daily (39) vs. placebo (38)	48 weeks	−0.9 vs. 0.2 ($P = 0.03$)		−0.1 vs. −0.8 ($P = 0.48$)	−2 vs. 1 ($P = 0.8$)	1 vs. 0 ($P = 0.38$)
Randomized, double-blind, placebo-controlled [17]	Average 13.8	Metformin 500 mg twice daily (36) vs. placebo (34)	6 months	0.07 vs. −0.31	−4.5 vs. −5.4	−0.45 vs. −1		
Randomized, controlled [12]	10–16	Metformin 1,500 mg daily and lifestyle (11) vs. lifestyle alone (14)	6 months	−1.8 vs. 0.5 ($P = 0.005$)	−3.6 vs. −9.5 (NS)	−0.5 vs. 2.53 (NS)	−0.52 vs. 0.2 ($P<0.05$)	0.09 vs. 0.12 (NS)
Randomized, double-blind, placebo-controlled [11]	9–17	Metformin 500 mg twice daily (90) vs. placebo (30)	6 months	−2.0 vs. 0.65 ($P < 0.01$)	−14.6 vs. −4 ($P = 0.003$)	−3.74 vs. −1.05 ($P = 0.008$)	Metformin effect ($P = 0.02$)	Metformin effect ($P = 0.044$)
Randomized, double-blind, placebo-controlled [20]	13–18	Metformin 1,500 mg daily (15) vs. placebo (13)	4 months	−0.9 vs. 1.1 ($P = 0.02$)	1.0 vs. 1.2 ($P = 0.4$)	1.0 vs. 1.2 ($P = 0.4$)	1.2 vs. 1.0 ($P = 0.3$)	−3.3 vs. −.01 ($P = 0.2$)

Study design	Age (year)	Treatment (n)	Duration	BMI	HOMA-IR	Fasting glucose	Fasting insulin	Triglycerides
Randomized, double-blind, placebo-controlled [15]	12–19	Metformin 850 mg twice daily (48) vs. placebo (16)	6 months	−0.16 vs. 0.63 ($P = 0.11$)	NS	NS		
Randomized, double-blind, placebo-crossover [16]	9–18	Metformin 1,000 mg twice daily vs. placebo (28)	6 months	Metformin effect −1.26 ($P = 0.002$)	Metformin effect −2.2 ($P = 0.011$)			
Randomized, double-blind, placebo-controlled [13]	12–19	Metformin 500 mg twice daily (14) vs. placebo (15)	6 months	−0.5 vs. 0.9 ($P < 0.02$)	−12.3 vs. −1.6 ($P < 0.9$)	($P < 0.01$)	−1.5 vs. −13.8 (NS)	0.8 vs. −1.4 (NS)
Randomized, double-blind, placebo-controlled [14]	15–16	Metformin 850 mg twice daily (12) vs. placebo (12)	2 months	Weight change −6.1 vs. −3.2 kg ($P < 0.01$)	−21 vs. 11 ($P < 0.05$)			−39 vs. −13 ($P < 0.05$)

NS not significant

0.9 ± 0.5 kg/m² in the metformin group compared to increase of 0.2 ± 0.5 kg/m² in the control group. However, the lowering effect in BMI among the metformin group disappeared at 12–24 weeks after discontinuation of treatment. No significant changes were found in HOMA-IR, triglycerides, HDL, or DXA fat mass, although this may have been related to an inadequate number of subjects studied [18]. Another study of metformin included lifestyle change in both the metformin-treated and control groups. BMI decreased by 1.8 kg/m², LDL and triglycerides decreased, and HDL increased in the metformin-treated group [12]. In a small, randomized, controlled study, the metformin-treated group had reduction in subcutaneous fat and decrease in leptin levels, but no change in visceral fat measured by MRI [20]. A meta-analysis of five RCTs (three from USA, one from Australia, and one from Turkey) with a total of 365 obese hyperinsulinemic participants ages 6–18 years was performed and supported benefit of metformin in reducing BMI by a mean of 1.42 mg/kg and HOMA-IR by 2 [21]. Effect on total cholesterol was small (0.26 SD), and it is unclear if the effect was related to weight loss or metformin. In summary, metformin reduces BMI and HOMA-IR and has some effect on improving triglycerides and HDL levels; however, the effect of metformin in preventing diabetes is still not certain.

Indications

Metformin should be considered as an option in children and adolescents with a BMI of at least 35 kg/m² and with increased risk of metabolic syndrome or diabetes, such risk having a family history of a first-degree relative with diabetes, elevated triglycerides, reduced HDL, hypertension, or a HgA1c greater than 6.0% [22]. The recommended starting dose is 500 mg daily with food; dose may be increased over several weeks by 500 mg increments up to a maximum dose of 2 g per day in two divided doses. Close monitoring for side effects and precautionary measure to prevent lactic acidosis are important in the therapy. Long-term effectiveness and safety studies are lacking.

Complications of Therapy and Contraindications

In clinical trials, side effects occur in up to 50% of patients treated with metformin [4]. Most common side effects were nausea and abdominal cramping which usually improved or resolved with continued treatment. Taking metformin with meals and slowly titrating dose over several weeks minimized gastrointestinal side effects. If side effects occur, decreasing the dose and waiting 1–2 weeks before increasing dose minimizes recurrent side effects. Metformin is associated with lactic acidosis. In vitro studies indicate that metformin may predispose to lactic acidosis through its inhibition of gluconeogenesis in the liver by inhibiting hepatic lactate uptake. Hence, metformin is contraindicated in renal disease, liver disease, acidosis, and dehydration which may increase patients' risk of lactic acidosis. It should be discontinued for surgical procedures or procedures requiring intravenous contrast. Metformin can be restarted after 48 h and when normal renal function is established. These precautions help avoid lactic acidosis in patients taking metformin. Monitoring and adjusting treatment is essential to managing side effects associated with metformin therapy.

Rosiglitazone

Rosiglitazone is a thiazolidinedione agent and a potent agonist for the peroxisome proliferator-activated receptor (PPAR-γ) which regulates the transcription of genes involved in adipogenesis and glucose metabolism. In adipose tissue, it increases expression of the glucose transporter GLUT-4 and improves glucose utilization in skeletal muscle and the liver. Plasma free fatty acid concentrations decrease, and changes in both free fatty acids and adipocytokines promote insulin sensitivity. In addition, the medication has a protective effect on pancreatic beta cell function and surveillance. Nonetheless, there are few randomized studies in adults evaluating efficacy in preventing diabetes. The DREAM (Diabetes Reduction Assessment with Ramipril and Rosiglitazone Medication) included 5,269 individuals with impaired fasting glucose or impaired glucose tolerance test. After 3-year follow-up, there was a 62% reduction in the incidence of diabetes in the treated group [23]. In a small randomized control study in obese children and adolescents with IFG and/or IGT receiving rosiglitazone or placebo for 4 months, almost 60% in the rosiglitazone group converted from IGT to NGT compared to 44% in the placebo. Peripheral insulin sensitivity increased along with levels of HMW-adiponectin. However, there was weight gain in the study group compared to placebo, although not significant [24]. Rosiglitazone is not yet approved for children.

Management of Obesity

Pharmacotherapy for obesity is only used for children and adolescents who have had intensive lifestyle modification but who continue to have severe obesity and comorbidities [3]. The American Academy of Pediatrics recommends pharmacological intervention when weight loss has not been achieved after 3 or 6 months of a formal weight loss program including dietary, lifestyle, and behavior modifications. The Endocrine Society recommends limiting pharmacological treatment to children with a BMI greater than the 95th percentile for age or children with severe comorbid conditions with a BMI greater than the 85th percentile. Pharmacological intervention should always be used in conjunction with continuing lifestyle modification and by a physician who is experienced in the use of antiobesity medications. Choice of treatment should be individualized. There should also be discussion of realistic expectations for outcome and risk for regaining weight after medications are discontinued. Close follow-up and monitoring of therapy must take into account potential side effects and treatment goals. If side effects occur or desired effects are not attained, discontinuation of medication must be considered.

Orlistat

Orlistat is the only FDA-approved medication for the treatment of obesity in the pediatric age group. It was approved by the FDA in 1998 for use in adults, and in 2003 for the use in children and adolescents over 12 years of age [9, 25].

Mechanism of Action

Orlistat, also known as tetrahydrolipstatin, irreversibly inhibits pancreatic and gastric lipases in the lumen of the gastrointestinal tract [26]. In healthy adults, 5% of fat in diet is excreted in feces [27]. In orlistat-treated individuals, intestinal absorption of dietary triglycerides decreases by up to 30% in a dose-dependent manner. However, orlistat does not inhibit other digestive enzymes, such as amylase or trypsin. Furthermore, its effect is limited to the gastrointestinal wall, hence there is no systemic activity. Ninety-seven percent of the medication is excreted in the stool (83% unchanged), complete excretion occurring over 3–5 days [26, 27].

Efficacy of Therapy

Only a few studies have determined safety and efficacy of orlistat in children and adolescents. The largest study to date was a multicentered, 54-week, randomized, double-blind study of 539 obese adolescents, 12–16 years of age [25]. This study used standard treatment doses of 120 mg orally three times per day with meals. Both the treated and placebo groups had a hypocaloric diet as well as exercise and behavioral therapy. After 52 weeks of treatment, the orlistat group had a decrease in BMI of 0.55 kg/m^2 from baseline, and the placebo group had an increase by 0.31 kg/m^2 from baseline. Smaller studies also indicated improvement in BMI over 3–15 months in children as young as 8 years old [28–30]. Meta-analysis of all randomized controlled trials involving obese adolescents showed a 0.76 kg/m^2 decrease in BMI after 6 months of orlistat [21]. However, Chanoine et al. found no differences in serum levels of lipids, and glucose or in the 2-h insulin levels in placebo and orlistat treatment groups over 1 year [25]. Orlistat does not affect long-term eating habits in adults treated with orlistat for 3 years.

Recommended Dose

Orlistat is recommended in combination with a hypocaloric diet with <30% of calories from fat. It should be taken during or up to 1 h after meals three times per day [26]. Orlistat 120 mg tablets are available by prescription, and 60-mg tablets are available over the counter. Efficacy is demonstrated at doses of 120 mg orally three times per day with meals.

Complications of Therapy and Contraindications

Side effects are typically related to increased fecal fat excretion. Studies in the adolescent population had a dropout rate of 2–30% due to gastrointestinal side effects [25, 30]. Common gastrointestinal effects include oily spotting (26.6%), flatus with discharge (23.9%), fecal urgency (22.1%), and fatty or oily stools (20%) [27]. Other gastrointestinal effects include abdominal pain, liquid stools, soft stools, flatulence without discharge, increased defecation, and fecal incontinence [26]. In a 3-month tolerability trial in adolescents, most gastrointestinal side effects were mild and resolved in the first 6 weeks of treatment [28]. Other potential side effects include altered gastrointestinal motility, vitamin absorption, and renal stone formation. With respect to gastrointestinal motility, orlistat initially accelerates gastric emptying after mixed meal tests. However, over the long term, gastric emptying is unchanged. In the short term, orlistat decreased cholecystokinin release, but results of long-term studies are inconsistent [31]. Data regarding GLP-1 and PYY are also inconsistent [31, 32]. Effects of orlistat on gastrointestinal hormones are still under investigation.

The absorption of vitamins D, E, and beta-carotene has been affected in studies of adults [26]. Among adolescents treated with orlistat, vitamin D levels decreased from baseline but were not significantly lower than placebo group after 3 months of therapy [29, 33]. No significant changes were seen in vitamins A, E, and K over 3 months in adolescents [28]. However, in light of a potential decrease in absorption of fat-soluble vitamins, careful monitoring of their blood levels during treatment is recommended [26]. Daily vitamin supplements should be taken and administered at least 2 h before or 2 h after taking orlistat to ensure their adequate absorption. Absorption of oxalate is increased during orlistat treatment, and there is increased risk of renal oxalate stone formation. Consequently orlistat should be used cautiously in patients with cholestasis, malabsorption syndromes, hyperoxaluria, and renal disease.

Growth and sexual maturation were not affected by orlistat treatment in adolescents during 1 year of treatment [25]. During 12 weeks of treatment in a study of 11 prepubertal obese children, no effect on growth was seen [29]. Although of limited duration, these studies suggest that the weight loss in obese children treated with orlistat does not negatively impact growth and pubertal development.

Sibutramine

Sibutramine was approved by the FDA for treatment of obesity in adolescents older than 16 years in 1997 but withdrawn from all markets in October 2010 because of an increased risk of nonfatal cardiovascular events, including stroke and myocardial infarction [34]. Nonetheless, we will review information from studies on mechanism of action and use of the drug.

Mechanism of Action

Sibutramine is a nonselective inhibitor of serotonin and norepinephrine reuptake. It promotes satiety after eating and increases energy expenditure.

Efficacy of Therapy

Patients treated with sibutramine (10–15 mg) and behavioral therapy intervention had a mean reduction of 2.2 kg/m^2 in BMI and 6-cm decrease in waist circumference when compared to placebo group receiving only behavioral therapy. However, there was no significant increase in HDL [35]. In another study of 498 adolescents aged 12–16 years treated with sibutramine (10 mg-day for 12 months), mean BMI decreased (2.9 kg/m^2) compared to placebo (0.3 kg/m^2), and 48% achieved a BMI loss of 10% [36]. In a Brazilian randomized control study of 60 adolescents using sibutramine (10 mg a day for 6 months), weight loss was of 10.3 ± 6.6 kg compared to 2.4 ± 2.5 kg in the placebo group. At least 50% of treated patients reduced weight by 10% in comparison to those in the placebo group [37]. In a controlled trial of 46 Mexican adolescents, sibutramine (10 mg for 6 months) resulted in weight loss of 7.3 kg compared to 4.3 kg, and waist circumference decreased by 8 cm compared to 3.8 cm in the placebo group. In summary, all of the controlled trials supported efficacy in adolescents including ethnic minorities. A meta-analysis looking at four randomized controlled trials with a total sample of 686 adolescents, three studies lasting 6 months and one 12 months, supported the efficacy of sibutramine [35].

Complications of Therapy

A number of studies in adults including those who had diabetes or who were treated for hypertension reported an increase of 1–3 mmHg in blood pressure. Nonetheless, another study with 6,360 patients reported a significant decrease in blood pressure [34]. The Sibutramine Cardiovascular Outcome Trial was the largest and longest adult study including almost 10,000 adults older than 55 years with cardiovascular disease and/or type 2 diabetes mellitus with at least one cardiovascular risk factor. The patients were followed for a mean of 3.4 years. All patients received sibutramine for the first 6 weeks and after were randomized to sibutramine 10 mg or placebo. Mean weight loss after 6 weeks was −2.7 kg with further weight loss of −1.7 kg in the group treated compared to weight gain of 0.7 kg in the placebo. Although this study indicated a 16% increased risk of cardiovascular events in the treated group (11.4% incidence in the sibutramine group versus 10% in the placebo), there was no difference on risk of cardiovascular death. However, weight loss did not decrease incidence of adverse cardiovascular disease, and sibutramine was withdrawn from the market. Cardiovascular side effects in adolescents were reported to be less than in adults. In the study by Daniels et al. in adolescents treated with sibutramine (10 mg for 12 months), adverse events were similar in the treated and in the placebo groups. In particular, there was no significant difference in diastolic blood pressure and systolic blood pressure, except for tachycardia which was 15% more common in the treatment group. It has been proposed that adolescents may have lower risk of cardiovascular side effects because greater weight reduction may mitigate the reported cardiovascular side effects of sibutramine or possibly that a different autonomic response in adolescents will lower risk of adverse cardiovascular events specifically due to differences in parasympathetic versus sympathetic systems [36]. However, sibutramine is no longer available for the treatment of pediatric or adult obesity.

Bupropion

Bupropion is an atypical antidepressant affecting norepinephrine and dopamine reuptake. It is FDA-approved for nicotine dependence, depression, and seasonal affective disorder in adults. In the pediatric age group, it is used for treatment of depression and attention deficit disorder. Bupropion has also been evaluated for obesity due to its side effect of reduced appetite and weight loss. Long-term trials indicated a modest weight loss with a plateau effect after 24 weeks. Bupropion induces weight loss by increasing POMC in the anorexigenic pathway of the arcuate nucleus. Because of its only modest effect on weight loss, bupropion is currently being evaluated for use in combination with other drugs such as naltrexone. Although the opioid antagonist naltrexone does not cause significant weight loss alone, the combination naltrexone and bupropion works synergistically to increase POMC and produce greater weight loss than with bupropion alone. With respect to bupropion, reported side effects include gastrointestinal disturbances, rash, and headache. Increased risk of seizure has also been reported. In 2004, the FDA placed a black box warning concerning potential risk of suicide with antidepressant use. This risk must be considered in the use of bupropion in the management of obesity [38].

Leptin

Leptin is an adipokine secreted by adipose tissue in proportion to adipose stores. The primary action of leptin is regulating energy homeostasis in the hypothalamus. Leptin receptors are expressed in several isoforms in the brain and in peripheral tissues. Leptin regulates appetite by activating anorexogenic neuropeptides and inhibiting orexigenic neuropeptides.

Leptin treatment normalizes plasma triglycerides and increases HDL. Improvement of insulin levels and insulin sensitivity are evident as early as 1 week after initiation of treatment, normalizing insulin levels by 6 months [39]. Pubertal children with congenital leptin deficiency had spontaneous puberty with normal progression through pubertal stages during treatment. Height velocity and bone mineral content are normal prior to treatment and remained unchanged during treatment [40]. Leptin therapy is effective for the management of weight and other conditions associated with congenital leptin deficiency. Recombinant leptin is given as a daily subcutaneous injection [39]. It can be given in the evening to mimic the normal circadian rhythm of leptin. Dose is calculated to provide 10% of predicted normal leptin concentration, based on age, sex, and body composition. Neutralizing antibodies may transiently impair responsiveness to therapy which can be overcome by increasing dose of recombinant leptin [40].

Lifestyle-induced obesity is associated with elevated levels of leptin, indicative of leptin resistance. Despite high pharmacological doses of recombinant leptin, weight loss did not occur in adults with lifestyle-induced obesity. During diet-induced weight loss, leptin levels normally decline. Treatment with leptin to maintain pre-weight-loss leptin levels is associated with maintenance of weight reduction. Leptin is not indicated for the treatment of lifestyle-induced obesity.

Exenatide

Mechanism of Action

Exenatide is a synthetic glucagon-like peptide (GLP-1) receptor analog. Exenatide in otherwise normal individuals is an incretin hormone secreted from L-cells of the jejunum, ileum, and colon following nutrient ingestion [41]. Secretion is particularly increased by carbohydrate and fat consumption. GLP-1 stimulates pancreatic insulin secretion in a glucose-dependent manner, inhibits postprandial glucagon production, and slows gastric empting. Endogenous GLP-1 has a short half-life of 1–2 min due to degradation by dipeptidyl peptidase IV (DPP-IV). Weight loss due to decreased caloric intake is mediated by vagal nerve activation in the peripheral nervous system and centrally in the hypothalamus. GLP-1 likely mediates sensory information from the gastrointestinal tract to vagal afferents, leading to slowed gastric empting. GLP-1 receptors are expressed in several regions of the brain and specifically the arcuate nucleus. Central nervous system effects on food consumption appear to be mediated through GLP-1 receptors in the paraventricular nucleus. Exenatide is resistant to DPP-IV degradation derived. Its half-life is 6 h and can be administered twice daily as a subcutaneous injection. Exenatide improves beta cell proliferation and restores first- and second-phase insulin secretion, improving postprandial hyperglycemia in adults with type 2 diabetes. Metformin works synergistically with GLP-1 to promote weight loss. Metformin upregulates GLP-1 receptor expression and enhances GLP-1 secretion. In addition to improvements in postprandial glucose regulation, exenatide is effective at decreasing caloric consumption and weight in adults.

Indications

Exenatide is approved as adjunctive treatment in the management of adults with type 2 diabetes. Exenatide is not approved for the use in children and adolescents.

Efficacy

Studies of exenatide in metabolic syndrome are limited. A retrospective study of the use of exenatide in adults with metabolic syndrome indicated a significant reduction in body weight. Seventy-six percent of the patients who lost weight had a decrease in triglycerides and blood pressure [42]. Weight loss with exenatide is progressive and persistent for up to 2 years.

Complications of Therapy

The most common side effect of exenatide is nausea, although the risk of nausea does not correlate with degree of weight loss. A less common but serious side effect is hemorrhagic or necrotizing pancreatitis.

Other GLP-1-Related Medication

Albiglutide is also a GLP-1 receptor agonist that is resistant to DPP-IV degradation with a half-life of 5 days and that is currently in clinical trials. GLP-1 analogs such as liraglutide and taspoglutide are also currently being investigated. Liraglutide decreases appetite in obese patients with type 2 diabetes. However, 25% of patients do not lose weight with liraglutide. Liraglutide is available as a once daily injection.

Topiramate

Topiramate is an antiepileptic approved for use in children over 10 years of age. Topiramate is associated with reduced appetite and weight loss [43]. In children with epilepsy, topiramate reduces food intake and reduces BMI in 10–40% of those treated [3]. Meta-analysis of randomized controlled trials indicated an average weight loss of 5.34 kg compared with placebo [43]. Weight loss is dose dependent and continues after 28 weeks of therapy. Side effects include paresthesia and hypoesthesia, change in taste, and psychomotor impairment. Currently topiramate is not indicated for weight loss, and use should be limited to treatment of epilepsy.

Potential New Agents for Treatment of Obesity

Amylin Analogs: Pramlintide

Amylin is co-secreted with insulin from beta cells. Amylin decreases food intake, slows gastric empting, and reduces postprandial glucagon release. Pramlintide is an amylin analog that is given subcutaneously before meals to patients with type 1 and type 2 diabetes. It improves postprandial glucose excursion, reduces meal time insulin dose, and is associated with improvement in hemoglobin A_1c. In obese patients, pramlintide can induce weight loss by increased satiety and hence decreased caloric intake. It is also associated with a decreased selection of foods in high-fat and high-sucrose content. Anorexic effects of pramlintide appear to be secondary to increased POMC expression in the arcuate nucleus. There is also indirect suppression of orexigenic genes in the hypothalamus. Approximately 50% of subjects achieved a 5% reduction in body weight after 4 months of treatment. Weight loss was maintained over a 12-month period [44]. Meta-analysis indicated a 2.27-kg weight loss using a dose of 120 mcg/dose [45]. Combination studies with amylin and leptin indicated a synergistic effect on weight loss in obese adults [46]. Twenty-four weeks of pramlintide and leptin treatment resulted in a 13% weight loss. Nausea is the most common side effect of pramlintide, but it is usually mild to moderate and improves with continued treatment. Pramlintide is not independently associated with hypoglycemia. However, patients taking both pramlintide and insulin are at greater risk for hypoglycemia. The insulin dose should be decreased by 50% when both medications are used, and glucose should be monitored carefully [45]. Pramlintide is currently only indicated for adults with type 1 or type 2 diabetics. Pramlintide has not been studied in the pediatric population.

Agents Targeting Lipid Abnormalities

In metabolic syndrome, dyslipidemia is characterized by abnormally high levels of plasma triglycerides and by subnormal levels of high-density lipoprotein cholesterol (HDL) [47]. Many patients also have elevated serum levels of small, dense LDL particles. Over 40% of obese children have a lipid abnormality [48]. Although lipid-lowering medications have traditionally targeted LDL, this may not be relevant in the treatment of metabolic syndrome where the dyslipidemia is not primarily associated with abnormally high serum LDL. Indeed, the low HDL and elevated triglycerides characteristic of metabolic syndrome are independent risk factors for cardiovascular morbidity.

The uses of lipid-lowering medications in children have been approved by the FDA only for the treatment of heterozygous familial hypercholesteremia. Indications for treating elevated LDL in pediatrics have been defined [49]. Therapy should be considered in addition to lifestyle modification after lifestyle modification has failed and LDL is ≥190 or ≥160 with two or more risk factors. Risk factors include family history of hyperlipidemia or early cardiovascular disease, diabetes mellitus, hypertension, obesity, end-stage renal disease, and smoking.

Only off-label use of lipid-lowering agents is available for the specific treatment of hypertriglyceridemia and low serum HDL of metabolic syndrome. Currently the most appropriate drug therapies for treating hypertriglyceridemia and low HDL are fibric acids and niacin. There are insufficient data to make specific recommendations for the treatment of low HDL and hypertriglyceridemia. Treatment should begin before triglycerides exceed 500 mg/dL due to increased risk of acute pancreatitis. Treatment can be started if triglycerides are persistently above 350 mg/dL or a random level greater than 700 mg/dL [50]. After acute coronary syndrome, maintenance of triglyceride levels below 150 mg/dL independently reduced risk of recurrent events [51]. Lipid-lowering medication should be started at the lowest dose and monitored for side effects. Treatment goals should be made at the beginning of therapy and treatment adjusted appropriately.

Fibric Acids

Fibric acids gemfibrozil and fenofibrate increase activity of hormone-activated nuclear receptor peroxisome proliferator-activated receptor-α (PPAR-α) (Fig. 16.2) [47]. Activation of PPAR-α stimulates oxidation of free fatty acids in the liver and decreases triglyceride synthesis by 30–50%. Fibrates also increase the expression of ApoAI and ApoAII and can increase HDL by 10–15%. Side effects include gastrointestinal symptoms such as abdominal pain, nausea, vomiting and diarrhea, and cholelithiasis. There is also increased risk of myopathy if used in conjunction with statins. Fibrate therapy in adults is associated with a significant reduction in cardiovascular events. The risk reduction for use of fibrates in children is unknown.

Nicotinic Acid

Niacin inhibits lipolysis in adipose tissue and thereby decreases hepatic production of very-low-density lipoprotein (Fig. 16.2) [47]. However, niacin is also an effective agent for increasing HDL and lowering both triglycerides and LDL. Side effects in children include flushing, impaired glucose tolerance, liver dysfunction, hyperuricemia, and myopathy [49]. Although flushing can be prevented in adults if niacin is taken with aspirin, aspirin use is contraindicated in children due to risk for Reye's syndrome.

Omega-3 Fatty Acids

Eicosapentaenoic and docosahexaenoic are both omega-3 fatty acids and have been used to lower triglyceride levels in adults (Fig. 16.2) [47]. Treatment is generally started at triglyceride levels between 180 and 450 mg/dL [52]. Fish oils contain

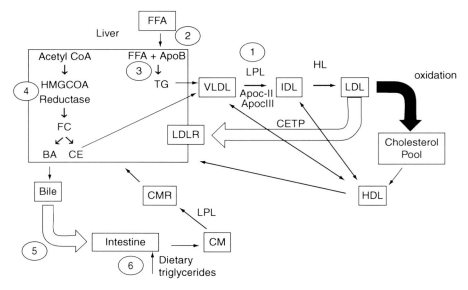

Fig. 16.2 Site of action of lipid-lowering medications. (1) Fibric acids, (2) nicotinic acid, (3) omega-3 fatty acids, (4) statins, (5) bile acid sequestrants, (6) ezetimibe. Free cholesterol (FC), bile acids (BA), free fatty acids (FFA), triglycerides (TG), very-low-density lipoprotein (VLDL), lipoprotein lipase (LPL), intermediate-density lipoprotein (IDL), hepatic lipase (HL), low-density lipoprotein (LDL), high-density lipoprotein (HDL), cholesterol ester transfer protein (CETP), LDL receptor (LDLR), chylomicron (CM), chylomicron remnant (CMR)

omega-3 fatty acids and can decrease triglycerides by up to 50% [53]. Omega-3 fatty acids decrease rate of growth of atherosclerotic plaques and reduce inflammation in adults. The standard adult dose is 4 g daily; this can be given once a day or divided twice daily with meals. It is available in 1-g tablets and liquid preparation. Currently there are no standard dosage recommendations for children and adolescents. Caution is needed in the treatment of subjects with markedly elevated triglycerides as high doses of omega-3 fatty acids may cause marked elevation in LDL cholesterol.

Statins

Statins inhibit 3-hydroxy-3-methyl-glutaryl-coenzyme A reductase, the rate-limiting step in cholesterol synthesis (Fig. 16.2) [47]. The decrease in cholesterol stimulates upregulation of LDL receptors and increases clearance of LDL. Statin use may result in a 20–65% reduction in serum LDL concentrations. Statins reduce triglycerides by 10–30% and increase HDL by 5–15%. Some of the statins have been approved for the treatment of familial hypercholesterolemia by the FDA for children as young as 8 years of age. Studies in children have evaluated statin use among individuals with heterozygous familial hypercholesterolemia. The longest study evaluating safety and efficacy of children is 2 years long [49]. As such, there is insufficient information regarding statin effect of growth and pubertal development in children. It is recommended to delay statin therapy until after Tanner stage II in male and after menarche in females. However, this may not always be possible. Therapy should begin at the lowest dose. If target LDL is not achieved by 4 weeks, the dose may be doubled and lipid evaluation be repeated after 4 weeks. Maximum dose has not been established in the pediatric population [53]. Creatinine kinase and liver enzymes should be monitored at baseline, 4 weeks, and then every 3–6 months after starting therapy. Growth and pubertal development should also be evaluated every 3–6 months. Patients and families should be counseled on potential side effects including myopathy and hepatic dysfunction and the potential of teratogenicity in pregnancy. Medication should be discontinued if CK reaches levels ten times the upper limit of normal or if liver enzymes rise above three times the upper limit of normal [49]. If side effects occur, drug should be discontinued and labs repeated in 2 weeks.

Bile Acid Sequestrants

Bile acid sequestrants prevent reabsorption of intestinal bile acids and as a consequence reduce hepatic cholesterol, reduce intracellular cholesterol concentrations, and increase LDL receptors (Fig. 16.2) [49]. Bile acid sequestrants effectively decrease LDL by 17%. Decreased intestinal fat absorption can cause constipation, bloating, and flatulence and has the potential to decrease absorption of fat-soluble vitamins. Newer bile acid sequestrants, such as colesevelam, have improved compliance due to less gastrointestinal side effects [49].

Ezetimibe

Ezetimibe inhibits intestinal cholesterol absorption at the small intestine brush border through the Niemann-Pick C1-Like 1 protein (Fig. 16.2) [49, 54]. It inhibits dietary cholesterol, plant sterols, and intestinal cholesterol reabsorption through bile [50]. It decreases LDL by 20% and in adults is used as adjunctive therapy with other lipid-lowering medications when monotherapy fails to reduce LDL to target range. It does not inhibit triglyceride absorption and does not interfere with the absorption of fat-soluble vitamins [49]. Ezetimibe appears to be safe and well tolerated in adults [50]. However, studies have yet to indicate a significant decrease in cardiovascular risk [49]. Studies in children are limited, but growth and pubertal development do not appear to be affected. Ezetimibe is FDA-approved for children ≥10 years of age with homozygous familial hyperlipidemia and sitosterolemia [54].

Pioglitazone

Pioglitazone is a PPAR-γ agonist primarily used for the treatment of adults with type 2 diabetes. It also decreases serum triglyceride concentrations through increased VLDL clearance secondary to increased lipoprotein lipase and reduction in ApoCIII production [47]. In adults with type 2 diabetes, pioglitazone has been demonstrated to improve left ventricular diastolic function and delay atheroma progression [55, 56]. Pioglitazone is not FDA-approved for the treatment of hypertriglyceridemia in adults or children. Currently studies in adolescents are directed toward the treatment of insulin resistance and polycystic ovarian syndrome.

Conclusion

Metabolic syndrome is prevalent in obese children and adolescents, and it correlates with cardiovascular disease and metabolic abnormalities in adulthood. Incidence of cardiovascular disease and type 2 diabetes mellitus is of great concern given the epidemic of pediatric obesity. Lifestyle and behavioral modifications are the most effective treatments but are not always sufficient. The use of metformin does not prevent the onset of type 2 diabetes mellitus; however, it does improve BMI and insulin sensitivity and might be considered in cases of severe insulin resistance. Further studies on efficacy and safety of metformin and other insulin sensitizers are needed in the pediatric population. Pharmacologic intervention for dyslipidemias may be indicated in specific situations.

References

1. Cook S, et al. Metabolic Syndrome rates in United States adolescents, from the National Health and Nutrition Examination Survey 1999–2002. J Pediatr. 2008;152:165–70.
2. Weiss R, et al. Obesity and the metabolic syndrome in children and adolescents. N Engl J Med. 2004;350(23):2362–74.
3. August G, et al. Prevention and treatment of pediatric obesity: an Endocrine Society clinical practice guideline based on expert opinion. J Clin Endocrinol Metab. 2008;93:4576–99.
4. Hundal RS, Inzucchi SE. Metformin new understanding, new uses. Drugs. 2003;63(18):1879–94.
5. Miller RA, Birnbaum MJ. An energetic tale of AMPK-independent effects of metformin. J Clin Invest. 2010;120(7):2267–70.
6. Boyle JG, Salt IP, McKay FA. Metformin action on MAP-activated protein kinase: a translational research approach to understanding a potential new therapeutic target. Diabet Med. 2010;27:1097–106.
7. Hardie DG. Role of AMP-activated kinase in the metabolic syndrome and in heart disease. FEBS Lett. 2008;582:81–9.
8. Grisouard J, et al. Mechanisms of metformin action on glucose transport and metabolism in human adipocytes. Biochem Pharmacol. 2010;80(11):1736–45.
9. Glandt M, Raz I. Present and future: pharmacologic treatment of obesity. J Obes. 2011;636181 [Epub 2011, Feb 8].

10. Sullivan SD, Ratner RE. Should the metabolic syndrome patient with prediabetes be offered pharmacotherapy? Curr Diab Rep. 2011;11(2):91–8.
11. Atabek ME, Pirgon P. Use of metformin in obese adolescents with hyperinsulinemia: a 6-month, randomized, double-blind, placebo-controlled clinical trial. J Pediatr Endocrinol Metab. 2008;21(4):339–48.
12. Clarson CL, et al. Metformin in combination with structured lifestyle intervention improved body mass index in obese adolescents, but did not improve insulin resistance. Endocrine. 2009;36(1):141–6.
13. Freemark M, Bursey D. The effects of metformin on body mass index and glucose tolerance in obese adolescents with fasting hyperinsulinemia and a family history of type 2 diabetes. Pediatrics. 2001;107(4):E55.
14. Kay JP, et al. Beneficial effects of metformin in normoglycemic morbidly obese adolescents. Metabolism. 2001;50(12):1457–61.
15. Love-Osborne K, Sheeder J, Zeitler P. Addition of metformin to a lifestyle modification program in adolescent with insulin resistance. J Pediatr. 2008;152(6):817–22.
16. Srinivasan S, et al. Randomized, controlled trial of metformin for obesity and insulin resistance in children and adolescents: improvement in body composition and fasting insulin. J Clin Endocrinol Metab. 2006;91:2080–6.
17. Wiegand S, et al. Metformin and placebo therapy both improve weight management and fasting insulin in obese insulin-resistant adolescents: a prospective, placebo-controlled, randomized study. Eur J Endocrinol. 2010;163(4):585–92.
18. Wilson DM, et al. Metformin extended release treatment of adolescent obesity. Arch Pediatr Adolesc Med. 2010;164(2):116–23.
19. Yanovski JA, et al. Effects of metformin on body weight and body composition in obese insulin-resistant children: a randomized clinical trial. Diabetes. 2011;60(2):477–85.
20. Burgert TS, et al. Short-term metabolic and cardiovascular effects of metformin in markedly obese adolescents with normal glucose tolerance. Pediatr Diabetes. 2008;9(6):567–76.
21. Park MH, et al. Metformin for obesity in children and adolescents: a systemic review. Diabetes Care. 2009;32(9):1743–5.
22. Aroda VR, Ratner R. Approach to the patient with prediabetes. J Clin Endcrinol Metab. 2008;93:3259–65.
23. Gerstein HC, et al. Effect of rosiglitazone on the frequency of diabetes in patients with impaired glucose tolerance or impaired fasting glucose: a randomized controlled trial. DREAM (Diabetes REduction Assessment with ramipril and rosiglitazone Medication) Trial Investigators. Lancet. 2006;368(9541):1096–105.
24. Cali AM, et al. Rosiglitazone improves glucose metabolism in obese adolescents with impaired glucose tolerance: a pilot study. Obesity. 2011;19(1):94–9.
25. Chanoine J, et al. Effect of orlistat on weight and body composition in obese adolescents a randomized controlled trial. JAMA. 2005;293(23):2873–83.
26. Heck A, Yanovski J, Calis K. Orlistat, a new lipase inhibitor for the management of obesity. Pharmacotherapy. 2000;3:270–9.
27. Wilding J. In: Wilding J, editor. Pharmacotherapy of obesity. Switzerland: Birkhauser Verlag; 2008.
28. McDuffie J, et al. Three-month tolerability of orlistat in adolescents with obesity-related comorbid conditions. Obes Res. 2002;10(7):642–50.
29. Norgren S, et al. Orlistat treatment in obese prepubertal children: a pilot study. Acta Paediatr. 2003;92:666–70.
30. Ozkan B, et al. Addition of orlistat to conventional treatment in adolescents with severe obesity. Eur J Pediatr. 2004;163:738–41.
31. Ellrichmann M, et al. Orlistat inhibition of intestinal lipase acutely increases appetite and attenuates postprandial glucagon-like peptide-1-(7–36)-Amide-1, cholecystokinin, and peptide YY concentrations. Endocrinol Metab. 2008;93:3995–8.
32. Sahin M, et al. The effect of single-dose orlistat on postprandial serum glucose, insulin and glucagon-like peptide 1 levels in nondiabetic obese patients. Clin Endocrinol. 2007;67(3):346–50.
33. Maahs D, et al. Randomized, double-blind, placebo-controlled trial of orlistat for weight loss in adolescents. Endocr Pract. 2006;12(1):18–28.

34. Scholze J. Sibutramine in clinical practice - a PMS-study with positive effects on blood pressure and metabolic parameters. Dtsch Med Wochenschr. 2002;127(12):606–10.
35. Viner RM, et al. Efficacy and safety of anti-obesity drugs in children and adolescents: systematic review and meta-analysis. Obes Rev. 2010:11(8):593–602.
36. Daniels SR, et al. Cardiovascular effects of sibutramine in the treatment of obese adolescents: results of a randomized, double-blind, placebo-controlled study. Pediatrics. 2007;120(1):147–57.
37. Godoy-Matos A, et al. Treatment of obese adolescents with sibutramine: a randomized, double-blind, controlled study. J Clin Endcrinol Metab. 2005;90(3):1460–5.
38. Daviss WB. Prescriptions into practice: bupropion - a guide to rational clinical use. J Child Adolesc Psychopharmacol. 2008;13(2):6–10.
39. Paz-Filho G, Wong M-L, Licinio J. Ten years of leptin replacement therapy. Obes Rev. 2011;12(5):e315–23.
40. Farooqui IS, et al. Beneficial effects of leptin on obesity, T cell hyporesponsiveness, and neuroendocrine/metabolic dysfunction of human congenital leptin deficiency. J Clin Invest. 2002;110(8):1093–103.
41. Bradley DP, Kulstad R, Schoeller DA. Exenatide and weight loss. Nutrition. 2010;26:243–9.
42. Bhushan R, et al. Exenatide use in the management of metabolic syndrome: a retrospective database study. Endocr Pract. 2008;14(8):993–9.
43. Kramer CK, et al. Efficacy and safety of topiramate on weight loss: a meta-analysis of randomized controlled trials. Obes Rev. 2011;12(501):e338–47.
44. Smith SR, et al. Sustained weight loss following 12-month pramlintide treatment as an adjunct to lifestyle intervention in obesity. Diabetes Care. 2008;31:1816–23.
45. Singh-Franco D, Perez A, Harrington C. The effect of pramlintide acetate on glycemic control and weight in patients with type 2 diabetes mellitus and in obese patients without diabetes: a systematic review and meta-analysis. Diabetes Obes Metab. 2011;13(2):169–80.
46. Chan JL, Roth JD, Weyer C. It takes two to tango: combined amylin/leptin agonism as a potential approach to obesity drug development. J Investig Med. 2009;57(7):777–83.
47. Raal FJ. Pathogenesis and management of the dyslipidemia of the metabolic syndrome. Metab Syndr Relat Disord. 2009;7(2):83–8.
48. Korsten-Reck U, et al. Frequency of secondary dyslipidemia in obese children. Vasc Health Risk Manag. 2008;4(5):1089–94.
49. O'Gorman CSM, O'Neil MB, Conwell LS. Considering statins for cholesterol-reduction in children if lifestyle and diet change do not improve their health: a review of the risks and benefits. Vasc Health Risk Manag. 2010;7:1–14.
50. McCrindle BW, et al. Drug therapy of high-risk lipid abnormalities in children and adolescents: a scientific statement from the American Heart Association Atherosclerosis, Hypertension, and Obesity in Youth Committee, Council of Cardiovascular Disease in the Young, with the Council on Cardiovascular Nursing. Circulation. 2007;115:14.
51. Miller M, et al. Impact of triglyceride levels beyond low-density lipoprotein cholesterol after acute coronary syndrome in the PROVE IT-TIMI 22 trial. J Am Coll Cardiol. 2008;51:724–30.
52. Manlhoit C, et al. Spectrum and management of hypertriglyceridemia among children in clinical practice. Pediatrics. 2009;123:458–65.
53. Brown WV, et al. The use of lipid-lowering drugs in children. J Clin Lipidol. 2010;4(6): 449–61.
54. Kwiterovich PO. Clinical and laboratory assessment of cardiovascular risk in children: guidelines for screening, evaluation, and treatment. J Clin Lipidol. 2008;2(4):248–66.
55. Nicholls S, et al. Lowering the triglyceride/high-density lipoprotein cholesterol ratio is associated with the beneficial impact of pioglitazone on progression of coronary atherosclerosis in diabetic patients: insights From the PERISCOPE (Pioglitazone Effect on Regression of Intravascular Sonographic Coronary Obstruction Prospective Evaluation) study. J Am Coll Cardiol. 2011;57(2):153–9.
56. Van der Meer R, et al. Pioglitazone improves cardiac function and alters myocardial substrate metabolism without affecting cardiac triglyceride accumulation and high-energy phosphate metabolism in patients with well-controlled type 2 diabetes mellitus. Circulation. 2009;119:2069–77.

Chapter 17
Bariatric Surgery to Reverse Metabolic Syndrome in Adolescents

Noor Kassira, Valerie Ann Marks, and Nestor de la Cruz-Muñoz

Abstract Adolescent obesity is a public health crisis with serious immediate and long-term health consequences. Currently, prevention is the best solution, but this may prove difficult in a world with a growing epidemic of childhood obesity. Bariatric surgery is the only proven intervention that provides sustained weight loss as well as improvement and resolution of obesity-related comorbidities. Prior to any surgical intervention, patients must go through a comprehensive evaluation phase. Available procedures are either restrictive or malabsorptive, with the most common being the Roux-en-Y gastric bypass and laparoscopic adjustable gastric banding. With the advent of laparoscopy, hospital stays have become short, but postoperative complications can still occur. The risks and benefits of operating on these obese adolescents with multiple comorbid conditions must be weighed and thoroughly discussed with patients and their families. According to published studies, there is a proven benefit to obese adolescents, even though most patients do not reach their ideal body weight. Almost all experience an improvement or resolution of comorbid conditions such as metabolic syndrome, diabetes, hyperlipidemia, hypertension, and sleep apnea. These results could have significant, long-lasting benefits on the adolescent patient. Given the young age of these patients, there should be an

N. Kassira, M.D.
Department of Surgery, Jackson Memorial Hospital, University of Miami,
Miami, FL, USA

V.A. Marks, B.A.
The DeWitt Daughtry Family Department of Surgery,
University of Miami Miller School of Medicine,
Miami, FL, USA

N. de la Cruz-Muñoz, M.D. (✉)
Division of Laparoendoscopic and Bariatric Surgery,
The DeWitt Daughtry Family Department of Surgery,
University of Miami Miller School of Medicine,
3650 NW 82nd Avenue, Suite 305, Miami, FL 33166, USA
e-mail: ndelacruz@med.miami.edu

emphasis on a multidisciplinary approach in their treatment in order to improve compliance. Bariatric surgery appears to be the most effective means of achieving sustained weight loss with improvement or resolution of obesity-related comorbidities in the adolescent population.

Keywords Bariatric surgery • Adolescents • Metabolic syndrome • Obesity • Comorbidities

Introduction

The rise of childhood obesity in recent years has brought a concomitant increase in obesity-related comorbidities. Obesity affects 17% of people aged 12–19 in the USA, and children are the fastest growing subgroup of the already booming obese population [1, 2]. Adolescent obesity is a public health crisis with serious immediate and long-term health consequences. Currently, there are no effective pharmacologic or behavioral treatments. Prevention gives children the best chance at growing up into healthy adults. Childhood obesity is a key predictor of adult obesity; up to 77% of obese children will grow up to be obese adults [3]. Until effective nonsurgical treatment is available for already morbidly obese patients, bariatric surgery is the only proven intervention that provides sustained weight loss as well as improvement and resolution of obesity-related comorbidities. Obesity results in a reduction in median survival of 8–10 years in adults with BMIs between 40 and 45 kg/m^2 [4]. Additionally, the various effects of morbid obesity encompass entire body systems, leading to the development of diabetes, hypertension, hyperlipidemia, sleep apnea, nephropathy, depression, and the metabolic syndrome.

This chapter will review options available for the surgical treatment of metabolic syndrome in the obese adolescent, the outcomes available in the published literature, and potential complications of surgery, which may be different than those in adults. Bariatric surgery appears to be the most effective means of achieving sustained weight loss with improvement or resolution of obesity-related comorbidities in the adolescent population.

Criteria for Surgical Intervention

Clinical guidelines for adolescent bariatric surgery have been proposed, but none are unanimously accepted. Indications for the surgical treatment of obesity in adults are based on the recommendations of the NIH Consensus Development Conference on Gastrointestinal Surgery for Severe Obesity [5]. Many in the field feel that bariatric surgery in adolescents should be offered with more strict guidelines than to adults because of several reasons. There are concerns about unknown long-term consequences of performing these procedures on developing adolescents. In addition, it is felt that the patients may not have the maturity to comply with the long-term requirements necessary for success, or be able to assent to the surgery. It has been proposed that adolescents who are candidates for surgery have a BMI of 40 kg/m^2 or more with serious comorbidities (e.g., type 2 diabetes mellitus, obstructive sleep apnea) or a BMI of 50 kg/m^2 or more with less severe comorbidities. A guideline published in Obesity Research in 2009 also advocates surgery in adolescents with less severe obesity (BMI > 35 kg/m^2) if significant comorbidities are present [6]. This is in contrast with the knowledge that surgery, when performed early, has the least operative risk. The outcomes at this time are likely to be the best possible, and the risk of repeating former undesirable behavior is lowest. Although some believe that surgery should be considered only after all other options have been exhausted, the surgical risks are highest when the patient's obesity is at its most severe and comorbidities have been long-standing and chronic. Studies have shown that gastric bypass is safer in young patients with lower BMIs and less serious comorbidities [2]. A patient who is heavier at the time of bariatric surgery will have less percent weight loss, a greater chance of weight regain, and a lower likelihood of comorbidities improving or resolving [7]. The main goal of bariatric surgery is not to restore the patient to an ideal body weight, but rather to improve their obesity-associated comorbidities and health-related quality of life as a result of the weight loss. Because cardiometabolic risk factors tend to be relatively stable through childhood to adulthood, it is imperative that children with signs of metabolic syndrome are recognized early [8].

Additional criteria, beyond simple BMI, factor into deciding if a patient is an appropriate candidate for bariatric surgery. The patient should have an extensive history of previous weight loss attempts prior to seeking surgery, with no history of unstable psychological conditions or substance abuse. When deemed a candidate based on all other criteria, patients should undergo routine psychological evaluation specifically for bariatric surgery. Most prospective patients have undergone a wide variety of nonsurgical interventions over the years, including exercise, behavior modification, and pharmacological therapy. Adolescents should have documented evidence of a nonsurgical weight loss program, followed for at least 6 months with unsatisfactory results. In addition, surgery should most likely be postponed until the epiphyseal plates have closed and mature bone length has been achieved. Rapid weight loss may adversely affect bone growth during this critical time of development due to the restricted caloric intake. Finally, the patient's family support system takes on an especially important role when operating on younger individuals. It is extremely rare for an individual at a young age to not be dependent on familial support. Thus, patient evaluation in adolescents strongly advocates for extensive evaluation of the patient's family and support network, as well.

The bariatric surgical patient should also not have severe organ dysfunction, which would make perioperative morbidity and mortality risks unacceptably high. In the adolescent population, this is rarely the case, and proponents of adolescent bariatric surgery reference the importance of preventing such severe end organ damage as a reason for proceeding (Table 17.1).

Table 17.1 Conservative criteria for adolescent bariatric surgery

BMI ≥ 40 kg/m^2 with
Type 2 diabetes
Moderate or severe obstructive sleep apnea
Pseudotumor cerebri
BMI ≥ 50 kg/m^2 with
Hypertension
Dyslipidemia
Venous stasis disease
Panniculitis
Nonalcoholic steatohepatitis
Urinary incontinence
Severe impairment in daily activities
Gastroesophageal reflux
Severe psychosocial distress
Significantly impaired quality of life
Weight-related arthropathies
Intertriginous soft tissue infection

One final consideration before bariatric surgery in adolescents is the advisability of restrictive (i.e., lap band) versus malabsorptive (i.e., biliopancreatic diversion or gastric bypass) procedures. Gastric bypass more permanently alters the patient's anatomy, while the laparoscopic adjustable band does not and can be more easily reversed. The long-term effects of either procedure in the adolescent population, however, are completely unknown. Patients should be offered bariatric surgery in centers offering a multidisciplinary team approach involving nutrition counseling, psychology, exercise physiology, bariatric surgeons, and experts in pediatric obesity, which will determine the prudence of surgical intervention. Although there remains a great deal to learn about adolescent bariatric surgery, this surgery plays an important role in combating the rapid rise of obesity in adolescents.

Bariatric Surgery Techniques

Surgical treatment of obesity began in the early 1950s when several groups proposed shortening the intestinal tract via a "bypass" procedure to produce a substantial decrease in the absorptive area. This was based on the observation that massive small bowel resections for treatment of other pathologic conditions resulted in weight loss followed by weight stabilization. Since that time, more than 30 different surgical techniques have been described for treating obesity. There are two main surgical approaches to obesity: reducing caloric absorption by a bypass of the small intestine and reducing caloric consumption by severely restricting gastric capacity. The most common surgical options for adolescents are Roux-en-Y gastric bypass (RYGB) and laparoscopic adjustable gastric banding (LAGB), with gastric bypass comprising more than 90% of US adolescent cases [9]. The procedures available are restrictive (laparoscopic sleeve gastrectomy and adjustable gastric banding), malabsorptive (biliopancreatic diversion and duodenal switch), or a combination of the two (Roux-en-Y gastric bypass). Many of these procedures can be performed laparoscopically, resulting in a shorter hospital stay, faster recovery, smaller scars, and less postoperative pain. However, not all patients are well-suited for laparoscopy; those who are extremely obese, have had previous abdominal surgery, or have complicating medical problems may require the open approach.

Restrictive procedures include the laparoscopic adjustable gastric banding and sleeve gastrectomy. LAGB has been associated with sustained weight loss and improved comorbidities in adults and also has the advantages of adjustability and reversibility. LAGB is also associated with a five- to tenfold lower mortality rate and threefold lower complication rate than gastric bypass [10]. Randomized controlled trials involving adults have shown gastric banding to be more effective and cost-efficient than optimal lifestyle treatment. Laparoscopic adjustable gastric bands have been used worldwide since the 1990s with FDA approval of two bands in the USA after 2001. There is little long-term data on LAGB in adolescents however, since the procedure is not yet FDA-approved for use in individuals under the age of 18 years, though there are now several studies published.

The adjustable gastric band restricts the stomach using a silicone band, which can be adjusted by addition or removal of saline through a port placed under the skin. This operation can be performed laparoscopically and is the least invasive of the bariatric procedures. Weight loss is predominantly due to the restriction of nutrient intake that is created by the small gastric pouch and the narrow outlet [7]. With a mortality rate of 0.05%, it is considered one of the safest bariatric procedures performed today [11]. The placement of the band creates a small pouch at the top of the stomach, which holds approximately 5% the capacity of a normal stomach. The band serves to slow the passage of food from the pouch to the distal portion of the stomach, decreasing the patient's sensation of hunger and increasing the feeling of satiety with less intake than prior to surgery. Patients tend to eat smaller portions and feel full quicker and longer, resulting in weight loss over time. As patients lose weight, the bands can be adjusted or refilled with saline through a port to ensure comfort and effectiveness. In the USA, two adjustable lap bands are approved by the FDA. No part of the digestive system is bypassed or transected, and therefore reversal is easily possible. Patients who desire a reversal undergo repeat laparoscopy and typically have substantial weight regain after removal of the band. In addition, adjustability of the band is thought to be an advantage, allowing increased durability of weight loss. Typically, patients who undergo adjustable gastric banding procedures lose less weight over the first 3.5 years than those who have Roux-en-Y gastric bypass, biliary pancreatic diversion, or duodenal switch surgeries, but results from a study by Maggard suggest that this difference decreases significantly over time [12]. Gastric banding patients lose an average of 47.5% of their excess weight, according to a meta-analysis by Buchwald [13]. Many see the gastric band as safer than other procedures, given its easier reversibility (Fig. 17.1 and Table 17.2).

Fig. 17.1 Roux-en-Y gastric bypass. *Arrows* note the flow bypassing part of the stomach and intestines (Courtesy Ethicon Endo-Surgery, Inc.)

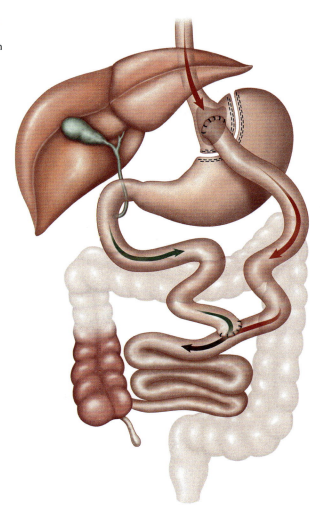

Table 17.2 Types of bariatric surgery

Restrictive
   Adjustable band
   Sleeve gastrectomy
Malabsorptive
   Biliopancreatic diversion
   Duodenal switch
Combination procedures
   Roux-en-Y gastric bypass
Investigational procedures
   Greater curvature plication
   Endoscopic procedures
      Intragastric balloon
      Duodenal-jejunal sleeve
      Endoluminal vertical gastroplasty

First described by Ren and colleagues, the sleeve gastrectomy evolved from the thought that a biliopancreatic diversion was best performed as a two-step procedure to decrease morbidity and mortality [14]. The sleeve gastrectomy reduces the stomach to approximately about 15% of its original size by the surgical removal of a large portion of stomach along the greater curvature. The procedure permanently reduces the size of the stomach; it can be performed laparoscopically and is not reversible. In its original inception, after 6–12 months of weight loss, and a decrease in operative risk, a second stage was performed. In this stage, the sleeve procedure can be converted to a gastric bypass or a biliopancreatic diversion laparoscopically. The two-step procedure is thought to be appropriate for patients with extremely high BMIs who may have greater risk than the less morbidly obese patient because longer time under general anesthesia increases both intra- and perioperative complications. Early experience with the sleeve gastrectomy has suggested that the weight loss induced by the first procedure alone, without performing the second stage, is significant enough to allow the sleeve to be used as a definitive one-stage procedure. A prospective, double-blind study in which the sleeve gastrectomy was compared with gastric bypass found that weight loss for the sleeve gastrectomy was better than the bypass (69.7% vs. 60.5% excess body weight lost 1 year after surgery) [15]. This result was associated with the finding that the gastric peptide ghrelin was significantly lower in the sleeve group compared with that of the GBP group, as was the patient's appetite. In addition, by avoiding the intestinal bypass, the chances of intestinal obstruction (blockage), anemia, osteoporosis, protein deficiency, and vitamin deficiency were significantly reduced. The data, however, is short-term, and some experts have stated concern that the gastric pouch of the sleeve may dilate over time and weight loss efficacy will be lost. Most other studies looking at weight loss have shown a greater weight loss with the bypass over the sleeve. Stomach volume is reduced but tends to function normally, so most food items can be consumed in small amounts (Fig. 17.2).

Malabsorptive procedures such as the biliopancreatic diversion and duodenal switch present other options for patients and their bariatric surgeon. The original biliopancreatic diversion is not often performed given the high incidence of malnutrition associated with it, and now it is usually performed with a modification known as a duodenal switch. The small bowel is divided 250 cm proximal to the ileocecal valve, and the distal small bowel limb is then anastomosed to the gastric remnant. The end of the proximal small bowel limb is anastomosed to the side of the distal small bowel limb 50 cm proximal to the ileocecal valve. This construction results in three small bowel limbs: a long biliopancreatic limb, a 200 cm alimentary limb, and a 50 cm common limb in which food and biliopancreatic secretions mix; most of the digestion and absorption of consumed food also occurs in this common limb (Fig. 17.3).

The surgeries also involve a restrictive portion in which 70% of the stomach is resected. In the biliopancreatic diversion, a subtotal gastrectomy is performed, resecting approximately 70% and leaving a pouch of the proximal stomach. The duodenal switch is a modification designed to prevent ulcers, increase the amount of gastric restriction, minimize the incidence of dumping syndrome, and reduce the

Fig. 17.2 Sleeve gastrectomy. Note the reduced volume of the stomach (Courtesy Ethicon Endo-Surgery, Inc.)

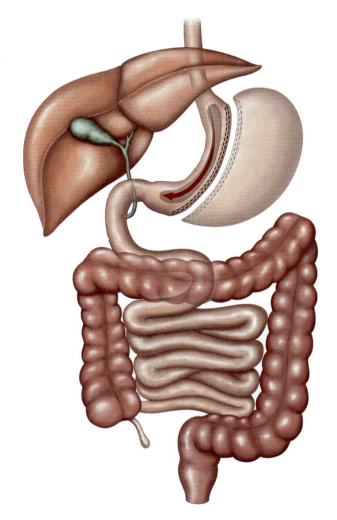

severity of protein/calorie malnutrition. In the duodenal switch, the stomach is fashioned into a sleeve (i.e., sleeve gastrectomy), preserving the pylorus, transecting the duodenum, and connecting the intestine to the duodenum proximal to where bile enters the intestine. Thus, the sleeve empties into a very short (2–4 cm) segment of the duodenum. Compared to the biliopancreatic diversion, the duodenal switch leaves a much smaller portion of stomach that creates a feeling of restriction similar to that of the gastric bypass. There is less likelihood of dumping syndrome as well given the pylorus is preserved in the duodenal switch. The weight loss in both is mostly induced by malabsorption. As described previously, the sleeve and malabsorptive portions of the procedure can be separated into two procedures. This combined approach can decrease the risk of weight loss surgery for specific groups of

Fig. 17.3 Biliopancreatic diversion with duodenal switch. Note both the restrictive (reduced stomach pouch) and malabsorptive (partially bypassed intestinal tract) aspects (Courtesy Ethicon Endo-Surgery, Inc.)

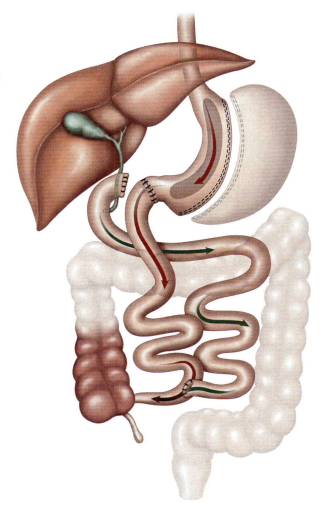

patients, even though the risk of the two surgeries is added. Most patients can expect to lose 30–50% of their excess body weight over a 6–12 month period with the sleeve gastrectomy alone. The timing of the second procedure varies according to the degree of weight loss, typically occurring after 6–18 months.

The gastric bypass, the most commonly performed bariatric surgery, was first described in the 1960s by Ito and Mason. Since then, it has been modified into its current form, using a Roux-en-Y limb of intestine. Approximately two thirds of bariatric procedures worldwide are both laparoscopic and open gastric bypasses. In this procedure, a 15–20 mL pouch is constructed and anastomosed to a Roux loop of the jejunum; this creates a short biliopancreatic limb through which bile and pancreatic secretions flow. It also comprises an alimentary limb of 100–200 cm in which food

Fig. 17.4 Adjustable gastric band. Port is placed for easy adjustment of band restriction (Courtesy Ethicon Endo-Surgery, Inc.)

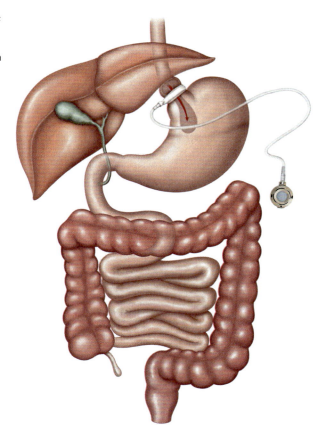

from the gastric pouch travels and a common limb that consists of the remainder of the small bowel located just distal to the anastomosis of the alimentary and biliopancreatic limbs. The majority of the stomach, the duodenum, and several centimeters of proximal jejunum are bypassed in this configuration. Thus, the procedure is traditionally said to combine both restrictive and malabsorptive features; however, in reality, there is very little, if any, malabsorption. The Roux-en-Y gastric bypass may also be performed laparoscopically, first published as a case series by Wittgrove and Clark in 1994. The subsequent reduction in ghrelin may also contribute to the weight loss efficacy of this procedure [15]. There is no difference in weight loss outcome between open and laparoscopic Roux-en-Y gastric bypass (Fig. 17.4) [16, 17].

There are several investigational procedures that have recently been developed. Gastric greater curvature plication is an alternative procedure that can be as restrictive as a sleeve gastrectomy with no staple line or prostheses. In a laparoscopic technique, the stomach is reduced by transecting the greater omentum and short gastric vessels, then the greater curvature is invaginated using multiple rows of nonabsorbable suture. At completion of the procedure, the stomach is shaped like a sleeve gastrectomy but slightly larger in size. Ramos et al. published their findings on 62 patients and at 2 years noted 8 patients to have 61% mean estimated excess weight loss, with all patients achieving at least a 10% initial excess weight loss [18]. Initial clinical reports by Talebpour and Amoli demonstrate satisfactory weight loss up to 3 years [19].

Several endoscopic procedures have been developed for weight loss, including both prosthetic and suturing/stapling devices, but human studies are limited. There has been extensive experience with the intragastric balloon published, but none are currently approved in the USA. In some cases, the balloon must be removed after 6 months because of patient intolerance with nausea and vomiting [20]. The duodenal-jejunal bypass sleeve was the first malabsorptive procedure using endoscopy. By placing the self-expanding implant to cover the mucosa of the duodenum and proximal jejunum, the device induces malabsorption and causes weight loss [21]. However, there is still limited human data, and the long-term safety and efficacy is unclear. New endoscopic suturing and stapling devices are also available that work using restrictive techniques. Endoluminal vertical gastroplasty employs sutures that are deployed in a continuous cross-linked fashion from proximal fundus to distal body so the gastric distension is limited [22]. Long-term follow-up to evaluate prolonged weight loss and stability of the gastric sutures is needed. Transoral gastroplasty creates a full-thickness plication in the proximal stomach and a gastric sleeve along the lesser curvature of the stomach [23]. A randomized study is currently ongoing to evaluate its efficacy and durability of the resulting weight loss. With any of these surgeries, patients must carefully follow postoperative guidelines with regard to diet, exercise, and band maintenance in order to maintain weight reduction.

Postoperative Care

In high-volume centers, the hospital stay for bariatric surgery patients varies from 1 to 3 days depending on the type of procedure performed. Laparoscopic gastric band patients are usually discharged within 24 h of surgery, while laparoscopic Roux-en-Y gastric bypass patients are generally discharged from the hospital in 2–3 days. Routine care during hospitalization focuses on providing pain control and ensuring adequate oral intake. Once these are stabilized, the patient can be safely discharged home. The diet is advanced through various "stages" over several weeks, and patients receive extensive education about maintaining hydration and consuming adequate protein (Table 17.3).

Benefits and Review of Outcomes in Literature

In the adult population, bariatric surgery procedures have been proven to induce significant excess weight loss in the very obese and improve obesity-related comorbidities. The benefits of bariatric surgery are well established in the adult population, and

Table 17.3 Complications of bariatric surgery

Immediate (general)
Pneumonia
Pulmonary embolus
Deep venous thrombosis
Wound infection
Long term (general)
Mild hair loss
Iron deficiency
Vitamin D deficiency
Hiatal hernia
Gastroesophageal reflux
Symptomatic cholelithiasis
Symptomatic nephrolithiasis
Adjustable band
Band slippage/pouch dilation
Esophageal dilatation/dysmotility
Gastric perforation
Band erosion
Mechanical malfunctions
Port displacement
Gastric bypass
Anastomotic leak
Strictures
Gastric ulceration

recent data are beginning to be published on adolescent outcomes. Substantial and sustained weight loss has been documented in adults, who average 61% of their excess body weight lost [24]. Even though most patients do not reach their ideal body weight, almost all experience an improvement or resolution of comorbid conditions such as metabolic syndrome, diabetes, hyperlipidemia, hypertension, and sleep apnea. Since bariatric surgery has limited experience in the adolescent population, the information involving long-term outcomes is scarce. There are several case series published that describe that the improvement of comorbidities and excess weight lost are similar to those in adults [14, 25]. O'Brien et al. studied adolescents in a prospective randomized trial with a LAGB versus those with a supervised lifestyle intervention. After 2 years, the LAGB group had an excess weight loss of 78.8% (34.6 kg) while the lifestyle group had an excess weight of loss of only 13.2% (3 kg) [26]. Nadler, et al. described their experience with 45 adolescents aged 14–17 who underwent LAGB; their excess weight loss after 2 years was 47±22%. Inge et al. detailed their experience with 61 obese adolescents undergoing Roux-en-Y gastric bypass. After 1 year, the BMI reduction was 37%, regardless of the baseline BMI [7]. Stanford et al. also noted similar success, with an 87% excess weight loss in adolescents undergoing gastric bypass. In a series by Strauss, 85–90% of adolescents had enduring weight loss after 4–6 years of follow-up [27]. Our work has shown that adolescents experience the same weight loss plateau that is seen in adult bariatric surgery patients. Interestingly, the weight

Table 17.4 Brief summary of results in literature

	n	Average age (years)	Average follow-up (months)	BMI reduction (%)	Metabolic syndrome resolution (%)	DM resolution (%)
O'Brien	40	41.8	12	19.9	93.3	
Nadler	47	15.8	12	34.3		57
Inge	61	17.2	12	37.4		88.9
Strauss	10	16.2	12	34.4		
Holterman	20	16	29	18.8	82	73.8

loss 4 years postoperatively was equivalent to that of the weight loss peak at 18 months [28]. We have also found that the ethnic groups we have studied experience the same improvements and resolution of obesity-related comorbidities, making bariatric surgery an effective option for adolescents of all demographics [28] (Table 17.4).

Major comorbidities in obese adolescents are significantly affected by bariatric surgeries. O'Brien et al. demonstrated significant reductions in metabolic syndrome after LAGB [24]. At baseline, 36% of gastric banding group and 40% of the lifestyle group had metabolic syndrome, but at 24 months, none of the gastric band group had metabolic syndrome while 22% of the lifestyle group still did. Nadler et al. describe a complete resolution of pre-existing comorbidities in 55% of patients 2 years post-surgery [7]. Holterman et al. described the first prospective trial in the USA assessing the role of LAGB as a bariatric procedure in pediatric weight loss [26]. All hypertensive patients had a normal systolic blood pressure at 12 months that was sustained at 18 months. Patients also were noted to have a significant increase in HDL and decrease in triglycerides, with 61% and 82% of those with dyslipidemia having resolution at 12 and 18 months, respectively. At 12 and 18 months, insulin resistance significantly decreased with resolution in 45% and 72% of patients, respectively. At 12 and 18 months, there was a resolution of metabolic syndrome of 63% and 82%. Interestingly, two patients at 12 months noted suboptimal weight loss but still experienced resolution of dyslipidemia and metabolic syndrome [29]. Inge et al. noted significant improvements in blood pressure, fasting insulin, and triglyceride levels, as well as type 2 diabetes remission after RYGB [27, 29]. In a series by Lawson, among 30 patients who underwent RYGB, there was a 37% reduction in BMI in adolescents with 1-year follow-up, with significant improvements in insulin resistance, fasting blood glucose, and dyslipidemia [30].

Insulin resistance decreases following bariatric surgery before significant weight loss occurs [31–33]. While the mechanism of the decrease in insulin resistance is still unclear, many studies have demonstrated changes in gut hormones and inflammatory mediators. In addition to increases in postprandial and fasting PYY, incretin and GLP-1 levels are also shown to have increased [34]. Both RYGB and sleeve gastrectomy reduce ghrelin levels [35]. A study by Ippisch noted significant benefits, including reversal in abnormalities of both left ventricular mass and cardiac function [36]. Obstructive sleep apnea has also been shown to improve significantly [37].

Psychological aspects have also been shown to improve in adolescents. In a small series by Loux, there was a significant improvement in quality of life [38]. A study by Collins demonstrated improvements in self-esteem, social functioning, and productivity in the school and workplace [39]. Holtermann noted a significant increase in the quality of life score in both adolescents and parents at 12- and 18-month follow-up visits [40].

Complications

As with any surgical procedure, complications may occur perioperatively and short- and long-term postoperatively. Rates vary with the type of procedure, length of follow-up, learning curve of the surgeon, and with the BMI and preoperative comorbidities of the patient. Perioperative complications can be both systemic and technical. Systemic complications include issues with the respiratory tract, cardiac, neurologic, thromboembolic, genitourinary tract, and multisystem complications. Bariatric surgery patients are already at a higher risk for systemic complications, given their obesity and associated comorbidities. Technical complications include unexpected reoperation due to surgical complications, splenic injury, hemorrhage, anastomotic leaks or abscesses, and wound complications.

Following gastric bypass, noted complications include anastomotic leak, pulmonary embolus, and strictures. There have been several complications noted for the gastric band: band slippage/pouch dilation, esophageal dilatation/dysmotility, erosion of the band into the gastric lumen, mechanical malfunctions (port leakage, cracking of the kink-resistant tubing, or disruption of the tubing connection from the port to the band), port site pain, port displacement, infection of the fluid within the band, bulging of the port through the skin, nausea/vomiting, gastroesophageal reflux, and dysphagia.

There are several case series for gastric bands or gastric bypasses with varying complication rates; long-term complication rates greater than 2 years post-surgery have not yet been established. O'Brien et al. noted that eight reoperations were needed in seven patients for revisional procedures for proximal pouch dilation or tubing injury over the 2-year follow-up [29]. Nadler et al. had an overall operative complication rate of 15% but described no intraoperative complications; however, two patients required band removal, one for restriction intolerance and at the patient's request [7]. The second patient had a gastric perforation after laparoscopic band replacement following band slippage. Seven procedures were performed on an outpatient basis; four band slips required laparoscopic repositioning, and three patients had laparoscopic repair of symptomatic hiatal hernia. One patient developed a postoperative wound infection, and one developed a port leak. Other complications included mild subjective hair loss, iron and vitamin D deficiencies, gastroesophageal reflux, cholelithiasis, and nephrolithiasis. Holtermann et al. describe few complications in their gastric band series: three wound explorations for tube- and port-related problems and two laparoscopic revisions for band malfunction and hiatal hernia repair [26].

Table 17.5 Recommended follow-up visits and laboratory tests for bariatric surgery patients

1 week postoperative and every month afterward
Behavioral/nutritional monitoring and counseling
Every 3 months
Psychological follow-up
Follow-up lab studies
At 3, 6, 9, and 12 months for the first year and every 6 months for the next 4 years:
Comprehensive metabolic panel
Hematological profile
Liver function tests
Fasting lipid profile
Vitamin D and parathyroid hormone levels
Band adjustments
Sixth postoperative week
Subsequently if criteria met:
Lack of feeling of restriction
Increased hunger sensation
Weight loss < 1–2 lb/week

In addition to technical issues, nutritional complications are especially significant in the adolescent population, given their young age and life expectancy. Gastric bypass produces minimal or no malabsorption of macronutrients, but patients are at risk for vitamin deficiencies due to the altered anatomy and rapid weight loss in the first year postsurgery. The most common deficiencies are iron, calcium, vitamin B12, and thiamine; therefore, patients are given multivitamins with iron, vitamin D, and calcium to assure bone health in the still-developing population (Table 17.5).

Specific Considerations for Doing Bariatric Surgery in Adolescents

As obesity continues to increase in the USA, more data will be made available regarding the safety and efficacy of the various bariatric surgeries available to this population; this will likely result in a subsequent increase in procedures performed. Given that noncompliance with medical regimens is common among adolescents with chronic illnesses, it is vital to ensure compliance to monitoring and follow-up to avoid complications [29]. Therefore, the decision to proceed with weight loss surgery during adolescence should include consideration of a patient's and parent's abilities to be compliant [6]. Patients and their parents need to demonstrate a willingness to adhere to lifestyle modification before surgery as well as an ability to understand potential nutritional and behavioral consequences after bariatric surgery. A psychological evaluation should also be completed to rule out an eating disorder, psychiatric illness, or exposure to child abuse. A supportive family structure should be present in order for the procedure to be as successful as possible.

Conclusion

Morbid obesity in adolescents has severe acute and chronic complications. With more data being published regarding bariatric surgery in this population, it is becoming clear that various procedures, especially the lap gastric band and gastric bypass, are safe for this population and provide benefits to the adolescent patient that may prolong their life such as resolution of major medical comorbidities, including metabolic syndrome. Cumulative data on bariatric surgery in adolescents suggests that lap band and gastric bypass procedures are as well tolerated as in adults when performed in centers with appropriate experience and adequate surgical volume. However, compliance with medication and follow-up may be more problematic in adolescents, and long-term outcomes greater than 2 years are not available. Therefore, any bariatric procedure in adolescents should be performed by experienced multidisciplinary teams with support for medical, surgical, nutritional, and psychological care, who then publish their data, so long-term outcomes can be evaluated. Bariatric surgery in obese adolescents is not a quick fix, but rather a lifelong commitment to physical and behavioral change that can provide patients with improved health and quality of life.

References

1. Levitsky LL, Misra M, Boepple PA, Hoppin AG. Adolescent obesity and bariatric surgery. Curr Opin Endocrinol Diabetes Obes. 2009;16(1):37–44.
2. Fielding GA, Duncombe JE. Laparoscopic adjustable gastric banding in severely obese adolescents. Surg Obes Relat Dis. 2005;1(4):399–405. discussion 405–7.
3. Freedman DS, Mei Z, Srinivasan SR, Berenson GS, Dietz WH. Cardiovascular risk factors and excess adiposity among overweight children and adolescents: the Bogalusa Heart Study. J Pediatr. 2007;150(1):12–17.e2.
4. Prospective Studies Collaboration, Whitlock G, Lewington S, Sherliker P, Clarke R, Emberson J, Halsey J, Qizilbash N, Collins R, Peto R. Body-mass index and cause-specific mortality in 900 000 adults: collaborative analyses of 57 prospective studies. Lancet. 2009;373(9669):1083–96.
5. Apovian CM, Baker C, Ludwig DS, Hoppin AG, Hsu G, Lenders C, Pratt JS, Forse RA, O'brien A, Tarnoff M. Best practice guidelines in pediatric/adolescent weight loss surgery. Obes Res. 2005;13(2):274–82.
6. O'Brien PE, Dixon JB, Laurie C, Skinner S, Proietto J, McNeil J, Strauss B, Marks S, Schachter L, Chapman L, Anderson M. Treatment of mild to moderate obesity with laparoscopic adjustable gastric banding or an intensive medical program: a randomized trial. Ann Intern Med. 2006;144(9):625–33.
7. Schauer PR, Burguera B, Ikramuddin S, Cottam D, Gourash W, Hamad G, Eid GM, Mattar S, Ramanathan R, Barinas-Mitchel E, Rao RH, Kuller L, Kelley D. Effect of laparoscopic Roux-en Y gastric bypass on type 2 diabetes mellitus. Ann Surg. 2003;238(4):467–84. discussion 84–5.
8. Messiah SE, Carrillo-Iregui A, Garibay-Nieto G, Lopez-Mitnik G, Cossio S, Arheart KL. Inter- and intra-ethnic group comparison of metabolic syndrome components among morbidly obese adolescents. J Clin Hypertens. 2010;12:645–52.
9. Xanthakos SA. Bariatric surgery for extreme adolescent obesity: indications, outcomes, and physiologic effects on the gut-brain axis. Pathophysiology. 2008;15(2):135–46.
10. Shikora SA, Kim JJ, Tarnoff ME. Nutrition and gastrointestinal complications of bariatric surgery. Nutr Clin Pract. 2007;22(1):29–40.
11. Freitas A, Sweeney JF. 20. Bariatric surgery. In: Banerjee B, editor. Nutritional management of digestive disorders. Boca Raton: CRC Press; 2010. p. 327–42.

12. Maggard MA, Shugarman LR, Suttorp M, Maglione M, Sugerman HJ, Livingston EH, Nguyen NT, Li Z, Mojica WA, Hilton L, Rhodes S, Morton SC, Shekelle PG. Meta-analysis: surgical treatment of obesity. Ann Intern Med. 2005;142(7):547–59.
13. Buchwald H, Avidor Y, Braunwald E, Jensen MD, Pories W, Fahrbach K, Schoelles K. Bariatric surgery: a systematic review and meta-analysis. JAMA. 2004;292(14):1724–37. Review. Erratum in: JAMA. 2005;293(14):1728.
14. Ren CJ, Patterson E, Gagner M. Early results of laparoscopic biliopancreatic diversion with duodenal switch: a case series of 40 consecutive patients. Obes Surg. 2000;10(6):514–23. discussion 524.
15. Karamanakos SN, Vagenas K, Kalfarentzos F, Alexandrides TK. Weight loss, appetite suppression, and changes in fasting and postprandial ghrelin and peptide-YY levels after Roux-en-Y gastric bypass and sleeve gastrectomy: a prospective, double blind study. Ann Surg. 2008;247(3):401–7.
16. Jones Jr KB, Afram JD, Benotti PN, Capella RF, Cooper CG, Flanagan L, Hendrick S, Howell LM, Jaroch MT, Kole K, Lirio OC, Sapala JA, Schuhknecht MP, Shapiro RP, Sweet WA, Wood MH. Open versus laparoscopic Roux-en-Y gastric bypass: a comparative study of over 25,000 open cases and the major laparoscopic bariatric reported series. Obes Surg. 2006;16(6):721–7.
17. Nguyen NT, Hinojosa M, Fayad C, Varela E, Wilson SE. Use and outcomes of laparoscopic versus open gastric bypass at academic medical centers. J Am Coll Surg. 2007;205(2):248–55.
18. Ramos A, Galvao Neto M, Galvao M, Evangelista LF, Campos JM, Ferraz A. Laparoscopic greater curvature plication: initial results of an alternative restrictive bariatric procedure. Obes Surg. 2010;20(7):913–8.
19. Talebpour M, Amoli BS. Laparoscopic total gastric vertical plication in morbid obesity. J Laparoendosc Adv Surg Tech A. 2007;17(6):793–8.
20. Spyropoulos C, Katsakoulis E, Mead N, Vagenas K, Kalfarentzos F. Intragastric balloon for high-risk super-obese patients: a prospective analysis of efficacy. Surg Obes Relat Dis. 2007;3(1):78–83.
21. Rodriguez-Grunert L, Galvao Neto MP, Alamo M, Ramos AC, Baez PB, Tarnoff M. First human experience with endoscopically delivered and retrieved duodenal-jejunal bypass sleeve. Surg Obes Relat Dis. 2008;4(1):55–9.
22. Fogel R, De Fogel J, Bonilla Y, De La Fuente R. Clinical experience of transoral suturing for an endoluminal vertical gastroplasty: 1-year follow-up in 64 patients. Gastrointest Endosc. 2008;68(1):51–8.
23. Devière J, Ojeda Valdes G, Cuevas Herrera L, Closset J, Le Moine O, Eisendrath P, Moreno C, Dugardeyn S, Barea M, de la Torre R, Edmundowicz S, Scott S. Safety, feasibility and weight loss after transoral gastroplasty: first human multicenter study. Surg Endosc. 2008;22(3):589–98.
24. Strauss RS, Bradley LJ, Brolin RE. Gastric bypass surgery in adolescents with morbid obesity. J Pediatr. 2001;138(4):499–504.
25. Nadler EP, Youn HA, Ren CJ, Fielding GA. An update on 73 US obese pediatric patients treated with laparoscopic adjustable gastric banding: comorbidity resolution and compliance data. J Pediatr Surg. 2008;43(1):141–6.
26. Inge TH, Jenkins TM, Zeller M, Dolan L, Daniels SR, Garcia VF, Brandt ML, Bean J, Gamm K, Xanthakos SA. Baseline BMI is a strong predictor of nadir BMI after adolescent gastric bypass. J Pediatr. 2010;156(1):103–108.e1.
27. Holterman AX, Browne A, Tussing L, Gomez S, Phipps A, Browne N, Stahl C, Holterman MJ. A prospective trial for laparoscopic adjustable gastric banding in morbidly obese adolescents: an interim report of weight loss, metabolic and quality of life outcomes. J Pediatr Surg. 2010;45(1):74–8. discussion 78–9.
28. de la Cruz-Muñoz N, Messiah SE, Cabrera JC, Torres C, Cuesta M, Lopez-Mitnik G, Arheart KL. Four-year weight outcomes of laparoscopic gastric bypass surgery and adjustable gastric banding among multiethnic adolescents. Surg Obes Relat Dis. 2010;6(5):542–7.
29. Inge TH, Miyano G, Bean J, Helmrath M, Courcoulas A, Harmon CM, Chen MK, Wilson K, Daniels SR, Garcia VF, Brandt ML, Dolan LM. Reversal of type 2 diabetes mellitus and improvements in cardiovascular risk factors after surgical weight loss in adolescents. Pediatrics. 2009;123(1):214–22.

30. Lawson ML, Kirk S, Mitchell T, Chen MK, Loux TJ, Daniels SR, Harmon CM, Clements RH, Garcia VF, Inge TH, Pediatric Bariatric Study Group. One-year outcomes of Roux-en-Y gastric bypass for morbidly obese adolescents: a multicenter study from the Pediatric Bariatric Study Group. J Pediatr Surg. 2006;41(1):137–43. discussion 137–43.
31. Coppini LZ, Bertevello PL, Gama-Rodrigues J, Waitzberg DL. Changes in insulin sensitivity in morbidly obese patients with or without metabolic syndrome after gastric bypass. Obes Surg. 2006;16(11):1520–5.
32. Morínigo R, Casamitjana R, Delgado S, Lacy A, Deulofeu R, Conget I, Barceló-Batllori S, Gomis R, Vidal J. Insulin resistance, inflammation, and the metabolic syndrome following Roux-en-Y gastric bypass surgery in severely obese subjects. Diabetes Care. 2007;30(7):1906–8.
33. Perugini RA, Quarfordt SH, Baker S, Czerniach DR, Litwin DE, Kelly JJ. Metabolic characterization of nondiabetic severely obese patients undergoing Roux-en-Y gastric bypass: preoperative classification predicts the effects of gastric bypass on insulin-glucose homeostasis. J Gastrointest Surg. 2007;11(9):1083–90.
34. Goldfine AB, Mun EC, Devine E, Bernier R, Baz-Hecht M, Jones DB, Schneider BE, Holst JJ, Patti ME. Patients with neuroglycopenia after gastric bypass surgery have exaggerated incretin and insulin secretory responses to a mixed meal. J Clin Endocrinol Metab. 2007;92(12):4678–85.
35. Ippisch HM, Inge TH, Daniels SR, Wang B, Khoury PR, Witt SA, Glascock BJ, Garcia VF, Kimball TR. Reversibility of cardiac abnormalities in morbidly obese adolescents. J Am Coll Cardiol. 2008;51(14):1342–8.
36. Cummings DE, Weigle DS, Frayo RS, Breen PA, Ma MK, Dellinger EP, Purnell JQ. Plasma ghrelin levels after diet-induced weight loss or gastric bypass surgery. N Engl J Med. 2002;346(21):1623–30.
37. Kalra M, Inge T, Garcia V, Daniels S, Lawson L, Curti R, Cohen A, Amin R. Obstructive sleep apnea in extremely overweight adolescents undergoing bariatric surgery. Obes Res. 2005;13(7):1175–9.
38. Loux TJ, Haricharan RN, Clements RH, Kolotkin RL, Bledsoe SE, Haynes B, Leath T, Harmon CM. Health-related quality of life before and after bariatric surgery in adolescents. J Pediatr Surg. 2008;43(7):1275–9.
39. Collins J, Mattar S, Qureshi F, Warman J, Ramanathan R, Schauer P, Eid G. Initial outcomes of laparoscopic Roux-en-Y gastric bypass in morbidly obese adolescents. Surg Obes Relat Dis. 2007;3(2):147–52.
40. Rianthavorn P, Ettenger RB. Medication non-adherence in the adolescent renal transplant recipient: a clinician's viewpoint. Pediatr Transplant. 2005;9(3):398–407.

Chapter 18
Moving Clinic- and Community-Based Practice into Policy to Address Child Healthy Weight (and Vice Versa)

Danielle Hollar, T. Lucas Hollar, and Michelle A. Lombardo

Abstract As mentioned in previous chapters, childhood obesity and the attendant clinical manifestations of metabolic syndrome and type 2 diabetes have a strong, negative effect on a child's organs, bones, sleep patterns, cancer risk, psychological health, and overall future cardiometabolic risk. And despite the fact that the prevalence of childhood overweight and obesity in the USA continues to grow, especially among underserved subgroups, there is hope for reversing these trends. One approach with much potential is a model of collaborative care for child healthy weight that uses a "hub and spoke" design whereby the school/child care center is a "hub" of good nutrition and healthy living in action, with messages and activities filtering out into the community organically through the "spokes" (clinics, after-school programs, grocery stores, etc.). This multi-sector, community contextually specific collaborative approach helps child healthy weight activities become embedded in clinical- and community-based practice and transforms policies to improve child health, which in turn provide ongoing guidance for practice implementation in all settings. Implementing evidence-based programming throughout the hub and the spokes, linking activities to sustainable, currently operationalized programs (such as the United States Department of Agriculture Supplementation Nutrition Assistance Program-Education, school wellness policies/Coordinated School Health

---

D. Hollar, Ph.D., MHA, M.S. (✉)
Department of Pediatrics, University of Miami School of Medicine,
881 NE 72nd Terrace, Miami, FL 33138, USA
e-mail: daniellehollar@gmail.com

T.L. Hollar, Ph.D.
Master of Public Health Program, Nova Southeastern University,
College of Osteopathic Medicine, Fort Lauderdale, FL, USA

M.A. Lombardo, DC
The OrganWise Guys Inc., Duluth, GA, USA

programming, etc.), and commencing strategic community-wide social marketing efforts, allows a wide variety of partnerships to develop that share consistent healthy messaging. The true power of this model lies in community collaborations of diverse organizations. It will take all of us working together to achieve healthy weight on our communities, the USA at large, as well as other countries that are struggling with similar challenges of keeping children at a healthy weight.

Keywords Public policy • Nutrition policy • School wellness policy • Evidence-based programming • Schools • United States Department of Agriculture • Child care centers • Clinics • Coordinated School Health • Community-based model • Social marketing

Introduction

As discussed in previous chapters, childhood obesity and the attendant clinical manifestations of metabolic syndrome and type 2 diabetes have a strong, negative effect on a child's organs, bones, sleep patterns, cancer risk, psychological health, and overall future cardiometabolic risk. And despite the fact that the prevalence of childhood overweight and obesity in the USA continues to grow, especially among underserved subgroups [1, 2], there is hope for reversing these trends. Through thoughtful, strategic, community-wide partnerships and supportive policies and environments, modifiable behavioral risk factors for childhood-onset overweight and obesity, including diets high in fat and calories [3, 4], reduced physical activity [3, 5, 6], and greater amounts of television (TV) viewing/computer use [7], can be addressed successfully. Through multi-sector, community contextually specific collaboration, clinical- and community-based practice can move to create policies to improve child health, which in turn provide ongoing guidance for practice implementation in all settings.

Multi-level, Multi-sector Strategies for Engaging Clinics and Communities

Because childhood overweight/obesity is a major public health problem with a complex network of etiological factors and associated comorbidities, a multi-level and multi-sectoral intervention approach that links primary care with public heath approaches and promotes behavioral change in conjunction with policy and environmental changes is needed. Such multi-level, multi-sector collaboration is required to address the multiplicity of factors affecting child healthy weight management and associated good nutrition and healthy living behaviors. A singular focus on individual behavior change in isolation from broader social, cultural, physical, economic, and political contexts has not worked. Instead, multi-level, multi-sector approaches are required that address the interpersonal level (feeding styles, family demands, family self-management skills, etc.), the community level (foods available in schools and other institutional cafeterias, presence of vending machines in schools and other public places, availability of fast food, lack of access to places for physical activity, etc.), and the governmental level (policies regarding food, education, urban design, marketing, etc.) [8] with a strategic goal to integrate the sectors that care for children at all levels.

In so doing, clinic- and community-based practice will transform policy, and policy, in return, will transform these practices, as supportive environments to address healthy weight among children are created that holistically address nutrition, physical activity behaviors, weight status, health-care service delivery and utilization, quality of life, and satisfaction among children and families, as well as ongoing changes to the policies and systems for addressing healthy weight. In our experience, a multi-level, multi-sector approach to healthy child weight has been successful when in the form of a "hub and spoke," whereby synergies of combining proven-effective programs, operated by multidisciplinary collaborators, are achieved using the school and/or early child care setting as the "hub" for community-based healthy weight activities, including a focus on prevention, but also on treatment as necessary, with activities' "spokes" reaching out to and engaging community-based practice partners. Schools and/or child care centers are ideal "hubs" of healthy weight activities because children generally attend school 5 days per week during 9 months of the school year and schools are located in communities of every socioeconomic and racial/ethnic group – thus, they provide ideal locales for interventions. Also, school-age children, particularly those from low-income backgrounds who participate in the United States Department of Agriculture (USDA) National School Lunch Program (NSLP) and the School Breakfast Program, receive a substantial proportion of their daily nutrient requirements at school, often resulting in as much as 51% of daily energy intake [9]. Additionally, due to the Supplemental Nutrition Assistance Program (SNAP) becoming electronic, fewer recipients go to offices and thus do not receive associated nutrition education. Therefore, providing SNAP Education (SNAP-Ed), recently renamed the Nutrition Education and Obesity Prevention Grant Program (NEOP), in schools and child care settings provides a strong healthy weight benefit for this particularly at-risk population. Finally, for many communities, schools/child care settings are the settings where children, families, and experts (educators and, hopefully increasingly, health personnel including nutritionists) come together often, daily as children are dropped off at school, and throughout the year during school orientation days, PTA meetings, school events, parent-teacher conferences, among other activities. Messages about healthy living and good nutrition behaviors that are promoted in these settings have a strong likelihood of crossing into other sectors including the home, after-school, clinic, and other settings that care for children.

> **Example of Messages Moving from School/Child Care Setting to the Home**
> The empowerment of children to feel confident in the selection of their food and their physical activity choices, cultivated in the "hub" of the child care center/school, can have a powerful effect on parent behaviors related to child healthy weight. Children can, and do, have influence on food items parents purchase. Through specific educational activities we see success in good nutrition and healthy living behavior messages reaching parents. For example, our work with The OrganWise Guys (OWG) [10][1] messaging, which is comprised of a set of simple but strong core messages (eating low-fat foods, eating high-fiber foods, drinking lots of water, and taking part in lots of daily exercise), shows parents of elementary schoolchildren increasingly are engaged with their children's nutrition and healthy food choices as a result of the OWG nutrition education resources provided through the schools [11]. Parents of children in early childhood settings that are part of a ~$1 million USDA-funded study of OWG and changes to meals in early childhood settings also report these good nutrition and healthy living messages reaching the home. For example, "When a parent told her child she had a stomach ache, the child asked the mom if she had eaten a lot of fruits & veggies. The parents told the child she had not, so the child told her mom she needs to eat lots of fruits and veggies because what 'Peri Stolic' says is good to go to the bathroom. The mom laughed, was shocked at her knowledge and told her child, she was right and she was going to eat more fruits and veggies" [12]. Another parent reported "hearing their children talk to their dolls friends about nutrition" [13]. We see, over and over again, the power of combining fun cartoon characters representing the body organs with science-based healthy weight messages. Teachers "were amazed how students were able to understand, retain and enjoy so much information about nutrition and wellness" [13]. This type of "character endorsement" causes messages to "stick" with children and adults in a way similar to that shown in the study by Lapierre et al. [14] which showed the influence of character presence on packaging had a strong impact on child taste assessments.

Our model of coordinated healthy weight activities engages multi-sector partners in coordinated action including elementary schools/child care centers, primary care clinics (federally qualified health centers, community health centers,

---

[1] The OWG has received a number of awards, including a gold rating by the Cooper Institute, an award based on an evaluation of over 300 childhood obesity projects around the country, sponsored by the Dell Foundation. They also won the United States Department of Health and Human Services 2005 Innovation in Prevention Award for a school-based prevention program. More recently, it was designated 4 out of 5 stars and thus one of the top programs based on a review of peer-reviewed literature regarding the most effective whole-system approaches to combating childhood obesity. See "What works in combating childhood obesity: an anthology of the literature on effective whole-system approaches" by Centre for Excellence and Outcomes in Children and Young People's Services (C4EO), Great Britain May 2011.

private practices), Cooperative (County) Extension (and their county nutrition educators), Area Health Education Centers (and their community health workers), nonprofit foundations and organizations (from all levels: local, state, regional, and/or national, as appropriate), professional associations (affiliates from the American Dietetic Association, American Academy of Pediatrics, School Nutrition Association, Society for Nutrition Education, American Public Health Association, etc.), state agencies (Agriculture, Education, and Health), federal agencies (USDA, Health and Human Resources [HHS], Centers for Disease Control and Prevention [CDC], etc.), national foundations (W.K. Kellogg Foundation), community-based service organizations (YMCAs, YWCAs, National Recreation and Parks Association and affiliated municipal park agencies, local foundations, etc.), and for-profit companies (Blue Cross/Blue Shield, Publix, Kroger, and other grocery stores, etc.). These multi-level, multi-sector partners bring a strong set of skills (including nutrition education and outreach, clinical care, program evaluation, dissemination of best practices/results, resources for ongoing programming, message dissemination outlets, etc.) and the potential for leveraging skills and resources, in a way that impacts policies and programs affecting the health of the diverse populations of children and families [15].

Theoretical Framework for the Model

The model for this type of an approach is a modification of Chronic Care Model for Childhood Obesity (CCMCO) [16], which focuses on health systems and primary care clinics, the community, resources, and policies using a family-centered approach, and includes a social change model for reducing childhood obesity similar to what was done in Somerville, MA [17]. The CCMCO recommends linking primary care with public heath approaches and promotes behavioral change in conjunction with policy and environmental changes to improve children's risk factors for obesity. Jacobson et al. [17] contend that if such models are utilized, the result may be a paradigmatic shift that acknowledges that childhood obesity is a chronic condition that can be prevented and managed. We agree and put the school/child care setting as the "hub" for the paradigmatic shift.

Our "hub" model places a stronger emphasis on the "community" component than found in the CCMCO model, which appears to have a stronger health-care institutional focus. Our approach utilizes a social change focus that is directed at a public health issue [17]. The model has its roots in other successful public health movements such as tobacco, seat belt use, etc. Accordingly, the call for social change results from a crisis, the one that is relevant to this chapter being the high prevalence of childhood obesity, and builds on a sound scientific base (school-based nutrition and healthy living programming, health-care delivery system and evidence-based protocols), recognizing the importance of economics (potential for health-care savings and leveraging of resources related to obesity prevention in many environments), through the development of coalitions and strong advocacy that uses government strategically (particularly salient during the current Child Nutrition Reauthorization [Healthy Hunger-Free Kids Act (HHFK) of 2010] [18] and Health Care Reform [Affordable Care Act (ACA) of 2010] [19]), including the engagement of mass/social communication coupled with environmental and policy changes to develop a clear plan for action to address child healthy weight. The aim of these collaborative activities is to *catalyze action* by creating a multi-sector, multi-level system of care to address child healthy weight that engages a multitude of socializing agents in the lives of children.

Overall, our model serves to address and include key aspects of a child healthy weight model, including (1) addressing components of the CCMCO [16] and social change models [17]; (2) providing child care- and school-based healthy weight education, utilizing evidence-based curricula and models, including specific information regarding healthy eating[2]; (3) linking these educational efforts to those in the community including clinical, nutrition, and physical activity resources; (4) identifying at-risk children through child care- and school-based screenings; (5) providing ongoing, coordinated support (in child care, school, and clinic, and other settings) to screened children and their families to reduce risk factors and promote the appropriate use of preventive, and treatment, services; (6) improving appropriate use of services for which medical assistance is available under Medicaid, State Child Health Insurance Program (SCHIP), and other health-care plan services; and, (7) informing change at the policy, system, and environmental levels to promote healthy lifestyles and behaviors that correlate with real anthropomorphic and physiologic improvements in child health.

A set of coordinated activities to address healthy weight for children, currently operationalized in a number of US locations, some of which are led by authors of this chapter, is described in Table 18.1. Many activities take place simultaneously, while others are integrated as feasible (such as summer camps during school break).

---

[2] A strong focus on healthy eating should be integrated strategically into the coordinated activities to reverse the overconsumption that is having such a negative impact on the healthy weight of children. As Swinburn and colleagues (2009) reported, "[a] reversal of the increase in energy intake of approximately …1500 kJ/d (350 kcal/d) for children would be needed for a reversal to the mean body weights of the 1970s" (to bring children back to a healthy weight), or an increase in daily physical activity of 110–150 min of walking per day, which is not reasonable for school-age children [20]. Thus, eating habits and food selection choices need to be front and center in our efforts, and merely changing foods in child care, schools, fast-food outlets, etc., may not produce the eating behavioral changes we seek. Instead, the nutritious changes should be made in conjunction with evidence-based nutrition educational activities, so children (and their families) know why changes are being made to meals served to them in various settings and why nutrient-rich foods should be consumed at home and in restaurants too. All the while, ongoing support for daily physical activity interventions should be commenced.

18 Moving Clinic- and Community-Based Practice into Policy

Table 18.1 Coordinated multi-sector, community-based activities to address child healthy weight

Child care- and school-based activities	School and child care institutions play a crucial role in improving the health of children. Because children generally attend school 5 days per week during 9 months of the school year and schools are located in communities of every socioeconomic and racial/ethnic group, they provide ideal locales for interventions. Also, school-age children, particularly those from low-income backgrounds who participate in the USDA NSLP and the School Breakfast Program, receive a substantial proportion of their daily nutrient requirements at school, often resulting in as much as 51% of daily energy intake [9]
	Evidence from projects in these settings, led by authors of this chapter, have been shown to improve health and academic achievement measures among children during the school year longitudinally [21–27]. Specifically, we report elsewhere that school- and child care- based interventions that include OWG nutrition and healthy living education [10], dietary changes to foods served in schools/child care centers, and increased levels of physical activity using WISERCISE! [28] result in statistically significant improvement in weight, waist circumference, and blood pressure measures, as well as higher average standardized test scores, among intervention children as compared to children not participating in the programming [11, 21–27]
	Programming in these settings often is facilitated, and sustained, through strategic collaboration with Land-grant Universities (especially Cooperative Extension), Department of Health, and other community-based health education entities that offer the USDA SNAP-Ed/NEOP program in low-income schools. SNAP-Ed nutrition educators are allowed, and encouraged, to use evidence-based OWG programming as they work with low-income children and families. They train teachers and child care providers on how to use the curricula that are matched to state core academic standards, and they provide ongoing technical assistance year after year through a combination of federal, state, and local funding sources. In locations where SNAP-Ed/NEOP is not provided, we train other community-based providers/teachers/staff using the same model and strategies for engaging teachers and children in daily nutrition and healthy living activities integrated into core subject lessons
	In addition to schools and child care centers being ideal locales for nutrition and healthy living interventions/education, they also are ideal locations for obesity screenings. This allows for the early identification of overweight with the ability to screen large numbers of children. Many states mandate collection of body mass index (BMI) data on children, even in the elementary school setting; thus, policy requirements of many states (and increasingly more each year) regarding mandatory recording of weight measures annually, such as FL (FL Statue 381.0056) [29], support screening and provide opportunities to identify at-risk children and refer them into clinical and dietetic care

Summer programs/camps	Although success in addressing obesity through school-based interventions for health improvement has been demonstrated, recent studies report children lose health benefits during summer [25, 30–32]. Reasons for the loss of health benefits during summer are not certain but may be attributed to the unstructured environments within which children live during summer. These environments may limit daily physical activity due to unsafe neighborhoods, limited access to venues for physical activity, and extreme weather conditions (hot temperatures) while allowing for increased consumption of calorie-dense, less-nutritious foods than those provided during the school day, and increased opportunities for snacking [30, 33, 34]
	To address issues related to the negative effects of summer break on the health of children and in collaboration with summer SNAP-Ed/NEOP programs, the National Recreation and Park Association (NRPA) and associated affiliates, and others, summer camps are offered that bring together nutrition and healthy living education. The camps include lots of fun, but also much instruction on good nutrition/healthy living, including at least one 1 hour of nutrition education using OWG to keep messages consistent across sectors from child care/schools to clinics to municipal camp locations. Camps also include many physical activity bouts, swimming a few days each week (for safety as well as lifelong physical activity), field trips that require physical activity, "messy" science projects (making whole grain pasta to cook at home), cooking instruction (sometimes in collaboration with local chefs, and Share Our Strength's Cooking Matters® program), camp and community gardening, staff role modeling, as well as experiential food education through collaboration with the USDA Summer Food Service Program (SFSP) meals. We encourage collaboration among food vendors and community dietitians to modify breakfast and lunch meals to include nutrient-dense foods that are the focus of camp education activities. Snacks provided in camps also follow this process
	One example of a successful camp partnership in Chicago takes place among the Chicago Park District and the University of Illinois-Chicago's Chicago Partnership for Health Promotion (CPHP). CPHP hosts interactive nutrition education programming and organized physical activity for school-age children during the summer to promote healthier food choices and increase physical activity in 36 locations throughout the city. The program is called "Become a Member of the Club." In this OWG Wellness Outreach Program, which takes place over six 6 weeks, an OWG character "Club Member" is highlighted each week and aligned with a health promotion topic of the week, such as Hardy Heart who teaches about the importance of heart-healthy low-fat food choices, including snacks, as well as daily physical activity. At the end of the summer program, each child receives an OWG Club membership card. This summer camp program extends CPHP in-school programming (conducted as part of the USDA SNAP-Ed/NEOP programming) and facilitates efficacy of seamless, year-round nutrition and healthy living programming to ameliorate the effects of this less-than-healthy time for children [15]

18 Moving Clinic- and Community-Based Practice into Policy

Primary care clinics	Current recommendations for the prevention, assessment, and treatment of child overweight/obesity call for primary care providers to be at the center of a nationwide effort to address obesity in the primary care setting [35, 36] and that effective, therapeutic approaches for overweight children that can be used in the primary care setting are urgently needed [37, 38]. However, research indicates traditional approaches in this setting do not work due to treatment options for pediatricians being limited by several factors, including having few resources for treatment, lack of time available for counseling, lack of reimbursement for such treatment, and lack of self-efficacy for helping patients achieve the behavioral changes needed for weight loss [39–41]. The Healthy Clinics-Healthy Kids (HCHK) model assists with clinic-based obesity prevention and treatment for children by providing clinicians with easy-to-use tools and educational materials that contain messaging and OWG characters that are consistent with activities in other intervention sectors (schools/child care, after-school, camps, etc.) to help messages "stick" with families. Through the fun characters of OWG, children are empowered by gaining the knowledge and motivation to help them prevent obesity, assisted by encouragement from their doctors and other medical providers. The kit is being piloted in IL, MI, and NM, with funding from the W.K. Kellogg Foundation and Blue Cross/Blue Shield entities in each of the three states
CLUB NUTRITION Cooking Schools	CLUB (Children Learning and Understanding Better) NUTRITION Cooking Schools, successfully pilot-tested during the $2 million, W.K. Kellogg Foundation-funded, six-state Healthy Opportunities for People through Extension 2 (HOPE2) project, focuses on teaching basic nutrition education, food safety, and physical fitness utilizing the OWG Pepto's Place curricula. Parents and project personnel serve as volunteers (and learners) to assist with CLUB NUTRITION. CLUB NUTRITION member children take home an identical set of food items and recipes to recreate/prepare the healthy meals at home, thus offering opportunities for parents to learn cooking skills as well. Typical venues for these activities are food banks, after-school program settings, summer camps, groceries, etc.
Grocery store activities to socially market good nutrition behaviors	In order to enhance the experiential learning of children and families regarding nutrient-rich foods, grocery store activities can be coordinated with healthy weight activities in other sectors as well as with overall social marketing efforts. For example, Publix Super Markets, Inc. in Brevard, FL, uses the OWG Foods of the Month (FoM) curriculum in their grocery stores whereby they post posters about nutrient-rich foods/food groups each month, disseminate information about nutrient-rich foods using FoM newsletters and activity sheets at checkout counters, and host experiential food events such as monthly food tastings, store tours, etc.
Community, child care center, and school gardens	Leveraging ongoing community garden activities and/or cultivating new gardening activities is an important part of helping communities take charge of some aspects of their healthy eating behaviors. In many cases, gardens are created in collaboration with local USDA Master Gardeners (MG) and are planted in community, child care center, and school locations. The aim is to expand experiential nutrition opportunities through gardens as children and adults are taught about agriculture production practices, diet, and nutrition through a multi-media, hands-on set of vegetable gardening/nutrition curricula including garden planting, harvesting, and tasting opportunities. Authors of this chapter pilot-tested school garden processes in the Healthier Options for Public Schoolchildren (HOPS) Study in five states with MGs and *Organic Gardening* (magazine) [11, 21–27]

Social Media as a community-wide communication Tool	Social media is emerging as a significant form of communication, with a strong impact on society. Around 74% of Americans have Internet access, 66% of US households have broadband connections, and 61% of adults look online for health information [42], and the Internet is increasingly used to affect health behavior change. Social marketing efforts to disseminate consistent prevention messages are crucial to promoting healthy weight for children. In addition to OWG healthy messages provided through Facebook (which allows linking with other "friends" interested in healthy weight issues and dissemination of health information quickly), Twitter (which also promotes information dissemination almost in "real time," including patient care reminders, daily health tips, and healthy eating tips/encouragement), and a free public web page (www.organwiseguys.com, where free apps that support the consistent messaging as well as child and parent blogs are available), we have worked with groups such as American Public Television, which provides free access to 70 OWG public service announcements (30- and 60-second videos) for local public television stations throughout the USA, to bring important nutrition and healthy living messages into the home. Also, local Comcast stations and school cable channels broadcast a variety of 15–20-minute OWG videos many days each week. Other media interventions for which we have found success include local radio talk shows, local television program presentations and interviews, web and print articles, etc. – all of which help push the messages that drive healthy weight management for children and families Social media is often successful when using gamification [43] whereby very specific natural human tendencies are targeted with game-like mechanisms to give people a sense that they are having fun while working towards a rewards-based goal. The aim is to reinforce positive behavioral change across a wide spectrum of non-game-related issues, such as health care, finance, general lifestyle, etc.[43] When social media activities include gamification, connections among families, clinics, community-based health educators/dietitians/supports, and other project partners often are amplified. For example, a "reward" program can be designed to provide incentive points for healthy behaviors, attending medical appointment, meeting with dietitians, etc. Points then can be used at local supermarkets to purchase nutrient-rich foods, etc. All of these social marketing activities help families have fun while staying on track
Minigrants for community-led and community-designed activities	An important aspect of successful community-wide healthy weight initiatives is the engagement of input from the community in regard to intervention design. This is made possible through the model of a self-developed "minigrant" program that has been piloted successfully in HOPE2 whereby community-based organizations design programming and apply for funds to support the activities they think will be the most powerful and effective in improving their communities' health. This programming may take place in any "spoke"/sector (churches, food banks, clinics, groceries, etc.) with the goal to continue consistent messaging originally presented at schools/child care settings (our "hubs") through use of OWG tools. Activities may include adult support programs (*Take Charge of Your Health*, a program for middle school-age children through adults about obesity, cardiovascular and diabetes, and other healthy living topics), cookbook creation, special food/physical activity events, etc., with guidance and approval from authors of this chapter

Strengthening Coordination Throughout the Multi-sector System Through Policy and Strategic Partnerships

Strengthening coordination throughout the multi-sector system of care for children includes the strategic use of policies that support healthy weight, the integration of existing activities, systems, and agencies, as well as the cultivation of new sets of activities, in support of coordinated care for child healthy weight. The current policy context supports such coordination in a variety of ways. For example, the Nutrition and WIC Reauthorization Act of 2004 [44] mandated, among other things, the development of wellness policies at every elementary school that participates in the USDA NSLP. These committees must be multidisciplinary and include community-based representatives, as well as parents. The recently released 2010 Dietary Guidelines for Americans [45], as well as the ChooseMyPlate.gov, promote across-sector attention to nutrient-rich foods that should be consumed by all people over the age of two. The proposed changes to school-provided meals put forth by the Institute of Medicine's Committee to Review the National School Lunch and School Breakfast Program Meal Patterns and Nutrient Standards [46], SNAP-Ed/NEOP [18], as well as increases in fresh fruit, vegetable, and whole grain offerings and education opportunities as part of the 2008 Farm Bill [47], support improvements in the nutrition well-being and knowledge of schoolchildren in multiple care settings. Finally, and somewhat not explicitly outlined for practice implementation, is the ACA [Health Care Reform] of 2010 [19] that, among other things, promotes preventive activities across sectors, with a strong emphasis on primary care-based healthy living activities.

Together, the policy initiatives from a variety of our governmental agencies enhance the meals and snacks provided to children through governmental programs and offer opportunities for children and families to become familiar with healthy eating habits. These efforts can play a strong role in addressing the childhood obesity crisis, child healthy weight, child nutrition status, food insecurity, and the attendant health and academic achievement implications.

The integration of existing activities, systems, and agencies, as well as the cultivation of new sets of activities, is supported through a variety of structures in place and to be created in response to policy mandates. For example, wellness committees at individual schools and/or at the school district level include school personnel associated with nutrition, health, and physical activity, as well as community-based members with relevant expertise, and parents. Engaging and/or expanding this school-based group, and perhaps linking them purposively with community-based groups already addressing child health to create a community-wide consortium addressing healthy weight, assists with coordination of interventions, reducing duplication, and leveraging resources. Together, these sectors can create and implement an integrated, comprehensive care model and assist with the paradigmatic shift that acknowledges that childhood obesity is a chronic condition that can be prevented and managed [16].

Through the process of coordinating new systems of care, it is likely that partners will need assistance with understanding how to seek out, and use, evidence-based healthy weight curricula and procedures. Thus, technical capacity for treating and preventing childhood obesity of medical providers and community-based support organizations may need to be enhanced through training courses appropriate to the disciplines of care takers/providers (which could also serve to provide continuing medical education [CME] and continuing educational units [CEU] for MDs, DOs, PAs, NPs, RDs, RNs, and others). In so doing, clinical and community-based *practice* would change as providers and caretakers have new understandings, tools, and protocols for caring for the overweight and/or obese child. A focus on family-based interventions in clinical and community settings should be central to these technical capacity-building efforts, so families can learn to manage healthy weight issues as well. A number of authors of this chapter have been assisting with this work through leveraging of partnerships, funding, and systems described in the text box below.

Existing Activities, Systems, and Policies to Build Upon in the City of North Miami

Many of us have been working in the City of North Miami (NM), FL, on childhood obesity, nutrition, and physical activity projects for a number of years and will use this as a primary example as such. We have found much success because we are well recognized and trusted in the community due to our long-standing community involvement and dedicated facilitation of bidirectional campus-community relationships in addition to a number of us actually living in this community. The City of NM has a strong coalition to address healthy weight of children facilitated through a CDC-funded "Action Communities for Health, Innovation and EnVironmental ChangE" (ACHIEVE), led by NM Parks and Recreation Department [P&R], that serves to help coordinate city-wide activities. This group coordinates existing activities, systems, and policies to address child healthy weight, for example:

Existing Activities

School-based nutrition education utilizing the OWG nutrition and healthy living programming, as well as physical activity and community/school gardening programs, are co-led by USDA SNAP-Ed/NEOP nutrition educators (county-, state-, and federal-funded) and the CDC-funded ACHIEVE coalition (federal- and city-funded), with additional financial support from the Blue Foundation for a Healthier Florida (corporate nonprofit) and the American Recovery Act, Communities Putting Prevention to Work physical activity programming grant (federal-funded). Additionally, school-based health services are provided to city schools through The Children's Trust HealthConnect program (local tax-supported) and the Miami-Dade Health Department (county-, state-, and federal-funded).

> **Existing Systems**
> Healthy weight assessment opportunities are possible for children in grades 1, 3, and 6 via the legislatively required [29] child body mass index (BMI) screenings led by HealthConnect and the Miami-Dade Health Department. Plans exist to link these screening activities with local primary care providers in FQHCs, CHCs, and other clinics that care for young children, particularly children qualified for Medicaid and SCHIP/FL KidCare. Additionally, a system for out-of-school child and family SNAP-Ed/NEOP and other USDA nutrition education and MG programs in the community exists to serve healthy weight management needs in NM. Finally, P&R has a set of activities focused on physical activity, including monthly mayor's bike rides, facilitated by ACHIEVE.

> **Existing Policies**
> Increasingly, federal- and state-level policies are supportive of preventive medicine as well as the expansion of treatment to address child healthy weight. Federal Health Care Reform [19], as well as FL Senate and House bills regarding SCHIP/FL KidCare and Medicaid currently under debate, have a strong focus on preventive services and the possibility of expansion for treatment of child weight issues. These likely can (and should) be connected to school- and child care-based screenings as referral agencies as needed. Additionally, federally required school wellness policies operated under guidance from the FL Department of Education's Office of Healthy Schools, as well as child care wellness policies, are part of The Children's Trust programming that help support healthy weight for children in the City of NM through institutional feeding and nutrition programs.

In an ideal situation, central to the coordination of efforts for an integrated system such as the one described above would be a cadre of multiethnic, professionally diverse, *obesity/healthy weight-trained* health workers (or other community-based coordinator/educator) who would guide children and their families through systems, social support groups, and community resources for nutrition and physical activity, as well as the health-care delivery and human resource systems at large – aimed at child healthy weight. One such network could be community health workers (CHWs) who operate in most states that could be retrained to understand, and thus provide assistance about, issues supportive of healthy weight. The CHW cadre, many of whom work with Departments of Health and/or Area Health Education Centers, is comprised of individuals with expertise in (1) helping families locate and connect to a full range of community resources related to a particular public health issue; (2) providing culturally appropriate direct education, counseling, and outreach to help families and communities take charge of their health and well-being; (3) delivering direct services – education, advocacy, and social support; (4) keeping families informed about important events, appointments, etc.; among other support and connecting activities. For example, in Florida, many CHWs have been part of the Florida Border Health Education and Training Centers (HETC) Program, in collaboration with the FL Area Health Education Centers (AHEC) Network that developed and implemented a statewide train-the-trainer program to maximize the contribution of CHWs in preventing disease and thus promoting well-being in FL communities, statewide [48].

As these models of collaborative care for child healthy weight expand, as they are doing in the USA and Canada [49], there is the need to understand what type – and which components – are the most efficacious. Thus, improving scientific knowledge, technical capability, and community-based and clinical practice regarding healthy weight comes to the forefront. Designing, implementing, and testing/evaluating multi-sectoral and multi-level intervention strategies will provide scientific knowledge about what type of contextually specific, ethnically/racially appropriate childhood obesity interventions in schools/child care centers, as well as in the clinical care facilities and other care settings ("spokes") in the footprints of the schools conducting healthy weight projects, are most efficacious. Investigative approaches to understanding multi-sector, multi-level impact likely would be enhanced by including community needs assessments prior to and during investigations, perhaps operationalized through the "Community Circles" model that would include the engagement of a wide variety of stakeholders in the care of young children including teachers, after-school providers, clinicians (MD, DO, PA, NP, RD, RN, CNA, etc.), mental health providers/counselors, community nutrition providers, policymakers, CHWs, as well as parents. Through this community-based participatory research process, an understanding of the system of care for healthy weight of children is possible, and key leverage points can be identified for addressing medical needs of children and the systems changes required to promote behavioral counseling for families and their children, as well as linkages to appropriate multi-sector organizations and resources related to childhood healthy weight.A number of recent funding opportunities support this type of investigation, such as:

- The CDC, National Center for Chronic Disease Prevention and Health Promotion, Division of Nutrition, Physical Activity, and Obesity; with the Health Resources and Services Administration, The Center for Medicare & Medicaid Services, and the Administration for Children and Families, as part of the ACA, recently released a funding opportunity announcement for Childhood Obesity Research Demonstrations that utilize an integrated model of primary care and public health approaches in the community to improve underserved children's risk factors for obesity (~$23,000,000 available). The CDC also is funding Community Transformation Grants aimed at coordinated policies and activities across sectors and levels in specific geographic areas. Approximately $102 million is available for fiscal year 2011 for these implementation grants that also were made available through the ACA [19].
- USDA National Institute for Food and Agriculture began funding a number of research projects in 2010 aimed at understanding the efficacy of nutrition and obesity prevention programming for children aged four to eight. Around

$80 million was provided during this round. Another set of proposals for understanding impact on older children currently are under review, with expected rollout in fall 2011, including about $33.5 million, with $8.5 million available for new awards.
- The National Blue Cross/Blue Shield Association has recognized, and created opportunities for leveraged funding to support, the evidence-based OWG nutrition and healthy living program [21–27]. As such, it is one of their premier obesity prevention examples whereby schools are the "hubs" of obesity interventions that reach out to clinics/doctors' offices, after-school programs, summer camps, grocery stores, and other places associated with socializing eating and physical activity behaviors.
- Health Care Service Corporation (Blue Cross/Blue Shield of IL, OK, and NM), Blue Cross/Blue Shield of Michigan, and the W.K. Kellogg Foundation recently funded a pilot program to provide OWG nutrition and healthy living programming in doctor's offices and Women, Infant, and Children (WIC) clinics that are located near schools that implement the OWG, with the aim to improve health outcomes of young children through coordinated messaging across sectors.

Conclusion

The child healthy weight "hub and spoke" model is created and sustained through community-based partnerships. With the school/child care center as a "hub" of good nutrition and healthy living in action, the messages filter out into the community organically, with assistance from the "spokes" (clinics, after-school programs, grocery stores, etc.). Using an evidence-based "umbrella" tool, such as the OWG, and linkages to sustainable, currently operationalized programs, such as the USDA SNAP-Ed/NEOP nutrition program, and strategic social marketing efforts, allows a wide variety of partnerships to develop to share consistent healthy messaging specific to each partner's organizational cause/service. Integration of a healthy weight program that fits strategically within established programs and agendas, including SNAP-Ed/NEOP and School Wellness Policies/Coordinated School Health programs, poses the greatest opportunity for community-wide healthy weight. The true power of this model lies in community collaborations of diverse organizations. We, along with our community-based collaborators, continue to test new components in our model with the aim of informing regulatory, programmatic, and policy change in nutrition education and feeding policies, health-care delivery, and community-based programming that serves children in and out of school time as well as their families. It will take all of us working together to achieve healthy weight on our communities, the USA at large, as well as other countries that are struggling with similar challenges of keeping children at a healthy weight.

Acknowledgments We would like to express our great appreciation and many thanks to Caitlin Heitz, MS, for all of your help with this chapter.

References

1. Olshansky S, Passaro D, Hershow RC, Layden J, Carnes BA, Ludwig DS. A potential decline in life expectancy in the United States in the 21st century. N Engl J Med. 2005;352:1138–45.
2. Ogden CL, Carroll MD, Curtin LR, Lamb MM, Flegal KM. Prevalence of high body mass index in U.S. children and adolescents, 2007–2008. JAMA. 2010;303(3):242–9.
3. Lee Y, Mitchell DC, Smiciklas-Wright H, Birch LL. Diet quality, nutrient intake, weight status, and feeding environments of girls meeting or exceeding recommendations for total dietary fat of the American Academy of Pediatrics. Pediatrics. 2001;107(6):E95.
4. Dowda M, Ainsworth BE, Addy CL, Saunders R, Riner W. Environmental influences, physical activity, and weight status in 8- to 16-year-olds. Arch Pediatr Adolesc Med. 2001;155(6):711–7.
5. Federal Interagency Forum on Child and Family Statistics. America's children: key national indicators of well-being. Washington, DC: U.S. Government Printing Office; 2007.
6. Katz DL, O'Connell M, Yeh MC, et al. Public health strategies for preventing and controlling overweight and obesity in school and worksite settings: a report on recommendations of the Task Force on Community Preventive Services. MMWR Recomm Rep. 2005;54(RR-10):1–12.
7. Dennison BA, Erb TA, Jenkins PL. Television viewing and television in bedroom associated with overweight risk among low-income preschool children. Pediatrics. 2002;109(6):1028.
8. Huang TTK, Glass TA. Transforming research strategies for understanding and preventing obesity. JAMA. 2008;300(15):1811–3.
9. Briefel RR, Wilson A, Gleason PM. Consumption of low-nutrient, energy-dense foods and beverages at school, home, and other locations among school lunch participants and nonparticipants. JADA. 2009;109:S79–90.
10. The OrganWise Guys, Inc. www.organwiseguys.com
11. Lombardo M. The Delta H.O.P.E. Tri-State Initiative. Presented at 2008 annual meeting of the American Public Health Association, San Diego, CA.
12. USDA University of Miami Child Care Study Listserv, March 2011, available from the authors.
13. USDA UM Listserv University of Miami Child Care Study Listserv, April 2011, available from the authors.
14. Lapierre MA, Vaala SE, Linebarger DL. Influence of licensed spokescharacters and health cues on children's ratings of cereal taste. Arch Pediatr Adolesc Med. 2011;165(3):229–34.
15. Lombardo M, Hollar D, Hollar TL, McNamara K. Schools as *Laboratories* for obesity prevention: proven effective models. In: Bagchi D, editor. Global view on childhood obesity: current status, consequences and prevention. London: Elsevier; 2010.
16. Jacobson D, Gance-Cleveland B. A systematic review of primary healthcare provider education and training using the Chronic Care Model for childhood obesity. Obes Rev. 2010. doi:10.1111/j.1467–789X.2010.00789.
17. Economos C, Brownson S, DeAngelis M, Foerster S, Tucker Foreman C, Kumanyika S, Pate R. What lessons have been learned from other attempts to guide social change. Nutr Rev. 2001;59(3):40–56.
18. Healthy, Hunger-Free Kids Act of 2010, S. 3307, 111th Cong. (2009–2010).
19. Patient Protection and Affordable Care Act, H.R. 3509, 111th Cong. (2009–2010).
20. Swinburn B, Sacks G, Ravussin E. Increased food energy supply is more than sufficient to explain the US epidemic of obesity. Am J Clin Nutr. 2009;90(6):1453–6. Epub 2009 Oct 14.
21. Hollar D, Messiah SE, Lopez-Mitnik G, Almon M, Hollar TL, Agatston AS. Effect of an elementary school-based obesity prevention intervention on weight and academic performance among low income children. Am J Public Health. 2010;100:646–53.
22. Hollar D, Messiah SE, Lopez-Mitnik G, Almon M, Hollar TL, Agatston AS. Effect of a school-based obesity prevention intervention on weight and blood pressure in 6–13 year olds. JADA. 2010;110(2):261–7.

23. Hollar D, Lombardo M, Lopez-Mitnik G, Almon M, Hollar TL, Agatston AS, Messiah SE. Effective multilevel, multi-sector, school-based obesity prevention programming improves weight, blood pressure, and academic performance, especially among low income, minority children. J Health Care Poor Underserved. 2010;21(2):93–108.
24. Hollar D, Lopez-Mitnik G, Hollar TL, Agatston AS, Lombardo M, Messiah SE. Elementary school-based obesity prevention intervention effect on waist circumference among multiethnic 6–13 year olds. Obesity. 2010;18(2):S127.
25. Hollar D, Messiah S, Hollar TL, Lopez-Mitnik G, Agatston AS. School-based obesity and related cardiovascular disease prevention intervention effect on weight and academic performance: three year results. J Am Coll Cardiol. 2009;53(10):A399.
26. Hollar D, Messiah S, Lopez-Mitnik G, Hollar TL, Agatston AS. Elementary-aged children lose weight and blood pressure improvements (achieved during the school year) during summer vacation. Circulation. 2009;119(10):e275.
27. Hollar D, Messiah SE, Lopez-Mitnik G, Almon M, Hollar TL, Lombardo M. Combining nutrition education, foodservice (feeding programs), and physical activity obesity prevention interventions for children: significant improvements in the health and academic achievement of young children. In: Bagchi D, editor. Global view on childhood obesity: current status, consequences and prevention. New York: Elsevier; 2010.
28. WISERCISE! www.organwiseguys.com
29. National Association of State Boards of Education. State level school health policies. (Florida Statute 381.0056). Alexandria: NASBE Center for Safe and Healthy Schools; 2009. Available at: http://www.nasbe.org/healthy_schools/hs/state.php?state=Florida. Accessed 19 June 2011.
30. von Hippel PT, Powell B, Downey DB, et al. The effect of school on overweight in childhood: gain in body mass index during the school year and during summer vacation. Am J Public Health. 2007;97(4):696–702.
31. Christodoulos AD, Flouris AD, Tokmakidis SP. Obesity and physical fitness of pre-adolescent children during the academic year and the summer period: effects of organized physical activity. J Child Health Care. 2006;10(3):199–212.
32. Carrel AL, McVean JJ, Clark RR, et al. School-based exercise improves fitness, body composition, insulin sensitivity, and markers of inflammation in non-obese children. J Pediatr Endocrinol Metab. 2009;22(5):409–15.
33. Smith DT, Bartee RT, Dorozynski CM, et al. Prevalence of overweight and influence of out-of-school seasonal periods on Body Mass Index among American Indian schoolchildren. Prev Chronic Dis. 2009;6(1):A20.
34. Kobayashi M, Kobayashi M. The relationship between obesity and seasonal variation in body weight among elementary school children in Tokyo. Econ Hum Biol. 2006;4(2):253–61.
35. Whitlock EP, O'Conner EA, Williams SB, Beil TL, Lutz KW. Effectiveness of primary care interventions for weight management in children and adolescents: an updated, targeted systematic review for the USPSTF [Internet]. Rockville: Agency for Healthcare Research and Quality (US); 2010 Jan. Report no.: 10-05144-EF-1. U.S. Preventive Services Task Force Evidence Syntheses, formerly Systematic Evidence Reviews.
36. National Association of Neonatal and Pediatric Nurse Practitioners. Identifying and preventing overweight in childhood clinical practice guideline part I. J Pediatr Health Care. 2006;20 Suppl 1:1–32.
37. US Preventive Services Task Force. Screening and interventions for overweight in children and adolescents: recommendation statement. Pediatrics. 2005;116:205–9.
38. Patrick K, Sallis JF, Prochaska J, et al. A multicomponent program for nutrition and physical activity change in primary care: PACE+ for adolescents. Arch Pediatr Adolesc Med. 2001;155:940–6.
39. Barlow SE, Dietz WH. Management of child and adolescent obesity: summary and recommendations based on reports from pediatricians, pediatric nurse practitioners, and registered dietitians. Pediatrics. 2002;110:236–8.
40. Jelalian E, Boergers J, Alday CS, Frank R. Survey of physician attitudes and practices related to pediatric obesity. Clin Pediatr. 2003;42:235–45.

41. Krebs NF. Screening for overweight in children and adolescents: a call to action. Pediatrics. 2005;116:238–9.
42. Pew Internet & American Life Project. Press release: 61% of American adults look online for health information. http://www.pewinternet.org/Press-Releases/2009/The-Social-Life-of-Health-Information.aspx. Posted June 11, 2009. Accessed 2 Apr 2011.
43. Mangalindan JP. Play to win: the game-based economy. CNN Money.Com. http://tech.fortune.cnn.com/2010/09/03/the-game-based-economy/. Posted September 3, 2010. Accessed 2 Apr 2011.
44. Child Nutrition and WIC Reauthorization Act of 2004 S. 2507, 108th Cong. (2003–2004).
45. U.S. Department of Agriculture and U.S. Department of Health and Human Services. Dietary guidelines for Americans, 2010. 7th ed. Washington, DC: U.S. Government Printing Offices, December 2010.
46. School meals: building blocks for healthy children. October 20, 2009. Institute of Medicine. Available at: http://www.iom.edu/Activities/Nutrition/SchoolMeals/2009-OCT-20.aspx. Accessed 19 June 2011.
47. H.R. 2419 [110th]: Food, Conservation, and Energy Act of 2008; http://www.govtrack.us/congress/billtext.xpd?bill=h110-2419. Accessed 19 June 2011.
48. Foster R, Legros J, Saldias G, Zucker S. CHWs addressing health disparities in cardiovascular disease. 130th Annual Meeting of American Public Health Association, November 12, 2002.
49. TROPIC (Treatment and Research of Obesity in Pediatrics In Canada). http://www.obesitynetwork.ca/pediatrics. Accessed 19 June 2011.

Index

A

Abdominal obesity, genomics, 247, 248, 256
Accelerated aging, evidence of, 70–71
Acute lung injury (ALI), 173–174
Acute respiratory distress syndrome (ARDS), 173–174
Adiponectin, 84, 98, 99, 162, 186, 203–204, 224
Adipose-derived hormones and bones, 185–187
Adipose tissue distribution, obesity-related changes, 201–202
Adjustable gastric band, 337, 342
Adolescents, metabolic syndrome
   monogenic forms of, 247
   prevalence of, 38, 42
   type 2 diabetes, 86, 87
Aerobic capacity. *See* Cardiorespiratory fitness
Affordable Care Act (ACA), 356
Alanine aminotransferase (ALT), 141, 142
Allostasis, 9
Ambulatory blood pressure (ABP) measurements, 125
American Academy of Pediatrics (AAP), 102
American Heart Association (AHA), 27–28, 102
America's Health Rankings®, 14
Amino acids availability, fetal undernutrition, 64
AMP-activated protein kinase (AMPK), 313–315
Amylin, 187
   analogs, pramlintide, 326
Angiotensin II type I receptor *(AGTR1)* gene, 259
Anthropometry, nutritional evaluation, 284–285

Apnea/hypopnea index (AHI), 167
Appetite suppressant drug, 208
ARDS. *See* Acute respiratory distress syndrome (ARDS)
Arginine and nitric oxide, in asthma, 164–165
Arthritis, 193
Asthma and obesity
   arginine and nitric oxide, 164–165
   childhood asthma, 166
   comorbidities, 164
   decreased medication response, 165–166
   epidemiology, 160–161
   genetic determinants, 163, 164
   hormonal differences, 165
   insulin resistance, 163
   lung mechanics and physiology, 162
   systemic inflammation, 162–163
   vitamin D, 164
   weight loss interventions, 166
Asymmetric dimethylarginine (ADMA), 164, 165
Atherogenic dyslipidemia, 247–250
Atherosclerosis
   in adolescents, 96, 97
   cardiovascular risk stratification and reduction, in children
      AHA/AAP, 102
      cancer therapies, 104
      cholesterol screening, 101
      dyslipidemia treatment, 104, 106
      for high-risk pediatric populations, treatment algorithm, 102, 103
      HIV infection, 104
      Kawasaki disease, 104
      NHLBI guidelines, 102
      population and individualized approach, 101

Atherosclerosis (*cont.*)
    treatment recommendations, 104–107
    components, of metabolic syndrome
        atherogenic dyslipidemia, 97
        cumulative effects, of multiple risk factors, 99
        high blood pressure, 98
        insulin resistance, 98
        obesity, 96
        PDAY risk score, 99, 100
        proinflammatory and prothrombotic states, 98–99
        smoking, 99
    epidemiology, 94–95
    pathogenesis, 95–96
    plaque, evolution of, 95

B
Bariatric surgery, metabolic syndrome
    adjustable gastric band, 337, 342
    adolescents, considerations for, 347
    biliopancreatic diversion, with duodenal switch, 339–341
    and bones, 193
    comorbidities, 334, 335, 345
    complications
        follow-up visits and laboratory tests for, 347
        gastric bands/gastric bypasses, 346
        nutritional complications, 347
        perioperative and technical complications, 346
    complications of, 344
    endoscopic procedures, 343
    greater curvature plication, 342
    LAGB, 337, 344
    obesity, 334
    outcomes in literature, 343–346
    postoperative care, 343
    Roux-en-Y gastric bypass, 338
    sleeve gastrectomy, 339, 340
    surgical intervention, criteria for, 334–336
    types of, 338
Beloranib, 208–209
β_3-adrenergic *(3-BAR)* gene, 259
Beta-cell
    hormones and bones, 187
    in type 2 diabetes, 88
Bile acid sequestrants, 329
Biliopancreatic diversion, with duodenal switch, 339–341
Bioelectrical impedance analysis (BIA), 288–289
Blood pressure (BP), 270
    elevated, 250–252, 258
    high blood pressure
        in atherosclerosis, 98
        and neurocognitive functioning, 232
    measurements, 125
    neurocognitive functioning, 232
    and physical activity, 275, 276
    and psychosocial functioning, 235
Blount's disease, 191
Body composition measurements, 269–270, 284–285
Body mass index (BMI), 285, 335
Body proportions, perinatal epidemiology, 67–68
Bone health and metabolic syndrome
    bone physiology, 184–185
    fat mass and bone density
        adipose-derived hormones, 185–187
        beta cell hormones, 187
        gut hormones, 188
    musculoskeletal effects, of obesity
        arthritis, 193
        bariatric surgery, 193
        bone mineral content (BMC), 188
        and fracture risk, 189–190
        and gait, 192
        musculoskeletal pain, 192
        and orthopedic complications, 190–191
Bone mineral density (BMD), 184, 185
    dual-energy X-ray absorptiometry, 287, 289
Breast cancer, 221–222
Bupropion, 323

C
Calcium, 299–300
Cancer risk and childhood metabolic syndrome
    adolescent, 219, 226
    biochemical factors, 223–224
    breast cancer, 221–222
    colorectal cancer, 221
    endometrial cancer, 222
    epidemiology, 218, 220
    esophageal cancer, 223
    International Diabetes Federation, 219
    kidney cancer, 222
    long-term survivors, of childhood cancer, 225
    National Health and Nutrition Examination Survey data, 226
    obesity-related, relative risk estimates

Index 371

in men, 220
in women, 221
obesity therapy and cancer prevention, 225
pancreatic cancer, 223
Cardiomyopathy and heart failure
adolescents, 200–202, 204, 208, 209
diagnosis
clinical presentation, 206
computed tomography, 207
echocardiography, 206–207
electrocardiography, 206
laboratory tests, 207
magnetic resonance cardiac imaging, 207
pathophysiology
adiponectin and inflammation, 203–204
obesity-related metabolic changes and lipotoxicity, 203
systemic response and hemodynamic changes, 204–205
pediatric, 209
treatment
pharmacotherapy, 208–209
weight control, 208
Cardiorespiratory fitness, 270–272
Cardiovascular complications and obstructive sleep apnea, 168
Cardiovascular disease, in childhood, 22
Cardiovascular risk stratification and reduction, in children
AHA/AAP, 102
cancer therapies, 104
cholesterol screening, 101
dyslipidemia treatment, 104, 106
for high-risk pediatric populations, treatment algorithm, 102, 103
HIV infection, 104
Kawasaki disease, 104
NHLBI guidelines, 102
population and individualized approach, 101
treatment recommendations, 104–107
Centers for Disease Control (CDC), 362, 364
Central body fat, perinatal epidemiology, 69–70
Child care-and school-based activities, 357
Child care centers, 353, 354, 359, 364, 365
Child healthy weight
clinics and communities, multi-level, multi-sector strategies for, 352–355
hub and spoke, 353
OrganWise Guys (OWG) messaging, 354

partners in, 354–355
school/child care setting, to home, 354
theoretical framework, for model aspects of, 356
CCMCO model, 355
community health workers (CHWs), 363, 364
coordinated multi-sector, community-based activities, 357–360
existing activities, systems, and policies, 362–363
funding opportunities support, 364–365
social change, 355
strengthening coordination, multi-sector system, 361–365
Childhood
factors, perinatal epidemiology
accelerated aging, evidence of, 70–71
central body fat, 69–70
diet during infancy, 69
path of growth, 69
obesity
bone health (*see* Bone health and metabolic syndrome)
cardiomyopathy and heart failure (*see* Cardiomyopathy and heart failure)
children out of balance, 8–11
epidemic, 16–17
prevalence of, 38, 42
respiratory diseases, 160
worldwide health emergency, 4–5
type 2 diabetes (*see* Type 2 diabetes)
Cholesterol
and neurocognitive functioning, 230–231
and psychosocial functioning, 234
screening, in atherosclerosis, 101
and triglycerides, genomics
dyslipidemia, 257–258
elevated blood pressure, 258
familial hypercholesterolemia, 257
insulin resistance, 258–259
Chronic Care Model for Childhood Obesity (CCMCO), 355
Chronic kidney disease (CKD), proteinuria, 126
Clinic-and community-based practice, into policy. *See* Child healthy weight
Colorectal cancer, 221
Community health workers (CHWs), 363, 364
Computed tomography (CT) scan, subcutaneous fat, 289–290
Coordinated School Health, 365
C-reactive protein (CRP), 66, 67

D

Diacylglycerol (DAG)-induced insulin resistance, 84
Diastolic function, myocardial functional changes, 202
Dietary intake, nutritional evaluation
    food frequency questionnaires (FFQ), 291
    24-h dietary recall, 291–292
    multiple-day food record, 291
    NDSR Report, 292
Dietary interventions, pediatric weight management
    altered macronutrient dietary approaches, 299
    balanced macronutrients diets, 297
    calcium, 299–300
    fiber, 301
    glycemic index (GI), 301–302
    guidelines, for Americans, 297–298
    Mediterranean-style diet (MSD), 298–299
    motivational and pharmacologic interventions, 303
    omega-3 fatty acids, 301
    psychological interventions, 302
    USDA food guide MyPlate, 298
    vitamin D, 300–301
Disposition index (DI), 87, 89
DNA methylation, 245
Dual-energy X-ray absorptiometry (DXA)
    BMD measurements, 184
    body fat levels, age and sex, 288
    bone mineral density, 287, 289
    principle, 287
    score for, 287
Duodenal switch, biliopancreatic diversion, 339–341
Dyslipidemia, 97, 104, 106
    genomics, 248, 249, 257–258

E

Echocardiography, 206–207
Economic urgency, of pediatric metabolic syndrome, 33–34
Ectopic fat deposition and insulin resistance, in obese child, 84–86
Electrocardiography, 206
Elevated blood pressure, 250–252, 258
Endometrial cancer, 222
Epidemiology of metabolic syndrome, in youth
    annual average charges, 51
    components of, 39
    definition, 40, 41
    ethnicity and prevalence, 42–43
    international prevalence estimates, 49
    NHANES prevalence estimates, 45–48
    pathophysiology of, 39
    population-based prevalence estimates, 44–45
    prevalence of obesity, in children and adolescents, 38, 42
    regional-based sample estimates, 48–49
    secular trends, lifespan, 49–50
    and socioeconomic status, relationship, 43–44
Epigenetics, 245, 246
    studies, perinatal epidemiology, 72
Esophageal cancer, 223
Evidence-based programming, 357, 365
Exenatide
    complications of therapy, 325
    indications and efficacy, 325
    mechanism of action, 324–325
Exercise
    interventions, for children, 276–277
    physiologic basis, 268, 269
    program designing, 277–278
Ezetimibe, 329

F

Familial hypercholesterolemia, 248, 257
Fat mass and bone density
    adipose-derived hormones
        adiponectin, 186
        estrogens, 187
        leptin, 185–186
        resistin, 186–187
        serotonin, 185
    beta cell hormones, 187
    gut hormones, 188
Fat mass and obesity-associated protein *(FTO)* gene, 256
Fatty liver disease, 25–26
Febuxostat, for kidney disease, 124
Fetal growth, perinatal epidemiology
    abnormal, measurement approaches, 60
    assessment, 58–59
    factors affecting, 59–60
    outcome, 59
    poor and excessive, causes of, 61
Fetal overnutrition, 66
Fetal undernutrition
    amino acids availability, 64
    chronic placental inflammation, 65
    lipid metabolism and liver function, 64–65
    renal morphology and function, 65

Fiber, 301
Fibric acids, 327
Fibrosis, in liver diseases, 140, 143, 148, 149
Fitness assessments, components of, 268–273
Flexibility, in fitness assessments, 273
Focal segmental glomerulosclerosis (FSGS), 122, 123
Food insecurity, 293
Fracture risk and obesity, 189–190
Free fatty acids (FFA), 144, 145
Fructose, in kidney disease, 123–124

G

Gait and musculoskeletal function, 192
Gastric band, in bariatric surgery, 337, 342
Gastric inhibitory peptide (GIP), 188
GCK mutation, 255
Gender effects, perinatal epidemiology, 68
Gene-mapping strategies, 242–246
Genomics, of pediatric metabolic syndrome
   abdominal obesity, 256
   cholesterol and triglycerides
      dyslipidemia, 257–258
      elevated blood pressure, 258
      familial hypercholesterolemia, 257
      insulin resistance, 258–259
   definition, 242
   gene environment interaction, 258, 260, 261
   gene-mapping strategies
      agouti yellow alleles (Avy), 246
      concepts, 242, 243
      deoxyribonucleic acid (DNA), sequence defects, 245
      epigenetic alterations, 245, 246
      family and population-based approaches, 244
      genome-wide association study (GWAS), 244
      multifactorial liability threshold model, of genetic inheritance, 245
      TNDM, 246
   heritability, 242
   intervention studies, fitness and physical activity for, 260
   monogenic forms
      in adolescent populations, 247
      GCK mutation, 255
      leptin and leptin-receptor deficiencies, 246
      MODY genes, 255
      mutations and polymorphisms, 248–254

      pro-opiomelanocortin *(POMC)* gene, 247
      rare mutation, 256, 257
Genuvalgum, 191
Gestational diabetes mellitus (GDM), 61
Gestational weight gain, perinatal epidemiology
   Collaborative Perinatal Project, 61
   IOM recommendations, 61–63
   LBW, 62
   maternal body fat, 63
   pattern of, 63
Ghrelin, 188
Glucagon-like peptide (GLP-1), 188, 324, 325
Glucocorticoid receptor, 165
Glucose sensitivity, of first-and second-phase insulin response, 89
Glycemic index (GI), 301–302
Glycemic load (GL), 301, 302
Gut hormones and bones, 188

H

Health and economic urgency, of pediatric metabolic syndrome, 33–34
Health-care crisis in children, importance, 14–15
Health-care system, 12, 13
Health promotion, mixed messages in, 12–13
Healthy Hunger-Free Kids Act (HHFK), 356
Heart
   failure (*see* Cardiomyopathy and heart failure)
   obesity-related anatomical changes in
      adipose tissue distribution, 201–202
      wall thickness and chamber dimensions, 201
Hemodynamic changes, cardiomyopathy, 204–205
Heritability, of metabolic syndrome, 242
High blood pressure/hypertension
   in atherosclerosis, 98
   and neurocognitive functioning, 232
Hip circumference measurements, 286
Human immunodeficiency virus (HIV) infection, in atherosclerosis, 104
HUPRA syndrome, 250, 258
Hypercholesterolemia, 97
Hyperfiltration theory, 122
Hyperlipidemia and physical activity, 276
Hypertension, multifactorial, 124–125
Hypertriglyceridemia, 97, 101, 249
Hyperuricemia, 123–124
Hypopnea, 167

I

Impaired glucose tolerance (IGT), 87–89
Inflammation, perinatal epidemiology, 66–67
Institute of Medicine (IOM), 61, 62
Insulin-like growth factor-1 (IGF-1), 120, 224
Insulinogenic index (IGI), 87
Insulin resistance
   and asthma, 163
   in atherosclerosis, 98
   and ectopic fat deposition, in obese child, 84–86
   genomics, 252–253, 258–259
   and neurocognitive functioning, 232–233
   pharmacological agents for
      metformin, 312–319
      rosiglitazone, 319–320
   and physical activity, 275
   and psychosocial functioning, 235
Insulin secretion, fall in, 88–89
International Diabetes Federation (IDF), 219
International pediatric metabolic syndrome prevalence estimates, 49
Intramyocellular lipid content (IMCL), 84
Iron deficiency, nutritional evaluation, 295

K

Kidney cancer, 222
Kidney disease
   central adiposity, 124
   early recognition of, 130
   evaluation and treatment
      allopurinol, 129
      assessment paradigm, 127, 128
      diagnosis and assessments, 127, 128
      dyslipidemia, 129
      formula calculations, 129, 130
      nutritional therapy, 127, 129
   evolution, two-hit hypothesis, 123
   fructose, 123–124
   hypertension, multifactorial, 124–125
   hyperuricemia, 123–124
   nephron endowment and obesity-related glomerulopathy, 121–123
   proteinuria, 126
   role, in metabolic syndrome
      endothelin-1, 120–121
      insulin effects, on glomerular function, 120
      insulin-like growth factor-1 (IGF-1), 120
      insulin resistance and hyperinsulinemia, 118
      mesangial phenotype, 120
      renal consequences of, 118, 119
   urolithiasis, 126
   vitamin D insufficiency, 127

L

Laparoscopic adjustable gastric banding (LAGB), 337, 344
Large for gestational age (LGA), 58, 59
Left ventricular mass, obesity-related changes, 201
Leptin, 99, 162, 185–186, 224, 246, 323–324
Liddle's syndromes, 250, 258
Lipid abnormalities, pharmacological agents for, 326
   bile acid sequestrants, 329
   ezetimibe, 329
   fibric acids, 327
   low HDL and hypertriglyceridemia, 327
   nicotinic acid, 327, 328
   omega-3 fatty acids, 327–328
   pioglitazone, 330
   site of action, 328
   statins, 328–329
Lipotoxicity and obesity-related metabolic changes, 203
Liver
   diseases
      cirrhosis, 140, 143, 148, 149
      diagnosis, in children, 149–150
      fibrosis, 140, 143, 148, 149
      liver enzymes, 149
      management of, 150–151
      NAFLD, 138–148 (*see also* Nonalcoholic fatty liver disease (NAFLD))
      obesity, 138
      ultrasonography, 139
Low birthweight (LBW), 59
Low-density lipoprotein *(LDLR)* receptor gene, 257
Lung mechanics and physiology, in asthma, 162

M

Macronutrient dietary approaches, 297, 299
Maternal hyperglycemia, 61
Maternal smoking effect, perinatal epidemiology, 67
Maternal weight gain, 61–63
Maturity onset diabetes of young (MODY) genes, 255
Maximal oxygen consumption (VO_2 max), 270–272
Mediterranean-style diet (MSD), 298–299

Melanocortin 4 receptor *(MC4R)*, 247, 256
Metabolic syndrome, pediatric age
  cardiovascular risk, 6
  challenges, 20–21
  clinical review and health issues, 29–30
  coronary atherosclerosis, 23
  as critical issue, 18–19
  definition, 20, 40, 41
  fatty liver disease, relation of, 25–26
  obesity, as societal issue, 31–32
  prevention approach, 7
Metformin, 209
  efficacy of therapy, 315, 318
  indications, 318
  in liver diseases management, 151
  mechanism of action, 313–315
  randomized control trials, 316–317
  therapy and contraindications, complications of, 318–319
Multi-sector system, strengthening coordination, 361–365
Muscular strength and endurance, 271, 273
Musculoskeletal effects, of obesity
  arthritis, 193
  bariatric surgery, 193
  bone mineral content (BMC), 188
  and fracture risk, 189–190
  and gait, 192
  musculoskeletal pain, 192
  and orthopedic complications, 190–191
Myocardial functional changes, obesity-related
  diastolic function, 202
  systolic function, 202–203
Myocardial strain imaging, 207

N
NAFLD. *See* Nonalcoholic fatty liver disease (NAFLD)
National Blue Cross/Blue Shield Association, 365
National Cholesterol Education Program (NCEP), 45, 49, 101
National Health and Nutrition Examination Survey (NHANES)
  advantages, 45
  1999-2002 dataset, 47
  1999-2004 dataset, 47
  1999-2006 dataset, 47
  NHANES III data, 45–46
  objectives of, 44
  population-based prevalence estimates, 44, 45
  waist circumference, 48

Nephron endowment and obesity-related glomerulopathy, 121–123
Neurocognitive correlates, of metabolic syndrome, 230
Neurocognitive functioning
  in children and adolescents, 229, 230, 232, 236, 237
  and cholesterol, 230–231
  and high blood pressure/hypertension, 232
  and insulin resistance, 232–233
  and overweight, 231–232
  research in, 237
NHLBI guidelines, atherosclerosis, 101, 102
Nicotinic acid, 327, 328
Nitric oxide, in asthma, 165
Nonalcoholic fatty liver disease (NAFLD), 25, 85
  adverse endocrine-metabolic milieu, 142
  definition, 138
  diagnoses of, 139–140
  epidemiological considerations, 141–142
  fibrosis, 140
  genetics of, 146–147
  histopathological features, 143–144
  liver transplantation, 140
  natural history of, 140, 148
  obesity, 142, 144, 145
  pathogenesis of
    hepatic steatosis, 144
    insulin resistance, 145
    oxidative stress, 145, 146
    thrifty phenotype hypothesis, 146
  prevalence, 138–139
Nonalcoholic steatohepatitis (NASH), 25, 26, 138, 140, 143
Normal glucose tolerance (NGT), 87–89
Nutritional evaluation
  anthropometry and body composition measurements, 284–285
  biochemical nutrition indicators, 293–294
  bioelectrical impedance analysis (BIA), 288–289
  body mass index (BMI), 285
  children, 284, 295, 303
  CT scans, 289–290
  dietary intake, 290–293
  dietary interventions, pediatric weight management
    altered macronutrient dietary approaches, 299
    balanced macronutrients diets, 297
    calcium, 299–300
    fiber, 301

Nutritional evaluation (*cont.*)
    glycemic index (GI), 301–302
    guidelines, for Americans, 297–298
    Mediterranean-style diet (MSD), 298–299
    motivational and pharmacologic interventions, 303
    omega-3 fatty acids, 301
    psychological interventions, 302
    USDA food guide MyPlate, 298
    vitamin D, 300–301
dual-energy X-ray absorptiometry, 287–289
food insecurity, 293
interventions
    components of, 296–297
    four-stage plan for treatment, of childhood obesity, 296
    and lifestyle interventions, 295
skinfold thickness (SFT), 286–287
vitamin and mineral deficiencies, 294–295
waist and hip circumference, 286
Nutrition and WIC Reauthorization Act of 2004, 361
Nutrition policy, 353, 365

O

Obesity
    ALI/ARDS, 173–174
    and asthma, 161 (*see also* Asthma and obesity)
    in atherosclerosis, 96
    cancer risk estimates
        in men, 220
        in women, 221
    cardiomyopathy
        definition, 200
        evidence of, 200–201
    gene mutations and polymorphisms, 248
    glomerulopathy, 122, 123
    and inflammation, perinatal epidemiology, 66–67
    myocardial functional changes, 202–203
    and perioperative adverse events, 171–173
    pharmacological agents for, 319
        albiglutide, 325
        amylin analogs, pramlintide, 326
        bupropion, 323
        exenatide, 324–325
        leptin, 323–324
        liraglutide, 325
        orlistat, 320–321
        sibutramine, 321–323
        topiramate, 325
    therapy and cancer prevention, 225
Obesity hypoventilation syndrome (OHS), 167–168
Obstructive sleep apnea (OSA)
    and cardiovascular complications, 168
    definition, 167
    and interventional studies, 170
    obesity and metabolic syndrome, interacting pathophysiology, 171
    and oxidative stress, 168–169
    and systemic inflammation, 169–170
Omega-3 fatty acids, 301, 327–328
Orlistat
    efficacy of therapy, 320
    mechanism of action, 320
    recommended dose, 320–321
    therapy and contraindications, complications of, 321
Orthopedic complications and obesity, 190–191
OSA. *See* Obstructive sleep apnea (OSA)
Osteoporosis, 185
Overweight. *See also* Obesity
    and neurocognitive functioning, 231–232
    and psychosocial functioning, 234–235
Oxidative stress and obstructive sleep apnea, 168–169

P

Pancreatic cancer, 223
Perilipin 4 (*PLIN4*) gene, 259
Perinatal epidemiology, of metabolic syndrome risk factors
    adiposity, 58, 66, 67
    body proportions
        reduced abdominal circumference, 68
        short and fat babies, 68
        symmetrically small newborn, 67
        thin newborn, 67–68
    childhood factors
        accelerated aging, evidence of, 70–71
        central body fat, 69–70
        diet during infancy, 69
        path of growth, 69
    cohort studies, 58
    epigenetic studies, 72
    fetal growth
        abnormal, measurement approaches, 60
        assessment, 58–59
        factors affecting, 59–60
        outcome, 59
        poor and excessive, causes of, 61

fetal origins, of adult disease, 58
fetal overnutrition, 66
fetal undernutrition, 63–65
gender effects, 68
gestational weight gain, 61–63
intergenerational effects, 72
maternal smoking, effect of, 67
obesity and inflammation, 66–67
socioeconomic effects, 71–72
z-scores/centile crossing changes, importance of, 71
Perioperative adverse events and obesity, 171–173
Pharmacological therapies, of metabolic syndrome
  insulin resistance
    metformin, 312–319
    rosiglitazone, 319–320
  lipid abnormalities, 326–330 (see also Lipid abnormalities, pharmacological agents for)
  obesity, 319–326 (see also Obesity, pharmacological agents for)
Physical activity assessment and intervention
  aerobic exercise, 275, 277
  exercise, 268, 269, 276–278
  fitness assessments, components of
    blood pressure, 270
    body composition, 269–270
    cardiorespiratory fitness, 270–272
    flexibility, 273
    metabolic laboratory values, 270
    muscular strength and endurance, 271, 273
  principles
    blood pressure, 275, 276
    duration of, 274
    frequency, of exercise sessions, 273–274
    hyperlipidemia, 276
    insulin resistance, 275
    intensity, 274
    weight management, 274–275
Pioglitazone, 330
Placental inflammation, chronic, 65
Plasminogen activator inhibitor 1 (PAI-1), 294
Population-based prevalence estimates of pediatric metabolic syndrome, 44–45
Pramlintide, amylin analogs, 326
Preeclampsia, 67
Primary pulmonary hypertension, 251
Proinflammatory and prothrombotic states, in atherosclerosis, 98–99

Proteinuria, 126
Psychological correlates, of metabolic syndrome, 233–234
Psychological interventions, pediatric weight management, 302
Psychosocial functioning
  and blood pressure, 235
  in children and adolescents, 234, 235, 237
  and cholesterol, 234
  and insulin resistance, 235
  and overweight, 234–235
  research in, 237
Public heath approaches, 352, 355, 364
Pulmonary arterial hypertension, 252

R
Regional-based sample estimates, of metabolic syndrome, 48–49
Renin-angiotensin-aldosterone system (RAAS), 120, 204
Resistin, 186–187
Rimonabant, 208
Rosiglitazone, 319
Roux-en-Y gastric bypass (RYGB), 193, 338

S
School wellness policy, 363, 365
Secular trends, in metabolic syndrome, 49–50
Sertraline, 208
Sibutramine
  complications of therapy, 322–323
  efficacy of therapy, 322
  mechanism of action, 322
Single-nucleotide polymorphisms (SNPs), 147, 163
Skinfold thickness (SFT), 286–287
Sleep-disordered breathing (SDB) and metabolic syndrome
  epidemiology, 166–167
  obesity hypoventilation syndrome (OHS), 167–168
  obstructive sleep apnea (OSA)
    and cardiovascular complications, 168
    definition, 167
    and interventional studies, 170
    obesity and metabolic syndrome, interacting pathophysiology, 171
    and oxidative stress, 168–169
    and systemic inflammation, 169–170
  upper airway resistance syndrome, 167

Sleeve gastrectomy, 339, 340
Slipped capital femoral epiphysis
  (SCFE), 190, 191
Small for gestational age (SGA), 58
Social marketing, 359, 360, 365
Social media, as community-wide
  communication tool, 360
Socioeconomic effects, perinatal
  epidemiology, 71–72
Socioeconomic status, 43–44
Statins, 328–329
Systemic inflammation
  and asthma, 162–163
  and obstructive sleep apnea, 169–170
Systolic function, myocardial functional
  changes, 202–203

T
Thiazolidinediones, 209
Topiramate, 325
Transient neonatal diabetes mellitus
  (TNDM), 246
Triglycerides, 257–259
Type 2 diabetes
  genetic studies, 90
  insulin resistance and ectopic fat
    deposition, in obese child
    hepatic steatosis, 85
    lipid partitioning, patterns of, 84
    metabolic patterns, 86
    NAFLD, 85
  obesity, metabolic complications, 84
  obstructive sleep apnea, 169
  in youth
    glucose sensitivity, of first-and
      second-phase insulin response, 89
    insulin secretion, fall in, 88–89
    metabolic staging, 86–87

U
Ultrasonography, fetal growth assessment, 59
United States Department of Agriculture
  (USDA), 353, 354, 362, 364–365
Urolithiasis, 126

V
Visceral adiposity, 124
Vitamin D
  in asthma, 164
  in cancer risk, 224
  deficiency, 294
  insufficiency, kidney disease, 127
  pediatric weight management, 300–301
Vitamin E, 294
  in liver diseases management, 151

W
Waist and hip circumference
  measurements, 286
Weight control, cardiomyopathy, 208
Weight loss interventions,
  in asthma, 166
Weight management and physical activity,
  274–275
Whole body insulin sensitivity
  index (WBISI), 86, 87
World Health Organization
  (WHO), 49
Worldwide health emergency,
  of childhood obesity, 4–5

X
Xanthine oxidase inhibitor, for
  kidney disease, 124

Y
Youth, type 2 diabetes
  insulin secretion, fall in, 88–89
  metabolic staging, 86–87

Z
Z-scores/centile crossing changes, perinatal
  epidemiology, 71